THE
HOME
GARDENER'S
SOURCE

Also by Solomon M. Skolnick

....

Seeds from a Secret Garden

Noah's Ark: A Retelling

A Garden of One's Own (with Marc Anello)

Photographed by Solomon M. Skolnick

....

The Window-Box Book, by Anne M. Halpin

Simple Gifts: The Shaker Song

THE HOME GARDENER'S SOURCE

Solomon M. Skolnick

RANDOM HOUSE • NEW YORK

Library of Congress Cataloging-in-Publication data is available.

ISBN 0-679-75477-6

Random House website address: http://www.randomhouse.com/
Printed in the United States of America on acid-free paper
9 8 7 6 5 4 3 2
First Edition

Book design by Lesley Ehlers, and Mullen & Katz

For Christel
and
Ettore Biagi

Acknowledgments

There once was an idea contained in a seed. The seed grew into a tree. This tree grew with a few oddly twisted branches. However, it survived and then thrived, and this is its fruit. This particular fruit came into its fullness because of the nurturing care and patience of a very long list of gardeners and stewards. I wish to thank them for their forbearance and faith, season after season after season, until finally this fruit did ripen.

I am forever grateful to Harry M. Evans, Walter Weintz, and Ann Godoff, each of whom has exhibited faith, exercised patience, and extended me a great deal of freedom in the belief that this would all come out right in the end. I hope that you are well pleased.

A bushel of thank yous go to Enrica Gadler, Page Dickinson, Amy Edelman, Martha Schwartz, Leah Weatherspoon, Tony Davis, and Joanne Barracca at Random House for their professionalism in seeing me–and this book–through to publication.

This book would not be much to look at if not for the design wizardry of Lesley Ehlers and Lana Veronica Mullen, the intuitive illustrations of Diana Minisci Appleton, and the cover art direction of Andy Carpenter. A bouquet of gratitude to each of you.

I wish to thank Jean Preller for her many months of dedicated and uncompromising work in helping to research this book, keyboarding the manuscript, and keeping me from becoming inextricably buried in catalogs, notes, and profiles.

Many thanks to the guest writers who lent their expertise and words: A. Richard "Dick" Brooks, Ken Cobb, Ron L. Engeland, Steve Miller, Rob Proctor, and Peter Schneider. And to Paulette Rickard of Capability's who provided a basic reading list for many of the plant material sections.

Thank you to my wife, Linda, and our children, Sophia and Jesse, for your love and sometimes idiosyncratic words of support while weathering the writing of this book. To Sophia, age eight, who has often asked, "Are you done yet?" and Jesse, age four and a half, who has demanded, not asked, "Papa, don't make words on the computer, draw me a train," I can now answer Sophia, "Yes, I am done," and Jesse, "Would you like a diesel train or a steam engine?"

Contents

Contents

$\mathcal{I}$ntroduction

$\mathcal{G}$ardening is a lifelong adventure.

NANCY BUBEL

$\mathcal{I}$ often fall in love in the garden. Most often, I fall in love with plants in other people's gardens.

If you show a gardener a plant, he'll probably want one—or more—of his own. The need to add to one's own garden can be met by the abundance of mail-order companies that cultivate for diversity. However, depending on finding an advertisement from a nursery or hearing about a really great source for a particular type of plant can prove limiting and time-consuming—time that could be happily spent reading catalogs, digging holes, enriching the earth, and admiring your garden through the seasons. The desire to have access to sources that specialize or offer a concentration in particular types of plants or products—"I want to find bulbs, daylilies, woodland flowers, ornamental grasses, tools and supplies," etc.—is what propelled me to write this book. The chapters are organized so that you can identify and compare, in succession, nurseries and other sources that offer similar material. You can revel in irises or peonies or lilacs. To help you make some prejudgments about whether it is worth your time and money to request a catalog, source profiles describe suppliers' offerings while at the same time giving a sense of what *they* say about their offerings. Profiles also include the number and nature of sources' catalog listings and the cultural and descriptive details provided.

The choice of sources in this book is mine. The inclusion of a source in the book, however, is not meant to be an endorsement; at the same time, omission is not a comment of any kind. A catalog was requested, read, and compared with the catalogs of others offering the same classification of plants bulbs, seeds, or materials. Notes were taken, then a profile form sent to the source asking for confirmation of information printed in the catalog and for any additional details and facts that would help distinguish sources from each other. After the signed profile was returned, there was a further culling to those that seemed to fit the bill as establishments eager to deal with private individuals, offering quantities and terms of sale that might make sense to folks just trying to grow their own gardens. The plant world is defined and enriched by bounty and diversity, and your garden can be too.

How to Read the Listings

There are three types of listings in *The Home Gardener's Source:*

The **Source** profiles are presented in alphabetical order within the category of material or goods that a vendor will supply, e.g., books and computer software, bulbs, daylilies, garden furniture and ornament, hosta, irises, roses, seeds, supplies, etc.

The **Geographical** index is organized alphabetically by state or province, then by city or town.

The **Alphabetical** index lists every source in the book.

How to Read a Source Profile

The information in italics is explanatory and does not appear in the actual listing.

Name of source: EDEN NURSERY
Year founded: 1900
Proprietor or contact: **Adam and Evie Furst**
Catalog: $2 (*recoverable, a credit issued against the price of the catalog usually with your first order*) (**FC**, *first class;* **FCS**, *first class stamp;* **LSASE**, *legal-size self-addressed stamped envelope*), **40 pp.**, **color photographs** (*based upon the most recent catalog reviewed*)
Narrative description: The source's specialty and a selection of material that you will find in their catalog. Where the number of items or varieties is quantified, it is an approximation based upon our own count in the most recent catalog reviewed. The notes regarding how a source describes stock is a characterization of the degree and nature of the details that you will find in that catalog. Guarantees satisfaction. Will replace or issue refund if returned within sixty days. *Their published guarantee.* See **Daylilies,** Hosta, Organics, **Supplies.** *Items outside the category that a source offers. A category in bold-face type indicates a separate descriptive entry appears in that section. Where there is no bold-face, the catalog offers other material in these categories, but there is no separate description for it in this book.*
Shipping season: April and May. September and October. *Knowing when a source ships living material will help you prioritize your ordering. Most sources will work with you so that plants arrive at the appropriate time (within a source's stated shipping season) for your area. This information is omitted for purveyors of nonliving material (and for most seed sources) that ship their goods throughout the year.*
No California or Hawaii. *States to which a vendor cannot or does not ship.*
Canada, Mexico, International. *Places outside of the United States to which a source ships. This information is omitted if a source ships domestically only or modified to specify which markets are served.*

Geographical Listing

State: **KANSAS**
City: **BOUNTIFUL 99999**
Source: **Eden Nursery**
Address: 101 Apple Orchard Way
Proprietor or contact: Adam and Evie Furst
Phone: 111-111-1111
Fax: 111-111-1112
On-site: Retail and wholesale
May through July. Monday, Wednesday, Thursday, 9:00–6:00.
By appointment. *The months, days of the week, times, and circumstances under which a source will welcome customers or visitors.*
NOTP. *Not open to the public.*

Alphabetical Listing

Name of the source: EDEN NURSERY
Mailing address: P.O. Box 1001
Bountiful, KS 99999
When the address for on-site sales or visits differs from the mailing address, it is noted in the geographical listing.
Phone: 111-111-1111
Fax: 111-111-1112
Catalog: $2
Method of payment: *The forms of payment that they honor.*
Terms: *At what point in the transaction they expect payment.* $25 minimum order. *The minimum purchase required. Does not include handling, shipping charges, or tax (where applicable).*
Daylilies, Hosta, Organics, Supplies. *Chapters where this source appears as a line listing or a profile.*

When requesting a catalog from a business in this book, please mention *The Home Gardener's Source,* published by Random House. If you are a supplier wishing to be considered for inclusion in the next edition of the *HGS,* please send your catalog to me c/o The Home Gardener's Source, P.O. Box 126, Pleasantville, NY 10570.

There is a time to sow, a time to read catalogs, a time to write this book, and now for me, finally, a time to go back into the garden.

Sol Skolnick
JANUARY 1997

Bulbs

$\mathcal{P}$lanting bulbs takes faith. So does ordering them by mail.

Bulbous plants have evolved to cope with the rigors of weather, storing nutrients in the structures we call bulbs, corms, tubers, or rhizomes. They go partly or completely dormant in response to various climatic factors such as cold, drought, or heat.

Bulb merchants and gardeners take advantage of this dormant period to harvest, ship, and replant bulbs throughout the year. Bulbs are the easiest plants to ship by mail, suffering little or no damage in transit. The trick is to order at the correct time of year, and to handle the bulbs properly once they arrive.

Spring-flowering bulbs are the largest group. Tulips, hyacinths, daffodils, and crocuses as well as lesser-known but lovely flowers such as squills, alliums, glory-of-the-snow, snowdrops, and bluebells herald the spring. These are to be planted between September and December, depending on local conditions. Ordering them in time for autumn planting is critical. Most bulb merchants send out their catalogs in the spring, while flowers still abound in the garden. It never hurts to order early while you can still evaluate your spring show (or lack of it). It is ideal to place orders by July, but avoid delaying beyond August.

Winter-flowering bulbs are also ordered during the summer and planted in the fall. These include amaryllises, paperwhite narcissi, and cyclamens, as well as clivias, freesias, veltheimias, and lachenalias.

Order summer-flowering bulbs—gladiolus, cannas, dahlias, and tuberous begonias—in winter and early spring. April through early June is the primary time to plant these tender bulbs. Most need to be dug up and stored in the fall before cold weather hits, although this need not apply to gardeners who experience little or no freezing temperatures.

Autumn-flowering bulbs are a small but important group. What would the garden be like without the September surprise of the blossoms of autumn crocuses, sternbergias, and colchicums? They display their flowers as the gardening season comes to an end in temperate areas. Their leaves appear briefly the following spring to store energy for the next season. You may wish to order these by midsummer to assure delivery in August. Plant them immediately upon arrival.

A few bulbous plants such as the fabled Madonna lily, *Lilium candidum*, is dormant only briefly in late summer and usually ships in August. After planting, it resumes growth almost immediately, holding a rosette of leaves over the winter that sends up flower stalks of pristine white trumpets in June.

Other lilies are shipped in either spring or fall. This is fortunate for gardeners who fancy these beautiful flowers, since most hardy bulbs are not so forgiving about their planting schedules.

When ordering bulbs, look for a guarantee that they are true to name, color, and variety. Many companies will not replace bulbs for failure to perform in your garden, since they can't be responsible for improper planting, poor drainage, wildlife or insect damage, or any number of variables.

Inspect your bulbs upon arrival. They should be firm and plump, with little sign of nicks or cuts from harvesting. Some bulbs, such as tulips, hyacinths, and lilies, may show a little blue mold. This is normal and will not affect the bulbs if they otherwise feel firm. Squishy bulbs or those that have dry rot should be replaced. Inform the company immediately.

If you cannot plant bulbs within a few days of their arrival, it is vital to store them properly. Spring-flowering bulbs require a cool, dark place such as a garage or basement. The refrigerator is also a possibility, especially for lilies. Make sure that the temperature never drops below freezing. Control the proliferation of mold by using a fungicide or a spray of diluted Lysol (a teaspoon for every gallon of water).

Tender bulbs that bloom in either summer or winter should be stored in a cool, dark place as well. Avoid humid, bright environments that will encourage them to sprout prematurely. Most can wait safely for several weeks to go into the soil. Bulbs have accommodating natures both in and out of the garden, but don't push it. Handled properly, they will reward your efforts and faith with a bounty of bloom.

—*Rob Proctor*

(Author, photographer, and botanical illustrator Rob Proctor teaches at the Denver Botanic Gardens. His books include *The Indoor Potted Bulb* and *The Outdoor Potted Bulb.*)

The number of offerings cited in each profile is based on information in the most recent catalog provided by the source. In this section, shipping season is for bulbs only. A selection of books about bulbs appears after the last listing.

QUICK FIND
The following sources are listed in this section:

LOUISIANA NURSERY
MARY MATTISON VAN SCHAIK
MCCLURE & ZIMMERMAN
MESSELAAR BULB COMPANY
NETHERLAND BULB COMPANY
OLD HOUSE GARDENS
OREGON TRAIL DAFFODILS
PARK SEED® CO.

PLEASANT VALLEY GLADS AND DAHLIAS
SCHIPPER AND COMPANY
SISTERS' BULB FARM
SKOLASKI'S GLADS AND FIELD FLOWERS
SUMMERVILLE'S GLADIOLUS WORLD-WIDE
TRANS-PACIFIC NURSERY

VAN BOURGONDIEN BROS.
VAN DYCK'S FLOWER FARMS, INC.
VELDHEER TULIP GARDENS, INC.
THE WAUSHARA GARDENS
WE-DU NURSERY
WHITE FLOWER FARM

BLOOMING PRAIRIE GARDENS
Circa 1930
J. P. Madson
Catalog: Free, 16 pp., color photographs
Carl Fischer, a preeminent hybridizer of gladiolus, offers ninety-five cultivars, the majority being his own introductions. Nine of the ten NAGC All-America selections offered by Noweta are Fischer's own. Hybridizer, year of introduction, size, color, conspicuous markings, number of days to bloom, nature of flowerhead and florets, size of bulb, and rich, charming descriptions. A substantial number of collections, composed of named but unlabeled varieties, are a feature of this catalog. Guarantees safe arrival.
Shipping season: February through May.

BONNIE BRAE GARDENS
1984
Jeanie McKillop Driver and Frank Driver
Catalog: 2 FCS
The Drivers grow true-to-name, standard, intermediate, and miniature show quality (novelty) daffodils. Many are also useful for landscaping. The catalog includes a thorough explanation of daffodil classifications, and the name, class, hybridizer, height, and season of bloom for each of their fifty offerings. Species bulbs are nursery propagated.
Shipping season: September and October.
Canada, International

BRECK'S
1818
Hans Van Amstel
Catalog: Free, 52 pp., color photographs
A broad selection of spring-flowering Dutch bulbs: allium, anemones, crocus, daffodils, hyacinths, lilium, and tulips. Descriptions, height, color, and season of bloom. Cultural and planting tips. Starter collections and assortments for naturalizing. Guarantees to bloom in your garden the first spring; will issue refund.
Shipping season: August through November.
Canada

BROOKESFIELD FARM
1987
Ric and Cathy Cavness
Catalog: Free, 20 pp., illustrations
The Cavnesses' bulbs are grown in a four-year crop rotation to control disease and maintain soil fertility in an "ideal climate" in western Washington. Daffodils include rock garden and Dutch Master early bloomers; midseason trumpets, small-cup, large-cup, and doubles. Hybrid tulips include: early-season *Fosterana*, *Kaufmanniana*, double and single early; midseason Darwin and Triumph; late-season fringe, lily, parrot, peony, and single forms. A few species are also listed. Guarantees safe arrival.
Shipping season: September and October.

THE BULB CRATE
1983
Alice Hosford
Catalog: $1 (recoverable), 8 pp.
A small nursery that hand-digs each order. Lilies: Aurelian, oriental, and Columbia-Platte asiatic and trumpet. Iris: Japanese, Siberian, dwarf bearded, and tall bearded, including several Dykes Medal winners. Fragrant peonies, including APS Gold Medal winner Coral Charm. Guarantees true to name, disease free, and in first-class condition; will replace or issue refund.
Shipping season: Early spring through late fall.

BUNDLES OF BULBS
1983
Kitty Washburne
Catalog: $2, 24 pp.
Bundles of Bulbs specializes in less well known bulbs, and some rare spring- and summer-flowering bulbs in the largest sizes for any particular variety. Offerings include one hundred tulips organized by season of bloom, eighty-five daffodils organized by division, *Allium*, *Anemone*, *Camassia*, *Crocus*, *Eranthis*, *Erythronium*, hyacinths, *Iris* (miniature), *Lilium*, *Scilla*, and *Triteleia*. Height, color, brief descriptions, and number of bulbs required to fill specific areas. Collections and spans of miniatures, fragrant types, daffodils that tend to naturalize, species tulips, and mixed starter gardens. Cultural notes.
Shipping season: October through January.

CASCADE BULB & SEED CO.
See Daylilies, **Seeds**.

CASCADE DAFFODILS
1986
Dave and Linda Karnstedt
Catalog: $2, 56 pp.
The Karnstedts list three hundred of the two thousand modern daffodil hybrids grown at Cascade. Numerous prizewinners for the collector and connoisseur. Catalog is organized by classification. Each listing includes hybridizer, year of introduction, season of bloom, color, awards received, and a detailed description. Several collections including two composed entirely of Wister Award winners. Guarantees true to name and pest and disease free.
Shipping season: September and October.
Canada, International

CHARLES H. MUELLER CO.
Circa 1940
Charles A. Fritz III
Catalog: Free, 18 pp.
Founded by Charles H. Mueller and entrusted upon his death in 1991 to Charles A. Fritz. Seventy varieties of daffodils, including four species. One hundred and twenty varieties of tulips, including six species. Organized by month of bloom. Height, color, and a brief description for each. Collections of named varieties for landscaping and the connoisseur. Spring-flowering bulbs, including *Allium*, *Anemone*, *Chionodoxa*, species and hybrid crocus, *Fritillaria*, hyacinth, *Lilium*, and *Scilla*. Small selection of varieties for forcing.
Shipping season: September through December.

THE DAFFODIL MART
1904
Brent and Becky Heath
Catalog: Free, 56 pp.
These third-generation bulb growers (and coauthors of *Daffodils for American Gardens*) offer twelve hundred hybrids and species from England, Holland, Israel, the United States, and their own fields. Organized by season of bloom, listed alphabetically by type within season. The Daffodil Mart catalog includes summer-flowering *Bletilla*, *Caladium*, *Canna*, *Crocosmia*, *Cyclamen*, *Gladiolus*, *Lilium*, *Oxalis*, *Tritonia*, and *Zantedeschia*; fall-flowering *Colchicum*, *Crocus*, *and Lycoris*; spring-flowering *Anemone*, *Camassia*, *Chionodoxa*, *Crocus*, daffodils, Dutch iris, *Eremurus*, *Erythronium*, *Fritillaria*, and tulips. The Heaths also list seventy varieties for forcing. Brief informative descriptions, cultural advice, and planning tips. Collections for landscaping, naturalizing, and show. Guarantees true to name, size, disease free, and will bloom in your garden in the first year. See **Booksellers, Supplies**.
Shipping season: March and April. September through November.

DUTCH GARDENS
1946
Henk van der Voort
Catalog: Free, 48 pp., color photographs
A long night's browsing. One hundred tulips, thirty daffodils, and a dozen hyacinths lead a catalog that also includes *Alium*, *Anemone*, *Chionodoxa*, *Crocus*, *Galanthus*, *Muscari*, and *Scilla*. Amaryllis and other varieties for forcing. Height, bulb size, hardiness and sun key, and description for each, as well as notation for best cut-flower types. Landscaping mixtures and collections. Planning information, including number of bulbs required to cover various areas. Guarantees bloom in your garden, will replace or issue refund. See Perennials.
Shipping season: Spring and fall.

FAR NORTH GARDENS
1962
Karen J. Combs
Catalog: $2 (recoverable), 52 pp.

Far North Gardens has a number of areas of concentration including Barnhaven primroses, rare flower seeds, wildflower plants and seeds, and "collector's bulbs" from the Caucasus, Greece, Middle Asia, Russia, and Turkey. One hundred and forty offerings, described by botanical name only, include several *Allium, Arum, Colchicum, Corydalis, Crocus, Cyclamen, Fritillaria, Galanthus, Iris, Muscari, Ornithogalum, Oxalis,* and *Polygonatum.* Guarantees safe arrival. See **Booksellers**, Grasses, **Perennials, Seeds, Wildflowers.**
Shipping season: March through June. September through November.
Canada, Mexico, International

FRENCH'S: BULB IMPORTER
1943
Robin Martin
Catalog: Free, 16 pp.
Dutch bulbs. Offerings include sixty varieties of tulips and fifty varieties of daffodils. Broad assortment of other spring- and autumn-flowering bulbs: *Allium, Amaryllis, Anemones, Colchicum, Crocus, Cyclamen, Freesia, Fritallaria, Muscari, Ranunculus,* and *Scilla.* Height, color, and description for each. Extensive notes highlight varieties that are suitable for forcing, and precooled bulbs. Guarantees success in your garden; will replace.
Shipping season: September through January.

GARDENIMPORT
Dugald Cameron
Catalog: $4, 64 pp., color photographs.
Separate catalogs for spring and fall.
Gardenimport, as their name implies, gathers plant materials from worldwide sources, and presents them in an exquisitely photographed catalog organized by botanical family. The summer/fall issue concentrates on spring flowering bulbs (80 percent of the book) and perennials that are easily planted in the fall. Recent offerings have included a broad range of *Allium, Amaryllis,* autumn *Crocus, Camassia, Colchicum, Crocus chrysanthus, Crocus vernus,* species *Crocus, Eremurus, Erythronium, Fritallaria, Galanthus,* hyacinths, *Iris* (bulbous), *Lilium, Muscari, Narcissus,* and tulips (species and hybrids). See **Booksellers**, Grasses, **Peonies**, Perennials.
Shipping season: Fall
Canada

GRANT E. MITSCH NOVELTY DAFFODILS
1927
Richard and Elise Havens
Catalog: $3 (recoverable), 28 pp., color photographs
A treasure for the daffodil collector. Catalog offers over three hundred varieties in twelve divisions that are grown on-site. Current year's introductions and other modern registrations. Many of the cultivars offered were bred by the Havens or Elise's father, Grant E. Mitsch. Specifications and rich descriptions. Cross-referenced by name and division. Pink and mixed collections, also seedlings.
Shipping season: September and October.
Canada, Mexico, International

GROWERS SERVICE CO.
1988
John K. Riordan
Catalog: $1, 40–56 pp. Subscription: $5 for five issues
Mr. Riordan describes his mail-order firm as a "wholesale bulb import club." Several hundred varieties of "exotic imported" and nursery-propagated native bulbs are purchased in lots and sold in varying quantities that permit landscapers, garden clubs, and individuals who subscribe to buy at off price. Selection is diverse and varies from issue to issue. Sample catalog is available for the price of postage to familiarize you with Growers Service's selection and tone. Guarantees true to name and disease and pest free. See **Perennials**, Waterscapes.
Shipping season: Spring and fall.
Canada, Mexico, International

HOLLAND BULB FARMS
1982
Sophie Langeveld
Catalog: Free, 40 pp., color photgraphs
Spring-flowering Dutch bulbs in collections for landscaping. Height, season of bloom, hardiness and sun key. Notes varieties that are best suited for cutting. Guarantees certificate of health. See also Netherland Bulb Co., offering virtually the same material but in different quantities.
Shipping season: September through December.

JIM DUGGAN FLOWER NURSERY
1990

Jim Duggan
Catalog: $2, 10 pp.
Duggan specializes in "bulbous plants" from South Africa. Catalog includes true bulbs, corms, and tuberous rootstocks that prefer excellent drainage and dry summers. The catalog lists two hundred of the five hundred varieties that Mr. Duggan currently has in cultivation. Organized alphabetically by botanical name. Description of characteristics by genus, including required growing conditions, and by species, including length of leaf, height of flower, common name, and a brief narrative. Guarantees disease free, pest free, and of flowering size.
Shipping season: June through September.
Canada, Mexico, International

JOHN SCHEEPERS, INC.
1911
Jan S. Ohms
Catalog: Free, 48 pp., color photographs
Offers 325 hybrid and species varieties for spring and for forcing. *Allium, Amaryllis, Anemone, Calla aethiopica, Camassia, Corydalis,* bunch and large flowering *Crocus,* daffodils, *Erythronium, Freesia, Galanthus nivalis,* hyacinth, *Iris* (Dutch and miniature), *Lilium, Muscari, Oxalis, Scilla,* eighteen varieties and classifications of tulips, and more. Cultural information, height, color, season of bloom, and description for each. Numerous collections for landscaping and naturalizing. Guarantees true to name, healthy, firm, and viable for planting; will replace or issue credit for failures in first growing season.
Shipping season: September through December

J. W. JUNG SEED & NURSERY CO.
1907
Richard J. Zondag
Catalog: Free, 76 pp., color photographs
This seed and nursery catalog for a wide range of interests offers forty types of gladiolus including Jung's exclusive giant exhibition varieties, All-America prizewinners (including miniatures), and "skyscrapers," producing scapes that are four to five feet tall. Also offers hardy Asiatic hybrid lilies, tiger lilies, Aurelian hybrids, Oriental mixed lilies, and spotted-leaf calla lilies. Descriptions include color of flower, height and nature of scape, and season of bloom. Guarantees true to name, safe ar-

rival, and will grow in your garden; will replace or issue credit. See **Fruit,** Garlic, **Kidstuff,** Perennials, **Seeds,** Supplies, **Trees,** Vegetables.
Shipping season: August through November.

LOUISIANA NURSERY
1950
Dalton E. Durio
Catalog: 70 pp., $3.50 (recoverable)
Louisiana Nursery occupies a fifty-six-acre complex. Five family members, all trained horticulturists, are currently involved in the business. One of six catalogs that they publish is "Crinums and Other Rare Bulbs." Over three hundred offerings are organized by botanical name (common name given). Included are numerous *Agapanthus, Alstroemeria, Amarcrinum, Amaryllis, Crinum, Hymenocallis, Lycoris, Richardia, Zantedeschia,* and *Zephyranthes.* Descriptions are rich in cultural information and in visualizing the form of the plant. See **Booksellers, Daylilies, Fruit, Grasses, Iris, Trees.**
Shipping season: All year.
Canada, Mexico, International

MARY MATTISON VAN SCHAIK
1948
Paula M. Parker
Catalog: $1 (recoverable), 12 pp.
Spring-flowering Dutch bulbs and an extensive selection for forcing. Catalog includes 125 species and hybrid tulips organized by season of bloom and fifty daffodils organized by division. *Allium,* miniature *Amaryllis, Anemone,* hybrid and species *Crocus, Galanthus,* hyacinths, *Muscari,* and *Scilla.* Height, color, and description. Miniature, naturalizing, and forcing collections. Guarantees true to name.
Shipping season: September and October.

MCCLURE & ZIMMERMAN
1980
Gloria Tamminga and Dick Zondag
Catalog: Free, 40 pp., illustrations
Six hundred spring, summer, fall, and suitable-for-forcing flowerbulbs. An eclectic catalog affording the home gardener an opportunity to diversify bulb choices. African corn lily, *Allium, Amaryllis, Anemone, Arum, Chionodoxa, Colchicum,* spring- and fall-flowering *Crocus, Cyclamen,* commercially propagated wild daffodils, *Eremurus, Erythronium,* hyacinths, *Ixia, Lilium, Lycoris, Oxalis, Pancratium, Puschkinia,* saffron, *Scilla,* squill, *Tecophilaea,* and commercially propagated wild tulips,

Veltheimia, wild ginger, and others. Genus, common name, size of bulb, uses, description of species and/or cultivar, height, season of bloom, hardiness zone, light requirements, and number of bulbs required per square yard. Cultural information and history. Numerous collections for landscaping. Guarantees true to name and safe arrival. **Shipping season: September through December. March.**

MESSELAAR BULB COMPANY
1946
Catalog: Free, 18 pp., color photographs
Two hundred and fifty (primarily) spring-flowering Dutch bulbs in various sizes: *Allium, Anemones, Crocus*, daffodils, hyacinths, Dutch and dwarf *Iris*, and tulips. Autumn-flowering *Colchicum*, and *Crocus, Sativus* and *Speciosus*. Identifies bulbs that are appropriate for forcing. Height, color, season of bloom, and brief description. Specializes in mixtures for landscaping. Many bulbs available in case quantities. Includes comparative season-of-bloom chart that is useful for planning succession. Guarantees safe arrival.
Shipping season: July through September.

NETHERLAND BULB COMPANY
1982
Peter Langeveld
Catalog: Free, 40 pp., color photographs
Spring-flowering Dutch bulbs in collections for landscaping. Height, season of bloom, hardiness and sun key. Highlights varieties that are well suited for cutting. Guarantees certificate of health. See also Holland Bulb Farms, offering virtually the same material but in different quantities.
Shipping season: September through November.

OLD HOUSE GARDENS
1993
Scott G. Kunst
Catalog: $1, 26 pp., illustrations
After ten years as a landscape historian, Scott Kunst founded Old House Gardens to help preserve historic bulbs by making them, and information about them, more widely available. Sixty-five rare, antique crocus, hyacinths, narcissus, tulips, and other spring-flowering bulbs dating from the 1500s through the 1920s are offered. Descriptions are rich in historical and cultural information. Scott works

with small-scale specialist growers to obtain and reintroduce antique flowerbulbs of merit that are no longer available through commercial merchants. Among Kunst's sources are Sisters' Bulb Farm (see listing), for which OHG is now the exclusive retail mail-order source. Guarantees true to name and safe arrival. See Heirlooms.
Shipping season: October.

OREGON TRAIL DAFFODILS
1988
Bill Tribe
Catalog: Free, 32 pp.
Family successors to Murray Evans Daffodils, continuing a four-generation tradition of breeding and growing exceptional daffodils for show and garden. All bulbs are grown, selected, and packaged on-site. Oregon Trail offers three hundred varieties bred by Murray Evans and Bill Pannill, as well as their own new hybrids. Classification, color, year of registration, season of bloom, height, and rich description. Precounted mixtures and custom collections.
Shipping season: September through November.
Canada, Mexico, International

PARK SEED® CO.
1868
J. Leonard Park and Karen Park Jennings
Catalog: Free, 48 pp., color photographs
Park Seed® bulb catalog includes over three hundred varieties of *Allium*, African *Amaryllis, Anemone, Colchicum*, spring- and fall-flowering *Crocus*, giant-flowered Dutch *Crocus*, species snow *Crocus, Cyclamen*, daffodils, *Freesia, Fritillaria*, hyacinths, Dutch *Iris, Lilium* (Asiatic and oriental hybrids), *Lycoris, Muscari, Scabiosa, Scilla* (squill and wood hyacinths), and tulips. Guarantees bulbs will grow and bloom for up to one year from delivery; will issue credit or refund. A feature of this catalog is the numerous collections: by color, season of bloom, price point, size of plant, and for recommended garden use, such as naturalizing or forcing. See **Garlic, Herbs**, Peonies, Roses, **Seeds, Supplies**, Vegetables.
Shipping season: Fall-flowering crocus: through September. Spring- and summer-flowering bulbs, fall.

Pleasant Valley Glads and Dahlias
1963
Roger Adams, Sr., and Gary Adams
Catalog: Whatever you please, 34 pp.
Roger Sr. started raising glads in 1920 at age fifteen. However, the Adamses, the only family in the NAGC with three accredited judges, didn't publish their first mail-order catalog until 1963. Features current introductions from these prizewinning exhibitors and other key breeders. General list composed of 300 large, 130 miniature, and 25 All-America modern gladiolus cultivars. Hybridizer, year of introduction, size, color, conspicuous markings, number of days to bloom, nature of flowerhead and florets, size of bulb, and narrative description. Three hundred and fifty giant, large, medium, small, miniature, ball, miniature ball, and pompon dahlias. Specifications, color, and brief description. Guarantees true to name and clean, healthy stock.
Shipping season: March through June.
Canada, Mexico, International

Schipper and Company
1912
Tim Schipper
Catalog: Free, 10 pp., color photographs
A third-generation bulb merchant, Tim Schipper introduces "colorblends" and "textureblends" for landscaping. He prepackages coordinated combinations of strong-performing spring flowerbulbs of various types and colors. Description focuses on overall landscape effect. Guarantees true to name.
Shipping season: September through November.

Sisters' Bulb Farm
1918
Celia Jones and Jan Jones Grigsby
Catalog: No longer published
Celia Jones lives on the farm where her grandmother started raising daffodils in 1918. She grows only old varieties that are not available through any other source. Empress, one of the varieties that has become unique to Sisters', was introduced in 1865 and was the standard against which other white-and-yellow trumpet daffodils were measured well into the twentieth century. Sisters' produced a mail-order catalog for several years but now devote their energies exclusively toward growing. Their heirloom daffodils are available through Scott Kunst's Old House Gardens (see Old House Gardens). See Heirlooms.

Skolaski's Glads and Field Flowers
1962
Stan and Nancy Skolaski
Catalog: Free, 20 pp.
Two hundred and twenty-five *Gladiolus*, hybrid *Lilium*, and a short list of summer-blooming bulbs. Current introductions from a select group of breeders and a general list of modern varieties. Hybridizer, year of introduction, size and color by NAGC classification, season of bloom, height, nature and shape of flowerheads and florets, and rich descriptions. Substantial number of unlabeled collections and mixtures. Guarantees safe arrival.
Shipping season: March through June.
Canada, Mexico, International

Summerville's Gladiolus World-Wide
Alex Summers
Catalog: Free, 32 pp.
Offers 250 modern cultivars. Features Summerville's current large-flowered and miniature introductions, and those of other key hybridizers. General list and All-America selections from select group of sources. Hybridizer, year of introduction, color, season of bloom, and detailed narrative descriptions. Season-of-bloom and show quality collections. Guarantees safe arrival.
Shipping season: February through May.
Canada, Mexico, International

Trans-Pacific Nursery
See **Booksellers**, Perennials, **Trees**, **Waterscapes**.

Van Bourgondien Bros.
1919
Deborah Van Bourgondien
Catalog: Free, 56 pp., color photographs
Spring, summer, and fall flowerbulbs for landscaping: *Allium, Anemone, Chionodoxa, Colchicum, Crocus* (spring and fall), daffodils, *Fritillaria*, hyacinths, *Iris* (English and Spanish), *Lilium, Lycoris, Ranunculus, Scilla*, tulips, winter aconite, wood hyacinths, and more. Height, season of bloom, and sun key. Strong on collections and mixtures. Daffodils by the bushel. See Perennials.
Shipping season: August through November.

VAN DYCK'S FLOWER FARMS, INC.
1989
Deborah DeMichiel
Catalog: Free, 72 pp., color photographs
A "wholesaler" to the home gardener. A pre-counted number of bulbs are put in packs, avoiding the cost of counting out bulbs for each order. Two hundred spring, summer, and fall flowerbulbs for landscaping: *Allium, Amaryllis* (indoor), *Anemone, Camassia, Crocus,* daffodils, *Fritillaria, Galanthus,* hyacinths, *Iris* (English and Spanish), *Lilium, Muscari, Ranunculus, Scilla,* tulips, and others. Height, season of bloom, and rich descriptions. Extensive offering of mixtures. Guarantees safe arrival.
Shipping season: Spring and fall.
Canada, Mexico, International

VELDHEER TULIP GARDENS, INC.
1951
Catalog: Free, 16 pp., color photographs
The Veldheer catalog is divided into eight bloom seasons. Within each season, several species are offered (e.g., "early spring blooming"): *Fosterana* and *Greigii* tulips, trumpet daffodils, *Muscari,* and *Puschkinia* are shown in color photographs.
Shipping season: September and October.
Canada

THE WAUSHARA GARDENS
1924
George Melk
Catalog: $1, 16 pp.
The catalog is written for both the home gardener and Waushara's trade customers purchasing gladiolus to be grown as cut flowers for resale. The florist, roadside stand, and county fair collections may entice you into daydreaming. Once you have disengaged from the dream, you will find eighty varieties of gladiolus in four sizes. Individual cultivars are organized by size and color according to NAGC classification. Hybridizer, year of introduction, season of bloom, height, nature and shape of flowerheads and florets, descriptions, and primary use. Prepaid mixtures for landscaping and noncommercial cut-flower gardens. See **Booksellers.**
Shipping season: February through June.
Canada

WE-DU NURSERY
1981
Dr. Richard E. Weaver and Rene A. Duval
Catalog: $2, 50 pp., illustrations
We-Du sits on a thirty-acre site abundant in water and with diverse terrain in Marion, North Carolina. The emphasis for most of their list are nursery-propagated southeastern natives and their Oriental counterparts. Recent bulb lists (10 percent of their six hundred offerings), however, included predominantly natives and imports from Argentina and Brazil and tender species from South Africa. Descriptions include botanical and common names, height at maturity, sun/shade requirements, color and form of flower. Bulbs are shipped as containerized growing plants in the spring except as noted. Guarantees true to name, correctly labeled, strong and healthy when shipped; will replace. See Iris, Perennials, **Wildflowers.**
Shipping season: Mid-February through mid-December.
No Arizona, California, or Hawaii

WHITE FLOWER FARM
1950
Steve Frowine
Catalog: Free, 146 pp., color photographs
White Flower Farm, a family-owned nursery in Litchfield, Connecticut, offers a wide range of ornamentals. Just under 20 percent of their spring book, and about a third of their fall edition, is devoted to bulbs. The White Flower catalog is beautifully presented and among the most clearly written that we've read. Spring planted varieties include begonias, *Crinodonna, Dahlia, Gladiolus,* late-flowering *Lilium, Ornithogalum, Sparaxis, Tritonia,* and *Zantedeschia.* Autumn-planted varieties include *Anemone, Erythronium,* hyacinths, species lilies and their hybrids, *Narcissus,* and a procession of tulips. Fully realized narrative descriptions accompany all of their offerings. Specifications including color, hardiness zone, height of mature plant, season of bloom, light and soil preference, spacing; fragrant varieties and suitability for use as a cut flower appear in a separate selection-and-planting chart. Guarantees true to name, in prime condition for growing, and delivered at the proper time for planting; will replace onetime only. See Fruit, **Perennials, Roses,** Supplies, Trees, **Waterscapes.**
Shipping season: Spring and fall.
Canada, no Hawaii

Selected Reading About Bulbs

The American Gardener's World of Bulbs, by Judith Glattstein. Toward developing the "New American Garden" from the bulb's point of view. Strategies for integrating hardy, tender, and native bulbous plants with perennials and shrubs in both formal and informal settings. Includes eighty color photographs.

Beautiful Bulbs: Simple Secrets for Glorious Gardens—Indoors and Out, by Georgeanne Brennan and Mimi Luebbermann. A gorgeous little book with terrific tips on forcing, growing bulbs in contained spaces, and integrating in the garden. Color photographs.

Bulbs: Taylor's Guide to Gardening. Part of an informative and critically well-regarded series. Includes information about three hundred types of bulbs for North American gardens. Over four hundred and fifty color photos.

Gardening with Bulbs: A Practical and Inspirational Guide, by Patrick Taylor. A selection of the best commercially available bulbous plants, including corms, tubers, and rhizomes. Entries describe each bulb's noteworthy qualities, offer cultural information, and suggest best uses in the garden. Two hundred color photographs.

The Random House Book of Bulbs, by Martyn Rix and Roger Phillips. Over one thousand bulbs (and three hundred photographs) organized by sequence and season of bloom. One in a highly regarded large-format series.

$\mathcal{P}$ERENNIALS

The number of offerings cited in each profile is based on information in the most recent catalog provided by the source. In this section, shipping season is for perennials only. A selection of books about perennials appears after the last listing.

QUICK FIND
The following sources are listed in this section:

ALPLAINS
See Seeds, **Wildflowers.**

AMBERGATE GARDENS
1985
Mike and Jean Heger
Catalog: $2, 68 pp., illustrations and color photographs
The Hegers, based in Waconia, Minnesota, offer two hundred uncommon and/or unusual native and exotic perennials hardy in zone 4. Mr. Heger is the author of *Perennials from A to Z,* based upon a series of articles that he wrote for the *Minnesota Horticulturist.* Forty percent of the Ambergate catalog lists perennials for sunny sites, 30 percent lists varieties for shady sites; just under 10 percent is devoted to ornamental grasses. Within each section, offerings are organized by botanical name. One of the varieties that they emphasize is Martagon lilies (they offer about a third of the thirty varieties that they grow), early blooming, shade-tolerant members of this genus that, according to the Hegers, are quite obscure in the nursery trade. Common name, color of flower, nature of foliage, season of bloom, height at maturity, cultural preferences and habits, companion planting tips, and notes about each variety's horticultural value are contained in the Hegers' thorough and accessible descriptive gems. Includes an extensive list of perennials with exceptional foliage quality and a list of those with long seasons of bloom. Ships bareroot. Guarantees state inspected, true to name, and healthy. See **Booksellers, Grasses.**
Shipping season: April and May. September and October.
Canada

AMERICAN DAYLILY & PERENNIALS
See **Daylilies,** Peonies.

ANDERSON IRIS GARDENS
See **Daylilies, Iris, Peonies.**

ANDRÉ VIETTE FARM & NURSERY
1920
Mark, André, and Claire Viette
Catalog: $3, 44 pp., color photographs
The Viettes are wholesalers (specify retail catalog) of over one thousand varieties of herbaceous perennials which are (primarily) propagated on-site by division and cutting. Their catalog lists 850 offerings including concentrations in *Achillea,*

Japanese anemone, *Aster, Astilbe, Buddleia, Cimicifuga, Coreopsis, Dianthus, Geranium* (cranesbill), *Liriope, Monarda, Phlox, Potentilla, Primula, Salvia, Thymus, Tricyrtis,* and *Veronica.* Descriptions include height at maturity, color of flower, and season of bloom. See **Daylilies, Hosta, Grasses.**
Shipping season: March through November.

ANTONELLI BROTHERS
1935
Skip Antonelli
Catalog: $1
The Antonellis' specialty is hybrid begonias. Recent introductions include a mini-strain with full double blooms and fragrant "hanging spice" varieties. Tubers sold through the mail. All plants dug, washed, and graded by hand. Precise instructions for care are included with the catalog. Guarantees to replace plants that fail. See Seeds.
Shipping season: Tubers, February through April. Seeds, November through July.
Canada, International

ARROWHEAD ALPINES
Bob and Brigitta Stewart
Plant catalog: $2, 88 pp. Seed catalog: $2, 62 pp.
The Stewarts describe their seed catalog, with four thousand listings, as the most extensive in the United States. Their plant catalog of two thousand woodland flowers, alpines, perennials, trees, and shrubs is equally impressive. Sixty-five percent of their catalog is devoted to perennials and rock plants, many of which are characterized as rare and unusual. Plants in this section are listed by botanical name only. Brief rich descriptions presuppose a knowledge of culture, site preference (for some), and hardiness range. See **Conifers,** Grasses, **Seeds,** Trees, Wildflowers.
Shipping season: March and April. August and September.

BEDFORD DAHLIAS
Eugene A. Woznicki
Catalog: 1 FCS, 20 pp.
Mr. Woznicki has been growing dahlias longer than he taught high school chemistry, which he did for forty-one years. He offers 110 varieties organized by cultivar. Descriptions include size classification, form of flower (such as anemone, ball, collarette, formal decorative,

etc.), season of bloom, and noteworthy characteristics for each listing. Features a list of the American Dahlia Society's "Winningest Dahlias in the United States," and a list of the world's best dahlias including trial garden scores and awards that they have won. Guarantees true to name.
Shipping season: January through May.
Canada

BIJOU ALPINES
1989
Mark Dusek
Catalog: $1, 18 pp.
Bijou Alpines, associated with Mount Tahoma Nursery until 1991, is a specialty nursery with 150 varieties of rare and unusual plants for the rock garden, scree, bog, water garden, and woodland. Lists twenty-five herbaceous perennials described in detail, including a key to placement within the garden environment. Encourages wish lists as the amount of material that they cultivate far exceeds the space to present it. The "Collector's Corner" is their forum for presenting either plants never before introduced or forms rarely encountered in the trade. Listed by botanical name, their descriptions include habit, shape and color of leaves and flower, and light requirements. All plants are nursery propagated. Custom propagation services available. See **Conifers, Trees, Waterscapes.**
Shipping season: March through May.
September and October.

BLUESTONE PERENNIALS
1972
William Boonstra
Catalog: Free, 80 pp., color photographs
The Bluestone catalog includes 550 herbaceous perennials, ferns, grasses, ground covers, herbs, and ornamental shrubs. Concentrations include *Achillea, Artemisia, Aster* (including dwarfs), *Campanula*, chrysanthemum, *Dianthus*, lupines, *Phlox, Sedum*, and *Viola*. Descriptions include height at maturity, spacing, sun/shade requirements, season of bloom, color and form of flower and foliage. Symbols highlight those varieties that are best for hot dry spots, moist soil, as ground covers, coldest areas (zones 3 to 4), the deep South, cut and/or dry easily, or are fragrant. Plants offered variously as liners, intermediate or mature potted sizes. Labeled collections include *Achillea, Astilbe, Di-*

anthus, Heuchera, Phlox, and *Veronica.* Pre-planned garden design collections for areas of 80 to 150 square feet include planting grid and instructions for borders, a shade garden, and a butterfly garden. Guarantees plants will grow; will replace or issue credit. See Grasses, **Trees.**
Shipping season: March through June.
Arizona, California, Idaho, Oregon: March and April.

BRAND PEONY FARM
See Heirlooms, **Peonies.**

BUSSE GARDENS
1977
Ainie Busse
Catalog: $2 (recoverable), 56 pp., illustrations
Busse's catalog includes two thousand cold-hardy perennials from their new location in Cokato, Minnesota. Offers extensive selections of *Achillea, Aconitum, Alchemilla, Anemone, Asters, Astilbe, Bergenia, Clematis, Dicentra, Geranium* (cranesbill), *Hemerocallis, Hosta*, ornamental grasses, peonies, poppies, *Phlox, Pulmonaria*, and *Veronica*, among others. Descriptions include detailed cultural information, garden uses, color of flower, height of plant, and notable characteristics of foliage. Extensive information about design, planting, and care as well as suggestions for grouping perennials by design principle, color, and shade and sun tolerance. Also offers unlabeled collections of *Asters, Astilbe*, poppies, and *Phlox*. Guarantees true to name, state inspected, and viable. See Daylilies, Grasses, **Hosta, Peonies,** Wildflowers.
Shipping season: May through October.
No California
Bareroot only: Arizona, Idaho, Kansas, Oregon, Washington

CANYON CREEK NURSERY
Susan Whittlesey
Catalog: $2, 32 pp.
The family Whittlesey grow five hundred types of perennials (including many they describe as less hardy or tender) in mild winter conditions in the foothills of the Sierra Nevadas. Selections include *Anthemis, Aquilegia, Aster* (including a late-flowering unnamed species), *Calamintha, Crambe, Diascia* (a South African native in the snapdragon family), *Erysimum, Euphorbia, Fuchsia, Lavandula, Lavatera*, rosemary, *Salvia, Stachys*, and *Viola* including Richard Cawthorne hybrids. Narrative

descriptions include color and form of leaves and flowers, height at maturity, some cultural requirements, and careful notes about tenderness/hardiness. Plants grown in 3¹/₂-inch to 5-inch pots, shipped bareroot. Guarantees satisfaction; will replace. See Grasses.
Shipping season: February through May. September through November.

CAPRICE FARM NURSERY
See **Daylilies,** Hosta, **Iris, Peonies.**

CARROLL GARDENS
1933
Alan L. Summers
Catalog: $3 (recoverable), 108 pp.
Carroll Gardens in Westminster, Maryland, devotes 70 percent of its catalog to seventeen hundred herbaceous perennials, ferns, ground covers, ornamental grasses, and rock garden plants. Areas of concentration include *Achillea* (including German hybrids), *Agapanthus, Ajuga, Artemisia, Aster, Astilbe* (including a six weeks of color collection), *Bergenia, Campanula,* chrysanthemums (including a hardy mum collection), *Dahlia, Delphinium, Dianthus, Dicentra, Digitalis, Epimedium, Geranium* (and a cranesbill sampler), *Geum, Gypsophila, Helianthus,* 160 *Hemerocallis* (including small-flowered, large-flowered, and landscape collections), *Heuchera* and *Heucherella,* 120 *Hosta* (including a fragrant hosta collection), *Iris,* Japanese iris, Siberian iris, *Kniphofia, Lavandula, Liatris, Lilium, Liriope, Monarda,* peonies, *Phlox* (including the perfume series and a garden phlox mixture), *Primula, Pulmonaria, Salvia, Sedum, Tradescantia* (including Kevin Vaughn's hybrids), *Veronica,* and *Viola.* Descriptions include cultural preferences, color of flower, sun/shade requirements, soil preference, height at maturity, spacing of plantings. Includes diagrams and plant variety suggestions for foolproof sun, shade, and partial shade perennial borders. Guarantees true to name, ready to grow, and safe arrival (California, Oregon and Washington true to name only); will replace one time only. See **Daylilies, Herbs, Hosta,** Iris, **Peonies, Roses, Trees.**
Shipping season: March through November. Canada

CLASSIC GROUNDCOVERS
1963
Wilbur C. Mull
Catalog: Free, 20 pp., color photographs
The plant materials offered by Mr. Mull and

company are an eclectic selection of perennials (including daylilies, hostas, phloxes, and sedums), creepers and vines such as ivies, myrtles, pachysandras, and periwinkles, ornamental grasses (including *Liriope, Lonicera,* and *Miscanthus*), and other plant materials that are of use as ground covers. Organized by botanical name descriptions include common name, sun/shade key, hardiness zone, color and texture of foliage, season of bloom, height and width at maturity, soil preference, and landscape or garden use. Plants are available variously as bareroot stock, 2¹/₄-inch pots, and as a Classic Pint™, with an established root system and pronounced foliage. Guarantees true to name; will replace. See Grasses.
Shipping season: All year

CLIFFORD'S PERENNIAL & VINE
See **Trees.**

COLLECTOR'S NURSERY
1990
Bill Janssen and Diana Reeck
Catalog: $2, 28 pp., illustrations
Seventy-five percent of Janssen and Reeck's diverse catalog (drawing from three thousand plants growing at their nursery) from worldwide sources is devoted to four hundred perennials. Areas of concentration include *Aconitum, Allium, Arisaema, Campanula, Clematis, Corydalis, Dodecatheon, Epimedium,* assorted ferns, *Heuchera,* abiqua hosta (see Walden West in **Hosta**), *Incarvillea, Meconopsis, Plantago, Pulmonaria, Tricyrtis,* and *Viola.* Catalog is organized by genera, genera organized by botanical name. Evocative descriptions, notes about origins of names, sources from which cultivars have been acquired, general cultural tips and site preferences. Ships in pots; some perennials shipped bareroot. Guarantees true to name, well rooted, and healthy. See **Conifers, Trees.**
Shipping season: March through May. September through November.

COOPER'S GARDEN
See **Daylilies, Iris.**

DABNEY HERBS
See **Booksellers, Herbs.**

DAISY FIELDS
1989
JoAnn Wiltrakis

Catalog: $2 (recoverable), 32 pp., illustrations
Daisy Fields (Daisy is the Wiltrakises' dog) specializes in old-fashioned cottage garden perennials (and a few biennials) grown from seed, cutting, or division in their own nursery/garden. Ms. Wiltrakis's 160 offerings are listed by botanical name in an airily designed intimately written catalog. Descriptions include common name, soil, site, and sun requirements, cultural habits, color of flower, season of bloom, height at maturity, and hardiness zone. Recent offerings included a diverse group of *Campanula* including *C. alliariifolia, C. garganica, C. pyramidalis* in blue and white varieties, *Crambe cordifolia* (colewort) whose height and spread can extend to seven feet, *Lychnis* 'Daisy Fields Pink', *Meconopsis betonicifolia* (Himalayan blue poppy), *Salvia forskaohlei* (in cultivation since 1800), and *Thalictrum Delavayi* which was introduced from China in 1890. Offers specially priced combinations of plants that complement each other in garden settings such as *Alchemilla* with *Campanula*, or *Thalictrum* with *Salvia*. Ships plants in soilless media in four-inch pots. Guarantees true to name and healthy; will replace or refund. See **Heirlooms.**
Shipping season: March through June.
No Hawaii

DAYSTAR
1970
Marjorie Walsh
Catalog: $1, 8 pp.
Daystar is a Maine nursery with rotating specialties. Recent catalogs featured 120 assorted perennials and primulas. They note botanical and common names and there is a brief description. Guarantees safe arrival; will replace. See **Conifers,** Trees.
Shipping season: April through June. September through November.
Canada

DIGGING DOG NURSERY
1978
Deborah Whigham and Gary Ratway
Catalog: $2, 66 pp., color illustrations
Gary, a landscape architect, and Deborah opened Digging Dog in 1978 because he had a difficult time finding plant material for his design jobs. Their first catalog dropped in 1993. Mail-order selections focus on those plants that they have observed over time, in Gary's land-

scapes and at the nursery. Presented as noteworthy for ease of care, long bloom periods, attractive year-round form, texture, color, and versatility are one hundred perennials, twenty ornamental grasses, and sixty shrubs, trees, and vines. Recent catalogs highlighted several anemones including *A. canadensis,* and *A.* × *hybrida* 'Queen Charlotte', a bevy of asters, a herbaceous clematis, hellebores including *H. argutifolius* (Corsican hellebore), a half dozen pulmonarias, and a member of the lily family native from Tennessee to Kansas and Texas commonly known as camas *(Zigadenus Nuttallii)*. Rich descriptions include height and spread, season of bloom, hardiness zone, sun and shade tolerance. See **Grasses, Trees.**
Shipping season: February through May. September through November.

DONAROMA'S NURSERY & LANDSCAPE SERVICES
1977
Mike Donaroma
Catalog: $1, 16 pp.
Donaroma's (on Martha's Vineyard) offers 360 garden perennials and wildflowers. Some plants are propagated from seed that has been wild-crafted. Areas of concentration include *Campanula, Coreopsis, Delphinium, Lobelia, Lupines, Penstemon, Platycodon,* Jacob's ladder *(Polemonium),* pincushion flower *(Scabiosa),* catch fly *(Silene),* and *Veronica.* Many of their offerings are appropriate for growing near the ocean shore. Aptly a number of these flowering plants, including butterfly weed, ox-eye daisy, common rose mallow, Queen Anne's lace, plains coreopsis, and Nippon daisy are included in their seaside collection. Descriptions are brief and include common name, hardiness zone, color, height at maturity, and size of plant being offered. Plants are sold in three-inch pots (minimum of five pots per variety). Guarantees true to name; will replace. See **Wildflowers.**
Shipping season: March through May.
Canada

DUTCH GARDENS
See **Bulbs.**

EASTERN PLANT SPECIALTIES
See **Conifers, Fruit, Rhododendrons, Trees, Wildflowers.**

EDGEWOOD FARM & NURSERY
See **Herbs.**

ENGLEARTH GARDENS
See **Daylilies, Hosta, Iris.**

EVERGREEN GARDENWORKS
See **Conifers,** Fruit, **Trees.**

FAR NORTH GARDENS
1962
K. J. Combs
Catalog: $2 (recoverable), 52 pp.
Far North Gardens has a number of areas of concentration among its 2,600 listings including wildflowers, rare flower seeds, bulbs, and perennials. Live plants that appeared in recent catalogs include Barnhaven primroses (specialty and Victorian *Polyanthus*, silver dollar, and *Acaulis*), native violets, and twenty types of ferns. Compact descriptions include botanical and common names, color and form of flowers, season of bloom, and occasional anecdotes about the derivation of common names. Guarantees safe arrival. See **Booksellers, Bulbs,** Grasses, **Seeds, Wildflowers.**
Shipping season: March through June. September through November.
Canada, Mexico, International

FARMER SEED & NURSERY
See **Garlic,** Seeds, **Vegetables.**

FLOWERPLACE PLANT FARM
Gail Barton, Richard Lowery, and Karen Partlow
Catalog: $3, 14 pp.
Flowerplace offers a carefully constructed selection of one hundred perennials that must past the owners' abuse test in humid conditions in Meridian, Mississippi. Richly drawn descriptions include color of flower, nature and color of foliage, occasional historical tidbits, common name, average height and spacing, and hardiness zone. Also notes Flowerplace's cultural category code assigned to each plant for one of five sets of conditions: full sun with well-drained soil, full sun and moisture-retentive soil, gentle sun and well-drained soil, woodland conditions, and dry areas. Stock grown outdoors in four-inch pots. See Herbs.
Shipping Season: All year.

FLOWERY BRANCH SEED CO.
See Herbs, **Seeds.**

FORESTFARM®
1974
Ray and Peg Pragg
Catalog: $3, 414 pp., illustrations and black-and-white photographs
The Praggs' catalog contains four thousand plants. Just under one hundred pages of the catalog are devoted to herbaceous perennials. Here is a teaser sampling of the eight hundred or so offerings in this section: you'll find ten *Achillea*, eleven *Anemone*, twelve *Campanula*, sixty-five *Clematis*, eight *Epimedium*, six *Gentiana*, thirteen *Heuchera*, seven *Lobelia*, twelve *Monarda*, eighteen *Penstemon*, eight *Pulmonaria*, seventeen *Sedum*, eighteen *Veronica*, and one *Zauschneria californica latifolia*. Their catalog is organized by botanical name but includes a common-name index that makes working with this in-depth catalog a pleasure. Adding to the manageability of this catalog is the excellent standardized descriptions that include genus, species, variety, common name, foliage habit, hardiness zone, origin, plant uses, cultural conditions, and a description of the plant's habits, form, and site preference. Ships in small tubes or one- and five-gallon containers depending on variety and availability. Guarantees true to name. See **Conifers,** Fruit, **Grasses, Roses, Trees.**
Shipping season: All year.
Canada

THE FRAGRANT PATH
See Heirlooms, Herbs, **Seeds,** Trees.

FREY'S DAHLIAS
Bob and Sharon Frey
Catalog: Free, 8 pp.
The Freys offer tubers for over two hundred named dahlias. Descriptions include color, size, and style of flower for all, year of introduction for most. Offers several collections by size or form of flower composed of named varieties chosen by the Freys. Guarantees true to name tubers with live eyes, state inspected; will replace during the following April.
Shipping season: April.
Canada

GARDEN PERENNIALS
1981
Gail Korn
Catalog: $1 (recoverable), 32 pp.
Although Ms. Korn is quick to tell you that

she's smitten with daylilies (and grows upward of 750 kinds of them) she's fairly deep into several hundred types of herbaceous perennials. Her plants are field grown in northeast Nebraska and subject to nearly every kind of weather imaginable—sometimes in the same day. Selections have been grown and observed on-site for at least three years before being included in her catalog. Recent offerings included nine forms of *Achillea*, *Antennaria tomentosa* (pussy-toes), a dozen types of button mums, cushion mums, and *Chrysanthemum maximum*, eight varieties of *Coreopsis*, and numerous *Phlox* and *Sedum*. The catalog is organized by botanical name with common name given. Descriptions include hardiness zone, sun/shade requirements, cultural habit, season of bloom, color of flower, and if a variety is especially useful as a cutting flower. Also offers a "Best Ever Dried Bouquet" assortment that she will select, but you do have to plant them and dry them. Guarantees true to name and state inspected; will replace. See **Daylilies**, Grasses.

Shipping season: April through June. September and October.

GARDEN PLACE
1974
Kathy Sneary
Catalog: $1, 24 pp.
This division of Springbrook Nurseries offers over six hundred types of perennial. Their selection is broad based. Highlights from recent catalog include a dozen *Achillea*, eight *Ajuga*, a dozen *Anemone*, a dozen *Aquilegia*, thirteen *Artemisia*, thirty *Aster*, fifteen *Campanula*, twenty *Dianthus*, nine *Gypsophila* (*paniculata* and *repens*), eleven *Heuchera*, five *Iberis*, twenty *Papaver*, six *Platycodon*, twenty-two *Phlox* (*paniculata* and *stolonifera*), five *Santolina*, seventeen *Sedum*, six *Thymus* that creep and five that do not. Plants are briefly decribed including hardiness zone, height at maturity; and color of foliage and flower. Symbols indicate sun/shade preference and suitability for the cutting garden. Includes cross-indexes that group plants by their color, height at maturity; foliage habit; partiality to sun, shade, or light shade; and their suitability as cut flowers. Guarantees true to name and healthy upon arrival; will replace those that prove untrue. See **Grasses**.

Shipping season: September through May. Canada, Mexico

GARDENIMPORT
See **Booksellers**, **Bulbs**, Grasses, **Peonies**.

GARDENS OF THE BLUE RIDGE
See **Trees**, **Wildflowers**.

GARDENS NORTH
See **Grasses**, **Seeds**, Wildflowers.

GILBERT H. WILD & SON
See **Daylilies**, Heirlooms, **Iris**, **Peonies**.

GILSON GARDENS
1947
Catalog: Free, 32 pp.
Gilson specializes in ground covers and container plants. Their 180 offerings include several choices of *Clematis*, *Dianthus*, *Hedera*, *Hosta*, *Lamium*, *Parthenocissus*, *Potentilla*, *Sedum*, *Sempervivum*, and *Vinca*. Descriptions include height at maturity, sun/shade preferences, color of flower, foliage characteristics, and merit when used as a ground cover. Their eight-page pamphlet, "A Guide to Selecting and Using Ground Covers," is an informative and clearly written guide to the basics. The pamphlet includes salient information about soil characteristics, the effects of sun and shade, planting and spacing, mulching, winter exposure, growth habits, mixing varieties of ground covers, choosing the appropriate time to plant, site preparation, trimming and fertilizing, as well as lists of recommended plants for slopes, shady areas, open sun, and in between stones. See Conifers, Trees.

Shipping season: April through October.

GOODWIN CREEK GARDENS
1977
Jim and Dotti Becker
Catalog: $1, 39 pp.
The Beckers, coauthors of *An Everlasting Garden*, specialize in the plants and seeds of herbs, everlasting flowers, scented geraniums, and other fragrant plants. Five hundred varieties are offered, with some emphasis on those that attract hummingbirds and butterflies, and nursery propagated natives. Plants are pot-grown and shipped in a soilless medium. Brief descriptions include habit, height at maturity, and life cycle for all; notation about uses and hardiness for many. Brief informative pieces about plant selection for creating butterfly and hummingbird gardens. See **Booksellers**, **Herbs**, **Seeds**.

Shipping Season: March through June.

GREER GARDENS
See **Booksellers, Conifers,** Fruit, **Grasses, Peonies, Rhododendrons, Trees.**

GROWERS SERVICE CO.
1988
John K. Riordan
Catalog: $1, 40 to 56 pp. Subscription: $5 for five issues
Mr. Riordan describes his mail-order firm as a "wholesale bulb and flower club." Offers eight hundred perennials and ground covers purchased in lots and sold in varying quantities that permit individuals who subscribe to buy at off price. Selection is diverse and varies from issue to issue. Perennials are described as number one grade plants (with hardiness zone specified) or hardy field grown northern types suitable for conditions throughout the continental United States, Alaska, and Canada. Recent catalogs featured lots of *Achillea, Aconitum, Ajuga,* dwarf hardy asters, *Astilbe, Centaurea* (bachelor buttons), daylilies, *Dicentra* (bleeding hearts), *Geranium* (cranesbill), *Heuchera, Hosta,* lupines, *Phlox, Pulmonaria,* and *Tradescantia.* Descriptions include minimum number of plants per variety required per order, hardiness zone, height at maturity, color of flower, and garden and landscape uses. Also offers numerous collections in bulk. (Sample catalog is available for the price of postage to familiarize you with Growers Service's selection and tone.) Guarantees true to name and disease and pest free. See **Bulbs,** Waterscapes.
Shipping season: Spring through fall.
Canada

HAUSER'S SUPERIOR VIEW FARM
1928
Jim and Marilyn Hauser, Jim Hauser, Jr.
Catalog: Free, 8 pp.
If you make it to Hauser's Superior View Farm overlooking Lake Superior in Bayfield, Wisconsin, you will have a chance to see their mail-order barn, as well as their collections of miniature tractors, rustic farm implements, hats, and cans. You can pick apples in the autumn from one (or all) of their two thousand trees or revel in one of the largest spreads of northern field-grown perennials. If you're disinclined to leave your own backyard you can peruse their catalog of 180 offerings, 25 percent of which is devoted to chrysanthemums.

They present a balanced list of low-growing, mid-height, and cushion types, and a small number of taller varieties. Cultivars include Hauser and Superior bronze. Also offers a diverse selection of *Achillea, Aquilegia, Campanula, Delphinium, Heuchera, Liatris, and Rudbeckia.* Notes sun/shade preference and color.
Shipping season: April through mid-June. September and October.
Canada

HENRY FIELD'S SEED & NURSERY CO.
See **Fruit, Garlic, Kidstuff,** Organics, **Seeds, Supplies, Trees, Vegetables.**

HERONSWOOD NURSERY LTD.
1987
Daniel Hinkley and Robert L. Jones
Catalog: $4, 220 pp.
Heronswood characterizes its mission as procuring and offering plant materials that have not previously been available to North American gardeners. (Many of the observations, ruminations, and diary-like entries laced throughout the catalog have also rarely been seen by American gardeners.) Mr. Hinkley (author of *Winter Ornamentals*) and Mr. Jones list over 2,000 trees, shrubs, perennials, and grasses. Approximately 1,200 perennials are listed and described, occupying about 50 percent of the Heronswood catalog. Plant families that Mr. Hinkley and Mr. Jones have highlighted in their recent offerings include *Allium, Arisaema, Aster, Diascia,* hardy *Fuchsia,* hardy *Geranium, Hellebore, Heuchera, Monarda,* and *Pulmonaria.* Descriptions that presuppose some knowledge of cultural requirements include provenance, hardiness zone, pot size, and a highly visual narrative of the plants' form, color, and size. Guarantees true to name, healthy upon departure; will accept claims filed within ten days of receipt. See **Conifers,** Fruit, **Grasses, Rhododendrons, Trees.**
Shipping season: March through mid-May. Mid-September through October.
Canada

HESCHKE GARDENS
1990
David Heschke
Catalog: Free, 14 pp.
Mr. Heschke offers over eight hundred perennials through his catalog, with the major attention to *Astilbe,* daylilies, *Hosta, Lilium,* and peonies. Recent catalogs included one hundred astilbe from among the *Arendsii, chinen-*

sis, japonica, simplicifolia, and *Thunbergii* hybrids. Notes cultivar name, color of flower, characteristics of foliage, and height at maturity. Also offers unlabeled mixtures from each of the astilbe groups. See **Daylilies,** Grasses, Hosta, **Peonies.**
Shipping season: April through June.

A HIGH COUNTRY GARDEN
1993
David, Meg, and Bill Salman
Catalog: Free, 47 pp., color photographs
The 175 plants offered by the Salmans are grown at Santa Fe Greenhouses in New Mexico at an elevation of 7,000 feet. Their perennials, shrubs, cactus, and ornamental grasses are acclimated to conditions that include cold dry winters, windy springs, and hot summers under a searing sun. The catalog is organized into categories such as xeric water-thrifty plants, rock garden perennials, hardy garden perennials, and ground covers. Plants are grouped within their category by season of bloom and listed by botanical name with common name given. Descriptions include color of flower, soil preference, height and width of plant after two to four years of growth, sun/shade preference, water requirements, and attractiveness to hummingbirds. Varieties that are very xeric are highlighted. Brief essays and lists regarding soil preparation, plants to use between flagstones, long blooming perennials, rabbit and deer resistant plants, and how to reduce transplant shock appear throughout the catalog. Includes an index of plants by horticultural name and a glossary of common names. Guarantees true to name, state inspected, and survival during first sixty days; will replace or issue a refund. See Cactus, Grasses.
Shipping season: Mid-February through May. September through mid-November.

HILDENBRANDT'S IRIS GARDENS
See Hosta, **Iris, Peonies.**

HILLARY'S GARDEN
1991
John Russo
Catalog: $3 (recoverable), 20 pp.
A family-owned and -operated perennial flower and organic herb nursery where even the pet goose (the real Hillary) got into the act. The catalog presents 225 offerings (10 percent herbs). including a number of PPA "Plant of the Year"

and "All American Selections" such as *Penstemon Digitalis* 'Husker's Red', *Achillea millefoilium* 'Summer Pastels', *Coreopsis lanceolata* 'Early Sunrise', *Lavendula angustifolia* ' Lavender Lady', *Leucanthemum superbum* 'Snow lady', and *Veronica longifolia* 'Sunny Border Blue'. Catalog is organized into sections for sun-loving and shade-loving perennials, and one for herbs. Descriptions include common name, color of flower, height at maturity, spacing between plants, sun/shade requirements, season of bloom, hardiness zone, cultural habits, and garden use. Stock is grown outdoors, overwintered in Warwick, New York, and shipped in quart containers (except to bareroot states noted below). Guarantees satisfaction; will replace or refund. See Herbs, Organics.
Shipping season: March through October.
Bareroot only to Arizona, California, Florida, Idaho, Nevada, New Mexico, Oregon, Texas, Washington

HOMESTEAD FARMS
See **Daylilies, Hosta,** Iris, Peonies.

HORTICO, INC.
Bill Vanderkruk
Perennials catalog: $3, 42 pp.
This Hortico catalog includes over sixteen hundred ferns, wildflowers, bog plants, grasses, bamboos, ground covers, herbs, and herbaceous perennials. Hortico carries an extensive selection of named varieties within many families. Highlights from their areas of concentration include *Aconitum, Ajuga, Anemone hupehensis* (Japanese anemone) and *A. Pulsatilla* (pasqueflower), *Aquilegia, Armeria, Artemisia, Aster, Bergenia, Campanula, Chelone, Cimicifuga, Delphinium, Dianthus, Dicentra, Digitalis, Doronicum, Epimedium, Erigeron, Gentian, Geranium* (cranesbill), *Gypsophila, Helenium, Heliopsis, Hemerocallis, Heuchera, Hosta, Iris, Ligularia, Lilium, Penstemon, Phlox* (*P. paniculata, P. stolonifera,* and *P. subulata*), *Potentilla, Primula, Rodgersia, Rudbeckia, Salvia, Saxifraga, Scabiosa, Sedum, Sempervivum, Thalictrum, Tradescantia, Trollius, Veronica,* and *Viola.* Descriptions are clear but spare and geared toward the trade; however, this nursery wholesaler invites retail orders by fax or mail. Plants shipped in four-inch pots. Guarantees true to name and healthy when shipped. See **Grasses, Roses,** Trees, Waterscapes.
Shipping season: November through May.
Canada, International (Europe)

JACKSON & PERKINS
See Heirlooms, **Roses**.

JASPERSON'S HERSEY NURSERY
See **Daylilies, Iris,** Organics.

JOY CREEK NURSERY
Mike Smith and Scott Christy
Catalog: $2, 52 pp. Extended list: LSASE
Joy Creek Nursery grows perennials and ornamental grasses from seeds, cuttings, and divisions on-site in Scappoose, Oregon, where they are also overwintered. Seedlings and cuttings are raised in a soilless mixture. Their catalog includes five hundred offerings and their extended list includes upwards of six hundred additional plants. Plant families that Mr. Smith and Mr. Christy have highlighted in their recent offerings include milkweed (*Asclepias*), *Aster*, butterfly bush (*Buddleia*), *Campanula, Delphinium, Dianthus*, foxglove (*Digitalis*), spurge (*Euphorbia*), *Fuchsia, Inula, Ligularia, Lobelia*, beard-tongue (*Penstemon*), Cape fuchsia (*Phygelius*), *Sedum*, toad lily (*Tricyrtis*), and *Verbascum*. Descriptions include common name, sun/shade preference, hardiness zone, color of flower, height at maturity, season of bloom, and intermittent comments and observations. Extended list (get out your reference books) are by botanical name only. Plants shipped out of their pots with rootball intact. Guarantees safe arrival; will replace or refund. See **Grasses**.
Shipping season: Late February through mid-November.

J. W. JUNG SEED & NURSERY CO.
See **Bulbs, Fruit,** Garlic, **Kidstuff,** Seeds, Supplies, **Trees,** Vegetables.

KLEHM NURSERY
See **Booksellers, Daylilies, Hosta, Peonies**.

KURT BLUEMEL, INC.
1964
Catalog: $3, 49 pp., illustrations and color photographs
Mr. Bluemel, who has been an important advocate for the propagation and use of ornamental grasses in the garden and landscape, devotes almost half of his catalog to ground covers and perennials. Among the four hundred offerings, areas of concentration include *Acanthus, Achillea, Agapanthus, Ajuga*, Japanese anemone, *Aruncus, Asters, Astilbe, Caryopteris, Cimicifuga, Coreopsis, Dicentra, Epimedium, Filipendula, Geranium* (cranesbill), *Hibiscus, Liriope, Lythrum, Monarda, Papaver* (oriental poppies),

Pulmonaria, Salvia, Sedum, Tradescantia, and *Verbascum*. Plants are field grown and shipped bareroot. Guarantees true to name; will replace (claims for stock that does not survive must be made within five days of receipt). See **Grasses, Waterscapes**.
Shipping season: March through first frost in Baldwin, Maryland.
California ($250 minimum and some restrictions)
Canada, International ($250 minimum)

LAKESIDE ACRES
See **Daylilies, Hosta**.

LAMB NURSERIES
Catalog: Free, 75 pp.
Lamb Nurseries, located in the eastern Washington desert (zone 5) offers nine hundred perennials, rock plants, flowering shrubs, and hardy vines. Areas of concentration include *Aconite; Ajuga; Androsace* (rock jasmine); Japanese and species anemone; species and hybrid asters; *Arabis; Artemisia; Aubrieta; Campanula;* chrysanthemums (species, spoon, giant-flowered, cushion, button, cascade, and daisy types, as well as an extra hardy hybrid developed at the University of Montana; *Dicentra; Dianthus; Epimedium; Eupatorium;* geraniums (cranesbill); *Geum; Heuchera; Hypericum; Monarda;* large-flowered, shrubby evergreen, and barbatus penstemons; *Potentilla;* primroses; *Salvia; Sempervivum;* dwarf creeping and upright sedums; *Veronica;* cuccullata and fragrant *Violas;* and two *Zauschneria*. Narrative descriptions include color of flower, nature of foliage, and height at maturity. Guarantees safe arrival; will replace if notified of failure within ten days. See Grasses, **Trees**.
Shipping season: Spring and fall.
Canada

LAURIE'S GARDEN
See **Iris,** Waterscapes.

LAURIE'S LANDSCAPE
See **Hosta, Peonies,** Trees.

LEDGECREST GREENHOUSES AND GARDEN CENTER
1974
Paul Hammer
Catalog: Free, 9 pp.
Dr. Hammer, a Ph.D. in florlculture, offers 150 types of perennials shipped in three-inch plastic pots. Descriptions include color and form of flower, season of bloom, sun and soil require-

ments. Also offers several assortments for various sites grown at his Storrs, Connecticut, location. Guarantees true to name, in good condition; will replace or refund.
Shipping season: March and October.

LEE GARDENS
1988
Janis Lee
Catalog: $2 (recoverable), 32 pp.
The daylilies, hostas, and three hundred other perennials in the Lee Gardens catalog are described as having proven hardy through extreme heat and cold, moisture and drought. Offerings include a number of the 'Galaxy' series achillea, Biedermeier and four other aquilegia; twenty-five astilbe from among *A. arendsii, A. chinensis, A. japonica,* and *A. simplicifolia;* four *Cimicifuga—acerina, racemosa, ramosa,* and *simplex;* five *Filipendula;* five named varieties of *Monarda;* eighteen types of early, meadow, and tall garden phlox; four toad lilies; and five *Trillium*—white, prairie, toad, *undulatum,* and yellow wood trillium. Descriptions are brief and include hardiness zone, height at maturity, color of flower, and (where appropriate) noteworthy foliage. Ships bareroot. Guarantees true to name and safe arrival. See **Daylilies, Hosta.**
Shipping season: April through first frost in Tremont, Illinois.

LILY OF THE VALLEY HERB FARM
1982
Paul and Melinda Carmichael
Catalog: $1 (recoverable), 32 pp.
The Carmichaels grow four hundred perennials and everlastings, four hundred herbs, and eighty scented geraniums on their farm in Minerva, Ohio. Areas of concentration include *Celosia,* columbine (*Aquilegia*), *Clematis, Dianthus,* cone flower (*Echinacea*), baby's breath (*Gypsophila*), globe amaranth, *Statice,* and straw flower. Brief descriptions include botanical name, life cycle, sun/shade requirements, and height at maturity. Seed packets (one hundred seeds per packet) are available for a few of their offerings and are so noted. Plants shipped on soilless medium in containers. Guarantees true to name and healthy. See **Herbs,** Seeds.
Shipping season: Mid-April through July.

MARYLAND AQUATIC NURSERIES, INC.
See **Waterscapes.**

MATTERHORN NURSERY, INC.
See **Conifers,** Grasses, **Rhododendrons, Trees, Waterscapes.**

MELLINGER'S
See **Booksellers, Furniture, Kidstuff, Seeds, Supplies,** Wildflowers.

MILAEGER'S GARDENS
1960
Kevin D. Milaeger
Catalog: $1, 84 pp., color photographs
A rich and diverse catalog of 1,100 herbaceous perennials that each seem to be presented with an even hand. Areas of concentration include *Aconitum, Anemone, Aquilegia, Aster, Astilbe, Bergenia, Campanula, Cimicifuga, Coreopsis, Delphinium, Digitalis, Echinacea,* ferns, *Geranium* (cranesbill), *Heuchera, Hosta, Liatris, Monarda, Penstemon, Phlox, Pulmonaria, Rudbeckia, Salvia, Sedum, Thalictrum, Tiarella,* and *Veronica.* Excellent cultural information, desirable characteristics, and natural history precede the descriptions of individual offerings that include hardiness zone, height and spread at maturity, color of flower, and sun/shade preference. Also offers a three-season cutting garden, a fernery collection, and numerous collections of the various perennial families. Guarantees true to name, disease free, and safe arrival; will replace. See **Booksellers, Grasses, Kidstuff,** Peonies.
Shipping season: April through September.

MINIATURE PLANT KINGDOM
1965
Don and Becky Herzog
Catalog: $2.50, 42 pp.
The two hundred perennials and alpines (comprising 30 percent of their catalog) offered by the Herzogs are miniature forms that are suitable for garden railroads, trough gardens, and screes. Descriptions (including general notes about hardiness) include site, sun/shade, and cultural requirements. Plants are available in $2^7/_8$-inch pots, some in larger sizes. See **Conifers,** Fruit, **Grasses, Trees.**
Shipping season: Spring and fall.
Canada, Mexico, International

MISSOURI WILDFLOWERS NURSERY
See Grasses, Seeds, **Wildflowers.**

MOSTLY NATIVES NURSERY
See **Grasses,** Trees, **Wildflowers.**

MT. TAHOMA NURSERY
1986
Rick Lupp
Catalog: $1, 24 pp.
Mr. Lupp is a hobbyist turned nurseryman who developed his interest in alpines, rock garden and woodland plants while hiking and climbing in the high areas of the Pacific Northwest and South America. Eighty-five percent of his catalog is devoted to four hundred perennials noted as suitable (variously) for bogs, rock gardens, screes, troughs, and the alpine house. The descriptions in this botanical name–only catalog includes sun/shade requirements, color and form of flowers, growth habit, and season of bloom. Most plants shipped in $2^1/_4$-inch by $3^1/_2$-inch rose pots. Some shipped out of pots with root ball intact. Guarantees safe arrival; will adjust for claims made within five days of receipt. See Grasses.
Shipping season: March through June. September through November.
Canada

NICHE GARDENS
See Trees, **Wildflowers.**

THE ONION MAN
See **Seeds.**

PERENNIAL PLEASURES NURSERY OF
VERMONT
1980
Judith and Rachel Kane
Catalog: $3 (recoverable), 64 pp.
The Kanes grow heirloom flowering plants and herbs using organic methods. Their catalog is organized into chapters covering the seventeenth through the twentieth centuries. One hundred and forty varieties of flowers are arranged according to their time of introduction or common appearance in American (eastern) gardens. Selected annuals and biennials that have been started in late winter are shipped in their packs in spring. Field-grown perennials that have overwintered in Vermont are shipped bareroot. Herbs in a separate section. Rich historical information, context of use, cultural information, and description of plant for each offering. Colonial dye plant, potpourri, and a collection of seventeenth-century "simples" are among the period and specialty assortments offered. Each contain perennials, prestarted annuals, seeds, planting instructions, and plans appropriate for an area

of twelve square feet. Guarantees true to name and healthy; will replace or issue refund at nursery's discretion. See **Booksellers**, Grasses, Heirlooms, **Herbs**, Organics, **Seeds.**
Shipping season: April and May. September and October.
No California

PLANT DELIGHTS NURSERY
1988
Tony and Michelle Avent
Catalog: $2, 117 pp., color illustrations and photographs
Plant Delights was started to support the test and demonstration gardens at Juniper Level Botanic Gardens. The purpose now is to search out new and better perennials and introduce this plant material into the trade. Plant Delights has five thousand varieties on site and is continuing to expand. If you can stop chuckling while reading their catalog (Mr. Avent could have a career in comedy writing if the nursery fails), you will find one of the most diverse and rich concentrations of plant life available to the home gardener. Perennials occupy about 75 percent of their annual book and it would be impossible here to list even the highlighted groups and families. Your gardening curiosity should be piqued (and rewarded) by the fact that they offer a dozen *Buddleia,* a rare climbing yellow flowered bleeding heart (*Dicentra scandens* 'Athens Yellow'), two dozen *Heuchera* and *Heucheralla,* eight *Lobelia,* and twenty-one *Salvia.* Descriptions are rich but even-handed and include sun/shade preference, hardiness zone, height at maturity, place of origin, nature of foliage and flower, season of bloom, cultural requirements, and site preference. Guarantees true to name and safe arrival. See **Conifers, Grasses, Hosta,** Trees.
Shipping season: March through November.
Canada, Mexico, International

PORTERHOWSE FARMS
1979
Don Howse
Catalog: $4 (recoverable), 80 pp., illustrations
Mr. Howse's collection emphasizes dwarf and unusual conifers, plants for bonsai culture, and nine hundred alpine and rock garden perennials—all nursery propagated in containers. Seventy-five percent of Mr. Howse's perennials listing are saxifrages, including mossy types *(Dactyloides),* silver and encrusted types *(Eu-*

aizoonia), kabschia and engleria (*Porophyllium*) and their hybrids, and other assorted varieties; as well as sedums, *Sempervivum,* and *Jovibarba.* Descriptions (many narrative, others in information-packed codes) includes hardiness zone; place of origin; color, form, and texture of flower and foliage; and size of plant being offered. Also offers collections of named sempervivum, alpines (for rock gardens, scree beds, and troughs), and bonsai companion plants. Guarantees true to name and safe arrival; will replace or refund for claims made within ten days of receipt. See **Conifers**, Trees.
Shipping season: March through June. September through November.
Canada, Mexico, International

POWELL'S GARDENS
1952
Loleta Kenan Powell
Catalog: $3.50 (recoverable), 60 pp.
There are over five thousand listings in this formidable catalog that includes daylilies, hostas, irises, and seventeen hundred other perennials with a southern flair owing to their Princeton, North Carolina location. Organized by botanical name (common name given for most), Powell's broad-based selection is strengthened by their concentrations in numerous families and groups, including *Achillea, Ajuga, Artemisia, Aster, Astilbe, Coreopsis, Dianthus,* ferns, *Heuchera, Kniphofia, Liriope, Lythrum, Monarda, Phlox, Pulmonaria, Salvia, Saponaria, Sedum, Thymus,* and *Verbena.* Information for each listing includes a key indicating border plant, rock garden plant, useful as a ground cover, and sun/shade preference. Descriptions range from a few words about color and height to those that are insightful and intimate. See Conifers, **Daylilies**, **Hosta**, **Iris**, Peonies, Trees.
Shipping season: March and April. September and October.
Canada, Mexico, International

PRAIRIE RIDGE NURSERY
See Grasses, Seeds, **Wildflowers**.

THE PRIMROSE PATH
1985
Charles and Martha Oliver
Catalog: $2, 48 pp., illustrations
The Olivers list 330 nursery propagated perennials, woodland and native plants, and alpines organized by botanical name. They list species and hybrids from the United States, Europe, Japan, and the Himalayas, while maintaining an active hybridization and breeding program of their own that has developed cultivars of *Heuchera* and *Tiarella.* Areas of concentration at Primrose Path include *Primula* in the vernales, oreophlomis, and candelabra groups; cranesbill; *Heuchera;* and border, meadow, and smaller woodland phlox. Broad cultural notes about those genera for which they offer a large selection. Descriptions are chatty and include common names, form and color of flower and foliage, height at maturity, and general habit. Guarantees true to name and healthy upon receipt. See Wildflowers.
Shipping season: March through May. September through December.

PUTNEY NURSERY, INC.
See Herbs, Seeds, **Wildflowers**.

REATH'S NURSERY
See **Peonies**.

ROBYN'S NEST NURSERY
1989
Robyn Duback
Catalog: $2 (recoverable), 32 pp., illustrations
A home-based nursery that features 300 hosta and 250 other perennials, ferns, and grasses for sun and shade, including: thirty-six forms of *Astilbe,* fifteen forms of cranesbill, a kaffir lily (*Schizostylis coccinea,* a fall blooming member of the iris family), three forms of toad lily (*Tricyrtis),* and a sun-drinking native of Tasmania, *Wahlenbergia saxicola.* Evocative descriptions complement clear cultural information and specifications. All native plants are nursery propagated. Guarantees true to name, certified pest and disease free. See **Hosta**, Grasses.
Shipping season: May through October.

ROSLYN NURSERY
1984
Dr. Philip Waldman
Catalog: $3, 76 pp., color photographs
Roslyn Nursery houses two thousand varieties of trees, shrubs, perennials, grasses, rhododendrons, and azaleas. Twenty percent of the catalog is devoted to 550 perennials. Areas of concentration include *Ajuga, Anemone, Arisaema, Astilbe, Campanula, Gentiana, Geranium* (cranesbill), *Heuchera, Lamium, Lobelia, Platycodon, Pulmonaria, Tiarella,* and *Viola.*

Brief narrative descriptions include plant's shape, color, habit, distinguishing characteristics, uses in the garden, and hardiness zone. Perennials shipped in 4$^{1}/_{2}$-inch pots. Guarantees true to name and healthy; will replace or issue a credit if plant fails within thirty days of receipt. See **Booksellers, Conifers, Rhododendrons, Trees.**
Shipping season: April through June. September through November. Bareroot (Arizona and California only), Mid-March Canada, Mexico, International

RUSSELL GRAHAM: PURVEYOR OF PLANTS
See **Wildflowers.**

SHADY OAKS NURSERY
1980
Dr. Clayton Oslund
Catalog: $1 (bulk) $2.50 FC, 46 pp., color photographs
The Oslunds found it a challenge to obtain perennials that would thrive under the shade of their spreading oak trees. Having done the research, and perceiving that the desire to establish attractive and diverse plantings in various degrees of shade was not unique to them, the Oslunds opened Shady Oaks. The catalog includes four hundred flowering garden and woodland perennials, ferns, and a concentration of hostas. Recent catalogs highlighted several varieties of monkshood (*Aconitum*), ten types of columbine (*Aquilegia*) including the 'Vivid Song Bird' series, three meadowsweet (*Filipendula*), seven lungworts (*Pulmonaria*) seven toad lilies (*Tricyrtis*), and four *Trilliums*. Descriptions include botanical and common names, shape and color of foliage and flowers, site and light conditions. The shade-tolerance guide describes five types of situations emphasizing that shade is a continuum and cannot be put into distinct categories. A number of essays, including one on deep-shade gardening, reinforce the diversity and flexibility of plant life in subtle light conditions. Guarantees true to name and successful in your garden if planted within appropriate hardiness zone; will replace, issue credit, or refund. See **Booksellers, Grasses, Hosta.**
Shipping season: March through September International: Bareroot or soilless media.
No California

SHOOTING STAR NURSERY

See **Grasses, Seeds, Waterscapes, Wildflowers.**

SISKIYOU RARE PLANT NURSERY
1963
Baldassare Mineo
Catalog: $2 (recoverable), 74 pp.
Siskiyou lists over eight hundred rock garden and alpine perennials, shrubs, wildflowers, ferns, and dwarf conifers of the four thousand plants under cultivation at the nursery. There are simply too many areas of concentration to list; however, some of the high spots (but not all) include a deep assortment of *Campanula, Dianthus, Draba,* cranesbill, *Lewisia,* penstemons, *Phlox, Potentilla, Saxifraga:* (silver, encrusted and porophyllum) and *Veronica.* Rich descriptions include color of flower and foliage, growth habit, uses in the rock garden. Culture codes note light requirements, scree, soil conditions (sandy, loam, or average), and moisture requirements. Offers collections for various needs and conditions. Will provide lists of recommended subjects for specific purposes: woodland, summer flowering, alpine house culture, troughs and containers, peat beds, drought tolerant, and silver- and gray-foliaged plants. Plants are grown from cuttings and raised in containers. Guarantees correctly labeled and safe arrival; must notify within five days of receipt if plant unsatisfactory. See **Booksellers, Conifers, Trees.**
Shipping season: All year.
Canada

SOUTHERN PERENNIALS & HERBS
1987
Barbara and Michael Bridges
Catalog: Retail: $3 (recoverable), 22 pp.
The Bridges specialize in herbaceous plants for the deep South. Almost all (97 percent by their reckoning) of their one thousand (plus) plant varieties are propagated at their Gulf South nursery in Tylertown, Mississippi. Descriptions are sensitive to performance in the South in addition to noting height, habit, season and profusion of bloom, and cultural requirements. Symbols denote sun/shade preference, dry site and bog plants, attractive to hummingbirds or butterflies, and if a plant is useful as a cut flower. See **Herbs.**
Shipping season: All year. (Not all types of plants available throughout the year. Check for availability).

STERRETT GARDENS
See **Daylilies**.

SUNNYBROOK FARMS
See Herbs, **Hosta**.

SURRY GARDENS
1978
James M. Dickinson
Catalog: $1.50, 8 pp.
Mr. Dickinson offers six hundred perennials, herbs, and grasses variously sown from seed or vegetatively propagated. The catalog is in chart form and differentiates plant materials as herbs, grasses, border, rock garden, and wild garden perennials. Areas of concentration include *Aquilegia, Campanula, Geranium* (cranesbill), *Primula,* and *Veronica.* Descriptive key notes hardiness zone, season of bloom, sun/shade requirements, height at maturity, soil preferences, color of flower and characteristics of leaves. Ships in 2$\frac{1}{2}$-by-3-inch pots. Guarantees true to name, safe arrival; will replace or refund. See **Grasses**.
Shipping season: May through June. September and October.

TISCHLER PEONY GARDEN
See **Peonies**.

TRANS-PACIFIC NURSERY
See **Booksellers**, Bulbs, **Trees, Waterscapes**.

TRIPPLE BROOK FARM
See Fruit, **Grasses**, Trees, **Wildflowers**.

VAN BOURGONDIEN BROS.
See **Bulbs**.

WAVECREST NURSERY AND LANDSCAPING
See **Booksellers, Conifers, Grasses, Trees**.

WAYSIDE GARDENS
See Fruit, Heirlooms, Grasses, **Roses**.

WE-DU NURSERY
See **Bulbs**, Iris, **Wildflowers**.

WEISS BROTHERS PERENNIAL NURSERY
1972
Martin Weiss
Catalog: Free, 24 pp., color photographs
Four hundred varieties of hardy perennials grown and shipped in pots. Recent catalogs highlighted *Achillea, Artemisia, Caryopteris, Centranthus, Deutzia, Dianthus, Euphorbia, Hibiscus, Iberis, Lobelia, Lupines, Platycodon, Teucrium,* and *Zauschneria.* Hardiness zone, height at maturity, color, season of bloom, sun/shade requirements for each listing. See Herbs, Grasses.
Shipping season: March through June.
August through October

WHITE FLOWER FARM
1950
Steve Frowine
Catalog: Free, 146 pp., color photographs
White Flower Farm is a family-owned nursery in Litchfield, Connecticut, whose catalog is beautifully presented and among the most clearly written that we've read. About 60 percent of their spring book, and about 40 percent of their fall edition, is devoted to four hundred hardy (some tender and some annuals) perennials. White Flower presents a broad range of perennial families for which (in most cases) they catalog a select number of varieties that seem well considered. Evocative descriptions accompany all of their offerings. Specifications including color, hardiness zone, height of mature plant, season of bloom, light and soil preference, spacing; fragrant varieties and suitability for use as a cut flower appear in a separate selection-and-planting chart. One of the many strengths of this catalog is the numerous collections and samplers that are not limited to offerings from the same family but accent garden design, and companion and complementary plantings such as their "Beginner's Border," "Welcome to Summer Collection," "A Garden Path," "A Garden of White and Purple Shades," "Moonbeams and Mallows," "A Northern Exposure Collection," and an all white "Moon Garden." Plants shipped variously bareroot and in pots. Guarantees true to name, in prime condition for growing, and delivered at the proper time for planting; will replace one time only any plant that has been properly cared for but failed to grow. See **Bulbs**, Fruit, **Roses**, Supplies, Trees, **Waterscapes**.
Shipping season: Spring and fall.
Canada

THE WILDWOOD FLOWER
circa 1980
Thurman Maness
Catalog: LSASE, 8 pp.

Among the sixty garden and or wildflowers, shrubs, and ferns in Mr. Maness's broadside are his own introductions including lobelia 'Ruby Slippers', which received wide attention soon after its introduction in 1989. His list includes other *Lobelia*, tricolored painted ferns, a half dozen cultivated *Phlox* and thirty hydrangeas. See Trees.
Shipping season: April through June.

WINDROSE
See **Trees**.

YORK HILL FARM
See **Daylilies**, Grasses, Heirlooms, **Hosta**, Iris.

YUCCA DO NURSERY AT PECKERWOOD GARDENS
See **Cactus, Conifers**, Grasses, Organics, **Trees, Wildflowers**.

Selected Reading About Perennials

Designing with Perennials, by Pamela Harper. Ms. Harper provides explanations about the principles of garden design and plant combinations as well as the use of color, depth, texture, and height in the creation of beds, borders, and foundations. Includes sections on mixed beds and the use of perennials as ground cover. Includes 300 color photographs.

English Cottage Gardening for American Gardeners, by Margaret Hensel. Foreword by Tasha Tudor. Using examples of successful adaptive planting in gardens created by nonprofessional gardeners Ms. Hensel offers plans and suggests appropriate plants for cottage gardens in diverse regions and under varying conditions. Includes over 200 color photographs.

Further Along the Garden Path: A Beyond-the-Basics Guide to the Gardening Year, by Ann Lovejoy. Using examples from backyard gardens that have been grown and maintained (primarily by their owners who are not gardening professionals), this volume gives practical advice on how to overcome gardening obstacles and offers a sophisticated eye toward plant selection. Includes 150 color photographs.

Gardening with Perennials Month by Month, by Joseph Hudak. This practical guide for North American gardeners includes monthly blooming schedules and growing requirements for over seven hundred species and their cultivars. Each month (March through September) of blooming perennials includes an extensive list of plant choices arranged by the color of their flower. Includes 435 color photographs.

Hardy Herbaceous Perennials, by Leo Jelitto, Wilhelm Schacht, and Alfred Fessler. Translated by Michael Epp. This two-volume masterwork covers 800 genera; 4,286 species, subspecies, varieties, and hybrids; and 3,600 cultivars. Considered by many in the plant world to be the most comprehensive and greatest perennial plant encyclopedia. Includes hardiness zones. 690 color photographs.

Herbaceous Perennial Plants: A Treatise on Their Identification, Culture, and Garden Attributes, by Allan M. Armitage. In-depth text on more than 2,600 types of herbaceous perennials includes scientific, common, and family names; size; ornamental characteristics; adaptability range; culture; propagation; and use. Ninety-six color photographs and 160 drawings.

Perennials: Toward Continuous Bloom, Edited by Ann Lovejoy. A symposium in book form moderated by Ms. Lovejoy. Gardeners from across the United States share information, inspiration, and memories pertaining to design, color, and climatic considerations in the planting and maintenance of perennials. Includes an index to over 700 plants.

Perennials for American Gardens, by Ruth Rogers Clausen and Nicolas H. Erikson. This A to Z volume (includes 3,000 plants in over 400 genera) notes height, spread, habit, color, season of bloom, sun/shade requirements, companion plantings, and propagation methods for each entry. Includes 360 color photographs.

Perennial Garden Plants, or The Modern Florilegium, by Graham Stuart Thomas. An insightful and very useful examination by a dean of gardening writers. Covers 2,000 perennials including spacing, color, season of bloom, propagation, and cultivation.

The Random House Book of Perennials: Volume I, Early Perennials, and *Volume II, Late Perennials*. by Roger Phillips and Martyn Rix. Each volume includes 1,250 species and superior varieties richly described in words and matching color photographs.

DAYLILIES

HEMEROCALLIS: THE DAYLILY

*P*opularity over several millennia has given rise to a modern-day dilemma for the genus *Hemerocallis*. Before the dawn of written history, the daylily's culinary and medicinal benefits were well known in China. Many centuries later, by way of Europe, early settlers carried daylilies across North America, where they naturalized them in the wild. Today, the daylily's image remains synonymous with the ancient lemon yellow or tawny orange species growing in roadside ditches, on railroad embankments, and beside great-grandmother's outhouse. Its very name suggests two misconceptions: that it is a brief-flowering perennial, and that it is a true lily bulb of the genus *Lilium*. The modern daylily is held hostage by its heritage. Don't be fooled!

True, its botanical name translates to "beauty-for-a-day," but bloom stalks (called scapes) of this fibrous-rooted perennial may have dozens of flower buds opening over a period of weeks. With many scapes per established clump, a well-branched variety can have hundreds of blooms a season. In addition, some have continuous or separate periods of rebloom. Modern hybrids, while generally peaking in midsummer, can bloom from late spring into autumn.

After decades of painstaking hybridization to unlock the hidden potential of the species, we see unprecedented progress today, mostly by amateur breed-ers. Vibrant-colored cultivars of the old "ditch lily" are now widely available: from near white, through all shades and blends of yellow, pink, melon, or-ange, scarlet, black-red, and lavender, to deep velvety purple. Dramatic pat-terns are emerging, too. Imagine a flower with a green throat radiating onto diamond-dusted cream petals, possibly surrounded by multiple bands of con-trasting colors, culminating in silver or gold edges with piecrust fluting. Exhil-arating!

The daylily's image is being revamped by selective breeding for height, form, and bloom size. Once very tall, most are now scaled to heights popular in home gardens, ranging from ten-inch edging plants to two or three feet for midborder. Narrow, pointy-petaled, trumpet-shaped blooms reminiscent of true lilies have generally given way to flatter, more rounded blooms with wider, overlapping petals. Diversity is served by peony style "doubles"; flam-boyant "spiders" with long, twisting, pinched flower segments; and flower diameters from under two inches to nearly dinner plate size.

Bareroot daylilies can safely ship for planting almost any time the ground is workable. In the northern climates, spring planting is usually preferable, with fall serving best elsewhere. Foliage habit, which ranges from dormant to evergreen, does not determine cold-hardiness. This makes it advisable to obtain plants and counsel from local specialists who will know those that adapt best to an area.

Light-colored daylilies prefer full- to half-day sun. The darker varieties welcome light afternoon shade. Most comfortable in fertile, well-drained, slightly acid soil (pH 6 to 6.5), they will, however, adapt to sandy or clay soils. Normally, a single spring application of a good perennial plant food will suffice, although an application of low-nitrogen fertilizer in early fall promotes good root growth and plant increase. They thrive on an inch of water per week. Pests and diseases do exist but are relatively easy to control without the use of chemicals.

Superb as individual specimens or in collections, there are few more versatile landscape plants. Envision sweeping masses of coordinated hot or cool colors undulating over the garden. Imagine the shimmering reflections of fragrant, nocturnal blossoms beside a pool at twilight. Consider that as foundation plantings they can complement the color of any dwelling. Container-grown plants open endless possibilities to the apartment dweller or to those who wish to force winter blooms in the greenhouse. The practical minded will see them as a ground cover for erosion control.

Daylilies love companions. Interplanted with daffodils, their emerging foliage conceals the fading spring bulbs. In season, enhance the daylily's smooth, slender, deep green foliage with complementary colors, shapes, and textures. Phlox, balloon flowers, daisies, coneflowers, artemisias, lamb's ear, stokesias, and hostas are just a few of the plants that look good in their company.

The ease with which one can breed daylilies is a seductive bonus. This can prolong the joy of the season as you plan your "pollen dabbing," make crosses, collect and plant seed, and anticipate your very own blooms in one to three years.

Purchasing hemerocallis from specialist sources will help you avoid un-named seedlings or decades-old staples of the trade. Many locales have clubs, an invaluable source of information and inexpensive—if not free—plants. The American Hemerocallis Society, to which most daylily specialists belong, is the ideal source for additional information. Long a culinary feast, it is the visual feast of the modern daylily that whets the appetite.

—Ken Cobb

(Ken Cobb is a recent president [1994–95] of the American Hemerocallis Society, director of its Carolina region, and an exhibition judge and clinic instructor. He has edited several AHS publications and is a frequent author of articles on the subject of daylilies.)

The cultivar count cited in each profile is based on information in the most recent catalog provided by the source. In this section, shipping season is for hemerocallis only. A selection of books about daylilies appears after the last listing.

QUICK FIND
The following sources are listed in this section:

ADAMGROVE
Eric and Bob Tankesley-Clarke
Catalog: $3 (two-year subscription), 68 pp.,
black-and-white and color photographs
The plants at Adamgrove endure the stresses
that are characteristic of "open winters": modest snow cover, temperatures that hover near
zero, and a windchill factor that replicates temperatures of 40 to 50 degrees below zero. Current introductions of the Tankesley-Clarkes'
large-flowered, small, miniature-flowered, and
double-flowered daylilies are presented in separate sections. Four hundred and fifty daylilies
(20 percent tetraploids) are well described.
Classification and cultural information is set
off from the main text. The glossary and basic
botanical illustrations are useful in clarifying
nomenclature. Hybridizer, year of introduction, height and season of bloom, foliage
habit, bloom diameter, and awards won noted
for all. Guarantees true to name and safe arrival. See **Iris.**
**Shipping season: May. August and Septem-
ber.**
Canada, Mexico, International

ALCOVY DAYLILY FARM
Jesse and Mary Lois Burgess
Catalog: Free, 14 pp.
Seven hundred cultivars (20 percent tetraploids) of the two thousand grown here are
listed in the catalog. Descriptions include
bloom size, color, height, time of bloom, and
foliage habit. Guarantees true to name and safe
arrival.
Shipping season: April through October.

AMERICAN DAYLILY & PERENNIALS
1976
Jack and Jo Roberson
Catalog: $3 (recoverable), 40 pp., color
photographs
American Daylily & Perennials introduced
'Black-eyed Stella', the first All-America daylily, a
hybrid noteworthy for its extremely long season
of bloom. Their informative catalog lists 145 (8
percent tetraploids) varieties of hemerocallis developed by the Robersons and by a select group
of breeders. Hybridizer, year of introduction for
most. Height, season of bloom, rebloom, and foliage habit precedes a detailed description and
cultural advice. Special notation for many cultivars specifying the number of days in bloom and
the number of divisions increased each year from

All-America test beds on-site. Supplementing the
alphabetical listing is an index that groups rebloomers, fragrant varieties, doubles, award winners, spider variants, miniatures, large bloomers,
and tetraploids. Offers several collections. Guarantees true to name, state inspected, and to grow
and bloom after one year; will replace. See **Peonies,** Perennials.
Shipping season: April through October.

THE AMERICAN HEMEROCALLIS SOCIETY
See **Horticultural Societies.**

ANDERSON IRIS GARDENS
1978
Sharol and George Longaker
Catalog: $1, 21 pp.
The main event in this catalog is the five hun-
dred-plus tall bearded iris. The Andersons do
offer fifty-five hybrid hemerocallis (30 percent
tetraploids). Name, color, and season of
bloom. See **Iris, Peonies,** Perennials.
Shipping season: July through September.

ANDRÉ VIETTE FARM & NURSERY
1920
Mark, André and Claire Viette
Catalog: $3, 44 pp., color photographs
The Viettes have been growing and selling
herbaceous perennials for over seventy years.
One hundred daylilies are offered in this rich
and varied catalog. Descriptions in the Viettes'
introductions are detailed. Descriptions for all
daylilies include hybridizer, size of flower, color,
and height of scape. Offers field-grown unlabeled assortments from their own breeding program (more than one hundred divisions) and
labeled assortments in quantities of twenty-five
or more divisions. Assortments shipped bareroot. See **Grasses, Hosta, Perennials.**
Shipping season: March through November.

APSHER'S PERENNIAL HAVEN
1987
Vern and Helen Apsher
Catalog $2, 20 pp.
Having retired from earlier careers, and traveled
much of the central and midwestern United
States, the Apshers settled down into what they
expected would be gardening-as-hobby. One
plant led to another, however, so they went into
the nursery business. Their catalog describes their
own current diploid introductions in detail. A
general section of six hundred modern hybrids

(60 percent tetraploids) from well-known breeders includes hybridizer, height, size of flower, and color.
Shipping season: April and May. August and September.

ARTEMIS GARDENS
1989
Cynthia E. Hyde
Catalog: $1 (recoverable), 23 pp., illustrations
Artemis Gardens specializes in small-flowered and miniature daylilies that are adapted to the cold winters and/or cool summer nights typical of some northern growing conditions. Daylilies grown here for several years are evaluated for winter-hardiness, the ability of foliage to withstand late spring frosts, vigor, the ability of flowers to open fully after cool summer nights (45 to 55 degrees), and beauty of bloom. Offers thirty cultivars. Notes hybridizer, year of introduction, height, foliage habit, size of bloom, descriptive and cultural information, and awards won. Guarantees true to name and success in your garden; will replace. See **Iris.**
Shipping season: May and June.
No Alaska or Hawaii

BARTH DAYLILIES
1971
Nicholas and Sandra G. Barth
Catalog: 1 FCS, 4 pp.
In the early 1950s, Dr. Joseph Barth became interested in the beauty and hardiness of the common orange daylily he observed on his farm in Alna, Maine. He began hybridizing, with the goal of cultivating the ultimate red tetraploid daylily. Beginning in 1971, hybridizing almost became his full-time avocation. Since Dr. Barth's death in 1988, eldest son Nicholas and his wife, Sandra, have continued hybridizing and growing hemerocallis. Seventeen Barth varieties are among the sixty registered daylilies in a catalog that primarily offers tetraploids. Hybridizer, bloom size, foliage, time of bloom, height, and date of registration are included. Collections of unnamed varieties are offered in four color groups.
Shipping season: May and June. August.

THE BLOOMING HILL
1986
Jerry and Lela Hadrava
Catalog: $1 (recoverable), 32 pp.

Soil conditions at The Blooming Hill range from almost pure sand to clay, from full sun to heavy shade. Daylilies and hostas are the main pursuit. Nine hundred hemerocallis varieties (50 percent tetraploids) occupy half the catalog. Offerings from numerous sources were registered in the 1970s, 1980s, and early 1990s. Hybridizer, year of introduction, foliage habit, height, bloom size, period of bloom, daily period of bloom, rebloom, and color noted for each. Offers a landscaping and a starter special composed of named cultivars. See **Hosta, Iris.**
Shipping season: May. August and September.

BLOOMINGFIELDS FARM
1969
Lee and Diana Bristol
Catalog: Free, 18 pp., illustrations
Bloomingfields is certified organic by the Northeast Organic Farming Association. The Bristols do not use herbicides or pesticides. The catalog offers 125 of the five hundred cultivars grown on trial at the farm. The Bristols had home gardeners in mind when they decided to organize their catalog by color group, sequentially listing cultivars in eight bloom seasons within each. Clear cultural and planting advice. Hybridizer, height, season and size of bloom, period of bloom. Evocative description for each offering. A wide range of collections and special offers for the collector and the landscaper. Guarantees true to name and will grow in your garden; will replace or issue refund. See **Organics.**
Shipping season: April through November.

BLOSSOM VALLEY GARDENS
1982
Sanford Roberts
Catalog: $1, 12 pp.
The catalog is accompanied by an engaging eight-page riff on music, art, culture in general, and the culture of the daylily specifically. Award-winning hybridizer Sanford Roberts offers two hundred cultivars (99.9 percent tetraploids), including an extensive selection of his own introductions. Specifications and creatively detailed descriptions for current and recent registrations. The general listing includes the previous introductions of a select group of hybridizers. Hybridizer, height, season of bloom, rebloom, foliage habit, color, and short description for each.

Shipping season: March through May.
September and October.

BUSSE GARDENS
See Grasses, **Hosta**, **Peonies**, **Perennials**, Wildflowers.

CAPE IRIS GARDENS
See **Iris**.

CAPRICE FARM NURSERY
1980
Dot, Al, and Rick Rogers, and Robin Blue
Catalog: $2 (recoverable), 36 pp., color
photographs
The Rogerses are members of the All-America Daylily Selection Council. They offer fifty carefully considered modern selections (15 percent tetraploids). Plants have grown for three to four years at Caprice before being offered. Hybridizer, extent of bloom and rebloom (as it applies), season of bloom, foliage habit, height, bud count, color, awards, and brief description for each. Also notes cultivars that typically open well after cool nights. Year of registration for some. Guarantees true to name and survival through first season; will replace. See Hosta, **Iris**, **Peonies**, Perennials.
Shipping season: April through October.
Canada, Mexico, International

CARROLL GARDENS
1933
Alan L. Summers
Catalog: $3 (recoverable), 108 pp.
Carroll Gardens in Westminster, Maryland, devotes 70 percent of its catalog to seventeen hundred perennials. One hundred and sixty daylilies, both new cultivars and time-tested standards, are offered. Descriptions include color and size of flower, season of bloom, and height at maturity. Offers a small-flowered and large-flowered collection, and a mixture of named, but unlabeled, varieties for landscaping. Guarantees true to name, ready to grow, and safe arrival (California, Oregon, and Washington true to name only); will replace one time only. See **Herbs**, **Hosta**, Iris, **Peonies**, Perennials, Roses, Trees.
Shipping season: March through November.
Canada

CASCADE BULB & SEED CO.
See Bulbs, **Seeds**.

CAT'S PAW GARDENS
1987
Tom and Gail Moore
Catalog: Free, 18 pp.
Yes, those are Jonah Moore's paw prints on the cover of the catalog. Catalog lists over half of the six hundred varieties (30 percent tetraploids) that the Moores grow. Description includes hybridizer, foliage habit, rebloom, length and season of bloom, height, and color and size of flower. Guarantees safe arrival.
Shipping season: April through August.

CHALYBEATE GARDENS
1988
George and Cathy Tolar
Catalog: Free, 30 pp.
The Tolars established Chalybeate in 1988, beginning commercial sales in 1991. The work of a wide range of hybridizers are represented here. The catalog is composed of twelve hundred selections (10 percent tetraploids), primarily introductions from the early 1970s through 1989. There are a few from the mid-1950s and as recent as 1995. Hybridizer, year of introduction, height, bloom time in season, foliage habit, size of bloom, and color and shape are noted. Guarantees true to name.
Shipping season: April through October.

CHARLES V. APPLEGATE
1980
Charles V. Applegate
Catalog: 1 FCS, 2 pp.
Mr. Applegate, who developed 'Blessing', an AHS Achievement Award winner in 1989, works toward breeding daylilies of quality for cold climates in modern forms—round, flat, and ruffled. Eighty-five of his introductions, primarily pink-, lavender-, and white-flowering diploids, appear in his flyer. Some specifications for recent introductions. Name and color only for the balance of the list.
Shipping season: August and September.

CHATTANOOGA DAYLILY GARDENS
1987
Lee and Jean Pickles
Catalog: $2 (recoverable), 24 pp.
The catalog features seventy introductions from Dr. C. E. Branch and D. Steve Varner. Detailed descriptions are provided. A general listing of 450 cultivars introduced in 1980 through the present from familiar names in

hybridizing, include basic specifications and a description of the bloom. Eighty spiders are described in their own section. Guarantees true to name and safe arrival.

Shipping season: April through October.
Canada, Mexico, International

COBURG PLANTING FIELDS
1984
Philipp Brockington and Howard J. Reeve, Jr.
Catalog: $2, 24 pp.
One third of the six hundred modern daylily cultivars grown by Brockington and Reeve (predominantly from mid- through late 1980s) are in their catalog. Hybridizer, year of introduction, height, bloom time, size of bloom, foliage habit, rebloom, and a brief description for each. The selection (55 percent tetraploids) includes plants developed at Coburg, "where temperatures consistently drop well below zero in the winter months."
Shipping season: May through September.

CONTEMPORARY GARDENS
1972
Perry Dyer
Catalog: $1, 30 pp. Display list: LSASE
The catalog includes 750 (45 percent tetraploids) of the 1,000 varieties of hemerocallis Perry Dyer grows. Selection from early 1980s through early 1990s, including many doubles, small, miniatures, and spider variants. Includes hybridizer, year of introduction, height, foliage habit, flower size, color, and a brief description. A master list with very limited quantities of the other varieties on display will be sent in return for an LSASE. Guarantees true to name, state inspected, and healthy on arrival. See **Iris.**
Shipping season: August and September.
Canada, Mexico, International

COOPER'S GARDEN
1992
Penny Aguirre
Catalog: $1 (recoverable), 41 pp.
Among Ms. Aguirre's perennial interests are daylilies. She lists thirty-five cultivars (30 percent tetraploids) described by height of plant, season of bloom, foliage habit, and size and color of flower. Hybridizer and year of introduction noted for all. Also offers a small customized collection that she will select within your stated preference for flower size, plant height, or color. See **Iris, Perennials.**
Shipping season: April and May. August and September.
Canada, Mexico, International

CORDON BLEU FARMS
1970
Bob Brooks
Catalog: $1, 48 pp., color photographs.
Spring price list: $1
One half of Mr. Brooks's catalog (and the entire spring price list) is devoted to hemerocallis. The catalog describes 325 (80 percent tetraploids) large, miniature, small-flowered, and double varieties. Emphasis is on registrations from 1980s through early 1990s. Mr. Brooks's recent tetraploids and the work of a diverse group of top breeders are richly described. Hybridizer, year of introduction, foliage habit, height, season of bloom, size of blossom, and AHS awards (where applicable) noted for all. Guarantees true to name and healthy on arrival; will replace any plant that does not survive the first season for the delivery fee. See **Iris.**
Shipping season: February through May.
July through November.
Canada, Mexico, International

CRINTONIC GARDENS
1987
Curt Hanson
Catalog: $1, 18 pp., color photographs
A one-man Eden, Crintonic specializes in cold-hardy daylilies grown in heavy clay soil. Mr. Hanson describes eighty current and recent introductions of his own in detail. A general list divided into sections includes 170 tetraploids, 90 diploids, and 30 spiders. Name of hybridizer, year of introduction, color, and basic specifications for each. Offers five special collections for the connoisseur. Guarantees safe arrival.
Shipping season: May through October.
Canada, Mexico, International

CROCHET DAYLILY GARDEN
1962
Clarence J. and Beth Crochet
Catalog: Free, 18 pp., black-and-white
photographs
Thirty-five Crochet introductions, almost all recipients of junior citations and/or honorable mentions from AHS, lead a catalog of nine hun-

dred cultivars. Mr. Crochet describes his list (10 percent tetraploids) as including "many of the great landscape plants as well as the latest introductions of the country's best hybridizers." Descriptions include hybridizer, year of introduction, foliage habit, height, bloom season, rebloom, and size of flower. A collection of miniatures suitable for landscaping is offered. Guarantees true to name and safe arrival.
Shipping season: March through November.
Canada, Mexico, International

DAYLILY DISCOUNTERS
1988
Tom Allin and Doug Glick
Catalog: $1, 76 pp., color photographs
Substantial space is devoted to daylily history, culture, propagation, placement, and botany. Each of the 185 cultivars offered is described in rich narrative detail. Hybridizer, height, bloom size, season, foliage habit, and awards. (Also the representatives for R. W. Munson, Jr., cultivars.) Offers four mixed landscape collections without name or identifying colors. Guarantees true to name and state inspected; will replace up to one year from date of shipment. See **Booksellers.**
Shipping season: All year.
Mexico, International

DAYLILY WORLD
1970
David Kirchhoff and Morton Morss
Catalog: $5 (recoverable), 28 pp., color photographs
Kirchhoff and Morss are award-winning hybridizers who create fifteen to twenty-five thousand seedlings each year. Their primary focus is double and single tetraploids that exhibit distinction, vigor, and hardiness. One hundred and thirty of their current and recent introductions described in detail, with specifications and cultural information. General listing of 450 cultivars from well-known hybridizers composed predominately of introductions from early 1980s through early 1990s: 85 percent tetraploids, some doubles, ponies, and miniatures. Hybridizer, year of introduction, height, season of bloom, rebloom, foliage habit, fragrance, extended opening time, and color. Five connoisseur and named collections are also offered. Guarantees safe arrival.
Shipping season: All year, but preferably February through October.
Canada, Mexico, International

DICKERSON DAYLILY GARDEN
1984
Jerry W. Dickerson
Catalog: $2 (recoverable), 22 pp.
Mr. Dickerson's recent introductions include sixty sun-hardy, very fertile, true spiders. An additional listing of six hundred cultivars (10 percent tetraploids) are line listed with specifications for height, bloom season, size of bloom, foliage habit, and color.
Shipping season: April through November.
International

EMILY GANDY'S DAYLILIES
1972
Emily Z. Gandy
Catalog: Free, 24 pp.
Emily Gandy will dig, label, and pack any of the eleven hundred cultivars (45 percent tetraploids) she has gathered from a diverse group of hybridizers. Year of introduction ranges from the early 1970s through the year before the catalog date. Hybridizer, year of introduction, size of bloom, description of features, height, time of bloom, rebloom, and foliage habit for each. "Daylilies without names" collections available in groups of fifty in yellow, red, or mixed colors. Guarantees true to name.
Shipping season: All year.

ENGLEARTH GARDENS
1931
The Herrema Family
Catalog: $1, 47 pp.
A family perennial farm growing over one thousand "Michigan hardy" hybrid daylilies. The catalog lists four hundred hemerocallis (25 percent tetraploids), including their own (primarily pink and yellow) introductions. Organized by chromosome count and listed by cultivar. Descriptions include hybridizer, season of bloom, foliage habit, color and size of flower, and height. Offers three assortments of unlabeled daylilies for early, mid-, and late season bloom. Guarantees true to name. See **Hosta, Iris,** Perennials.
Shipping season: April through November.
Canada

THE FLOWER LADY'S GARDEN
1953
Agnes Miller
Catalog: $2 (recoverable), 15 pp.
Agnes Miller arrived in Granite City, Illinois, from Evansville, Indiana, with two hundred rosebushes

and three hundred iris in tow. She planted her treasures in the 15 degree weather and The Flower Lady's Garden began. A dear friend kept sending daylilies as gifts. Although Agnes didn't care much for daylilies, she planted them to avoid disappointing her friend. One morning, after a certain daylily struck her as being beautiful, nothing was to be the same. Ms. Miller now has 800 daylilies. A brief list of her own introductions leads a catalog that includes 250 named cultivars from about sixty hybridizers. Descriptions include height, season, size, color of bloom, and hybridizer. Over one hundred inexpensive landscape varieties are also available.
Shipping season: April and May. August through October.
Canada, International

FLOYD COVE NURSERY
1978
Grace and Patrick Stamile
Catalog: $2 (recoverable), 36 pp., color photographs
The Floyd Cove catalog features thirty of the Stamiles' own introductions (99.9 percent tetraploids) from the current and previous year. Each is described in rich detail. The color photographs are among the best you'll find in any daylily catalog. Five hundred (50 percent tetraploids) of the one thousand hemerocallis varieties grown at the garden are also offered. Name of hybridizer, height, bloom season, foliage habit, and color as registered. The Stamiles acquire approximately 125 new cultivars each year while deleting an equal number. Guarantees safe arrival.
Shipping season: All year.
International

FORESTLAKE GARDENS
Fran Harding
Catalog: Free, 16 pp.
List contains four hundred plants (40 percent tetraploids), primarily introductions from the late 1970s through mid-1980s. Brief descriptions for some; height, season of bloom, flower size, hybridizer, and year of introduction for all.
Shipping season: March through June

FULTS GARDEN SHOP
1969
Bertha Fults
Catalog: LSASE, 1 p.
The shop is adjacent to Ms. Fults's home on a Texas Century Farm settled in 1850 by her great-grandfather James Robert Boyd. Ms. Fults

has registered eight cultivars since she began hybridizing in 1988. Her major effort is toward the development of a "perfect" large pink diploid. Her own introductions (all but one is pink) are briefly described. A selection of daylily seedlings are also offered. Guarantees true to name and safe arrival.
Shipping season: All year.

GARDEN PATH DAYLILIES
1992
Jean Duncan
Catalog: $1 (recoverable), 24 pp.
Specializing in newer cultivars, Jean Duncan hybridizes (in a subtropical environment) for exceptional early season daylilies with increased bud count and rebloom, along with beauty and refinement of form. Breeding for clear pinks is her passion. Offers other hybridizers' cultivars from early 1980s through year prior to the catalog date. Hybridizer, year of introduction, foliage habit, bloom time, fragrance, rebloom, height, and size of flower for over three hundred offerings (90 percent tetraploids). Plants grown in raised beds. Guarantees true to name and safe arrival.
Shipping season: March through May. October and November.
Canada, Mexico, International

GARDEN PERENNIALS
1981
Gail Korn
Catalog: $1 (recoverable), 32 pp.
Garden Perennials is not a daylily nursery per se; however, Gail Korn's passion for hemerocallis has led to the acquisition of 750 cultivars. Over 250 varieties (35 percent tetraploids), including a substantial number of miniatures, are available by mail. Height, season of bloom, bloom size, foliage habit, awards, and a brief description for each. Daylily basics presented in question-and-answer format. Plants are grown for three years before they are offered, making for mature, ready-to-bloom specimens. Offers special large-flower and miniature collections. See Grasses, **Perennials**.
Shipping season: April through June. September and October

GILBERT H. WILD & SON
1885
Greg Jones
Catalog: $3 (recoverable), 75 pp., color photographs
One hundred–plus years of experience pro-

vides the material for a catalog that includes old, new, borrowed, but no blue. Over one thousand cultivars. Hybridizer, year of introduction, height, bloom size, tendency to rebloom, foliage habit, color, and substantive descriptions for new Wild introductions and general listings. Dozens of collection, off-price, and mix-and-match offerings for the landscaper and collector. Guarantees true to name and healthy on arrival. See Heirlooms, **Iris**, **Peonies**, Perennials.

Shipping season: March through September. Canada, Mexico, International

GREENTHUMB DAYLILY GARDENS
1978
Bill and Joyce Green
Catalog: Free, 21 pp.
The Greens feature the new introductions of Wyatt LeFever. The general listing contains one thousand cultivars (25 percent tetraploids). Concentration on late 1970s through late 1980s. Hybridizer, year of introduction, height, season of bloom, rebloom, color, and foliage habit for every listing. A pick-your-own budget assortment can be selected from one hundred named varieties. Guarantees true to name and state inspected.

Shipping season: April through October

G.R.'S PERENNIAL FARM
1988
G. R. Burningham
Catalog: $1 (recoverable), 20 pp.
G.R.'s Perennial Farm is an AHS display garden. G. R. Burningham has won numerous state and national awards as a flower exhibitor. The catalog includes six hundred named cultivars (25 percent tetraploids) grown in a variety of conditions and soils in the Bountiful, Utah, area. Selection represents introductions from the 1960s, 1970s, and 1980s. Awards, hybridizer, year of introduction, bloom size, season, foliage habit, height, and color included for all.

Shipping season: April through June. August and September.

HESCHKE GARDENS
1990
David Heschke
Catalog: Free, 14 pp.
Mr. Heschke offers over eight hundred perennials through his catalog with the major attention to astilbes, daylilies, hostas, *Lilium*, and peonies. Recent catalogs included four hun-

dred daylily cultivars. Notes name of hybridizer, height at maturity, nature of foliage, season of bloom, and size and color of flower. See Grasses, Hosta, **Peonies**, **Perennials**.

Shipping season: April through October

HOBBY GARDEN, INC.
1967
Lee E. Gates and Mary C. Schexnaydre
Catalog: Free, 6 pp.
Lee Gates and Mary Schexnaydre sell only their own introductions bred to exhibit a wide range of colors, tones, and hues. Plants are offered as capable of performing well in all regions with frequent rebloom. Sixty cultivars (10 percent tetraploids) are described in vivid detail with full specifications. Catalog is organized by year of introduction. Guarantees true to name and state inspected.

Shipping season: June through September.

HOLLY LANE IRIS GARDENS
Jan and Jack Worel
Catalog: $1, 24 pp.
As a complement to their extensive iris collection, the Worels offer 120 daylily cultivars, described by name and color. Guarantees true to name and healthy on arrival. See Heirlooms, Hosta, **Iris**.

Shipping season: August and September.

HOMESTEAD FARMS
1984
Ron Vitoux
Catalog: Free, 32 pp.
Homestead Farms is not just another evocative name. The Vitouxes live in a log home built with natural resources harvested from their property. Once their home was completed, the development of nursery stock began in earnest. This small, rapidly expanding operation offers 225 daylily varieties (35 percent tetraploids). Hybridizer and year of introduction for most; height, season of bloom, foliage habit, size, and color of flower for all. Notes rebloom and awards. Rich descriptions. Landscape collections by color and size. Guarantees true to name, healthy, and safe arrival. See **Hosta**, Iris, **Peonies**, Perennials.

Shipping season: April through October.

IRON GATE GARDENS
1960
Van M. Sellers and Vic Santa Lucia
Catalog: $2 (recoverable), 40 pp., color photographs

Award-winning hybridizers Sellers and Santa Lucia also introduce Pauline Henry's "Siloam" series through Iron Gate. Each new variety is briefly described and specifications are noted. Bits of advice are sprinkled throughout the catalog. A section of "musings" include some helpful cultural tips. There is a strong focus on the newest varieties from other breeders. Approximately three hundred cultivars are acquired, and a similar number dropped, each year. Sixteen hundred varieties are grown at Iron Gate, with eight hundred (45 percent tetraploids) appearing in the catalog. Hybridizer, foliage habit, height, season of bloom, and color are noted. See **Hosta**.
Shipping season: April through June.
Canada, Mexico, International

ISABEL HIBBARD GARDENS
1980
Isabel Hibbard
Catalog: $1 (recoverable), 3 pp.
Isabel Hibbard specializes in the best of the older standard varieties and many new and rare plants from a select group of hybridizers, as well as her own creations. Hibbard's recent introductions are briefly described and include specifications. The balance of the list is organized by color and size. Hybridizer and height are noted.
Shipping season: April through October.
Canada

JAGGERS BAYOU BEAUTIES
Leroy and Fran Jaggers
Catalog: Free, 20 pp.
Four hundred and forty (45 percent tetraploids) modern daylilies from the mid-1970s through current catalog year. Hybridizer, year of introduction, height, season of bloom, foliage habit, and short description provided for each cultivar. Guarantees true to name and state inspected.
Shipping season: February through June.
September through November.

JASPERSON'S HERSEY NURSERY
1989
Lu Jasperson
Catalog: $1, 6 pp.
Lu Jasperson strives to stay organic in all gardening practices. She evaluates daylilies for hardiness, good growth, and reliable bloom. "If the flower itself is beautiful, that's okay too," writes Lu. Fifty varieties. Notes foliage habit, size of bloom, and color. See **Iris**, **Organics**, **Peonies**, **Perennials**.

Shipping season: August and September.

JERNIGAN GARDENS
1955
Winifred Jernigan Williams
Catalog: $1 (recoverable), 16 pp.
Bettie Godwin, Ms. Williams's mother, planted her first flower, a peony, here in 1925. Jernigan Gardens came into being as a business in 1955 when Bettie and her husband, Noble Jernigan, took an ad in *The Progressive Farmer*. Ms. Williams offers 250 (50 percent tetraploids), including a number of "Jernigan's own." Hybridizer, year of introduction, height, season of bloom, rebloom, foliage habit, size of bloom, and color for each. Guarantees true to name and state inspected. Does not ship daylilies every year. See **Hosta**.
Shipping season: April through October.

JOHNSON DAYLILY GARDEN
1991
Jeff and Linda Johnson
Catalog: Free, 6 pp.
The Johnsons' focus is AHS Achievement Award winners and popularity poll favorites. Offers 250 cultivars (25 percent tetraploids) introduced in the late 1970s through the mid-1980s by top hybridizers. Name of cultivar, hybridizer, year of introduction, height, time, size, shape, and nature of bloom noted for each offering. Guarantees true to name and safe arrival.
Shipping season: March through October.
Canada

KIRKLAND DAYLILIES
1989
Marjorie C. Kirkland
Catalog: Free, 18 pp.
Marjorie Kirkland's nursery specializes in daylily varieties with blooms that are seven inches and larger. List of over 450 cultivars includes hybridizer, color, size of bloom, season of bloom, height, and foliage habit. Kirkland offers a number of assortments, including nonlabeled but registered, labeled, a landscaping selection, and named varieties by budget.
Shipping season: April through September.

KLEHM NURSERY
1852
Kit C. Klehm
Catalog: $4 (recoverable), 104 pp., color
photographs and illustrations

Five generations of Klehms have tilled the soil and tended plants. Their catalog is a work of art blending full-color photographs, artwork, and exceptional design. Their daylily selection favors Illinois-area hybridizers developing varieties that have proven hardy through vigorous winters. Descriptions of two hundred cultivars (50 percent tetraploids) includes hybridizer, height, bloom size, color, and narrative detail. Numerous named collections and a tetraploid mixture for landscaping. Guarantees true to name; will replace up to one year after purchase. See **Booksellers, Hosta, Peonies**, Perennials.
Shipping season: April through November. Canada, Mexico, International

LADY BUG BEAUTIFUL GARDENS
1982
Ra Hansen
Catalog: $2 (recoverable), 36 pp., black-and-white photographs
Located on one of the largest daylily properties in Florida, Lady Bug sells only hybrids developed within the past fifteen years. Ra Hansen's enthusiasm and knowledge effervesce from the pages of her catalog. Specifications are provided for 1,040 cultivars (15 percent tetraploids), predominantly AHS prizewinners. Most are described in unique detail. All guaranteed true to name. Lady Bug introductions replaced if they do not thrive and bloom; other introductions guaranteed to arrive healthy or replaced.
Shipping season: March through October.

LAKESIDE ACRES
1957
Mary Chastain
Catalog: $2 (recoverable), 18 pp.
The daylily selection in the Lakeside Acres catalog includes 160 named varieties (1 percent tetraploids). Bloom size, color, and tendency toward rebloom are noted. Guarantees state inspected and safe arrival. See **Hosta**, Perennials.
Shipping season: May through October. International

LEE GARDENS
1988
Janis Lee
Catalog: $2 (recoverable), 32 pp.
The daylilies (15 percent tetraploids) at Lee Gardens have proven to be hardy through extreme heat and cold, moisture and drought. One hundred and ten modern hybrid varieties are repre-sented in Ms. Lee's catalog. Hybridizer, season of bloom, height, bloom size, color for all, and re-bloom when appropriate. Year of introduction not noted. Ships bareroot. Guarantees true to name and safe arrival. See **Hosta, Perennials.
Shipping season: April to first frost in Tremont, Illinois.**

LENINGTON GARDENS
1952
Robert L. Lenington
Catalog: 2 FCS, 24 pp.
This is the oldest commercial daylily garden in the Kansas City area, established in 1952 by George and Lucille Lenington, developers of over two hundred introductions. The nursery operated from 1984 to 1990 as the Lenington-Long Gardens. The business closed after the deaths of George Lenington and Don Long in 1990. George's son Bob reopened the nursery under its original name in 1992. The catalog offers over one thousand "commercial time-tested and proven" cultivars (25 percent tetraploids). Hybridizer, height, season of bloom, rebloom, flower size, and color for each variety. The hybridizing program is small after being restarted; however, a number of older Lenington cultivars are offered. Guarantees safe arrival.
Shipping season: April through June. August through October.

THE LILLY PLACE NURSERY
1984
Echo Larsen
Catalog: 1 FCS, 10 pp.
Echo Larsen describes the Lilly Place as "a working, growers nursery (and a hybridizer's garden) located in the lush Willamette Valley at the foothills of the Coast Range." Originally an herb farm, the nursery has now been given over almost entirely to the nurturing of seven hundred registered cultivars and several hundred newly hybridized seedlings. Catalog includes three hundred offerings (85 percent tetraploids), with a wide representation of introductions from the early 1970s through the current year. Prizewinners are noted as part of a description that includes foliage habit, hybridizer, year of introduction, fragrance, bloom habit, height, size and color of bloom, and whether the plant has a tendency to re-bloom.
Shipping season: April and May. August and September.

LITTLE RIVER FARM DAYLILIES
1984
Mel Oliver, Jr.
Catalog: $2, 18 pp.
Little River Farm operated as a full-line perennial and specialty plant nursery from 1984 to 1991. A partner's illness forced a change in direction in late 1991. Since that time, Mel Oliver, Jr., has operated the daylily garden primarily as a mail-order business. Plant material for the home gardener seeking older specimens and newer varieties. Six hundred (50 percent tetraploids) of the eight hundred cultivars grown here are listed. Hybridizer, height, rebloomer, season of bloom, bloom size, and color. A landscape mixture is offered. State inspected. Guarantees safe arrival.
Shipping season: March through May.
August through October.

LOUISIANA NURSERY
1950
Dalton E. Durio
Catalog: $4 (recoverable), 98 pp., color and black-and-white photographs
Louisiana Nursery occupies a fifty-six-acre complex that was founded by Ken Durio. Five family members, all trained horticulturists, are currently involved in the business. Half of this catalog is a presentation of twenty-five hundred daylily varieties (20 percent tetraploids). New Durio introductions are richly described. The general listing includes previously introduced cultivars from the Durios and a select group of familiar breeders. Hybridizer, foliage habit, bloom season, flowering habit, height, bloom size, and awards for all. Fuller narrative description for many. Over a dozen collections, labeled for the connoisseur and the collector, and unlabeled for the landscaper. Cultural and hybridizing tips. This catalog includes two dozen books on daylilies, iris, and general and southern interest. State and U.S. government inspected. Guarantees true to name and healthy on departure. See **Booksellers, Bulbs, Fruit, Grasses, Iris, Trees.**
Shipping season: February through June.
Canada, Mexico, International

LOVE GARDENS
1985
Bob Love
Catalog: $2 (recoverable)
Bob Love offered his first four introductions in

1994. The catalog includes two hundred modern cultivars (35 percent tetraploids) selected from the thousand growing at the garden. Hybridizer, season, height, foliage habit, bloom size, and color noted for each.
Shipping season: April through June. August through October.

MAPLE TREE GARDEN
1960
Larry L. Harder
Catalog: $1 (recoverable), 26 pp.
Mr. Harder began his nursery with irises but now devotes almost half of his catalog to daylilies. Four hundred and fifty cultivars (20 percent tetraploids) from the late 1970s through the end of the 1980s are listed with hybridizer, year of introduction, height, season, size, and color of bloom. Offers starter collections based on your budget. See **Iris.**
Shipping season: July through September.
Canada

MARIETTA GARDENS
1982
John, Faye, and Elizabeth O. Shooter
Catalog: Free, 24 pp., black-and-white photographs
The Shooters' catalog describes in detail diploids from their own hybridizing program and recent miniature introductions developed by John and Faye's daughter, Elizabeth. The general listing of nine hundred cultivars (20 percent tetraploids) grown at Marietta (developed by the Shooters and others) identifies hybridizer, year of introduction, bloom size, height, foliage habit, color, and each is described. Two hundred and fifty cultivars from the AHS display garden at Marietta are described by name only. Guarantees state inspected.
Shipping season: March through November.

METAMORA COUNTRY GARDENS
1992
Pat and Larry Salk
Catalog: Free, 20 pp.
The temperature drops well below zero in Metamora, where the evergreen varieties the Salks sell have grown for at least one year. Five hundred and fifty cultivars (15 percent tetraploids) are available for purchase. Hybridizer, height, season of bloom, foliage habit, bloom size, rebloom, and color noted for each

plant. Guarantees true to name, state inspected, and safe arrival. See Hosta, **Iris.**
Shipping season: May. August and September.
No Hawaii

MID-AMERICA GARDEN
1979
Paul Black
Catalog: $3, 42 pp.
Paul Black founded Mid-America Iris, now Mid-America Garden, with the bearded iris as the main focus. Two years of devastating rains in the early 1990s substantially diminished his stock. A change of focus, and name, have ensued. One third of the catalog now features daylilies. Four hundred modern large varieties (30 percent tetraploids) and one hundred small-flowered (four-inch and under) cultivars are listed. Hybridizer, height, size of bloom, and foliage habit for each. Plants are field grown, shipped bareroot. Guarantees true to name and safe arrival. See **Hosta, Iris.**
Shipping season: May. August and September.
Canada, Mexico, International

MONARCH DAYLILY GARDEN
1984
George and Melba Fain
Catalog: Free, 24 pp.
A small selection of the Fains' own diploids are briefly listed in a catalog that includes thirteen hundred varieties (25 percent tetraploids). Hybridizer, height, season of bloom, rebloom, foliage habit, and size and color of bloom for each plant. Guarantees safe arrival.
Shipping season: March through October.

OAK HAVEN FARMS NURSERY
1990
Glenn and Yolanda "Lonnie" Ward
Catalog: $2 (recoverable), 17 pp., color photographs
The Oak Haven catalog features the Wards' current and recent introductions, with specifications and descriptions. General listing of 760 varieties (10 percent tetraploids) primarily from late 1970s through mid-1980s. Specifies hybridizer, year of introduction, height, bloom season, size of bloom, color, and foliage habit. Four collections of registered plants are offered. Guarantees state inspected.
Shipping season: March through June.

September through November.
Canada, Mexico, International

OAKES DAYLILIES
Stewart Oakes
Catalog: $2 (recoverable), 32 pp., color photographs
Collector's catalog of 800 cultivars: $1, black-and-white photographs
Three generations of the Oakes family tend to their modern hybrid daylilies and their seven-acre display garden. A selection of ninety cultivars (40 percent tetraploids) feature All-America Daylily Selection Council Regional Favorites, and a bevy of AHS Achievement Award winners, including the Oakeses' own introductions. Catalog is organized by size and nature of bloom: large-flowered, small-flowered, miniatures, and doubles. Descriptions include hybridizer, height of mature plant, size and color of flower, season of bloom, tendency to rebloom, and foliage habit. Offers a collection for beginners, several by color or size, and one very substantial grouping composed of every cultivar in their catalog (for those who want it all!). Guarantees satisfaction; will replace or issue refund.
Shipping season: March through October.
Canada, Mexico, International

OLALLIE DAYLILY GARDENS
1982
Christopher and Amelia Darrow
Catalog: $1, 22 pp.
In 1981, Dr. George Darrow (a chief horticulturist for the USDA until 1957) began transferring daylilies here from his collection at Olallie Farm in Maryland. His collection is the basis for this operation managed by his grandson and his wife. The Darrows list one hundred daylily cultivars and six species, all characterized as being adaptable. The plants tolerated warm Maryland summers but have thrived for over a decade in a zone that experiences temperatures as low as minus 25 degrees. Included are many of Dr. Darrow's fifty-nine registered cultivars. Catalog is arranged by color of bloom. Height, season of bloom, foliage habit, color, awards, and description for each variety. Offers early and extended bloom collections, and mixtures by color. Guarantees safe arrival.
Shipping season: May through September.
Canada, Mexico, International

PINECLIFFE DAYLILY GARDENS
1989
Donald C. and Kathy Smith
Catalog: $2, 31 pp.

The Smiths list fifteen hundred of the two thousand cultivars in residence at Pinecliffe. Selection from mid-1970s to the year prior to date of catalog. Hybridizer, year of introduction, color, height, size of bloom, season of bloom, foliage habit, fragrance, rebloom, and awards noted for all. The Smiths have introduced twenty-five cultivars, primarily midseason bloomers, that are fully described.

Shipping season: March through November.
Canada, Mexico, International

PINEGARDEN
Patricia Seaman
Catalog: $1 (recoverable), 8 pp.

Patricia Seaman has recently started to offer her own ruffled diploid introductions. Specifications and narrative description for each of these cultivars. General listing of four hundred varieties (15 percent tetraploids), primarily introductions from the 1980s, includes hybridizer, year of introduction, bloom size, and color.

Shipping season: March through May.
September through November.

POWELL'S GARDENS
1952
Loleta Kenan Powell
Catalog: $3.50 (recoverable), 60 pp.

One quarter of the book is devoted to twelve hundred daylily cultivars. Includes seventy-five of Powell's own introductions from the past twenty years, nine hundred other large-flowered cultivars from a broad range of hybridizers, and a separate section for "little stars"—miniature flowering varieties. Hybridizer, year of introduction, season of bloom for many; height, bloom size, and color for all. See Conifers, Hosta, Iris, Peonies, Perennials, Trees.

Shipping season: April through September.
Canada, Mexico, International

RAMONA GARDENS
1984
Linda Moore
Catalog: $1 (recoverable), 18 pp., color photographs

Two hundred varieties (50 percent tetraploids), mostly registrations from the mid-1970s through mid-1980s. Hybridizer, year of introduction, height, season of bloom, foliage habit, bloom size, and color. Guarantees true to name, state inspected, and healthy when shipped.

Shipping season: April through June. September and October.
Canada, Mexico, International

RENAISSANCE GARDENS
1979
Judith and Robert Weston
Catalog: $1 (recoverable), 22 pp., black-and-white photographs

Growing, hybridizing, and introducing modern daylilies is the exclusive business of Renaissance Gardens, which began in Detroit in 1979. The nursery has been in its current location since 1986. Twenty-five of the Westons' current and recent introductions are richly described. The general listing of 350 cultivars (40 percent tetraploids) includes hybridizer, foliage habit, size and season of bloom, height, and color.

Shipping season: April through October.
Canada, Mexico, International

ROBIN MEADOW FARM
1989
Ralph H. Maiwaldt
Catalog: $1 (recoverable), 32 pp.

Mr. Maiwaldt's offering covers an expanse of eight hundred modern hybrid daylilies (45 percent tetraploids). Organized by cultivar, his descriptions include hybridizer, year of introduction, season of bloom, rebloom, foliage habit, fragrant varieties, height, size of bloom, and length of bloom time. His perennial interests include a wide range of herbaceous companion plants that are not included in the Robin Meadow Farm catalog. He encourages you to drop him a card inquiring after special requests that grow in zone 6. Guarantees true to name.

Shipping season: April and May. September and October.

ROYCROFT DAYLILY NURSERY
1984
Bob Roycroft
Catalog: Free, 12 pp.

An AHS display garden, Roycroft Daylily Nursery specializes in award-winning modern hybrid daylily cultivars. They acquire thirty to fifty new cultivars each year and discontinue a similar number. Approximately 90 percent of the 350

offerings (15 percent tetraploids) are prizewinners. Very useful explanation of AHS awards and eligibility. Prices vary by the number of fans (one, two, or three) per plant. Hybridizer, year of introduction, bloom size, foliage habit, season, rebloom, height, and description.
Shipping season: March through November.
Canada, Mexico, International

R. SEAWRIGHT
1976
Bob and Love Seawright
Catalog: $2 (recoverable), 28 pp.
Bob Seawright's love affair with the daylily started when he was twelve years old. His catalog lists four hundred (35 percent tetraploids) of the one thousand registered varieties grown at the garden. Mr. Seawright adds and deletes fifty to sixty new cultivars each year. The collection concentrates on the 1970s through the current year, including his own introductions. Hybridizer, year of introduction, height, season of bloom, foliage habit, size of bloom, and color, as well as brief but rich description of each plant and its habits. A special introductory collection based on the customer's budget is available. Guarantees true to name, state inspected, and safe arrival. See **Hosta**.
Shipping season: May through September.

SAXTON GARDENS
1945
S. E. Saxton
Catalog: $1, 8 pp., color photographs
The Saxtons' original nursery was in the Adirondack Mountains of New York. This led them to develop a series of extremely cold-hardy plants, fifty of which are offered here as the "Adirondack Strain." They have originated more than 280 cultivars. The catalog contains two hundred varieties in all (15 percent tetraploids), featuring the Saxtons' current and previous introductions organized by color. Specifications include height, size of bloom, bloom season, rebloom, fragrance, color of throat, and prizes won. Description includes cultural characteristics. Landscape assortments offered.
Shipping season: April through June.
Canada, International

SERENDIPITY GARDENS
1989
Becky Stegall and Shirley Farmer
Catalog: Free, 28 pp.

Serendipity began as the private garden of mother and daughter Shirley Farmer and Becky Stegall. They offer twelve hundred (35 percent tetraploids) of the fifteen hundred cultivars growing in their garden. Choice selections from the 1940s, 1950s, and 1960s, with a major concentration in the 1970s through the mid-1980s. Hybridizer, year of introduction, height, bloom season, rebloom, foliage habit, size of bloom, and color noted for all. Two collections of named varieties and one landscape collection of unnamed seedlings from named parents. Guarantees state inspected.
Shipping season: April through October.

SKYLAND GARDENS
1971
Bob Hale
Catalog: LSASE
Skyland Gardens features Bob Hale's current and recent introductions, which are equally divided between tetraploids and diploids. Specifications and some description for his own cultivars. The general list offers 325 varieties (40 percent tetraploids), providing name of hybridizer, bloom size, and color. Guarantees true to name, state inspected, and safe arrival.
Shipping season: August through October.
Canada, Mexico, International

SOULES GARDEN
1979
Marge Soules
Catalog: $2 (recoverable), 36 pp.
More than thirty years ago, Marge Roberts Soules began working with plants and developing her hybridizing techniques. Today, Marge is among the leaders in creating and developing modern hemerocallis. One half of her catalog is devoted to 450 daylily cultivars (45 percent tetraploids), including many of her own. Concentration is from the mid-1980s through the current year. Hybridizer and year of introduction for most; height, season of bloom, foliage habit, color, and awards for all. See **Hosta**.
Shipping season: April through October.

STERRETT GARDENS
1987
Richard and Rikki Sterrett
Catalog: Free, 10 pp.
The eight hundred cultivars at this official AHS display garden are the beneficiaries of

sandy soil, plenty of irrigation, and a moderate climate tempered by the Chesapeake Bay. The catalog of five hundred varieties (25 percent tetraploids), primarily registered in the 1970s through late 1980s, includes the name of the hybridizer, year of introduction, height, season of bloom, rebloom, bloom size, foliage habit, and awards. A collection of ten named varieties, the Sterretts' choice, is available by color preference. See Perennials.
Shipping season: April through September.

STOVER MILL GARDENS
Arthur M. and Ruth E. Kroll
Catalog: Free, 10 pp.
A specialized nursery and private garden that evaluates and propagates twelve hundred recent high-quality daylilies from leading hybridizers. The collection at Stover Mill is described by the Krolls as one of the most comprehensive in the eastern United States. Catalog features their own current introductions, with specifications and extensive descriptions. The general listing of five hundred cultivars (35 percent tetraploids) includes hybridizer, year of introduction, bloom size, color, and foliage habit. Guarantees true to name and state inspected.
Shipping season: April through June. August through October.
International (Europe only)

SUNNYRIDGE GARDENS
1983
Geraldine Couturier
Catalog: $1.50 (recoverable), 23 pp.
Geraldine Couturier grows several thousand daylily cultivars. She devotes three quarters of her catalog to eight hundred plants (15 percent tetraploids). Ms. Couturier's introductions, primarily spiders and spider variants, include specifications and descriptions. The general listing, introductions from the 1940s through the mid-1980s, includes hybridizer, year of introduction, and full specifications. Offers a named variety collection and an unnamed landscape collection. Guarantees true to name, state inspected, and safe arrival. See Iris, Heirlooms.
Shipping season: April through October.

SWANNS' DAYLILY GARDEN
1988
Jean and Mark Swann

Catalog: Free
An AHS display garden. Seven hundred (20 percent tetraploids) of the thirteen hundred cultivars grown by the Swanns are available through their catalog. Introductions from 1960 through the early 1990s (with emphasis on the 1980s) from a diverse group of breeders. Hybridizer, year of introduction, height, size of bloom, season of bloom, foliage habit, fragrance, throat color, extended bloom, nocturnal habit, for every plant. The Swanns employ biological pest control in lieu of chemical sprays. Guarantees true to name and state inspected.
Shipping season: March through September.
Canada, Mexico, International

T & M GARDENS
1989
Terah George and Mae Snow
Catalog: $1 (recoverable), 28 pp.
Terah George and Mae Snow offer eleven hundred (27 percent tetraploids) varieties from a diverse group of hybridizers. Specifications include hybridizer, height, size of bloom, foliage habit, color, and rebloom. A collection of labeled varieties of T & M's choice is available. Guarantees true to name, state inspected, and safe arrival.
Shipping season: April through October.

THOMAS GARDENS
1984
Dale Thomas
Catalog: Free, 24 pp.
Mr. Thomas hybridizes and grows tetraploids. His own efforts are toward red flowers and late bloomers. All plants on offer have been fed organically for at least three years. Catalog lists one hundred cultivars from early 1970s through current introductions from Thomas and other hybridizers. Detailed descriptions and cultural information for most offerings. Hybridizer, year of introduction, height, time and size of bloom, and foliage habit for all. Seven special collections of named varieties, both labeled and unlabeled. Guarantees safe arrival. See Organics.
Shipping season: April and May. August through October.

THUNDERING SPRINGS DAYLILY GARDEN
1972
Elmer and Ivelyn Brown
Catalog: $1 (recoverable), 20 pp.

An AHS display garden since 1986. The Browns offers seven hundred cultivars (25 percent tetraploids), including some double-flowering varieties. Hybridizer, height, season and size of bloom, rebloom, and color included. Several landscaping collections.
Shipping season: All year.

TRANQUIL LAKE NURSERY
1970
Philip Boucher and Warren Leach
Catalog: $1, 45 pp., color photographs.
Supplemental lists: LSASE
Tranquil Lake is an AHS display garden and a member of the All-America Daylily Selection Council that is involved in the testing and evaluation of daylilies. Boucher and Leach provide hardy plants for the northern gardener, selling only those plants that have performed well at their nursery. Two thirds of their catalog is devoted to three hundred daylilies (60 percent tetraploids) from diverse sources. Special attention to the work of Bill and Eleanor Lachman and other select New England hybridizers. Hybridizer, height, foliage habit, season of bloom, and awards noted for each listing. Special collections for the beginner through the connoisseur are available. Guarantees true to name and safe arrival. See **Iris.**
Shipping season: April through October.
Canada, Mexico, International

WATER MILL DAYLILY GARDEN
1990
Dan and Jane Trimmer
Catalog: Free
The Trimmers' list nearly all of the three hundred newer, named cultivars (50 percent tetraploids) that they have for sale. Included among the work of two dozen breeders are a small number of their own introductions from a nascent hybridizing program. Hybridizer, height, foliage habit, season of bloom, and color for each plant.
Shipping season: April through November.
Canada, Mexico, International

WILDWOOD GARDENS
1984
Will and Tracy Plotner
Catalog: $2 (recoverable), 36 pp.
One third of the catalog is devoted to 120 types of daylily (50 percent tetraploids). Cultivars primarily from the early to mid-1970s; a select few from the 1950s, 1960s, and 1980s.

Hybridizer, year of introduction, height, bloom size, tendency to rebloom, foliage habit, and brief description of color and habit. See Hosta, Iris.
Shipping season: April and May. August through October.
Canada, Mexico, International

WIMBERLYWAY GARDENS
1950
Ida and Bill Munson, Betty Hudson
Catalog: $2 (recoverable), 64 pp., color photographs
Bill Munson, author of *Hemerocallis: The Daylily*, has been hybridizing for over forty years. A pioneer in tetraploids, he is credited with having introduced several hundred significant cultivars. This beautifully produced catalog describes in detail over two hundred varieties (99.9 percent tetraploids) introduced by Bill and Ida Munson. Numerous prizewinners. A half dozen doubles bred by Betty Hudson are also fully described. Foliage habit, bloom season, height, and year of introduction are provided for every offering. Guarantees true to name and healthy arrival.
Shipping season: March through September (later in the South).
Canada, International

YORK HILL FARM
1990
Darlyn C. Springer
Catalog: $1.50, 30 pp., black-and-white photographs
York Hill's plants are field grown and presented as "hardy, tried-and-true," having performed well in "New England's varied and sometimes difficult climate." A quarter of the York Hill catalog is devoted to hemerocallis. Ms. Springer, a professional daylily garden judge, is involved in a hybridizing program with Irene Melin, whose work (with her late husband) is featured. The general listing of two hundred cultivars (55 percent tetraploids) introduced in the 1980s includes hybridizer, year of introduction, height, foliage habit, and bloom color and size for most offerings. A selection of cultivars from York Hill's breeding program are included for the benefit of amateur hybridizers. Guarantees true to name and state inspected. See Grasses, Heirlooms, Hosta, **Iris,** Perennials.
Shipping season: Mid-April through mid-June. September and October.

Selected Reading About Daylilies

Daylilies, by A. B. Stout. The classic work on hemerocallis through the early part of this century. Published in 1934; updated in 1986 by Dr. Darrel Apps.

Daylilies: The Perfect Perennial, by Lewis Hill and Nancy Hill. Includes information on basics of selection, planting, and maintenance. Description and habits of two hundred popular hybrids. Color photographs.

Eureka! National Daylily Locator, by Ken and Kay Gregory. Lists thirty-five thousand individual cultivars and sources. Annual revised edition published in February.

Hemerocallis: The Daylily, by R.W. Munson, Jr. The successor to Stout's book. Includes an extensive list of desirable modern varieties, arranged by color, and illustrated with photographs throughout. Munson, of Wimberlyway Gardens, is considered a dean of modern hybridizers.

IRIS

The plant count cited in each profile is based on information in the most recent catalog provided by the source. In this section, shipping season is for iris only. A selection of books about iris appears after the last listing.

QUICK FIND
The following sources are listed in this section:

ADAMGROVE
Eric and Bob Tankesley-Clarke
Catalog: $3 (two-year subscription), 68 pp., black-and-white and color photographs
The plants at Adamgrove endure the stresses that are characteristic of "open winters": modest snow cover, temperatures that hover near zero degrees, and a windchill factor that replicates temperatures of 40 to 50 degrees below zero. Nine hundred irises—arilbred, border bearded, intermediate bearded, miniature dwarf bearded, miniature tall bearded, standard dwarf bearded, tall bearded, species bearded, and species crested—fill nearly three quarters of the catalog. Current introductions of the Tankesely-Clarkes and other notable hybridizers make for a list with a substantial number of prizewinning cultivars. Insightful classification and cultural information is set off from the main text. The glossary and basic botanical illustrations are useful in clarifying nomenclature. Guarantees true to name and safe arrival. See **Daylilies.**
Shipping season: Bearded irises, July and

August. Beardless irises, August and September.
Canada

AITKEN'S SALMON CREEK GARDEN
1978
Terry and Barbara Aitken
Catalog: $2, 50 pp., color photographs
Terry and Barbara Aitken's primary objective is to hybridize award-quality plants across a wide variety of iris types. The catalog features introductions from the Aitkens, Carol Lankow, Marky Smith, and Ken Fisher; richly described. The general listing—twelve hundred varieties of border bearded, Louisiana, Japanese, miniature dwarf bearded, miniature tall bearded, Pacific Coast, Siberian, standard dwarf bearded, spuria, and tall bearded irises—is diverse. Emphasis on the mid-1980s through the mid-1990s. Hybridizer, year of introduction, brief description and awards noted for each offering. There is also a separate section of Dykes Medal winners. Several species iris are available. Collections of bearded iris are

available to garden clubs. Guarantees true to name and safe arrival.

Shipping season: Bearded irises, July through August. Beardless irises, August through October.

Canada, International

AMBERWAY GARDENS
1988
Sue and Ken Kremer
Catalog: $1, 32 pp.

A rebloomer fan's dream come true from a nursery that came into being by happenstance. In 1988, the Kremers had a row of hybrid irises in their yard that they wanted to thin out. They casually put up an Iris for Sale sign on the side of the road. The plants in this tag sale sold out in two weeks. Applying for a tax number and a nursery license put them in business almost overnight. Amberway has come far from those not too long ago early days. Their catalog offers over 1,150 bearded and beardless cultivars. The majority of this nursery's plants are rebloomers, including many Monty Byers introductions and plants with Byers parentage. Catalog includes border bearded, intermediate bearded, Japanese, Louisiana, miniature dwarf bearded, miniature tall bearded, standard dwarf bearded, species, and tall bearded irises; hybridizer, year of introduction, a brief description, the likelihood of rebloom by zone, and awards noted for each. Offers four species iris, including a rare typhifolia Siberian from China. Guarantees true to name, registered with AIS, pest and disease free, and safe arrival.

Shipping season: July through September.

THE AMERICAN IRIS SOCIETY
See **Horticultural Societies.**

ANDERSON IRIS GARDENS
1978
Sharol and George Longaker
Catalog: $1, 21 pp.

Five hundred and fifty tall bearded irises occupy almost the entire catalog. The Longakers' recent introductions are featured and described. A general list filled with Award of Merit and Dykes Medal winners includes the year the prize was awarded, season of bloom, and a shorthand description for each plant. A special collection for the connoisseur and another for the landscaper are offered. Guarantees true to name and state

inspected. See **Daylilies, Peonies,** Perennials.

Shipping season: July through September.

ARTEMIS GARDENS
1989
Cynthia E. Hyde
Catalog: $1, 23 pp., illustrations

Artemis Gardens specializes in standard dwarf bearded irises and small-flowered daylilies that are adapted to the cold winters and/or cool summer nights typical of many northern growing conditions. One hundred and twenty-five irises from the late 1970s through early 1990s, including numerous award winners. Hybridizer, year of introduction, plant height, and a rich description of each characterize a catalog that offers substantial cultural information. Guarantees true to name and successful in your garden. See **Daylilies.**

Shipping season: July and August.

No Alaska or Hawaii

BAY VIEW GARDENS
1964
Joseph Ghio
Catalog: $2, 18 pp.

A wish book for the connoisseur and collector. Award-winning hybridizer Joseph Ghio introduces his own iris creations of all types as well as the Dunn Louisiana iris and Corlew spuria. Catalog of four hundred cultivars features an up-to-date Pacifica iris listing, releases from the Ghio Pacifica strain, and recent varieties from other top breeders. Hybridizer, year of introduction, color, and rich description for each. Offers a number of mix-and-match collections of named varieties and surprise packages.

Shipping season: Bearded irises, July and August. Beardless irises, September and October.

Canada, Mexico, International

THE BLOOMING HILL
1986
Jerry and Lela Hadrava
Catalog: $1 (recoverable), 32 pp.

Soil conditions at The Blooming Hill range from almost pure sand to clay, from full sun to heavy shade. Species *pseudacorus*, twenty hybrid Louisiana, and fifty Siberians are offered. Information for cultivars includes hybridizer, year of introduction, season of bloom, height, and a quick description of color. See **Daylilies, Hosta.**

Shipping season: Bearded irises, July and August. Beardless irises, August and September.

BLUEBIRD HAVEN IRIS GARDEN
1985
Mary and John Hess
Catalog: $1, 20 pp. Antique varieties: $1, 20 pp.
The range of introduction in Ms. Hess's two catalogs is broad. The catalog of 260 modern varieties is peppered with introductions from the 1950s through the 1980s. The antique catalog (three hundred iris) has historic and vintage cultivars from the 1930s through the 1960s. Hybridizer, year, class, height, bloom time, color, and description given for each entry in both lists. Border bearded, intermediate bearded, miniature dwarf bearded, miniature tall bearded, standard dwarf bearded, and tall bearded varieties available. Guarantees true to name and safe arrival. See Heirlooms.
Shipping season: July and August.

CAPE IRIS GARDENS
1967
Dave Niswonger
Catalog: $1, 32 pp., color photographs
Cape Iris Gardens is primarily for the specialist and collector. Award-winning hybridizer Dave Niswonger includes among his prizes the Dykes Medal. Almost half of the catalog of fifteen hundred varieties are his own, and they include well-described introductions. Potential rebloomers are noted. Cultivars from other sources. Border bearded, intermediate bearded, miniature dwarf bearded, miniature tall bearded, Siberian, standard dwarf bearded, tall bearded, and species varieties available. See Daylilies.
Shipping season: July through October.
Canada, International

CAPRICE FARM NURSERY
1980
Dot, Al, and Rick Rogers, and Robin Blue
Catalog: $2 (recoverable), 36 pp., color photographs
Caprice offers a brief selection of carefully chosen Japanese, Siberian, and water irises. All of their plants are propagated and grown at Caprice. Realistic cultural information and concise narrative descriptions characterize a catalog that is informed and informative. Guarantees true to name and survival through first season; will replace. See Daylilies, Hosta, Peonies, Perennials.
Shipping season: April and May. August through October.
Canada, Mexico, International

CARROLL GARDENS
See Daylilies, Herbs, Hosta, Peonies, Perennials, Roses, Trees.

COMANCHE ACRES IRIS GARDENS
1981
Jim and Lamoyne Hedgecock
Catalog: $3 (recoverable), 24 pp., color photographs
The Hedgecocks introduce their own new varieties (including numerous prizewinners) and offer a selection from other key hybridizers, with a primary focus on the mid-1980s through the mid-1990s. Year of introduction, hybridizer, class, height, color, detailed description, and AIS awards included for each of 160 varieties. A substantial number of assortments for the collector and landscaper are included in a lush and detailed catalog. Border bearded, Louisiana, tall bearded varieties available. Guarantees true to name, disease free, and safe arrival.
Shipping season: July through September.

CONTEMPORARY GARDENS
1972
Perry Dyer
Catalog: $1, 30 pp.
Award-winning hybridizer Perry Dyer (elected president of the Society for Louisiana Irises in 1995) offers a collector's catalog that includes over 225 Louisiana and 200 tall bearded irises. The balance of the selection is composed of arilbred, Border bearded, intermediate bearded, miniature dwarf bearded, miniature tall bearded, and standard dwarf bearded varieties. Hybridizer, year of introduction, color, prizes won, and a brief description for each. Guarantees true to name, state inspected, and healthy on arrival. See Daylilies.
Shipping season: Bearded irises, July and August. Louisiana irises, August and September.
Canada, Mexico, International

COOLEY'S GARDENS
1928
Richard Ernst

Catalog: $4 (recoverable), 80 pp., color photographs

A family operation that also happens to be the world's largest grower of irises. A single iris planted in the Ernsts' backyard in 1923 led to the issuing of their first catalog in 1928. They now grow more than seven million rhizomes annually. Their award-winning catalog is published as *The Iris Fanciers Reference Book*. Three hundred named tall bearded varieties, Cooley's and those of other top hybridizers, are pictured in photographs. Hybridizer, year of introduction, height, awards, tendency to rebloom, and a richly detailed narrative description for each. Dozens of theme collections. Excellent cultural and hybridizing information. Unique "Gardener's Nightmare Insurance" (at an additional charge) protects your irises against such extraordinary occurrences as damage by a neighbor's livestock or children, flood, tornado, the freeze of the century, etc. Guarantees true to name, pest and disease free, and safe arrival.

Shipping season: July through September.
Canada, Mexico, International

COOPER'S GARDEN
1992
Penny Aguirre
Catalog: $1 (recoverable), 41 pp.

Penny Aguirre assumed the stewardship of this garden from founder Joan Cooper. Offers one hundred bearded and beardless species irises; includes height, season of bloom, and color. Hybrid irises include forty Siberian and twenty Louisiana varieties; height, season of bloom, rebloom, hybridizer, and year of introduction provided for each. Collections of labeled surplus offered for both. Japanese hybrids are available only as part of a collection. Guarantees true to name and healthy on arrival. See **Daylilies**, Perennials.

Shipping season: August and September. Siberian irises, May and June.
Canada, Mexico and International ($100 minimum)

CORDON BLEU FARMS
1970
Bob Brooks
Catalog: $1, 48 pp., color photographs

Specializing in daylilies and irises for the collector, Mr. Brooks's offerings include 120 Louisiana and 70 spuria irises. Good general cultural information. Descriptions include hy-

bridizer, year of introduction, color and form of flower and plant, and awards. Guarantees true to name and healthy on arrival; will replace any that fails in the first year for the delivery fee. See **Daylilies**.

Shipping season: August through mid-October.
Canada, Mexico, International

ENGLEARTH GARDENS
1931
The Herrema Family
Catalog: $1, 47 pp.

The main events in the Englearth catalog are the four hundred daylilies and two hundred hostas. However, the Herremas offer several "Michigan hardy" naturalizing mixtures of bearded, Japanese, and Siberian irises in quantities of ten to one hundred per group. Guarantees true to name. See **Daylilies, Hosta**, Perennials.

Shipping season: April through November.
Canada

ENSATA GARDENS
1983
Bob Bauer and John Coble
Catalog: $2

Over the past decade, Bauer and Coble have collected all known available varieties to make Ensata the largest commercial Japanese iris garden in the United States. Upward of 450 varieties are grown, 250 are currently listed in the catalog, and over 1,000 seedlings are planted each year. Extensive cultural information is followed by hybridizer, year of introduction, and succinct descriptions for each plant. Ensata's first Japanese iris was introduced in 1993, their first Siberian in 1994. Ensata is a resource for the collector that also offers several groupings tailored for the beginner.

Shipping season: May and June. July through October.
Canada, Mexico, International

FRIENDSHIP GARDENS
1991
Joan and Ken Roberts
Catalog: $1, 46 pp.

The Robertses assumed the catalog service of Dr. Lloyd Zubrigg (Avonbank Gardens), a hybridizer noted for his work with rebloomers. They list three hundred border bearded, intermediate bearded, standard dwarf bearded, and

tall bearded irises registered primarily in the early 1980s through the early 1990s, including Dr. Zubrigg's own registrations. Hybridizer, year of introduction, height, season of bloom, rebloom (including location and hardiness zone where a given cultivar has rebloomed), and description for each.
Shipping season: July and August.

GILBERT H. WILD & SON
1885
Greg Jones
Catalog: $3 (recoverable), 75 pp., color photographs
The emphasis in Wild's catalog is a selection of three thousand daylilies. Having withdrawn irises from their offerings in the late 1980s they reappeared in 1994. Wild currently offers forty hybrids from the 1970s and mid- to late 1980s, from well-known breeders. Offerings available individually or in several collections. Guarantees true to name and healthy on arrival. See **Daylilies**, Heirlooms, **Peonies**, Perennials.
Shipping season: August through mid-October.
Canada, Mexico, International

HILDENBRANDT'S IRIS GARDENS
1956
Les and Toni Hildenbrandt
Catalog: 2 FCS., 16 pp.
The Hildenbrandts offer a list of seven hundred arilbred, border bearded, dwarf, miniature, and tall bearded varieties, primarily from the mid-1980s through the current year. They do not grow a large number of any single variety and they consistently add new choices. Hybridizer, year of introduction, short description, and awards for main list. Guarantees true to name, state inspected, and healthy on arrival. See Hosta, **Peonies**, Perennials.
Shipping season: July through September.
Canada, Mexico, International

HOLLY LANE IRIS GARDENS
Jan and Jack Worel
Catalog: $1., 24 pp. (separate historical list)
Holly Lane offers 415 hybrid and 20 species iris. Hybridizer, year of introduction, color, and rebloom noted for each border bearded, intermediate bearded, miniature tall bearded, Siberian, and tall bearded listing in the catalog. The Worels provide full descriptions, including season of bloom, of cultivars that they have

bred and introduced in Minnesota. Surplus stock of named varieties in several classifications comprise their reduced-rate collections. A separate list of historical irises is also available. Guarantees true to name and healthy on arrival. See **Daylilies**, Heirlooms, Hosta.
Shipping season: July through September.

HOMESTEAD FARMS
See **Daylilies**, **Hosta**, Peonies, Perennials.

IRIS COUNTRY
1966
Roger R. Nelson
Catalog: $1 (recoverable), 6 pp.
A small number of Mr. Nelson's own cultivars, bred for vigor and hardiness, are fully described. An eclectic selection of ninety bearded irises is also offered. Hybridizer, year of introduction, and quick description for each. A dozen beardless hybrids, spuria, and Siberians round out the catalog.
Shipping season: July through September.
Canada

THE IRIS POND
1984
Clarence Mahan
Catalog: Free, 8 pp.
When not tending his garden, Clarence Mahan writes articles on the iris for *Flower & Garden*, *The American Horticulturist*, and *American Cottage Gardener* magazines. The Iris Pond offers an eclectic mix of 180 irises, including modern Japanese introductions, historic bearded (frequently including the 1797 odoratissima), miniature dwarf bearded, reblooming bearded, tall bearded, Siberian, and ten species beardless. Hybridizer, year of introduction, and short descriptions for all bearded irises; more detail for the beardless. Guarantees true to name and healthy on arrival; will replace any that fails in the first year. See Heirlooms.
Shipping season: Bearded irises, June through August. Beardless irises, August and September.
Canada, Mexico, International

JASPERSON'S HERSEY NURSERY
1989
Lu Jasperson
Catalog: $1, 6 pp.
Ms. Jasperson strives to stay organic in all gar-

dening practices. She offers sixty tall bearded, intermediate bearded, and Siberian irises. Brief description and color for each. Collections of named and unnamed cultivars available. See **Daylilies**, Organics, Perennials.
Shipping season: Siberian irises, August and September. Tall bearded irises, July.

KEITH KEPPEL
1958
Keith Keppel
Catalog: $1, 32 pp.
Noted hybridizer Keith Keppel offers 780 border bearded, intermediate bearded, standard dwarf bearded, and tall bearded irises primarily to the collector seeking new cultivars. His own new introductions, in all three classes, are described in rich detail. Hybridizer, year of introduction, season of bloom, color, and some description for general listings. Also grows "Tempo Two" varieties from Australia.
Shipping season: July and August.

LAURIE'S GARDEN
1964
Lorena M. Reid
Catalog: 1 FCS, 8 pp.
Grower and breeder of beardless irises, specializing in Japanese, Siberian, and interspecies types. Three hundred and fifty offerings fill Ms. Reid's catalog. Hybridizer, year of introduction, height, season of bloom, and copious specifications provided for most. Also offers water and species irises. Guarantees true to name and healthy on arrival. See Perennials, Waterscapes.
Shipping season: July through October.

LONG'S GARDEN
1905
Catherine Long Gates
Catalog: Free, 18 pp.
Four hundred irises, including arilbred, border bearded, intermediate bearded, miniature dwarf bearded, standard dwarf bearded, and tall bearded, registered in the early 1970s through the year prior to catalog date. Hybridizer, year of introduction, color, and Dykes Medal winners noted. Current year's introductions from a select group of Colorado breeders includes description. Rainbow beginners collection of labeled plants. Guarantees true to name; will replace any that fails in the first year.

Shipping season: July and August.

LOUISIANA NURSERY
1950
Dalton E. Durio
Catalog: $4 (recoverable), 98 pp, color and black-and-white photographs
Louisiana Nursery occupies a fifty-six-acre complex that was founded by Ken Durio. Five family members, all trained horticulturists, are currently involved in the business. The Durios publish six specialty catalogs. A portion of this catalog includes eight hundred blue flag, hardy native, hybrid native, hybrid Louisiana, Japanese, species Lousiana, spuria, and water irises. Descriptions include hybridizer, year of introduction, season of bloom, color, height, and awards. Collections of mixed hybrid, hybrid, and species irises, and by color group, with an emphasis on landscaping. The catalog includes two dozen books on daylilies, irises, and general and specifically southern plant interest. Guarantees true to name and healthy on departure, state and U.S. government inspected. See **Booksellers**, **Bulbs**, **Daylilies**, **Fruit**, **Grasses**, **Trees**.
Shipping season: August through October.
Canada, Mexico, International

MAPLE TREE GARDEN
1960
Larry L. Harder
Catalog: $1, 26 pp.
Half of Mr. Harder's catalog is devoted to 750 irises: aril, arilbred, border bearded, intermediate bearded, miniature dwarf bearded, miniature tall bearded, standard dwarf bearded, and tall bearded varieties. Selection concentrates on introductions from 1980s through mid-1990s. Hybridizer, year of introduction, and color for each. Offers customized collections based on your budget. See **Daylilies**.
Shipping season: July through September.
Canada

MARYOTT'S GARDENS
1978
Bill Maryott and Marilyn Harlow
Catalog: $1
Bill Maryott and Marilyn Harlow are both American Iris Society judges. Their catalog includes their own introductions and a general list of over 550 varieties described by hybridizer, year of introduction, height, season of

bloom, and color. Separate sections for intermediate, standard dwarf bearded, and antiques, including a pair of hybrids from the mid-ninteenth century. The Collector's Corner offers five special groupings, including the tried-and-true for beginners. Border bearded, intermediate bearded, miniature dwarf bearded, miniature tall bearded, standard dwarf bearded, and tall bearded varieties available. All of Maryott and Harlow's plants are guaranteed to thrive in your garden. Should a cultivar fail, they will send a replacement with your order the following year.

Shipping season: July and August.

MAXIM'S GREENWOOD GARDENS
1954
Georgia Maxim
Catalog: $2, 24 pp.
Georgia Maxim began growing irises in 1942. She commenced commercial operations twelve years later. Her late husband Paul was a hybridizer and his work is well represented here. The current catalog includes over eleven hundred varieties from a who's who of iris breeders. Hybridizer, year of introduction, color, a brief description, and award winners (which are numerous) noted. Special sections include novelty (Space Age) iris, water iris, winter bloomers, rebloomers, fragrant varieties, and Dykes Medal winners. Arilbred, border bearded, intermediate bearded, Japanese, Louisiana, miniature dwarf bearded, miniature tall bearded, Pacific Coast, Siberian, spuria, tall bearded varieties available. Rainbow collections of tried-and-true named varieties and a classic tall bearded collection are available.

Shipping season: Bearded irises, July through December. Louisiana and Siberian irises, September. Japanese and spuria irises, October through December.

MCALLISTER'S IRIS GARDEN
1991
Sharon McAllister
Catalog: $1 (recoverable), 24 pp.
Arilbreds are McAllister's specialty. The ones grown here have adapted to the stress of temperature variations of 30 to 40 degrees between daytime and night. Aimed at collectors and aspiring hybridizers, McAllister's catalog includes 150 offerings: her own introductions, her collaborations with Gene Hunt and Gus Seligman, and the registrations of a small group of other breeders. Arilbreds, arilbred medians, and regelia species and cultivars are described in depth. Hybridizer and year of introduction included where appropriate. Sampler packages (rhizomes), the "Gene Pool" collection (seedlings), and a "Breeders" collection are available. Cultural information sprinkled throughout. Guarantees true to name, state inspected, and healthy on arrival. Ms. McAllister has written two 32-page booklets, "Hybridizing" and "Varietal Tips for Hybridizers," that can be ordered through her catalog. See **Booksellers**.

Shipping season: July through September.
Canada, International

METAMORA COUNTRY GARDENS
1992
Pat and Larry Salk
Catalog: Free, 20 pp.
Metamora Country Gardens offers ninety hybrid tall bearded irises, 550 hybrid daylilies, and a "Hosta Room" with thirty-five named varieties; also, many seedlings and other perennials. See **Daylilies**, Hosta.

Shipping season: May. August through September.

MID-AMERICA GARDEN
1979
Paul Black
Catalog: $3, 42 pp.
Paul Black opened Mid-America Iris, now Mid-America Garden, with the bearded iris as the main focus. Two years of devastating rains in the early 1990s destroyed many plants and substantially diminished his stock. A change of focus—and name—have ensued. Ships bareroot. Guarantees true to name and safe arrival. See **Daylilies**, Hosta.

Shipping season: August and September.
Canada, Mexico, International

PLEASURE IRIS GARDEN
1979
Luella Danielson
Catalog: $1, 21 pp.
Irises only at this pleasure garden, where many of the plants are originated by Luella or Henry Danielson. One hundred and fifty arilbreds, oncocyclus hybrids and species, regeliocyclus hybrids, and regelia species. Color and technical descriptions. Introductory-level essay on aril/arilbred history and culture. Also offers

small selection of border bearded, intermediate bearded, standard dwarf bearded, and tall bearded rebloomers. Guarantees true to name, and safe arrival.

Shipping season: July through September. Japanese irises, September and October. Canada, Mexico, International ($50 minimum)

POWELL'S GARDENS
1952
Loleta Kenan Powell
Catalog: $3.50 (recoverable), 60 pp.
One quarter of the book is dedicated to thirteen hundred iris varieties. Includes one hundred of Ms. Powell's own tall bearded introductions. A general list of border bearded, intermediate bearded, Japanese, miniature tall bearded, Siberian, and tall bearded varieties from numerous hybridizers provides hybridizer, year of introduction for some, and color for all. See Conifers, **Daylilies**, **Hosta**, Peonies, **Perennials**, Trees.
Shipping season: July and August. Canada, Mexico, International

RORIS GARDENS
Catalog: $3 (recoverable), 72 pp., color photographs
Over three hundred modern tall bearded, irises from the mid-1970s though the current catalog year, developed by well-known breeders. Hybridizer, year of introduction, description, awards, height, and season of bloom for each. Designer, Dykes Medal, and value-priced collections. Planting and care notes. Guarantees true to name and pest and disease free; will replace any that fails in first year with the next season's reorder.
Shipping season: July through September. Canada ($25 minimum), Mexico, International ($50 minimum)

SCHREINER'S IRIS GARDENS
1925
David Schreiner
Catalog: $4 (recoverable), 76 pp., color photographs
The recepient of six Dykes Medals, the first Wister Medal, and numerous other awards, Schreiner's began in St. Paul, Minnesota, as a hobby during World War I. The main feature of the catalog is three hundred tall bearded irises. Hybridizer, year of introduction, season of bloom, height, color, description, and

awards for each. Numerous collections for various needs and fancies. A complementary selection of arilbreds, border bearded, and dwarf and intermediate bearded. Guarantees true to name, pest and disease free, and safe arrival; will replace any that fails in the first year.
Shipping season: July through October. Canada, Mexico, International

SHEPARD IRIS GARDEN
1972
Don and Bobbie Shepard
Catalog: 2 FCS, 24 pp.
Features new border bearded, and tall bearded introductions, fully described, from Don Shepard and Bernard Hamner, new spuria from Charles Jenkins and Floyd Wickencamp. General list of four hundred Louisiana, spuria, and tall bearded varieties from a broad range of breeders. Hybridizer, year of introduction, color and rebloom noted. Brief cultural notes. Guarantees true to name and safe arrival.
Shipping season: July through September Canada

SOCIETY FOR JAPANESE IRISES
See **Horticultural Societies.**

SOCIETY FOR LOUISIANA IRISES
See **Horticultural Societies.**

SOCIETY FOR SIBERIAN IRISES
See **Horticultural Societies.**

SOURDOUGH IRIS GARDENS
1984
Maurine K. Blackwell
Catalog: LSASE, 4 pp.
Sourdough offers 110 dwarf, miniature, and tall bearded varieties that have survived the high altitude and cold weather conditions of the northern Rockies for up to twenty-five years. Catalog organized by color. Brief description and award winners noted.
Shipping season: July and August

THE SPECIES IRIS GROUP OF NORTH AMERICA (SIGNA)
See **Horticultural Societies.**

SPRUCE GARDENS
1988
Cal Reuter
Catalog: $1 (recoverable), 27 pp.

Spruce Gardens offers eleven hundred of the fifteen hundred varieties of irises grown here, ranging from late 1970s through current catalog year. Nine hundred tall bearded varieties, the balance being border bearded, intermediate bearded, miniature dwarf bearded, miniature tall bearded, and standard dwarf bearded irises. Hybridizer, year of introduction, a brief description, and Dyke Medal winners provided for each. Surprise assortments for the value conscious are shipped toward the end of the season and are Mr. Reuter's choice. Guarantees true to name, state inspected, and healthy on arrival. **Shipping season: August and September. Canada, Mexico, International**

STOCKTON IRIS GARDENS
1973
James McWhirter
Catalog: Free, 50 pp., color photographs
The principals owned the Cottage Gardens in San Francisco and are now in the former location of Keith Keppel's iris nursery, which relocated to Salem, Oregon. Over one thousand bearded irises are offered from a wide range of sources. Hybridizer, year of introduction, a brief description, and awards won provided for each. There are separate sections for rebloomers within various classifications. Special collections sold by price point to entice those who are new to iris culture. Border bearded, intermediate bearded, miniature dwarf bearded, miniature tall bearded, standard dwarf bearded, and tall bearded varieties available. Guarantees true to name and safe arrival.
Shipping season: July and August.

SUNNYRIDGE GARDENS
1983
Geraldine Couturier
Catalog: $1.50, 23 pp.
One quarter of the Sunnyridge catalog contains 260 bearded, dwarf bearded, intermediate bearded, miniature tall bearded, tall bearded, and beardless Japanese, Siberian, and species irises. Full specifications including hybridizer and year of introduction for each listing. Some historical varieties. Discounted collection available. Guarantees true to name, state inspected and safe arrival. See **Daylilies**, Heirlooms.
Shipping season: April through October.

TRANQUIL LAKE NURSERY
1970

Philip Boucher and Warren Leach
Catalog: $1, 24 pp., color photographs
Supplemental list: LSASE
Tranquil Lake is a display garden for the Society for Japanese Irises. Boucher and Leach provide hardy plants for the northern gardener, selling only those plants that have performed well in their nursery. Catalog includes sixty Siberian and forty Japanese irises. Hybridizer, specifications, awards, and a brief but rich description for each cultivar. Also offers two species irises. Guarantees true to name and safe arrival. See **Daylilies**.
Shipping season: April and May. August through October.
Canada, Mexico, International

WE-DU NURSERY
See **Bulbs**, Perennials, **Wildflowers**.

WICKLEIN'S WATER GARDENS
See Booksellers, Supplies, **Waterscapes**.

WILDWOOD GARDENS
1984
Will and Tracy Plotner
Catalog: $2, 36 pp.
Wildwood started with Will Plotner's first introductions offered through a two-page flyer. Two thirds of the current catalog includes 535 irises. Rich descriptions of the Plotners' new tall bearded introductions. General listing of tall bearded focuses on varieties from the late 1980s and early 1990s. Hybridizer, year of introduction, height, color, descriptive and cultural information, and awards won for each. Numerous choices for mix-and-match collections include plant name and a brief description. Select choices of Japanese and Siberian irises, including a number of vintage cultivars. Starter collections of "Early Little Ones" and Siberians. See **Daylilies**, Hosta.
Shipping season: Spring, late summer, and fall (depending on plant variety). Canada, Mexico, International

YORK HILL FARM
1990
Darlyn C. Springer
Catalog: $1.50, 30 pp., black-and-white photographs
A specialty nursery offering irises, daylilies, and hostas, especially those plants considered hard to find or new introductions. Plants are

field grown and presented as hardy, tried-and-true, having performed well in New England's "varied and sometimes difficult" climate. A quarter of York Hill's catalog includes 130 Japanese, Louisiana, Siberian, species, and miscellaneous irises. Hybridizer, year of introduction, height, and description for most. Cultural information sprinkled throughout. Guarantees true to name and state inspected. See **Daylilies**, Grasses, Heirlooms, **Hosta**, Perennials.

Shipping season: Mid-April through mid-June. September and October.

Selected Reading About the Iris

The Genus Iris, the 1913 classic by William R. Dykes. Dykes, in whose honor the medal awarded by AIS was established, described and made rational the modern classifications for this flower.

Iris, by Fritz Kohlein. A complete modern survey (1987) of two hundred species and cultivars.

The Iris, by Brian Mathew. Devoted to the wild species iris, with descriptions and information on cultivation.

The Iris Book, by Molly Price. Written with the North American gardener in mind. Describes numerous hybrid and species varieties that bloom from late winter through summer. Includes information on planning, planting, season of bloom, and general culture. Illustrations.

The Louisiana Iris: The History and Culture of Five Native American Species and Their Hybrids, by Marie Caillet and Joseph K. Mertzweiller. Prepared by members of the Society for Louisiana Iris, this work includes the history of this iris, hybridizing techniques, recommended cultivars, and in-depth cultural information. Includes color and black-and-white photographs and line drawings.

$\mathcal{P}$EONIES

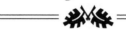

The plant count cited in each profile is based on information in the most recent catalog provided by the source. In this section, shipping season is for peonies only. A selection of books about the peony appears after the last listing.

QUICK FIND
The following sources are listed in this section:

AMERICAN DAYLILY & PERENNIALS
See **Daylilies**, Perennials.

AMERICAN PEONY SOCIETY
See **Horticultural Societies**.

ANDERSON IRIS GARDENS
1978
Sharol and George Longaker
Catalog: $1, 21 pp., black-and-white
photographs
Tall bearded irises occupy almost the entire catalog; however, the Andersons (being located in that part of peony paradise known as Minnesota) also offer sixty varieties of herbaceous peony. Season of bloom, color, brief description. Guarantees true to name and state inspected. See **Daylilies**, **Iris**, Perennials.
Shipping season: September and October.

BRAND PEONY FARM
1870
Irene or Gerald Lund
Catalog: $1 (recoverable), 12 pp.
Walking most of the way from Fond du Lac, Wisconsin, Oliver F. Brand, a nursery salesman, arrived in Faribault, Minnesota, in 1867. Three years later, he established the nursery that became known as Brand Peony Farm. Oliver's son, A. M. Brand, took over the business in 1911, took on a former schoolteacher, Miss Myrtle Gentry, as a partner in 1919, and continued in the business until he died in 1953. In 1956, A. P. and R. W. Tischler (see Tischler Peony Garden) purchased the nursery from Miss Gentry. One hundred and ten years after it all began in Faribault the stock, bought by the Lunds, was

moved to St. Cloud, Minnesota. Brand Peony Farm now grows herbaceous singles, doubles, Japanese, and bomb types that include old named varieties developed by the Brands and others as well as their own new introductions. Catalog of 110 offerings indicates hybridizer, year of introduction for most, shape, color of flower, season of bloom, and growth habit. See **Heirlooms**, Perennials.
Shipping season: September through November.

BUSSE GARDENS
1977
Ainie Busse
Catalog: $2 (recoverable), 56 pp., illlustrations
Busse's highly informative catalog includes two thousand cold-hardy perennials from their new location in Cokato, Minnesota. Offers fifty herbaceous peony cultivars including their own and the work of Auten, Bigger, Brand, Glasscock, and Kreckler. Descriptions of their selection of singles, semi-double, double, and anemone flowering types, include hybridizer, height at maturity, season of bloom, and color. Also offers landscape collection of unlabeled varieties. Guarantees true to name, state inspected, and viable. See **Daylilies**, **Grasses**, **Hosta**, Perennials, **Wildflowers**.
Shipping season: September and October.
No California
Bareroot only: Arizona, Idaho, Kansas, Oregon, Washington

CAPRICE FARM NURSERY
1980

Dot, Al, and Rick Rogers, and Robin Blue
Catalog: $2 (recoverable), 36 pp., color
photographs
Al Rogers is the author of the recently published *Peonies*. Caprice offers fifty considered
varieties of peony within the herbaceous, interspecies (*Itoh*) hybrids, and tree peony
groups. Realistic cultural information and
concise narrative descriptions characterize a
catalog that is informed and informative.
Caprice offers a beginners' sampler and a
choice of collections that are tailored to your
preference of color or season of bloom. Guarantees true to name and survival through first
season; will replace.
See **Daylilies**, Hosta, **Iris**, Perennials.
**Shipping season: September through No-
vember.**
Canada, Mexico, International

CARROLL GARDENS
1933
Alan L. Summers
Catalog: $3 (recoverable), 108 pp.
Carroll Gardens in Westminster, Maryland,
devotes 70 percent of its catalog to seventeen
hundred perennials. The peony section (80
herbaceous types) includes extensive information about peony flower forms, spacing, site
preparation, planting, fertilization, seasonal
care, cutting of the plant and cutting the flowers for decorative use. Descriptions include
flower's characteristics, color, and season of
bloom. Also offers tree (*Paeonia suffruticosa*)
and double fern-leaf (*tenuifolia Rubra Plena*)
types. Guarantees true to name, ready to grow,
and safe arrival (California, Oregon and Washington true to name only); will replace one
time only. See **Daylilies**, Herbs, **Hosta**, Iris,
Perennials, Roses, Trees.
**Shipping season: All peonies September and
October. Selected cultivars year-round.**
Canada

GARDENIMPORT
Dugald Cameron
Catalog: $4, 64 pp., color photographs.
Separate catalogs for spring and fall.
Gardenimport, as their name implies, gathers
plant materials from worldwide sources, and
presents them in an exquisitely photographed
catalog organized by botanical family. The sum-
mer/fall issue concentrates on spring flowering
bulbs and perennials that are easily planted in

the fall. Recent catalogs have included sixteen
named herbaceous and tree peonies including
singles, doubles, and Japanese cultivars. Features the "rare and unusual" Golden Peony
(*Paeonia mlokosewitschii*). Descriptions include
color and form of flower, and season of bloom.
See **Booksellers, Bulbs,** Grasses, Perennials.
Shipping season: Fall.
Canada

GILBERT H. WILD & SON
1885
Greg Jones
Catalog: $3 (recoverable), 75 pp., color
photographs
The Wild's catalog includes three thousand
daylilies, a selection of irises, and over one hundred herbaceous peonies. The peonies represented here include named cultivars from the
mid-nineteenth century through the 1980s. The
selection includes the introductions of Auten,
Glasscock, Nicholls, Saunders, and Wild's own.
Descriptions include hybridizer, year of introduction, color, quality of fragrance, height of
plant, season of bloom, and classification of
bloom described as double, Japanese, single, or
semi-double. Plants sold as three-eye divisions,
or larger upon request. Offers numerous collections grouped by color, fragrance, season of
bloom, and varieties well suited for the South.
Guarantees true to name and healthy on arrival.
See **Daylilies**, Heirlooms, **Iris**, Perennials.
Shipping season: Fall.

GREER GARDENS
1955
Harold E. Greer
Catalog: $3, 148 pp., illustrations and color
photographs
A specialist in rhododendrons and azaleas, Mr.
Greer has over time expanded to include
twenty-five hundred ornamental trees, shrubs,
fruit-bearing plants, perennials, ornamental
grasses, books, and videotapes. Offers thirteen
container-grown tree peonies and twenty
herbaceous cultivars shipped in gallon pots.
Rich descriptions include cultivar name, hardiness zone, color and texture of foliage, use in
the garden, and height and spread at maturity.
A cross-referenced list highlights those offerings that have a pleasing fragrance, exceptional
color, thrive in the shade, or are even obnoxious to deer. Guarantees quality stock, true to
name, and safe arrival; will replace plants one

time only. See **Booksellers, Conifers,** Fruit, Grasses, Perennials, **Rhododendrons, Trees.** **Shipping season: All year (September through May recommended).** **Canada, Mexico, International**

HESCHKE GARDENS
1990
David Heschke
Catalog: Free, 14 pp.
Mr. Heschke offers over eight hundred perennials through his catalog with the major attention to *Astilbe,* daylilies, *Hosta, Lilium,* and peonies. Recent catalogs included fifty herbaceous peonies. Notes cultivar name, color of flower, and height at maturity. See **Daylilies,** Grasses, Hosta, **Perennials.**
Shipping season: April. October and November.

HILDENBRANDT'S IRIS GARDENS
1956
Les and Toni Hildenbrandt
Catalog: 2 FCS, 16 pp.
Forty-five varieties including Klehm Estate Peonies and a number of Japanese cultivars. Season of bloom, flower type, and color. Guarantees true to name, state inspected, and healthy on arrival, See Hosta, **Iris,** Perennials.
Shipping season: September.
Canada, Mexico, International

HOMESTEAD FARMS
1984
Ron Vitoux
Catalog: Free, 32 pp.
Among the perennials the Vitouxes care for, when not lounging around their homemade log cabin, are herbaceous peonies. They offer twenty named varieties. Descriptions include hybridizer, year of introduction for most, prevalence of fragrance, season of bloom, form (bomb, single, double, or Japanese), suitability for use as cut flowers, and awards won where appropriate. Offers several small collections. Guarantees true to name, healthy, and safe arrival. See **Daylilies, Hosta,** Iris, **Perennials.**
Shipping season: August through October.

KLEHM NURSERY
1852
Kit C. Klehm
Catalog: $4 (recoverable), 104 pp., color photographs and illustrations

Five generations of Klehms have tilled the soil and tended plants. Their catalog is a work of art, blending full color photographs, artworks, and exceptional design and detailed cultural information. Peonies are a passion here. Flower forms include single, double, Japanese, and bomb type. Three hundred herbaceous varieties, including their own "Estate Peony" introductions, are in their catalog. Hybridizer, description, flower type, height, and main color included. Ninety tree peonies are also on offer. Hybridizer, description, type of flower, and main color is noted. Guarantees true to name; will replace any plant that fails up to one year from purchase. See **Booksellers, Daylilies, Hosta,** Perennials.
Shipping season: Herbaceous peonies, September through November. Tree peonies, March through November.
Bareroot only to California and Washington.
Canada, Mexico, International

LAURIE'S LANDSCAPE
1987
Laurie Skrzenta
Catalog: $1 (recoverable), 6 pp.
Laurie's garden has graced the pages of several publications. Her brief list of "rare" peonies includes two intersectional hybrids, 'Bartzella' and 'First Arrival'. Descriptions, color, flower type and size, and plant habit and size provided. A general list of thirty herbaceous varieties includes flower type, bloom time, color and size of flower, and plant height. See **Hosta,** Perennials, Trees.
Shipping season: September through November.

MILAEGER'S GARDENS
See **Booksellers, Grasses, Kidstuff, Perennials.**

MOUNTAIN MAPLES
1989
Don and Nancy Fiers
Catalog: $1, 36 pp.
The Fierses, whose Mountain Maples nursery specializes in *Acer palmatum* cultivars and species, and the cultivars of other *Acer* species, recently added eight Moutan (or Chinese) tree peonies, cultivars of *Paeonia suffruticosa,* to their catalog. A thorough introduction to this cultivar precedes individual descriptions. Notes include height, spread, and season of

bloom. Guarantees true to name and healthy. See **Booksellers, Trees.**
Shipping season: October.

PARK SEED® CO.
See **Bulbs, Garlic, Herbs**, Roses, **Seeds, Supplies**, Vegetables.

POWELL'S GARDENS
See Conifers, **Daylilies, Hosta, Iris, Perennials**, Trees.

REATH'S NURSERY
1971
David, Eleanor, R. Scott, and Elizabeth Reath
Catalog: $2, 24 pp., color photographs
The Reath farm was designated as one of Michigan's "Centennial Farms" in 1974, having been owned and tended by the family for one hundred years. The Reaths, who hybridize as a well as grow the introductions of other breeders, include 150 peonies in their catalog. Specialties include the Daphnis series, Itoh-Smirnow hybrid tree peonies, Chinese (or Moutan), Reath's own cultivars, and species peonies. Tree peonies are sold as three- and four-year grafts. Herbaceous varieties, sold as

three- to five-eye divisions include a number of ninteenth-century cultivars but are dominated by the work of breeders such as Brand, Fay, Glasscock, Glasscock-Falk, Murawska, and Saunders. See Perennials.
Shipping season: September and October.
Canada, International

TISCHLER PEONY GARDEN
1976
R. W. Tischler
Catalog: Free, 4 pp.
Mr. Tischler retired from the peony business in 1976—well, sort of. Mr. Tischler purchased the Brand Peony Farm in Faribault (see Brand Peony Farm) from Miss Myrtle Gentry in 1956. He sold out in 1976 in order to retire, which, by his own account, didn't last too long. His current forum includes seventy double, single, Japanese and hybrid peonies. Many of the introductions are his own as well as those of Bigger, Brand, Glasscock, and Lemoine. Descriptions include hybridizer, color and form of bloom, season of bloom, and plant's growth habit. See Perennials.
Shipping season: August and September.
Canada, Mexico, International

Selected Reading About Peonies

The Official Handbook of the American Peony Society. Peony basics including planting, culture, care, disease and pest control, hybridizing, and propagation. Features brief lists of herbaceous and tree peonies categorized by type and color.

Peonies, by Allan Rogers. Mr. Rogers of Caprice Farm Nursery, includes detailed information on peony history, lore, propagation, hybridizing, and cultivation. Describes 1,300 modern cultivars; includes 140 color photographs.

The Peony, by Alice Harding. This combined edition of the author's previously published works is organized, updated, and commented upon by Roy G. Klehm (of Klehm Nursery). *The Peony* represents a selection of Ms. Harding's writings that includes a substantial amount of survey and historical information about both herbaceous and woody peonies. Includes twenty-five color photographs.

H OSTA

The plant count cited in each profile is based on information in the most recent catalog provided by the source. In this section, shipping season is for hosta only. A selection of books about the genus Hosta *appears after the last listing.*

QUICK FIND

The following sources are listed in this section:

AMERICAN HOSTA SOCIETY
See **Horticultural Societies.**

ANDRÉ VIETTE FARM & NURSERY
1920
Mark, André, and Claire Viette
Catalog: $3, 44 pp., color photographs
The Viettes have been growing and selling herbaceous perennials for over seventy years. Their catalog includes one hundred hosta listed by cultivar name. Brief descriptions include color and form of leaves, color of flowers, height and spread at maturity, and relative tolerance to sun. See **Daylilies, Grasses, Perennials.**
Shipping season: March through November.

BANYAI HOSTAS
1984
Bruce and Lois Banyai
Catalog: Free, 8 pp.
The late Pauline Banyai founded the nursery, now owned and operated by her sons and their families. The Banyais continue to propagate for strong floral impact. Eighty cultivars, the creations of Banyai and other hybridizers, are offered. Descriptions are brief. Most of the plants in the catalog are registered with the AHS. Information regarding three hundred additional varieties is available upon request. Guarantees true to name and pest and disease

free; will replace plants that fail within the year.
Shipping season: April through October.

THE BLOOMING HILL
1986
Jerry and Lela Hadrava
Catalog: $1 (recoverable), 32 pp.
Soil conditions at The Blooming Hill range from almost pure sand to clay, from full sun to heavy shade. Hosta and daylilies are the main pursuit. Two hundred and seventy hosta varieties occupy one third of the Hadravas' catalog. Each briefly described, including size of clump at maturity and color of foliage and flower. See **Daylilies, Iris.**
Shipping season: May through September.

BRIDGEWOOD GARDENS
1994
Catalog: Free, 8 pp.
Bridgewood, a recently formed division of Crownsville Nursery specializing in hosta, sends out a newsletter of their offerings two or three times a year. Twenty-five to thirty plants are described in rich detail. An order sheet included with the newsletter provides brief descriptions, flower color, fragrance (when appropriate), and standard plant height and width for 150 varieties. Bridgewood currently grows over 300 varieties

and encourages inquiries.
Shipping season: April and May. September and October.
Bareroot only to Arizona, California, Oregon, and Washington

BUSSE GARDENS
1977
Ainie Busse
Catalog: $2 (recoverable), 56 pp., illustrations
Busse's informative catalog includes two thousand cold-hardy perennials from their new location in Cokato, Minnesota. Among the 200 hosta that they offer, 150 are listed as "select" including cultivars bred by Aden, Avent, Savory, Smith, Summers, Walters, Williams, and under the auspices of the American Hosta Society. Descriptions include hybridizer, color and characteristics of leaves, height at maturity, color of flower, and notes varieties that are sun tolerant. Offers a landscape collection of unlabeled plants that are suitable for underplanting and use as ground cover. Guarantees true to name, state inspected and viable. See Daylilies, Grasses, Peonies, Perennials, Wildflowers.
Shipping season: May through October.
Bareroot only: Arizona, Idaho, Kansas, Oregon, Washington
No California

CAPRICE FARM NURSERY
See Daylilies, Iris, Peonies, Perennials.

CARROLL GARDENS
1933
Alan L. Summers
Catalog: $3 (recoverable), 108 pp.
Carroll Gardens in Westminster, Maryland, devotes 70 percent of its catalog to seventeen hundred perennials. One hundred and twenty hostas, both new cultivars and time-tested standards, are offered. Descriptions include mature clump diameter; height of the foliage mound; height from ground to the tip of the flower stalk; shape, size, and color of leaves; color of flower; and season of bloom. Most of Carroll Gardens' hostas are grown in gallon pots and removed for shipment. Also grows numerous hostas (not listed in catalog) for collectors, and a collection of fragrant hostas that exhibit a diverse range of leaf forms and flower colors. Guarantees true to name, ready to grow, and safe arrival (California, Oregon and Washington true to name only); will replace

one time only. See Daylilies, Herbs, Iris, Peonies, Perennials, Roses, Trees.
Shipping season: March through November.
Canada

ENGLEARTH GARDENS
1931
Ken Herrema and Holly DeShane
Catalog: $1, 47 pp.
A family perennial farm offering two hundred "Michigan hardy" *Hosta* cultivars including their own (primarily small) introductions. Organized by cultivar. Brief description includes plant size, foliage texture, and color. Offers three assortments for naturalizing in the shade. Guarantees true to name. See Daylilies, Iris, Perennials.
Shipping season: May.
Canada

HESCHKE GARDENS
See Daylilies, Grasses, Peonies, Perennials.

HILDENBRANDT'S IRIS GARDENS
See Iris, Peonies, Perennials.

HOLLY LANE IRIS GARDENS
See Daylilies, Heirlooms, Iris.

HOMESTEAD DIVISION OF SUNNYBROOK FARMS
1980
Pete and Jean Ruh
Catalog: $2, $3.50 international (recoverable), 32 pp., 16 color photographs
Hosta seed list: LSASE
Pete and Jean Ruh took over and renovated Sunnybrook Farm in 1946. The Ruhs "retired" to the Homestead Division in 1980, where their focus is a collection of thirteen hundred hostas, the largest in North America. Their catalog presents 250 cultivars, including a select group of natural divisions from the Ruhs' personal collection, introductions from Homestead and Mark Zilis, and Eric Smith's 'Tardiania'. Concise descriptions include color, season of bloom, and leaf form. Ships bareroot. Separate hostas seed list offers twelve hundred varieties.
Shipping season: April through October.
Seeds, January through June.
Canada, International ($100 minimum)

HOMESTEAD FARMS
1984
Ron Vitoux

Catalog: Free, 32 pp.
Homestead Farms is not just another evocative name: the Vitouxes live in a log home built with natural resources harvested from their property. Once their home was completed, the development of nursery stock began in earnest. Offers one hundred hostas organized by color of foliage. Leaf size, plant size, description, and cultural observations included. Guarantees true to name, healthy, and safe arrival. See **Daylilies,** Iris, **Peonies,** Perennials.
Shipping season: April through October.

IRON GATE GARDENS
1960
Van M. Sellers and Vic Santa Lucia
Catalog: $2 (recoverable), 40 pp., color photographs
Although Sellers and Santa Lucia's primary focus is *Hemerocallis* (90 percent of their catalog and their fax number are devoted to it), there are plenty of hostas here. The catalog offers 160 cultivars, including several of Iron Gate's own introductions. Brief description of leaf color and form. See **Daylilies.**
Shipping season: April through June.
Canada, Mexico, International

JERNIGAN GARDENS
1955
Winifred Jernigan Williams
Catalog: $1 (recoverable), 16 pp.
Bettie Godwin, Winifred Jernigan Williams's mother, planted her first flower, a peony, here in 1925. Jernigan Gardens came into being as a business in 1955 when Bettie and her husband, Noble Jernigan, took an ad in *The Progressive Farmer.* One hundred and sixty hostas, including Jernigan Gardens' introductions. Size, leaf form and color, and brief description included. A few award winners tucked into the list. Guarantees true to name and state inspected. See **Daylilies.**
Shipping season: April through October.

KLEHM NURSERY
1852
Kit C. Klehm
Catalog: $4 (recoverable), 104 pp., color photographs and illustrations
Five generations of Klehms have tilled the soil and tended to their plants. The Klehm Nursery catalog is a work of art, blending full-color photographs, artwork, exceptional design, and substantial cultural information. One hundred and twenty-five *Hosta* varieties offered. Hybridizer, height, width, leaf color and form, bloom color, and description included. Guarantees true to name; will replace plant that fails up to one year from purchase. See **Booksellers, Daylilies, Peonies,** Perennials.
Shipping season: March through November.
Canada, Mexico, International

KUK'S FOREST NURSERY
1986
Bob Kuk
Catalog: $2 (recoverable), 21 pp.
Hostas only need apply at KFN. Bob Kuk's first seedling selection was in 1979 with *H.* 'Bizarre'. His cultivar 'Gray Cole' won a major award in 1986, coinciding with the opening of Kuk's nursery. A catalog of 225 species and hybrid *Hosta* includes over two dozen of Kuk's introductions, as well as those of other key breeders. Hybridizer, size, leaf form and color, bloom color, habit, and description. Collection of Kuk's introductions for the connoisseur. "Create a Border" and "Create a Slope" collections for quick landscaping. Guarantees true to name, pest and disease free, and state inspected.
Shipping season: April through October.
Canada ($100 minimum), International ($250 minimum)

LAKESIDE ACRES
1957
Mary Chastain
Catalog: $2 (recoverable), 18 pp.
One fourth of the Lakeside catalog is dedicated to 180 hostas. A few have been bred here. Size, leaf color and form, a brief description, and occasional cultural information included. Guarantees state inspected and safe arrival. See **Daylilies,** Perennials.
Shipping Season: May through October.
International

LAURIE'S LANDSCAPE
1987
Laurie Skrzenta
Catalog: $1 (recoverable), 6 pp.
Laurie's garden has graced the pages of several publications. Seventy-five tissue culture container-grown hostas from a variety of sources are offered. Leaf color and form, size, habit, and short description provided for each. See

Peonies, Perennials, Trees.
Shipping season: May through September.

LEE GARDENS
1988
Janis Lee
Catalog: $2 (recoverable), 32 pp.
The hostas at Lee Gardens have proven to be hardy through extreme heat and cold, moisture and drought. Descriptions for 230 listings include size, color and form of leaf, and color of flower for each. Guarantees true to name and safe arrival. Ships bareroot. See **Daylilies, Perennials.**
Shipping season: April to first frost in Tremont, Illinois.

METAMORA COUNTRY GARDENS
See **Daylilies, Iris.**

MID-AMERICA GARDEN
Circa 1979
Paul Black
Catalog: $3, 42 pp.
Paul Black founded Mid-America Iris, now Mid-America Garden, with the bearded iris as the main focus. Two years of devastating rains in the early 1990s destroyed many plants and diminished his stock. A change of focus—and name—ensued. Ten percent of the catalog now features 185 hostas. Description of each offering includes size, leaf form, color, and habit. Guarantees true to name and safe arrival. See **Daylilies, Iris.**
Shipping season: May. August and September.
Canada, Mexico, International

PLANT DELIGHTS NURSERY
1988
Tony and Michelle Avent
Catalog: $2, 117 pp.
Plant Delights was started to support the test and demonstration gardens at Juniper Level Botanical Gardens. The purpose now is to search out new and better perennials and introduce them to the trade. Plant Delights has a number of areas of concentration among the five thousand varieties on site. Hostas are a "special" specialty. An extensive breeding program and the fruits (er, foliage) of the Avents' labors have culminated in the offering of two hundred species and hybrid hostas. If you can stop chuckling while reading this catalog (the author could have a career in comedy if the nursery fails), you will find hybridizer, year of introduction, light preference, hardiness zone, height, and a rich description for each hosta. Chart of hostas grouped by foliage and flower color. Guarantees true to name and safe arrival. See **Conifers, Grasses, Perennials,** Trees
Shipping season: March through November.
Canada, Mexico, International

POWELL'S GARDENS
1952
Loleta Kenan Powell
Catalog: $3.50 (recoverable), 60 pp.,
Hosta specimen list: LSASE
Ms. Powell's catalog includes eight hundred hostas, covering almost every conceivable garden situation. This section features current and recent Powell introductions that are richly described. The general list has an intense variety of plants from a range of sources. Size and leaf form and color for all; bloom color, hybridizer, and year of introduction for many. A limited specimen list of Powell's finest hostas planted in display pots is also available. See **Conifers, Daylilies, Iris,** Peonies, **Perennials, Trees.**
Shipping season: April through September.
Canada, Mexico, International

ROBYN'S NEST NURSERY
1989
Robyn Duback
Catalog: $2 (recoverable), 32 pp., illustrations
Robyn Duback has amassed what she believes to be the largest collection of West Coast hosta hybrids in North America. New and recent introductions from select sources in the Northwest, including Caprice Farm, Collector's Nursery, and Walden West are a feature. Also showcases the introductions of British hybridizer Eric Smith. The Robyn's Nest catalog, which includes planting and cultural instructions, offers over three hundred varieties of hostas. Information for each listing includes hybridizer, plant size, leaf form and color, and a thorough and intimate description. Notes award winners. Offers collections for color, fragrance, and form. Guarantees true to name, and pest and disease free. See **Grasses, Perennials.**
Shipping season: May through October.
Canada, International

R. SEAWRIGHT
1976
Bob and Love Seawright
Catalog: $2 (recoverable), 28 pp.

One quarter of the Seawright's catalog is devoted to 175 varieties of hostas. Height, leaf size, detailed description of foliage and flower, habit, and cultural information for each listing. Guarantees true to name, state inspected, and safe arrival. See **Daylilies**.
Shipping season: May through September.

SAVORY'S GARDENS, INC.
1946
Bob, Arlene, and Dennis Savory
Catalog: $2, 34 pp., color photographs
The Savory's catalog offers 270 of the 1,200 varieties grown in their garden. Selection includes 30 hybrids developed by the Savorys and AHS popularity poll winners. Descriptions include size, color, leaf form, and season of bloom. Offers separate collections of blue and gold varieties. Guarantees true to name and state inspected. Ships bareroot. See **Supplies**.
Shipping season: April and May. September and October.
Canada ($100 minimum), Mexico, International ($250 minimum)

SHADY OAKS NURSERY
1980
Dr. Clayton Oslund
Catalog: $1 (bulk), $2.50 (FC), 46 pp., color photographs
The nursery evolved out of need. The Oslunds found it a challenge to obtain perennials that would thrive under the shade of their spreading oaks. Having undertaken the research, and believing that the desire to establish diverse plantings in various degrees of shade was not unique to them, they opened Shady Oaks. Organized by color of foliage, the hosta section contains over 250 varieties. Subsections feature types with variegated foliage, dwarfs, fragrant plants, those with high resistance to slug attack, popularity poll winners, and hosta "babies" produced from tissue culture. Size, leaf form, and description for each variety. The Oslunds share substantial cultural information from their "shady" experiences. Guarantees true to name and successful in your garden if planted within appropriate hardiness zone; will replace or issue credit or refund. See **Booksellers, Grasses, Perennials.**
Shipping season: March through September. No California.
International (bareroot or nonsoil media)

SOULES GARDEN
1979
Marge Roberts Soules
Catalog: $2 (recoverable), 36 pp.
Ms. Soules has a passion for hybridizing and growing hostas. She devotes half of her catalog to 350 of the 700 varieties grown in her garden. Current year's introductions and a general list of modern varieties. Size, height, and color of bloom and leaf. See **Daylilies**.
Shipping season: May through October.

SUNNYBROOK FARMS
1928
Tim Ruh
Catalog: $1 (recoverable), 34 pp., color photographs
Founded by Tim's grandfather, Dr. Harold Ruh, Sunnybrook has access to the largest collection of hostas in North America. This collection, under the stewardship of Tim's parents (see Homestead Division), maintains thirteen hundred cultivars. The Sunnybrook catalog contains concise descriptions, including size, color, leaf form, and season of bloom for 150 varieties. Ships bareroot. Guarantees state inspected and safe arrival. See **Herbs, Perennials.**
Shipping season: March through June. September and October.

WALDEN WEST
1982
Dr. Charles Purtymun and Jay Hyslop
Catalog: $1, 12 pp.
Catalog features 240 of the 500 hostas grown at Walden West, including their own 'Abiqua' introductions that have been tested on site for seven or eight years. Size, leaf color and form, bloom color, and a brief description for each. Guarantees true to name, disease free, and state inspected.
Shipping season: May through September.
Canada, some European countries

WILDWOOD GARDENS
See **Daylilies, Iris.**

YORK HILL FARM
1990
Darlyn C. Springer
Catalog: $1.50, 30 pp., black-and-white photographs
A specialty nursery offering hard-to-find varieties and new introductions. Plants are field

grown and presented as "hardy, tried-and-true," having performed well in "New England's varied and sometimes difficult climate." The York Hill catalog includes sixty varieties of hostas. Hybridizer and description for each offering. Guarantees true to name and state inspected. See **Daylilies**, Grasses, Heirlooms, **Iris**, Perennials.

Shipping season: Mid-April through mid-June. September and October.

Selected Reading About Hosta

The Gardener's Guide to Growing Hostas, by Diana Grenfell. Advice on cultivation, propagation, and garden uses. An alphabetical plant listing describes four hundred varieties. Seventy-five color photographs.

Genus Hosta, by W. George Schmid. A comprehensive scientific and horticultural study. Includes detailed descriptions of named species, cultivars, and nonregistered classic variations. Two hundred color photographs.

The Hosta Book, edited and compiled by Paul Aden. An ensemble work incorporating the writings of distinguished contributors. Valuable information on hosta culture and landscape use. Two hundred color photographs.

GRASSES, SEDGES, RUSHES, AND BAMBOOS

The plant count cited in each profile is based on information in the most recent catalog provided by the source. In this section, shipping season is for bamboos and ornamental grasses only. A selection of books about grasses, sedges, rushes, and bamboos appears after the last listing.

QUICK FIND:
The following sources are listed in this section:

AMBERGATE GARDENS
ANDRÉ VIETTE FARM & NURS-
ERY
ARROWHEAD ALPINES
BALDWIN SEED CO.– SEEDS OF
ALASKA
BEAVER CREEK NURSERY
BERLIN SEEDS
BLUESTEM PRAIRIE NURSERY
BLUESTONE PERENNIALS
BURT ASSOCIATES BAMBOO
BUSSE GARDENS
CANYON CREEK NURSERY
CATTAIL MEADOWS LTD.
CLASSIC GROUNDCOVERS
COMSTOCK SEED
COUNTRY WETLANDS NURSERY
& CONSULTING
DEGIORGI SEED COMPANY
DIGGING DOG NURSERY
D. LANDRETH SEED COMPANY
EARTHLY GOODS LTD.
EDGE OF THE ROCKIES "NATIVE
SEEDS"
FAR NORTH GARDENS
FEDER'S PRAIRIE SEED COM-
PANY
FORESTFARM®
FROSTY HOLLOW ECOLOGICAL
RESTORATION
GARDEN CITY SEEDS
GARDEN PERENNIALS
GARDEN PLACE
GARDENIMPORT
GARDENS NORTH
GIRARD NURSERIES

GREEN HORIZONS
GREENLEE NURSERY
GREER GARDENS
HAMILTON SEEDS & WILD-
FLOWERS
HERONSWOOD NURSERY LTD.
HESCHKE GARDENS
A HIGH COUNTRY GARDEN
HOMAN BROTHERS SEED
HORTICO, INC.
IOWA PRAIRIE SEED COMPANY
JAPONICA WATER GARDENS
JOHNNY'S SELECTED SEEDS
JOY CREEK NURSERY
KURT BLUEMEL, INC.
LAMB NURSERIES
LANDSCAPE ALTERNATIVES, INC.
LARNER SEEDS
LAS PILITAS NURSERY
LIMEROCK ORNAMENTAL
GRASSES, INC.
LOCKHART SEEDS, INC.
LOUISIANA NURSERY
MATTERHORN NURSERY, INC.
MILAEGER'S GARDENS
MINIATURE PLANT KINGDOM
MISSOURI WILDFLOWERS
NURSERY
MOSTLY NATIVES NURSERY
MT. TAHOMA NURSERY
NATIVE AMERICAN SEED
NATIVE GARDENS
NEW ENGLAND BAMBOO CO.
ORAL LEDDEN & SONS
OTTER VALLEY NATIVE PLANTS

PEACEFUL VALLEY FARM &
GARDEN SUPPLY
PERENNIAL PLEASURES NURSERY
OF VERMONT
PLANT DELIGHTS NURSERY
PLANTS OF THE SOUTHWEST
PRAIRIE MOON NURSERY
PRAIRIE NURSERY
PRAIRIE RIDGE NURSERY
PRAIRIE SEED SOURCE
RAINTREE NURSERY
ROBYN'S NEST NURSERY
ROSWELL SEED COMPANY, INC.
SEEDS TRUST: HIGH ALTITUDE
GARDENS
SHADY OAKS NURSERY
SHARP BROS. SEED CO.
SHOOTING STAR NURSERY
STEVE RAY'S BAMBOO GARDENS
STOCK SEED FARMS
SURRY GARDENS
THOMPSON & MORGAN
TRADEWINDS BAMBOO NURS-
ERY
TRIPPLE BROOK FARM
WAVECREST NURSERY AND
LANDSCAPING
WAYSIDE GARDENS
WEISS BROTHERS PERENNIAL
NURSERY
WILD EARTH NATIVE PLANT
NURSERY
WILD SEED, INC.
YORK HILL FARM
YUCCA DO NURSERY AT PECK-
ERWOOD GARDENS

AMBERGATE GARDENS
1985
Mike and Jean Heger
Catalog: $2, 68 pp., illustrations and color
photographs
The Hegers, based in Waconia, Minnesota, offer
two hundred uncommon and/or unusual native

and exotic perennials hardy in zone 4. Mr. Heger
is the author of *Perennials from A to Z*, based
upon a series of articles that he wrote for the
Minnesota Horticulturist. Just under 10 percent of
the catalog is devoted to ornamental grasses, with
a concentration of what Mr. Heger describes as
the most ornamental of the reed grasses. Within

each section offerings are organized by botanical name. Common name, color of flower, nature of foliage, season of bloom, height at maturity, cultural preferences and habits, companion planting tips, and notes about each variety's horticultural value are encased in the Hegers' thorough and accessible descriptive gems. Ships bareroot. Guarantees state inspected, true to name, and healthy. See **Booksellers, Perennials.**
Shipping season: April and May. September and October.
Canada

ANDRÉ VIETTE FARM & NURSERY
1920
Mark, André, and Claire Viette
Catalog: $3, 44 pp., color photographs
The Viettes have been growing and selling perennials for over seventy years. Their catalog includes fifty ornamental grasses organized by botanical name. Descriptions include common or cultivar name and a brief mention of foliage color and characteristics and height at maturity. See **Daylilies, Hosta, Perennials.**
Shipping season: March through November.

ARROWHEAD ALPINES
See **Conifers, Perennials, Seeds,** Trees, **Wildflowers.**

BALDWIN SEED CO.–SEEDS OF ALASKA
See Seeds, **Wildflowers.**

BEAVER CREEK NURSERY
See **Conifers,** Trees.

BERLIN SEEDS
See **Booksellers, Fruit, Garlic, Kidstuff, Seeds, Supplies,** Vegetables.

BLUESTEM PRAIRIE NURSERY
See Seeds, **Wildflowers.**

BLUESTONE PERENNIALS
See **Perennials,** Trees.

BURT ASSOCIATES BAMBOO
1990
Albert Adelman
Catalog: $2 (recoverable), 16 pp.
Burt's "Bamboo: A Guide for the Home and Garden" is an enlightening short course in the nature of bamboo, bamboo anatomy, and how to grow it indoors and out. Catalog organized by botanical name, updated lists organized into tall,

short, and collectible (specimens in limited quantities) varieties. Describes about fifty varieties but welcomes inquiries about additional offerings. Stock-in-trade includes Buddha Belly (*Bambusa ventricosa*), *Chimonobambusa quadrangularis* (square bamboo), *Chusquea coronalis,* and several *Fargesia, Phyllostachys, Pleioblastus* (Japanese running type), and *Sasa.* Information about growth habit, suitability for bonsai or other container cultures, height at maturity and, color and characteristics of culms and leaves. All plants are grown and shipped in their containers.
Shipping season: All year.
No Hawaii
Canada

BUSSE GARDENS
See Daylilies, **Hosta, Peonies, Perennials,** Wildflowers.

CANYON CREEK NURSERY
See **Perennials.**

CATTAIL MEADOWS LTD.
See **Wildflowers.**

CLASSIC GROUNDCOVERS
See **Perennials.**

COMSTOCK SEED
1985
Ed and Linda Kleiner
Catalog: Free, 4 pp.
The Kleiners collect most of their drought-tolerant seeds in the Great Basin area of the Far West. The Comstock catalog lists (intermittently by common or botanical name) wildflowers and forbs; legumes, trees and shrubs; and fifty grasses, sedges, and rushes including alkalai grass, bluegrass, brome, carex, fescue, needle grass, wheat grass, and wild rye. Price by weight on request. Guarantees correctly labeled. See Seeds, Trees, **Wildflowers.**
Shipping season: All year.
Canada, Mexico, International

COUNTRY WETLANDS NURSERY & CONSULTING
1987
Jo Ann Gillespie
Catalog: $2, 16 pp., illustrations and black-and-white photographs
Ms. Gillespie fully describes the wetland restoration and management services that her company

provides. She also explains the characteristics of the natural communities for which Country Wetlands' plants are appropriate. One hundred and twenty species of plants and 135 seeds suitable for wetlands, prairie, and woodlands of the greater Midwest, including grasses, rushes, and sedges. Selection includes *Andropogon, Carex, Eleocharis* (spikerush), *Glyceria, Juncus, Scripus* (bulrush), and *Spartina.* Listings organized by botanical name; includes common name, level of availability, and native community. Seeds sold by weight. Guarantees viable and true to name. See **Booksellers**, Seeds, Waterscapes, **Wildflowers**.
Shipping season: All year.

DeGiorgi Seed Company
See **Booksellers, Garlic**, Herbs, **Kidstuff, Seeds**, Vegetables.

Digging Dog Nursery
1978
Deborah Whigham and Gary Ratway
Catalog: $2, 66 pp., color illustrations
Gary, a landscape architect, and Deborah opened Digging Dog in 1978 because he had a difficult time finding plant material for his design jobs. Their first catalog dropped in 1993. Mail-order selections are those plants that they have observed over time, in Gary's landscapes and at the nursery. Presented as noteworthy for ease of care, long bloom periods, attractive year-round form, texture, color, and versatility are one hundred perennials, twenty ornamental grasses, fifty shrubs, and a dozen trees and vines. Rich descriptions include height and width estimates, bloom times, hardiness and sun/shade tolerance. See **Perennials, Trees.**
Shipping season: February through May.
September through November.

D. Landreth Seed Company
See Garlic, Heirlooms, Herbs, **Seeds**, Vegetables.

Earthly Goods Ltd.
See **Furniture**, Seeds, **Wildflowers**.

Edge of the Rockies "Native Seeds"
See Seeds, **Wildflowers**.

Far North Gardens
See **Booksellers, Bulbs, Perennials, Seeds, Wildflowers**.

Feder's Prairie Seed Company
See Seeds, **Wildflowers**.

Forestfarm®
1974
Ray and Peg Pragg
Catalog: $3, 414 pp., illustrations and black-and-white photographs
The Praggs' catalog, containing some four thousand plants and including an ornamental grasses and sedges section that accounts for eight pages and sixty offerings, is organized by botanical name but also includes a common-name index that makes working with it a pleasure. Excellent standardized descriptions include genus, species, variety, common name, foliage habit, hardiness zone, origin, plant uses, cultural conditions, and a description of the plant's habits, form, and site preference. Ships in small tubes or one- and five-gallon containers depending on variety and availability. Guarantees true to name. See **Conifers, Fruit, Perennials, Roses, Trees.**
Shipping season: All year.
Canada

Frosty Hollow Ecological Restoration
See Seeds, Trees, **Wildflowers**.

Garden City Seeds
See **Booksellers, Garlic**, Herbs, Organics, **Seeds, Supplies**.

Garden Perennials
See **Daylilies, Perennials**.

Garden Place
1974
Kathy Sneary
Catalog: $1, 24 pp.
This division of Springrbrook Nurseries offers over six hundred types of perennial including thirty-five ornamental grasses primarily from the *Deschampia, Festuca, Miscanthus* and *Pennisetum* species. Plants are briefly described including hardiness zone, height at maturity, color of foliage and flower, and suggested garden uses. Symbols indicate sun/shade preference and suitability for the cutting garden. Includes cross-indexes that group plants by their color; height at maturity, foliage habit; partiality to sun, shade, or light shade; and their suitability as cut flowers. Guarantees true to name and healthy upon arrival; will replace those that prove untrue. See **Perennials**.

Shipping season: September through May.
Canada, Mexico

GARDENIMPORT
See Booksellers, Bulbs, Peonies, Perennials.

GARDENS NORTH
1991
Kristl Walek
Catalog: $4, 100 pp.
Gardens North's purpose is to offer perennial seed that will be hardy for the majority of Canadian gardeners. Ms. Walek offers over eight hundred types of perennial (and biennial) flowering plants and nearly fifty ornamental grasses, rushes, and sedges developed (primarily) on site using only organic methods. Rich descriptions highlighted by insightful personal observations and anecdotes provide the commentary to match the substance of her offerings in what is one of the best written seed catalogs you are likely to encounter. Descriptions include common name, season of bloom and other seasons of interest, cultural habits, germination methods and tips, and hardiness information based on the experiences and reports of Ms. Walek's network of growers and gardeners. Seed sold by the packet with a specified number of seeds per packet, and by weight. See Perennials, Seeds, Wildflowers.
Canada, International

GIRARD NURSERIES
See Conifers, Rhododendrons, Seeds, Trees.

GREEN HORIZONS
See Booksellers, Seeds, Wildflowers.

GREENLEE NURSERY
1985
John Greenlee and Kathy Reeder
Catalog: $5, 34 pp.
The Greenlee catalog is a mini-education in ornamental grasses and grassy-looking plants. Mr. Greenlee reassuringly takes the home gardener through various points about habit, flowering, water requirements, planting, fertilization, disease and pest management, and pruning and maintenance. Over 225 offerings include *Acorus*, *Andropogon* (blue stems), *Arundo* (giant reeds), *Boutela*, *Calamagrostis* (reed grasses), *Carex* (sedges), *Cortaderia* (pampas grass), *Cyprus* (including papyrus), *Deschampsia*, *Elymus* (rye), *Festuca*, *Juncus* (rushes), *Luzula* (wood rushes), *Miscanthus*,

Molinia and *Sesleria* (moor grasses), *Panicum* (switch grasses), *Pennisetum* (fountain grasses), *Typha* (cattails), and *Vetiver Zizanoides* (*Vetiver-Khus-Khus-Khas-Khas*), which has been sought for its aromatic oil since the time of Marco Polo. Organized by botanical name, descriptions for the individual listing are thorough and even-handed and include provenance, common name, hardiness zones, height, spread, appropriate garden and landscape uses, seasonal foliage color changes, and nature of flower. A guide for quick reference includes lists of grasses that provide fall color, colored foliage; are shade, drought, or moisture tolerant; flower in the spring, flower in the summer; are suitable for cut flowers; and are useful as beach plantings, as ground cover in sun, or in varying degrees of shade. Guarantees true to name.
Shipping season: With dirt, June through September. Bareroot, October through May.

GREER GARDENS
1955
Harold E. Greer
Catalog: $3, 148 pp., illustrations and color photographs
Originally a specialist in rhododendrons and azaleas, Greer over time has expanded to include ornamental trees, shrubs, conifers, fruiting plants, rock garden plants, perennials, ground covers, bonsai specimens, books, and videos. The catalog offers thirty-five grasses, including *Carex*, *Cortaderia*, *Miscanthus*, and fifteen bamboo types, including *Fargesia*, *Phyllostachys*, and *Pleioblastus*. Guarantees quality stock, true to name, and safe arrival, will replace plants (one time only) that have been properly cared for but do not survive.
See Booksellers, Conifers, Fruit, Peonies, Perennials, Rhododendrons, Trees.
Shipping season: all year (recommends September through May).
Canada, Mexico, International

HAMILTON SEEDS & WILDFLOWERS
1981
Rex and Amy Hamilton
Catalog: Free, 15 pp., color photographs
The Hamiltons offer forty-five perennial wildflowers and ten grasses native to Missouri and the Midwest, including big bluestem, broom sedge, prairie dropseed, river oats, switch grass, and wild rye. Grasses are organized by relative height and listed by common name. Descriptions include botanical name, height at matu-

rity, sun and shade requirements, and preferred soil type. Bareroot plants are two to five years old. Seeds are two hundred to a packet or sold by weight. See Seeds, **Wildflowers**.
Shipping season: Bareroot, March and April. Seeds, all year.

HERONSWOOD NURSERY LTD.
1987
Daniel Hinkley and Robert L. Jones
Catalog: $4, 220 pp.
Heronswood characterizes its mission as procuring and offering plant materials that have not previously been available to North American gardeners. Mr. Hinkley (author of *Winter Ornamentals*) and Mr. Jones list over two thousand trees, shrubs, perennials, and ornamental grasses. Among the seventy grasses that Mr. Hinkley and Mr. Jones have offered in their recent catalogs are three *Acorus*, three *Calamagrostis*, eighteen *Carex*, three *Luzula*, fifteen *Miscanthus*, four *Pennisetum*, a pair of *Stipa*, one *Unicinia unciniata*, and a single *Xerophyllum tenax*. Descriptions include provenance, hardiness zone, site preference, pot size, and a highly visual narrative of the plants' form, color, and size. Guarantees true to name, healthy upon departure; will accept claims filed within ten days of receipt. See **Conifers**, Fruit, **Perennials, Rhododendrons, Trees**.
Shipping season: March through mid-May.
Mid-September through October.
Canada

HESCHKE GARDENS
See **Daylilies**, Hosta, **Perennials, Peonies**.

A HIGH COUNTRY GARDEN
See Cactus, **Perennials**.

HOMAN BROTHERS SEED
See Seeds, Trees, **Wildflowers**.

HORTICO, INC.
Bill Vanderkruk
Perennials catalog: $3, 42 pp.
This Hortico catalog includes over sixteen hundred ferns, wildflowers, herbaceous perennials, bog plants, ground covers, herbs, grasses, and bamboos. Hortico carries one hundred types of bamboo, ornamental grasses, rushes and sedges. Recent catalogs included meadow foxtail (*Alopecurus*), quaking grass (*Brizza*), *Carex*, *Deschampsia*, blue lyme grass (*Elymus*), sheep's fescue (*Festuca*), *Miscanthus*, moor grass (*Molinia*),

and fountain grass (*Pennisetum*), and cord grass (*Spartina*). Descriptions are clear but spare and geared toward the trade; however, this nursery wholesaler invites retail orders by fax or mail. Plants shipped in six-inch or one gallon pots. Guarantees true to name and healthy when shipped. See **Perennials, Roses**, Trees, Waterscapes.
Shipping season: November through May.
Canada, International (Europe)

IOWA PRAIRIE SEED COMPANY
See Seeds, **Wildflowers**.

JAPONICA WATER GARDENS
See **Waterscapes**.

JOHNNY'S SELECTED SEEDS
See **Booksellers, Garlic**, Heirlooms, **Herbs**, Organics, **Seeds, Supplies**, Vegetables.

JOY CREEK NURSERY
Mike Smith and Scott Christy
Catalog: $2, 52 pp. Extended list: LSASE
Joy Creek Nursery grows perennials and ornamental grasses from seeds, cuttings, and divisions on site in Scappoose, Oregon, where they are also overwintered. Seedlings and cuttings are raised in a soilless mixture. Their catalog includes five hundred offerings and their extended list includes upwards of six hundred additional plants. A little more than 5 percent of their combined lists are devoted to ornamental grasses including a number of *Carex*, *Festuca*, *Miscanthus*, *Panicum*, and *Pennisetum*. Descriptions include common name, sun/shade preference, hardiness zone, color of flower, height at maturity, season of bloom, and intermittent comments and observations. Extended list (get out your reference books) are listed by botanical name only. Plants shipped out of their pots with rootball intact. Guarantees safe arrival; will replace or refund. See **Perennials**.
Shipping season: Late February through mid-November.

KURT BLUEMEL, INC.
1964
Catalog: $3, 49 pp., illustrations and color photographs
Mr. Bluemel has been an important advocate of the propagation and use of ornamental grasses in the garden and landscape. His catalog includes 270 grasses, sedges, rushes, and over a dozen bamboos

such as *Acorus calamus, A. gramineus, Agropyon, Andropogon, Arundo, Bouteloua, Calamagrostis, Carex* (including a mop-headed sedge grass called 'The Beatles'), *Cortaderia, Deschampsia, Equisetum, Festuca, Holcus, Koeleria, Luzula, Miscanthus* (most available in specimen five gallon size and larger), *Molinia, Panicum, Pennisetum, Phalaris, Pharagmites, Poa, Partina, Stipa, Typha,* and *Zizania latifolia.* Descriptions include hardiness zone, whether a plant requires spring or fall planting, and salient features of each type. Plants are field grown and shipped bareroot. Catalog includes a list of grasses for specific purposes such as: specimens, cut flowers, screening, seashore, and natural landscapes, and a list of those with desirable traits such as fall color, shade, drought, or moisture tolerance, and those with spring or summer inflorescens. Also offers a comprehensive video dictionary of ornamental grasses, slide sets, and a color poster of forty (labeled) grasses in their natural settings. Guarantees plants true to name; will replace (claims for stock that does not survive must be made within five days of receipt). See **Perennials, Waterscapes.**
Shipping season: March through frost in Baldwin, Maryland.
Canada, International/$250 minimum

LAMB NURSERIES
See **Perennials, Trees.**

LANDSCAPE ALTERNATIVES, INC.
1986
Karl Ruser
Catalog: $2, 16 pp.
Mr. Ruser offers 150 native and other low-maintenance cold-hardy grasses and forbs. Plants are nursery propagated from stock originally collected within a hundred-mile radius of St. Paul, Minnesota. Catalog is organized by conditions: full sun/dry, full sun/dry to mesic, full sun/mesic to moist on through grasses for full shade/mesic. Descriptions include common and botanical names, color, height at maturity, and suggestions for use in the garden. The catalog poses a series of questions to encourage the reader to evaluate site and conditions in order to select the right plant for the right location. A considerable amount of space is devoted to precise planting guidelines and to describing the benefits of naturalizing the landscape. Offers preplanned assortments for prairie gardens (forbs and grasses) as well as native and ornamental grass packages. Guarantees true to name. See **Wildflowers.**
Shipping season: April through September.

LARNER SEEDS
1978
Judith Lowry
Catalog: $2, 45 pp., illustrations
Larner specializes in California native plants, including twenty-five western bunchgrasses. Offerings have included California oat grass, bottlebrush grass, and meadow barley; coastal hair grass; and the state grass of California, purple needlegrass (*Stipa pulchra*). The emphasis here is backyard restoration gardening that encourages existing natives and reintroduces others appropriate to a given site. Rich descriptions include botanical and common name, height at maturity, growth habit, sun and soil preferences, and appropriate use in the garden. Grass seed sold by the packet or by weight. Also offers flats of fifty plants and half-flats of twenty-five plants, including an erosion mixture composed of three perennial bunchgrasses available by weight only. See **Booksellers, Seeds, Trees, Wildflowers.**
Shipping season: All year.

LAS PILITAS NURSERY
See Trees, **Wildflowers.**

LIMEROCK ORNAMENTAL GRASSES, INC.
1980
Norm and Phyllis Hooven
Catalog: $3 (recoverable), 28 pp., illustrations
The Hoovens hold that their gardening philosophy is to "enjoy gardening without having to be on their hands and knees all the time." Therefore, they characterize the plants they have chosen to sell as being drought resistant, needing infrequent dividing, flowering well for an extended period of bloom, being disease and insect resistant, and thriving under neglect. Their catalog includes one hundred ornamental grasses, rushes, and sedges from a variety of families with the largest selection among the fescues and miscanthuses. Other highlights include giant and feather reed grasses, several of their own introductions, and a patented Ebony Knight–Mondo Grass (*Ophiopogon planiscapus*). Evocative descriptions include shape, texture, and color of foliage; growth habit; seasonal interest; hardiness zone; and space between plants designated by group numbers assigned to all of the stock at Limerock. Special notation for varieties that have proven to be drought resistant in their fields in Port Matilda, Pennsylvania. To complement the individual listings, the Hoovens group ties together grasses for specific landscape uses such as borders, rock gardens, ground covers, edgings,

tall background plants, woodland settings, beach house (salt air) environments, waterside plantings, cool and warm season grasses, and fall color. Will replace plants (one time only) if they die within the season they were shipped.

Shipping season: Bareroot, March through May. Bareroot cool season grasses, August through November. Bareroot warm season grasses, October and November. Container shipments, June through November.
Bareroot only to Alabama, Arizona, Florida, Hawaii, Idaho, Kansas, Minnesota, Nevada, Oregon, South Carolina, Tennessee, Utah, Washington
No California

LOCKHART SEEDS, INC.
See **Garlic**, Seeds, **Vegetables**.

LOUISIANA NURSERY
1950
Dalton E. Durio
Bamboo and Ornamental Grasses Catalog:
$3 (recoverable), 12 pp.
Louisiana Nursery occupies a fifty-six-acre complex that was founded by Ken Durio. Five family members, all trained horticulturists, are currently involved in the business. "Bamboos and Ornamental Grasses," one of six catalogs, describes sixty-five bamboos and thirty other grasses and grasslike plants. Descriptions include growth habit, garden use, sun/shade requirements, hardiness expressed in minimum average temperature, hardiness zone, height at maturity, and size of culms and leaves. Plant material shipped variously bareroot or in containers of various sizes. See **Booksellers**, **Bulbs**, **Daylilies**, **Fruit**, **Iris**, **Trees**.
Shipping season: All year.
Canada, Mexico, International

MATTERHORN NURSERY, INC.
See **Conifers**, Perennials, **Rhododendrons**, **Trees**, **Waterscapes**.

MILAEGER'S GARDENS
1960
Kevin D. Milaeger
Catalog: $1, 84 pp., color photographs
A rich and diverse catalog of eleven hundred herbaceous perennials that each seem to be presented with an even hand. Milaeger's offers thirty ornamental grasses, including representatives from the *Andropogon, Bouteloua, Briza, Calamagrostis, Carex, Chasmanthium, Erianthus, Festuca, Hakonechloa,*

Helictotrichon, Miscanthus, Molina, Panicum, and *Pennisetum.* Excellent cultural information, desirable characteristics, and natural history precede the descriptions of individual offerings that include hardiness zone, height and spread at maturity, color of flower, sun/shade preference. Guarantees true to name, disease free, and safe arrival; will replace. See **Booksellers**, **Kidstuff**, Peonies, **Perennials**.
Shipping season: April through September.

MINIATURE PLANT KINGDOM
1965
Don and Becky Herzog
Catalog: $2.50, 42 pp.
The thirty-five bamboos, ornamental grasses and sedges offered by the Herzogs are miniature forms that are suitable for garden railroads, trough gardens, and screes. Descriptions (including general notes about hardiness) include site, sun/shade, and cultural requirements. Plants are available in $2^7/_8$-inch pots, some in larger sizes. See **Conifers**, Fruit, **Perennials**, **Trees**.
Shipping season: Spring and fall.
Canada, Mexico, International

MISSOURI WILDFLOWERS NURSERY
See Perennials, Seeds, **Wildflowers.**

MOSTLY NATIVES NURSERY
1984
Walter Earle and Margaret Graham
Catalog: $3, 20 pp., illustrations
Although Mr. Earle and Ms. Graham grow plants from near and far, they catalog and sell only California coastal and drought-tolerant natives by mail. Their stock also includes perennials, shrubs, and ground covers. They consistently have highlighted tufted reed and hair grass, giant rye grass, California fescue, bunchgrass, and manzanitas. They also write about such plant communities as the northern coastal forests, scrub and prairie, southern coastal sage, scrub and chaparral, and oak woodlands. Descriptions of individual offerings (botanical and common names given) include provenance, habit, and cultural information. A tolerance chart specifies season of bloom, flower color, sun/shade preferences, waterscapes and heat requirements, and hardiness zone. See Perennials, Trees, **Wildflowers.**
Shipping season: March through May.
September through November.

MT. TAHOMA NURSERY
See **Perennials**.

NATIVE AMERICAN SEED
See **Booksellers**, Seeds, **Wildflowers**.

NATIVE GARDENS
See Seeds, Trees, **Wildflowers**.

NEW ENGLAND BAMBOO CO.
Catalog: $1, 12 pp., Collector's list: LSASE
The New England Bamboo Company specializes in the propagation of bamboo proven hardy for zones 4 through 8. Lists thirty bamboos including *Arundinaria, Phyllostachys, Pleioblastus, Sasa,* and *Fargesia*. Descriptions laid out in a consistent format including maximum height, maximum diameter, type (running or clumping), sun/shade, minimum average temperature followed by a narrative describing leaf form and size, color and nature of culms, seasonal interest, and form of plant. Collector's list of rare and unusual bamboos available for an LSASE.
Shipping season: April and May.
Canada, Mexico, International

ORAL LEDDEN & SONS
See **Garlic**, Heirlooms, **Seeds**, **Supplies**, Vegetables.

OTTER VALLEY NATIVE PLANTS
See Seeds, **Wildflowers**.

PEACEFUL VALLEY FARM & GARDEN SUPPLY
See **Booksellers**, **Garlic**, Organics, Seeds, **Supplies**, **Wildflowers**.

PERENNIAL PLEASURES NURSERY OF VERMONT
See **Booksellers**, Heirlooms, **Herbs**, Organics, **Perennials**, Seeds.

PLANT DELIGHTS NURSERY
See **Conifers**, **Hosta**, **Perennials**, Trees.

PLANTS OF THE SOUTHWEST
1977
Gail Haggard
Catalog: $3.50, 103 pp., color photographs
Plants of the Southwest offers 450 trees, shrubs, wildflowers, chilies, vegetables, and grasses that are native or have adapted to the conditions of the American Southwest. Offers the seed for forty grasses characterized either as alternatives for lawns, useful for meadow and reclamation, or as ornamental subjects. Orna-

mentals include big bluestem, silver beardgrass, bamboo and bush muhly, New Mexico feather grass, and thread grass. Descriptions include growth habit and nature, color, height, and form of spikes, seedheads, or blades. Specifies cool or warm season grass, sun or part shade, medium, low, or very low waterscapes required, and hardiness zone for each listing. Lawn, meadow, and reclamation grasses sold by weight; amount of seed required for a thousand square feet or per acre specified. Ornamental grasses sold by the packet with number of seeds specified. Guarantees viable, true to name and variety; and will grow in your garden if you follow their instructions; will replace if seed fails. See **Booksellers**, Heirlooms, Seeds, Trees, **Vegetables**, **Wildflowers**.
Shipping season: Seed, all year.

PRAIRIE MOON NURSERY
1982
Alan Wade
Catalog: $2, 30 pp.
Prairie Moon specializes in native plants and seeds of the wetlands, prairies, and woodlands of Minnesota and the upper midwestern United States. Natives are defined here as plants that were indigenous prior to European settlement. Plants are organically grown on-site in outdoor nursery beds. The catalog includes 40 grasses, sedges, and rushes; 225 forbs; and 40 trees, shrubs, and vines listed by scientific name. Descriptions include common name, germination code, soil moisture requirements, sun preferences, height at maturity, and cool or warm season grass. Notes aggressive varieties. Extensive information on site preparation, seeding, sowing, cover crops, packing, watering, weeding, burning, and successional restoration. Seed sold by the packet (number of seeds not specified) or by weight. See **Booksellers**, Organics, Seeds, Trees, **Wildflowers**.
Shipping season: April and May. October and November.
Canada

PRAIRIE NURSERY
See **Booksellers**, Seeds, **Wildflowers**.

PRAIRIE RIDGE NURSERY
See Perennials, Seeds, **Wildflowers**.

PRAIRIE SEED SOURCE
See **Booksellers**, Seeds, **Wildflowers**.

RAINTREE NURSERY
1974
Sam Benowitz
Catalog: Free, 74 pp., black-and-white and color photographs
Raintree Nursery offers five hundred edible plants from worldwide sources. They specialize in disease-resistant varieties of fruits, nuts, and berries for home gardeners. They also offer a dozen carefully chosen hardy bamboo of the *Arundinaria, Fargesia, Phyllostachys,* and the *Sasa* species. Descriptions include each offering's usefulness as food, a screen, timber, or in specific landscape situations. This brief but informative section of the Raintree catalog includes information about how to use bamboo in the kitchen and landscape, cultural and botanical facts, and how to grow, harvest, and restrict bamboo. Guarantees true to name, safe arrival, and will survive first year; will replace plants that fail if you believe that mortality is due to Raintree's error; will accept unconditionally the return of any item for a full refund up to thirty days after delivery. See **Booksellers, Fruit.**
Shipping season: Bareroot, January through mid-May. Potted plants, all year.

ROBYN'S NEST NURSERY
See **Hosta, Perennials.**

ROSWELL SEED COMPANY, INC.
See Garlic, Seeds, **Vegetables.**

SEEDS TRUST: HIGH ALTITUDE GARDENS
Bill McDorman
Catalog: Free, 44 pp.
Seeds Trust is a bioregional company that acquires and tests seeds from diverse sources that are acclimated to cold, short-season use and, in the case of this firm, growing at six thousand feet above sea level. The native grasses section of this catalog (twenty-five offerings) is organized by color (blond, red, blue) and by growth habit or use (drought tolerant sod forming, bunch grasses, and reclamation grasses). Seeds sold by weight. Guarantees satisfaction; will replace or issue a refund. See **Booksellers,** Garlic, Heirlooms, Organics, Seeds, **Vegetables, Wildflowers.**
Canada, Mexico, International

SHADY OAKS NURSERY
See **Booksellers, Hosta, Perennials.**

SHARP BROS. SEED CO.
1958
Gaile Sharp
Catalog: $4 (recoverable), 12 pp., illustrations
Specializes in seeds of native grasses. One hundred offerings are organized as warm season grasses including numerous varieties of bluestem, grama, Indiangrass, switch grass, love grass, dropseed, and buffalograss; cool season grasses: crested, bluebunch, slender, western streambank, tall, and beardless wheatgrass, smooth and meadow bromegrass, fescue, foxtail, and needlegrass; and a number of legumes, and lawn grasses. Descriptions include botanical name, height at maturity, and a rich descriptive paragraph explaining the characteristics, life expectancy, care requirements, landscape, ecological and livestock uses, drought resistance, and winter hardiness of each offering. Seed sold by weight. See Seeds.
Shipping season: All year.
Canada, Mexico, International

SHOOTING STAR NURSERY
1989
Sherri and Marc Evans
Catalog: $2 (recoverable), 25 pp., illustrations
Shooting Star is the plant materials division of Ecological Stewardship Services, whose specialty is ecological landscaping, restoration, and stewardship planning. The Evanses' catalog focuses on 250 species of plants native to forests, prairies, and wetlands of the eastern United States. Plants are nursery propagated; seeds are nursery collected and wild-crafted. Offers twenty-seven grasses, sedges, and rushes variously available as live plants, in seed packets, or in bulk. Recent offerings included Elliott's broom sedge, wild cane, Frank's sedge, fox sedge, dwarf bamboo, bur reed, and eastern gama grass. Listed by botanical name. Descriptions include common name, form and size of plant, color and shape of plume or leaf, moisture preference, light preference, the type of wildlife a given species attracts, whether the plant is suitable for the xeric garden, postharvest uses, whether shipped bareroot, in pots, or available as seeds by the packet or in bulk. Guarantees healthy and viable; will replace plants that fail through the first season. See Perennials, Seeds, **Waterscapes, Wildflowers.**
Shipping season: Seeds, all year. Potted plants, April through October. Bareroot, November through April.
Canada

STEVE RAY'S BAMBOO GARDENS
1970
Steve and Janie Ray
Catalog: $2, 24 pp., black-and-white photographs

The Rays grow over one hundred types of bamboo (including many cold hardy varieties) on their fifty-acre site. Their range includes small variegated groundcovers, low-growing greens and blacks, as well as wine colored, yellow, and gray. They also grow twenty giants. Thirty-five offerings are pictured in the catalog. Rich descriptions are born of observation including height at maturity, diameter, color and density of culms, suggested uses in the garden, and hardiness expressed in minimum average temperature. Twenty-five percent of the catalog is devoted to cultural information including expectations of cold tolerance, soil and site requirements, sun/shade preferences, planting mulching, fertilizing, and cultivation. Guarantees healthy and viable when shipped.
Shipping season: September through mid-April.

STOCK SEED FARMS
1957
Lyle, Margaret, Dave, and Linda Stock
Catalog: Free, 26 pp., color photographs and black-and-white illustrations

The Stocks specialize in the seeds of prairie grasses and wildflowers. They catalog thirty types of native prairie grasses, nonnative grasses, and legumes including Cody buffalograss, bluestems, switchgrass, wild ryes, and sand lovegrass. Organized by common name (botanical name also provided), the Stocks' descriptions include color of blades, seasonal interest, height at maturity, special site uses, number of square feet a pound of seed will cover, and extensive information on seeding, soil preparation, care after planting, special sites such as shaded and sandy areas, and the virtue of patience in establishing and growing prairie grasses. Also offers mixtures for reclaiming or re-creating prairies, and for use in flood plains, cool season pastures, shady sites, and a sampler (sold in packets) for ornamental use. Seed sold by weight. See Seeds, **Wildflowers**.
Shipping season: All year.

SURRY GARDENS
See **Perennials**.

THOMPSON & MORGAN
1855
Bruce Sangster
Catalog: Free, 224 pp., color photographs

If you have a passion for seeds, plan to take a month off from work, ignore your family and friends, and generally dispense with any other responsibilities before sitting down to read the Thompson & Morgan catalog, which includes seed for over one thousand varieties of flowering plants and vegetables. The selection of ornamental grass seed alone includes ten annuals, seven perennials, a mixture of annuals, and a mixture of perennial grasses. Listed by botanical name, with common name given, information includes height, hardiness, sun/shade preferences, uses in the garden and post harvest, and the number of seeds per packet. See **Garlic**, Heirlooms, **Seeds**, **Vegetables**.
Shipping season: All year.
Canada, International

TRADEWINDS BAMBOO NURSERY
1986
Gib and Diane Cooper
Catalog: $2 (recoverable), 17 pp., Price list: LSASE

Tradewinds was established following the dissolution of Panda Products Nursery in Northern California, in which Mr. Cooper was a partner. The catalog includes nearly one hundred dwarf, shrub, tall shrub, and timber bamboo plants, and bamboo seedlings. Offerings are listed within their sections by botanical name, common name given in Chinese, English, Japanese, or Thai. Symbols indicate sun/shade preference, height at maturity, culm diameter, minimum average temperature, hardiness zone, if suitable for indoor and container use, and whether the plant has a running or clumping habit. Description includes native habitat and locale, general look of plant as it matures, culm and foliage characteristics, landscape and postharvest use. Ships containerized plants in a soilless mixture.
Shipping season: All year.
Canada, Mexico, International

TRIPLE BROOK FARM
Catalog: Free, 60 pp., illustrations

Tripple Brook offers over five hundred native (east of the Rockies) and introduced perennials, groundcovers, shrubs, bamboos, and grasses, almost all of which are propagated at their

Southampton, Massachusetts, nursery. Forty grasses, rushes, and sedges (including *Carex*, fescue, *Miscanthus*, and *Pennisetum*) are listed within the main body of the catalog sequenced with their other offerings by botanical name. Descriptions include common name, life cycle, height at maturity, hardiness zones, garden and landscape uses, where it originated, color and characteristics of foliage. Forty bamboos (mostly for temperate regions) are presented in a separate section, preceded by an extended introductory essay about this plant. Their catalog represents the *Arundinaria, Bambusa, Indocalamus, Pseudosasa, Sasa, Sasaella,* and *Semiarundinaria* species; however, their most in-depth selection is from among tall to very tall evergreen, woodystemmed *Phyllostachys*, and the low growing *Pleioblastus*. Descriptions include usefulness as a screen or hedge, adaptability to container culture, maximum height, maximum culm diameter, minimum average temperature, clumping or running habit, nature of leaves, and color and characteristics of culms. Plants shipped in pots. Guarantees true to name and safe arrival; will replace or refund. See Fruit, Perennials, Trees, **Wildflowers.**
Shipping season: March through December. Bareroot or sterile soil mix to Arizona, California, Minnesota, Oregon, Washington. Canada

WAVECREST NURSERY AND LANDSCAPING
1959
Carol T. Hop
Catalog: $1 (recoverable), 24 pp.
Wavecrest sits on the shore of Lake Michigan, providing the plants grown there with a milder climate than much of zone 5. Ms. Hop lists twenty-four ornamental grasses, grown at Wavecrest, whose large clumps, according to Ms. Hop, are ready to plump up. Recent offerings included Karl Forster's feather reed grass (*Calamogrostis × acutiflora*), a hardy nonspreading Ravenna grass (*Erianthus ravennae*), various maiden grasses, and a black mondo grass (*Ophiopogon planiscapus*) 'Black Knight'. Offerings listed first by botanical name/common

name; includes a brief, effective description of color and form and specifies size of container or sleeve. Must notify upon arrival if plants are unsatisfactory. See **Booksellers, Conifers,** Perennials, **Trees.**
Shipping season: March through May.
Canada, Mexico, International

WAYSIDE GARDENS
See Fruit, Heirlooms, Perennials, **Roses.**

WEISS BROTHERS PERENNIAL NURSERY
See Herbs, **Perennials.**

WILD EARTH NATIVE PLANT NURSERY
1990
Richard Pillar
Catalog: $2, 26 pp.
Mr. Pillar is a certified landscape architect who propagates native wildflowers, ferns, and grasses. Recent offerings included palm sedge, black blooming sedge, river oats, Japanese blood grass, and a local (to Freehold, New Jersey) Indian grass that is shorter than most midwestern strains. Descriptions include botanical and common names, form and color of flower and foliage, growth and cultural habits, and site preferences. Consistent symbols indicate moisture requirements, height and spread, hardiness zones, sun/shade preference, and size of plant and container being offered. Guarantees true to name and healthy. See Seeds, **Wildflowers.**
Shipping season: April through October.

WILD SEED, INC.
See **Booksellers, Kidstuff,** Seeds, Trees, **Wildflowers.**

YORK HILL FARM
See **Daylilies,** Heirlooms, **Hosta, Iris,** Perennials.

YUCCA DO NURSERY AT PECKERWOOD GARDENS
See **Cactus, Conifers,** Organics, Perennials, **Trees, Wildflowers.**

Selected Reading About Grassses, Sedges, Rushes, and Bamboos

Bamboos, by Christine Recht and Max F. Wetterwald. A survey of bamboo in a historical and cultural context as well as practical material about uses in the home and home garden. Information about morphology, genera, species, cultivars, and specific recommendations for garden use. Includes one hundred photographs and drawings.

Encyclopedia of Ornamental Grasses, by John Greenlee. Each of the 225 entries includes a description of the plant and varieties, color photographs, use in design, planting and propagation, and hardiness zone. Two hundred and fifty color photographs.

Grasses: An Identification Guide, by Lauren Brown. Takes the worry out of identifying and collecting northeast and midwestern grasses. Drawings and description of 135 species include distinguishing traits, height, habitat, season of bloom, natural history, and lookalikes. Three hundred and eighty-six line drawings.

Manual of Grasses, Rick Darke, consulting editor. Based on the *Royal Horticultural Society Dictionary of Gardening,* this work describes grasses, sedges, and bamboos in authoritative detail. Information about the natural history of grasses, rich descriptions, and cultural information. Thirty line drawings.

Ornamental Grass Gardening: Design, Ideas, Function and Effects, by Reinhardt, Reinhardt, and Moskowitz. How to plant, cut, and divide grasses. Profile of fifty "top" species and varieties, including suggestions and methods for use in borders, as accent plants, and in the waterscape. Over one hundred color photographs.

Ornamental Grasses: Brooklyn Botanic Garden Handbook. An introduction to ornamental grasses and bamboos including charts with sources, landscape use, and how to start seeds.

Waterscapes

The plant count cited in each profile is based on information in the most recent catalog provided by the source. Many of the businesses in this section sell plant material, pond fish, and the supplies and products necessary to establishing and maintaining these life-forms in an aquatic environment. The shipping seasons for live materials are noted separately from the supplies that are available year-round. A selection of books about gardening in and near the water appears after the last listing.

QUICK FIND
The following sources are listed in this section:

AQUACIDE COMPANY
1956
Mr. Marhoe
Catalog: Free, 30 pp., illustrations and black-and-white photographs
This firm sells a full line of aquatic herbicides and tools for removal of weeds. Describes problems and appropriate solutions from their product line. Catalog includes a quick reference chart of weed susceptibility and another of water restriction use after treatment. See **Supplies.**
Shipping season: All year.

BIJOU ALPINES
1989
Mark Dusek
Catalog: $1, 18 pp.
Bijou Alpines is a specialty nursery with 150 varieties of rare and unusual plants for the rock garden, scree, bog, water garden, and woodland. Approximately 10 percent of their recent offerings include water and bog plants, with an emphasis on hardy water lilies. Listed by botanical name, the descriptions include habit, shape and color of leaves and flower, and light requirements. See **Conifers, Perennials, Trees.**
Shipping season: March through May. September and October.

COUNTRY WETLANDS NURSERY & CONSULTING
See **Booksellers,** Grasses, Seeds, **Wildflowers.**

GROWERS SERVICE CO.
See **Bulbs, Perennials.**

HERMITAGE GARDENS
1946
Russell A. Rielle
Catalog: $1 (recoverable), 8 pp., color photographs
Mr. Rielle established Hermitage Gardens to provide material to build aquatic and Japanese-style gardens. His manufactured products include preformed pools, pond liners, pool connectors, bridges, faux rock waterfalls, waterwheels, pumps, lights, and fountainheads. See Supplies.
Shipping season: All year.
Canada, Mexico, International

HORTICO, INC.
See **Grasses, Perennials, Roses,** Trees.

INTERNATIONAL WATER LILY SOCIETY
See **Horticultural Societies.**

JAPONICA WATER GARDENS
1991
William and Ron Howes
Catalog: LSASE, 28 pp.
The Howeses' catalog of 285 varieties of plants that grow in and around water include hardy bog plants, tropicals, floating plants and lilies (organized by color of flower), moisture-loving perennials (including *Iris ensata*), oxygenating plants, and sixty bamboo. Descriptions include botanical name, common name, size and color of leaves, site and soil preferences, color and fragrance of flower where appropriate. Information for bamboo includes maximum height, cumulative diameter, minimum temperature required, sun and shade requirements, and growth habit (running or clumping type). Guarantees true to name; will replace any plant that fails to grow within thirty days of planting. See Grasses.
Shipping season: April through September. Lotus, April through early May.

KURT BLUEMEL, INC.
1964
Catalog: $3, 49 pp., illustrations and color photographs
Included among the seven hundred ornamental grasses, sedges, rushes, bamboo, ferns, perennials, and ground covers are fifty plants characterized as water and moisture loving. Mr. Bluemel's offerings include *Acorus* (sweet flag), *Glyceria* (manna grass), *Phragmites* (australis), and *Scirpus* (bullrush). Descriptions in this section of the catalog include the depth below the surface that the plant is rooted (shallow and deep water), plants that are rooted in moist area just above the surface, floating types, height of plant, shape and color of foliage and other characteristics, hardiness zones. Plants are field grown and shipped bareroot. Guarantees true to name; will replace (claims for stock that does not survive must be made within five days of receipt). See Grasses, Perennials.
Shipping season: March to first frost in Baldwin, Maryland.
California $250 minimum and some restrictions
Canada, International ($250 minimum)

LAURIE'S GARDEN
See Iris, Perennials.

LILYPONS WATER GARDENS®
1930
Charles Thomas
Catalog: Free, 100 pp., color photographs
In 1917, G. Leicester Thomas, Sr., turned his goldfish hobby into a business. In 1930, he began to sell the water lilies that he had been growing and hybridizing for his fishponds. The subsequent success of this aspect of his venture required the establishment of a post office to handle his business. In the pre–zip code era, each post office had to be named. Mr. Thomas proposed Lily Pons, in honor of his favorite diva. The postal service preferred that the town have a single-word name . . . Lilypons. This comprehensive water gardener's catalog includes extensive offerings of pool and pond liners, filtration systems and pumps, water treatments, fish, scavengers, bog plants, hardy and tropical water lilies, hardy and tropical marginals, lotus, and iris. Descriptions are richly detailed. Information for plants include growth habit, height, water depth, sun and shade requirements, bloom season, color of flower, and hardiness zone. Instructions and tips about pool and pond installation, maintenance, plant and live material selection, care, preferences, and growing requirements abound. Guarantees vary for supplies and live material. See Booksellers, Supplies.
Shipping season: Supplies, all year. Live material, inquire Lilypons regional outlet.

MARYLAND AQUATIC NURSERIES, INC.
1986
Kelly Billing
Catalog: $5 (recoverable), 43 pp., color photographs
MAN is both a nursery and a manufacturer of patio gardens, fountain gardens, and pond filtration systems. Their catalog offers 60 hardy and tropical water lilies, 15 lotus, 20 iris, 115 floating plants and oxygenators, shallow-water plants, and 10 miniature lilylike aquatics. Also offers 25 moisture-loving perennials and grasses that are noted but not shown or described. Ships potted and bareroot. See Perennials.
Shipping season: All year.

MATTERHORN NURSERY, INC.
1981
Matt and Ronnie Horn
Catalog: $5, 102 pp., illustrations

Ten percent of the Matterhorn catalog, listing perennials, ornamental grasses and bamboo, trees, and shrubs, is devoted to aquatic plants. Offerings include fifty hardy water lilies, fifteen tropical water lilies and lotus, thirty-five hardy (twelve tropical) marginal and bog plants, and fifteen floating and oxygenating types. A simple illustration of the relative placement of these plants within and around the water is a welcome aid. Listed by botanical name, the descriptions include common name, height of plant, maximum depth for planting, shape of foliage, and light requirements. Guarantees true to name. See **Conifers**, Grasses, Perennials, **Rhododendrons, Trees.**
Shipping season: Please inquire.

PARADISE WATER GARDENS
1950
Paul Stetson, Jr.
Catalog: $3 (recoverable) 66 pp., color illustrations, black-and-white and color photographs
The Stetsons offer New England–grown hardy water lilies (including Slocum and Strawn introductions) among the two hundred aquatic plants in their catalog. Additional selections include hardy lotus, tropicals, water iris, shallow-water marginals, rushes, grasses, and floating and oxygenating plants. Live supplies include scavengers and fish. Other supplies include liners, pools, TetraPond products, waterfalls, water courses, pumps, fountainheads, and tubs. Guarantees true to name; will replace any plant that fails to grow within thirty days of planting. See **Booksellers**, Supplies.
Shipping season: Plants (other than tropical lilies), April through September. Tropical lilies, Mid-May through October delivered to the South; June through September delivered to the North. Supplies, all year.
Canada

RESOURCE CONSERVATION TECHNOLOGY, INC.
1984
Catalog: Free, 17 pp., illustrations
RCT manufactures and sells EPDM (ethylene propylene diene monomer polymer) and Butyl pond liners and liner-protection fabric. Offers an extensive selection of weights, shapes, and sizes, with scrupulously detailed descriptions and explanations of their materials and its uses. More than half of the catalog shows how to install liners, secure edges, seaming, and do repairs. Offers a twenty-year limited warranty.
Shipping season: All year.
Canada, Mexico, International

SHOOTING STAR NURSERY
1989
Sherri and Marc Evans
Catalog: $2 (recoverable), 25 pp., illustrations
Shooting Star is the plant materials division of Ecological Stewardship Services, whose specialty is ecological landscaping, restoration, and stewardship planning. The Evanses' catalog lists 250 species of nursery-propagated plants native to the wetlands, forests, and prairies of the eastern United States. Ten percent of their offerings are recommended for waterscaping. Descriptions include form and size of plant, color and shape of flower, site and light preferences, the type of wildlife a species attracts, and season of bloom. Guarantees healthy and viable; will replace plants that fail the first season. See **Grasses**, Perennials, Seeds, **Wildflowers.**
Shipping season: Potted plants, April through October. Bareroot, November through April.
Canada

SLOCUM WATER GARDENS
Catalog: $3, 60 pp., color photographs
P. D. Slocum
1940
Slocum Water Gardens' plant list includes two hundred types of hardy, tropical, and dwarf water lilies (including Slocum introductions), shallow-water and bog plants, lotus, dwarf lotus, and floating and oxygenating plants. Water lilies are organized by color within time of bloom and life cycle designations. Descriptions include habit and size of plant. Cultural information provided for each group of plants. The catalog also includes fish and scavengers, fish food and care products, rigid ponds and tubs, underliners, water and pool care products, pumps, filters, and a few books. Guarantees plants to be of blooming size and healthy; will replace if notified within thirty days of receipt. Guarantees live delivery of fish and scavengers; will replace if notified within ten days of receipt.
Shipping season: Plants, April through June. Supplies, all year.

STIGALL WATER GARDENS
1990
Trent Stigall
Catalog: Free, 42 pp., illustrations
A water garden specialist offering one hundred varieties of hardy and tropical water lilies, lotus, bog plants, and a selection of floating and oxygenating plants. Very rich descriptions include color and form of flower and leaves, plant spread, cultural requirements, and light preferences. The second half of their catalog includes scavengers and a full line of manufactured supplies: liners, tubs, containers, pumps, fountainheads, preformed ponds, water and fish treatments, and a brief list of books. Mr. Stigall punctuates his catalog with clear advice and instructions that lend it a reassuring tone. Guarantees true to name and healthy; will exchange or issue a refund if notified within fourteen days of receipt. Supplies subject to manufacturers' guarantees. See **Booksellers**, Supplies.
Shipping season: Hardy plants, April through September. Tropicals, June through September. Lotus, April and May. Supplies, all year.

TRANS-PACIFIC NURSERY
Jackson Muldoon
Catalog: $2, 44 pp.
Mr. Muldoon specializes in the rare, unusual, hard-to-find, and exotic specimens from all over the world, with an emphasis on the southern hemisphere and Pacific Rim. Trans-Pacific sponsors collecting expeditions to far-flung destinations such as Mt. Kilimanjaro and Yunnan, China, to which customers can subscribe and gain first access to newly introduced plants. Catalog runs to over 450 selections. Recent offerings included water lettuce (*Salvinia auriculata*), zebra rush (*Schoenoplectus lacustris*), and papyrus (*Cyperaceae*) species: sparkler grass, umbrella plants, McCoy grass, and Egyptian papyrus reed, from which paper was first made, and the bullrushes of Moses fame. Information for offerings include the nature of a plant's natural habitat and cultural requirements as well as a fully realized description. Plants are shipped in four-inch pots unless otherwise specified. Notes those plants that are suitable for bogs and ponds. See **Booksellers**, Bulbs, Perennials, **Trees**.
Shipping season: All year (preferably not December or January).
Canada, Mexico, International

VAN NESS WATER GARDENS
1932
William C. Uber
Catalog: $2, 55 pp., color photographs
Robert Van Ness, having given up his trade as a plasterer for health reasons, began raising goldfish, partially on the strength of an article in the *Saturday Evening Post* entitled "Gold in Goldfish." Robert's wife, Edith, an avid gardener, began decorating their ponds with water lilies that pleased their customers as much as their fish. International recognition came two decades later when Ted and Louella Uber began introducing the water lilies of Martin Randig, a reclusive breeder. William C. Uber, the current owner, is the author of *Water Gardening Basics*. Live material in this catalog includes sixty-five types of plants (oxygenating, tropical and hardy water lilies, tropical night bloomers, lotus, and aquatic bog plants), and five varieties of fish. Supplies include ponds and liners, waterfalls and fountains, filtration systems, pumps, and pond and fish care products. Complementing the rich descriptions is a detailed two-month pond setup schedule. Guarantees true to name, viable, and healthy; will replace up to ninety days after receipt. See **Booksellers**, Supplies.
Shipping season: Hardy lilies, all year. Tropical lilies, May through July. Supplies, all year.
Canada, Mexico, International

WATERFORD GARDENS
1895
John A. Meeks
Catalog: $5, 40 pp., color photographs
William Tricker, one of the earliest propagators of water lilies in the United States, established this wet nursery at the close of the nineteenth century. In 1926, his son Charles relocated the facility to its present site. John A. Meeks, a prominent landscape architect, acquired Waterford Gardens in 1985 from Bill Schmidlin, son-in-law of Charles Tricker. Aquatic plants offered in the catalog include fifty-three tropical and hardy water lilies and lotus, thirty-five hardy and tropical marginals (including water iris), and ten floating and oxygenating plants. Description for lilies include color, bloom habit, light requirements, spread of plant, and color of leaves. Descriptions for other plants include flower color and plant habit, height of plant, and range of depth for planting. Supplies include pond liners (including installation tips), waterfalls, pre-

formed ponds, fish, fish care products, fountain-heads, pumps, filters, and water conditioners. Guarantees plants in prime growing condition and live delivery for fish and scavengers; will replace or issue refund within thirty days of delivery. See **Booksellers**, Supplies.
Shipping season: Plants, April through October. Supplies, all year.
Canada, Mexico, International

WATER WAYS NURSERY
1986
Sally Kurtz
Catalog: $2, 19 pp., illustrations
Just under half of Ms. Kurtz's catalog of aquatics, water lilies, and native perennials is devoted to fifty types of submerged, floating, emergent, and underwater plants with floating leaves. Descriptions include depth of planting, height of plant, color of leaves and flowers, soil preference, and landscape use. Guarantees true to name and viable; will replace or issue a refund. See **Wildflowers**.
Shipping season: April through July

THE WATERWORKS®
1975
Todd Schaffer
Catalog: $4 (recoverable), 36 pp., illustrations and black-and-white photographs
The firm began as a landscaper of residential properties with water garden pond construction as their specialty. They opened their aquatic division in 1984. One third of the WaterWorks® catalog offers hardy and dwarf water lilies, tropicals, bog plants, and oxygenating varieties. A phone call is required to find out which tropicals are available, since they are not listed by name in the catalog or the annual price list. The balance of the catalog includes seven varieties of fish, and other live material, as well as nonliving supplies: pools, nets, liners, pumps, filtration systems, pool, fish, and plant maintenance products. See **Booksellers**, Supplies.
Shipping season: Plants, April through October. Lotus, May and June. Supplies, all year.

WHITE FLOWER FARM
1950
Steve Frowine
Catalog: Free, 146 pp., color photographs
White Flower Farm, a family-owned nursery

in Litchfield, Connecticut, offers a wide range of ornamentals: annuals, perennials, shrubs, bulbs, and recently added water gardening kits and plants. Offers complete kits including plants and materials for a pond, three variations on a pond in a kettle, a preformed pool, a whiskey-barrel water container, faux granite pools, and water lilies in a pot. Also offers six types of water lilies and a number of accessories. Guarantees true to name, in prime condition for growing, and delivered at the proper time for planting; will replace one time only any plant that fails. See **Bulbs**, Fruit, **Perennials**, **Roses**, Supplies, Trees.
Shipping season: Bareroot plants shipped to arrive on four preselected Fridays in May and June. Nonliving components shipped in early March.
No Hawaii
Canada

WICKLEIN'S WATER GARDENS
1954
Walt Wicklein
Catalog: $2, 24 pp.
Mr. Wicklein's aquatic gardening catalog includes forty-five hardy water lilies, eleven lotus, one hundred hardy marginal and bog plants, twenty water irises, thirty tropical bog plants, and fifteen floating and oxygenating plants. Water lilies are organized by color. Descriptions of water lilies and lotus include size, color, light requirements, hardiness zone, and occasional comments. Information for other plants, organized by botanical name, include common name, flower and foliage, height, depth of planting, light requirements, and hardiness zone. Supplies are line listed without further description in Wicklein's price list and include pool liners, preformed pools, pumps, fountainheads, filters, water treatments, test kits, fertilizer, nets, underwater lighting, fish food, planting containers, and books. Guarantees plants for one growing season; will replace those that fail. See Booksellers, Iris, Supplies.
Shipping season: All year.
Canada, Mexico, International

WILLIAM TRICKER, INC.
1895
Richard Lee
Catalog: $3, 52 pp., color photographs
This wet nursery also traces its roots to the pio-

neering water lily hybridizer William Tricker (see Waterford Gardens). Mr. Lee characterizes its selection of aquatic lilies as the largest in the United States, with over 135 varieties (including many Tricker-bred cultivars) and numerous collections. Describes sixty-five shallow-water and bog plants, lotus, floating plants, and oxygenating plants. Full descriptions for most, historical and hybridizing notes for many. Also offers fish and scavengers and a full line of manufactured supplies: liners, tubs, containers, pumps, fountainheads, preformed ponds, water and fish treatments, and a brief list of books. Guarantees satisfaction for plants and live delivery of fish; will replace if notified within thirty days of receipt.

Shipping season: Plants, April through June. Supplies, all year.

WINDY OAKS AQUATICS
1980
Marilyn Buscher
Catalog: $1, 10 pp., illustrations
Ms. Buscher will design water gardens through the mail for a fee that is refundable with the purchase of a liner. Offers an unspecified number of named hardy and tropical water lilies and *Nelumbo* (lotus), sixty hardy and tropical marginals, and a select group of perennials and *Clematis* for planting at the water's edge. Descriptions for plants (other than lilies and lotus) include shape and color of foliage and flower, height of plant, and range of depth for planting. Also offers pumps, filters, pond forms, water treatments, koi and other pond fish, food for fish, and aquatic plants.
Shipping season: All year.
Canada

Selected Reading About Waterscapes

A Fishkeeper's Guide to Fancy Goldfish, by Dr. Chris Andrews. A guide to maintaining and breeding unusual and exotic goldfish. One hundred color photographs.

A Fishkeeper's Guide to Koi, by Barry James. A how-to guide for raising koi. Includes substantial information about constructing and maintaining a balanced pond. One hundred color photographs and black-and-white illustrations.

Gardening with Water, by James van Sweden. How award-winning designers Wolfgang Oehme and James van Sweden integrate water features into environments of all sizes. Includes practical planning and building instructions and an extensive guide to plant selection, and guidance on gathering additional advice and assistance. Color photographs and black-and-white illustrations.

John Dawes's Book of Water Gardens, by John Dawes. How to choose a site and prevent errors in the placement and construction of pools and contained waterscapes. Design ideas and wise words about installation, pond edging, plant materials.

The Pond Doctor, by Helen Nash. Prevention and problem solving for maintaining a healthy water garden. Color photographs.

Water Gardening, Water Lilies and Lotuses, by Perry D. Slocum and Peter Robinson. Practical information for designing, building, planting, and maintaining a water garden, combined with a comprehensive encyclopedia of water lilies and lotuses. Color photographs and black-and-white illustrations.

Waterscaping: Plants and Ideas for Natural and Created Water Gardens, by Judy Glattstein. Ms. Glattstein emphasizes native and adaptable nonnative plants for water gardens and moist conditions around aquatic environments, both natural and created. Fifty color photographs.

Waterside Planting (previously published as *At the Water's Edge*), by Philip Swindells. A comprehensive work on the selection and culture of bog and marginal plants. Forty color photographs.

Cactus and Succulents

The plant count cited in each profile is based on information in the most recent catalog provided by the source. Although most sources in this section will ship year-round, many advise caution in requesting that plants be transported to colder climates during the winter months. A selection of books about cactus and succulents appears after the last listing.

QUICK FIND
The following sources are listed in this section:

BURKS' NURSERY

THE CACTUS AND SUCCULENT
SOCIETY OF AMERICA

DESERTLAND NURSERY

DESERT MOON NURSERY

DESERT NURSERY

GRIGSBY CACTUS GARDENS

THE HAWORTHIA SOCIETY

HENRIETTA'S NURSERY

A HIGH COUNTRY GARDEN

K & L CACTUS & SUCCULENT
NURSERY

LIVING STONES NURSERY

MESA GARDEN

MIDWEST CACTUS

NORTHRIDGE GARDENS

PLANTASIA CACTUS GARDENS

REDLO CACTI

SCHULZ CACTUS GROWERS

THE SEED SHOP

SOUTHWESTERN NATIVE SEEDS

SQUAW MOUNTAIN GARDENS

STRONG'S ALPINE SUCCULENTS

SUNRISE NURSERY

YUCCA DO NURSERY AT PECK-
ERWOOD GARDENS

BURKS' NURSERY
1988
Lois Burks
Catalog: $1 (recoverable), 16 pp.
Ms. Burks specializes in nursery-propagated haworthia and gasteria. Her catalog includes two hundred *Haworthia* and thirty-five *Gasteria, Astroloba,* and *Astroworthia.* Compact descriptions include hybridizer, leaf and plant form, flower color, and plant's habit. Location data provided for many offerings. Ships bareroot.
Shipping season: Late April through November. December through mid-April at customer's risk.
Canada, International

THE CACTUS AND SUCCULENT SOCIETY
OF AMERICA
See **Horticultural Societies.**

DESERTLAND NURSERY
1976
David and Lupina Guerra
Catalog: $1, 4 pp.
The Guerras grow five thousand types of desert plants. Their "Aztekakti" seed list offers four hundred types of Mexican and North American cactus, South American plants, desert and subtropical trees, and a variety of succulents. Botanical name given without further description. Seeds are nursery collected and wild-crafted. Seed sold by count. See Seeds.
Shipping season: All year.
Canada, Mexico, International

DESERT MOON NURSERY
1988
Hodoba Family
Catalog: $1, 30 pp. Seed list: 6 pp.
Desert Moon specializes in the plants and trees of the Chihuahuan desert. Ted Hodoba, the author of *Growing Desert Plants: From Windowsill to Garden,* encourages and provides suggestions for the use of these plants in nondesert environments. About eighty of the plants in their main catalog are cactus and other succulents primarily from this region. Descriptions include common name, plant and flower form and habit, and hardiness zone. Guarantees true to name and healthy; will replace up to ten days after delivery. See **Seeds,** Wildflowers.
Shipping season: April through October.

DESERT NURSERY
1977
Laszlo and Shirley Nyerges
Catalog: 1 FCS, 7 pp.
The Nyergeses organize their catalog of 260 offerings into winter-hardy (sometimes down to 0 degrees Fahrenheit in Deming, New Mexico), semihardy (grown in a cold greenhouse), and greenhouse-hardy plants. They focus on *Coryphantha, Echinocactus, Echinocereus,* a large selection of *Opuntia* (sold as unrooted pads or joints), *Mammillaria, Euphorbia,* and *Haworthia.* Information includes botanical name, size of plant, and original location for some.
Shipping season: Late April through mid-November. Late November through mid-April at customer's risk.

GRIGSBY CACTUS GARDENS
1965
M. Lee
Catalog: $2 (recoverable), 24 pp.,
black-and-white photographs
Grigsby specializes in rare plants for collectors, show specimens, and other large- to medium-sized plants. Offers three hundred varieties of *Agave, Alluadia, Aloe, Ceropegia, Dorstenia, Euphorbia, Haworthia, Sansevieria, Cereus, Ferocactus*, and *Mammillaria* grown on their three-acre nursery. Rich descriptions include form and shape of plant and approximate size of material that you will receive. Issues three to five "wish letters" each year to active customers, listing limited to rare and specimen plants. Guarantees safe arrival for air shipments; will issue credit or refund for plants returned within ten days.
Shipping season: All year.

THE HAWORTHIA SOCIETY
See **Horticultural Societies**.

HENRIETTA'S NURSERY
1958
Jerry and Sylvia Hardaway
Catalog: $1, 48 pp., black-and-white
photographs
The Hardaways characterize their holdings as making up one of the larger collections of cactus and succulents in the world, with over twelve hundred varieties; offered as seedlings to mature plants several feet tall. They specialize in cold-hardy plants that will adapt to the northern areas of the United States, Christmas cactus, orchid cactus, and South African succulents. Descriptions are informal but provide a clear sense of the plant's form, habit, and potential size. Also offers collections of aloe, South African natives, hybrid *Echinopsis, Mammillaria*, a group suitable for rock gardens, and another group for hanging baskets. Guarantees safe arrival; will replace up to twenty days of receipt. See **Booksellers**.
Shipping season: All year.

A HIGH COUNTRY GARDEN
See **Grasses, Perennials**.

K & L CACTUS & SUCCULENT NURSERY
1970
Keith and Lorraine Thomas
Catalog: $2 (recoverable), 28 pp.,
black-and-white and color photographs

The Thomases specialize in flowering desert and jungle cactus and succulents. Their catalog has 260 varieties, including *Ariocarpus, Astrophytum, Cereus, Echinopsis, Ferocactus, Rebutia, Lithops, Mesembryanthemum, Melocactus, Stapelia, Haworthia*, yuccas, aloes, *Trichocereus*, and *Trichonopsis*. Brief description of plants for all, size noted for some. Also offers twenty-one seed mixtures of varieties from within the same family containing fifty seeds per packet. Guarantees safe arrival. See **Booksellers, Seeds**.
Shipping season: All year. Orders received from colder areas between December 1 and April 1 will be held.
Canada, Mexico, International

LIVING STONES NURSERY
1987
Jane Evans and Gene Joseph
Catalog: $2 (recoverable), 34 pp.,
black-and-white photographs
Ms. Evans and Mr. Joseph acquired Ed Storm's highly regarded succulent collection. Their catalog of nursery-propagated plants from seeds and cuttings contains over nine hundred offerings. What is striking about the catalog is that descriptions and offerings make easy transitions between plants and collections for the beginner (including a concise glossary) to those for the connoisseur. Includes extensive cultural information for each of the families represented in an alphabetical arrangement. Plant size describes the pots for which they are suited. Offers collections of *Aloinopsis*, aloes, new world cactus, *Cheiridopsis*, Desmond T. Cole *Lithops, Conophytum, Euphorbia, Faucaria, Glottiphyllum, Haworthia, Mesembryanthemum, Pleiospilos*, and starter sets with diverse components. Ships bareroot.
Shipping season: All year.
Canada, Mexico, International

MESA GARDEN
1976
Steven Brack
Catalog: Seed list, $1, 87 pp., plant list, 16 pp.
Mesa Garden offers 150 types of succulents and cactus plants and the seeds of four thousand varieties. Nursery-propagated plants and gathered seeds from known (attributed) sources and locations. Includes extensive germination and cultural notes. Descriptions are brief. Seeds sold by packet of specified quantities or in bulk lots of one hundred and five hundred seeds. See Seeds.
Shipping season: Seeds, all year. Plants,

April through November.
Canada, Mexico, International

MIDWEST CACTUS
1985
Chris Smith
Catalog: $1, 18 pp., black-and-white
photographs
Mr. Smith offers forty-four cold-hardy cactus
suitable for the Midwest and those temperate
climates common to the highly populated regions of the United States and Europe. Features
beginner and intermediate-level collections tailored to designated hardiness zones, and individual specimens of *Opuntia* or more common
prickly pear varieties. Descriptions include tolerance to moisture, hardiness zone, plant form,
and color of flowers. Brief cultural notes.
Shipping season: May through September.
Canada, International

NORTHRIDGE GARDENS
1991
Arnie and Susan Mitchnick
Catalog: $1, 34 pp., black-and-white
photographs
The Mitchnicks are the successors to Singers'
Growing Things, having acquired the Singers'
complete inventory upon their retirement. The
Northridge Gardens catalog lists two hundred
succulents, including but not limited to the following genera: *Aloe, Brachychiton, Bursera, Euphorbia, Ficus, Fockea, Haworthia, Jatropha,
Monadenium, Othonna, Pachypodium, Pelargo-
nium, Sansevieria* (send LSASE for separate list),
Senecio, and *Tylecodon.* Information for each
plant includes size, whether a caudex will form or
is well developed, preferred light and moisture
levels, and whether plant is a winter or summer
grower. Brief but rich descriptions of plant and
flower form and habit. Offers collections by
genus, a diversified starter set, an odds-and-ends
collection, and a winter-growing collection.
Guarantees satisfaction; will issue credit or refund if notified within ten days of receipt.
Shipping season: March through November.
December through February at customer's
risk.

PLANTASIA CACTUS GARDENS
1992
LaMar N. Orton
Catalog: LSASE with 2 FCS, 8 pp.
Plantasia sells only winter-hardy cactus grown

out-of-doors in temperatures that dip to 10 degrees below zero. All of their plants are cultivated
from cuttings or started from seeds, not wild-
crafted. The majority of their seventy offerings
are *Opuntia* and *Cylindropuntia.* Plantasia is also
in the process of brush-pollinating seeds from
ball and hedgehog cactus hoping to make rare
species and varieties available to collectors. Descriptions include form of plant and flower, cultural preferences, and habitat of origin.
Shipping season: April through November.
Canada, Mexico, International

REDLO CACTI
1982
Lorne E. Hanna
Catalog: $2 (recoverable), 30 pp.
The Redlo catalog offers 280 of the 550 cactus
and succulents in cultivation at Mr. Hanna's
nursery. Several pages of enlightening cultural
information and care suggestions. Plants from
diverse genera and families are grown from
stock or purchased from other growers. A small
number are field collected under written permits. Descriptions are brief but full, including
plant's form, habit, and color and nature of
flower. Offers *Lithops* collection.
Shipping season: All year.

SCHULZ CACTUS GROWERS
1980
Ernst Schulz
Catalog: Free, 10 pp.
Mr. Schulz offers three hundred types of green-
house-grown cactus and other succulents. Plants
are started from seeds or propagated from offsets.
Selection includes *Corypantha, Echinocereus,
Echinofossulocactus, Mammillaria, Melocactus,
Notocactus, Parodia, Rebutia, Thelocactus, Wein-
gartia,* and *Lithops.* Lists Latin name without ad-
ditional description. Ships bareroot.
Shipping season: All year.

THE SEED SHOP
1988
Jim and Barbara Linaburg
Catalog: $2, 29 pp.
The Linaburgs list the seed of two hundred
species of desert and tropical cactus and succulents from worldwide sources, both nursery
propagated and wild-crafted. In addition to general germination instructions, there is extensive
information about plant and seed culture for
each of the genera listed. Descriptions include

size, form, and color of plant and flower and the number of seeds per packet. See Seeds.
Shipping season: All year.
Canada, Mexico, International

SOUTHWESTERN NATIVE SEEDS
See Seeds, Trees, **Wildflowers.**

SQUAW MOUNTAIN GARDENS
1983
Joyce Hoekstra, Janis and Arthur Noyes
Catalog: Free, 44 pp.
The folks at Squaw Mountain in Estacada, Oregon, grow alpines and rock garden plants including 1,100 *Sempervivum*, 450 *Sedum*, 150 tender succulents (including *Crassula, Echeveria, Gasteria, Haworthia, Kalanchoe,* and *Senecio*), and a select group of hardy ferns, ground covers, grasses, and ivies. The catalog is arranged by botanical name. Descriptions include color and characteristics of flower and foliage, size of plant. Hybridizer and year of introduction are noted for new issues. Also offers a number of samplers and collections. See **Booksellers.**
Shipping season: March through mid-October.
Canada, International

STRONG'S ALPINE SUCCULENTS
1989
Shirley Strong
Catalog: $2 (recoverable), 8 pp.
Ms. Strong tends to two hundred varieties of hardy (they all live out-of-doors) plants in the Arizona high country. Her catalog is filled with *Sempervivums* (bareroot), *Sedums,* and a few *Jovibarbas.* Descriptions of plant's color and form are supplemented by several pages outlining the shapes of the leaves. Started to offer a few book titles in 1995.
Shipping season: June through September.
Canada, Mexico, International

SUNRISE NURSERY
1991
Tim and Kathy Springer
Catalog: Free, 20 pp.
All of the Springer's plants are vegetatively propagated, most are started from seeds and a few from cuttings. None are field collected. The catalog lists four hundred types of plants with areas of concentration among the *Corypantha, Echinocereus, Escobaria, Ferocactus, Mammillaria, Opuntia,* and *Wilcoxia* cactus; and agaves, aloes, *Aloinopsis, Dorstenia, Euphorbia, Haworthia, Lithops, Monadenium,* and *Pachypodium* succulents. Succinct descriptions provide plant form and the color and nature of flower.
Shipping season: March through November.
December through February at customer's risk.

YUCCA DO NURSERY AT PECKERWOOD GARDENS
1988
John Fairey and Carl Schoenfeld
Catalog: $3, 45 pp.
A nursery using only organic methods in cultivating seeds and cuttings of the natives of Texas, Mexico, and Asia. Most varieties offered are hardy in zones 7, 8, and 9. Offerings include seventy types of cactus and other succulents, many noted as being introduced into the trade as a result of expeditions into Mexico by the folks at Yucca Do. Succulents are predominantly *Echeverias;* Cactus includes *Corypantha, Echinocereus, Mammillaria,* and *Opuntia.* Descriptions include location of find, and color and form of flowers and foliage. Guarantees safe delivery; will replace or issue refund if notified within ten days of receipt. See **Conifers,** Grasses, Organics, Perennials, Trees, **Wildflowers.**
Shipping season: January through June.
October through mid-December.
International

Selected Reading About Cactus and Succulents

Beautiful Cacti, by Gerhard Groner and Erich Goetz. A basic guide with information about watering, fertilizing, plant placement, potting and repotting, and tips on care. Sixty-five color photographs.

Cacti, by Clive Innes. A basic introduction with practical information and guidance. Step-by-step information for easy-to-grow genera. Twenty-five color photographs.

The Encyclopedia of Cacti, by Willy Cullmann, Gerhard Groner, and Erich Goetz. A comprehensive guide to cacti and their cultivation. Describes 750 species. Four hundred color photographs.

Growing Desert Plants: From Windowsill to Garden, by Theodore Hodoba. Includes information on cactus, succulents, wildflowers, shrubs, and trees. Detailed information for 101 plants, including propagation and care in nondesert regions.

Succulents, by Clive Innes. A basic introduction with practical information and guidance. Forty-seven color photographs.

Succulents: The Illustrated Dictionary, by M. Sajeva and M. Constanzo. Descriptions and cultural and historical information on 195 genera. 1,212 color photographs.

Fruit- and Nut-Bearing Plants and Trees

The number of plants cited in each profile is based on information in the most recent catalog provided by the source. In this section, shipping season is for fruit- and nut-bearing varieties only. A selection of books about these plants and home orcharding appears after the last listing.

QUICK FIND
The following sources are listed in this section:

ALLEN PLANT COMPANY
AMES' ORCHARD & NURSERY
BEAR CREEK NURSERY
BERGESON NURSERY
BERLIN SEEDS
BLUEBIRD ORCHARD NURSERY
BOSTON MOUNTAIN NURSERIES
BRITTINGHAM PLANT FARMS, INC.
BRUDY'S TROPICAL EXOTICS
BUCKLEY NURSERY GARDEN CENTER
BURFORD BROTHERS
BURNT RIDGE NURSERY & ORCHARDS
CEDAR VALLEY NURSERY
CHESTNUT HILL NURSERY
CLOUD MOUNTAIN FARM
COLD STREAM FARM
COLVOS CREEK NURSERY
COOLEY'S STRAWBERRY NURSERY
DEGRANDCHAMP'S BLUEBERRY NURSERY
DYKE'S BLUEBERRY FARM & NURSERY
EASTERN PLANT SPECIALTIES
EDIBLE LANDSCAPING
ENOCH'S BERRY FARM
EVERGREEN GARDENWORKS
FAIRWEATHER GARDENS
FEDCO TREES
FINCH BLUEBERRY NURSERY

FORESTFARM®
FOUR WINDS TRUE DWARF CITRUS GROWERS
FOWLER NURSERIES, INC., GARDEN CENTER
FRUIT TESTING ASSOCIATION NURSERY, INC.
GARDEN OF DELIGHTS
GIANT WATERMELONS
GOLDEN BOUGH TREE FARM
GREENMANTLE NURSERY
GREER GARDENS
GRIMO NUT NURSERY
HEIRLOOM SEED PROJECT— LANDIS VALLEY MUSEUM
HENRY FIELD'S SEED & NURSERY CO.
HERONSWOOD NURSERY LTD.
HIDDEN SPRINGS NURSERY
HIGHLANDER NURSERY
HOLLYDALE NURSERY
INDIANA BERRY & PLANT CO.
JOHNSON NURSERY
J. W. JUNG SEED AND NURSERY CO.
LAWSON'S NURSERY
LIVING TREE NURSERY
LONG HUNGRY CREEK NURSERY
LOUISIANA NURSERY
MILLER NURSERIES
MINIATURE PLANT KINGDOM
MUSSER FORESTS
NORTH STAR GARDENS

NORTHWIND NURSERY AND ORCHARDS
NOURSE FARMS, INC.
OIKOS TREE CROPS
PACIFIC TREE FARMS
PAMPERED PLANT NURSERY
PENSE NURSERY
PLUMTREE NURSERY
RAINTREE NURSERY
ROCKY MEADOW ORCHARD & NURSERY
ST. LAWRENCE NURSERIES
SAVAGE NURSERY CENTER
SCHLABACH'S NURSERY
SMITH NURSERY COMPANY
SONOMA ANTIQUE APPLE NURSERY
SOUTHERN SEEDS
SOUTHMEADOW FRUIT GARDENS
STARK BRO.'S
SWEDBERG NURSERIES, INC.
TEC
TRIPPLE BROOK FARM
THE URBAN HOMESTEAD
VAN WELL NURSERY
VERNON BARNES AND SON NURSERY
WAYSIDE GARDENS
WHITE FLOWER FARM
WHITMAN FARMS
WILEY'S NUT GROVE NURSERY
WOMACK'S NURSERY CO.

ALLEN PLANT COMPANY
1885

Catalog: Free, 15 pp., color photographs

The Allen Plant Company lists twenty-five varieties (in ripening order) of field-grown, registered, certified virus-free strawberry plants. Descriptions of individual varieties are rich and clear regarding hardiness, attributes, and weakness, noting also types that are best suited for home growers. A chart of test results notes size of berry, flesh firmness, skin firmness, dessert quality, freezing quality, and resistance to four diseases. Explains planting basics and lists suggested planting dates for various regions in the United States. Also offers high bush blueberries (eight types), red and black raspberries, and thornless blackberries. Guarantees safe arrival and satisfactory growth; will fully replace plants up to forty-five days after receipt, then half that up to one year.

Shipping season: February through June. November through May to southern states.

AMES' ORCHARD & NURSERY
1983
Guy Ames and Carolyn Falge Ames
Catalog: Free, 24 pp., illustrations
The Ameses, both with a master's degree in horticulture, specialize in growing disease-resistant fruit plants that are adapted to conditions east of the Rockies. Their stock includes grafted apples, pears, late-blooming peaches, plums, grapes, raspberries, blueberries, strawberries, and thornless blackberries. Offer thirty types of apples grafted onto MM-111 rootstock, listed in approximate ripening order. Descriptions include provenance, taste and nature of fruit, attributes, and vulnerabilities. Includes a section on disease resistance by region, including a chart indicating size and use of fruit and susceptibility and resistance to five diseases. They adhere to a low spray apple pest management program. Guarantees safe arrival; will replace or issue refund. See Heirlooms, Trees.
Shipping season: February through mid-April. Mid-November through December.

BEAR CREEK NURSERY
1977
Hunter and Donna Carleton
Catalog: $1 (recoverable), 80 pp., illustrations
You'll want to set aside some quality reading and dreaming time when you sit down with the Carletons' catalog of two hundred apple varieties and more. It's packed with practical information on choosing fruit trees, planting and pruning, budding, and whip grafting. Fully realized descriptions include provenance and year a variety was first described; time of ripening; color, shape, texture, and taste of fruit, postharvest uses; and characteristics of the tree or plant. Here is a taste of the stone fruit, nuts, grapes, and berries that grow beyond the apples at Bear Creek: sweet and tart cherries, peaches, plums and apricots and their crosses ("plumcots"and "peachcots"), European and Asian pears, blueberries, currants, elderberries, boysenberries, chestnuts, walnuts, filberts and hazelnuts and their crosses ("filazels" and "trazels"). Stock is cold and drought hardy and most selections are available as bench grafts, budded trees, scionwood, summer budwood, and whips. Charts specify time of bloom and time of ripening, suitability for long-term storage, lists pollinators and nonpollinators as well as the degree of resistance to four diseases. Includes a plant

purpose reference guide. Guarantees true to name and safe arrival; will replace for shipping charge only if plant fails to grow first season. See **Booksellers**, Heirlooms, **Trees**.
Shipping season: March through June. Ten percent premium for shipments in October and November.

BERGESON NURSERY
1937
Paul and Glenda Bergeson
Catalog: Free, 26 pp.
Eric Bergeson, the third generation to work at the nursery, would like to set the record straight: Despite the name of their town being Fertile, Minnesota, they are situated in "the most hostile climate in the lower forty-eight states." It should not be surprising, therefore, that he characterizes their stock, which survives in temperatures of 40 degrees below zero, as cold hardy. Nor is it surprising that a portion of this catalog is devoted to fruit-bearing plants, since the sharing of food has been an important theme in the history of this nursery. The founder, Melvin Bergeson, had painful memories of an employer who had him work twelve hours straight without being allowed to eat. Mr. Bergeson insisted that his nursery's crew be fed three times a day! At one point, so much food was being prepared and served to the staff and customers that the nursery employed two full-time cooks. If you're interested in growing your own, however, Bergeson offers cranberries, grapes, raspberries, strawberries, ten types of apple, crabapples, plums, and cherry-plum hybrids. Brief clear descriptions include approximate ripening season, degree of fruit bearing, and intermittent cultural notes. See Conifers, **Trees**.
Shipping season: Potted plants, March through October. Bareroot, March through mid-June.
Canada

BERLIN SEEDS
1984
Edward and Brenda Beachy
Catalog: Free, 60 pp., illustrations and color photographs
A general seed catalog selling commercial quality vegetable seed, Ball and Burpee brand flower seed, nineteen types of primarily midseason strawberry plants, and four hybrid blueberry bushes. Description for plants concentrate on

taste and culinary uses. Presupposes some knowledge as to whether a given fruit is appropriate for conditions in your garden. Guarantees satisfaction; will replace if notified by July 1 of the year of purchase. See **Booksellers, Garlic,** Grasses, **Kidstuff, Seeds, Supplies,** Vegetables. **Shipping season: Late March through mid-June.**
Canada

BLUEBIRD ORCHARD NURSERY
1984
Tim Strickler
Catalog: Free, 6 pp.
Mr. Strickler offers sixty varieties of apples on rootstocks, ranging from the very dwarf (10 percent of standard size) to the semidwarf (80 percent of standard size), three types of pear, and a quince. Fruits are described by name only; notes when variety ripens. Mr. Strickler recommends other publications for descriptions. Will custom graft. Also sells scionwood. Guarantees true to name; will replace. See Trees.
Shipping season: March and April. October and November.

BOSTON MOUNTAIN NURSERIES
1970
Gary Pense
Catalog: 1 FCS, 18 pp., illustrations
The Penses were the Farm Family of the Year in 1966, an accolade that they shared gladly with the family's lone mule, Old Red. The mule is now gone, but the fields remain fertile and productive. Boston Mountain specializes in small fruit plants for the commercial grower and the home gardener. They list fifty types of brambles and berry plants and twenty types of grapes. Their fruit list includes: thornless and thorny blackberries, boysenberries, tayberry (a Scottish cross between a red raspberry and a blackberry), currants, strawberries, blueberries, table and juicing grapes. Fully realized descriptions include: provenance, shape, texture, and color of fruit, time of ripening, varieties that have proven adaptable to various climatic conditions, uses in the garden, and culinary uses. Makes recommendations of cultivars that are most rewarding for home gardeners. Planting chart indicates distance between rows, distance between plants in rows, interval from planting to fruiting, life expectancy of individual plants, height of mature plant, and time of ripening. Blueberry bushes are two-year plants, twelve to eighteen inches; grapes are one-year, field-grown plants. Ships during dormancy only. Guarantees true to name, number one grade, state inspected, and safe arrival; will replace or issue refund within ten days of receipt.
Shipping season: Mid-October through mid-April.

BRITTINGHAM PLANT FARMS, INC.
1945
Wayne I. Robertson
Catalog: $1, 32 pp., color photographs
Brittingham offers twenty-three types of strawberries organized by time of ripening: early, early midseason, midseason, late, and day neutral. Notes hybrid's lineage, developing organization, nature of flesh and skin, taste, disease resistance, and postharvest uses. Also offers red rhubarb, brambles, grapes, and eight blueberry cultivars. Extensive cultural, planting, and growing information appears in a separate section. Chart shows depth to work soil, depth to set plants, types of fertilizer required, preferred pH levels, pruning requirements, distance between rows, yield at maturity, and life expectancy. Guarantees growth during first season; will replace or issue a refund before August 1 of the year of purchase.
Shipping season: January through October.

BRUDY'S TROPICAL EXOTICS
1968
Mike Stich
Catalog: Free, 52 pp., illustrations and black-and-white photographs
The plants in this catalog are tropical in nature and most can be grown in your greenhouse or in containers indoors in the winter, outdoors in the summer. Since Brudy's stock-in-trade is rarities, offerings and availability vary from year to year. Recent catalogs include banana corms; grafted citrus trees; orange, lime, and lemon trees; kumquats; fig trees; pomegranates; and the rhizomes of edible ginger. Descriptions include cultural information; size, color, and taste of fruit, height at maturity; hardiness; and growth habit. If not satisfied, will replace or issue refund. See Conifers, **Seeds,** Trees.
Shipping season: April through September.

BUCKLEY NURSERY GARDEN CENTER
1922
Don Marlow
Catalog: Free, 8 pp.
Two thirds of this catalog is devoted to fruiting plants and trees. Organized by family and time of ripening, nineteen dwarf and semidwarf apples are offered as three-year trees; ten semidwarf cherries as three-year trees; nectarine (standard-size and miniature), peach (standard-size and miniature), eighteen pear (including Asian) as three-year semidwarfs; eight dwarf and semi-dwarf plums and prunes; standard-size two-year persimmon, quince, almond, filbert, walnut, fig, brambles, strawberries, and blueberries; and ten types of table, jelly, and wine grapes available as two-year plants. They also offer a grafted semi-dwarf three-year tree called a "four-of-a-kind" that bears apples, pears, cherries, and plums. See Trees.
Shipping season: February through April.

BURFORD BROTHERS
1980
Thomas Burford
Catalog: $2 (recoverable), 16 pp. *Apples: A Catalog of International Varieties,* **$12, 48 pp.**
If you are fortunate enough to be near Charlottesville, Virginia, in October, you can sample a few of the Burford Brothers' heirloom and modern apple varieties during the Saturdays in the Garden series conducted at Thomas Jefferson's home at Monticello. Don't be too down-hearted, however, if that destination is not on your itinerary; Burford's sales catalog includes a nearly complete inventory of their holdings, offering descriptions of fifty of the 440 types listed. Descriptions, in alphabetical order, include date and locality of origin, original name (if documented), skin and flesh color, taste, postharvest uses, and time of ripening. A portion of their list is offered as one-year-old nursery stock, the balance may be preordered for spring shipment as bench grafts; available on four types of rootstock: full size, 80 percent of standard, 65 percent of standard, and 50 percent of standard. Thomas Burford's *Apples: A Catalog of International Varieties* is an in-depth companion piece to the sales catalog. This apple fancier's delight includes a definition of terms, prototypical illustrations of fruit and tree shapes, an alphabetical listing of their holdings, brief histories of a half dozen "lost" varieties, charming and informative eighty- to one-hundred-word profiles for each of 440 apples. Guarantees true to name and state inspected. See Heirlooms, Trees.
Shipping season: March and April. October through December.

BURNT RIDGE NURSERY & ORCHARDS
1980
Michael Dolan and Carolyn Cerling-Dolan
Catalog: 1 FCS, 8 pp.
The Burnt Ridge catalog features 150 nut-bearing and fruiting trees, shrubs, two-year certified grapevines, and minor fruits such as pawpaw, jujube, persimmon, and mayhaw that are appropriate for temperate zone locations. Recent catalogs featured nine chestnut varieties available as two- to five-foot trees grafted onto their own seedlings or as one- and two-year seedlings, twelve types of hazelnut offered as two-year layered transplants, and English and Persian walnut, pecan, hickory, and almond trees. Fruit-bearing varieties include a selection of semidwarf grafted Asian and European pears, dwarf and semidwarf apples, cherries, plums, and figs. A featured list for Northwest natives include salal, blue and red elderberry, evergreen huckleberry, chokecherry, and salmonberry. Notes growth habit, physical characteristics, flavor of fruit or nut, and disease resistance. See Trees.
Shipping season: All year.

CEDAR VALLEY NURSERY
1979
Charles C. Boyd
Catalog: Free, 6 pp.
Mr. Boyd specializes in fruit-bearing bushes produced from tissue culture. Lists eight varieties of Northwest raspberries and fourteen blackberries. Raspberry chart notes fruit bearing on first- and second-year canes (primocane or everbearing types) or on second-year canes only (floricane types), time of fruiting, berry size and color, and if virus indexed. Blackberry chart notes the presence or absence of thorns, time of first harvest, berry size and firmness, growth habit, winter-hardiness, and if virus indexed. Ships plants in pots. Guarantees true to name and healthy when shipped; will replace or issue refund.
Shipping season: April through November.
Canada, Mexico, International

CHESTNUT HILL NURSERY
R. D. Wallace
Catalog: Free, 19 pp., color photographs

Chestnut Hill specializes in named chestnut cultivars developed by Dr. Robert T. Dunstan, the present owner's grandfather. Selections include: 'Revival' (the first chestnut to be granted a plant patent), 'Carolina', 'Willamette', 'Heritage', 'Carpentar', and 'Alachua'. Also offers seventeen types of astringent and nonastringent Kaki persimmons, several types of fig, and cold-hardy citrus. The catalog contains substantial information about the history of the chestnut tree, its revival, and its culture. Descriptions of individual cultivars include patent number, size and characteristics of tree and foliage, volume of crop, and culinary and landscaping uses. Ships bareroot. Guarantees true to name and healthy when shipped; claims must be made within three days of receipt, although will consider written requests for replacements for trees that do not leaf out through July 1 of the year of purchase. See Trees.
Shipping season: January through March (some potted stock such as figs available at other times).

CLOUD MOUNTAIN FARM
1978
Tom and Cheryl Thornton
Catalog: $1, 46 pp., illustrations and black-and-white photographs
Half of the Cloud Mountain catalog is devoted to fruit- and nut-bearing trees and plants that have been grown in western Washington. The balance of the material in the catalog is available only at the nursery, not through mail order. The catalog features seventeen apple varieties (on five types of rootstock), including eight that are described as scab resistant. Also offers European and Asian pears, peaches, apricots, mulberries, northern persimmons, pawpaw, elderberry, and miniature peach and nectarines for container culture or the small garden. Features seven types of cherry available on Gisela dwarf and semidwarf colt rootstock. In addition to European and Japanese plums, the Thorntons grow "pluots," a plum-apricot cross. The balance of this section includes dayneutral and June-bearing strawberries, raspberries, blackberries, highbush, compact highbush, and dwarf blueberries, currants and gooseberries, dessert and wine grapes, native *Vacciniums* (cranberries and huckleberries), kiwi, walnuts, and hazelnuts. Cultural information, apple and pear pollination charts, information about the spindle bush training method, and other tips and instructions com-plete a catalog that provides full descriptions and specifications for each item offered. Guarantees true to name and safe delivery; will replace or issue a credit or refund within ninety days of receipt.
Shipping season: February through May.

COLD STREAM FARM
1978
Mike Hradel
Catalog: Free, 6 pp.
The Hradels currently grow seventy-three mostly native species of trees, conifers, and berry plants that are useful in reforestation, wildlife habitat, and the yard. Offers black elderberry, highbush cranberry, nannyberry, chokecherry, sand cherry, and wild black cherry; American chestnut; and hazelnut, black and English walnut. Stock is not described other than to indicate sizes of stock available. See Conifers, Trees.
Shipping season: April and November.

COLVOS CREEK NURSERY
See Conifers, Trees.

COOLEY'S STRAWBERRY NURSERY
1983
James Cooley
Catalog: Free, 10 pp.
Cooley's grows and sells strawberries exclusively. Mr. Cooley offers eighteen varieties including: 'Allstar', 'Arking', 'Cardinal', 'Dunlap', 'Guardian', 'Honeoye', 'Midway', 'Ozark Beauty', 'Sparkle', and 'Tribute'. He is straightforward and precise in describing geographical areas for which each cultivar is best suited, the plant's appearance, time of ripening, disease resistance, color, and taste. Guarantees true to name, safe arrival, and initial growth; will replace.
Shipping season: January through mid-June.

DEGRANDCHAMP'S BLUEBERRY NURSERY
1955
Mike DeGrandchamp
Catalog: $1, 14 pp.
DeGrandchamp's, a participating nursery in Michigan's "Virus Tested" blueberry program, offers twenty-five types of container-grown blueberries, including early-ripening 'Bluetta', 'Duke', 'Patriot', and 'Spartan'; mid-season-ripening 'Bluecrop', 'Bluejay', 'Sierra', and 'Toro'; mid- to late-season-ripening 'Berkeley'

and 'Nelson'; and 'Elliott', a late-season variety. Specifications are presented in a chart including virus testing, postharvest uses, easiest method for picking, cold-hardiness, disease resistance, productivity, size of berry, size of bush at maturity, space between plants and between rows. Blueberry plants available as rooted microshoots, three- to six-inch one-year, seven- to twelve-inch one-year field-ready, and two-year container plants. Also lists ten types of cranberries available as rooted plugs or potted plants, and five lingonberries sold as rooted microshoots and one-year container plants. Guarantees true to name; will replace or issue refund.
Shipping season: March through May. September through December. Canada, Mexico, International

DYKE'S BLUEBERRY FARM & NURSERY
1977
Jeff Nelson
Catalog: Free, 8 pp.
Dyke's is a pick-your-own blueberry and blackberry farm that also operates a nursery for highbush blueberries. They grow and sell 'Blueray', 'Berkeley', and 'Coville' cultivars as two-year plants in half-gallon containers. Their informative catalog is for pick-your-own growers, home gardeners interested in the blueberry's food and landscaping potential, and stewards concerned with wildlife planning and land reclamation. Cultural information, garden use suggestions, planning and planting instructions. Plant descriptions include cold-hardiness, sun and soil requirements, how the fruit tastes, and the plant's height at maturity. Guarantees true to name, state inspected, and in vigorous growing condition; will replace or issue refund.
Shipping season: All year. Canada

EASTERN PLANT SPECIALTIES
1985
Mark Stavish
Catalog: $3 (recoverable), 28 pp., illustrations
Mr. Stavish's New England–hardy plant material includes highbush and lowbush blueberries with ornamental value, mountain and bog cranberries, lingonberry, pawpaw, and an American chestnut. Descriptions include height at maturity, growth habit, time of ripening, characteristics of berry

and foliage. A cross-referenced index notes light preference, tolerance of wet or dry soil, fragrance, autumn color, attractive berries, or distinctive bark. See **Conifers**, Perennials, **Rhododendrons**, **Trees**, **Wildflowers**.
Shipping season: March through June. September through November.

EDIBLE LANDSCAPING
1981
Michael McConkey
Catalog: Free, 14 pp., illustrations and color photographs
Mr. McConkey's specialty is ornamental trees and shrubs for home landscape use that require low to no spray regimens while displaying attractive flowers and bearing edible fruit. Recent catalogs featured eleven varieties of dwarf citrus (both grafts and own-root varieties) that are suited for container culture, cherries, edible dogwoods, hardy kiwis, oriental persimmons, five nut-producing pines, raspberries, thornless blackberries and currants, peaches, eleven varieties of fig, mulberry, jujube, pawpaw, dwarf pears, blueberries, strawberries, juneberry, apples, crabapple, plums, and seven kinds of grapevine. Descriptions include some cultural notes but focus on taste and look of the fruit and the esthetic characteristics of the plant. Ships potted plants. See Trees.
Shipping season: All year.

ENOCH'S BERRY FARM
1978
A. B. Enoch
List: Free, 1 p.
Offers three kinds of patented blackberries: 'Navaho' (available as plants, crowns, or root cuttings), and 'Choctaw' and 'Shawnee' (available as crowns or root cuttings).
Shipping season: December through March.

EVERGREEN GARDENWORKS
See **Conifers**, Perennials, **Trees**.

FAIRWEATHER GARDENS
See **Conifers**, Rhododendrons, Trees.

FEDCO TREES
1979
Roberta and John Bunker
Catalog: $2, 32 pp., illustrations
A cooperative that offers plant materials ac-

quired from worldwide sources that have performed well in Maine's cold-shortened growing season. Seventy-five percent of Fedco's catalog is devoted to fruit-bearing plants. Their most popular apple is 'Black Oxford', once grown throughout Maine but on the verge of extinction when they began propagating it. Offerings, including an increasing number of endangered cultivars for which the Bunkers have multiplied stock, now number one hundred varieties of apple, crabapple, pear, cherry, peach, plums, blueberry, grape, raspberry, strawberry, rhubarb, highbush cranberry, elderberry, and nut-bearing trees. Descriptions include basic cultural information for each family. Individual entries include breeder, year of introduction and parentage where appropriate, growth and cultural habits, time of ripening, hardiness, and postharvest uses. Stock consists of small, well-rooted trees. Ships bareroot except as noted. Fedco encourages group orders but will accept individual orders. Guarantees safe arrival; will replace or issue a credit or refund. See **Booksellers, Conifers,** Heirlooms, Trees.

Shipping season: January through March.

FINCH BLUEBERRY NURSERY
1951
Rudy Perry
Catalog: Free, 6 pp.
Mr. Perry's catalog features forty-seven varieties. Among the eighteen rabbiteye types are 'Bluebelle', 'Delite', 'Tifblue', and 'Choice'. Among the highbush offerings are ten southern (including 'Cooper', 'Misty', and 'Sharpblue') and seventeen northern (including 'Blue Ray', 'Bluechip', 'Duke', 'Elliot', 'Northland', and 'Patriot'). He also propagates two creeping ornamentals: 'Bloodstone' and 'Well's Delight'. Stock sold as two- and three-year plants; bareroot runners for creepers. Mr. Perry shares recommendations about site selection, planting, and maintenance. Descriptions are straightforward, covering size, color, and nature of fruit, time of ripening, and ornamental characteristics of the bush where appropriate.

Shipping season: October through April.
Canada, Mexico, International

FORESTFARM®
1974
Ray and Peg Pragg
Catalog $3, 414 pp., illustrations and black-and-white photographs

The Praggs' catalog contains four thousand plants. The fruit bearers include fifteen apple, seven cherry, three peach, five pear, and a representation of apricot, plum, blueberry, currant, boysenberry, and blackberry selections. Their catalog is organized by botanical name but includes a common-name index that makes working with this in-depth catalog a pleasure. Descriptions are standardized to include genus, species, variety, common name, foliage habit, hardiness zone, origin, plant uses, cultural conditions, and narrative about the plant's habits, form, and site preference. Ships in small tubes and one- and five-gallon containers, depending on variety and availability. Guarantees true to name. See **Conifers, Grasses, Perennials, Roses, Trees.**

Shipping season: All year.
Canada

FOUR WINDS TRUE DWARF CITRUS GROWERS
1946
Don and Mary Ann Dillon
Catalog: LSASE, 16 pp., black-and-white photographs
Floyd C. Dillon switched careers in 1946, from department store executive to amateur gardener with a purpose, and the fruits of that decision were, literally, fruits. He developed true dwarf citrus whose ultimate size in the ground is eight feet (somewhat smaller when grown in a container outside or in a solarium and greenhouse). The nursery, now operated by Dillon's son Don and Don's wife, Mary Ann, offers thirty-one varieties of these grafted dwarves bearing full-sized fruit, including orange, mandarin, lemon, grapefruit, lime, tangelos, and kumquats. The Dillons write reassuringly about care and culture; descriptions of individual cultivars include taste, bearing habits, and season of ripening. Ships in containers. See Trees.

Shipping season: All year.
International

FOWLER NURSERIES, INC., GARDEN CENTER
1912
Dick Fowler
Catalog: $4, 42 pp.
At the turn of the century, Placer County, California, was rich with commercial fruit or-

chards. One hundred and twenty years after the establishment of the first orchard there, Fowler Nurseries stands as the county's sole surviving fruit tree nursery. Fowler annually ships more than 800,000 trees to commercial orchardists throughout the United States. Their home orchard selection guide includes three hundred varieties of plants primarily for the greater northern California (zones 2–5) fruit-growing region. Twenty-three varieties of apple, particularly suited to California's gold country, are available on EMLA 111, EMLA 7 semidwarf, and M 27 dwarf rootstock, ten apricots on Marianna 2624 and Lovell full-size rootstocks, and three-quarter-size trees on citation rootstock. Also offers "aprium," (an apricot-plum cross), "peachcot," and "plumcot." Other fruiting trees include Asian pear and pear, cherry, fig, jujube, nectarine, peach, persimmon, plum, pomegranate, quince, and an assortment of a dozen miniatures. Nut-bearing trees include eight types of almond and several varieties each of chestnut, filbert, pecan, and walnut. Shrubs and vines include blackberries, highbush blueberries, currants, raspberries, kiwi, strawberries, and twenty-one types of table grapes, including cabernet sauvignon, chenin blanc, pinot chardonnay, and zinfandel for wine making. Fowler's catalog includes a section with bareroot planting hints, an illustrated pruning guide, and a map noting chilling requirements. Descriptions include nature and taste of fruit, skin, and flesh, growth habit, and time of ripening. Ships bareroot during dormancy. Guarantees true to name and growth during first season. If plant proves untrue during first fruiting season, Fowler's will replace it. If a plant fails to grow, they will replace it if notified by August 1 of the year of receipt. See Heirlooms, Trees.

Shipping season: February through April.

FRUIT TESTING ASSOCIATION NURSERY, INC.
1918
Helen Van Arsdale
Catalog: Free (included in $10 membership), 40 pp., illustrations
The Fruit Testing Association Nursery is a nonprofit cooperative established to market test varieties developed at the New York State Agricultural Experiment Station at Geneva as well as cultivars developed at other testing stations throughout the United States. Their catalog of new and noteworthy fruit includes three

hundred varieties of apple, crabapple, pear, sweet and tart cherry, plum, peach, nectarine, apricot, seedless table grapes, wine grapes, white and red French hybrid wine grapes, Northern highbush and half-high blueberries, brambles, strawberries, elderberries, and Asian pears. An extensive collection of rootstocks is also offered. Charts show spacing for rootstocks; other charts list comparative ripening seasons, place of cultivar's origination, year of introduction, and relative vigor. Descriptions and cultural information are very thorough, as you might expect from a catalog that doubles as a research tool. Guarantees true to name; will replace stock if notified by August 1. See **Horticultural Societies**, Trees.
Shipping season: March through May.
Budwood, August.
No plum, peach, nectarine, or apricot to Arizona, California, Idaho, Oregon, or Washington
Canada

GARDEN OF DELIGHTS
1980
Murray Corman
Catalog: $2 (recoverable), 10 pp. Specialty catalogs available upon request: *Islandia: Fruits of the Caribbean; Frutales: Fruits of Latin America; Jambure: Fruits of Asia; and Bombabies: Fruits of India*
Mr. Corman conducted post-entry inspections of tropical fruit plants for the Florida Department of Agriculture during the late 1970s that made him aware of a need for a source of "ethnic botanicals." Collecting germ plasm and propagating exotics has allowed him to establish a list of two hundred species and hybrids, over half of which bear edible fruit. Recent offerings include: *Acca (Feijoa) sellowiana* (pineapple guava), *Anacardium occidentale* (cashew nut), *Bombax glabra* (French peanut), *Carica papaya* (papaya), *Cocoloba ivifera* (pigeon plum), *Eriobotrya japonica* (loquat), *Litchi chinensis* (litchi), *Manihot esculenta* (tapioca), *Pereskia aculeata* (Barbados gooseberry), *Pouteria hypoglauca* (cinnamon apple), *Rubus niveus* (Mysore raspberry), *Synsepalum dulcificum* (miraculous fruit), and *Ziziphus mauritiana* (Indian jujube). Lists plants by genus and species, gives common name, and specifies size of growing container. Ships bareroot. See Seeds, Trees.
Shipping season: All year.
Canada, Mexico, International

GIANT WATERMELONS
See **Seeds**, Vegetables.

GOLDEN BOUGH TREE FARM
See Conifers, Trees.

GREENMANTLE NURSERY
1983
Ram and Marissa Fishman
Fruit catalog: $3, 28 pp., illustrations
Homesteaders who settled in Humboldt County, California, made extensive plantings of fruit and nut trees in an attempt to establish a viable agrarian economy. Although their efforts were successful through the first third of this century, infestations of coddling moths and competition from large-scale growers contributed to the decline of their orchards as commercial enterprises. The foundation of the Greenmantle fruit tree list (over 110 offerings) consists of plant material that the Fishmans have collected from these old orchards in southern Humboldt while working with others in a new generation of homesteaders to promote a responsible and sustainable agricultural base. The Fishmans focus on their own bioregion, with the expectation that their stock will also adapt to conditions in the Pacific Northwest and northern California. The Fishman's organically grown pesticide-free trees include fifty-five apple varieties organized by time of ripening (including a unique astrological division of the apple harvest season), from midsummer to mid- to late autumn; sixteen pear and Japanese pear, seven plum, three peach, eighteen cherry and sour cherry, as well as fig and chestnut varieties. They list a hundred additional apples that they will propagate to order. The descriptions of the trees and rootstocks border on poetry, all the while presenting specifications, cultural habits, historical notes, postharvest uses, and other essential information about each variety. An extensive discussion of rootstock, variety, and nursery stock selection, planning, planting, pruning, and pests make this a reassuring and informative catalog. Ships one-year bareroot trees and dormant whip grafts. Guarantees true to name, healthy, viable, and safe arrival; return unsatisfactory plants immediately. See Heirlooms, Organics, **Roses**, Trees.
Shipping season: January through March.

GREER GARDENS
See **Booksellers, Conifers, Grasses, Peonies**, Perennials, **Rhododendrons**, Trees.

GRIMO NUT NURSERY
Ernie Grimo
Catalog: $2 (recoverable, two-year subscription), 8 pp., illustrations
Mr. Grimo specializes in nut-bearing trees that are most hardy for Canadian conditions. Offers fourteen Persian walnut, eight black walnut, three "alpricot", (almond-apricot crosses producing both fruit and nuts), eight heartnut (a sport of the Japanese walnut), five butternut, "buartnut" (a butternut-heartnut cross), four pines with edible nuts, a female ginkgo, thirteen hazelnut, seventeen Chinese chestnut, three American chestnut, a pair of hickories, and a number of northern pecan. Rich descriptions of each family precede spare comments for individual offerings. Stock sold variously as seedlings and grafts from one to six feet high, potted and bareroot. Guarantees stock to grow; up to 100 percent replacement allowance for stock that does not leaf out and grow. See Trees.
Shipping season: Early spring.
Canada

HEIRLOOM SEED PROJECT—LANDIS VALLEY MUSEUM
1987
Steve Miller and Nancy Pippart
Catalog: $2.50, 52 pp., illustrations
The Landis Valley Museum's Heirloom Seed Project was the recipient in 1991 of the American Association for State and Local History's Award of Merit. The project and its historic gardens program are nonprofit organizations oriented toward education on environmental and cultural living history. For a brief time each year, they make available the scionwood of heirloom apple trees. Varieties that have been available include: 'Baldwin Woodpecker', 'Cox's Orange Pippin', 'Jonathan', 'Smokehouse', 'Stayman Winesap', and 'Summer Rambo'. Vintage descriptions of apple trees are based on those that were originally published in 1905 in *The Apples of New York*, by S. A. Beach. See Heirlooms, Organics, Seeds, Trees, **Vegetables.**
Shipping season: Late March through early April.
Canada

HENRY FIELD'S SEED & NURSERY CO.
1892
Orville Dragoo
Catalog: Free, 87 pp., color photographs

A full-line seed and nursery catalog that offers fruit- and nut-bearing trees, vines, and shrubs including their own-grown apples (eighteen varieties), nine pear, eight plum, ten peach, ten apricot, "plumcots," and nectarines available variously as standard or dwarf trees and at shipping heights from three to five feet. Offers fourteen bush and tree cherries; several walnut, pecan, chestnut, butternut, hazelnut, and almond trees; eleven raspberries; eight blackberries; fifteen strawberries; twelve grape vines; and five blueberry bushes. Descriptions include size, color, and shape of fruit, and season of ripening. Guarantees plants will grow; will replace or issue credit. See **Garlic, Kidstuff,** Organics, Perennials, **Seeds, Supplies, Trees, Vegetables.**
Shipping season: February through June.

HERONSWOOD NURSERY LTD.
See **Conifers, Grasses, Perennials, Rhododendrons,** Trees.

HIDDEN SPRINGS NURSERY
1979
Hector, Susie, and Annie Black, and Diana Lalani
Catalog: $1, 14 pp. Apple and pear gift list: LSASE
Hidden Springs was originally a wholesale grower of herbs and fuchsias. But soil conservation and food propagation concerns caused them to reorient their efforts toward providing plant material for edible landscaping. Their catalog describes forty-plus offerings from worldwide sources, including autumn olive (*Elaeagnus umbellata*), buffaloberry (*Shepherdia argentea*), melon tree (*Cudrania tricuspidata*), five types of European medlar (*Mespilus germanica*), as well as blueberries, cranberries, kiwi, cherries, gingkoes, pomegranates, apples, pears, and quince. Origin of plants, distinguishing characteristics of fruit, foliage, and bark, height at maturity, cultural and growth habits for all. Hardiness zones for many. Send an LSASE for their list of fifty varieties of apple and twenty varieties of pear that you can order as custom grafts. See Trees.
Shipping season: November through June.
Canada, Mexico, International

HIGHLANDER NURSERY
Lee and Louise McCoy
Catalog: Free, 10 pp.

Highlander sells six early and midseason northern highbush blueberry cultivars that are ready to bear. Also lists two southern highbush types ('Avonblue' and 'O'Neal'), two ground covers ('Bloodstone' and 'Wells Delight'), a fruiting ornamental ('Tophat'), two late-ripening bushes ('Burlington' and 'Coville'), and a half-high ('Northland'). Descriptions include height at maturity, growth habit, and general observations about hardiness, fruit size, and color. Provides detailed cultural information and recommendations about site selection and plant care. Ships bareroot. Guarantees satisfaction; will replace or issue refund. See Trees.
Shipping season: Mid-October through May.

HOLLYDALE NURSERY
1986
Dale Bryan
Catalog: Free, 4 pp.
Hollydale is a peach (127 varieties, that is) of a fruit tree nursery. They also grow nineteen varieties of plum, nine nectarine, seven pear (including the 'Bradford' flowering type), and seventeen apple. Stock available on Lovell and Nemaguard rootstock; apples and pears also grown on semidwarf rootstock. Chart of specifications for peach varieties listed in ripening sequence includes flesh color, stone freeness, chilling hours to break dormancy, and number of days to ripen relative to the Elberta peach. Trees shipped in six height ranges from twelve to eighteen inches through four to five feet. Guarantees true to name and shipped in good condition. If tree proves untrue, notify Hollydale during first fruiting season for a refund or replacement at their option. Notify nursery within ten days of receipt if stock is damaged. See Trees.
Shipping season: January through March.
Canada, Mexico, International

INDIANA BERRY & PLANT CO.
1993
Carol Chappell and Jeff Altmeyer
Catalog: Free, 32 pp., black-and-white and color photographs
I. B. & P. offers thirty-three strawberry varieties, summer red raspberries, fall-bearing raspberries, black, yellow, and purple raspberries, four tame and eight thornless blackberries, eleven midwestern and eastern blueberries, grapes, kiwi, currant, gooseberries, saskatoon, elderberries, and rhubarb. Rich descriptions (listings only for

some strawberries) include parentage, regions in which particular varieties have proven consistently successful, cultural and site selection information, flavor, and uses. Charts for strawberries include fruiting season, relative size of fruit, firmness, skin quality, dessert quality, usefulness for processing or freezing, susceptibility and resistance to leaf spot, leaf scorch, red stele, and verticillium wilt. The grower's guide to raspberry and blackberry cultivars in the catalog specifies fruiting season, grade of flavor, hardiness, cane height, disease resistance, and size of fruit. Guarantee true to name, disease free, and vigorous; will issue refund.
Shipping season: All year.

JOHNSON NURSERY
1980
Elisa and Bill Ford
Catalog: Free, 22 pp., black-and-white photographs
The Fords describe their enterprise as the largest grower of fruit trees in Georgia. Apples are their strongest suit, with twenty-six new and antique varieties. Trees available variously as semidwarf and dwarfs; graded as premium, super premium, two-year, and three-year trees. They have recently added figs, "plumcots," muscadines, strawberries, Asian persimmons, and Asian pears to their selection of nectarines, peaches, cherries, plums, grapes, pears, blackberries, raspberries, and rabbiteye blueberries. Information provided includes a home orchard spraying schedule. Cultural notes for each type of tree or plant precedes full descriptions that include color, shape, and size of fruit, growth habit, hardiness zones, and postharvest uses. Ships bareroot. Guarantees safe arrival of live material in plantable condition that will leaf out and grow. Will replace stock that arrives in unacceptable condition if notified within seven days of receipt. Will replace or issue a credit at half the purchase price if plant does not leaf out or dies before July 1 in the year that it is received. See Heirlooms, Trees.
Shipping season: December through April.

J. W. JUNG SEED AND NURSERY CO.
1907
Richard J. Zondag
Catalog: Free, 76 pp., color photographs
Ten percent of this wide-range-of-interests seed and nursery catalog is devoted to fruit-bearing plants and trees. Jung offers eleven virus-free strawberries, including three everbearing cultivars, five northern-grown raspberries, a hardy kiwi, and assorted brambles, lowbush, highbush, and half-high hardy blueberries, seven types of cherry tree, plums, rhubarb, apples, pears, dwarf peaches, an apricot, and grapes. Descriptions are clear and thorough, including age and approximate size of plants (varies with type) offered for mail-order shipment. Offers collections of elderberries, strawberries, raspberries, super-dwarf apple trees, hardy grapes, and north country blueberries. Guarantees true to name, safe arrival, and will grow in your garden; will replace or issue credit. See Bulbs, Garlic, Kidstuff, Perennials, Seeds, Supplies, Trees, Vegetables.
Shipping season: March through mid-June.
No Alaska, Arizona, California, Hawaii, Idaho, Nevada, New Mexico, Oregon, or Washington.

LAWSON'S NURSERY
1965
James and Bernice Lawson
Catalog: Free, 36 pp.
The Lawsons catalog 115 apple varieties, including a substantial number of heirlooms. Apple trees are offered on various rootstocks, including: EMLA Oregon-certified virus-free types, EMLA 9 (about 40 percent of the size of a standard tree), EMLA 106 (65 percent), and EMLA 111 (75 percent). Descriptions are informal, including historical information, year of first description, color and nature of skin and flesh, time of ripening, taste, and postharvest uses. A separate list specifies the rootstock onto which each variety has been grafted, the age of the trees being offered, and availability of individual varieties at the time the catalog was issued. Lawson's also grows edible crabapples, pears for fruit and ornament, peach, plum, and cherry trees and bushes, southern rabbiteye blueberries, strawberries, fig, muscadine, and walnut. Will make custom bench grafts of a single specimen or in quantity. See Heirlooms, Trees.
Shipping season: November through April.
No Arizona or California.

LIVING TREE NURSERY
1979
Jesse Schwartz
Catalog: $4, 30 pp., illustrations and black-and-white photographs

Dr. Schwartz's "Living Tree Catalog of Historical and Biblical Fruits" is a time capsule for fruit fanciers. Forty heirloom apples are organized by season of harvest. Also sells pears, figs, apricots, nectarines, peaches, plums, quince, almonds, grape, and jujube. Descriptions include historical information, attributions to plantsmen and horticulturists who have developed or rediscovered particular heritage varieties, shape, color, and postharvest uses of fruit; intermittent coverage of culture and hardiness. Trees are one-year whips on two-year root systems. Offers a collection of biblical fruit and nut-bearing trees and plants described according to their place in Scripture. See Heirlooms, Trees.
Shipping season: January through May.
Canada, Mexico, International

LONG HUNGRY CREEK NURSERY
1980
Jeff Poppen
Catalog: Free, 4 pp.
Jeff Poppen and Debby Beaver steward a seventy-acre biodynamic vegetable and cattle farm in Red Boiling Springs, Tennessee. Their primary interest is in making available apples and small fruit suitable for the home orchardist (with emphasis on those in the Southeast) who employs little or no spraying. The fourteen old-time and eight modern apple varieties on their list are chosen with attention to high resistance to fire blight, scab, cedar apple rust, and mildew, and with tendencies toward productivity, flavor, and late blooming. Brief descriptions for some, name of cultivar only for others. Highlights 'Arkansas Black' and 'Liberty' as particularly responsive to organic methods. Trees are available on EMLA 111 virus-free rootstock as one-year whips (three to five feet) and two-year well-branched trees that are five feet tall or better. Guarantees healthy; will replace. See Heirlooms, Organics, Trees.
Shipping season: November through April.

LOUISIANA NURSERY
1950
Dalton E. Durio
Catalog: $3.50 (recoverable), 62 pp.
Louisiana Nursery occupies a fifty-six-acre complex that was founded by Ken Durio. Five family members, all trained horticulturists, are currently involved in the business. The Durios' catalog "Fruiting Trees, Shrubs and Vines"

(one of six that they publish) includes four hundred listings: thirty-five kiwi species and cultivars, ten pawpaws, thirty citrus, twenty-five persimmons, forty figs, and a broad selection of bananas, blueberries, chinquapins, crabapples, gumis, jujubes, quince, mulberries, chestnuts, filberts/hazelnuts, and black walnuts. Cultural notes: soil and drainage, watering requirements, fertilization, pest control, weeding and mulching. Descriptions include botanical and common names, look and size of leaves, color and qualities of flowers and fruit, season of ripening, origins, site preferences, and hardiness zone. Ships bareroot and potted plants, depending on variety. See **Booksellers, Bulbs, Daylilies, Grasses, Iris, Trees.**
Shipping season: All year.
Canada, Mexico, International

MILLER NURSERIES
1884
John E. Miller
Catalog: Free, 60 pp., color photographs
Miller has its origins as a grape grower and vintner circa 1884 and became a direct-to-the-gardener mail-order business in 1936. Their catalog includes ground covers, conifers, shrubs, perennials, and supplies, but the overwhelming feature here is the two hundred fruit- and nut-bearing plants and trees—a balance between the tried-and-true and the new and unusual. Unique cultivars include combination trees: a three-on-one cherry tree with 'Black Tartarian', 'Emperor Francis', and 'Windsor' types; a three-on-one pear tree with 'Anjou', 'Bartlett', and 'Clapps' varieties; a three-on-one Asian pear bearing 'Chojuro', 'Hosui', and 'Shinseiki' fruit; a five-on-one modern and a five-on-one antique apple tree. Some of their fruit trees are available as Miller's Compspur compact types; semidwarfs that are characterized in their catalog as very winter-hardy and prolific. Other offerings include eight cherry trees, fifteen dwarf and standard plums, twenty-eight No Ladder® semidwarf hybrid apples, twenty-nine antique apples, nineteen standard apples, nine dwarf hybrid pear, ten dwarf and standard pears, twenty-one dwarf and standard peaches, four dwarf apricot, two standard apricot, three dwarf nectarine, eleven strawberries, eleven raspberries, and a selection of blueberries, blackberries, currants, persimmons, chestnut, walnut, heartnut, butterheart nut, and butter-

nut. Miller's original crop, grapes, is represented by thirty varieties listed by season of ripening. Descriptions vary from brief to the fully realized and very rich. Emphasis on hardiness and nature of fruit. Age and size of plant specified. The catalog includes a chart noting approximate bearing age, distance between plants, and pollination habit for all families of plant material that they sell. Guarantees Canandaigua Quality™ stock to be vigorous and ready to grow. Will replace or issue credit or refund (at their discretion) if plant material does not survive the first year in your garden. See Heirlooms, Trees.

Shipping season: March through May. October and November.

MINIATURE PLANT KINGDOM
See **Conifers, Grasses, Perennials, Trees.**

MUSSER FORESTS
See **Conifers, Trees.**

NORTH STAR GARDENS
1983
Kyle D. Haugland
Catalog: Free, 48 pp., color photographs
Raspberries are the mainstay at this nursery in Marine on St. Croix, Minnesota, with almost thirty varieties being offered. Although the catalog is written to answer the needs of commercial growers and pick-your-own operations, the backyard gardener should find the information and selection enlightening and exciting. The catalog is organized by berry type, then within type by season of ripening. North Star's raspberry offerings include fourteen red summer-bearing types, seven red fall-bearing varieties, three purple and six black that are summer-bearing varieties, and two bushes that produce yellow fruit. North Star's stock also includes nine thornless and thorny blackberries, nine black and red currants, gooseberries, a jostaberry, and several blueberries. Individual narrative descriptions include year of introduction, parentage, location where developed, size, shape, and taste of berry, disease susceptibility and resistance, nature and size of canes, and hardiness. A chart compares time of ripening, best postharvest uses, flavor, vulnerability to specific maladies, spininess, height of canes at maturity, hardiness zone, and recommendations as to the coldest areas for which a variety should be

used. Specifies spacing between rows and between plants. Guarantees true to name, viable, and in good condition at time of shipment. See Booksellers.

Shipping season: January through May. Canada, Mexico, International

NORTHWIND NURSERY AND ORCHARDS
1983
Frank Foltz
Catalog: $1 (recoverable), 35 pp., illustrations. "Fruit Collection" list: LSASE.
The Foltz family are growers of northern-hardy, organically grown fruit trees and plants cultivated without the use of pesticides or chemicals. A keynote of their catalog is self-reliance and practicability for small-scale orchardists and backyard growers. The Foltzs offer many fruits that have been released from the University of Minnesota Horticultural Research Center, including 'Centennial', 'Keepsake', 'Lakeland', and 'State Fair' apples; 'Summercrisp' and 'Parker' pears; and 'Lakeland', 'Nordic', and 'Redwing' raspberries. Northwind's selection includes thirty-six apple varieties balanced between summer, fall, and winter bearers available as standard trees (ten are available on semidwarfing rootstock); seven European and Asian pears; seven juicing, table, and dessert grapes; twelve Japanese, American, and European plums; cherry plums; apricots; blueberries; raspberries; fruiting shrubs; crabapple; and nut trees. Brief effective descriptions include size and nature of fruit, postharvest uses, hardiness, and cultural habits. Fruit rated according to productivity, reliability, hardiness, storage life, and cooking/processing quality. Ships small and medium bareroot stock. For a complete scionwood list, request "The Fruit Collection" and include an LSASE. See **Booksellers**, Organics, **Supplies**, Trees.

Shipping season: April and May. October and November. Dormant scionwood, November and December.

NOURSE FARMS, INC.
1933
Anne Kowaleck
Catalog: Free, 10 pp., color photographs
Nourse Farms specializes in the propagation of virus-free small fruit developed through tissue culture. Offers twenty-five strawberries (early season, early midseason, midseason, late midseason, and everbearing), raspberries (eleven summer red, four everbearing, black, yellow, and purple), thornless and thorny blackber-

ries, and nine blueberries. Descriptions include parentage, size, shape, and texture of fruit, cultural and growth habit, and disease resistance. Notes distance between rows and distance between plants in rows. A variety guide highlights individuals from their offerings that excel in flavor, largeness of fruit, response to freezing, ease of growing, and largest yield. Extensive site preparation, planting, feeding, and cultural instructions abound in a catalog that reassures the home gardener while providing larger growers with the key facts they require. Guarantees true to name.

Shipping season: March through June.
Canada, International

OIKOS TREE CROPS
1985
Ken Asmus
Catalog: $1, 46 pp., illustrations, black-and-white and color photographs
Mr. Asmus specializes in low-maintenance trees and bushes, many providing fruit and nuts for humans and wildlife. Offers edible natives (native to Michigan) including tree and apple serviceberry, Michigan saskatoon, Viking black chokeberry, pawpaw, bearberry honeysuckle, American persimmon, prairie crabapple, and golden currant. Thirty fruiting plants of various origins include flowering quince, date plum, silk mulberry, dwarf ground cherry, several cotoneasters, Chinese stranvaesias, and Manchurian viburnums. Nut trees include: hybrid and species chestnuts, walnuts, pecans, hickories, and hazelnuts and their crosses ("filazels," "hazelberts," and "trazels"). Stock available variously in paper pots, flats, and as one- and two-year seedlings. Descriptions include nature and use of fruit, age of plant for first fruit, hardiness, preferred soil and site, height at maturity, and spacing. Guarantees healthy and true to catalog description. See **Trees.**

Shipping season: Potted plants, February through December. Bareroot, March through May. October and November.
No chestnuts to Florida, no chestnuts or filberts to Oregon or Washington, no nuts or persimmons to California, no walnuts to Arizona
Canada, Mexico, International

PACIFIC TREE FARMS
William L. Nelson
Catalog: $2, 20 pp.
Mr. Nelson offers 350 container-grown trees and shrubs from diverse sources. Approximately 70

percent are fruit and nut bearing. Recent lists featured *Acacia chinensis* ('Chico', 'Hayward', 'Matua', and 'Tomuri' kiwi); *Carya illonoinensis* ('Cheyenne', 'Choctaw', 'Mohawk', and 'Wichita' pecan); *Citrus limon* ('Eureka', 'Sungold' variegated, sweet lemon); *Citrus reticulata* ('Algerian Clementine'); daisy, kara, kinnow, and ponkin mandarins; and *Vitis vinifera* (European grape: golden muscat, lamento, muscadine, and ruby seedless). Stock is listed by botanical name and cross-referenced by common name, without further description. Varieties that are available on alternate rootstocks are noted. Ships most in five-gallon pots; some are bareroot only. See **Conifers, Trees.**

Shipping season: Potted plants, all year.
Bareroot, January through mid-March.
No citrus to Arizona, Florida, Louisiana, or Texas
Canada, Mexico, International

PAMPERED PLANT NURSERY
1992
Douglas Armstrong
Catalog: LSASE, 8 pp.
Mr. Armstrong's list is dominated by edibles. Northern selections are grown on-site in Illinois. Those designated as southern selections are grown in Tennessee. He offers figure-grained and fast-growing black walnut varieties, butternut, heartnut, Persian walnut, pecan, shagbark and shellbark hickory, hican, filbert, chestnut, American and Oriental persimmon, pawpaw, jujube, mulberry, Japanese raisin tree, cornelian cherry, saskatoon, hawthorn/mayhaw, kiwi, and hardy kiwi. Plants are listed by common name (botanical name given) and are offered variously as one-, two-, three-year, and older seedlings, grafted/budded plants, rooted cuttings, scionwood, and green cuttings. Mr. Armstrong also provides custom grafting/budding and seed germination services. See Trees.

Shipping season: Primarily spring and fall.
Canada

PENSE NURSERY
1981
Phillip D. Pense
Catalog: Free, 8 pp.
This branch of the Pense family has been specializing in small fruit plants under this name since 1981. Contract growers for many other large mail-order nurseries, they will gladly sell directly to you. Offers four thornless and six

thorny blackberries, thornless and thorny boysenberry, 'Austin' and 'Lucretia' dewberries, nine raspberries, gooseberry, red currant, eight seedless grapes, elderberry, and six blueberries. Brief descriptions include hardiness and size and flavor of fruit. Guarantees safe arrival and healthy; will replace or issue refund. See Trees.
Shipping season: October through April.
Canada, Mexico, International

PLUMTREE NURSERY
1985
Lee Reich
Catalog: $1, 8 pp., illustrations
Lee Reich is the author of *Uncommon Fruits Worthy of Attention: A Gardener's Guide* and *A Northeast Gardener's Year*. His specialty is a selective offering of organically grown rare fruit: alpine yellow strawberries, musk strawberries, consort European black currant, clove currant, maypops, and Nanking cherry. Descriptions are intended to make the unfamiliar become familiar, noting origins, flavor, and growth habit. See Organics.
Shipping season: April through June. September and October.

RAINTREE NURSERY
1974
Sam Benowitz
Catalog: Free, 74 pp., black-and-white and color photographs
Raintree Nursery offers five hundred edible plants from worldwide sources. They specialize in disease-resistant varieties of fruits, nuts, and berries for home gardeners. Range of selection includes apple, apricot, blackberry, blueberry, cherry, citrus, edible crabapple, cranberry, currant, elderberry, fig, grape, gooseberry, jujube, lingonberry, loquat, nectarine, pawpaw, pear, pineapple guava, plum, "plumcot," pomegranate, strawberry, chestnut, filbert, walnut, and edible ground covers. Descriptions are thorough and include season of ripening, flavor, growth habit, and hardiness for most, rootstock for many. Pollination charts (where applicable) by cultivar within families. A sidebar within each section includes kitchen and landscape uses, size at maturity, sun/shade preference, space between plants, time of harvest, origin, life expectancy, soil requirements, pruning, thinning, and pests. Provides an index and map of varieties that will thrive in your area by family and

name. Guarantees true to name, safe arrival, and will survive first year. Will replace plants that fail if you believe that mortality is due to Raintree's error. Will accept unconditionally the return of any item for a full refund up to thirty days after delivery. See **Booksellers, Grasses.**
Shipping season: Bareroot, January through mid-May. Potted plants, all year.

ROCKY MEADOW ORCHARD & NURSERY
1974
Ed Fackler
Catalog: $1, 18 pp., illustrations.
Scionwood list: LSASE
Rocky Meadow Orchard & Nursery offers nursery stock to home gardeners and commercial orchardists. Varieties are represented as having two or more of the following attributes: unique superior flavor and texture, desirable tree manageability, productive early and annual cropping, and disease resistance. The catalog includes twenty-eight apple varieties, three crabapple, eleven pear, and seven plum. Varieties recommended for backyard enthusiasts include 'Ashmead's Kernal', 'Cox's Orange', 'Kerry', 'Newtown Pippin', and 'Spitzenburg' apples; 'Bierschmitt' and 'Worden' pears; and 'Hollywood' and 'Pearl' plums. Descriptions include origin, shape and color of skin and flesh, ripening time, degree of vigor, growth habit, and intermittent notations about the zones in which a variety has done best. Lists fifteen rootstocks for home use and a custom propagation service for larger orders. A list of scionwood is available for an LSASE. Guarantees true to name, state inspected, and will survive the first season in your garden. If instructions are followed and you are not satisfied, notify Rocky Mountain by July 1 of the year plant was received for an adjustment. See Trees.
Shipping season: November through May.
No plums to Arizona, California, Oregon, or Washington

ST. LAWRENCE NURSERIES
1920
Bill and Diana MacKentley
Catalog: Free, 30 pp., illustrations and black-and-white photographs
The MacKentleys sell stock grown in zone 3 where winter temperatures have chilled to minus 50 degrees Fahrenheit. Their catalog lists 127 heirloom and modern standard apple trees, fifteen pear, and a number of plums,

cherry plums, sour cherries, blueberries, lingonberries, raspberries, bush cherries, juneberries, grapes, black walnuts, and other nut trees. A separate section features edible ornamentals: currants, jostaberry, rhubarb, buffaloberry, Siberian pea shrub, and American highbush and true bog cranberries. Includes cultural information, hardiness, parentage, color, season of ripening, postharvest uses, and resistance to diseases. Guarantees state inspected and will survive the first year in your garden; will replace. See **Booksellers**, Heirlooms, Organics, Trees.

Shipping season: April and May. October and November.

Canada, International

SAVAGE NURSERY CENTER
1942
Jim Savage
Catalog: Free, 4 pp., color photographs
Mr. Savage offers twenty-nine standard, semidwarf, and dwarf apples. Standard-size trees of other fruits include four plums, three pears, seven peaches, six cherries, selected figs, apricots, and a nectarine. Lists twenty-four fruits on dwarfing rootstock, including peach, pear, apricot, nectarine, cherry, and plum. Concord, catawba, 'Fredonia', and 'Niagara' grapevines offered with seeded and seedless fruit. Lists nine types of mid- and late midseason blueberry cultivars and a dozen nut-bearing trees including 'Halls' hardy almond, 'Thomas' black walnut, American and European filberts, Mahan pecan, and Chinese and sweetheart chestnuts. Compact informative descriptions for most, including fruit's taste and color, time of ripening, current height and height at maturity. Guarantees safe arrival and survival the first year in your garden. Will replace plants that arrive in unsatisfactory condition free of charge. Those that fail will be replaced for half the original price. See Conifers, **Trees.**

Shipping season: January through May. October through December.

SCHLABACH'S NURSERY
1990
David Schlabach
Catalog: Free, 4 pp.
Schlabach's is an Amish family-run fruit- and nut-tree nursery specializing in the propagation and preservation of old-time favorites from the area around Millersburg, Ohio. Lists

twenty-four varieties of apple, three peaches, and three pears on virus-free dwarf and semidwarf rootstock. Brief descriptions include growth habit, color of fruit, season of ripening, and a key attribute for each tree. Also offers Chinese chestnut, heartnut, Ohio 'Thomas' black walnut, and concord and 'Fredonia' grapes. Ships bareroot. Additional lists furnished upon request: scionwood, one hundred varieties of apples, pears, and peaches, cherries, and nuts. Custom grafting for heirloom varieties. Mr. Schlabach's only channel of communication is the written word. Guarantees healthy; will replace or issue refund. See Heirlooms, Trees.

Shipping season: March through May.

SMITH NURSERY COMPANY
See Seeds, Trees.

SONOMA ANTIQUE APPLE NURSERY
1979
Carolyn and Terry Harrison
Catalog: Free, 37 pp., illustrations
The Harrisons' nursery is certified organic and their catalog includes over two hundred primarily antique apple, crabapple, pear, plum, peach, and fig varieties that are budded and trained on-site. Heirlooms include 'Calville Blanc D'Hiver' (1598), 'Duchess of Oldenburg' (1700), 'Golden Noble' (1820), 'Kerry Irish Pippin' (1802), 'Northern Spy' (1800), 'Rhode Island Greening' (1650), and original winesap (1817) apples. Charts, organized by season of ripening, denote season of bloom, best climatic conditions, hardiness, pollination, storability, and size of tree for apples; season of bloom, resistance to fire blight, pollination, storability, and size of tree for pears; resistance to leaf curl, climatic preference, method of pollination, size of tree, and showiness of blossoms for peaches; pollenizers, size of tree and country of origin for plums, prunes, and "pluots." Narrative descriptions include provenance, year of introduction or first reference, color, texture, culinary uses, characteristics of its taste, and cultural habits. Scionwood available for most of their list. Additional selections of fruit, nuts, berries, table and wine-making grapes cultivated by other nurseries are also listed. Also specializes in espaliered plants trained in fan or informal shapes: sixteen apples, five figs, eleven pears, three persimmons, two plums, seven ornamentals, and 'Wonderful Pom' pomegranates. A few apple and pear varieties are also available as multitiered cordons. Guarantees

true to name and that stock will grow if planted according to instructions; will replace any tree that proves to be untrue or does not survive in your garden through July 1 of the year following delivery. See Heirlooms, Organics, Trees.
Shipping season: Mid-January through March.

SOUTHERN SEEDS
See **Booksellers**, Garlic, Organics, **Seeds**, Vegetables.

SOUTHMEADOW FRUIT GARDENS
1950
Theo, Catharina, and Peter Grootendorst
Catalog: $9, 112 pp., illustrations and black-and-white photographs
Southmeadow Fruit Gardens is the result of an outgrowth of an article about Robert A. Nitschke's fruit garden in *Flower and Garden* magazine. The volume and intensity of inquiries that came Mr. Nitschke's way from people interested in acquiring the varieties described sent him in search of a nurseryman (who he found in the person of Theo C. J. Grootendorst) to effectively propagate these varieties on suitable, size-controlling, early-bearing rootstocks. The catalog includes 190 apples on dwarf rootstock, thirty-eight dwarf pears, twenty-three peaches, three nectarines, nine apricots, thirty European and Japanese plums, fourteen sweet cherries, a quince, sixty grapes, twenty gooseberries, currants, and nineteen winter-hardy fruits for wildlife. Descriptions include historical, cultural, and culinary information. See Heirlooms, Trees.
Shipping season: February through May. November and December.

STARK BRO.'S
1816
Walter C. Logan II
Catalog: Free, 56 pp., color photographs
Stark Bro.'s are fruit tree specialists. They grow all of their own trees and focus on developing new (many disease resistant) and exclusive varieties. Offers thirty apples, fifteen peaches, thirteen pears, twelve sweet and sour cherries, thirteen plums, ten apricots, "apriums," and "pluots," and an assortment of persimmons, kiwi, figs, jostaberry, tayberry, pawpaw, and seven strawberries. Fifteen nut trees available variously from seed and grafts. Several fruiting trees are Starkspur® types, described as a nat-

ural semidwarf that bears fruit in clusters from the trunk out. Enthusiastic descriptions include time of ripening, hardiness zones, culinary uses, and specific attributes of their own cultivars. Charts compare time of ripening for optimal selection. Trees available variously on dwarf, semidwarf, and standard rootstocks. Numerous collections within families emphasize staggered and overlapping time of ripening and planting of small-scale home orchards in limited space. Guarantees satisfaction; will replace or issue refund. See Conifers, Trees.
Shipping season: February through May. October through December.
No nuts (except filberts and hazelnuts) to Arizona, California, or New Mexico
No filberts or hazelnuts to Oregon and Washington

SWEDBERG NURSERIES, INC.
Catalog: Free, 14 pp., color photographs
Swedberg Nurseries, located in Battle Lake, Minnesota, devotes half of their catalog to fruit-bearing trees and plants. Their list of hardy apple trees includes Canadian varieties 'Goodland', 'Norland', 'Parkland', and 'Westland'. Highlights a number of large (eight-foot) and big (eight- to ten-foot) apple trees and assorted one-year-old grafts. Also available are hardy Canadian and Minnesota apricots ('Moongold', 'Scout', and 'Sungold') and hardy Canadian and Minnesota pears ('Luscious', 'Parker', 'Patton', 'Summercrisp', and 'Ure'). Offers crabapple, tree and bush cherries, plums, berries, hardy Minnesota blueberries, June-bearing and everbearing strawberries, grapes, and 'Arctic Beauty' kiwi. Concise descriptions emphasize time of ripening, culinary attributes, and current height of stock. Guarantees will grow through first season; will replace plants one time only at half the original price if claim is filed prior to August 1 of the year of purchase. See Conifers, Trees.
Shipping season: Spring.

TEC
See **Conifers, Trees.**

TRIPPLE BROOK FARM
See **Grasses**, Perennials, Trees, **Wildflowers.**

THE URBAN HOMESTEAD
1992

Tim and Donna Hensley
Catalog: Free, 8 pp.
Originally a part-time endeavor for the Hensleys supplying old and hard-to-find apples, the addition of a landscape service in 1994, favoring the use of native plants, turned this into a full-time venture. The catalog includes 139 apples grafted onto Antanovka or Domestica full-sized rootstocks. Many are also available as early bearing semidwarfs. Among those apples in their collection that the Hensleys characterize as rare are 'Bramley's Seedling' (1809), 'Buff', 'Golden Sweet' (1832), 'Hoover', 'Queen Pippin', and 'Ruben'. Descriptions include year of introduction or first citation, provenance, season of ripening, and postharvest uses for most; name only for others. Stock available variously as husky four- to six-foot whips, three- to five-foot whips, and two- to three-foot whips. Also lists (without description) forty fruiting, nut-bearing, and edible trees and plants. See Heirlooms, Trees.
Shipping season: November through May.

VAN WELL NURSERY
1946
Pete Van Well, Jr.
Catalog: $1, 28 pp., color photographs
In 1996, the Van Well family celebrated their fiftieth anniversary as a purveyor of fruit trees to commercial growers and backyard orchardists. They specialize in modern cultivars, including fifty-four apples, twenty cherries, fifteen pears, eight nuts, six nectarines, thirty-two peaches, twelve apricots, and thirteen European and Japanese plums and prunes. Recent catalogs featured 'Oregon Spur® II', 'Scarlet Spur™', and 'Super Chief® Red Delicious' apples; 'Bing' and 'Sweetheart™' cherries; 'Bartlett' and 'Golden Russet Bosc' pears; 'Arctic Glo' nectarines; early (improved) 'Elberta' peaches; 'Blenheim' ('Royal') and 'Wenatchee Moorpark' apricots, 'Duart' plums; and Italian prune/plums. Organized by order of ripening within family, each offering is richly described including color and texture of skin and flesh, culinary uses (noting those varieties that are best for fresh eating and home canning), and pollination requirements. Extensive charts and lists of harvest dates, planting distances, pollination interaction, variety/rootstock combinations, and shipping height of stock. Ships bareroot. Guarantees true to name. Will replace or issue refund if untrue with verified written claim by November 1. Claims for incorrect count or sizes must be made within ten days of receipt. Claims for mortality must be made by September 1 following the date of delivery. See Trees.
Shipping season: Mid-November through early June.

VERNON BARNES AND SON NURSERY
1948
James V. Barnes, Jr.
Catalog: Free, 32 pp., color photographs
Barnes offers standard-size peach, apple, cherry, pear, apricot, nectarine, and plum trees. Most are one- and two-year-old trees that are two to four feet tall. Also offers ten varieties of semidwarf apple and one- and two-year dwarf (maturity at six to eight feet) peach, apple, cherry, and pear trees. Catalog includes selected pecan and walnut trees, five grapevines, blueberry bushes, raspberries, thorny blackberries, and ten kinds of virus-free strawberries. Descriptions include hardiness, bearing month, and postharvest uses. See Conifers, Trees.
Shipping season: January through April. October through December.

WAYSIDE GARDENS
See Grasses, Heirlooms, Perennials, Roses.

WHITE FLOWER FARM
See Bulbs, Perennials, Roses, Supplies, Trees, Waterscapes.

WHITMAN FARMS
1980
Lucile Whitman
Catalog: $1 (recoverable), 10 pp.
Lucile Whitman is a wholesale grower of unusual ornamental deciduous trees and shrubs for the landscape and retail nursery trade. However, the retail mail-order edition of her catalog features unusual fruit- and nut-bearing plant material: currant, gooseberry, kiwi, pawpaw, chestnut, hazelnut, walnut, mulberry, elderberry, and jujube. Brief descriptions of fruit and habit. Ships bareroot. Guarantees true to name and safe arrival; will replace any plant that dies within six months of delivery. See Trees.
Shipping season: Mid-November through April.

WILEY'S NUT GROVE NURSERY
1950
Robert F. Wiley and Chris Pataky

Catalog: 1 FCS, 6 pp.
Wiley's develops and grows northern-hardy nut-bearing trees. Selection includes: butternuts, sweet-eating Chinese chestnut, hybrid filberts, hickory, 'Colby' northern-hardy pecans, persimmons, pawpaws, black walnuts ('Ohio', 'Thomas', and 'Elmer Myers'), and Carpathian walnuts ('Broadview', 'Hansen', 'Fatley', and 'McKinster'). Offerings by name only. Catalog includes general guidance on planting, fertilizing, and care of young nut-bearing trees. Stock available variously as seedlings, seedling trees, and grafts. Guarantees true to name; will replace. See Trees.
Shipping season: Spring and fall.

WOMACK'S NURSERY CO.
1959
Larry J. Womack
Catalog: Free, 32 pp., black-and-white photographs
In the early years of his career, James H. Womack, the nursery's founder, often sold fruit trees out of the back of a pickup truck while traveling the roads of central and western Texas. His son Larry J. and grandson Larry Don sell fruit- and nut-bearing plants adapted to southern conditions from their nursery, located between DeLeon and Gorman, Texas. The Womacks offer eastern and western pecans ('Caddo', 'Cheyenne', 'Choctaw', 'Kiowa', 'Maramec', 'Mohawk', 'Oconee', 'Pawnee', 'Podsednik', 'Sioux', and 'Wichita'). The catalog also describes thirty-eight peaches on Nemaguard rootstock ('Belle of Georgia', 'Floridaking', 'Tex Royal', and 'Tex Star'), and a selection of nectarines, apples, apricots, figs, persimmons, pears, plums, berries, and grapes. Descriptions include parentage, taste, shape and size of nut, nuts per pound, growth habit, and area of the South for which a pecan is best suited. Descriptions for fruit include characteristics and color of flesh, bearing habit, number of chilling hours (where required), and origin for most. Guarantees true to name, safe arrival, and to leaf out. Will replace or issue refund if untrue. Notify within seven days of receipt if stock arrives damaged. Will replace or issue credit for half of the purchase price for mortality if notified by June 30 in the year of purchase. See Trees.
Shipping season: Mid-December through March.

Selected Reading About Fruit- and Nut-Bearing Trees and Plants

The Backyard Berry Book, by Stella Otto. The berry, bramble, and vine companion to Ms. Otto's *The Backyard Orchardist.* Instructions for site preparation, soil conditioning, overwintering, irrigation, and pest and disease troubleshooting and control. Features individual sections for blackberries, blueberries, grapes, kiwis, lingonberries, raspberries, strawberries, and more. Includes a calendar of seasonal maintenance and care.

The Backyard Orchardist, by Stella Otto. Highly recommended by many as the complete guide to growing fruit trees at home. Includes a thorough glossary and the answers to hundreds of questions about care, growth, maintenance, diseases, postharvest uses, and storage techniques.

The Book of Apples, by Joan Morgan and Alison Richards. A survey of over two thousand apple varieties. Includes an apple directory with detailed notes on taste, historical, geographical, and botanical specifications. Also includes advice on growing and using apples.

Citrus: How to Select, Grow and Enjoy, by Richard Ray and Lance Walheim. How to determine the right varieties for your climate and tastes, with some attention to growing citrus outside of the citrus belt. Includes a selection guide for choosing produce and culinary suggestions.

Designing and Maintaining Your Edible Landscape Naturally, by Robert Kourik. A whole earth approach that recommends edible plants that add fertility to your soil, attract beneficial insects, and minimize the effects of erosion, and offers techniques for enriching your soil and other strategies for providing food through the cultivation of low-maintenance plants.

Fruits and Berries for the Home Garden, by Lewis Hill. How to select the appropriate fruits to grow, how and when to plant them, and techniques for pest control. Good attention to the basics.

"Grow the Best Blueberries," by Louise Riotte. A Garden Way booklet that helps you get the basics down cold: when, how, and where to plant and cultivate blueberries.

"Grow the Best Strawberries," by Louise Riotte. Another Garden Way booklet that helps you get the basics down fruitfully.

Growing Fruits and Nuts in the South: The Definitive Guide, by William D. Adams and Thomas R. LeRoy. A respected guide to numerous fruits that can be grown from southern Virginia to Florida to Texas.

The Orchard Almanac: A Spraysaver's Guide, by Steve Page and Joe Smillie. A handbook organized by season that offers organic and IPM solutions that stress low toxicity in maintaining the health of your home orchard. Also includes tips on planting, pruning, fertilization, restoring old trees, harvesting, and storage.

CONIFERS

The plant count cited in each profile is based on information in the most recent catalog provided by the source. In this section, shipping season is for conifers only. A selection of books about conifers appears after the last listing.

QUICK FIND
The following sources are listed in this section:

THE AMERICAN CONIFER SOCIETY
See **Horticultural Societies.**

AMERICAN FORESTS: FAMOUS AND HISTORIC TREES
See Heirlooms, Kidstuff, **Trees.**

APPALACHIAN GARDENS
1985
Tom McCloud
Catalog: $2, 38 pp., illustrations
This Wayne, Pennsylvania, nursery offers 375 ornamental trees, shrubs, and conifers. Among the conifers, areas of concentration include arborvitae, cypress, juniper, pine, and yew. Plants are listed by genus and species, common name, height, spread, shape, flower color and prominence, fruit, and color of needles, and presented in consistent order and uniform language. Shape (shown in silhouette for each listing), habit, site preference, and required care are well detailed. Stock is characterized as well established, two years or older, started from cuttings or seeds; grafts appear separately. Guarantees true to

name and safe arrival; will replace or issue refund or credit. See **Rhododendrons, Trees.**
Shipping season: March through December.
Bareroot (dormant), December through February.
No juniper to California. No pine to Arizona, California, Colorado, New Mexico, or Nevada

ARBORVILLAGE FARM NURSERY
1978
Lanny, Sue, and Derrick Rawdon
Catalog: $1, 56 pp.
The Rawdons' nursery, located in zone 5, offers a thousand woody trees and shrubs. Thirty-five conifers, including fir, ginkgoes, spruce, and pine, are presented in a separate part of their catalog. Organized by genus and species, listings also include common names, a few words about growth habit, expected size of plant after five years, and current size of plant. Plants are two to six feet on one- to three-gallon-sized root systems. Will replace or issue credit or refund within five days of receipt. See **Trees.**

Shipping season: February through May. September through December.
Canada, Mexico, International

ARROWHEAD ALPINES
Bob and Brigitta Stewart
Seed catalog: $2, 62 pp. Plants: $2, 88 pp.
The Stewarts' plant catalog includes almost two thousand varieties of shrubs, trees, perennials, and wildflowers, complementing their seed list of four thousand offerings. Two hundred and twenty conifers, including the rare and unusual, are propagated here and by other highly regarded growers and are offered as transplants and/or rooted cuttings. Listed strictly by botanical name, they include arborvitae, *Cryptomeria,* false cypress, hemlock, juniper, spruce, *Thujopsis,* and yew. Brief descriptions that touch on color and form presuppose a knowledge of culture, site preference, and hardiness range. Ships bareroot. See Grasses, **Perennials, Seeds,** Trees, Wildflowers.
Shipping season: May.

BEAVER CREEK NURSERY
1986
Mike Stansberry
Catalog: $1, 22 pp.
Beaver Creek Nursery of Knoxville, Tennessee, lists two hundred dwarf conifers, trees, shrubs, and grasses. Recent catalogs offered nursery-grown hemlock, including dwarfs, weeping types, and a large Carolina. Listed by botanical name, descriptions include common name, color and habit of foliage, growth habit, and height at maturity for most. Ships in containers of one gallon or larger. Guarantees true to name and nursery grown; if not satisfied, notify within seven days. See Grasses, **Trees.**
Shipping season: October through April.
No California, Oregon, or Washington

BERGESON NURSERY
See **Fruit, Trees.**

BIJOU ALPINES
1989
Mark Dusek
Catalog: $1, 18 pp.
Bijou Alpines, until 1991 associated with Mount Tahoma Nursery, is a specialty nursery with 150 varieties of rare and unusual plants for the rock garden, scree, bog, water garden, or woodland. Dwarf trees and shrubs are described in detail, including a key to placement in the garden. Among the genera of conifers that have been featured are *Abies, Chamaecyparis, Cryptomeria japonica, Podocarpus,* and various *Taxus.* The "Collector's Corner" is their forum for presenting plants either never before introduced or forms rarely encountered in the trade. All plants are own-root and nursery propagated; custom propagation services available. See **Perennials, Trees, Waterscapes.**
Shipping season: March through May. September and October.

BRUDY'S TROPICAL EXOTICS
See **Fruit, Seeds,** Trees.

COENOSIUM GARDENS
Robert L. Fincham
Catalog: $3 (recoverable), 43 pp.
Coenosium Gardens' orientation is toward rare and unusual plants, emphasizing conifers: arborvitae, cedar, false cypress, fir, hemlock, juniper, pine, and spruce. They produce a new catalog, with seven hundred offerings organized by botanical name, every three years. During the intervening years, they publish interim lists with new selections, price changes, and any other pertinent information. Descriptions include common name, growth habit, color, and ultimate height. About 20 percent of their catalog lists shrubs and trees other than those that are coniferous. Most plants are sold as new grafts. Guarantees plants to be in good condition on leaving nursery but cannot guarantee survival once in transit and will consider cases only if notified in writing. See Trees.
Shipping season: June.

COLD STREAM FARM
1978
Mike Hradel
Catalog: Free, 6 pp.
The Hradels currently grow seventy-three mostly native species of trees, conifers, and berry plants for reforestation, wildlife habitat, and yard. Their list of conifers, organized by common name, includes white cedar, northern-hardy bald cedar; balsam, Douglas fir; Austrian pine, jack pine, Scotch pine, red pine, and eastern white pine; giant sequoia; and blue spruce, Norway spruce, and white spruce. Stock is not described other than to indicate current size of tree. See **Fruit, Trees.**
Shipping season: April. September and October.

COLLECTOR'S NURSERY
1990
Bill Janssen and Diana Reeck
Catalog: $2, 28 pp., illustrations

Mr. Janssen and Ms. Reeck continue to work on developing a display garden for their three thousand species and varieties of shrubs, trees, and perennials. While you may not get to Battle Ground, Washington, to see their collection, Janssen and Reeck list five hundred plants that are ready to make their way to your garden, including thirty-five conifers organized by botanical name. Highlights include *Picea sitchensis* 'Sugar Loaf', a dwarf pyramidal form discovered in the Coast Range in 1985; *Microbiota decussata*, a hardy Siberian ground cover; and *Pinus Wallichiana* 'Zebrina', a pine with variegated needles. Descriptions include growth habit, color of needles, recommended use in the garden, and hardiness zone. Plants that are offered as grafts are so noted. Ships in pots. Guarantees true to name, well rooted, and healthy. See **Perennials, Trees.**
Shipping season: March through May. September through November.

COLVOS CREEK NURSERY
1977
Michael Lee
Catalog: $2 (recoverable), 23 pp.

Michael Lee, a registered landscape architect, is the steward of this part-time business specializing in Northwest and West Coast natives and other plants adapted to dry summer climates. Among the six hundred shrubs, trees, and perennials listed by botanical name in Mr. Lee's catalog, cedar, cypress, fir, hemlock, juniper, pine, and spruce are well represented. Descriptions include nature of needles, color and form of flower and fruit where appropriate, uses in the garden, and hardiness zone. Container-grown plants shipped in liners or gallons filled with a mix of sand and composted sawdust; bareroot shipments available for an additional charge. Guarantees true to name and safe arrival; will replace or issue credit or refund for any plant that falters or fails during the first month in your garden. See Fruit, **Trees.**
Shipping season: All year.
Bareroot only to Hawaii
Canada, Mexico, International

DAYSTAR
1970
Marjorie Walsh
Catalog: $1, 8 pp.

Daystar is a Maine nursery with rotating specialties. Recent catalogs featured ericaceae, northern-hardy perennials, primulas, trees, shrubs, and thirty-five conifers, including Hinoki and Sawara cypress, blue Pacific juniper, and several compact and prostrate hemlocks. Notes botanical and common names and there is a brief description. Guarantees safe arrival; will replace. See **Perennials, Trees.**
Shipping season: April through June. September through November.
Canada

EASTERN PLANT SPECIALTIES
1985
Mark Stavish
Catalog: $3 (recoverable), 28 pp., illustrations

Mr. Stavish's New England–hardy plants include wildflowers, trees, shrubs, rhododendrons, woodland plants, and forty conifers. Recent catalogs offered weeping larch, cedar of Lebanon, table pine, pond cypress, and Sargent's weeping hemlock. Highlights common name but organized by botanical name. Notes size and texture of needles, growth habit, hardiness, and current height of plant. A cross-referenced index includes light preference, tolerance to wet or dry soil conditions, fragrance, if any, autumn color, and attractive berries or distinctive bark. See **Fruit**, Perennials, **Rhododendrons, Trees, Wildflowers.**
Shipping season: March through June. September through November.

ECCLES NURSERIES, INC.
1940
Michael A. Birocco
Catalog: Free, 6 pp.

The Biroccos offer twelve types of seedlings (two-, three-, and four-year, depending on the conifer) in groups of five, ten, and twenty-five plants. Among these are Scotch, white, red, Japanese black, mungo, and Ponderosa pine, Norway and Colorado blue spruce, concolor and Douglas fir. Notes only age and size of seedling. The balance of the list is for the trade, sold in lots of one hundred or more seedlings. See Trees.
Shipping season: March through May. September through November.

EVERGREEN GARDENWORKS
1989
Brent Walston
Catalog: $2, 53 pp.
Mr. Walston propagates 650 types of shrubs, and trees, favoring dwarfs and semidwarfs. Coniferous plants in his catalog, organized by genus with an index of botanical names, include blue Atlas cedar, conica spruce, several *Cryptomeria japonica*, shore pine, and five needle pine organized by botanical name. Fully realized descriptions include common name, height at maturity, shape and nature of plant and needles, cultural requirements, light requirements, water requirements, suitability for bogs or wetlands, minimum temperature tolerance, and use as a landscape, rock garden, or bonsai specimen. Plants are from well-rooted cuttings, seedlings, or divisions shipped in 2¹/4-inch pots unless otherwise noted. See Fruit, Perennials, Trees.
Shipping season: Potted plants, all year.
Bareroot, dormant, to Alabama, Arkansas, Louisiana, Mississippi, North Carolina, Oregon, South Carolina, Tennessee, Texas, Virginia, and Washington, October through March. Florida, first Monday in December and first Monday in March.

FAIRWEATHER GARDENS
1989
Robert Hoffman and Robert Popham
Catalog: $3, 60 pp., illustrations, black-and-white and color photographs
Messrs. Hoffman and Popham offer conifers, trees, and shrubs that they characterize as having significant merit, shipped in sizes that usually allow for immediate placement in your garden. They list twenty-seven conifers, including monkey puzzle tree, Japanese plum yew, goldenthread *Chamaecyparis*, golden Leyland cypress ('Castlewellan Gold'), Koyama spruce, bald cypress, and the emerald green eastern white cedar 'Smaragd'. Full narrative descriptions, written in an informal, familiar tone, include botanical and common names, form, native areas, shape and size of branches and needles, seasonal habit, sun and soil requirements, and hardiness zone. Guarantees safe arrival. See Fruit, Rhododendrons, Trees.
Shipping season: March and April. September through November. Shorter shipping season to Arizona, California, Idaho, Minnesota, Nevada, Oregon, Utah, and Washington.
Canada

FEDCO TREES
1979
Roberta and John Bunker
Catalog: $2, 32 pp., illustrations
A cooperative that offers plant materials acquired from worldwide sources that have performed well in Maine's cold-shortened growing season. Selection varies from year to year; a recent list of a dozen conifers included arborvitae, fir, pine, and spruce. Notes hardiness zone, size of tree at time of shipment and at maturity, historical information, provenance, shape and color of branches, needles, and cones, and site preference. Stock consists of small, well-rooted trees. Ships bareroot except as noted. Fedco encourages group orders but will accept individual orders. Guarantees safe arrival; will replace or issue credit or refund. See Moose Growers Supply. See also Booksellers, Fruit, Heirlooms, Trees.
Shipping season: April.

FOREST SEEDS OF CALIFORNIA
See Seeds, Trees.

FORESTFARM®
1974
Ray and Peg Pragg
Catalog $3, 414 pp., illustrations and black-and-white photographs
Yes, the Praggs' catalog really is over four hundred pages and contains four thousand plants. Conifers appear throughout the catalog and we made no attempt to count them. Varieties of arborvitae, cedar, cypress, false cypress, fir, juniper, pine (ten pages), and spruce abound. Their catalog is organized by botanical name but includes a very thorough index of common names that makes working with this in-depth catalog a simple pleasure. Standardized descriptions include genus, species, variety, common name, foliage habit, hardiness zone, origin, plant uses, cultural conditions, and a description of the plant's habits, form, and site preference. Ships in small tubes or one- and five-gallon containers depending on variety and availability. Guarantees true to name.
See Fruit, Grasses, Perennials, Roses, Trees.
Shipping season: All year.
Canada

GILSON GARDENS
See Perennials, Trees.

GIRARD NURSERIES
1944
Peter Girard, Jr.
Catalog: Free, 23 pp., color photographs
Girard grows and hybridizes azaleas and rhododendrons, flowering shrubs and trees, broadleaf evergreens, ornamental and shade trees, and 150 conifers. Selections include globe, pyramidal, dwarf, and upright arborvitae, weeping and false cypress, fir, hemlock, juniper, larch, pine (including Japanese), and spruce. Highlights rare and collectible specimens, as well as varieties that readily lend themselves to bonsai culture. Rich descriptions include common and botanical names, growth habit, form, foliage habit and color, and landscaping and garden uses. Offers numerous collections by family and age. Ships potted plants, seedlings, and transplants; also offers seed packets for fifty types of arborvitae, fir, juniper, pine, and spruce. Guarantees safe arrival; will replace stock lost to extreme heat or cold (or possibly customer neglect or lack of experience) for half the purchase price if a claim is made within thirty days of receipt. See Grasses, **Rhododendrons, Seeds**, Trees.
Shipping season: Mid-March through June. September to first frost.

GOLDEN BOUGH TREE FARM
See Fruit, **Trees**.

GREER GARDENS
1955
Harold E. Greer
Catalog: $3, 148 pp., illustrations and color photographs
Originally a specialist in rhododendrons and azaleas, Harold Greer over time has expanded to include twenty-five hundred ornamental trees, shrubs, fruit-bearing plants, plants for the rock garden, perennials, ground covers, ornamental grasses, bamboo, and bonsai specimens. He also sells books. Two hundred and twenty-five conifers, organized by botanical name, include arborvitae, *Cryptomeria japonica* 'Elegans', Leyland cypress, Oregon blue false cypress, corkbar fir, Arizona glauca, Skyrocket juniper, larch, Brewer's weeping spruce, hemlock, lace bark pine, and giant sequoia. All are presented with rich descriptions that include common name, hardiness zone, color and texture of foliage and bark, use in the garden, annual growth, and height of plant at shipment and at maturity. A cross-referenced list highlights those offerings that have a pleasing fragrance, have exceptional color, thrive in the shade, or are even obnoxious to

deer. Guarantees quality stock, true to name, and safe arrival; will replace one time only. See **Booksellers**, Fruit, **Grasses, Peonies**, Perennials, **Rhododendrons**, Trees.
Shipping season: All year (recommends September through May).
Canada, Mexico, International

HABITAT PLANTS
See **Trees**.

HERONSWOOD NURSERY LTD.
1987
Daniel Hinkley and Robert L. Jones
Catalog: $4, 220 pp.
Heronswood characterizes its mission as procuring and offering plant materials that have not previously been available to North American gardeners. Mr. Hinkley (author of *Winter Ornamentals*) and Mr. Jones list fifteen hundred trees, shrubs, perennials, and grasses. One hundred and thirty conifers, listed by botanical name, include arborvitae, *Cryptomeria*, false cypress, hemlock, *Podocarpus* (from Australia, New Zealand, China, and Chile), yew, and singular offerings of rare and exotic specimens of other varieties. Descriptions that presuppose some knowledge of cultural requirements include provenance, hardiness zone, pot size, and a highly visual narrative of the conifer's form, color, and size. Guarantees true to name, healthy upon departure; will accept claims filed within ten days of receipt. See Fruit, **Grasses, Perennials, Rhododendrons**, Trees.
Shipping season: March through mid-May. Mid-September through October.
Canada

MATSU-MOMIJI NURSERY
1976
Steve Pilacik
Catalog: $2, 8 pp.
Mr. Pilacik, a bonsai artist and teacher, is the author of *Japanese Black Pine*. He lists fifty trained trees, primarily Japanese black and Japanese white pine, as well as untrained stock plant material, grafted specimens, Japanese black pine seedlings, and maples from cuttings. All offerings are briefly described. See Trees.
Shipping season: All year.
Canada, Mexico, International

MATTERHORN NURSERY, INC.
1981
Matt and Ronnie Horn
Catalog: $5, 102 pp., illustrations

Matterhorn offers a wide range of ornamentals, including perennials, ferns, bamboo and ornamental grasses, conifers, deciduous trees, shrubs, and aquatic plants. The Horns offer 250 conifers (15 percent of their catalog), representing a balanced list of arborvitae, cedar, false cypress, fir, hemlock, juniper, pine, and spruce. The conifer section is organized by botanical name and notes shape, habit, landscape use, light and soil preferences, and height at maturity. Guarantees true to name. See Grasses, Perennials, **Rhododendrons**, **Trees**, **Waterscapes**.
Shipping season: Please inquire.

MINIATURE PLANT KINGDOM
1965
Don and Becky Herzog
Catalog: $2.50, 42 pp.
Dwarf conifers predominate in this part of the kingdom, comprising 15 percent of the Herzogs' catalog. They are as proud and emphatic about how small their plants will be at maturity as most catalogs are about how large theirs will be. Most of this section is made up of arborvitae (American and Chinese), false cypress, *Cryptomeria*, and spruce (black, Colorado, Norway, Sitka, and white). Also offers Japanese and golden larch, dawn redwood, and bald cypress. Fully realized descriptions include color and texture of foliage, site preferences, suitability for bonsai culture, rate of growth, and height at maturity. See Fruit, **Grasses**, **Perennials**, **Trees**.
Shipping season: All year.
Canada, Mexico, International

MUSSER FORESTS
1928
Nancy Musser
Catalog: Free, 10 pp., color photographs
Musser Forests began with the purchase of six hundred acres of abandoned farmland that the Mussers planted with pine and spruce for Christmas trees and timber. Their expansion into the nursery business was propelled in part by their successful introduction of the Scotch pine as a viable Christmas tree in the mid-1930s. They currently produce over 55 million seedlings, transplants, and rooted cuttings each year. Conifers include fifty types of arborvitae, fir, hemlock, juniper, pine, spruce, and yew available as two-, three-, and four-year seedlings and transplants of various ages. Some offerings are "precision sown"—that is, grown in perfectly spaced rows that encourage superior rooting,

branching, and uniformity. Descriptions include height at maturity, best time to transplant, color and texture of needles, culture and care, light and site preferences, and landscape use. Guarantees true to name. See Fruit, **Trees**.
Shipping season: Potted plants, all year.
Bareroot, March through May. September through November.
Canada

PACIFIC COAST SEED COMPANY
See Trees, **Seeds**.

PACIFIC TREE FARMS
William L. Nelson
Catalog: $2, 20 pp.
Mr. Nelson offers 350 container-grown trees and shrubs from sources worldwide. Conifers comprise 10 percent of his catalog; recent lists featured Brazilian, bunya bunya, big cone, Himalayan white, and corkbar pine. Stock is listed by botanical name and cross-referenced by common name without further description. Ships in five-gallon pots. See **Fruit**, **Trees**.
Shipping season: Potted plants, all year.
Bareroot, January through mid-March.
Canada, Mexico, International

PLANT DELIGHTS NURSERY
1988
Tony and Michelle Avent
Catalog: $2, 117 pp., color illustrations and photographs
Plant Delights was started to support the test and demonstration gardens at Juniper Level Botanical Gardens. The purpose now is to search out new and better perennials and introduce them to the trade. Conifers are not the main draw in this in-depth catalog, however; the Avents have carefully selected forty offerings of arborvitae, *Cryptomeria*, false cypress, and juniper. Descriptions include light requirements, hardiness zone, height at maturity, and their trademark narrative descriptions that inform fully while entertaining always. Guarantees true to name and safe arrival. See **Grasses**, **Hosta**, **Perennials**, Trees.
Shipping season: March through November.
Canada, Mexico, International

PORTERHOWSE FARMS
1979
Don Howse
Catalog: $4 (recoverable), 80 pp., illustrations
Mr. Howse is a collector of plants, with empha-

sis on dwarf and unusual conifers (35 percent of his catalog), plants for rock gardens, and plants for bonsai culture—all nursery propagated in containers. Mr. Howse presents a broad, balanced list of 370 conifers in separate sections for specimens propagated from root cuttings or seedlings and varieties that are grafted; all organized by botanical name within their sections. Varieties offered have included spreading star silver fir, Himilayan cedar 'Aurea', false cypress 'Blue Feathers', *Cryptomeria japonica* 'Pygmaea', 'Blue Alps' juniper, dwarf conica Alberta spruce, 'Torulosa' pine, a prostrate giant redwood, and the Humphrey Welch hemlock. Hardiness zone precedes a fully realized narrative description of plant's origin (where known), form, color, habit, and size at maturity. Ships plants in the pots in which they are grown (size noted in description). Guarantees true to name and healthy upon departure; requires written notification within ten days of receipt to replace plant or issue refund. See **Perennials**, Trees.

Shipping season: March through June. September through November. Grafted plants, June.

Canada, Mexico, International

POWELL'S GARDENS

See **Daylilies**, **Hosta**, **Iris**, Peonies, **Perennials**, Trees.

RARE CONIFER FOUNDATION–RARE CONIFER NURSERY

1991

Darshan Mayginnes

Catalog: Free, 28 pp.

The Rare Conifer Foundation is a public charity that works to protect conifers in their native habitats. They specialize in providing seeds and seedlings to groups and horticultural organizations for planting. However, their Rare Conifer Nursery division sells one hundred types directly to home gardeners (request their plant list). RCF, located at three thousand feet elevation, borders an old-growth national forest and receives seventy inches of precipitation annually. Their climate and locale allows them to grow numerous temperate conifers under conditions that they characterize as ideal. *The Rare Conifer Handbook* explains the foundation's programs, and in a section organized by botanical name provides hardiness zone, place of origin, historical notes, height at maturity, and descriptions of the tree's shape, color, foliage, pods and cones for 160 conifers. Trees grown in containers in nonsoil

media, fed with natural supplements and fertilizers. Specimens on RCN's list are available variously as plugs or liners or in one- to five-gallon containers. See **Booksellers**, **Kidstuff**, Trees.

Shipping season: All year.

Canada, Mexico, International

ROSLYN NURSERY

1984

Dr. Philip Waldman

Catalog: $3, 76 pp., color photographs

Roslyn Nursery grows two thousand varieties of trees, shrubs, perennials, grasses, rhododendrons, and azaleas. Fifteen percent of their catalog contains 175 conifers that Dr. Waldman believes are noteworthy for their unusual foliage colors and their suitability for small garden schemes. He grows a number of Alaskan, Himalayan, and Japanese cedars, Hinoki cypress, Sawara false cypress, juniper, Norway spruce, Colorado spruce, eastern white pine, and Canadian hemlock. Brief narrative descriptions include plant's shape, color, habit, distinguishing characteristics, uses in the garden, and hardiness zone. The "Woody Plants for Special Uses" section includes plants for wet and dry conditions, plants that will tolerate shade, and those that are unattractive to deer. Guarantees true to name and healthy; will replace or issue credit if plant fails within thirty days of receipt. See **Booksellers**, **Perennials**, **Rhododendrons**, **Trees**.

Shipping season: April through June. September through November. Bareroot only to Arizona and California, mid-March.

Canada, Mexico, International

SAVAGE NURSERY CENTER

See **Fruit**, **Trees**.

SHEPHERD HILL FARM

See **Rhododendrons**, Trees.

SISKIYOU RARE PLANT NURSERY

1963

Baldassare Mineo

Catalog: $2 (recoverable), 74 pp., illustrations and color photographs

Siskiyou lists over eight hundred rock garden and alpine perennials, shrubs, wildflowers, ferns, and seventy-five dwarf conifers. Siskiyou's conifers are slow-growing dwarfs and miniatures. Mr. Mineo characterizes his stock as "ever changing" in the false cypress, *Cryptomeria*, juniper, *Podocarpus*, yew, and hemlock. Rich descriptions include height and width after ten years, provenance, fo-

liage features, growth habit, and hardiness. Culture codes note light requirements, scree, soil conditions (sandy, loam, or average), and moisture requirements. Offers collections for various needs and conditions. Will provide lists of recommended subjects for specific purposes: woodland, summer flowering, alpine house culture, troughs and containers, peat beds, drought tolerant, and silver- and gray-foliaged plants. Plants are grown from cuttings and raised in containers. Guarantees correctly labeled and safe arrival; must notify within five days of receipt if plant unsatisfactory. See **Booksellers, Perennials,** Trees.
Shipping season: All year.
Canada

SPRINGVALE FARM NURSERY
1980
Will and Jeanne Gould
Catalog: $3 subscription, 12 pp.
"The Avid Gardener™" catalog from Springvale Farm Nursery features dwarf, rare, and unusual conifers, flowering shrubs, and ground covers organized by botanical name. The Goulds focus their selection of two hundred midwestern-hardy (tolerant of cold and extreme summer heat) conifers on plants for collectors, bonsai artists, and operators of garden railways. They recently featured *Chamaecyparis nootkatensis* 'Pendula' (a cypress with wet feet), 'Old Gold' juniper, *Picea Abies* 'Nidiformis' (bird's-nest spruce), 'Papoose' Sitka spruce, 'Hillside Creeper' (a prostrate pine), and 'Gentsch White' (a white-tipped hemlock). Listing for each offering includes hardiness zone, if it has potential as a bonsai or railway garden specimen, size (current or at maturity), and size of container. Plants shipped in their growing containers. Guarantees true to name; will replace or issue refund for any misnamed plant. If dissatisfied with a plant for other reasons, notify within ten days of receipt. See **Trees.**
Shipping season: March through May.
October and November.
No Alaska, Arizona, California, or Hawaii

STARK BRO.'S
See **Fruit,** Trees.

SWEDBERG NURSERIES, INC.
See **Fruit, Trees.**

TEC
1975
Catalog: Free, 4 pp.

Half of TEC's Minnesota-grown tree and shrub list is composed of twenty-five conifers. They also offer seedlings: pine (Norway, Scotch, and white), fir (balsam, Douglas, Fraser, and concolor), eastern red and northern white cedar, larch (tamarack, European, and Siberian), and spruce (black or swamp, Colorado blue, Serbian, white, and Black Hills). Lists botanical name and size when shipped. Guarantees viable upon departure from nursery. See **Fruit, Trees.**
Shipping season: April and May.

VERNON BARNES & SON NURSERY
1948
James V. Barnes, Jr.
Catalog: Free, 32 pp., color photographs
Barnes offers a basic assortment of 250 ornamentals, shrubs, fruiting plants, hedges, and wildflowers. About 10 percent of the catalog contains conifer seedlings (mostly collected) of hemlock, juniper, pine, and yew. Brief descriptions include hardiness zones. Ships bareroot. See **Fruit, Trees.**
Shipping season: January through April.
October through December.

WASHINGTON EVERGREEN NURSERY
1980
Jordan Jack
Catalog: $2, 36 pp.
Washington Evergreen Nursery is really located in Leicester, North Carolina, the only confusing item in this otherwise well-organized catalog of 220 conifers and kalmias. Half of the listings are from the *Chamaecyparis* or false cypress, including Lawson and Hinoki or Sawara cypress. The balance includes about twenty varieties each of arborvitae, hemlock, juniper, pine, spruce, and yew. General notes about each precedes individual entries listed by botanical name, then common name, including hardiness zone. Descriptions of foliage color and texture, growth habit, uses in the garden, current size (cross-referenced to a price list in the index), and size at maturity. Guarantees true to name and safe arrival; must notify within ten days if plant is mislabeled or arrives in unsatisfactory condition. See **Rhododendrons,** Trees.
Shipping season: April through June. September and October. Prefers to ship orders to southern states in April and October.
No California
Canada, International

WAVECREST NURSERY AND LANDSCAPING
1959
Carol T. Hop
Catalog: $1 (recoverable), 24 pp.
Wavecrest sits on the shore of Lake Michigan, providing the plants grown there with a milder climate than much of zone 5. Fifty conifers make up 20 percent of their catalog. Recent offerings include a plum yew that Ms. Hop notes deer won't eat, four types of *Ginkgo biloba*, Thompson's blue spruce, 'Sherwood Frost' (a white-margined arborvitae), and 'Jeddeloh' (a dwarf hemlock described as cascading like a waterfall). Offerings listed first by botanical name, then common name; includes a brief, effective description of color and form and specifies size of container. Must notify upon arrrival if plants unsatisfactory. See **Booksellers**, **Grasses**, Perennials, **Trees**.
Shipping season: March through May.
Canada, Mexico, International

YUCCA DO NURSERY AT PECKERWOOD GARDENS
1988
John Fairey and Carl Schoenfeld
Catalog: $3, 45 pp.
A nursery using only organic methods in cultivating seeds and cuttings of the natives of Texas, Mexico, and Asia. Offers forty-five conifers that are hardy in zones 7, 8, and 9. Lists *Cephalotaxus* that have adapted well to heat and humidity of the southern United States; *Cryptomeria* that grows well at Yucca Do in rich sandy soil and high-filtered shade; a blue form of Leyland cypress, unusual in the trade since it is difficult to propagate and slow to grow; several juniper and pine from the Mexican high country; and an African cypress that is comfortable in hot, dry sites. Descriptions include where the specimen was found, as well as the color and form of flowers and needles. Will replace or issue refund if notified within ten days of receipt. See **Cactus**, Grasses, Organics, Perennials, **Trees**, **Wildflowers**.
Shipping season: January through May.
October through December.
International

Selected Reading About Conifers

Conifers: The Illustrated Encyclopedia, by D. M. van Gelderen and J. R. P. van Hoey Smith. The nucleus of this book is van Gelderen and van Hoey Smith's *Conifers*, published in 1986. This new work, however, covers sixty-five genera and is characterized as containing the most complete collection of photographs of conifers ever assembled. Information for each genus includes geographical distribution, botanical characteristics and classification, and species of merit. The 2,300 photographs display details of bark, cones, and needles as well as general habit.

A Garden of Conifers: Introduction and Selection Guide, by Robert A. Obrizok. A guide to dwarf and slow-growing conifers. Includes information for 2,550 plants that is essential to understanding the habits, shapes, growth rates, and seasonal color changes of conifers used in garden planning. Includes fifty color photographs.

The Pruning of Trees, Shrubs and Conifers, by George E. Brown; updated by John Bryan. An encyclopedic volume on the best pruning methods for 450 genera of trees, shrubs, conifers, and woody vines. One hundred and fifty black-and-white photographs and illustrations.

TREES, SHRUBS, AND VINES

The plant count cited in each profile is based on information in the most recent catalog provided by the source. In this section, shipping season is for trees and shrubs only. A selection of books about trees, shrubs, and vines appears after the last listing.

QUICK FIND
The following sources are listed in this section:

The Urban Homestead

Van Veen Nursery

Van Well Nursery

Vernon Barnes & Son Nursery

Washington Evergreen Nursery

Wavecrest Nursery and Landscaping

Wedge Nursery

White Flower Farm

Whitman Farms

Whitney Gardens & Nursery

Wild Seed, Inc.

The Wildwood Flower

Wiley's Nut Grove Nursery

Windrose

Womack's Nursery Co.

Yucca Do Nursery at Peckerwood Gardens

American Forests: Famous and Historic Trees
1875
Susan T. Corbett
Catalog: Free, 16 pp., illustrations and black-and-white photographs

American Forests, a nonprofit citizen's conservation organization sponsors the Famous & Historic Trees project. The project grows trees (from seed) that are direct descendants of those that are associated with significant people or historic events. Among the specimens listed are tulip poplar and American holly from George Washington's home at Mount Vernon; silver maple and catalpa from Thomas Jefferson's home at Monticello; overcup oak and black walnut from Abraham Lincoln's birthplace in Hardin County, Kentucky; various species from Civil War battlefields; Franklinia and river birch from the garden of John Bartram, the Father of American Botany; an oleander from Thomas Edison's winter home in Fort Myers, Florida; and trees that shaded Henry David Thoreau's cabin at Walden Pond. Historical notes about the trees and their significance abound in this catalog. Information organized in chart form includes flower, desirable foliage traits, soil requirements, tolerance to high heat, tolerance to shade, spread, and rate of growth. Each tree kit includes a one- to three-foot container plant, planting instructions, a photodegradable tree shelter, fertilizer, bird safety net, certificate of authenticity, and instructions for overwintering indoors. Also offers historic groves. Guarantees tree will grow for one year; will replace for shipping charges. See Conifers, **Kidstuff,** Heirlooms.
Shipping season: All year.
Canada

Ames' Orchard & Nursery
See **Fruit,** Heirlooms.j

Appalachian Gardens
1985
Tom Mc Cloud
Catalog: $2, 38 pp., illustrations

Appalachian Gardens offers 375 ornamental trees, shrubs, and conifers. Plants are listed by genus and species, common name, height, spread, shape, flower color and prominence, fruit, and color of foliage. Descriptions of shape, habit, site preference, and care are well detailed. Silhouette of plant's shape for each listing. Plants are characterized as well established, two years or older, started from cuttings or seeds; grafts noted separately. Guarantees true to name and safe arrival; will replace or issue a credit or refund. See **Conifers, Rhododendrons.**
Shipping season: March through December. Bareroot to California, Florida, Oregon and Washington, December through February.

Arborvillage Farm Nursery
1978
Lanny, Sue, and Derrick Rawdon
Catalog: $1, 56 pp.

The Rawdons, located in hardiness zone 5, offer a thousand woody trees and shrubs. Organized by genus and species, listings also provide common names, comments about growth habits, expected size of plant after five years, and current size of plant. Ships plants that are two to six feet in one- to three-gallon-size root system. Will replace plants injured in transit or issue credit or refund if claim is filed within five days of receipt. See **Conifers.**
Shipping season: February through May. September through December.
Canada, Mexico, International

Arrowhead Alpines
See **Conifers,** Grasses, **Perennials, Seeds,** Wildflowers.

ARROWHEAD NURSERY
1986
Linda Cardinal Schneider
Catalog: $2, 10 pp.
Ms. Schneider's nursery, located in the mountains of western North Carolina, offers a mix of natives, the cultivars of natives, and Asian varieties with a penchant for flowering. Recent features among the forty-five trees and shrubs in her catalog have been Chinese stewartia, Japanese serrated styrax, numerous magnolias, and the Ben Franklin Tree, first identified along the banks of the Altamaha River by John Bartram in 1765. Fully realized descriptions include provenance and history, form and habit of foliage, flower, and plant, height and spread at maturity, and hardiness zones. Plants shipped in containers.
Shipping season: All year.

BEAR CREEK NURSERY
1977
Hunter and Donna Carleton
Catalog: $1 (recoverable), 80 pp., illustrations
You'll want to set aside some quality reading and dreaming time when you sit down with the Carletons' catalog. The very big feature at Bear Creek are the edibles (see **Fruit**); however, their "Plants of Many Uses" section includes aspen, red Japanese barberry, purple beech, hardy catalpa, caragana (Siberian pea shrub), clethra, saucer magnolia, eastern redbud, and fragrant sumac. Fully realized descriptions include mature height and spread, precipitation required at maturity, age of plant being offered, current height and caliper, color, shape, and display of foliage, and landscape and postharvest uses. Includes a plant purpose reference guide. Guarantees true to name and safe arrival; if plant fails to grow within first season, will replace for shipping charge only. See **Booksellers, Fruit**, Heirlooms.
Shipping season: March through June. October and November.

BEAVER CREEK NURSERY
1986
Mike Stansberry
Catalog: $1, 22 pp.
Beaver Creek Nursery of Knoxville, Tennessee, lists two hundred dwarf conifers, trees, shrubs, and ornamental grasses. Recent catalogs featured a Kentucky coffeetree, *Fothergilla* 'Mt. Airy' selected for the arboretum of that name

by Dr. Michael Dirr; five butterfly bushes, including a purple *Buddleia alternifolia;* and a semi-evergreen southeastern native, dusty blue zenobia, that is characterized as being seldom offered in cultivation. Listed by botanical name, descriptions include common name, color and habit of foliage, growth habit, and height at maturity for most. Ships in containers of one gallon or larger. Guarantees true to name and nursery grown; if not satisfied, notify within seven days. See **Conifers**, Grasses.
Shipping season: October through April. No California, Oregon, or Washington

BERGESON NURSERY
1937
Paul and Glenda Bergeson
Catalog: Free, 26 pp.
Eric Bergeson, the third generation to work at the nursery, would like to set the record straight: Despite the name of their town being Fertile, they are situated in "the most hostile climate in the lower forty-eight states." It should not be surprising, therefore, that he characterizes their stock, which survives in temperatures of 40 degrees below zero, as cold-hardy. Their non-food-bearing stock includes shade and ornamental trees, shrubs, and plants for windbreaks. Features whips of the fast-growing green Bergeson ash. Other trees offered variously from twelve-inch pot plants up to eight-foot whips include cutleaf weeping and paper birch, Ohio buckeye, American linden, European and Fertile (Minnesota) Mountain Ash, and several willow. Among their shrubs are potentillas and spireas. Brief clear descriptions include size of plants, attractive characteristics, and ultimate height. See Conifers, **Fruit**.
Shipping season: Potted plants, March through October. Bareroot, March through mid-June. Canada

BIJOU ALPINES
1989
Mark Dusek
Catalog: $1, 18 pp.
Bijou Alpines, until 1991 associated with Mount Tahoma Nursery, is a specialty nursery with 150 varieties of rare and unusual plants for the rock garden, scree, bog, water garden, or woodland. Thirty-six dwarf trees and shrubs are described in detail, including a key to placement in the garden.

The "Collector's Corner" is their forum for presenting either plants never before introduced or forms rarely encountered in the trade. Also offers conifers, ferns and other perennials, water and bog plants. All plants are own-root and nursery propagated; custom propagation services available. See **Conifers, Perennials, Waterscapes.**
Shipping season: March through May.
September and October.

BLUEBIRD ORCHARD NURSERY
See **Fruit.**

BLUESTONE PERENNIALS
1972
William Boonstra
Catalog: Free, 80 pp., color photographs
Among Bluestone's five hundred and fifty offerings is a broad selection of ninety ornamental shrubs. They characterize their shrubs as small established plants "to grow on" requiring one or two years in your garden to become showy. Offers numerous types with one or two (for most) selections of each. Includes a sampling of *Buddleia* (butterfly bush), *Clethra, Hydrangea, Hibiscus, Salix, Spiraea, Viburnum,* and assorted arborvitae, junipers, and yews. Descriptions include height at maturity, spacing, hardiness zone, sun/shade requirements, season of bloom, and color and form of flower and foliage. Symbols highlight those varieties that are best for hot dry spots, moist soil, coldest areas (zones 3–4), the deep South, cut and/or dry easily, or are fragrant. Guarantees plants will grow; will replace or issue credit. See Grasses, **Perennials**
Shipping season: March through June.
Arizona, California, Idaho, Oregon: March and April.

BRIARWOOD GARDENS
See **Rhododendrons.**

BROKEN ARROW NURSERY
See **Rhododendrons.**

BRUDY'S TROPICAL EXOTICS
See Conifers, **Fruit, Seeds.**

BUCKLEY NURSERY GARDEN CENTER
See **Fruit.**

BURFORD BROTHERS
See **Fruit,** Heirlooms.

BURNT RIDGE NURSERY & ORCHARDS
See **Fruit.**

CAPE COD VIREYAS
See **Rhododendrons.**

CARLSON'S GARDENS
See **Rhododendrons.**

CARROLL GARDENS
1933
Alan L. Summers
Catalog: $3 (recoverable), 108 pp.
Carroll Gardens in Westminster, Maryland, devotes 20 percent of its catalog to woody plants, 70 percent to perennials, and just under 10 percent to roses. Selections from a broad range of genera: paperbark and Japanese maple, bottlebrush buckeyes, twenty butterfly bush, four boxwood, six blue spiraea (carpinus), seven clethra, shrub and tree dogwood, nine witch hazel, eighteen heather (*Calluna vulgaris*), seven heath (*Erica carnea*), twenty-two hydrangea, fourteen deciduous and fifteen evergreen holly, twenty crape myrtle (distinguished by various heights at maturity), twenty-five magnolia, seven andromeda, and fifty lilac (including hyacinthiflora), Preston (Canadian) lilac, dwarf Korean, French hybrid, and Japanese tree lilac. Descriptions include botanical and common names, hardiness zone, color, size and form of flower, growth habit, foliage form and color, soil and light preferences. Size of growing container prior to shipment is specified. Guarantees true to name, ready to grow, and safe arrival. California, Oregon and Washington trueness to name only. Will replace one time only any plant that is determined after flowering not to be true to name. See **Daylilies, Herbs, Hosta,** Iris, Peonies, Perennials, Roses.
Shipping season: March through November.
Canada

CHESTNUT HILL NURSERY
See **Fruit.**

CLIFFORD'S PERENNIAL & VINE
Catalog: Free, 14 pp.
Clifford's offers three dozen clematis. Part of their selection is differentiated by color, and within color by cultivar name. Also offers Montana clematis and a group of small varieties. Descriptions include color and form of

flower for all, size of flower for many. Plants shipped in 2¹/₂-inch pots. See Perennials.
Shipping season: April and May.

COENOSIUM GARDENS
See **Conifers**.

COLD STREAM FARM
1978
Mike Hradel
Catalog: Free, 6 pp.
The Hradels currently grow seventy-three mostly native species of trees, conifers, and berry plants for reforestation, wildlife habitat, and yard. Their list of trees and shrubs, organized by common name, includes European mountain, green, and white ash; American beech; paper and river birch; black locust; Amur maple; burr, English, live, white, and red oak; hybrid poplar; red Japanese barberry; flowering white, silky, and red dogwood; tartarian and Amur honeysuckle; and staghorn sumac. Stock is not described other than to indicate current size of tree. See **Conifers**, **Fruit**.
Shipping season: April and November.

COLLECTOR'S NURSERY
1990
Bill Janssen and Diana Reeck
Catalog: $2, 28 pp., illustrations
Mr. Janssen and Ms. Reeck continue to work on developing a display garden for their three thousand species and varieties of shrubs, trees, and perennials. While you may not get to Battle Ground, Washington, to see their collection, Janssen and Reeck list five hundred plants that are ready to make their way to your garden, including fifty ornamentals primarily from among the *Acer, Buxus, Cornus kousa, Hamamelis, Lonicera, Salix,* and *Wisteria.* Evocative descriptions include growth habit, color of foliage and flowers, recommended use in the garden, hardiness zone, ultimate height for some, and particular attention to those specimens that are appropriate for bonsai culture. Plants that are offered as grafts are so noted. Ships in pots. Guarantees true to name, well rooted, and healthy. See **Conifers**, **Perennials**.
Shipping season: March through May.
September through November.

COLVOS CREEK NURSERY
1977
Michael Lee

Catalog: $2 (recoverable), 23 pp.
Michael Lee, a registered landscape architect, is the steward of this part-time business specializing in Northwest and West Coast natives and other plants adapted to dry summer climates. Among the six hundred shrubs, trees, and vines listed by botanical name in Mr. Lee's catalog are crape myrtle, twenty *Cotoneaster,* bamboo leaf oak and water oak, jetbead, various osmanthus, numerous (including species) ivies, redtwig willow, Chinese elm, and California and Mexican fan palms. Descriptions include nature of foliage, color and form of flower and fruit where appropriate, uses in the garden, and hardiness zone. Container-grown plants shipped in liners or gallons filled with a mix of sand and composted sawdust; bareroot shipments available for an additional charge. Guarantees true to name and safe arrival; will replace or issue credit or refund for any plant that falters or fails during the first month in your garden. See **Conifers**, Fruit.
Shipping season: All year.
Canada, Mexico, International

COMSTOCK SEED
See **Grasses**, Seeds, **Wildflowers**.

DAVE & SUE'S AQUARIUMS AND GREENHOUSE
1983
David Lowman
Catalog: $1 (recoverable), 18 pp., illustrations and black-and-white photographs
Mr. Lowman is a potter and a bonsai artist. His catalog (no fish to be found) includes the tools of the trade, and a selection of prepared bonsai and deciduous material for indoor and outdoor culture. Brief clear descriptions of plants. Guarantees satisfaction; will issue refund. See **Booksellers**, **Supplies**.
Canada, Mexico, International

DAYSTAR
See **Conifers**, Perennials.

DIGGING DOG NURSERY
1978
Deborah Whigham and Gary Ratway
Catalog: $2, 66 pp., color illustrations
Gary, a landscape architect, and Deborah opened Digging Dog in 1978 because he had a difficult time finding plant material for his design jobs. Their first catalog dropped in 1993.

Mail-order selections are those plants that they have observed over time, in Gary's landscapes and at the nursery. Presented as noteworthy for ease of care, long bloom periods, attractive year-round form, texture, color, and versatility are one hundred perennials, twenty ornamental grasses, fifty shrubs, and a dozen trees and vines. Rich descriptions include height and width estimates, bloom times, hardiness, sun and shade tolerance. See **Grasses, Perennials.**
Shipping season: February through May. September through November.

 EASTERN PLANT SPECIALTIES
1985
Mark Stavish
Catalog: $3 (recoverable), 28 pp., illustrations
Mr. Stavish's New England–hardy plant material includes two hundred trees and shrubs. Recent catalogs included thirty heaths (*Erica carnea*) and heathers (*Calluna vulgaris*), dwarf shadblow, groundsel bush (tolerant of wet spots and heavy salt spray), dwarf hummingbird summersweet, several *Fothergilla*, eight winterberry hollies, and fly honeysuckle, as well as trees that are characterized as rare or having special attributes: David's maple, autumn brilliant shadblow, gold birch, dove tree, Irigi tree, and Korean mountain ash. Highlights common name but organized by botanical name. Notes size, color, and texture of foliage, growth habit, hardiness, and current height of plant. A cross-referenced index includes light preference, tolerance to wet or dry soil conditions, fragrance, if any, superior autumn color, and distinctive bark. Notes groups of trees and shrubs that are particularly useful for wet areas and those tolerant of consistently dry spots. See **Conifers, Fruit,** Perennials, **Rhododendrons, Wildflowers.**
Shipping season: March through June. September through November.

ECCLES NURSERIES, INC.
See **Conifers.**

EDIBLE LANDSCAPING
See **Fruit.**

ERICACEAE
See **Rhododendrons.**

EVERGREEN GARDENWORKS
1989
Brent Walston

Catalog: $2, 53 pp.
Mr. Walston propagates 650 types of shrubs, trees, and conifers, favoring dwarfs and semi-dwarfs. Woody plants in his catalog, organized by genus with an index of botanical names, include forty-two maple, four wormwood, seven birch, twenty-five flowering quince, twenty-three crabapple, ten willow, sixteen elm, and various dogwood, beech, tea tree, sweetgum, magnolia, oak, and lilac. Fully realized descriptions include common name, height at maturity, shape and nature of plant, flower and foliage, cultural requirements, light requirements, water requirements, suitability for bog or wetland, minimum temperature tolerance, and use as a landscape, rock garden, or bonsai specimen. Plants are from well-rooted cuttings, seedlings, or divisions shipped in 2¼-inch pots unless otherwise noted. See **Conifers,** Fruit, Perennials.
Shipping season: Potted plants, all year. Bareroot (dormant) to Alabama, Arkansas, Louisiana, Mississippi, North Carolina, Oregon, South Carolina, Tennessee, Texas, Virginia, and Washington, October through March. Florida, first Monday in December and first Monday in March.

FAIRWEATHER GARDENS
1989
Robert Hoffman and Robert Popham
Catalog: $3, 60 pp., illustrations, black-and-white and color photographs
Messrs. Hoffman and Popham offer ornamentals that they characterize as having significant merit, shipped in sizes that usually allow for immediate placement in your garden. Recent offerings have included thirty-seven magnolia, forty-six viburnum, thirty-two camellia, nineteen dogwood, eight Japanese maple, fourteen hydrangea, twelve butterfly bush, thirteen witch hazel, and numerous winter hazel, crape myrtle, hawthorn, European beech, *Fothergilla,* and American, Chinese, Japanese, evergreen, and deciduous holly. Narrative descriptions, written in an informal, familiar tone, include botanical and common names, form, native areas, shape and size of branches and foliage, seasonal habit, sun and soil requirements, and hardiness zones. Guarantees safe arrival. See **Conifers,** Fruit, **Rhododendrons.**
Shipping season: March and April. September through November.
Shorter shipping season to Arizona, California, Idaho, Minnesota, Nevada, Oregon,

Utah, and Washington.
Canada

FEDCO TREES
See **Booksellers, Conifers, Fruit,** Heirlooms.

FOLIAGE GARDENS
1976
Sue and Harry Olsen
Catalog: $2, 12 pp.
Sue Olsen specializes in hardy and exotic ferns,
Harry in Japanese maple cultivars with an unusual cornus kousa variety occasionally thrown
in. Sue has been growing ferns from spore (no
collected plants) since the late 1960s and
Harry has been propagating maples since retir-
ing from his engineering job at Boeing in
1990. The catalog, about a fifty-fifty proposi-
tion, includes seventy-five richly and carefully
described ferns and forty-five grafted Japanese
maples. Descriptions include growth habit,
shape, color and habit of foliage, hardiness
zones, and height at maturity.
**Shipping season: April through June. Sep-
tember and October.**
Canada, International

FOREST SEEDS OF CALIFORNIA
See Conifers, **Seeds.**

FORESTFARM®
1974
Ray and Peg Pragg
Catalog $3, 414 pp., illustrations and black-
and-white photographs
The Praggs' catalog contains four thousand
plants. Trees and shrubs abound and we have
made some attempt to count them. At the very
least, you'll find ninety-eight maple, ten alder,
twenty-four birch, twenty-five butterfly bush,
six boxwood, four camellia, eleven hornbeam,
six catalpa, eleven redbud, forty-five dogwood,
nine beech, fifteen ash, twelve witch hazel,
twenty-six hydrangea, forty-five holly, thirteen
crape myrtle, forty-eight oak, forty-eight willow, etc. Their catalog is organized by botanical name but includes a common-name index
that makes working with this in-depth catalog
a pleasure. Adding to the manageablity of this
catalog is the excellent standardized descriptions that include genus, species, variety, common name, foliage habit, hardiness zone,
origin, plant uses, cultural conditions, and a
description of the plant's habits, form, and site

preference. Ships in small tubes or one- and
five-gallon containers depending on variety
and availability. Guarantees true to name. See
Conifers, Fruit, Grasses, Perennials, Roses.
Shipping season: All year.
Canada

FOUR WINDS TRUE DWARF CITRUS
GROWERS
See **Fruit.**

FOWLER NURSERIES, INC., GARDEN
CENTER
See **Fruit,** Heirlooms.

THE FRAGRANT PATH
See Heirlooms, Herbs, Perennials, **Seeds.**

FRED & JEAN MINCH
See **Rhododendrons,** Seeds.

FROSTY HOLLOW ECOLOGICAL RESTORA-
TION
See Grasses, Seeds, **Wildflowers.**

FRUIT TESTING ASSOCIATION NURSERY,
INC.
See **Horticultural Societies, Fruit.**

GARDEN OF DELIGHTS
See **Fruit,** Seeds.

GARDENS OF THE BLUE RIDGE
1892
Edward and Robyn Fletcher
Catalog: $3 (recoverable), 31 pp., color
photographs
This Pineola, North Carolina, nursery dates back
to 1892, and the Fletchers are great-grandsons of
the nursery's cofounder. Gardens of the Blue Ridge
offers perennial woodland wildflowers and ferns
and twenty-five hardy native deciduous trees and
shrubs. Offerings have included *Calycanthus
floridus* (common sweet shrub), *Clethra alnifolia*
(summersweet), *Cytisus scoparius* (Scotch broom),
Rhus copallina (shining sumac), and *Xanthorhiza
simplicissima* (yellowroot). General planting instructions precede listings in botanical order. Descriptions include common name, foliage habit,
maximum height under ideal conditions, description of flower, fruit, and foliage, sun/shade and site
preference, and season of bloom. Most plants are
shipped bareroot. Guarantees true to name. See
Perennials, **Wildflowers.**

Shipping season: March through May.
September through December.
Canada, Mexico, International

GILSON GARDENS
See Conifers, **Perennials**.

GIRARD NURSERIES
See **Conifers**, Grasses, **Rhododendrons**, Seeds.

GOLDEN BOUGH TREE FARM
Catalog: $2, 17 pp.
A tree farm in Marlbank, Ontario (zone 5A), offering a considered selection of forty shade and flowering trees, fruit- and nut-bearing trees, decorative shrubs, and conifers. Recent catalogs have included European lime; thornless honey locust; littleleaf linden; Japanese, Amur, silver, sugar, and hedge maple; and a Japanese tree lilac. Descriptions include botanical and common name, hardiness zone, original locale, color and ornamental features of foliage and flower, historical notes, landscape, garden, and wildlife uses, site preference, and size of stock being offered. Although no sightings of the King of the Woods have been reported in Marlbank recently, the catalog from Golden Bough conveys a sensitive (but sensible) tone of reverence for each of the trees described. Guarantees plants will grow; will replace with next order. See Conifers, Fruit.
Shipping season: March through May.
September through November.
Canada

GOSSLER FARMS NURSERY
Marjory and Roger Gossler
1962
Catalog: $2, 26 pp.
The Gosslers were farmers of sweet corn and peppermint when they began the nursery in 1962. They put aside farming in 1986 when the nursery became a full-time business. The catalog includes four hundred offerings from the four thousand that they grow in their garden. A Gossler specialty, among the numerous hamamelis, maple, redbud, dogwood, eucalyptus, *Fothergilla*, and hydrangea, are some eighty magnolia. Highlights in recent catalogs include all eight Kosar-DeVos hybrids, *Magnolia denudata* (hardy white-flowering), which they characterize as *the* magnolia that they would grow if they could grow only one; and cutting-grown named cultivars of *Magnolia soulan-*

giana, and a *Magnolia stellata* 'Centennial' from the Arnold Arboretum. Descriptions include provenance, extensive cultural observations, color of flowers, and nature and habit of foliage. They pointedly do not include hardiness zones or ultimate sizes but recommend several reference works (also available from them) for further guidance. See Booksellers.
Shipping season: October through December.
February through April.
Canada

THE GREENERY
See **Rhododendrons**.

GREENMANTLE NURSERY
See **Fruit**, Heirlooms, Organics, **Roses**.

GREER GARDENS
1955
Harold E. Greer
Catalog: $3, 148 pp., illustrations and color photographs
Mr. Greer, a specialist in rhododendrons and azaleas, has over time expanded to include twenty-five hundred ornamental trees, shrubs, fruit-bearing plants, perennials, ground covers, ornamental grasses, bamboo, books, and videotapes. Greer's woody plants, trees, and vines include ninety maple, sixty magnolia, forty camellia, forty dogwood, forty clematis, thirty hydrangea, seventeen lilac, and numerous burning bush, birch, redbud, boxwood, witch hazel, beech, sumac, and others. Rich descriptions include common name, hardiness zone, color and texture of foliage and bark, use in the garden, and height of plant at shipment and at maturity. A cross-referenced list highlights those offerings that have a pleasing fragrance, have exceptional color, thrive in the shade, or even obnoxious to deer. Guarantees quality stock, true to name, and safe arrival; will replace plants one time only that have been properly cared for (except maples, which will be replaced if loss occurs during the first sixty days on a half-price basis) but do not survive. See **Booksellers**, **Conifers**, Fruit, **Grasses**, Peonies, Perennials, **Rhododendrons**.
Shipping season: All year (recommends September through May).
Canada, Mexico, International

GRIMO NUT NURSERY
See **Fruit**.

HABITAT PLANTS
1992
Greg Smith
Catalog: Free, 8 pp.
North of Coeur d'Alene, Idaho, east and up a bit from Spokane, Washington, sitting fifty miles south of the border with British Columbia, is Sandpoint, Idaho, home to Habitat Plants, where trees and shrubs are grown in containers for at least one year while overwintering in unheated cold frames. Mr. Smith focuses on trees and shrubs that exhibit strong features such as unusual leaf shape or color, intricate branching patterns, striking flowers, and textured bark for multiseasonal interest when creating his list of seventy-five offerings. Among his selections are whitespire birch, butterfly bush 'Black Knight' (which he recommends treating like a herbaceous perennial in cold climates), February daphne, European beech 'Purple Fountain', Persian parrotia, hankow willow 'Scarlet Curls', and *Xanthoceras sorbifolium*, also called yellowhorn or popcorn tree. Rich descriptions include botanical and common names, height at maturity, color and duration of flowers, color and habit of foliage. Specifies size of plant available and notes grafts where appropriate. Ships in growing containers. Guarantees true to name and safe arrival. See Conifers.
Shipping season: Please inquire.

HAMMOND'S ACRES OF RHODYS
See **Rhododendrons**.

HEARD GARDENS LTD.
1928
Mary Anne Rennebohm
Catalog: $2, 12 pp.
Lilacs, lilacs, and more lilacs, please. Heard Gardens offers forty-plus own-root varieties from dwarf to full-size, in all colors listed in the *International Register of Cultivar Names in Genus Syringa*. Catalog is organized by color of bloom, and varieties are listed alphabetically by common name within color. A sampler of their offerings: white 'Edith Cavell', violet 'Pocahontas', blue 'President Grevy', lilac 'Victor Lemoine', pink 'James MacFarlane', and reddish purple 'Charles Joly'. Descriptions include year of introduction, botanical name, an evocative characterization of flower color and cluster, fragrance, growth habit, historical anecdotes, and range of height at maturity. The catalog includes a useful lilac sequence of bloom chart, and Ms. Rennebohm highlights those lilacs useful in warm climates requiring minimum winter chill. Helpful diagrams and notes about proper planting and pruning. Ships bareroot when dormant. See Heirlooms.
Shipping season: March and October.

HEIRLOOM SEED PROJECT–LANDIS VALLEY MUSEUM
See **Fruit**, Heirlooms, Organics, Seeds, **Vegetables**.

HENRY FIELD'S SEED & NURSERY CO.
1892
Orville Dragoo
Catalog: Free, 87 pp., color photographs
A full-line seed and nursery catalog, including twenty ornamental shade trees, thirteen flowering trees, numerous varieties of windbreaks, and fifty shrubs, hedges, and vines. Descriptions include foliage habit, height and spread at maturity, and size of plant being offered. Guarantees plants will grow; will replace or issue refund. See **Fruit**, **Garlic**, **Kidstuff**, Perennials, Organics, **Seeds**, **Supplies**, **Vegetables**.
Shipping season: February through June.

HERONSWOOD NURSERY LTD.
1987
Daniel Hinkley and Robert L. Jones
Catalog: $4, 220 pp.
Heronswood characterizes its mission as procuring and offering plant materials that have not previously been available to North American gardeners. (Many of the observations, ruminations, and diarylike entries laced throughout the catalog have also rarely been seen by American gardeners.) Mr. Hinkley (author of *Winter Ornamentals*) and Mr. Jones list two thousand trees, shrubs, vines, ornamental grasses, and perennials. Recent catalogs have featured a diverse range of *Acer, Buddleia, Clematis, Cistus, Helianthemum, Halimium,* × *Halmiocistus, Hydrangea,* and *Rhododendron,* among the 450 shrubs, 100 vines, and 100 trees being offered. Descriptions include provenance, hardiness zone, pot size, and a highly visual narrative of the plant's form, color, and size. A supplementary list, without descriptions, of "choice" shrubs that are in short supply follows the descriptive section. Guarantees true to name, healthy upon departure; will accept claims filed within ten days of

receipt. See **Conifers**, Fruit, **Grasses**, **Perennials**, **Rhododendrons**.
Shipping season: March through mid-May.
Mid-September through October.
Canada

HIDDEN SPRINGS NURSERY
See **Fruit**.

HIGHLANDER NURSERY
See **Fruit**.

HOLLY RIDGE NURSERY
1990
Paul Hanslik and Lucinda Little
Catalog: Free, 4 pp. (specify retail mail-order catalog)
A wholesaler of *Ilex* offering seventy-five varieties to home gardeners from among the following: American, Japanese, Inkberry, Longstalk, Meservae, Winterberry-Michigan, yellow fruited, dwarf, and variegated English holly. Descriptions include color and form of foliage, growth habit, color of fruit, whether male or female and varieties it will pollinate, size of specimen available, height at maturity, and cold-hardiness. Guarantees safe arrival; will issue refund.
Shipping season: March through December.
No Arizona, California, Oregon, or Washington
Canada

HOLLYDALE NURSERY
See **Fruit**.

HOMAN BROTHERS SEED, INC.
See Grasses, Seeds, **Wildflowers**.

HORTICO, INC.
See **Grasses**, **Perennials**, **Roses**, Waterscapes.

JOHNSON NURSERY
See **Fruit**, Heirlooms.

J. W. JUNG SEED & NURSERY CO.
1907
Richard J. Zondag
Catalog: Free, 76 pp., color photographs
Fifteen percent of this seed and nursery catalog for a wide range of interests is devoted to hardy ornamental and dwarf shrubs and hedges, including barberry, privet, highbush cranberry, French and other hybrid lilacs; and to flowering trees, including eight types of flowering

crabapple, shade and ornamental trees, and hardy climbing vines. Descriptions include common and botanical names, hardiness zone, color and habit, height or age of stock being offered, and height at maturity. See **Bulbs**, Fruit, Garlic, **Kidstuff**, Perennials, **Seeds**, Supplies, Vegetables.
Shipping season: January through June.
August through November.

KELLEYGREEN RHODODENDRON NURSERY
See **Rhododendrons**.

LAMB NURSERIES
Catalog: Free, 75 pp.
Lamb Nurseries, located in the eastern Washington desert (zone 5), offers nine hundred perennials, rock plants, flowering shrubs, and hardy vines. Featured shrubs and vines include ten types of butterfly bush (*Buddleia*), four flowering quince (*Chaenomeles*), numerous ivies (*Hedera*), and over thirty large-flowered and other hybrid clematis. Narrative descriptions include color of flower, nature of foliage, and height at maturity. Guarantees safe arrival; will replace if notified of failure within ten days. See Grasses, **Perennials**.
Shipping season: Spring and fall.
Canada

LARNER SEEDS
1978
Judith Lowry
Catalog: $2, 45 pp., illustrations
Larner specializes in the seed of California native plants, including thirty-five shrubs and vines and fifteen trees. The emphasis here is on backyard restoration gardening as practiced by encouraging existing natives and reintroducing others appropriate to a particular niche. Recent catalogs have included California sagebrush, California mugwort, Santa Cruz Island buckwheat, flannel bush, California buckeye, redwood alder, Gowan's cypress, and canyon live oak. Descriptions are brief but rich, including botanical and common name, height of plant at maturity, sun and soil preference, and growing habit. Seed for shrubs and vines offered in regular packets and larger trade packets. Also packets for some individual specimens of large seeds. See **Booksellers**, **Grasses**, Seeds, **Wildflowers**.
Shipping season: All year.

LAS PILITAS NURSERY
See Grasses, **Wildflowers**.

LAURIE'S LANDSCAPE
See **Hosta, Peonies,** Perennials.

LAWSON'S NURSERY
See **Fruit**, Heirlooms.

LIVING TREE NURSERY
See **Fruit**, Heirlooms.

LONG HUNGRY CREEK NURSERY
See **Fruit**, Heirlooms, Organics.

LOUISIANA NURSERY
1950
Dalton E. Durio
Catalogs: Hydrangeas: $3.50, Magnolias: $6
(recoverable), 146 pp.
Louisiana Nursery occupies a fifty-six-acre complex that was founded by Ken Durio. Five family members, all trained horticulturists, are currently involved in the business. "Magnolias and other Garden Aristocrats" features 225 deciduous and evergreen hollies, 120 hydrangeas, 200 fragrant plants, 30 oleanders, 30 wisteria, 100 ornamental vines, and this catalog's centerpiece, 500 magnolias. "Hydrangea Species and Cultivars" is a separate fully descriptive catalog showcasing 120 offerings ranging from dwarf shrubs of eighteen to twenty-four inches to giants that can reach thirty feet at maturity, including twenty oak-leaf types. Brief descriptions characterize plant habit, shape, height, color, and hardiness. Plant material shipped variously bareroot or in a range of container sizes. See **Booksellers, Bulbs, Daylilies, Fruit, Grasses, Iris**.
Shipping season: All year.
Canada, Mexico, International

MATSU-MOMIJI NURSERY
See **Conifers**.

MATTERHORN NURSERY, INC.
1981
Matt and Ronnie Horn
Catalog: $5, 102 pp., illustrations
Matterhorn offers a wide range of ornamentals. Fifteen percent of the Horns' catalog is devoted to 150 deciduous trees and 25 percent is devoted to 250 shrubs, including an extensive collection of rhododendron and azalea. Trees include twenty-four Japanese maple, of which ten are thread-leaf cultivars, nine birch, eight dogwood, fifteen crabapple as well as beech, birch, and oak. Highlights of the shrub section include twenty-nine heather (*Calluna vulgaris*) that are organized by color of foliage within their genus, a dozen heath (*Erica carnea*), eight *Potentilla*, and numerous witch hazels and hollies. Trees and shrubs are listed in alphabetical order by botanical name in their respective sections. Information given for each offering includes common name, description of plant and landscape use, sun/shade and soil preferences, and a range for height at maturity. Guarantees true to name. See **Conifers**, Grasses, Perennials, **Rhododendrons, Waterscapes**.
Shipping season: Please inquire.

MILLER NURSERIES
See **Fruit**, Heirlooms.

MINIATURE PLANT KINGDOM
See **Conifers**, Fruit, **Grasses, Perennials**.

MOSTLY NATIVES NURSERY
See **Grasses**, Perennials, **Wildflowers**.

MOUNTAIN MAPLES
1989
Don and Nancy Fiers
Catalog: $1, 36 pp.
The Fierses offer over two hundred *Acer palmatum* cultivars and species, cultivars of other *Acer* species, beech trees, and Chinese tree peonies. Catalog is organized by group: deeply divided or dissectum, dwarf, linearilobum, and palmate maple, other *Acer* species, and maple particularly suited to container and bonsai culture. Distinguishing characteristics of each group are enumerated; descriptions include name of cultivar or species, height after ten years in container culture, and height after ten years in landscape use, color and features of foliage, growth habit, age of specimens available. See **Booksellers, Peonies**.
Shipping season: February through May. November.

MUSSER FORESTS
1928
Nancy Musser
Catalog: Free, 10 pp., color photographs.
Specify retail catalog
Musser Forests currently produces over 55 million seedlings, transplants, and rooted cuttings for ornamentals, hardwoods, shrubs, and

conifers each year. Varieties offered variously as one-, two-, and three-year seedlings include European beech; black, European white, gray, Japanese white, paper white, and river birch; catalpa; Chinese, gray, silky, and white-flowering dogwood; locusts; Japanese, red, silver, and sugar maple; and black, English, pin, red, scarlet, sawtooth, and white oak. Some offerings are "precision sown"—that is, grown in what Musser characterizes as perfectly spaced rows that encourage superior rooting, branching, and uniformity. Descriptions include height at maturity, the best time to transplant, color and texture of leaves, culture and care, light and site preferences, and landscape use. Guarantees true to name. See **Conifers**, Fruit.
Shipping season: Potted plants, all year. Bareroot, March through May. September through November.
Canada

NATIVE GARDENS
See Grasses, Seeds, **Wildflowers**.

NICHE GARDENS
See Perennials, **Wildflowers**.

NORTHWIND NURSERY AND ORCHARDS
See **Booksellers**, **Fruit**, Organics, **Supplies**.

OIKOS TREE CROPS
1985
Ken Asmus
Catalog: $1, 46 pp., illustrations, black-and-white and color photographs
Mr. Asmus prefers low-maintenance trees and bushes. Half of his catalog is devoted to fruit- and nut-bearing plants. One third of his catalog includes hybrid oak for timber, mast, and horticultural value, evergreen oak, deciduous oak, and native and other species from diverse sources worldwide. In the section called "A few other good plants . . . ," he offers buckeye, Montpelier maple, Russian rock birch, gray birch, and Tibetan birch. Plants are listed alphabetically in their section by genus and species. Stock available variously in paper pots, flats, and as one- and two-year seedlings. Descriptions include hardiness, preferred soil and site, spacing, and height at maturity. Guarantees healthy and true to catalog description. See **Fruit**.
Shipping season: Potted plants, February through December. Bareroot, March through

May. October and November.
No oak to California
Canada, Mexico, International

PACIFIC COAST SEED COMPANY
See Conifers, **Seeds**.

PACIFIC TREE FARMS
William L. Nelson
Catalog: $2, 20 pp.
Mr. Nelson offers 350 container-grown trees and shrubs. Approximately 70 percent are fruit and nut bearing; conifers comprise another 10 percent of his catalog. Other plant materials include a variety of palm and oak, and an eclectic selection from diverse sources. Stock is listed by botanical name and cross-referenced, without further description by common name. Ships in five-gallon pots; some (noted) are shipped bareroot only. See **Conifers**, **Fruit**.
Shipping season: Potted plants, all year. Bareroot, January through mid-March.
Canada, Mexico, International

PAMPERED PLANT NURSERY
See **Fruit**.

PEN Y BRYN NURSERY
1946
Catalog: $2.95, 58 pp., illustrations
A nursery for coniferous, deciduous, fruiting, and exotic plant material appropriate to bonsai culture. Offers two hundred specimens. Evocative, thorough narrative descriptions of tree's form, flower's color and shape, foliage's features and habits, seasonal changes, pest and disease problems and resistance, and height at maturity if grown without restriction. Notes hardiness, age of specimen, current height, and size of traveling container. Includes an index of common names keyed to catalog page number. See **Booksellers**, **Rhododendrons**, **Supplies**.
Shipping season: April through mid-December.

PENSE NURSERY
See **Fruit**.

PLANT DELIGHTS NURSERY
See **Conifers**, **Grasses**, **Hosta**, **Perennials**.

PLANTS OF THE SOUTHWEST
See **Booksellers**, **Grasses**, Heirlooms, Seeds, **Vegetables**, **Wildflowers**.

PORTERHOWSE FARMS
See **Conifers, Perennials**.

POWELL'S GARDENS
See Conifers, **Daylilies, Hosta, Iris,** Peonies, **Perennials**.

PRAIRIE MOON NURSERY
See **Booksellers, Grasses,** Organics, Seeds, **Wildflowers**.

RARE CONIFER FOUNDATION–RARE CONIFER NURSERY
See **Booksellers, Conifers, Kidstuff**.

ROCKY MEADOW ORCHARD & NURSERY
See **Fruit**.

ROSLYN NURSERY
1984
Dr. Philip Waldman
Catalog: $3, 76 pp., color photographs
Roslyn nursery grows two thousand varieties of trees, shrubs, perennials, grasses, rhododendron, and azalea. About 40 percent of their catalog contains three hundred ornamental vines, trees and shrubs. Areas of concentration include *Acer, Buddleia, Camellia, Clethra, Clematis, Cornus, Daphne, Hamamelis, Hydrangea, Lonicera, Magnolia,* and *Viburnum*. Brief narrative descriptions include plant's shape, color, habit, distinguishing characteristics, uses in the garden, and hardiness zone. The "Woody Plants for Special Uses" section includes plants for wet and dry conditions, plants that will tolerate shade, and those that are unattractive to deer. Guarantees true to name and healthy; will replace or issue credit if plant fails within thirty days of receipt. See **Booksellers, Conifers, Perennials, Rhododendrons**.
Shipping season: April through June. September through November. Bareroot (Arizona and California only), mid-March.
Canada, Mexico, International

ST. LAWRENCE NURSERIES
See **Booksellers, Fruit,** Heirlooms, Organics.

A SANDY RHODODENDRON
See **Rhododendrons**.

SAVAGE NURSERY CENTER
1942
Jim Savage
Catalog: Free, 4 pp., color photographs

Mr. Savage offers ornamental, shade, and fruit-bearing trees and twenty-five flowering shrubs. Recent catalogs have included European, Japanese, and white paper birch, saucer and soulangeana magnolia, smoke tree, golden rain tree, mimosa, and hydrangea. Compact informative descriptions for most include shape and ultimate height, color and season of bloom for flowering varieties, current height and height at maturity. Guarantees safe arrival and to survive the first year in your garden. Will replace plants that arrive in unsatisfactory condition free of charge; those that fail will be replaced for half the original price. See Conifers, **Fruit**.
Shipping season: January through May. October through December.

SCHILD AZALEA GARDENS AND NURSERY
See **Rhododendrons**.

SCHLABACH'S NURSERY
See **Fruit,** Heirlooms.

SHEPHERD HILL FARM
See Conifers, **Rhododendrons**.

SISKIYOU RARE PLANT NURSERY
See **Booksellers, Conifers, Perennials**.

SMITH NURSERY COMPANY
1962
Bill Smith
Catalog: Free, 8 pp.
Primarily a wholesale grower, Smith will accept small orders at adjusted prices as noted. Offers four hundred hardy northern-grown (Charles City, Iowa) landscape shrubs and shade trees, including many natives. Recent selections included twelve spirea, three forsythia, seventeen lilac, three euonymus, ten viburnum, eleven maple, eleven dogwood, as well as a variety of cotoneaster, witch hazel, privet, honeysuckle, magnolia, smoke tree, sumac, willow, ash, birch, elm, locust, linden, oak, and poplar. Lists botanical and common names and size of plant available, variously nine to twelve inches, twelve to twenty-four inches, or as seedlings. Also lists seed for one hundred types of shrubs and trees sold in quarter-pound measures and more. Guarantees safe arrival. See Fruit, Seeds.
Shipping season: Mid-February through mid-June.
Canada

SONOMA ANTIQUE APPLE NURSERY
See **Fruit**, Heirlooms, Organics.

SOUTHMEADOW FRUIT GARDENS
See **Fruit**, Heirlooms.

SOUTHWESTERN NATIVE SEEDS
See Cactus, Seeds, **Wildflowers**.

SPRINGVALE FARM NURSERY
1980
Will and Jeanne Gould
Catalog: $3 (subscription), 12 pp.
The Avid Gardener™ catalog published by Springvale Farm Nursery features dwarf, rare, and unusual flowering shrubs, ground covers, and conifers organized by botanical name. The Goulds focus their selection of midwestern-hardy (tolerant of cold and extreme summer heat) ornamentals on plants for collectors, bonsai artists, and operators of railway gardens. They recently featured fourteen Japanese maple, four barberry, five boxwood, eight holly, and five spirea. Information about each offering includes hardiness zone, potential for bonsai, as a patio container plant, or as railway garden specimen, its size at maturity, and the size of the container. Notes grafted stock. Plants shipped in their growing containers. Guarantees true to name; will replace or issue refund for any misnamed plant. If dissatisfied with a plant for other reasons, notify within ten days of receipt. See **Conifers**.
Shipping season: March through May.
October and November.
No Alaska, Arizona, California, or Hawaii

STARK BRO.'S
See Conifers, **Fruit**.

SUNLIGHT GARDENS
See **Wildflowers**.

SWEDBERG NURSERIES, INC.
Catalog: Free, 14 pp., color photographs
Swedberg Nurseries, located in Battle Lake, Minnesota, devotes just under half of its catalog to trees and shrubs for shade, windbreaks, hedges, and snowcatch. Their list of fast-growing hardy trees includes 'Siouxland' poplar, 'Theves' poplar, and a cottonless cottonwood developed by the South Dakota Plant Pathology Department. Swedberg's shrub list features twenty dwarf varieties: crimson pygmy barberry, rosy glow barberry, Korean dwarf lilac, spirea, daphne, goldflame and goldmound, and taller named varieties, including hydrangea, spirea, and French lilac. Organized by height at maturity, listed by common name. Concise descriptions note growth habit, site preference, season of bloom, color of flower and foliage, and current size. Ships bareroot unless noted. Guarantees will grow through first season; will replace plants one time only at half the original price if claim is filed prior to August 1 of the year of purchase. See Conifers, **Fruit**.
Shipping season: Spring.

TEC
1975
Catalog: Free, 4 pp.
Half of TEC's Minnesota-grown plant list is composed of shrubs, hardwoods, and nut trees. Offers transplants and seedlings of ash, white paper birch, river birch, red, sugar, and silver maples, black walnut, American chestnut, highbush cranberry, and mulberry. Lists botanical name and size of specimen. Guarantees viable upon departure from their nursery. See **Conifers**, Fruit.
Shipping season: April and May.

TRANS-PACIFIC NURSERY
Jackson Muldoon
Catalog: $2, 44 pp.
Mr. Muldoon specializes in rare, unusual, hard-to-find, and exotic specimens from all over the world, with an emphasis on the southern hemisphere and Pacific Rim. Trans-Pacific sponsors collecting expeditions to far-flung destinations like Mount Kilimanjaro and Yunnan, China, to which customers can subscribe and gain first access to newly introduced plants. Catalog runs to over 450 stunningly diverse selections. Recent offerings included thirty Japanese maples (*Acer japonicum* 'Aconitifolium'), coral trees (*Erythrina*), fourteen types of eucalyptus (*Myrtaceae*), tender Arabian jasmine (*Jasminum sambac*), and a Namibian native, Hottentot's bean tree (*Schotia afra*). Information for offerings include a plant's natural habitat and cultural requirements as well as a fully realized description. Plants are shipped in four-inch pots unless otherwise specified. See **Booksellers**, Bulbs, Perennials, **Waterscapes**.
Shipping season: All year (prefers not to ship

in December or January).
Canada, Mexico, International

TRIPLE BROOK FARM
See Fruit, **Grasses**, Perennials, **Wildflowers**.

THE URBAN HOMESTEAD
See **Fruit**, Heirlooms.

VAN VEEN NURSERY
See **Booksellers, Rhododendrons**.

VAN WELL NURSERY
See **Fruit**.

VERNON BARNES & SON NURSERY
1948
James V. Barnes, Jr.
Catalog: Free, 32 pp., color photographs
Barnes provides a basic assortment of 250 one-
and two-year-old ornamentals including flowering shrubs: Persian, French, and old-fashioned lavender lilacs; green and red barberry;
Japanese snowballs; twenty flowering trees, including American redbud and pink and red
flowering dogwood; and eighteen shade trees,
including pin, red, scarlet, and willow oak,
sweetgum, and sassafras. Notes specimens that
have been collected. Descriptions include ultimate height, flower and foliage characteristics,
sun/shade preference, size of plant being offered, and hardiness zones. Ships bareroot. See
Conifers, Fruit.
Shipping season: January through April.
October through early December.

WASHINGTON EVERGREEN NURSERY
See **Conifers, Rhododendrons**.

WAVECREST NURSERY AND LANDSCAPING
1959
Carol T. Hop
Catalog: $1 (recoverable), 24 pp.
Wavecrest sits on the shore of Lake Michigan,
providing the plants grown there with a milder
climate than much of zone 5. Fifty percent of the
catalog includes 150 trees, shrubs, and vines. Recent catalogs included paperbark maple (*Acer
griseum*), tricolor vine (*Actinidia kolomikta*),
weeping Japanese Katsura (*Cercidiphyllum mag-
nificum* 'Pendulum'), a dwarf burning bush (*Euonymus alata* 'Rudy Haag'), sixteen varieties of
magnolia, and a white-bloomed Japanese hydrangea vine (*Schizopragma hydrangeoides*). Of-

ferings listed by botanical name and common
names; includes a brief effective description of
color and form; specifies size of container or
sleeve. Must notify upon arrival if plants are unsatisfactory. See **Booksellers, Conifers, Grasses,**
Perennials.
Shipping season: March through May.
Canada, Mexico, International

WEDGE NURSERY
1878
Bradford D. Wedge
Catalog: Free, 8 pp.
Lilacs white, lilacs bluish, lilacs pinkish, lilacs
purple, and magenta too, please. Mr. Wedge,
thanks in part to his forebears, offers ninety-
five own-root hybrid French lilac (*Syringa vulgaris*), twenty *Syringa hyacinthiflora,* and a
selection of later-blooming Preston (Canadian) hybrids (*Syringa × Prestoniae*) and
Josikaea. Also offers several species and miscellaneous hybrids including the Japanese tree
lilac 'Ivory Silk' and 'Summer Snow'. Catalog
is organized alphabetically by name of cultivar.
Descriptions include colors as listed in the *International Register of Cultivar Names in Genus
Syringa,* whether a single or double, noteworthy characteristics, form, growth habit, and
season of bloom.
Shipping season: Bareroot, March and April.
Pots, April and May.

WHITE FLOWER FARM
See **Bulbs**, Fruit, **Perennials, Roses**, Supplies,
Waterscapes.

WHITMAN FARMS
1980
Lucile Whitman
Catalog: $1 (recoverable), 10 pp.
Lucile Whitman is a wholesale grower of unusual ornamental deciduous trees and shrubs
for the landscape and retail nursery trade.
However, the retail mail-order edition of her
catalog includes a special section of seventy-
five unusual maple and magnolia species and
graftlings. Listed by botanical name with common name given. Notes size and age of tree.
Ships in pots. Guarantees true to name and
safe arrival; will replace any plant that dies
within six months of arrival if you believe it is
due to Ms. Whitman's error. See **Fruit.**
Shipping season: May and June.

WHITNEY GARDENS & NURSERY
See **Rhododendrons**.

WILD SEED, INC.
See **Booksellers**, Grasses, **Kidstuff**, Seeds, **Wildflowers**.

THE WILDWOOD FLOWER
See **Perennials**.

WILEY'S NUT GROVE NURSERY
See **Fruit**.

WINDROSE
1993
M. Nigel Wright
Catalog: $3 (recoverable), 72 pp.
The trademarked phrase at Windrose is "Diversity not Adversity." In keeping with their motto, 85 percent of their catalog is devoted to 650 trees, shrubs, and vines, with major stops for birch, butterfly bush, clematis, dogwood, ivy, hydrangea, holly, honeysuckle, magnolia, oak, spirea, and viburnum. Consistently formatted descriptions include botanical and common names, hardiness zone, origin, size of plant in its container, range for height at maturity, foliage habit, sun/shade preference, soil requirements. Guarantees true to name and healthy; will replace or issue credit for misnamed stock. See Perennials.
Shipping season: March through June.
August through November.

WOMACK'S NURSERY CO.
See **Fruit**.

YUCCA DO NURSERY AT PECKERWOOD GARDENS
1988
John Fairey and Carl Schoenfeld
Catalog: $3, 45 pp.
A nursery using only organic methods in cultivating seeds and cuttings from the natives of Texas, Mexico, and Asia, which have been gathered on expeditions by the folks at Yucca Do. Most varieties offered are hardy in zones 7, 8, and 9. Offerings include 180 trees and shrubs. Recent introductions into their catalog include *Clethra pringlei* 'White Water' found in Tamaulipas, Mexico, a Chinese tulip tree (*Liriodendron chinense*), a Mexican relative of the southern big leaf magnolia, a nonhybridized *Mahonia lanceolatus,* and *Styrax glabrescens* var. *pilosus*. Descriptions include location of find and color and form of flowers and foliage. Will replace or issue a refund if notified within ten days of arrival. See **Cactus, Conifers**, Grasses, Organics, Perennials, **Wildflowers**.
Shipping season: January through May.
October through December.
International

Selected Reading About Trees, Shrubs, and Vines

Manual of Climbers and Wall Plants, Charles J. K. Burras, consulting editor. Adapted from the *Royal Horticultural Society Dictionary of Gardening*, this book includes a comprehensive listing of climbing plants by genus with information about cultivation, habits, and landscape uses. Fifty black-and-white illustrations.

Manual of Woody Landscape Plants: Their Identification, Ornamental Characteristics, Culture, Propagation, and Uses, by Michael Dirr. A standard reference for American landscape-worthy trees, shrubs, and vines. Includes three hundred genera, several hundred species, and two thousand cultivars. Copious information about propagation, care, size, characteristics, and landscape uses. Illustrated.

Ornamental Shrubs, Climbers, and Bamboos, by Graham Stuart Thomas. Thousands of species for special purposes and with desirable features are listed and explained. Includes cultural habits, size, hardiness, seasonal interest, and propagation. Two hundred black-and-white and color photographs.

Plants That Merit Attention Volume I: Trees, edited by Janet Meakin Poor. Includes 143 trees deemed noteworthy by the Garden Club of America. The text describes each tree, its cultural requirements, and landscape uses. Three color photographs of each tree focus on details of bark, leaf, flowers, fruit or cones, and growth habit. Over four hundred color photographs.

Plants That Merit Attention Volume II: Shrubs, edited by Janet Meakin Poor and Nancy Peterson Brewster. Includes 750 native and non-native species and cultivars deemed noteworthy by the Garden Club of America for their beauty, pest- and disease-resistance, and tolerance of environmental changes. Includes cultural requirements, landscape uses, and gardens or parks where the shrubs can be observed. Seven hundred color photographs.

The Pruning of Trees, Shrubs and Conifers, by George E. Brown; updated by John Bryan. An encyclopedic volume on the best pruning methods for 450 genera of trees, shrubs, conifers, and woody vines. One hundred and fifty black-and-white photographs and illustrations.

The Tree and Shrub Expert, by Dr. D. G. Hessayon. Features one thousand flowering shrubs, deciduous trees, climbers, and conifers. Each entry is illustrated and includes recommendations about top varieties, site and soil requirements, care, and propagation. Five hundred color illustrations.

Trees and Shrubs for Temperate Climates, by Gordon Courtright. Eight hundred color photographs of mature woody plants in landscape settings permit the reader an opportunity to understand what their young trees will look like after years of growth. A valuable tool for planning a landscape.

The Year in Trees: Superb Woody Plants for Four-Season Gardens, by Kim E. Tripp and J. C. Raulston. The authors, having participated in the North Carolina State University Arboretum's trials of more than 9,000 woody plants, offer information and observation about 150 unusual and underused woody plant materials suitable for North American gardens. Two hundred color photographs.

$\mathcal{R}$HODODENRONS, $\mathcal{A}$ZALEAS, AND $\mathcal{K}$ALMIAS

*F*ew genera of woody plants provide such diversity of form, habit, leaf, and flower as *Rhododendron*. This genus (which also contains plants commonly referred to as azaleas) includes sixty- to eighty-foot trees, dense-growing shrubs only a few feet high, and still other types that at maturity are only a few inches tall and with a spreading, mat-forming habit.

Leaves can vary from 2 1/2 feet to scarcely 1/2 inch in length, providing a wide range of textures in the garden. Some kinds have fuzzy leaves, beset with fine hairs; others are glossy on the upper surface but covered underneath with a thick velvety coating called indumentum. Still others are deciduous, and may furnish a brilliantly colored flourish to the autumn landscape.

Rhododendron and azalea flowers provide a diversity of sizes and shapes, from huge scented trumpets six inches across, to elegant pendant bells, to tiny stars barely one quarter inch in diameter. They can be had in all the colors of the rainbow except true blue and green.

Of course, not all these characteristics are available to gardeners in all climates. Rhododendrons come from a tremendous range of habitats extending from Arctic tundra to tropical rain forests. The most important factor in selecting a particular plant is its tolerance of your climatic conditions.

There are hundred of species and cultivars that will flourish in many parts of the world. Their possible uses in landscape are as diverse as their individual characteristics suggest; some of the more common uses include:

Background, screen, or hedge planting; the taller growing kinds would be most suitable here. For year-round screening evergreen types are preferable.

Mass planting in a shrub border, flanking a drive or a walk or framing a vista; depending on the scale of the garden, these might be medium- or low-growing type. In certain settings, those with smaller foliage would prove more suitable. Depending on your selection, each cultivar could provide a two-week extravaganza of color any time from early spring to midsummer.

An individual plant with rare or unique features, such as variegated foliage or unusually colored flowers, might be selected as an attention-attracting specimen for a focal point in a landscape.

Smaller types, with a mature height of two feet or less, can be used in front of taller rhododendrons or azaleas to "face down" or mask leggy stems. These low-growing kinds are also valuable subjects for gardens where space is at a premium.

For the rock garden, there are many alpine rhododendrons and azaleas that grow slowly and feature tiny leaves and flowers. A number of this type make excellent subjects for the bonsai artist.

In a natural woodland setting, rhododendrons with an informal habit of growth, such as many of the azaleas native to North America, make a springtime picture of unrivaled grace, in hues ranging from delicate to flamboyant.

Although the multitudes of rhododendrons and azaleas have quite different ranges of climatic tolerance, they do share some common requirements for soil, moisture, and other cultural factors.

Good drainage is essential. No rhododendron can survive long with its roots submerged in water or in heavy, wet soil. Ideally, the soil should be open and porous, with a high percentage of organic material, and should definitely be on the acid side. Although they will not tolerate wet feet, rhododendrons need a steady supply of moisture. Watering during prolonged summer dryness is a must. A coarse organic mulch (bark, oak leaves, rotted wood chips, etc.) is highly desirable; it will conserve soil and moisture and insulate the shallow root systems against extremes of heat and cold.

A partially shaded location is best for large-leafed rhododendrons, while the smaller-leafed kinds and azaleas not only tolerate full exposure but bloom more profusely because of it.

Getting to know the many diverse members of this genus through books and catalogs is a pleasure in itself, but the real joy comes from actually growing them and finding the ideal location for each in your garden.

—Dick Brooks

The plant count cited in each profile is based on information in the most recent catalog provided by the source. In this section, shipping season is for rhododendron, azaleas, and mountain laurel only. A selection of books about rhododendrons, azaleas, and kalmias appears after the last listing.

QUICK FIND
The following sources are listed in this section:

APPALACHIAN GARDENS
1985
Tom McCloud
Catalog: $2, 38 pp., illustrations
This Wayne, Pennsylvania, nursery offers forty species and hybrid evergreen and deciduous azaleas (including Robin Hill's cultivars), rhododendrons, and mountain laurel. Information for azaleas includes color, bloom size, form, season of bloom, and growth habit. Descriptions of rhododendrons and kalmias include common name, height, spread, shape, flower color and prominence, fruit, and foliage. Shape (shown in silhouette for each listing), habit, site preference, and required care are well detailed; natives are highlighted. Stock is characterized as well established, two years or older, started from cuttings or seeds. Guarantees true to name and safe arrival; will replace or issue refund or credit. See **Conifers, Trees.**
Shipping season: March through December. Bareroot (dormant), December through February.

BRIARWOOD GARDENS
1980
Kevin Shinn
Catalog: $2, 10 pp.
Briarwood Gardens positions itself as the largest specialized rhododendron nursery in New England. The nursery grew out of plans to propagate the distinctive cultivars of Charles Dexter from nearby Heritage Plantation (formerly the Dexter Estate) in Sandwich, Massachusetts. Briarwood works with the Heritage collection to offer over one hundred Dexter hybrids and other named varieties of proven merit, promising cultivars created by local hybridizers, the work of Jack Cowles, and introductions from their own breeding program. Most of Briarwood's plants are propagated and field grown at the nursery. Descriptions include name of hybridizer, color and shape of flower, nature of leaves, growth habit, minimum temperature to which a plant is hardy, height after ten years, season of bloom, and size of plants available. Guarantees true to name and safe arrival; will replace or issue refund within thirty days of receipt. See Trees.
Shipping Season: April through June. Canada

BROKEN ARROW NURSERY
1984
Richard A. Jaynes
Catalog: $2, 8 pp. Current price list: LSASE

Dr. Jaynes is the author of *Kalmia: The Laurel Book II.* His list includes thirty mountain laurel, one hundred hybrid and species rhododendrons and azaleas, and 150 other trees and shrubs. The majority of the kalmias offered have been selected and named by Dr. Jaynes including: 'Bridesmaid', 'Elf', 'Minuet', 'Pinwheel', 'Snowdrift', and 'Yankee Doodle'. Naturalizing grade mountain laurel are available at lower prices. Compact descriptions include color, growth habit, size and characteristics of foliage, hybridizer, and size of plants available by mail order. Rhododendrons and kalmias from Broken Arrow are generally branched, two-year, four- to ten-inch specimens that have overwintered once in outdoor beds (zone 6), and are shipped with their root balls intact. See Trees.
Shipping season: April and May. October and November.
No Arizona or California.

CAPE COD VIREYAS
1988
Richard Chaikin
Catalog: $3, 12 pp.
Dr. Chaikin offers one hundred named Vireya rhododendrons from Australia, Borneo, New Zealand, Papua New Guinea, and Sumatra. These tropicals, grown in containers, are available primarily as rooted cuttings and one-year plants. Enthusiastic descriptions include parentage, color of flower, growth habit, and season of bloom. See Trees.
Shipping season: March through October.
Canada, Mexico, International

CARLSON'S GARDENS
Bob Carlson
Circa 1975
Catalog: $3, 52 pp.
A two-year subscription to Mr. Carlson's chatty (and poetic) catalog will also find you intermittently receiving what he describes as cue cards sporting color photographs (and original verse) of selected specimens from among the two thousand varieties he grows in South Salem, New York. Mr. Carlson's catalog of northern-grown and -acclimated rhododendrons, azaleas, and *Kalmia latifolia* includes nursery-propagated natives, Knaphill-Exbury crosses, evergreen varieties developed by Robin Hill, Gartrell, Northern Tisbury, Glenn Dale, Joseph Gable, Mr. Carlson, and summer-blooming 'Postscript' azaleas. Rhododendrons

include small-leafed types propagated by Mezitt and Gable & Nearing, and large-leafed plants from numerous propagators including Dexter hybrids. Descriptions include hybridizer, color and form of flower and foliage, season of bloom, and the size of plants offered. A cross-reference to Carlson's photographs is noted where appropriate. Guarantees safe arrival. See Trees.

Shipping season: March through November.

No California

EASTERN PLANT SPECIALTIES
1985
Mark Stavish

Catalog: $3 (recoverable), 28 pp., illustrations

Mr. Stavish's New England–hardy, Maine-grown offerings include seventy-five hybrid and species rhododendrons, thirty evergreen and deciduous azaleas, and fifteen kalmias. Recent catalogs highlighted Dexter hybrids 'Janet Blair', 'Parker's Pink', and David Leach's 'Tow Head', species rhododendrons *Dauricum alba* and *Hippophaeiodes*, evergreen azaleas *kiusianum* var. *album* and 'Linda Stuart', the deciduous *Rhodora canadense* and *canadense* var. *alba*, and Vaseyi 'White Find', and *Kalmia poliifolia* (bog laurel). Descriptions include bud hardiness, color, season of bloom, height after eight to ten years, parentage, and age and size of plants being offered. A sidebar groups rhododendrons that are most cold hardy, heat tolerant, cool summer tolerant, and noteworthy for their attractive foliage. An index with cross-references denotes light preference, tolerance to wet or dry soil, fragrance, and autumn color. See **Conifers, Fruit,** Perennials, **Trees, Wildflowers.**

Shipping season: March through June. September through November.

ERICACEAE
Matt Zack

Catalog: Free, 4 pp.

Mr. Zack grows ericaceous plants that are well suited for the Northeast coast. He specializes in rhododendrons developed by Dr. David C. Leach, characterized as well-branched two- and three-year plants (approximately eight to ten inches high) grown in six-inch containers under drip irrigation. Mr. Zack also offers the kalmia of Dr. Richard A. Jaynes as two-year, six- to ten-inch plants grown under the same conditions. Descriptions of Leach cultivars are rich and precise, including parentage, height at

maturity, minimum temperature at which they are hardy, form and habit, character of foliage, color of flowers, number of flowers per truss, and season of bloom. Descriptions of Dr. Jayne's kalmias include color of flower, whether it is a dwarf or a full-size plant, and hardiness zone for some. A brief selection of *Calluna vulgaris* is also represented. See Trees.

Shipping season: March through June. August through November.

Canada, Mexico, International

FAIRWEATHER GARDENS
1989
Robert Hoffman and Robert Popham

Catalog: $3, 60 pp., illustrations, black-and-white and color photographs

Messrs. Hoffman and Popham offer plants that they characterize as having significant merit, shipped in sizes that usually allow for immediate placement in your garden. They offer ten deciduous azaleas, and a selection of Aromi hybrids that are the result of breeding English Exbury stock with heat-resistant North American natives. Also offer eight *Kalmia latifolia* that are appropriate for zones 5 through 8. Descriptions include cultural information, color of flower, growth habit, and height of specimens available for shipping. Guarantees safe arrival. See **Conifers,** Fruit, **Trees.**

Shipping season: March and April. September through November.

Shorter shipping season to Arizona, California, Idaho, Minnesota, Nevada, Oregon, Utah, and Washington.

Canada

FRED & JEAN MINCH
Circa 1970
Fred and Jean Minch

Catalog: Free, 5 pp. Seed list: 5 pp.

Fred Minch is a prizewinning hybridizer of rhododendrons and deciduous azaleas. Jean is a prizewinning photographer of plants and the self-described assistant weeder and head bookkeeper at their nursery. Together the Minchs live amid over 150,000 plants on three acres in Puyallup, Washington. Although not everything that grows on the Minch's property is for sale by mail, they do offer 520 azalea and rhododendron seedlings, including 'Yakushimanum' and their hybrids, species rhododendrons and azaleas, and deciduous azaleas. Seedlings are listed by name and, where appropriate, by cross. A separate list of 450 varieties of rhododendron and azalea seeds, sold fifty seeds to the packet, is also available. See Seeds, Trees.

Shipping season: All year.

GIRARD NURSERIES
1944
Peter Girard, Jr.
Catalog: Free, 23 pp., color photographs
Girard grows and breeds azaleas and rhododendrons, flowering shrubs and trees, ornamental and shade trees, broadleaf evergreens, and conifers. Offers Girard® evergreen azaleas, hardy deciduous, Korean, and *Schlippenbachii* (native to Korea and Manchuria) azaleas, English Exbury and Naphill hybrid seedlings, hardy North American native rhododendrons, hybrid seedlings from named and unnamed varieties, and Girard® rhododendron cultivars. Rich descriptions include common and botanical names, growth habit, form, foliage habit and color, and landscaping and garden uses. Provides extensive cultural information, and offers numerous collections. Ships potted plants. Also offers seed packets for twenty-five types of azaleas and rhododendrons. Guarantees safe arrival; will replace stock lost to extreme heat or cold (or possibly customer neglect or lack of experience) for half the purchase price if a claim is made within thirty days of receipt. See **Conifers**, Grasses, **Seeds**, Trees.

Shipping season: Mid-March through June. September to first frost.

THE GREENERY
1964
Lynn and Marilyn Wats
Catalog: $2, 21 pp.
The Watses list 325 species rhododendrons and 175 hybrids. Information for each offering includes botanical name (parentage for hybrids), method of propagation, foliage habit, color of flower, foliage color and/or texture where it represents a particularly desirable characteristic, season of bloom, minimum temperature to which a variety is hardy, and relative height expressed as dwarf, low, medium, and tall. Plants are offered in steps at between one to two inches in height through fifteen to eighteen inches. The Watses suggest that you inquire about current pricing and stock levels to determine if the size that you require is available. The Greenery brokerage service will locate and acquire landscape-size plants on your behalf. Guarantees true to name, healthy, and well rooted. See Trees.

Shipping season: March through June. September and November. Will ship at other times at customer's risk.

GREER GARDENS
1955
Harold E. Greer
Catalog: $3, 148 pp., illustrations and color photographs
A specialist in rhododendrons and azaleas, Mr. Greer over time has expanded to include twenty-five hundred ornamental trees, shrubs, fruit-bearing plants, plants for the rock garden, perennials, ground covers, ornamental grasses, bamboo, and bonsai specimens, as well as books and videotapes. His offerings include 100 deciduous and 120 evergreen azaleas, 400 hybrid and 120 rhododendron species. Recent offerings include 'Apple Tree Pink', 'Debutante', 'Yellow Mollis', 'Kazan', 'Renee Michelle', 'Extraordinaire', 'Hachmann's Polaris', 'Ingrid Melquist', 'Red Delicious', and 'Vincent Van Gogh'. Greer's descriptions include common name, hardiness zone, color and texture of foliage and bark, use in the garden, annual growth, and height of plant at shipment and at maturity. Cultural tips and growing hints for rhododendrons and azaleas include soil conditioning, watering, sun/shade preferences, fertilization, pest and disease prevention and control, planting procedures, and a straightforward discussion about hardiness. A cross-referenced list highlights those offerings that have a pleasing fragrance, exceptional color, thrive in the shade, or are obnoxious to deer. A feature in the Greer catalog is the "Frugal-dendron" and "Frugal azalea" lists, selected varieties (six to ten inches) offered at reduced prices. Guarantees quality stock, true to name, and safe arrival; will replace plants one time only that have been properly cared for but do not survive. See **Booksellers, Conifers**, Fruit, **Grasses**, **Peonies**, Perennials, **Trees**.

Shipping season: All year (recommends September through May).
Canada, Mexico, International

HAMMOND'S ACRES OF RHODYS
1976
Dave and Joan Hammond
Catalog: $2, 32 pp.
The Hammonds offer 680 hybrid, and 80 species rhododendrons from their collection of 3,000 varieties acquired from worldwide sources. Information given includes parentage, season of bloom, ARS rating, lowest tempera-

ture a plant can withstand with minimal damage, and expected height in ten years. Descriptions include color of flowers, color and shape of leaves, and notable characteristics and tolerances. Plants are variously one- through six-year plants from three to six inches through thirty to thirty-six inches. The Hammond's catalog includes a brief list of deciduous and evergreen azaleas and *Kalmia latifolia*. See Trees.
Shipping season: Spring and fall.

HERONSWOOD NURSERY LTD.
1987
Daniel Hinkley and Robert L. Jones
Catalog: $4, 220 pp.
Heronswood characterizes its mission as procuring and offering plant materials that have not previously been available to North American gardeners. Mr. Hinkley (author of *Winter Ornamentals*) and Mr. Jones list over two thousand trees, shrubs, perennials, and grasses. Their rhododendron list includes cultivars from the 'Northern Lights' series among their thirty offerings. Descriptions include provenance, hardiness zone, pot size, growth habit, color, and height at maturity. Guarantees true to name and healthy upon departure; will accept claims filed within ten days of receipt. See **Conifers**, Fruit, **Grasses**, **Perennials**, **Trees**.
Shipping season: March through mid-May.
Mid-September through October.
Canada

KELLEYGREEN RHODODENDRON NURSERY
1979
Jan D. Kelley
Catalog: $2, 28 pp., 30 color photographs
The Kelleys assumed the stewardship of Hall's Rhododendrons in the late 1980s. Their catalog includes 460 hybrid and 300 species rhododendrons and 100 evergreen and deciduous azaleas. Kelleygreen also offers thirty container-grown rhododendron giants (at least thirty inches in diameter) organized by color. Information includes parentage, height after ten years, hardiness rating, season of bloom, and ARS quality ratings for the beauty of flower and the habit of the plant. Descriptions include color and characteristics of flower, growth habit, number of flowers on each truss and (for some) scent, and age (variously two, three, four, and five years) of plants that are being offered. Sidebars highlight

Kelley's ten favorites (characterized as having excellent flowers, foliage, and form), thirteen easy-to-grow varieties for novices living in the East, and a similar number for those in the West. Varieties that have been consistent performers within seven geographical regions are identified. The "Tried 'n' True Something New" section offers favorite standard rhododendrons in multiples of five plants at reduced prices. Guarantees satisfaction. See Trees.
Shipping season: September through June.
Canada, Mexico, International

MATTERHORN NURSERY, INC.
1981
Matt and Ronnie Horn
Catalog: $5, 102 pp., illustrations
Among the 250 shrubs listed by the Horns are 66 named azaleas, evergreen and deciduous) and 50 rhododendron cultivars. Plants listed alphabetically by name. Descriptions include foliage and growth habit, suggestions for landscape use, light and soil preferences, and a range of height at maturity. Guarantees true to name. See **Conifers**, Grasses, Perennials, **Trees**, **Waterscapes**.
Shipping season: Please inquire.

PEN Y BRYN NURSERY
1946
Catalog: $2.95, 58 pp., illustrations
Among the two hundred specimens suitable for bonsai culture, Pen Y Bryn offers forty *Kaempferi, kiusianum, kurume,* and *satsuki* azaleas. Consistently formatted descriptions include name of cultivar, size and color of flower, growth habit, hardiness zone, age of plant, current height, and size of container. See **Booksellers**, Conifers, **Supplies**, **Trees**.
Shipping season: April through mid-December.

ROSLYN NURSERY
1984
Dr. Philip Waldman
Catalog: $3, 76 pp., color photographs
Dr. Waldman and his staff hybridize and cultivate rhododendrons and azaleas among their two thousand varieties of conifers, trees, shrubs, perennials, and grasses. The catalog includes 235 elepidotes (large-leafed), 50 lepidote (small-leafed) types, and 80 species rhododendrons. The azalea selection includes 100 evergreen and 48 deciduous varieties. Information

in these sections of the catalog (which differ in presentation from those for other plants) uniformly includes parentage, ARS hardiness ratings, bloom time, and height after ten years. Descriptions include foliage habit, intimate characterizations of flower's color and nature, and intermittent comments about awards, growth habit, and sun and site preferences. A section of "Woody Plants for Special Uses" lists rhododendrons that are superhardy, heat tolerant, accept wet or shady situations, fragrant, and have very attractive foliage. Among the sixty-five titles on Roslyn's book list are several about rhododendron and azaleas. Guarantees true to name and healthy; will replace or issue credit if plant fails within thirty days of receipt. See Booksellers, **Conifers**, Perennials, **Trees**. **Shipping season: April through June. September through November. Bareroot to Arizona and California only during one week in mid-March.**
Canada, Mexico, International

A SANDY RHODODENDRON
1989
Christopher J. Hoffman
Catalog: $2, 40 pp. Seasonal supplements include color photographs
Mr. Hoffman grows three hundred species and three hundred hybrid rhododendrons that he characterizes as most rare and sought after. Listings include bud hardiness to low temperature, height in ten years, season of bloom, hybridizer, a point system rating flower, foliage, and plant performance for species only, and a narrative describing foliage, habit, and color and nature of bloom for varietal types. The main catalog features a list of plants for zones 4 and 5 and selections with "best" characteristics, such as best pinks, blues, blotches, flower structure, indumentum, as well as largest leaves, easiest and hardest to grow, etc., without consideration of climate zone. Informally written advice on planting sites, soil requirements, fertilization, pruning, deadheading, pests and diseases, and reference reading is included. Guarantees true to name and disease and pest free. See Trees.
Shipping season: All year.
Canada, International

SCHILD AZALEA GARDENS AND NURSERY
1988
Joseph E. Schild
Catalog: $1 (recoverable), 12 pp.

Offers sixty nursery-propagated U.S. natives, Asian species, and hybrid deciduous azaleas, species rhododendron, and *Kalmia latifolia*. Rich descriptions of foliage and flower shape, form, and habit are complemented by consistent shorthand notations for hardiness zone, height in ten years, season of bloom, and size of plants being offered. Mr. Schild's "Breeder's Corner" is a list of his own crosses between species and hybrid rhododendrons, and between species and species rhododendrons. Guarantees true to name and satisfaction for one year; will issue refund. See Trees.
Shipping season: Mid-September through May.

SHEPHERD HILL FARM
1985
Gerry Bleyer
Catalog: Free, 56 pp.
Shepherd Hill Farm grows rhododendrons, azaleas, conifers, and Japanese maple. Eighty percent of their catalog is devoted to plants in the azalea family. Recent catalogs included one hundred large-leafed rhododendrons (with emphasis on the cultivars of Charles Dexter, Joseph Gable, and David Leach), twenty Yakushimanum and Yakushimanum hybrids, fifty small-leafed rhodies (predominantly species and Mezitt hybrids), twenty-eight evergreen azaleas (including those bred by Girard, Glenn Dale, Robin Hill, and North Tisbury), and a brief offering of deciduous azaleas native to the eastern United States. Descriptions include height after ten years, minimum temperature before floral buds damaged, season of bloom, hybridizer, color and texture of flowers, shape and texture of foliage, plant's habit, and current size. Guarantees true to name and satisfactory arrival. See Conifers, Trees.
Shipping season: All year.
No Arizona, California, Oregon, or Washington.

VAN VEEN NURSERY
1926
Ted Van Veen
Catalog: $5 (recoverable), 15 pp. Price list: Free
Van Veen Nursery is a wholesale grower of rhododendrons that as a courtesy will fill retail orders for ARS members. Rhododendrons were introduced to the nursery in 1930 by Theodore Van Veen, Sr., a pioneer in the technique of growing them on their own roots. Van Veen

currently offers four hundred field-grown rhododendrons of which 20 percent are species. Hybrids, organized by color and described by name, ARS hardiness rating, and current size, are primarily the work of Charles Dexter, Joseph Gable, David Leach, Halfdan Lem, Tony Shammarello, Theodore Van Veen, and William Whitney. Guarantees true to name and satisfaction. See **Booksellers**, Trees.

Shipping season: Juniors, June. Yearlings, October through April. Budded plants, please inquire.
Canada

WASHINGTON EVERGREEN NURSERY
1980
Jordan Jack
Catalog: $2, 36 pp.
Washington Evergreen Nursery is really located in Leicester, North Carolina, the only confusing item in this otherwise well-organized catalog that includes seventeen kalmia, including dwarf *Kalmia angustifolia* (sheep laurel), and *Kalmia myrtifolia* 'Elf', 'Minuet', and 'Tiddlywinks'. Descriptions include foliage and flower color and texture. Guarantees true to name and safe arrival; must notify within ten days if plant is mislabeled or arrives in unsatisfactory condition. See **Conifers**, Trees.

Shipping season: April through June. September and October. Prefers to ship to southern states in April and October.
No California
Canada, International

WHITNEY GARDENS & NURSERY
1955
Anne Sather
Catalog: $4 (recoverable), 75 pp., color photographs
Whitney Gardens & Nursery sprawls over a seven-acre site in Brinnon, Washington. Lush photographs and an enticing map of bloom times at the nursery may be as close as you get to Brinnon, but the catalog goes a long way toward making you feel that you are there and, of course, can have a little (or a lot) of what's there sent to you. Recent catalogs included four hundred hybrid rhododendrons, ninety deciduous azaleas (with a strong representation of cultivars from Arneson, Exbury, Ghent, Knap Hill, and the University of Minnesota), one hundred evergreen azaleas (from a diverse group of breeders), twenty-two *Kalmia latifolia*, one hundred rhododendron species (primarily from China, Nepal, Tibet, and Japan), and two hundred Yakushimanum hybrids. Information for hybrids includes sun and shade requirements, height in ten years, season of bloom, color of flower, parentage, and hardiness. Narratives describe plant's habit, form of flower, hybridizer, and size of plants being offered. Description of species substitutes notes about place of origin (when known) for propagator. Descriptions and specifications for mountain laurel are less detailed than for other offerings. Guarantees true to name and healthy. See Trees.

Shipping season: All year. September through April preferred.
Canada, International

Selected Reading About Rhododendrons, Azaleas, and Kalmias

Azaleas, by Fred C. Galle. Considered by many plantsmen to be the definitive reference work about azaleas. Covers 6,000 species and cultivars. Black-and-white photographs, color photographs, and line drawings.

The Book of Rhododendrons, by Marianna Kneller. Experts write about their favorite species to the visual accompaniment of paintings by the artist-in-residence at Exbury Gardens. Ms. Kneller's paintings explore the detail of a flowering branch, bud, flower division, new leaf growth, and seedhead.

Cox's Guide to Choosing Rhododendrons, by Peter A. Cox and Kenneth N. E. Cox. Recommends the "best" rhododendrons and azaleas for planting in moderate-climate gardens. Provides cultural information and suggests varieties with a range of favored characteristics. Profiles one hundred species and two hundred hybrid rhododendrons and numerous deciduous and evergreen azaleas. Color photographs.

Kalmia: The Laurel Book II, by Richard A. Jaynes. A thorough reference work on the mountain laurel written by a most influential figure in his field. Color photographs.

Rhododendron Hybrids, by Homer E. Salley and Harold E. Greer. A guide to the parentage of registered hybrids. Includes all new registrations from 1985 through 1992. This updated edition of a previous work contains all-new color photographs.

The Rhododendron Species (in four volumes), by H. H. Davidian.
>   *Volume I: Lepidotes*
>   *Volume I: Elepidotes (Arboreum–Lacteum)*
>   *Volume II: Elepidotes (Neriiflorum–Thomsonii, Azaleastrum and Camtschaticum)*
>   *Volume IV: Azaleas*
The major taxonomic treatment of the genus including historical background and meticulous descriptions of the species growing in cultivation and the wild. Color photographs.

Success With Rhododendrons and Azaleas, by H. Edward Reilly. A hands-on practical work offering detailed information pertaining to site selection, landscape design, planting, and care. Color and black-and-white photographs.

Vireya Rhododendrons, by J. Clyde Smith. An appreciation and reference work (published by The Australian Rhododendron Society) of Vireyas. Includes a comprehensive list of species and cultivars, propagation techniques and tips, and pest and disease identification and control. Color photographs and black-and-white drawings.

Roses

*A*fter years of confinement in secluded cutting gardens, roses have reemerged as a plant that can answer nearly every landscaping need. Thanks to the efforts of contemporary rose breeders, the hybrid tea no longer arrives on a gaunt, spindly plant, and several new developments provide interest for those whose taste in roses is not limited to the classic, high-centered form of the hybrid tea. Specialist nurseries provide a full range of the latest rose introductions as well as hundreds of resurrected old garden roses.

Miniature roses make useful pot plants, and low-growing varieties (such as 'Beauty Secret' and 'Spice Drop') are ideal window box specimens. Be sure to study catalogs closely, however: while producing petite flowers, many miniature rose plants can grow more vigorously than one might expect, especially when planted in the same beds as larger roses. Miniature roses do not benefit from the same rich diet of plant food generally offered to hybrid teas.

Climbing miniatures, such as 'Jeanne Lajoie' and 'Laura Ford', are excellent for covering privacy fences in town house and condominium gardens and in other settings where the need is for vertical interest in a limited space.

With a growth habit between that of the traditional miniature rose and that of the floribunda, the patio rose is not restricted to container culture. Many of these roses—including my favorites, 'Hakuun' and 'Regensberg'—make excellent foundation planting and can be thought of as replacements for the ubiquitous geranium.

Floribunda roses generally produce the greatest color impact in the garden and they are most effective when planted in groups of three or more. Some of the most exciting and trouble-free recent rose introductions have been floribundas, including 'Ainsley Dickson', 'Sexy Rexy', and 'Trumpeter'.

Today's new shrub roses, such as the Meidiland series, are often advertised as "low maintenance." And so they are compared to the more demanding hybrid tea. All require sunlight, regular watering, and good drainage, however, and will do best if planted where air circulation is good and root competition from trees and more vigorous shrubs is at a minimum. These shrub roses are generally the best choices for those who want to grow roses without the aid of chemical pesticides.

Northern gardeners have welcomed the series of "Explorer" roses bred by the Canadian Department of Agriculture. Including shrubs and a few modest climbers, and limited so far to varieties in the pink and red color range, the series has literally taken modern roses where they have not grown before.

David Austin's English roses, combining the fragrance and form of old garden roses with the enhanced capacity for repeated blooming, have reintroduced many gardeners to roses. Some of the smaller Austins, such as 'Fair Bianca' and 'Wife of Bath', make excellent bedding plants, while the larger varieties, including 'Gertrude Jekyll' and 'The Countryman', are best when grown either as specimen plants or as part of the traditional shrub border.

Some of the largest ground-cover roses, such as 'Immensee' and 'White Immensee', can be planted on six-foot centers, providing low-maintenance and economical color over large areas. Less rampageous varieties of this rose are suitable for difficult sunny areas in smaller suburban gardens and can make an attractive, cascading accent when planted in a half barrel or other large container.

While most nurseries offer miniature roses only as own-root plants, and modern classifications such as floribundas and hybrid teas only as grafted specimens, old garden roses are generally available either way, depending on the nursery you choose. One form is not superior to the other. Grafted plants will generally get off to a quicker start in your garden, while own-root plants may demonstrate more winter-hardiness in northern zones. Old garden roses such as gallicas that can sucker invasively may be best as grafted specimens.

Specialist nurseries offer a range of standard (or tree) roses far beyond what may be available locally. Standard roses can be very effective in the landscape when used judiciously. Rose varieties with a round, bush, or trailing habit make the most striking standards; those that grow bolt upright are generally less effective garden ornaments when budded as standards.

There are over eight thousand rose varieties in commerce today, and with a little research it should not be difficult to find the ones that are right for you.

—*Peter Schneider*

(Peter Schneider is the editor and compiler of *The Combined Rose List*, which aims to chronicle all known roses in commerce worldwide, and *The Akron Rose Rambler,* the newsletter of the Akron Rose Society.)

The number of roses cited in each profile is based on information in the most recent catalog provided by the source. In this section, shipping season is for roses only. A selection of books and videos about roses appears after the last listing.

QUICK FIND
The following sources are listed in this section:

THE AMERICAN ROSE SOCIETY
See **Horticultural Societies.**

THE ANTIQUE ROSE EMPORIUM
1983
G. Michael Shoup
Catalog: $5, 80 pp., color photographs
Mr. Shoup is a charter member of the Texas Rose Rustlers, coauthor (with Liz Druitt) of *Landscaping with Antique Roses,* and is passionate about the reintroduction of old garden roses. His catalog includes well-crafted essays on old garden and found roses, culture, bed preparation, planting, mulching, watering, training, and feeding. A selection of 320 varieties, grown on their own roots, are organized as follows: found roses, species, old European, China, Noisette, Bourbon, tea, hybrid perpetual, early hybrid tea, polyantha and floribunda, rugosa, shrub, hybrid musk, climbing, and rambling. Rich narrative descriptions for each offering are completed by shorthand notations indicating approximate height at maturity, hardiness zone, bloom time, fragrance, hip display, and color of flower. Includes year of introduction when known. Ships bareroot during dormancy. Active roses shipped in two-gallon containers. Guarantees true to name; will refund money or replace plant one time only for up to three months after receipt. See **Booksellers,** Heirlooms.
Shipping season: Bareroot, December through February. Container, March through May
Canada, International

ARENA ROSE COMPANY
1991
John and Sylvester Arena
Catalog: $5, 32 pp., color photographs
This father-and-son team began their venture as propagators of antique roses. They have expanded their offering of 120 varieties to include over 60 English (which they believe to be the most extensive offering of field-grown English roses in the United States) and 60 exhibition roses. Their exuberant and beautiful catalog includes an extensive introduction to antique roses and their classification. Included among the varieties offered: damask, China, moss, Portland,

Bourbon, hybrid perpetual, tea, Noisette, hybrid musk, early floribundas, and species and hybrid rugosas. A thorough description of each offering includes year of introduction, color of flower, height and spread at maturity, a description of the plant's form, parentage, and suggestions for care and placement. See Heirlooms.

Shipping season: December through April.

BLOSSOMS & BLOOMERS
1988
Geraldine Krueger
Catalog: $1, 12 pp.

Ms. Kreuger describes the location of her nursery and two-acre display garden in the foothills of the Rockies as being in serious winter country. The constant loss of her own hybrids due to the effects of cold weather led her to try old garden roses. She now grows over three hundred varieties, most of which were introduced prior to 1900. The Blossoms & Bloomers catalog lists sixty varieties of first-year rooted cuttings. Information for each offering includes year of introduction, height at maturity, a narrative description of the plant's form and fragrance, and the color of its flowers. Guarantees true to name and healthy. See Heirlooms.

Shipping season: April and May.
No Hawaii

BRIDGES ROSES
1982
Dennis A. Bridges
Catalog: Free, 10 pp, color photographs

Bridges offers one hundred miniature roses developed by a select group of hybridizers. A substantial number of their offerings are ARS Award of Excellence winners and All America Rose Selections. There are twenty hybrid teas and grandifloras in the catalog. Includes hybridizer, description of the plant and its flowers, and size range expressed as short (twelve inches or less), medium (twelve to twenty-four inches), or tall (twenty-four to thirty-six inches). Miniatures shipped in three-inch pots. Hybrid teas and grandifloras are one-year own-root roses.

Shipping season: Hybrid tea roses, spring, after last frost. Miniatures, all year

BUTNER'S OLD MILL NURSERY
1953
Charles E. Amtil
Catalog: Free, 5 pp.

Mr. Amtil lists 150 hybrid teas, floribundas,

grandifloras, climbers, and shrubs. Two-year-old field-grown plants are listed by name, American Nurseryman's standard grade point, and color. Ships bareroot. Guarantees roses will grow and bloom in your garden; if they do not leaf out or die by October 1, a replacement will be sent to you the following spring.

Shipping season: Spring.

CARLTON ROSE NURSERIES
1938
Jerry Strahle
Catalog: Free, 6 pp., color photographs

The Strahles, fourth-generation rose growers, specialize in developing and producing rosebushes that commercial greenhouses resell to florists as fresh-cut flowers. They offer eight of their patented varieties to home gardeners. Plants are one-year field grown. Brief, colorful descriptions for each offering. According to Jerry Strahle, these plants require no more care than other roses of their classification. Guarantees plants will grow and bloom in your garden.

Shipping season: January through June.

CARROLL GARDENS
1933
Alan L. Summers
Catalog: $3 (recoverable), 108 pp.

Carroll Gardens, in Westminster, Maryland, devotes 70 percent of its catalog to perennials, 20 percent to woody plants, and just under 10 percent to one of its long-standing specialties, roses. Offers 220 varieties organized as old and new hybrid teas and grandifloras, landscape roses (patio, floribunda, shrub, rugosa hybrid, and old garden), David Austin's English roses, and climbing and pillar roses. Descriptions include color and form of flower, notable fragrance, nature of foliage, growth habit, and height at maturity. Ships roses bareroot. Guarantees true to name, ready to grow, and safe arrival (California, Oregon, and Washington, trueness to name only); will replace one time only any plant that after flowering is determined not to be true to name. See **Daylilies, Herbs, Hosta, Iris, Peonies, Perennials, Trees.**

Shipping season: March through November.
Canada

DONOVAN'S ROSES
1983
Tom and Kathy Schimschock
Catalog: Free, 3 pp.

Donovan's is the retail outlet for Cooperative Rose Growers. Their list includes eighty hybrid tea, grandiflora, floribunda, shrub, and climbing roses. New and recent introductions include a bevy of AARS prizewinners and world-class varieties. A description of the flower's form, color, and the nature of its fragrance is provided for all varieties. Ships bareroot.
Shipping season: January through April.

EDMUNDS' ROSES
1949
Kathy and Phil Edmunds
Catalog: Free, 20 pp., color photographs
Fred Edmunds, Sr., was the curator of the Washington Park Rose Test Gardens in Portland, Oregon. Fred Jr. leased forty acres in Wilsonville and started growing roses. The nursery was moved to its present site in 1961. Fred's son Phil and daughter-in-law Kathy assumed the stewardship of the nursery in 1992. Edmunds' specializes in modern garden roses and European and exhibition varieties and many of their offerings are AARS prizewinners. They offer 120 hybrid teas, floribundas, grandifloras, and climbers. Rich narrative description, height at maturity, nature of fragrance, hybridizer, and year of introduction are provided for all roses. Ships bareroot, two-year, field-grown plants. Guarantees true to name and will grow and bloom the first spring after receipt. Guarantee waived on fall shipments. See **Supplies.**
Shipping season: November through May.
Canada, Mexico, International

FLOWERS N' FRIENDS MINIATURE ROSES
Dick and Kathy Gruenbauer
Catalog: Free, 10 pp., color photographs
The Gruenbauers' catalog of 120 hardy hybrids is organized into miniature, microminiature, miniature tree, and climbing miniatures. Descriptions include hybridizer, color of flower, size range (short, medium, tall, extra tall), and recommended placement. Ships in $3^1/2$-inch containers. These roses are dormant or semidormant from November through March. Guarantees satisfaction during the first growing season if planted outdoors; will replace or issue refund.
Shipping season: All year.

FORESTFARM®
1974
Ray and Peg Pragg

Catalog $3, 414 pp., illustrations and black-and-white photographs
Yes, the Praggs' catalog really is 414 pages (plus or minus in a given year) and contains four thousand plants. They offer thirty-five roses. Descriptions in the catalog are standardized to include the following: genus, species, variety, common name, leaf retention, hardiness zone, origin, plant uses, cultural conditions, and a few words of commentary. Ships in small tubes and in one- and five-gallon containers, depending on variety and availability. Guarantees true to name. See **Conifers, Fruit, Grasses, Perennials, Trees.**
Shipping season: All year.
Canada

GILES RAMBLIN' ROSES
1983
James and Mary Giles
Catalog: LSASE, 4 pp.
The Gileses' list includes 260 offerings, primarily hybrid teas, floribundas, and old garden roses. Notes name of variety and color. Ships bareroot. See **Heirlooms.**
Shipping season: March through May.
September through November.
No California

GREENMANTLE NURSERY
1983
Ram and Marissa Fishman
Catalog: $3, 28 pp. Rose list: LSASE, 4 pp.
Greenmantle Nursery is a husband-and-wife enterprise that began as an outgrowth of their respective horticultural interests. The Fishmans grow plants organically without chemical fertilizers or pesticides. The rose collection includes over three hundred different varieties chosen to represent the diversity of the genus *Rosa*. The rose list has 165 classic and modern roses (without descriptions), including numerous rare species, under the following classifications: sweet briers, species, rugosas, gallicas, damasks, Albas, centifolias, mosses, Bourbons, hybrid perpetuals, rambling, bedding, Chinas, teas, hybrid musks, and shrubs. There are sixty varieties, described with passion, in the main catalog. Many roses are useful for potpourri gathering and rose hip harvests. Own-root roses are shipped with a wrapped root ball; budded plants are shipped bareroot. Guarantees true to name, healthy, viable, and safe arrival; return unsatisfactory plants immediately. See **Fruit,** Heirlooms, Organics, Trees.
Shipping season: January through March.

HARDY ROSES FOR THE NORTH
1991
Barry Poppenheim
Catalog: $3 (recoverable), 72 pp., color photographs
Offers 160 roses, including: the "Explorer" series that combines extreme hardiness with long repeat blooming periods and resistance to mildew and blackspot; the "Parkland" series, a hardy shrub developed for the prairies and similar climates; David Austin's English roses; and selected old garden and miniature roses. Mr. Poppenheim's fully realized descriptions give special attention to hardiness, disease resistance, the habit of individual varieties, and their most advantageous placement and use. Hybridizer, year of introduction, height at maturity, and color and form of flower noted for all offerings. Ships own-root roses in quart pots. Plants that cannot be shipped to U.S. customers from this Canadian source are clearly indicated in the catalog. Guarantees stock for the first five weeks in your garden; will replace.
Shipping season: March through October.
Canada

HEIRLOOM OLD GARDEN ROSES
1986
John and Louise Clements
Catalog: $5, 112 pp., color photographs
The Clementses' catalog offers 650 of the thousand types of roses grown at Heirloom Old Garden Roses. The catalog is organized into thirty classifications that include: Alba, Bourbon, China, damask, English, ground cover, hand painted, American and Canadian hardy, large-flowered climbers, Noisettes, Portland, rambling, species, tree, and miniature varieties. Narrative descriptions are full of historical tidbits and cultural information, as well as habit, flower color, height at maturity, and year of introduction or provenance. Grows own-root roses shipped in six-inch pots. Ships dormant in the winter, leafed out during all other seasons. Guarantees true to name and safe arrival. See **Booksellers**, Heirlooms.
Shipping season: All year.

HERITAGE ROSE GARDENS
1982
Virginia Hopper and Joyce Demits
Catalog: $2, 18 pp.
According to sisters Virginia Hopper and Joyce Demits, they opened their nursery to offer old-fashioned, rare, and species roses nationally (mail order) before these roses underwent their current renaissance. Ms. Hopper and Ms. Demits are also active in the noncommercial preservation of old roses, having established an endowment fund for the Historical Rose Collection at the Mendocino Coast Botanical Gardens. Three hundred roses are described in the HRG catalog, including six species roses native to California. Some of the other classifications include: gallica, damask and perpetual damask, Alba, moss, China and hybrid China, tea, hybrid tea, climbing tea, rugosa, old and new shrubs, and floribunda. Descriptions focus on the color and form of the flower, and notes height at maturity. Indicates year of introduction or provenance when known. Ships two-year bareroot stock, most of which have been field grown. Guarantees live delivery west of the Rockies; guarantees same east of the Rockies only if second-day air service used. See Heirlooms.
Shipping season: January and February.
International

HIDDEN GARDEN NURSERY
1986
Wayne and Kathy Lauman
Catalog: LSASE, 10 pp.
The Laumans specialize in miniature roses, including numerous exhibition and award-winning varieties. They began their own hybridizing program in 1990 and now offer their cultivars for sale. Descriptions of seventy-five miniatures include hybridizer, approximate height, color of flower, awards, and tips on uses in the garden. They offer a discount to current members of rose societies.
Shipping season: March through October.

HISTORICAL ROSES
1983
Ernest J. Vash
Catalog: LSASE, 8 pp.
Sixty of the 120 varieties on the Historical Roses list are categorized as old-fashioned shrub and landscape plants. The balance of Mr. Vash's stock is composed of Dr. Griffith Buck's shrubs, hybrid perpetuals, floribundas, climbers, and hybrid teas. Brief descriptions provide classification, year of introduction, fragrance, and recurrent bloom. All of Mr. Vash's plants are two years old and field grown, budded on multiflora rootstock. See Heirlooms.
Shipping season: October through April.

HORTICO, INC.
Bill Vanderkruk
Rose catalog: $3, 42 pp., color photographs
Hortico is a nursery wholesaler whose specialties include roses. The catalog is clear but spare and geared toward the trade; however, Hortico invites retail orders by fax or mail. Seven hundred varieties are offered under the following classifications: David Austin's English, agriculture Canada (hardy "Explorer" and "Parkland"), hybrid teas, antique, and miniatures. Guarantees true to name and healthy when shipped. See **Grasses**, **Perennials**, Trees, Waterscapes.
Shipping season: November through May.
Canada

HOWERTOWN ROSE NURSERY
1949
Jane A. Schrantz
Catalog: Free, 10 pp.
Howertown offers modern varieties: one hundred hybrid teas, thirteen grandiflora, thirty-six floribunda, and sixteen climbers. Brief notes include color, fragrance, and whether the plant is patented. Requires that orders be placed by mid-October for shipment during the current year.
Shipping season: November.

INGRAHAM'S COTTAGE GARDEN
1989
Jill Ingraham and Alan Ingraham
Catalog: $1, 12 pp.
One third of Ingraham's list of ninety plants is made up of old garden roses from several classifications. Also offers modern hybrid teas, floribundas, David Austin's English roses, and a few climbers, ramblers, and scramblers. Description includes color and form of flower, occasional notations about height and habit, and year of introduction for most. Two-year, field-grown plants. Ships bareroot. See Heirlooms.
Shipping season: February and March.
International

JACKSON & PERKINS
1872
Robert Van Diest
Rose catalog: Free, 60 pp., color photographs
The area of high expertise here is modern hybrid teas, including many developed by Jackson & Perkins. A selection of David Austin's English, floribundas, rugosas, miniatures, hardy ('Morden'), antique, shrub, and tree roses round out the 120 offerings. Information includes height, color of flower, shape of buds, size of bloom, number of petals, texture of foliage, length of stems, and fragrance. Ships two-year, bareroot plants. Guarantees satisfaction; will replace or issue credit or refund if notified within sixty days. See Heirlooms, Perennials.
Canada

JUSTICE MINIATURE ROSES
1983
Jerry, June, and Tara Justice
Catalog: Free, 31 pp., color photographs
Two hundred and sixty miniatures are arranged alphabetically on separate lists. The plants with descriptions are more expensive than those that are only listed. Hybridizer and color are given for all plants. Plants shipped in full leaf or in bud, blooming from April through September.
Shipping season: March through October.
Canada

LOWE'S OWN-ROOT ROSES
Mike Lowe
Catalog: $2, 17 pp.
Lowe's specialty is custom growing historic roses on their own roots or on *canina* and multiflora understicks. Many of their one thousand varieties come from the collections of such distinguished rosarians and collectors as Peter Beales, David Austin, Wilhelm Kordes, Ellen and Hugo Lykke, Leonie Bell, and Karl Jones. A number of their species roses are obtained through the Arnold Arboretum in Boston. Grabbing a piece of rose history from Lowe's requires some planning on your part: orders must be placed prior to May of the current year for shipment in October and November of the following year. There are 250 varieties to choose from in their basic list; ordering from their full master list can be done only with large orders. Descriptions in their basic catalog for Alba, centifolia, China, damask, damask perpetual, eglanteria, gallica, rambler, species, and shrub roses list color and year of introduction. The descriptions of Bourbons, which they consider to be their strong suit, contain additional detail. See Heirlooms.
Shipping season: October and November.
Canada, International

McDaniel's Miniature Roses
1973
Carol L. Gladson
Catalog: Free, 2 pp.
One hundred and twenty miniature roses are organized by color, with half the list composed of pinks and reds. Description of flower form and color for all plants. Guarantees roses to be healthy when shipped; report damage within seven days.
Shipping season: All year.

Mendocino Heirloom Roses
1990
Alice Flores and Gail Daly
Catalog: $1, 32 pp.
The lumber town of Mendocino, where Ms. Flores and Ms. Daly live, saw great economic growth in the eighties (the 1880s, that is). Among the finer things that were brought to town were cultivated roses. The survivors from that time provided the plant material for the first cuttings these rosarians propagated. They specialize in own-root roses descended from varieties that predate the ascendancy of the hybrid teas. Their selection of 125 varieties favors species, very old found roses, old hybrids, hybrid musks, hybrid perpetuals, and ramblers. Descriptions are personal, thorough, richly textured in language, and make the reader feel already familiar with the variety he or she is about to order. No pesticides or fungicides are used at MHR. Ships bareroot. See Heirlooms, Organics.
Shipping season: December through March.
Canada

The Mini-Rose Garden
1983
Michael and Betty Williams, Valerie Jackson
Catalog: Free, 18 pp., color photographs
Did you know that 150 years ago miniature roses were called fairy roses? That the first mini introduced into the Western world came from Mauritius? This catalog offers these tidbits of mini-rose lore, as well as seventy-five modern varieties of miniature rose. Information for each cultivar includes hybridizer, color and form of flower, habit of plant, and ARS awards received. Ships in pots. Guarantees plants during first outdoor growing season, from planting to first frost; will replace or issue refund.
Shipping season: All year.

Nor' East Miniature Roses, Inc.
1970
Barbara Blackhall
Catalog: Free, 30 pp., color photographs
Fully describes eighty miniature introductions, including ARS prizewinners, and those from Nor' East's own hybridizing program. Lists an additional forty varieties that are either too recent to have undergone full evaluation or are being phased out. Nor' East lists twelve miniature tree roses that have been grafted onto eighteen- to twenty-inch understock. Ships in pots. Guarantees live arrival, true to name, and disease free; will replace plants that fail within ninety days of receipt.
Shipping season: All year.

Oregon Miniature Roses, Inc.
1974
Nick, Katie, and Ray Spooner
Catalog: Free, 16 pp., color photographs
The Spooners offer two hundred miniature varieties, including microminis, ground covers, climbers, moss, and shrubs. Hybridizer, color, height (expressed as small, medium, or tall), habit, appropriate uses, and awards received. Plants grown and shipped in four-inch pots.
Shipping season: All year.

Park Seed® Co.
See **Bulbs, Garlic, Herbs,** Peonies, **Seeds, Supplies,** Vegetables.

Pickering Nurseries
Catalog: $3, 64 pp., color photographs
Pickering offers seven hundred varieties of roses, of which many are very winter-hardy, having been grown in Pickering, Ontario. General notes about hardiness and disease resistance by classification: hybrid teas, grandifloras, floribundas, polyanthas, patio, hybrid perpetuals, climbers, David Austin's English, shrub, rugosa, and thirteen classes that generally fall under those that are considered antique or rare. Descriptions, including height, ARS rating, fragrance, and color, are brief by design. Color photographs of over 40 percent of their offerings fill much of the catalog. Ships two-year, bareroot plants. See Heirlooms.
Shipping season: March and April. October and November.
Canada, International

Roses & Wine
1992
Wayne and Barbara Procissi

Catalog: LSASE, 2 pp.

Ms. Procissi is a landscape architect who through her use of roses in her designs has come to the cultivation of roses for resale. Roses & Wine is developing a palette of old-fashioned roses that are characterized by repeat bloom, fragrance, and hardiness. Ms. Procissi is expanding her selection of trailing and semi-procumbent varieties for use as ground covers. One hundred and twenty roses are on her list. Description specifies classification and color. See Heirlooms.

Shipping season: January and February.

ROSES OF YESTERDAY AND TODAY
Circa 1935
Patricia Stemler Wiley and Kathryn Wiley Minier
Catalog: $3 (third-class mail), $5 (first-class), 76 pp., black-and-white photographs
Roses of Yesterday and Today has had its own share of yesterdays, having been known under three previous names: the Francis Lester Rose Gardens, Lester and Tillotson, and Will Tillotson's Roses of Yesterday & Today, from which Tillotson's name was dropped in 1978. Dorothy Stemler was the owner from 1957 to 1976. She died in 1976, leaving the business to Patricia Wiley, her daughter, who with Kathryn Wiley Minier, Patricia's daughter, shares stewardship today. Their signature cover, a bevy of their cut blooms with a translucent overlay (that lets you identify each variety shown), wraps this catalog of 320 old, rare, unusual, and modern roses. This is among the best-written and most thorough rose catalogs that you are likely to find. The history of roses and the development and discovery of various classifications acts as a springboard into the listings. Classification, year of introduction, height at maturity, season of bloom, history, descriptions of the flower and plant, and a generous sprinkling of comments from satisfied customers included. Ships dormant, bareroot plants. Guarantees true to name and healthy upon arrival; will replace plants that fail to grow through July 1 of the year received. See Heirlooms.

Shipping season: January through May.
Canada, International

ROSES UNLIMITED
1988
Bill Patterson
Catalog: Free, 8 pp.
Mr. Patterson offers 350 primarily old garden

varieties from among the following classifications: Bourbon, China, hybrid perpetual, Noisette, species, tea, shrub, hybrid musk, rugosas, hybrid tea, grandiflora, and floribunda. List includes color and year of introduction. All roses are grown on their own roots. Ships in one-gallon containers. See Heirlooms.

Shipping season: March through June.

ROYALL RIVER ROSES AT FOREVERGREEN FARM
1983
David King
Catalog: $1, 48 pp., black-and-white photographs
The catalog lists 325 gallica, damask, Alba, centifolia, moss, Bourbon, David Austin's English, Dr. Griffith Buck, J. Benjamin Williams, shrub, agricultural Canada (northern-hardy), rugosa, climbing, rambling, and species roses. Information provided includes alternate name, location and date of origin, parentage, height and width, hardiness zone, whether own-root or grafted stock, a description of the plant's habit, and the flower's color and form. An easy-to-understand section of cultural information precedes a guide entitled "Roses for Particular Applications" that sorts Royall's offerings by suggested use, e.g., fragrance, picking, containers, shady sites, etc. Ships bareroot. Guarantees true to name and healthy; will replace one time only or issue credit or refund up to ninety days from receipt. See **Booksellers**, Heirlooms, **Supplies**.

Shipping season: March through June.
Canada

SEQUOIA NURSERY—MOORE MINIATURE ROSES
1937
Ralph Moore
Catalog: Free, 20 pp., color photographs.
Supplementary list of old, rare, and unusual (primarily nonminiature) varieties: Free
The primary focus of the Sequoia catalog is the miniature creations of award-winning hybridizer Ralph Moore. One hundred and twenty offerings from Moore and other breeders, including a few small specimens from within other classifications, are thoroughly described. Information includes flower color, size, fragrance, height of plant, classification, habit, and tips on uses. Ships miniatures in 2 1/2- and 3-inch pots; others ship in 4-inch pots.

Shipping season: All year.

SPRING HILL NURSERIES
1849
Theresa W. Lusch
Rose catalog: Free, 24 pp., color photographs
The rose catalog of Spring Hill Nurseries, a mail-order source for a variety of nursery stock, lists fifty offerings. Classifications primarily include hybrid tea, climbing, tree, and miniature roses. Information includes height of plant, size, color, and form of bloom, a narrative description, and recommended uses and placement. Guarantees satisfaction; will replace or issue refund through July of the year that plant was purchased.
Shipping season: February through May.

STANEK'S NURSERY
1913
Stanek Family
Catalog: Free, 4 pp.
Stanek's could be the entertainment capital of the rose world: modern hybrids that they offer include 'Dolly Parton', 'Ingrid Bergman', 'Audrey Hepburn', 'Elizabeth Taylor', 'Lucille Ball', 'Lynn Anderson', and 135 other "celebrities." Their hybrid teas are organized by color. Other classifications: grandiflora, floribunda, climbers, country garden, standard tree, and David Austin's English. Colorful descriptions include ARS rating and height of plant. Ships two-year bareroot plants unless specified otherwise. Guarantees plants to be alive when sold and, given proper care, to grow; will allow purchase price as credit for replacement. See Heirlooms.
Shipping season: March and April.

TATE ROSE NURSERY
1942
Bobbie Tate
Catalog: Free, 4 pp.
The Tates list eighty modern hybrid teas, grandifloras, floribundas, polyanthas, and climbers. Brief descriptions highlight color and form of flower, height of plant, and awards (which are numerous here). Ships two-year, bareroot plants. Guarantees true to name and will bloom first spring in your garden; if not, notify the Tates by July 1 and they will send you a replacement the following spring.
Shipping season: January through April.

TINY PETALS NURSERY
1973
Pat and Sue O'Brien
Catalog: Free, 16 pp., color photographs
The Tiny Petals catalog of 140 miniatures emphasizes the work of the nursery's founder, Dee Bennett. Narrative descriptions of each offering are rich and convey an easy familiarity with each variety. Includes hybridizer, color, and height of plant. List includes a brief section of microminis and climbers.
Shipping season: January through December.
No Hawaii or Alaska

VINTAGE GARDENS
Gregg Lowery
Catalog: $5, 80 pp., illustrations
Vintage gardens publishes an ambitious catalog every second year, listing two thousand antique and extraordinary roses grown on their own roots; supplements are mailed out in between when stocks becomes available. Classifications include Alba, Bourbon, China, damask, eglantine, floribunda, gallica, hybrid, Bourbon, China, musk, perpetual, tea, climbing hybrid tea, moss, miniature, Noisette, polyantha, rambler, and shrub roses. Descriptions in catalog include color, rebloom, fragrance, year of introduction, form of flower, height of plant, and historical notes. Supplements include color and year of introduction only. Guarantees true to name, healthy, and ready to grow when shipped. See Heirlooms.
Shipping season: Bareroot, January and February. Containers, March through May. September through mid-November.

WAYSIDE GARDENS
1920
Karen P. Jennings
Rose catalog: Free, 46 pp., color photographs
The rose catalog of Wayside Gardens, a mail-order source for a wide range of nursery stock, includes 225 varieties. Offerings include Alba, Bourbon, centifolia, climber, damask, floribunda, gallica, hybrid musk, hybrid tea, miniature, shrub, moss, David Austin's English, patio standard, rambler, rugosa, and species roses. Descriptions include hybridizer, year of introduction, height and width of plant, color and form of flower, season of bloom, and growth habit. Guarantees satisfaction for one year if planted within recommended zone; will replace stock or issue credit or refund. See Fruit, Grasses, Heirlooms, Perennials.
Shipping season: January through May.

WEE GEMS
Ted LeBoutillier
Catalog: Free, 16 pp.
Offers the work of numerous breeders of miniature rose cultivars, listing 135 "Little Jewels of the Rose World." Narrative descriptions include color; the amount of additional description varies from listing to listing. Plants grown and shipped in four-inch containers.
Shipping season: All year.

WHITE FLOWER FARM
1950
Steve Frowine
Catalog: Free, 146 pp., color photographs
White Flower Farm, a family-owned nursery in Litchfield, Connecticut, offers a wide range of ornamentals: annuals, perennials, shrubs, and bulbs. In addition to their own expertise, the folks in Litchfield have enlisted rosarian Suzy Verrier, author of *Rosa Rugosa* and *Rosa Gallica*, as an advisor in matters *Rosa*. They offer a high spot selection of antique, modern (including a sampling of David Austin's English), rugosa, climbing, standard, and species roses. General cultural requirements of the rose precede rich narrative descriptions for each offering: height at maturity, form and color of flower, growth habit, and uses in the garden. Guarantees true to name, in prime condition for growing, and delivered at the proper time for planting; will replace one time only any plant that has been properly cared for but has failed to grow. See **Bulbs**, Fruit, **Perennials**, Supplies, Trees, **Waterscapes**.
Shipping season: Spring and fall.
Canada.
No Hawaii

WITHERSPOON ROSE CULTURE
1951
David and Rhonda Pike
Catalog: Free, 12 pp., black-and-white and color photographs
With the retirement of A. Paul and Sarah Hjort, resulting in the closing after ninety-five years in business of Thomasville Nurseries, the Pikes of Witherspoon became a major mail-order source for Weeks roses. Witherspoon offers three hundred modern hybrid tea, grandiflora, floribunda, climbing, David Austin English, tree, and miniature varieties. Also has a selection of old country garden types. Narrative descriptions include color and form of flower, plant's habit, and awards (they are numerous here). Roses grafted on Dr. Huey understock unless otherwise noted. Plants are dormant and bareroot. Guarantees true to name and will grow and bloom during the plant's first season in your garden.
Shipping season: January through March.

Selected Reading About Roses

The Combined Rose List, compiled and edited by Peter Schneider. A 160-page annual that aims to chronicle all known roses in commerce worldwide. In addition to the individual listings, it includes a rose registration update and a section on hard-to-find roses and where to find them.

The Graham Stuart Thomas Rose Book, by Graham Stuart Thomas. Thomas, a key figure in reviving interest in old garden and other roses that time had appeared to pass by, has revised and updated three earlier works–*Old Shrub Roses, Shrub Roses of Today,* and *Climbing Roses Old and New*–combining them into an omnibus volume. Includes 158 color photographs and 21 drawings.

Growing Good Roses, by Rayford Clayton Reddell. This award-winning rosarian's opinionated commentary and practical advice is highly valued and sure to assist you in your quest to grow healthy and beautiful roses. See "Growing Good Roses," in "Selected Videos About the Rose," on the next page.

Hardy Roses: An Organic Guide to Growing Frost- and Disease-Resistant Varieties, by Robert Osborne. Excellent information and insight for gardeners who work with harsh winter climates. Includes two hundred descriptions and comprehensive charts. Seventy photographs.

The Heritage of the Rose, by David Austin. The creator of David Austin's English roses, a category unto themselves, describes over nine hundred varieties including his own. Includes a history of the rose and its many uses in the garden.

Landscaping with Antique Roses, by Liz Druitt and G. Michael Shoup. The authors explain how roses can be used in developing landscape plans. The form and shape of each of the eighty varieties presented here are described not just as the possessors of beautiful blooms but as landscaping tools. Photographs show the rose plants in the context of the garden, as well as the expected portraits of their flowers.

Modern Roses 10, by the American Rose Society. Lists sixteen thousand registered varieties in the United States. Information includes name and alternate names, classification, bloom and growth habit, form, and fragrance.

The Old Rose Advisor, by Brent C. Dickerson. A thorough guide to the reblooming old rose varieties. Includes 274 color illustrations.

The Random House Guide to Roses, by Roger Phillips and Martyn Rix. A particularly beautiful volume in this large-format series. Includes color photographs of fourteen hundred varieties taken in groups, highlighting their relative sizes, shapes, and colors, and a description for each one.

Rosa Gallica, by Suzanne Verrier. Advice on the care and use of these nineteenth-century roses that are of compact growth, cold-hardy, and highly disease resistant. Includes an annotated, descriptive index of eighteen hundred "lost" Gallicas, their names and history. Includes sixty photographs.

Rosa Rugosa, by Suzanne Verrier. Ms. Verrier's book is the first one devoted to rugosa roses. Includes descriptions and insightful characterizations of the habit, form, and bloom of each. Also includes fifty photographs.

The Rose Expert, by Dr. D. G. Hessayon. Listed in numerous sources as the best-selling book on roses. Useful both for the beginner and the master gardener. Describes over three hundred types of roses and illustrates them in color. Includes practical advice on diagnosing and treating plants that are in need of care.

Roses: An Illustrated Encyclopedia and Grower's Handbook of Species Roses, Old Roses and Modern Roses, Shrub Roses and Climbers, by Peter Beales. Once you decide that you cannot live without roses in your garden, this becomes the book that you cannot live without in your home. Includes detailed descriptions of two thousand varieties and nearly eleven hundred color photographs.

Selected Videos About the Rose

A Celebration of Old Roses, by Peter Beales and Vivian Russell. Roses: the epic film. The history of roses brought to video in the most English setting of Norfolk. Great stories and exquisite flowers.

For the Love of Roses, by the staff of the Brooklyn Botanic Garden. Behind the scenes through the seasons at the Cranford Rose Garden in Brooklyn.

Growing Good Roses, by Rayford Clayton Reddell. Hosted by the author in his garden with a cast of six thousand . . . rosebushes. A lush tour of rose culture filled with good advice on caring for your friend *Rosa*.

SEEDS

Sources that offer flower or flower and vegetable seeds appear in this section. Sources offering vegetable seed only (and in some cases live plants) appear in the chapter on vegetables. A source characterizing its seed holdings as predominantly native plants and/or wildflowers is to be found in the Wildflower section.

The number of offerings cited in each profile is based on information in the most recent catalog provided by the source. Sources ship seed year-round unless otherwise noted. A selection of books about seed starting, planting, care, and seed saving appears after the last listing.

QUICK FIND
The following sources are listed in this section:

PUTNEY NURSERY, INC.
REDWOOD CITY SEED COMPANY
R. H. SHUMWAY, SEEDSMAN
RICHTERS
RONNIGER'S SEED POTATOES
ROSWELL SEED COMPANY, INC.
SALT SPRING SEEDS
THE SANDY MUCH HERB NURSERY
SEED SAVERS EXCHANGE–SEED SAVERS PUBLICATIONS
SEED SHARES™
THE SEED SHOP
SEEDS BLÜM
SEEDS OF CHANGE®
SEEDS TRUST: HIGH ALTITUDE GARDENS
SEEDSCAPES

SELECT SEEDS–ANTIQUE FLOWERS
SENECA HYBRIDS
SEYMOUR'S SELECTED SEEDS
SHARP BROS. SEED CO.
SHARP BROS. SEED CO.— WILDFLOWER DIVISION
SHEPHERD'S GARDEN SEEDS
SHOOTING STAR NURSERY
SMITH NURSERY COMPANY
SOUTHERN EXPOSURE SEED EXCHANGE®
SOUTHERN SEEDS
SOUTHWESTERN NATIVE SEEDS
"SOW ORGANIC" SEEDS
STOCK SEED FARMS
STOKES SEEDS
SUNRISE ENTERPRISES

TERRITORIAL SEED COMPANY
THE THOMAS JEFFERSON CENTER FOR HISTORICAL PLANTS
THOMPSON & MORGAN
TINMOUTH CHANNEL FARM
TOMATO GROWERS SUPPLY CO.
TOTALLY TOMATOES
VAN DYKE ZINNIAS
VERMONT BEAN SEED COMPANY
VERMONT WILDFLOWER FARM
VESEY'S SEEDS LTD.
WILD EARTH NATIVE PLANT NURSERY
WILD SEED, INC.
WILDSEED FARMS, INC.
WILLHITE SEED CO.
WILLIAM DAM SEEDS
WOOD PRAIRIE FARM

ABUNDANT LIFE SEED FOUNDATION
1975
Susan Herman
Catalog: $2 (recoverable), 64 pp., black-and-white photographs
A nonprofit organization that acquires, propagates, and preserves native and naturalized seeds. ALSF also disseminates information about seed culture and use. The catalog lists 600 varieties of true-to-parentage, open-pollinated, untreated seed: 115 vegetables, legumes, and grains, 65 herb, 80 garden and wildflowers, and a selection of shrubs and trees, including heirloom and heritage varieties. Rich descriptions, number of days for germination (vegetables), life cycle, range and elevation (wildflowers, trees, shrubs), and year of introduction when known. Quantifies number of seeds by weight or minimum number of seeds per packet. Regional mixtures and special purpose collections. Sells mounted and unmounted seed-cleaning screens. Guarantees true to name; will exchange or issue refund. See **Booksellers**, **Garlic**, Heirlooms, Herbs, Organics, Vegetables.
Canada, Mexico, International

ALFREY SEEDS
See **Vegetables**.

ALLEN, STERLING, & LOTHROP
1911
Catalog: $1 (recoverable), 40 pp., illustrations
The Allen, Sterling, & Lothrop seed catalog contains a selection of lawn covers and three hundred varieties of vegetables, flowers, and herbs that have adapted to the climate of northern New England.

Cultural information and detailed descriptions for each variety. Planting guide includes depth to plant seeds, number of seeds per foot, distance between plants and rows, number of days for germination, soil preference, transplanting timetable, and days to maturity. Seeds sold by the packet or by weight. Flower and herb seed primarily by packet with an unspecified number of seeds. Guarantees true to name. See **Garlic**, Herbs, Organics, **Supplies**, Vegetables.

ALPLAINS
See Perennials, **Wildflowers**.

ANTONELLI BROTHERS
See **Perennials**.

ARROWHEAD ALPINES
Bob and Brigitta Stewart
Seed catalog: $2, 62 pp.
The Stewarts describe their seed catalog, with four thousand listings, as the most extensive in the United States. This massive selection, including many varieties noted as rare and unusual, offers the seeds of wildflowers, alpines, perennials, trees, shrubs, and grasses that dovetail with the Stewarts' two thousand plants and rooted cuttings offered in their plant list. Each variety, from *Acacia iteaphylla* to *Zigadenus venenosus*, is presented in informative one-line descriptions. Sold by the packet with an unspecified number of seeds. See **Conifers**, Grasses, **Perennials**, Trees, Wildflowers.
Shipping season: November through March.
Canada, Mexico, International

BALDWIN SEED CO.–SEEDS OF ALASKA
See Grasses, **Wildflowers**.

BERLIN SEEDS
1984
Edward and Brenda Beachy
Catalog: Free, 60 pp., illustrations, black-and-white and color photographs
The Beachys sell commercial-quality vegetable seeds to the home gardener. Also carries one hundred types of Burpee and Ball brand flower seeds. Height and color for all, brief description for some. Warrants purity and vitality of seeds. Guarantees seeds to grow; will issue credit or refund. See **Booksellers, Fruit, Garlic**, Grasses, **Kidstuff**, Organics, **Supplies**, Vegetables.
Shipping season: Mid-February through late spring.
Canada

BLUESTEM PRAIRIE NURSERY
See Grasses, **Wildflowers**.

BOOTHE HILL WILDFLOWERS
See Organics, **Wildflowers**.

BOUNTIFUL GARDENS
1972
Bill and Betsy Bruneau
Catalog: Free, 72 pp., illustrations and black-and white photographs Rare seeds catalog: $2, 30 pp.
The Bountiful Gardens catalog is published by Ecology Action, a nonprofit organization that practices and teaches organic biointensive methods. The main catalog includes three hundred untreated, open-pollinated varieties of vegetable, herb, composting crop, grain, and flower seeds. Herb and flower listings include cultural information and postharvest uses, life cycle, height of mature plant, spacing, and seeds per packet. AAS selections are highlighted. Guarantees that seeds are vital at time of shipment and meet or exceed federal minimum germination standards. See **Booksellers, Garlic**, Heirlooms, Herbs, **Kidstuff**, Organics, **Supplies**, Vegetables.
Canada, Mexico, International

BOWMAN'S HILL STATE WILDFLOWER PRESERVE
See **Horticultural Societies, Wildflowers**.

BRUDY'S TROPICAL EXOTICS
1968

Mike Stich
Catalog: Free, 52 pp., illustrations and black-and-white photographs
All of the plants in this catalog are tropical in nature and most can be grown in your greenhouse or in containers indoors in winter, outdoors in the summer. Forty percent of the catalog is devoted to seeds. Catalogs have included the seeds of asparagus ferns, acacia, laceleaf Japanese maple, baobab tree, strawberry tree, African wisteria, Illiwarra flame tree, blue bush, Kaffir plum, giant rose mallow, and true Irish shamrock. Descriptions are rich in detail and cultural requirements, including instructions for germination. Also offers a sampler of ten exotics. Guarantees true to name; if not satisfied, Mr. Stich will replace seeds one time only or issue refund. See Conifers, **Fruit**, Trees.
Canada, Mexico, International

BUTTERBROOKE FARM
See **Booksellers**, Organics, **Vegetables**.

CASCADE BULB & SEED CO.
1980
Dr. Joseph C. Halinar
Catalog: 1 FCS, 4 pp. Computer disk: $1.50, $2
Dr. Halinar emphasizes disease resistance and garden worthiness in his hybridizing work. He offers seeds for one hundred varieties of lily, hemerocallis, and allium. Technical description and seeds per packet. A larger seed list, hybridizing information, and Dr. Halinar's published articles on lily, daylily, and allium is available in DOS format computer disk only. Guarantees lily and daylily seeds are true to name. Guarantees other seeds to be from stated parent. See Bulbs, Daylilies.
Shipping season: November through April.
Canada, Mexico, International

CLYDE ROBIN SEED CO.
See **Wildflowers**.

COMPANION PLANTS
1982
Peter Borchard
Catalog: $3, 44 pp.
Mr. Borchard thinks of plants, particularly the herbs (or useful plants) that are his specialty, as companions. His catalog of 550 plants includes 250 for which he offers seeds, too. Most of the seeds are gathered from Mr. Borchard's own herbs,

some varieties are wild. Catalog is organized by common name. Information includes botanical name, height, hardiness, life cycle, sun/shade preference, growth habit, and postharvest uses. Seeds sold by the packet, quantities (described as generous) vary according to size of seeds. Guarantees true to name and viable. See Herbs.
Canada, Mexico, International

COMSTOCK SEED
See **Grasses**, Trees, **Wildflowers**.

THE COOK'S GARDEN
1983
Ellen and Shepherd Ogden
Catalog: $1, 112 pp., color and black-and-white illustrations
The Cook's Garden has its origin in the Ogdens' work as organic market gardeners. They are the coauthors of the award-winning seed-to-table book *The Cook's Garden*. Their catalog is brimming with cultural information, gardening tips, and recipes. Four hundred varieties of modern and heirloom seeds for flowering annuals and perennials, cutting gardens, everlastings, herbs, salad greens, cover crops, vegetables, and a small group of edible plants. Descriptions are extensive and precise. Heirloom varieties noted. A large number of collections and mixtures are offered. Seeds sold by the packet with seed count or weight specified for each. Guarantees satisfaction; will issue refund. See **Booksellers**, **Garlic**, Heirlooms, **Herbs**, Kidstuff, Organics, **Supplies**, Vegetables.
Canada

COUNTRY WETLANDS NURSERY & CONSULTING
See **Booksellers**, Grasses, Waterscapes, **Wildflowers**.

D. LANDRETH SEED COMPANY
1784
Shirley, Charlotte, Dottie, Gloria, and Ben
Catalog: $2, 47 pp., vintage illustrations and black-and-white photographs
"A fresh importation of choice garden seeds, by a person lately arrived from London, who, from a thorough knowledge of the Gardening Business, hopes to establish himself in or near the city, as a Nurseryman, Seedman and Florist . . ." announced D. Landreth in his first advertisement printed in a Philadelphia newspaper on May 21, 1784. Landreth's selection has increased substantially over the past two hundred years, from when

their clients included Thomas Jefferson, George Washington, James Madison, and Joseph Bonaparte. They offer modern hybrid and heirloom seeds for three hundred types of vegetables, thirty herbs, and sixty flowers. (You may well think of this firm when you see zinnias, as they are credited with having introduced this ubiquitous flower to the States in 1798.) Descriptions are precise and thorough (and often appear charmingly clipped and pasted from vintage catalogs), tinged with commonsense suggestions and a reverence for the seeds and soil. Sold by the packet or by weight. Guarantees satisfaction; will issue refund. See Garlic, **Grasses**, Heirlooms, Herbs, Vegetables.
Shipping season: September through May.

DAN'S GARDEN SHOP
1977
Dan Youngenberg
Catalog: Free, 30 pp., illustrations
Mr. Youngenberg offers the seeds for eighty vegetables, an equal number of flowers, and a dozen herbs. Descriptions are rich and include cultural advice, site selection, distance between plants, number of days for germination and maturity, and postharvest uses. Number of seeds per packet and by weight. See **Booksellers**, Organics, **Supplies**, Vegetables.

DEGIORGI SEED COMPANY
1905
Duane and Monte Thompson
Catalog: $2 (recoverable), 75 pp.
The DeGiorgi company originated in Council Bluffs, Iowa, where it remained until 1988. Some of the earliest versions of the catalog were printed in Czech, the native language of the two founding brothers. The Thompsons, the current stewards of the company, are both from Nebraska farm families. Their catalog contains fourteen hundred varieties of seeds for flowering annuals, perennials, herbs, regional wildflowers, ornamental grasses, and vegetables. DeGiorgi features a number of cultivars described as unique or difficult to find. Rich descriptions of most varieties include cultural information, ease of care, and germination requirements. All varieties sold by the packet, some by weight. Seeds per packet noted. Number of days to maturity included in description of vegetables. Guarantees satisfaction; will replace or issue refund. See **Booksellers**, **Garlic**, **Grasses**, Herbs, **Kidstuff**, Vegetables.

DESERT MOON NURSERY
1988
Hodoba family
Catalog: $1, 30 pp. Seed list: 6 pp.
Desert Moon specializes in the plants and trees of the Chihuahuan desert. Ted Hodoba, the author of *Growing Desert Plants: From Windowsill to Garden,* encourages and provides suggestions for the use of these plants in nondesert environments. The Hodoba's include their seed list of forty desert ornamentals as an insert in the Desert Moon catalog. Includes information on stratification; descriptions note botanical name, common name, form and color of foliage and flower, cultural notes, and germination requirements for each. Sold by the packet; number of seeds unspecified. See **Cactus**, Wildflowers.
Shipping season: April through October.
Canada, Mexico, International

DESERTLAND NURSERY
See **Cactus**.

DoRoCo SEED COMPANY
See **Herbs**.

DOWN ON THE FARM SEED
See **Garlic**, Heirlooms, Herbs, **Kidstuff**, Organics, **Vegetables**.

EARTHLY GOODS LTD.
See **Furniture**, Grasses, **Wildflowers**.

EDGE OF THE ROCKIES "NATIVE SEEDS"
See Grasses, **Wildflowers**.

ELIXIR FARM BOTANICALS
See **Booksellers, Herbs**, Organics.

FAR NORTH GARDENS
1962
K. J. Combs
Catalog: $2 (recoverable), 52 pp.
Far North Gardens has a number of areas of concentration among its 2,600 listings including Barnhaven primroses, rare flower seeds, and bulbs. The collector's seed list includes 800 varieties of perennials and wildflowers described by name and available by the packet. Seeds pop up throughout the catalog, including in sections of cut flowers, colonial flowers, trees, shrubs, ornamentals, alpines, and woodland plants. Several hundred offerings including twenty primulas are available wholesale to the general

public. Number of seeds per packet not noted. Guarantees safe arrival. See **Booksellers, Bulbs**, Grasses, **Perennials, Wildflowers**.
Canada, Mexico, International

FARMER SEED AND NURSERY
See **Garlic**, Perennials, **Vegetables**.

FEDCO SEEDS
1979
Joann Clark
Catalog: $2, 46 pp., illustrations
A cooperative that offers untreated seeds acquired from worldwide sources that have performed well in Maine's cold-shortened growing season. The catalog contains six hundred varieties of annual and perennial flowers, everlastings, herbs, and vegetables. Descriptions include cultural and germination information and tips on use and placement. Organically grown varieties are noted. A chart with planting and cultural requirements for vegetables is useful for design and planning crop succession. Seeds per packet and by weight for each listing. Fedco encourages group orders but will accept individual orders. See **Booksellers**, Garlic (see Moose Growers Supply), Heirlooms, Herbs, Organics, Vegetables.
Shipping season: January through March.

FEDER'S PRAIRIE SEED CO.
See Grasses, **Wildflowers**.

FISHER'S GARDEN STORE
1957
Kenneth J. Fisher and Judy Fisher
Catalog: Free, 19 pp., black-and-white photographs
Mr. Fisher breeds and grows hybrid and open-pollinated seeds suitable for high altitudes and short growing seasons. The Fishers' catalog includes 170 vegetable and eighty flowering varieties. Descriptions for vegetables include number of days to maturity, size, shape, and form of mature plants. Descriptions for flower seeds include height for some, color only for most. Seeds available by the packet, many also by weight. See **Garlic**, Vegetables.
Canada

FLOATING MOUNTAIN SEEDS
See Garlic, Heirlooms, Herbs, **Vegetables**.

FLOWER AND HERB EXCHANGE
See **Horticultural Societies**.

FLOWERY BRANCH SEED CO.
1989
Dean Pailler
Catalog: $3, 100 pp., illustrations
Flowery Branch whose first offering numbered thirty herbs, now catalogs an enormous number (1,125 and counting) of common and unusual perennials, herbs, everlastings, and wildflowers from diverse sources worldwide. Mr. Pailler favors open-pollinated, fragrant, and unusual varieties, often available in an assortment of colors. Each listing specifies the botanical name, an explanation of the botanical name, the common name, life cycle, and hardiness. Descriptive passages includes tidbits of historical information, plant size, flower size and color, sun requirements, cultural information, and habit. An index of common names is provided. Approximate number of seeds per packet noted. Guarantees that seeds conform to label descriptions. See Herbs, Perennials.
Canada, Mexico, International

FOREST SEEDS OF CALIFORNIA
1984
Bob Graton
Catalog: Free, 4 pp.
Mr. Graton, a registered professional forester, likes to climb trees (especially in California) to collect and clean seeds. His list includes seeds for 140 varieties, including cedar, cypress, eucalyptus, fir (including Douglas), hemlock, juniper, sequoia, spruce, and numerous hardwoods and forest shrubs, including California buckeye, California redbud, coast and interior live oak, California nutmeg, and mountain whitehorn. Seeds sold by weight. See Conifers, Trees.
Canada, Mexico, International

FOX HOLLOW HERB & HEIRLOOM SEED CO.
See Garlic, Heirlooms, **Herbs, Vegetables.**

THE FRAGRANT PATH
1982
E. R. Rasmussen
Catalog: $2, 40 pp.
An eclectic assortment of five hundred types of seeds for fragrant annuals, perennials, biennials, prairie flowers, grasses, herbs, trees, and shrubs. Other seeds, not necessarily fragrant but considered by E. R. Rasmussen to be of merit, include rare and unusual vines, annuals, perennials, and exotics (for growing under controlled conditions). Rasmussen's rich descriptions suggest intimate and enthusiastic knowledge of the varieties being offered but are a bit shy of specific growing requirements, in turn suggesting that you will need supplementary information to judge which selections are appropriate for conditions in your own garden. See Heirlooms, Herbs, Perennials, Trees.
Canada

FRED & JEAN MINCH
See **Rhododendrons**, Trees.

FROSTY HOLLOW ECOLOGICAL RESTORATION
See Grasses, Trees, **Wildflowers.**

GARDEN CITY SEEDS
1982
Susan Wall-MacLane
Catalog: $1, 75 pp., illustrations and black-and-white photographs
Garden City Seeds is a subsidiary of the non-profit Down Home Project, Inc., which supports self-reliant living. GCS offers 350 untreated, northern-acclimated vegetable, flower, and herb seeds. The catalog includes a "Green Resource Guide" with sources of information about sustainable agriculture, as well as articles on mulching, storage of harvests, and seed saving. Descriptions of 260 vegetables include cultural advice, soil temperature and composition preferences, season and time of germination, companion plants, susceptibility to pests and solutions, and specific seed-saving techniques. Description for each variety includes number of days to maturity, size of plant and vegetable, and postharvest uses. Symbols indicate heirlooms, cold-hardiness, All America selections, and the organization that has certified that a specific variety has been grown by organic methods. Flowers and herbs organized by life cycle. Describes flower and plant, season of bloom, number of days for germination, and culture. Symbols indicate light preference and cold-hardiness. Sold by the packet with specified number of seeds and by weight. Guarantees true to name and satisfaction; will issue refund. See **Booksellers, Garlic**, Grasses, Herbs, Organics, **Supplies.**
Canada

GARDEN OF DELIGHTS
See **Fruit**, Trees.

GARDENS NORTH
1991
Kristl Walek
Catalog: $4, 100 pp.
Gardens North traces its beginnings to Ms. Walek's dining room (in her then home) in the city of Ottawa where she gardened on a five-hundred-square-foot lot. Ms. Walek's seed house is now located on a private eight-acre site south of her original location. Her purpose is to offer perennial seed that will be hardy for the majority of Canadian gardeners. Gardens North offers over eight hundred types of perennial (and biennial) flowering plants and a major gathering of ornamental grasses from international sources as well as those developed on-site using only organic methods. Rich descriptions highlighted by insightful personal observations and anecdotes provide the commentary to match the substance of her offerings in what is one of the best-written seed catalogs you are likely to encounter. Descriptions include common name, season of bloom and other seasons of interest, cultural habits, germination methods and tips, and hardiness information based on the reports of Ms. Walek's network of growers and gardeners. Specialties include species native to Alaska. Seed sold by the packet with a specified number of seeds per packet, and by weight. Also offers a seed search service for perennials not listed in her catalog. Will confirm availability and price prior to acquiring seeds for special orders. See **Grasses**, Organics, Perennials, Wildflowers. **Canada, International**

GIANT WATERMELONS
Catalog: Free, 2 pp.
The growers at Giant sell seeds that will produce Carolina Cross and Blue Rind variety watermelons capable of bearing fruit that weighs from 120 to 200 pounds. Giant also sells the seeds of Colossal variety cantaloupe that can produce melons that weigh over forty pounds. Seeds sold by the dozen. They offer a sixty-four-page booklet about growing watermelons for competition. See Fruit, Vegetables.
Canada

GIRARD NURSERIES
1944
Peter Girard, Jr.
Catalog: Free, 23 pp., color photographs
Girard breeds azaleas and rhododendrons, flowering shrubs and trees, ornamental and shade trees, broadleaf evergreens, and conifers. They also offer the seeds of selected azaleas, rhododendrons, broadleaf evergreens, fir, cypress, juniper, spruce, pine, Oriental arborvitae, and other ornamentals. Seeds sold by the packet with the number of seeds unspecified. See **Conifers**, Grasses, **Rhododendrons**, Trees.

GLECKLER'S SEEDMEN
See Heirlooms, Organics, **Vegetables**.

GOODWIN CREEK GARDENS
1977
Jim and Dotti Becker, Laurie and Gracie Richer
Catalog: $1, 39 pp.
A small family farm specializing in the seeds and plants of herbs, everlastings (the Beckers coauthored *An Everlasting Garden*), scented geraniums, and other fragrant plants. Seeds for one hundred of the five hundred plants to be found in their catalog are offered by the packet. Brief descriptions include habit, height at maturity, and life cycle for all; notation about uses and hardiness for many. Includes short informative pieces about starting seeds and creating gardens to attract butterflies and hummingbirds. Seeds per packet specified. See **Booksellers, Herbs, Perennials.**
Canada

THE GOURMET GARDENER™
See **Booksellers**, Garlic, **Herbs**, Vegetables.

GREEN HORIZONS
See **Booksellers**, Grasses, **Wildflowers**.

GURNEY'S SEED & NURSERY CO.
1866
Donald L. Kruml
Catalog: Free, 64 pp., color photographs
This generalist's catalog includes 325 varieties of vegetable seeds and 120 flowering types (mostly annuals). Extensive selection of bush bean, cabbage, carrot, corn, cucumber, radish, pole bean, sweet pepper, hot pepper, pumpkin, and squash seed. Vegetable description includes number of days to maturity, nature of yield, disease resistance, and All America selections. Listing for flowers includes color and height of plant. Specifies seeds per packet. Vegetables also by weight. Guarantees seeds for one year from date of shipment; will issue credit or refund. See **Garlic, Kidstuff**, Organics, **Supplies**, Vegetables.

HALCYON GARDEN HERBS
See **Herbs.**

HAMILTON SEEDS & WILDFLOWERS
See **Grasses, Wildflowers.**

HARRIS SEEDS
1879
Richard (Dick) Chamberlin
Catalog: Free, 81 pp., color photographs
Founder Joseph Harris was the editor of *The Genesee Farmer* and *The Rural New Yorker* and the first head of the Department of Agriculture at Cornell University (1867). The business remained in his family for a hundred years until the death of his grandson (and namesake) in 1979. Still privately owned, Harris offers two hundred vegetables, one hundred flowers, and fifteen herbs in the home garden version of their catalog. Many of their hybrids are exclusive to Harris. Will provide a free growing guide with order and encourages your participation in their test program of new varieties. Vegetable listings include description of plants and produce, number of days to maturity, culinary taste and uses, and broad cultural tips. Number of seeds per packet and per ounce are noted. Description includes color of flowers and height of plant. Charts for flowering annuals and perennials include sun/shade requirements, postharvest uses, and seed-starting tips. Approximate number of flower seeds per packet noted. If not satisfied with the plants that grow from their seed, Harris will accept empty seed packets for refund or credit. See **Garlic,** Herbs, **Supplies,** Vegetables.

HEIRLOOM GARDEN® SEEDS
1979
Warren Raysor
Catalog: Free, 37 pp., illustrations and black-and-white photographs
This catalog begins with adonis (*Adonis aestivalis)* and ends with zinnia, stopping along the way for butterfly weed, carnation, desert star (*Mentzelia lindleyi*), mimosa, and two hundred other heirloom herbs and flowers. Mr. Raysor gives thorough historical and cultural information for each offering. Also includes life cycle; when and how to sow, transplant, fertilize, mulch, and harvest; time and conditions for germination; setting distance; landscape, wildlife, and postharvest uses; and color. Includes an accessible essay on growing plants from seed. Offers fourteen theme collections

including ones for window boxes, old English cottage gardens, fence climbers, salad gardens, and a cut-flower garden. Seeds sold by the packet; weight specified. Guarantees true to name, untreated, and disease free; will exchange unsatisfactory seeds within sixty days. See **Booksellers,** Heirlooms, Herbs, **Kidstuff. Canada**

HEIRLOOM SEED PROJECT–LANDIS VALLEY MUSEUM
See **Fruit,** Heirlooms, Organics, Trees, **Vegetables.**

HEIRLOOM SEEDS
See Heirlooms, **Vegetables.**

HENRY FIELD SEED & NURSERY CO.
1892
Orville Dragoo
Catalog: Free, 87 pp., color photographs
A full-line seed and nursery company for the home gardener offering sixty flowering annuals and the seed and selected plants for three hundred vegetables. Selection includes hollyhock, impatiens, morning glory, petunia, veronica, and zinnas. Descriptions for annuals include size and color of flowers, number of seeds per packet, and height of plants. See **Fruit, Garlic, Kidstuff,** Organics, Perennials **Supplies, Trees., Vegetables.**

HOLLAND WILDFLOWER FARM
See **Booksellers,** Herbs, **Wildflowers.**

HOMAN BROTHERS SEED, INC.
See Grasses, Trees, **Wildflowers.**

HORTICULTURAL ENTERPRISES
See **Vegetables.**

IOWA PRAIRIE SEED COMPANY
See Grasses, **Wildflowers.**

J. L. HUDSON, SEEDSMAN
1911
J. L. Hudson and Sheri Calkins
Catalog: $1, 95 pp., illustrations. Four supplements (published at irregular intervals): $2
The firm was founded by Harry E. Saier. The pseudonymous (and pointedly phoneless) J. L. Hudson and his or her partner in seedsmanship, Ms. Sheri Calkins, have been the proprietors since around 1973. "The Ethnobotanical

Catalog of Seed" is what, on many levels, sets Hudson apart from other seed catalogs. It is laced with essays, quotes, epigrams, and aphorisms invoking freedom of choice, independence, and diversity. It also offers fifteen hundred varieties of open-pollinated seeds for flowers, vines, herbs, shrubs, vegetables, and other plant material (much of it rare or unusual) from worldwide sources. Descriptions are aggressively rich with cultural and historical color. Information includes soil and site preferences, hardiness, life cycle, form and color of flowers or fruit, plant habit, and instructions for care and germination. Seeds sold by the packet; varieties available in bulk noted. See **Booksellers**, Garlic, Heirlooms, Herbs, Vegetables.

Canada, Mexico, International

JOHNNY'S SELECTED SEEDS
1973
Robert L. Johnston, Jr.
Catalog: Free, 136 pp., color photographs
The 700 types of seeds offered by Johnny's are grown using primarily organic methods and nonchemical pest deterrents at their Albion, Maine, trial grounds and seed farm. Listings for 550 vegetables include description, culinary uses, and disease resistance. Highlights heirlooms as well as vegetables that are easy to grow. The catalog is deep in cultural information, helpful hints, and charts. Includes a planting planner for direct seeding of vegetables and a supplemental chart for transplants. The flower index and culture guide for 85 varieties, organized by common name (botanical name included), starting methods, germination information, spacing, months to bloom, and light requirements. Offers fifty annual and perennial herbs for culinary, medicinal, and ornamental use. Johnny's has devised a code to accommodate and clarify the different cultural requirements for each species of herb. Specifies number of seeds sold by the packet or by weight. Germination standards are noted for all seeds. Guarantees satisfaction; will replace or issue refund. See **Booksellers, Garlic**, Grasses, Heirlooms, Herbs, Organics, **Supplies**, Vegetables.
Canada, Mexico, International

J. W. JUNG SEED & NURSERY CO.
1907
Richard J. Zondag
Catalog: Free, 76 pp., color photographs
This wide range of interests seed and nursery cata-

log offers three hundred types of annual flower seeds. Features include celosia, cosmos, hybrid geraniums, hybrid impatiens, marigolds (including "Sophia" series, 'Espana', Jung's goldilocks, gems, super brocade), petunias, pansies, and verbena. Offers mixed flower selections: rainbow flower garden for bedding and cutting, winter flower (everlastings) garden, and everblooming cutting flowers. Offers a balanced selection of seeds for 350 vegetables and melons. Many varieties are noted as exclusive to Jung and a generous number are All America selections. Descriptions include size of fruit, postharvest use, and number of days to maturity. Seeds offered variously by the packet; number of seeds specified for most, the rest by weight. Also offers several theme garden seed mixtures in cans (coverage expressed in square feet): songbird meadow, hummingbird garden, butterfly garden, and native American wildflowers. See **Bulbs, Fruit**, Garlic, **Kidstuff**, Perennials, Supplies, **Trees**, Vegetables.

K & L CACTUS AND SUCCULENT NURSERY
See **Booksellers, Cactus.**

KIDS IN BLOOM SPECIALTY SEEDS
See Heirlooms, Herbs, **Kidstuff**, Vegetables.

KILGORE SEED COMPANY
1918
J. H. Hunziker
Catalog: $1 (recoverable), 24 pp.
Kilgore specializes in seeds for gardeners in Florida and areas with similar growing conditions. Offerings include 240 vegetables, 20 herbs, and 60 types of flowering annuals. Descriptions for vegetables includes number of days to maturity, growth habit, taste, and culinary uses. The catalog includes specific dates to sow vegetable seeds in Florida. Also for Floridians, a reference table for vegetables that includes hardiness, number of seeds per row in running feet, and the number of seeds or plants required to feed a family; also specifies depth to cover seeds, space between rows, distance to set plant from seedbed, and approximate time to produce a harvestable crop. A separate table for flowers includes height, hardiness, when to plant, time from sowing to bloom, space between rows, landscape, postharvest use, and preferred site for sowing seed. Seeds sold by the packet or by weight. See **Booksellers**, Garlic, Herbs, Vegetables.
Canada, Mexico, International

KITAZAWA SEED CO.
See **Vegetables**.

LARNER SEEDS
See **Booksellers, Grasses, Trees, Wildflowers**.

LE JARDIN DU GOURMET
See Booksellers, Garlic, Herbs, **Vegetables**.

LILY OF THE VALLEY HERB FARM
See **Herbs, Perennials**.

LONG ISLAND SEED COMPANY
See Garlic, Heirlooms, **Vegetables**.

MELLINGER'S
1927
Phil Steiner
Catalog: Free, 104 pp., illustrations and color photographs
Mellinger's home, farm, and garden catalog describes over four thousand garden-related items, including three hundred types of vegetable, herb, garden, and wildflower seeds. Flower seeds (mostly mixtures) listed with name, color, and preferred soil pH level. Vegetable offerings include specialty sections for gourmet and oriental vegetables and for organically grown heirlooms. Description for eatables includes number of days to maturity, vegetable taste, and form. All seeds sold by the packet; with number of seeds specified; most vegetables also offered by weight. See **Booksellers, Furniture,** Herbs, **Kidstuff,** Perennials, **Supplies,** Wildflowers.
Canada, Mexico, International

MESA GARDEN
See **Cactus**.

MIDWEST WILDFLOWERS
See **Wildflowers**.

MISSOURI WILDFLOWERS NURSERY
See Grasses, Perennials, **Wildflowers**.

MOON MOUNTAIN WILDFLOWERS
See **Wildflowers**.

NATIVE AMERICAN SEED
See **Booksellers,** Grasses, **Wildflowers**.

NATIVE GARDENS
See Grasses, Trees, **Wildflowers**.

NATIVE SEEDS, INC.
See **Wildflowers**.

NATIVE SEEDS/SEARCH
See **Booksellers,** Garlic, **Kidstuff, Vegetables,** Wildflowers.

NEW ENGLAND WILD FLOWER SOCIETY
See **Booksellers, Horticultural Societies, Kidstuff, Wildflowers**.

NICHOLS GARDEN NURSERY
1950
Rose Marie Nichols McGee
Catalog: Free, 72 pp.
Nichols Garden Nursery sells the seeds for 150 garden flowers, everlastings, and wildflowers, 120 varieties of herbs, and 470 vegetables. Separate listings for garden flowers, wildflowers, everlastings, pansies, and edibles. Flowers organized by common name; information includes botanical name, life cycle, height of mature plant, cultural hints, and postharvest uses. Seeds sold by the packet or by weight; number of seeds per packet noted. See **Booksellers, Garlic, Herbs,** Organics, Supplies, **Vegetables,** Wildflowers.

NITRON INDUSTRIES, INC.
See **Kidstuff,** Organics, **Supplies, Vegetables**.

NORTHPLAN/MOUNTAIN SEED
1975
Loring M. Jones
Catalogs: Garden seed, $1 (recoverable).
Native seed, $1 or LSASE
Flower and vegetable garden seeds featuring short season vegetables adapted for cooler climates. Offers both hybrid and nonhybrid seeds and some heirloom varieties. Also tree, shrub, and forb (wildflower) seeds of primarily inland northwest wildland species, although many others are listed as well.
Canada, Mexico, International

NORTHWEST NATIVE SEED
See **Wildflowers**.

THE ONION MAN
Mark McDonough
Catalog: $1, 10 pp.
Mr. McDonough offers the seeds for one hundred true to name *Allium* species and their cultivars. The catalog is introduced with clear and

useful information about *Allium* seed germination. Descriptions include botanical names, size and color of flower, form and habit of plant. Number of seeds per packet is specified for most listings. See Perennials.
Canada, Mexico, International

ORAL LEDDEN & SONS
1904
Don Ledden
Catalog: Free, 55 pp., black-and-white photographs
A traditional family-owned and -operated seed house that stocks new hybrids and many hard-to-find heirloom varieties gathered from diverse sources. Two hundred flowering annuals and perennials organized by common name, with brief descriptions of plant, flower, and recommended uses. All America selections are highlighted. The descriptions of four hundred vegetable varieties include sowing dates and number of days to maturity. A planning chart specifies planting rate per one hundred feet and per acre, space between rows, distance after thinning, depth and time of planting for open ground, soil temperature range, days for germination, and days to harvest. Seeds per packet noted; also available by weight. Guarantees safe arrival; will replace or issue refund. See **Garlic**, Grasses, Heirlooms, **Supplies**, Vegetables.
Canada, Mexico, International

OSC SEEDS
1900
Catalog: Free, 72 pp., color photographs
OSC specializes in seeds obtained from diverse sources that are suitable for Canadian climatic conditions and short growing seasons. OSC lists seeds (primarily untreated) for 275 types of vegetables (strong on beans, corn, and peas), 200 annual and perennial flowers, and brief sections for herbs and grasses. Descriptions are thorough and clear, including specifications and growing conditions for each variety. Cultural notes, germination, and planting recommendations throughout. Highlights numerous All America and Fleuroselect winners. Seeds sold by the packet or by weight. Guarantees purity and vitality of seeds; will issue refund for seeds returned within ten days of receipt. See Garlic.
Canada, International

OTIS S. TWILLEY SEED COMPANY
Arthur Cobb Abbott
Catalog: Free, 98 pp., color photographs

Over 500 vegetable, 280 flower, and 60 herb seeds for the roadside stand or home gardener who desires new treated hybrid varieties. The Twilley catalog highlights All America selections and their own proprietary professional seed series that they believe to be the best in its class. Includes vivid maps recommending vegetable varieties that are well suited for your geographical area, including separate ones for tomatoes and corn. Descriptions are thorough and include number of days to maturity, plant and fruit form and characteristics, and the area of the United States for which each is best suited. Seeds sold by the packet or by weight. Guarantees true to name; will issue refund if reported within thirty days of receipt. See Garlic, Herbs, Vegetables.
Canada, International

OTTER VALLEY NATIVE PLANTS
See Grasses, **Wildflowers**.

P & P SEED COMPANY
1984
Ray Waterman
Catalog: LSASE, 2 pp.
Established to support the World Pumpkin Federation (see Horticultural Societies) by supplying the seed of record-setting specimens and varieties. Forty-five types of seeds, including Atlantic giant pumpkin and 'Show King' giant green squash, are among the offerings with a potential to grow to over seven hundred pounds. Also offers seed for oversized watermelons, gourds, corn, sunflowers, tomatoes, beets, cucumbers, and onions. Descriptions emphasize potential size. Seeds sold by count. See Horticultural Societies, Vegetables.
Canada, Mexico, International

PACIFIC COAST SEED COMPANY
Catalog: $1, 4 pp.
Purveyor of needle-bearing evergreen, maple, and birch seeds: spruce (Black Hills, Colorado blue, Norway, and white), pine (piñon nut, ponderosa, mugho, Scotch, and white), fir (concolor, Douglas, European silver, Fraser, Korean, and west Himalayan), Canadian hemlock, coast redwood, and American giant arborvitae; and non-needle-bearing maple (Amur, flame Amur, Norway, paperbark, red, sugar, Tatarica, and trident), and Japanese white birch. Descriptions include botanical name, seasonal foliage, growth habit, out-

standing ornamental features, and height at maturity. Seeds sold variously by the packet of a specified number of seeds or by weight. Notes number of years seeds will retain their viability when stored properly. See Conifers, Trees.
Shipping season: All year.
Canada, Mexico, International

PARK SEED® CO.
J. Leonard Park and Karen Park Jennings
1868
Catalog: Free, 76 pp., color photographs
Founded by G. W. Park in the living room of his Libonia, Pennsylvania, home, Park Seed currently describes its business as the oldest and largest family-owned seed company in America. The catalog presents the seeds for two hundred vegetables, two hundred flowers, and eighty kitchen and landscape herbs from its list of two thousand varieties gathered from worldwide sources and developed here. A number of flowering types are also offered as live plants. Highlights All America selections and Park's High Performers that have consistently tested superior at their trial grounds. Descriptions are compact but rich in detail. Includes number of days to maturity, habit, form and taste for vegetables, height of plant, and color of bloom for flowers. A separate guide supplements individual descriptions with bloom season, germination time, and cultural notations. Specifies number of seeds per packet. Guarantees satisfaction for one year from date of delivery; will replace or issue credit or refund. See **Bulbs, Garlic, Herbs,** Peonies, Roses, **Supplies, Vegetables.**
Canada

PEACEFUL VALLEY FARM & GARDEN SUPPLY
See **Booksellers,** Garlic, Grasses, Organics, **Supplies, Wildflowers.**

THE PEPPER GAL
See **Vegetables.**

PERENNIAL PLEASURES NURSERY OF VERMONT
1980
Judith and Rachel Kane
Catalog: $3 (recoverable), 64 pp.
The Kanes grow heirloom flowering plants and herbs using organic methods. Their catalog is organized into chapters covering the seventeenth through the twentieth century. Sixty-eight varieties of perennial seeds are offered, arranged according to their time of introduction or common appearance in (eastern) American gardens. Herbs appear in a separate section. Rich historical information, context of use, cultural information, and description of mature plant for each offering. Seeds harvested from species. Packets contain one hundred or more seeds. Period and specialty collections include seeds and plants. Guarantees true to name; will replace or issue refund. See **Booksellers,** Grasses, Heirlooms, **Herbs,** Organics, **Perennials.**
Canada, Mexico

PINETREE GARDEN SEEDS
1979
Dick Meiners
Catalog: Free, 152 pp., illustrations and color photographs
Pinetree offers seven hundred types of hybrid and open-pollinated seeds, primarily in a natural, untreated state, packaged in small-count, inexpensive packets suitable for the home gardener. Flowering annuals include asters, calendulas, celosias, cosmos, flowering kales and cabbages (not the first kind that you'd run to eat), nasturtiums, nicotinias, poppies, and sunflowers. Other flowering varieties include perennial aquilegias and pansies and an expanding section of everlastings. Thorough descriptions. Number of flower seeds per packet not specified. Guarantees satisfaction; will replace or issue refund. See **Booksellers,** Garlic, **Herbs, Kidstuff,** Organics, **Supplies, Vegetables.**
Canada, Mexico, International

P. L. ROHRER & BRO.
1919
Jim Gamber
Catalog: Free, 40 pp., illustrations and color photographs
Rohrer & Bro. describe their selection of seeds for farmers and home gardeners as tested varieties typical to the area in which they are situated, Lancaster County's Pennsylvania Dutch country. Their catalog includes 280 vegetables, 30 herbs, and 75 flowers. Descriptions include practical cultural advice for vegetables, clear basic descriptions of habit and taste, and number of days to maturity. Their home garden planting chart, weighted for a family of five people, denotes planting dates (indoors and out), spacing of plants in rows, and number of seeds or plants per

row foot. Seeds sold by the packet or by weight. Guarantees satisfaction; will issue refund. See Garlic, Herbs, Organics, Supplies, Vegetables.

PLANTS OF THE SOUTHWEST
See **Booksellers, Grasses**, Heirlooms, Trees, **Vegetables, Wildflowers**.

PRAIRIE MOON NURSERY
See **Booksellers, Grasses**, Organics, Trees, **Wildflowers**.

PRAIRIE NURSERY
See **Booksellers**, Grasses, **Wildflowers**.

PRAIRIE RIDGE NURSERY
See Grasses, Perennials, **Wildflowers**.

PRAIRIE SEED SOURCE
See **Booksellers**, Grasses, **Wildflowers**.

PUTNEY NURSERY, INC.
See Herbs, Perennials, **Wildflowers**.

REDWOOD CITY SEED COMPANY
See **Booksellers**, Garlic, Heirlooms, Herbs, **Kidstuff, Vegetables**.

R. H. SHUMWAY, SEEDSMAN
1870
Catalog: Free, 55 pp., black-and-white and color illustrations
Shumway's first mail-order catalog was published in 1870 under the name "The Pioneer American Seedsman." Many of the seven hundred offerings are pictured in vintage and vintage-style engravings. Ninety garden flowers, both old fashioned and noteworthy recent introductions, are described briefly. Seventy-five ornamental, fragrance, tea, and culinary herbs organized by life cycle, common name (botanical name included), height of plant, and uses in garden and postharvest. Number of seeds noted within a broad range. Guarantees seeds to grow, will issue one-time refund at seller's discretion. (For six hundred flowers from a division of R. H. Shumway, see Seymour's Selected Seeds.) See **Garlic**, Heirlooms, Herbs, **Vegetables**.
Canada, International

RICHTERS
See **Booksellers**, Heirlooms, **Herbs**, Organics, Vegetables.

RONNIGER'S SEED POTATOES
See **Booksellers, Garlic**, Heirlooms, Organics, Vegetables.

ROSWELL SEED COMPANY, INC.
See Garlic, Grasses, **Vegetables**.

SALT SPRING SEEDS
See Garlic, Heirlooms, **Kidstuff**, Organics, **Vegetables**.

THE SANDY MUSH HERB NURSERY
See **Booksellers, Herbs**.

SEED SAVERS EXCHANGE–SEED SAVER PUBLICATIONS
See **Booksellers**, Heirlooms, **Horticultural Societies**, Vegetables.

SEED SHARES™
1992
Jeff McCormack
Catalog: $2
Seed Shares™, a sister company to Southern Exposure Seed Exchange®, collects and distributes vegetable, flower, and herb seeds that are not in general circulation but have a special interest or usefulness. See Heirlooms, Vegetables.
Canada

THE SEED SHOP
See **Cactus**.

SEEDS BLÜM
1981
Jan Blüm
Catalog: $3 (first-class mail, $4.50), 99 pp., illustrations
Seeds Blüm (yes, it's pronounced *bloom*) was begun and continues as a direct answer to Jan Blüm's concern about maintaining biodiversity. The catalog presents 600 vegetable, 50 herb, and 230 ornamental and edible flowering varieties of open-pollinated, nonhybrid seeds organized by botanical family. Ms. Blüm's catalog integrates cultural and practical information about seeds, seed saving, and growing with a strong message about biodiversity and cooperative self-reliance. She contracts small-scale growers to provide seeds and maintains a "garden to garden network" for home gardeners to test and cultivate seed. Plants are described by family name and flower. Listings for vegetables include evocative but precise descriptions, pollination information, genus and species,

when to plant, number of days to harvest, spacing, rows, number of seeds per packet, and a notation for heirlooms that have been on record for at least a hundred (a few, seventy-five) years. Descriptions for herbs include life cycle, height of plant, color of flower, garden and culinary uses. Flowers include life cycle, hardiness, shape and habit of plant, light requirements, when to sow, soil conditions, and color of flower. Offers fifteen mixtures of wildflower seeds by weight only. See **Booksellers**, **Garlic**, Heirloom, Herbs, **Kidstuff**, Vegetables, Wildflowers
Canada, Mexico, International

SEEDS OF CHANGE®
1989
Frank Connelly
Catalog: Free, 66 pp., color photographs
Seeds of Change® positions itself as the only national company whose seeds are 100 percent organically grown. Seeds are acquired through a network of farmers whose practices are certified organic in accordance with the Oregon tilth standards. Seeds that are not certified have been wild-crafted or obtained from Native Americans whose methods are organic but who do not seek outside certification. All seeds are open pollinated and untreated. Several in-depth essays regarding seedsmanship and biodiversity underscore the company's commitment to sound practices and the preservation of traditional and other heirloom varieties. Offers four hundred vegetable, sixty herb, and fifty flowering varieties. Descriptions include historical background, soil preference and culture, height of plant, form and consistency of fruit, number of days to maturity, amount of moisture required, sun/shade preference, and minimum number of seeds per packet. Guarantees satisfaction: will issue refund. See **Booksellers**, Heirlooms, Organics.
Canada

SEEDS TRUST: HIGH ALTITUDE GARDENS
See **Booksellers**, Garlic, **Grasses**, Heirlooms, Organics, **Vegetables**, **Wildflowers**.

SEEDSCAPES
1986
Karen Tefft and Kathryn Alexander
Catalog: Free, 6 pp.
Ms. Tefft and Ms. Alexander will deliver to you a list of plants, a layout, growing guidelines for each recommended plant, a gardening manual, a monthly calendar, and suggestions as to where to

buy recommended seeds. They offer a vegetable garden, three types of herb gardens, four annual flower gardens, a butterfly garden, a wildflower garden, and two shades of everlasting gardens. Guarantees satisfaction; will replace or issue refund.
Canada

SELECT SEEDS–ANTIQUE FLOWERS
1986
Marilyn Barlow
Catalog: $3 (first-class mail, $3.75), 27 pp.
Select Seeds is a source for gardeners wishing to cultivate a period flower garden. Ms. Barlow offers seed for 160 species and antique cultivars. General information pertaining to site selection, soil preparation, and seed starting and saving precedes the flower list. Cultural information is interspersed with thorough descriptions of the individual offerings. Each listing, headed by common and botanical names, includes the date by which a variety became commonly available, life cycle, color and form of flower, cultural requirements, sun and soil preferences, hardiness zone, and height. Many descriptions contain historical notes and the derivation of the given flower's name. Varieties that are fragrant, attract butterflies, and are suited to drying are highlighted. Seeds sold by the packet; seeds per packet not specified. Guarantees true to name and satisfaction; will replace or issue credit or refund. See **Booksellers**, Heirlooms.
Canada

SENECA HYBRIDS
See **Vegetables**.

SEYMOUR'S SELECTED SEEDS
1993
James Harrison
Catalog: Free, 64 pp., color photographs
Seymour's offers six hundred varieties of primarily imported seeds of flowering plants suitable for creating English-style cottage gardens. An eclectic selection of annuals, biennials, perennials, and shrubs that include the expected (marigolds, impatiens, zinnias) and the unexpected (asarinas, Himalayan blue poppies, nemophilas). Descriptions include color of flower, height of plant, cultural preferences, site selection, and varieties that are preferred as cut flowers. Seeds sold by the packet or by weight; seeds per packet specified. Guarantees satisfaction; will replace or issue credit or refund.
Canada, Mexico, International

SHARP BROS. SEED CO.
See **Grasses**.

SHARP BROS. SEED CO.–WILDFLOWER
DIVISION
See **Wildflowers**.

SHEPHERD'S GARDEN SEEDS
1984
Renee Shepherd and Beth Benjamin
Catalog: $1, 108 pp., illustrations
Shepherd's positions itself as providing seeds from worldwide sources to the gardener who loves to cook with especially fine-tasting vegetables and culinary herbs. But that doesn't preclude a glorious offering of 140 flowers focusing on old-fashioned varieties, soft colors, and graceful shapes for cutting, everlastings for drying, and edibles. Recent features included Shepherd's fragrant sweet pea renaissance and the reintroduction of seventeenth-, eighteenth-, and nineteenth-century "Heritage" sweet peas, 'Cupani', 'Painted Lady', and 'America'. Numerous collections regularly adorn this catalog. Recent entries include a collection (with instructions) to attract beneficial insects, as well as a butterfly, fragrant flower, hummingbird, songbird, and a white garden collection. Number of seeds per packet specified. Guarantees satisfaction; will accept seed packets for credit or refund up to six months after purchase. See **Booksellers**, **Garlic**, Heirlooms, Herbs, **Kidstuff**, **Supplies**, **Vegetables**. **Canada**

SHOOTING STAR NURSERY
See **Grasses**, Perennials, **Waterscapes**, Wildflowers.

SMITH NURSERY COMPANY
See Fruit, **Trees**.

SOUTHERN EXPOSURE SEED EXCHANGE®
See **Booksellers**, **Garlic**, Heirlooms, Herbs, **Supplies**, **Vegetables**.

SOUTHERN SEEDS
See **Booksellers**, Fruit, Garlic, Organics, **Vegetables**.

SOUTHWESTERN NATIVE SEEDS
See Cactus, Trees, **Wildflowers**.

"SOW ORGANIC" SEEDS
See Garlic, Heirlooms, Herbs, Organics, **Vegetables**.

STOCK SEED FARMS
See Grasses, **Wildflowers**.

STOKES SEEDS
1881
Catalog: Free, 112 pp., color photographs
Stokes is a seed catalog to savor. There are one thousand varieties of annuals, perennials, cut flowers, and everlastings; and nine hundred choices for vegetables (including oriental and gourmet types), with many variations. The catalog is steeped in cultural information for groups of vegetables and flowers as well as information specific to individual hybrids and open-pollinated varieties. Some of Stokes seed is now available untreated. Rich full descriptions are precise and include specifications for the flower, fruit, and plant as well as sowing, germination, and care instructions. Number of seeds per packet and per ounce are specified. See **Garlic**, **Supplies**, Vegetables.
Canada, Mexico, International

SUNRISE ENTERPRISES
See **Booksellers**, Garlic, **Vegetables**.

TERRITORIAL SEED COMPANY
See **Booksellers**, **Garlic**, Herbs, **Kidstuff**, Organics, **Supplies**, **Vegetables**.

THE THOMAS JEFFERSON CENTER FOR
HISTORICAL PLANTS
1987
Catalog: $1, 4 pp., illustrations and black-and-white photographs
The TJCHP at Jefferson's home in Monticello collects, preserves, and distributes historic plant varieties and promotes an appreciation for the origins of garden plants. They offer fifty types of seeds harvested from the gardens of Monticello and seeds packaged by the Center for Historic Plants at Tufton Nursery. Recent catalogs have included hollyhock, native columbine, cockscomb, tassel flower, bachelor's buttons, English lavender, and perennial pea. Descriptions include the date that a variety was first grown in American gardens and the date of the first reference in Jefferson's garden books. Also includes hardiness zone, color and size of flowers, and height of plant. Offers a Jefferson sampler with ten varieties known to have been grown by him, a kitchen herb sampler, and a mallow garden sampler. See **Booksellers**, **Furniture**, Heirlooms.

THOMPSON & MORGAN
1855
Bruce Sangster
Catalog: Free, 224 pp., color photographs
If you have a passion for seeds (flowers for sure), you'd better plan to take a month off from work, ignore your family and friends, and generally dispense with any other responsibilities before sitting down to read the Thompson & Morgan catalog. There are over 900 flowering plants and 120 vegetables in this catalog that counts among its inactive customers Charles Darwin and Claude Monet. Information for their A to Z of flower seeds includes life cycle, hardiness, All America selections, Royal Horticultural Society Award of Merit, National Council for the Conservation of Plants and Gardens, height and spread of mature plant, ease of germination, ease of aftercare, soil and sun requirements, and number of seeds per packet. Guarantees satisfaction; will replace or issue credit. See **Garlic**, Heirlooms, **Grasses**, **Vegetables**.
Canada, International

TINMOUTH CHANNEL FARM
See **Herbs, Kidstuff**, Organics.

TOMATO GROWERS SUPPLY CO.
See **Booksellers**, Heirlooms, **Supplies**, Vegetables.

TOTALLY TOMATOES
See **Supplies, Vegetables**.

VAN DYKE ZINNIAS
1992
Mickey Van Dyke
Color photo: LSASE
A specialist's specialist, Mrs. Van Dyke offers her own 'Supreme' variety zinnia that took a decade to develop. Grows three to five feet in height and comes in assorted colors. Sold by the packet with the number of seeds unspecified.
Canada, Mexico, International

VERMONT BEAN SEED COMPANY
See **Garlic**, Heirlooms, Herbs, **Vegetables**.

VERMONT WILDFLOWER FARM
See **Wildflowers**.

VESEY'S SEEDS LTD.
1939
Allen Perry
Catalog: Free, 126 pp., black-and-white and color photographs
A purveyor of seeds, primarily untreated, with headquarters on Prince Edward Island, specializing in varieties for short growing seasons. Trial gardens and germination tests on-site. Three hundred types of vegetable, fifteen herb, and one hundred flower seeds comprise 80 percent of the catalog. Rich descriptions include soil, feeding, water, light, and spacing requirements, planting and harvest times, and pests and problems. Descriptions include number of days to maturity for vegetables. Four assortments of easy-to-grow vegetables and herbs, five flower collections (biennials and perennials, everlastings, an old-fashioned cutting garden, a rock garden, and a selection characterized by strong colors), and four wildflower mixtures (for the Northeast, shady sites, low-growing varieties, and a meadow of favorite flowers from Lucy Maud Montgomery's book *Anne of Green Gables*). Most seeds offered by the packet or by weight, some by weight only. Specifies either seeds per packet or amount of seed required to plant a measured area. See **Booksellers, Garlic**, Herbs, **Supplies**, Vegetables, Wildflowers.
Canada

WILD EARTH NATIVE PLANT NURSERY
See Grasses, **Wildflowers**.

WILD SEED, INC.
See **Booksellers**, Grasses, **Kidstuff**, Trees, **Wildflowers**.

WILDSEED FARMS, INC.
See Herbs, **Wildflowers**.

WILLHITE SEED CO.
See **Garlic, Vegetables**.

WILLIAM DAM SEEDS
1949
Rene W. Dam
Catalog: $2., 63 pp., color photographs
Offers over one thousand varieties of vegetable, herb, flower, tree, shrub, and vine seeds. Over half of the catalog is devoted primarily to hybrid short-season vegetable seeds from Canada, the United States (including All America selections), and Europe (including Fleuroselect Medal winners). Information includes varieties that are best for selling at market, best for preserving, seeds per gram, seeds per packet, number of days to maturity outdoors, and

substantial cultural information. Offers fifty varieties of herbs and several hundred varieties of flowering annuals, perennials, and everlastings. Seeds sold by the packet or by weight. Guarantees satisfaction; will replace or issue refund within calendar year of purchase. See **Book**-sellers, **Garlic**, Herbs, Vegetables, Wildflowers. **Canada, International**

WOOD PRAIRIE FARM
See **Garlic**, Vegetables.

Selected Reading About Seeds

From Seed to Bloom, by Eileen Powell. How to propagate over five hundred types of flowering plants from seed. Includes a resource and source list for finding information and for finding seeds.

Garden Flowers from Seed, by Christopher Lloyd and Graham Rice. Written in the form of a dialog between two well-known experts, this volume offers advice on which seed-raised flowers to grow, how to germinate and care for them, and recommended uses in the garden. Includes thousands of flowering plants from over two hundred genera.

The New Seed-Starters Handbook, by Nancy Bubel. If you ask ten gardeners to recommend a book about how to get seeds started, you are likely to have this one recommended eleven times. In addition to the procedures for starting, transplanting, growing, and harvesting, there is an encyclopedic listing for two hundred plants with details about how to start each one from seed.

Park's Success with Seeds, by Ann Reilly. How to grow plants (mostly flowers and herbs) from seed. Includes germination requirements and pictures the developing seedlings and mature plants for over four hundred species. Color photographs.

Saving Seeds: The Gardener's Guide to Growing and Storing Vegetable and Flower Seed, by Marc Rogers. The basics on producing your own seeds. Includes information on harvesting, drying, storing, and testing.

Secrets of Plant Propagation, by Lewis Hill. Mr. Hill explains the basic techniques of propagation: divisions, seeds, layering, cuttings, grafting, and budding for flowers, vegetables, fruits, berries, shrubs, and trees. Clear, easy-to-follow illustrations.

Seed to Seed: Seed Saving Techniques for the Vegetable Gardener, by Suzanne Ashworth. A complete guide for saving the seeds of 160 vegetable varieties. A primer for the basics of seed saving and small-scale seed production. Includes a source list for hard-to-find seed-saving supplies. Photographs.

WILDFLOWERS AND NATIVES

PLANTS AND SEEDS

A source's criteria for designating a plant or seed as wildflower, native (including trees, shrubs, and vines), or adapted native helped determine its placement in this section or the perennial section. The number of offerings cited in each profile is based on information in the most recent catalog provided by the source. In this section, separate shipping seasons are noted for plants and seeds. A list of books about wildflowers and natives appears after the last listing.

Quick Find
The following sources are listed in this section:

ALPLAINS
1989
Alan D. Bradshaw
Catalog: $2 (recoverable), 54 pp., color photographs
Alplains offers seven hundred varieties of seeds from desert to alpine natives that are particularly useful in rock gardens. Seeds are collected worldwide, with emphasis on natives of the American Northwest and Rocky Mountain areas. Most varieties offered by Alplains are expected to be drought tolerant and suitable for xeric gardens. Each listing includes plant name, family name, height and spread at maturity, hardiness zone, life cycle, seed pretreatment code, germination code, color, and description. An explanation of pretreatment and germination procedures precedes the seed list. Descriptions of seeds that have been wildcrafted include their original location and elevation. Packets contain a minimum of thirty seeds. Guarantees satisfaction; will replace. See Perennials, Seeds.
Shipping season: All year.
Canada, Mexico, International

ARROWHEAD ALPINES
See **Conifers**, Grasses, **Perennials**, **Seeds**, Trees.

BALDWIN SEED CO.–SEEDS OF ALASKA
Richard Baldwin
Circa 1955
Catalog: $3, 32 pp.
Baldwin's has been collecting the seeds of Alaskan wildflowers for four decades. The catalog includes fifty-three varieties that are appropriate for gardeners in northern regions but not recommended for the South. Cultural and climatic information about the seeds and plants of this area makes for entertaining reading even if you ultimately decide not to commit to undertaking the extra care many of these varieties require. Descriptions include common and botanical names, plant height, and color of flower for most. Baldwin lists, but does not describe, 130 Russian and Siberian forbs, shrubs, trees, and grasses. Seeds sold by the packet; number of seeds not specified. See Grasses, Seeds.
Shipping season: All year.

BLUESTEM PRAIRIE NURSERY
1985
Ken Schaal
Catalog: Free, 19 pp.
Mr. Schaal lives at the ecozone between the grand prairie of Illinois and the eastern deciduous forest. From his avocation of saving Illinois tall grass prairie species, he found himself growing a surplus of plants. Inquiries about the sale of these plants grown from seed, cutting, or division evolved into Bluestem. The catalogue lists 100 one- and two-year-old forbs, 175 forb seeds, and 60 grass and sedge seeds. Organized by botanical name (common name also provided), the brief listings include color, habitat, height, and a notation for species of the Illinois ecotype. Ships dormant bareroot plants. Seeds sold by the packet, with a minimum count of one hundred. Seed orders must be placed by February. Guarantees true to name and safe arrival. See Grasses, Seeds.
Shipping season: Plants, March and April. Seeds, October through February.

BOOTHE HILL WILDFLOWERS
1988
Nancy Easterling
Catalog: Free, 12 pp., illustrations

Boothe Hill specializes in native and naturalized flowering species that perform well in the southern United States and should adapt to other areas of the country. Plants are organically grown and nursery propagated. Twenty-six varieties, mostly for sunny settings, have been selected for their ease of culture, durability, and beauty. Life cycle, height, color, bloom time, cultural requirements, and description for each. Plants shipped in containers; seeds sold by the packet. A mixture of annuals for open areas, and another particularly suited to the Southeast offered by the packet and by weight. See Organics, Seeds.
Shipping season: Plants, spring. Seeds, All year

BOWMAN'S HILL WILDFLOWER PRESERVE
1934
Tom Stevenson
Catalog: $1, 6 pp.
Bowman's Hill Wildflower Preserve is an eighty-acre tract of woodland in Bucks County, Pennsylvania, where the appreciation of native plants and conservation practices have been nurtured for over sixty years. Offers 104 varieties of seeds harvested at the preserve that are appropriate for a wide range of conditions. Botanical name, common name, germination requirements, and preferred habitat are noted for each variety. Seeds sold by the packet. Guarantees true to name. See **Horticultural Societies**, Seeds.
Shipping season: All year.
Canada, International

BUSSE GARDENS
See Daylilies, Grasses, **Hosta**, Peonies, **Perennials**.

CATTAIL MEADOWS LTD.
1993
Ed Tuhela and Laura and Steve Tuhela-Reuning
Catalog: Free, 15 pp.
This trio specializes in nursery propagated (some bulldozer-crafted) native perennials. Compatible nonnatives are clearly identified. Plants grown here (northern Ohio) have proven hardy through fluctuations in temperature from 20 degrees below zero to 100 degrees above. The catalog offers sixty varieties organized by botanical name. Listings include common name, hardiness zone, description of

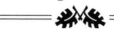
foliage and flower, site preference, cultural requirements, and habit. Ships in soil or bare-root depending upon requirements of the plant. Also offers shade, wetland, and wildlife garden collections chosen from among their most popular plants. Guarantees correctly labeled. See **Grasses**.
Shipping season: March through May.
August through November.

CLYDE ROBIN SEED CO.
1934
Stew Atwoun
Catalog: Free, 24 pp., color photographs
Clyde Robin sells wildflower seed mixtures and collections for specific regions and purposes (to deter pests or attract butterflies and hummingbirds) or a particular variety of flower in assorted colors. Mixtures sold in prepackaged containers; individual flower varieties sold by the packet or by weight. Guarantees satisfaction. See **Seeds**.
Shipping season: All year.
Canada, Mexico, International

COMSTOCK SEED
1985
Ed and Linda Kleiner
Catalog: Free, 4 pp.
The Kleiners collect most of their drought-tolerant seeds in the Great Basin area of the Far West. The Comstock catalog lists one hundred wildflowers and forbs, fifty grasses, eight legumes, and fifty trees and shrubs. Price by weight on request. Guarantees correctly labeled. See **Grasses, Seeds, Trees**.
Shipping season: All year.
Canada, Mexico, International

COUNTRY WETLANDS NURSERY & CON-
SULTING
1987
Jo Ann Gillespie
Catalog: $2, 16 pp., illustrations and black-
and-white photographs
Ms. Gillespie fully describes the wetland restoration and management services that her company provides. She also explains the characteristics of the natural communities for which Country Wetlands's plants are appropriate. One hundred and twenty species of plants and 135 seeds suitable for wetlands, prairie, and woodland of the greater Midwest are organized by botanical name. Listing includes common name, level of

availability, and native community. Offers a pre-selected package (fifty-seven plants) for ponds and a smaller package (six plants) for garden pools or water containers. Seeds sold by weight. Guarantees viable and true to name. See **Booksellers, Grasses**, Seeds, Waterscapes.
Shipping season: All year.

DESERT MOON NURSERY
See **Cactus, Seeds**.

DONAROMA'S NURSERY & LANDSCAPE
SERVICES
See **Perennials**.

EARTHLY GOODS LTD.
1990
Ann Streckfus and Stephen Brown
Catalog: $2 (recoverable), 17 pp., illustrations
Ms. Streckfus and Mr. Brown offers seeds for 110 varieties of wildflowers, native flowering plants, and grasses. The presentation of each variety includes an illustration, a detailed description, cultural requirements, historical notes, color of flower, height, life cycle, pounds per acre, and sun and soil requirements. Special notations highlight varieties that are native and those that are particularly attractive to birds and butterflies. Seeds sold by the packet or by weight; seeds per packet not specified. An extensive list of regional mixtures available by weight only includes the area, elevation, and climate for which each selection is best suited. Guarantees satisfaction; will issue refund up to thirty days from date of purchase. See **Furniture**, Grasses, Seeds.
Shipping season: All year.
Canada, Mexico, International

EASTERN PLANT SPECIALTIES
1985
Mark Stavish
Catalog: $3 (recoverable), 28 pp.,
illustrations
Mr. Stavish's New England–hardy plant material includes nursery-grown wildflowers. Among his fifty-five offerings are blue and yellow flag iris, Dutchman's breeches, Jack-in-the-pulpit, double bloodroot, yellow lady's slipper, and four trilliums. Descriptions include common and botanical name, height at maturity, color of flower, degree of difficulty to grow, and preferred sites and conditions. See **Conifers, Fruit**, Perennials, **Rhododendrons, Trees**.

Shipping season: March through June.
September through November.

EDGE OF THE ROCKIES "NATIVE SEEDS"
1991
Susan Komarek
Catalog: $2.50, 25 pp.
Susan Komarek wild-crafts and harvests seeds
from patches that she has developed in the
Four Corners region of the southern Rocky
Mountains. Ms. Komarek's catalog provides
information about establishing, sowing, watering, weeding, and nurturing the seeds that she
sells. Mixtures from seven plant communities
in this region, thoroughly described, are sold
in bulk packets that will cover from 50 to 250
square feet each. Seventy-five varieties available in individual packets are organized by
habitat. Description, range of native habitat,
annual precipitation, soil and sun preference,
stratification requirements, and seeds per
packet for each. Guarantees true to name. See
Grasses, Seeds.
Shipping season: All year.
Canada, International

FAR NORTH GARDENS
1962
K. J. Combs
Catalog: $2 (recoverable), 52 pp.
Far North Gardens has a number of areas of
concentration. Fifteen percent of Ms. Combs's
catalog is devoted to wildflowers offered as
plants and seeds. Native flowering plants include white baneberry, mayapple, foamflower,
and twin-leaf. Woodland setting plants include
trillium rhizomes, yellow trout lily corms, wood
leek corms, and squirrel corn. Plant assortments
include a showy wildflower sampler, an assortment of violets, a woodland walking tour assortment, and a fern potpourri. Species offered
as seed only include fifteen violets, blazing star,
black-eyed Susan, and thimble weed. Compact
descriptions include botanical and common
names, color and form of flowers, season of
bloom, and occasional anecdotes about the derivation of common names. Seeds sold by the
packet, with count or weight unspecified. Guarantees safe arrival. See Booksellers, Bulbs,
Grasses, Perennials, Seeds.
Shipping season: Seeds, all year. Plants,
March through June. September through
November.
Canada, Mexico, International

FEDER'S PRAIRIE SEED COMPANY
1989
Wayne and Lynda Feder
Catalog: Free, 4 pp.
The Feders specialize in native prairie wildflower
and grass seeds. They offer sixty varieties by
weight or thirty-six seeds per packet. Price list includes name of variety and required soil type.
Feder's offers four standard forb and prairie grass
mixtures. Customized mixtures and consulting
services are also available. See Grasses, Seeds.
Shipping season: Various, please inquire.

FROSTY HOLLOW ECOLOGICAL RESTORA-
TION
1982
Steve Erickson and Marianne Edain
Catalog: LSASE, 4 pp.
As an adjunct to its primary business, consultation on ecological restoration in the Pacific
Northwest, Frosty Hollow provides wild-crafted
native seeds from the area. Organized by botanical name (common name also provided) are the
seeds of forty trees and shrubs; ten grasses, sedges,
and rushes; and ninety herbaceous perennials,
wildflowers, and ground covers. Frosty Hollow
requires that gardeners order by the dates specified
since seed is collected based on orders received.
Seeds sold by weight. Guarantees true to name
and in good condition when shipped. See
Grasses, Seeds, Trees.
Shipping season: All year by preorder.
Canada, International

GARDENS OF THE BLUE RIDGE
1892
Edward and Robyn Fletcher
Catalog: $3 (recoverable), 31 pp.,
color photographs
The Fletchers are great-grandsons of the nursery's
cofounder, and their grandparents worked here in
Pineola, North Carolina, for the entirety of their
sixty-two-year marriage. The catalog offers 130
herbaceous perennial woodland wildflowers and
ferns as well as native trees and shrubs. General
planting instructions precede listings that are in
botanical order; descriptions include common
name, foliage habit, maximum height under ideal
conditions, description of flower and foliage,
sun/shade and site preferences, and season of
bloom. Guarantees true to name. The Fletchers
like to "keep our good rich North Carolina soil," so
most plants are shipped bareroot. See Perennials,
Trees.

Shipping season: March through May.
September through December.
Canada, Mexico, International

GARDENS NORTH
See Grasses, **Seeds**, Perennials.

GREEN HORIZONS
1970
Sherry Miller
Catalog: LSASE, 12 pp.
Green Horizons offers fifty-four individual varieties of Texas wildflower seeds, including four types of scarified bluebonnet (*Lupinus texensis*). Also prepares six mixtures for autumn sowing: "East Texas," "Gulf Coast," "Hill Country," "Native Texas Wildflowers," "Roadside" (for open sunny areas), and "Perennial" (for nine months of bloom). All are available by the packet; most also available by weight. Number of seeds per measure specified. Carries buffalo grass and a local turf blend sold by the pound. See **Booksellers**, Grasses, Seeds.
Shipping season: All year.
Canada, Mexico, International

HAMILTON SEEDS & WILDFLOWERS
1981
Rex and Amy Hamilton
Catalog: Free, 15 pp., color photographs
The Hamiltons' business began by harvesting prairie grass seeds for ranching and wildlife purposes. Struck by the beauty of the wildflowers that grew on the ever-changing prairie, they began harvesting wildflower seeds. Offers forty-five perennial wildflowers native to Missouri and the Midwest. Organized by common name, descriptions include color of flower, height at maturity, sun/shade requirements, and preferred soil type. Offers glade-dry soil mixes and prairie-deep soil mixes as seed, bareroot, and potted plants. Bareroot plants are two to five years old; field-grown plants are shipped in four-by-four-inch pots; seeds are two hundred to the packet or by weight. See **Grasses**, Seeds.
Shipping season: Bareroot, March and April. Potted plants, March through May. Seeds, all year.

HOLLAND WILDFLOWER FARM
Bob and Julie Holland
Catalog: $4.25, 32 pp., illustrations
Price list: LSASE (with 2 FCS), 4 pp.

The Hollands sell nursery-propagated wildflowers and seeds, grown and harvested on their farm in the Ozarks. Their catalog is sold as a guidebook to wildflower gardening and includes sections on wildflower terms, planning and design, seeding versus planting, soil conditioning, growing wildflowers from seed, and creating a wildflower meadow. Descriptions of one hundred plants, primarily natives of the southeastern United States, include sun/shade requirements, color of flower, season of bloom, height at maturity, and garden uses. Natives, cutting flowers, ground covers, and wildflower cultivars are so noted. Separate price lists for plants and seeds list those varieties that are currently being offered. Sold by the packet, with an unspecified number of seeds, or by weight. See **Booksellers**, Herbs, Seeds.
Shipping season: Seeds, all year. Plants, March through June. September through November.
Canada, Mexico, International

HOMAN BROTHERS SEED, INC.
1980
Nathan Young
Price list: Free, 3 pp.
Homan Brothers offers 125 types of flower, grass, tree, and shrub seeds native to Arizona. Twenty-five percent of their list is flowers: from Arizona lupine, to deer vetch, to wild pink penstemon. Thirty-five percent of the list covers trees and shrubs, including Apache plume, cliffrose, mountain mahogany, Texas mountain laurel, and turpentine bush. The balance of their seeds is grasses, including blue panic grass, desert Indian wheat, fluff grass, and Sodar streambank whitegrass. Organized by botanical name; descriptions include common name, life cycle, planting time, color of flower, height at maturity, number of seeds per pound, number of pounds per acre, and brief comments about use and habit. Seeds sold by weight. See Grasses, Seeds, Trees.
Shipping season: All year.

IOWA PRAIRIE SEED COMPANY
1988
Daryl F. Kothenbeutel
Catalog: $2, 12 pp.
Mr. Kothenbeutel specializes in native prairie grasses and wildflowers, most requiring full sun. Offers thirty types of wildflowers (perennials) and grass species (nursery–propagated from Iowa ecotype seed) as live plants. Seed list of 120 offerings

includes five types of milkweed, eight asters, four gentians, a narrow-leafed and a broad-leafed cattail, and twenty-four grasses. The catalog, organized by botanical name, includes common name, natural habitat (wetland, wet prairie, medium prairie, dry prairie, and woodland), and seed treatment. Seeds sold by the packet, with an unspecified number per packet, or by weight. Offers custom-blended prairie wildflower mixtures on request, assistance in controlled burning of fields, and on-site planning and consultation services. See Grasses, Seeds.
Shipping season: Seeds, all year. Plants, April through June.

LANDSCAPE ALTERNATIVES, INC.
1986
Karl Ruser
Catalog: $2, 16 pp.
Mr. Ruser offers 150 native and other low-maintenance cold-hardy forbs and grasses. Plants are nursery propagated from stock originally collected within a hundred-mile radius of St. Paul, Minnesota. Catalog is organized by characteristics: forbs for full sun and dry conditions, forbs for full sun and dry to mesic conditions, forbs for full sun and mesic to moist conditions, etc., through forbs for full shade and mesic conditions. Descriptions include common and botanical names, color, height at maturity, and suggestions for use in the garden. The catalog poses a series of questions to encourage you to evaluate your site and conditions in order to select the right plant for the right location. A considerable amount of space is devoted to precise planting guidelines and to describing the benefits of naturalizing your landscape. Offers preplanned assortments for the creation of prairie gardens of two hundred square feet, one thousand square feet, and larger. Guarantees true to name. See Grasses.
Shipping season: April through September.

LARNER SEEDS
1978
Judith Lowry
Catalog: $2, 45 pp., illustrations
Larner specializes in the seeds of California native plants, including sixty-five wildflowers, twenty-five grasses, thirty-five shrubs and vines, and fifteen trees. The emphasis here is on backyard restoration gardening as practiced by encouraging existing natives and reintroducing others appropriate to a particular area. Descriptions are brief

but rich, and include botanical and common names, height of plant at maturity, sun and soil preferences, and growth habit. Annuals sold by the ounce or in swathe quarter pounds. Perennial seeds sold by the packet; larger trade packets also available. Six mixtures for a variety of site locations and conditions available by the packet or by weight. See Booksellers, Grasses, Seeds, Trees.
Shipping season: All year.

LAS PILITAS NURSERY
1979
Celeste Wilson
Catalog: $6. Availability list: $1, 10 pp.
Las Pilitas grows plants that are native to California (some also growing throughout the West) and maintains stock in over five hundred species grown in one-gallon or larger containers as part of their restoration and consulting business. Their catalog, "A Manual of California Natives," is a thorough reference work with ecological and cultural information along with descriptions of some nine hundred species and varieties. See Grasses, Trees.
Shipping season: All year.
Canada, Mexico, International

MELLINGER'S
See Booksellers, Furniture, Kidstuff, Perennials, Seeds, Supplies.

MIDWEST WILDFLOWERS
1969
Leroy and Diane Busker
Catalog: $1, 14 pp., illustrations.
The Buskers, operating a mail-order business from their home in Rockton, Illinois, specialize in the seeds of species that are common to the midwestern United States. Seeds are collected with the permission of the owners of private meadows and woods. The Buskers' catalog offers highly detailed profiles including history, culture, and uses for a dozen species. Their seed list (common name and botanical name only) includes 120 species. Number of seeds per packet varies according to the size of individual seeds. See Seeds.
Shipping season: All year.
Canada, Mexico, International

MISSOURI WILDFLOWERS NURSERY
1985
Mervin Wallace
Catalog: $1, 18 pp., color photographs

MWN propagates plants that have their genetic origin within the state of Missouri 99 percent of the time. Offers one hundred wildflowers and a sampling of grasses and shrubs grown from seeds or cuttings. Descriptions include botanical name, common name, sun/shade preference, season of bloom, color, height at maturity, moisture requirements, spacing when sowing, life cycle, and comments about special requirements or qualities. Includes clear instructions for preparation of beds before planting or sowing. Bareroot plants are one to five years old; potted plants (shipped in quart or gallon pots) are one and two years old; packets usually contain one hundred seeds; also sells in bulk. Guarantees species to be true to name and to arrive in good condition. See Grasses, Perennials, Seeds.
Shipping season: Bareroot, March and April. Potted plants, March through June. Seeds, all year.

Moon Mountain Wildflowers
1986
Becky L. Schaff
Catalog: $3, 32 pp.
Moon Mountain's wildflower seed is native to, and suitable for, a wide range of climates. Ms. Schaff lists sixty species and provides, in a uniform format, information about ease of growth, culture (sun/water preferences), color and size of flower and stem, period of bloom, the area to which a species is native, and the range of geographic and climatic areas to which it can be adapted. Provides extensive cultivation instructions. A strong feature of the catalog is the lists of moisture-loving and drought-tolerant flowers for shady and sunny spots, those that grow in clay soils, those that promote erosion control, flowers for planting in existing grassland, for cutting gardens, and the best bets for extended seasonal bloom. Ms. Schaff also has numerous prepared mixtures for specific locales: an Alaska wildflower mix, six for California, and seven specifying states for which they are most appropriate. Species seed packets cover fifteen square feet; a half ounce of seeds covers 125 square feet. See Seeds.
Shipping season: All year.
Canada, Mexico, International

Mostly Natives Nursery
1984
Walter Earle and Margaret Graham
Catalog: $3, 20 pp., illustrations

Although Mr. Earle and Ms. Graham grow plants from near and far, they catalog and sell (by mail) only California coastal and drought-tolerant natives. Just under 50 percent of their stock, which includes bunchgrasses, ground covers, and shrubs, are perennials. They have consistently highlighted several types of *Eriogonum* (buckwheat) and *Heuchera* (alum root). The catalog includes extensive writings about plant communities: northern coastal forests, scrub and prairie, southern coastal sage scrub and chaparral, and oak woodlands. Descriptions of individual offerings (botanical and common names provided) include provenance, habit, and culture. A tolerance chart specifies season of bloom, flower color, sun/shade preference, water and heat requirements and tolerance, and hardiness zone. See Grasses, Perennials, Trees.
Shipping season: March through May. September through November.

Native American Seed
1986
Jan and Bill Neiman
Catalog: $1, 20 pp., color photographs
The Neimans specialize in twenty-five types of native wildflower and grass seeds harvested from the gene pool of the Texas-Oklahoma bioregion. Uniformly presented descriptions include height, time of bloom, planting rate for seeds per one hundred square feet and per acre, location of seed harvest, and references to specific books for additional culture and care information. Harvested seeds available by weight. Also offers wildflower tubers (number of tubers per packet listed) and conservancy seed packets that each cover twenty to twenty-five square feet. See Booksellers, Grasses, Seeds.
Shipping season: All year.

Native Gardens
1983
Meredith and Ed Clebsch
Catalog: $2, 26 pp.
This Greenback, Tennessee, propagator of natives lists 150 herbaceous perennials, 30 trees, shrubs, and vines, and a smaller number of ferns and grasses. Plant material is available variously as seeds (some collected) and as plants in 3 1/2-by-3 1/2-inch containers or quart and gallon sizes. The first section of the catalog presents charts organized by botanical name (common name also provided), with information about sun/shade preference, growth and habit, moisture requirements, season of bloom, color of flower, soil preference, hardiness zone, and

size at maturity. The cultural reference section, also organized by botanical name, provides multiple common names by which a species may be known, provenance prior to naturalizing in the United States, a thorough physical description of the plant, garden and landscape uses, companion plants, use as a deterrent to pests (where applicable), when to divide, and other facts specific to an individual species. Guarantees plants shipped in good condition and true to name. Condition of orders shipped west of the Rockies guaranteed only when shipped by second-day air. See Grasses, Seeds, Trees.
Shipping season: All year.
No Arizona, California, Oregon, or Washington

NATIVE SEEDS, INC.
1979
Dr. James A. Saunders
Catalog: Free, 5 pp.
Thirty-five species of wildflower are organized by common name. Description includes botanical name, life cycle, cultural advice, height of plant, intermittent historical notes, and postharvest uses. Offers general North American mixture, Northeast, South, and West (including the desert Southwest) mixes, one of natives, and another of species that have been naturalized in North America for at least a century. Seed packets appropriate for one hundred square feet. Bulk seed sold in weights of a quarter pound or more. Guarantees true to description. See Seeds.
Shipping season: All year.
Canada, Mexico, International

NATIVE SEEDS/SEARCH
See **Booksellers**, Garlic, **Kidstuff**, Seeds, Vegetables.

NEW ENGLAND WILD FLOWER SOCIETY
1900
Catalog: $2.50, 22 pp.
NEWFS promotes the conservation of temperate North American plants through horticulture, education, research, habitat preservation, and advocacy. Most of their 230 species of seeds and twelve spores from plants in the Garden in the Woods (also offers a brief selection of wild collected seeds) are native to eastern North America. Prairie and western species are noted and can be referenced in a guide for the central states or western regions. Many of the species in this catalog are uncommon in cultivation but are characterized by NEWFS as worthy of

attention. All species are noted as hardy to at least zone 5. Catalog is organized by botanical name. Descriptions include common name, sun/shade preferences, season of bloom, color of flower, height at maturity, and foliage characteristics. Extensive germination information is given for all seeds. Packets contain an unspecified number of seeds. See **Booksellers**, **Horticultural Societies**, **Kidstuff**, Seeds.
Shipping season: January through March.

NICHE GARDENS
1986
Kim Hawks
Catalog: $3, 30 pp., color photographs
Niche Gardens is located near Chapel Hill in the Piedmont region of North Carolina. The flora flourishing in the roadside ditches, open fields, and nearby woodlands there had a special appeal to Kim Hawks when over a decade ago, faced with unemployment, she decided instead to create a business that offered nursery-propagated wildflowers. Ms. Hawks's catalog of natives, adapted natives, and wildflowers includes 180 herbaceous plants and 30 trees and shrubs. Niche has introduced several "new" plants from the wild, including *Helianthus giganteus* 'Sheila's Sunshine', *Lobelia cardinalis* 'Heather Pink', and, jointly with the North Carolina Botanical Gardens, *Baptisia* 'Purple Smoke', and *Solidago rugosa* 'Fireworks'. Descriptions include botanical name (with pronunciation key); common name, rich observations on habit, culture, companions, and landscape uses; and legends indicating light preference, height and spread of mature plants, whether attractive to or provider for birds, butterflies, and wildlife, noseworthy fragrance, cutting or dried flower use, and hardiness zone. See Trees, Perennials.
Shipping season: February through November.

NICHOLS GARDEN NURSERY
See **Booksellers**, **Garlic**, **Herbs**, Organics, Seeds, Supplies, **Vegetables**.

NORTHWEST NATIVE SEED
1992
Ron Ratko
Catalog: $1, 40 pp.
Mr. Ratko originally started collecting native seed for seed exchanges but quickly found that he had amassed a sufficient diversity of species to establish a mail-order catalog. He offers wild collected seeds from the western United States, emphasizing infrequently offered species suitable for the

rock garden, perennial border, or the alpine house. His list of one thousand types of seeds include those found in habitats from the desert alkaline flats to alpine fellfields in the remote regions of California, the northern Rockies, and the Great Basin region of Nevada and Utah. The catalog is organized by botanical name. Mr. Ratko identifies the location and notes the elevation and exposure of the harvest site; he also describes the prevalent geographical and climatic conditions at the site. Plant descriptions are finely detailed and graphic. Packets contain twenty-five seeds unless otherwise noted. See Seeds.

Shipping season: November through April.
Canada, Mexico, International

OTTER VALLEY NATIVE PLANTS
Gail Rhynard
Catalog: $2, 9 pp.
Otter Valley is a highly focused nursery trading in the native and native adapted plants and seeds of, and for use only in, southern Ontario. Ms. Rhynard's list of seventy-five species includes primarily perennial wildflowers, grasses, sedges, and a brief mention of vines and shrubs. All species offered are available as live plants; seed is available for about 20 percent of her list. Descriptions include color of flower, height at maturity, time of bloom, sun/shade preference, soil moisture preference, whether seeds are also available, and brief comments noting a particular need or characteristic of a species. See Grasses, Seeds.

Shipping season: Seeds, all year. Plants, mid-April through mid-May. Mid-September through October.
Southern Ontario only

PEACEFUL VALLEY FARM & GARDEN SUPPLY
1976
Kathleen Fenton
Catalog: Free, 120 pp., illustrations and black-and-white photographs
This full-service catalog is packed with seeds, supplies, and tools for organic gardeners and farmers of all sizes. PVF & GS offers three native species wildflower mixes from NPI: native California, native Northwest, native Southwest, and eight regional mixes: California central valley, California coast range, the Midwest, Northeast, Pacific Northwest, Southeast United States, the desert Southwest, and mountain. Mixtures for broader use include a blue-and-gold blend, a col-

lection of twenty-two annuals, and mix of wildflowers that will grow in partial shade. Also lists ten individual varieties including four lupines. Sells seeds by weight. See **Booksellers, Garlic, Grasses, Organics, Seeds, Supplies.**

Shipping season: All year.
Canada, Mexico, International

PLANTS OF THE SOUTHWEST
1977
Gail Haggard
Catalog: $3.50, 103 pp., color photographs
Plants of the Southwest offers the seed and live plants of 450 wildflowers, trees, shrubs, chilies, vegetables, and ornamental grasses that are native to or have been adapted to the conditions of the American Southwest. Two hundred and twenty wildflowers available variously as four- to six-inch plants or as seeds include a concentration in primroses (*Oenothera*), penstemons, and unusual collections for cutting and drying. Organized by botanical name, descriptions include common name, color and shape of flowers, season of bloom, growth habit, and seed-sowing suggestions. Specifies sun or part shade, medium, low, or very low water required, and hardiness zone for each listing. Indicates method of stratification (if any) a seed requires. Catalog includes a thorough "Where, When, & How to Plant Natives" section. Offers mountain meadow shady, high plains piñon juniper, high desert, California coast and foothills, low desert, Texas prairie, as well as annual seed mixtures. Mixtures sold by the ounce, with number of square feet covered per ounce specified. Seeds sold by the packet, with a specified number of seeds, or by weight. Plants are four- to six-inch starts. Guarantees seeds are viable, true to name, and will grow in your garden if you follow instructions; will replace. Guarantees live delivery of plants; will replace. See **Booksellers, Grasses,** Heirlooms, Seeds, Trees, **Vegetables.**

Shipping season: Seeds, all year. Plants, April through June. September and October.

PRAIRIE MOON NURSERY
1982
Alan Wade
Catalog: $2, 30 pp.
Prairie Moon specializes in native plants and seeds of the wetlands, prairies, and woodlands of Minnesota and the upper midwestern United States. Natives are defined here as plants that were indigenous prior to European settlement. Plants are organically grown on-site in outdoor

nursery beds. Extensive information on site preparation, seeding, sowing, cover crops, packing, watering, weeding, burning, and restoration. The catalog includes 225 forbs, 40 trees, shrubs, and vines, and forty grasses, sedges, and rushes listed by botanical name. Descriptions for forbs include common name, germination code, soil moisture requirements, sun preference, height at maturity, color of flower, and season of bloom. Shipped bareroot. Seeds sold by the packet (number of seeds not specified) or by weight. Mr. Wade has developed twelve mixtures for areas under a thousand square feet. Named varieties within each of the twelve mixtures are listed by weight. Also offers eight mixtures for areas over thirty-five hundred square feet. See **Booksellers, Grasses**, Organics, Seeds, Trees.

Shipping season: Seeds, all year. Plants, April and May. October and November. Canada

PRAIRIE NURSERY
1972
Neil Diboll
Catalog: $3, 48 pp., color photographs
Mr. Diboll specializes in native plants for ecological gardening for soil, water, and habitat conservation. He groups plants by site and condition, such as clay busters (species that will establish themselves in heavy clay soils), moist meadow gardens, dry and medium soil short grass prairies, and tall grass prairies. Most stock is grown in the ground in Westfield, Wisconsin (except for some grasses and rhizomatous flowers), before being dug and barerooted for shipment. Over half of the catalog is devoted to individual species organized by common name with botanical name given. Species are richly described with detailed information about color of flowers, height, season of bloom, soil preferences, and sun/shade requirements. One hundred wildflowers, grasses, and sedges available as one-year (some older) bareroot transplants, and 125 species offered as seeds sold by weight. Guarantees true to name, healthy and vigorous. See **Booksellers**, Grasses, Seeds.

Shipping season: Plants, April through June. September through November. Seeds, all year. Canada (plants)

PRAIRIE RIDGE NURSERY
1974
Joyce A. Powers
Catalog: $3 (recoverable), 23 pp.

Prairie Ridge Nursery's specialty is native midwestern herbaceous plants for environmental restoration, landscape, and garden use. Prairie Ridge began with the sun-loving prairie species of Wisconsin but have since added wetland and woodland plants to its offerings. Seeds are wild ecotype; all plants are propagated at the nursery. One hundred and thirty species organized as forbs, grasses, and sedges; description includes habitat, height, color, season of bloom, postharvest uses, and attractiveness to birds and butterflies. Seeds sold by weight; number of seeds per measure available upon request. Offers seven plant collections for sites of twenty-five to one hundred square feet and seven seed mixtures for a thousand square feet or more. Offers consulting, planning, planting, and management services under the name of CRM Ecosystems Services. Guarantees true to name and safe arrival; will replace or issue refund or credit. See Grasses, Perennials, Seeds.

Shipping season: Plants, April and May. October and November. Seeds, February through November. Canada

PRAIRIE SEED SOURCE
1974
Robert Ahrenhoerster
Catalog: $1, 18 pp.
Mr. Ahrenhoerster's specialty is the seed of southeastern Wisconsin prairie genotypes and related ecosystem members. Seeds are collected locally from natural sites and designated restoration areas. The PSS catalog is one of the most straightforward and easy to understand that you are likely to read. One hundred and sixty-five species are organized and illustrated (with graphs that show comparative height) by the month of bloom. Within the month are descriptions of genus, species, common name, dried-flower usage, color, moisture requirement, and identification as a grass, shrub, or forb. Each packet covers ten square feet. Guarantees safe arival. See **Bookseller**, Grasses, Seeds.

Shipping season: All year. Canada, International

THE PRIMROSE PATH
See **Perennials**.

PUTNEY NURSERY, INC.
1928
Ruth and C. J. Gorius

Catalog: Free, 16 pp., color photographs
The Putney Nursery woodland wildflower gardens were started by George D. Aiken, senator from Vermont, the governor of that state, and the author of *Pioneering with Wildflowers*. The Goriuses list eighty-five of the two hundred varieties of wildflowers, perennials, and alpines that they propagate and from which they collect seeds. Descriptions include botanical name, common name, a broad range for height at maturity, color of flower, and season of bloom. Offers a mixture containing only annuals for a quick flush of color, a perennial mix, a shady meadow mix, mixes that are appropriate for the midwestern and southeastern United States, and a New England wildflower meadow mix. Individual varieties available by the packet (number of seeds not specified), one-ounce "Flower-Up" packets (covering up to eighteen hundred square feet depending upon the type of seed) and mixtures by weight. See Herbs, Perennials, Seeds.
Shipping season: April through December.
Canada

RUSSELL GRAHAM: PURVEYOR OF PLANTS
1980
Yvonne and Russell Graham
Catalog: $2 (recoverable), three-year subscription; 32 pp.
The Grahams grow five hundred "unordinary hardy herbaceous species perennials" (including hardy ferns), with an emphasis on Northwest and North American natives. They characterize their selections of four hundred offerings as (mostly) requiring little or low maintenance. Areas of concentration and recent highlighted selections include *Acorus* (sweet flag), *Alcea* (hollyhock), *Allium* (ornamental onions), hardy cyclamen, true perennial digitalis, *Eremurus* (foxtail lily, desert candles, king's spears), cranesbill, *Meconopsis* (Welsh poppy, Himalayan poppy), *Polemonium* (Jacob's ladder), primula, *Thalictrum* (meadow rue), *Verbascum* (moth mullen), and American species and English bedding viola or violets. Descriptions include color of flower, height of plants at maturity, and hardiness zone. Notes Northwest and North American natives. Ships bareroot. Guarantees true to name and healthy. See Perennials.
Shipping season: February through April.
August through November.

SEEDS BLÜM
See **Booksellers, Garlic,** Heirlooms, Herbs, **Kidstuff, Seeds,** Vegetables.

SEEDS TRUST: HIGH ALTITUDE GARDENS
Bill McDorman
Catalog: Free, 44 pp.
Seeds Trust is a bioregional company that acquires and tests seeds from diverse sources that are acclimated to cold, short-season use and, in the case of this firm, growing at six thousand feet above sea level. Guarantees satisfaction; will replace or issue refund. See **Booksellers,** Garlic, **Grasses,** Heirlooms, Organics, Seeds, **Vegetables.**
Canada, Mexico, International

SHARP BROS. SEED CO.–
WILDFLOWER DIVISION
1985
Judith Rogers
Catalog: Free, 17 pp., watercolors
The emphasis here is the seed of midwestern wildflowers. Forty-five species offered, listed by common and botanical names; extensive information provided regarding proper height of plant, form and color of flowers, season of bloom, and life cycle. Lists contents of several mixtures for Great Plains, Midwest, and wet and dry conditions. Seeds sold by the packet or by weight. See Seeds.
Shipping season: All year.
Canada, Mexico, International

SHOOTING STAR NURSERY
1989
Sherri and Marc Evans
Catalog: $2 (recoverable), 25 pp., illustrations
Shooting Star is the plant materials division of Ecological Stewardship Services whose specialty is ecological landscaping, restoration, and stewardship planning. The Evanses' catalog focuses on 250 species of plants native to forests, prairies, and wetlands of the eastern United States. Plants are nursery propagated; seeds are nursery collected and wildcrafted. Perennial wildflowers are organized by botanical name followed by common name. Descriptions include form and size of plant, color and shape of flower, site and light preferences, the type of wildlife a species attracts, season of bloom, whether a plant is suited to xeric gardens, postharvest uses, whether shipped bareroot or in pots, and availability of seeds by the packet and bulk. Number of seeds per packet noted. Offers native grass seed, prairie seed, and wildflower seed meadow mixtures by weight for areas under four thousand square feet. Includes a chart of appropriate prairie forbs for dry, mesic, and wet soils. Naturescapes™ packets for butterfly, prairie patch, hummingbird, bird and butterfly, and woodland edge sites of up to 125

square feet. Guarantees healthy and viable; will re-place plants that fail the first season. See **Grasses**, Perennials, Seeds, **Waterscapes**.

Shipping season: Seeds, all year. Potted plants, April through October. Bareroot, November through April.

Canada

SOUTHWESTERN NATIVE SEEDS
1975
Sally and Tim Walker
Catalog: $1, 7 pp.
The majority (over 200) of the 350 species for which the Walkers have collected the seed of shrubs, succulents, and wildflowers are native to their Arizona–New Mexico area. Also offers a smaller number from California, Colorado, Idaho, Mexico, Montana, Texas, Utah, and Wyoming. Will provide growing instructions for desert plants, as well as a bibliography of useful publications about growing and identifying southwestern natives, upon request. Seeds sold by the packet. See Cactus, Seeds, Trees.
Shipping season: November through March. May.
Canada, International

STOCK SEED FARMS
1957
Lyle, Margaret, Dave, and Linda Stock
Catalog: Free, 26 pp., color photographs and black-and-white illustrations
The Stocks specialize in the seeds of prairie grasses and wildflowers. About 35 percent of their cata-log is devoted to forty types of prairie and natu-ralized wildflowers. Organized by common name (botanical name also provided), the Stocks' de-scriptions include color and form of flower, sea-son of bloom, special site uses, height at maturity, life cycle, and amount of seeds required for a thousand square feet. Extensive information on planting or seeding, bed preparation, care after planting, special sites such as shaded and sandy areas, and the virtue of patience in establishing and growing wildflowers. Seed sold by the packet (sufficient for ten to fifteen square feet) or by weight. See **Grasses**, Seeds.
Shipping season: All year.

SUNLIGHT GARDENS
1982
Andrea Sessions and Marty Zenni
Catalog: $3.00 (two-year subscription), 29 pp., illustrations

Sunlight Gardens offers two hundred nursery-prop-agated and -grown wildflowers, ferns, and shrubs that are native to the southeastern United States. Ms. Sessions and Mr. Zenni's definition of natives is nondogmatic as they offer (and identify as such) plants that originated elsewhere and have natural-ized here over an extended period or that are horti-cultural selections of native plants. The catalog is organized by botanical name (with common name also provided). Highlights plants that are easy to es-tablish and, based on their observations during the drought of 1988, those that need less water. The narrative descriptions are thorough and very acces-sible, including information on flower color, leaf formation, growth habit, sun and site preferences, cultural notes, pleasing companion plants, expected height and width at maturity, and hardiness zone. Offers collections suitable for sunny or shady loca-tions, and damp or dry meadows. Guarantees true to name, healthy, and safe arrival; will replace or issue refund at customer's choice. See Trees.
Shipping season: September through May.

TRIPPLE BROOK FARM
Catalog: Free, 60 pp., illustrations
See Fruit, **Grasses**, Perennials, Trees.

VERMONT WILDFLOWER FARM
1981
Chy and Ray Allen, and Rob Towne
Catalog: Free, 16 pp.
VWF offers seed mixtures for six geographical re-gions within specific states and provinces; also of-fers partial-shade, all-perennial, drought-tolerant, and low-growing mixtures for use across regions. Varieties listed by botanical and common names; description includes height at maturity, season of bloom, life cycle, and color. Forty varieties sold by the packet listed by common and botanical names. Description includes color, sun/shade preference, season of bloom, height at maturity, and area of origin. Seeds per packet not noted. Offers thirty-minute instructional video, *How to Create Your Own Wildflower Meadow*. Guarantees seeds will grow (if not subjected to drought, ex-treme temperatures, or "acts of God"); will replace or issue credit or refund. See Seeds.
Shipping season: All year.
Canada

VESEY'S SEEDS LTD.
See **Booksellers, Garlic**, Herbs, **Seeds, Sup-plies**, Vegetables.

WATER WAYS NURSERY
1986
Sally Kurtz
Catalog: $2, 19 pp., illustrations
Just over half of Ms. Kurtz's catalog of aquatics and perennials (primarily) native to the eastern United States is devoted to one hundred plants that she identifies as "terrestrials." Organized by the number of hours of sunlight a plant requires daily (and listed by botanical name), Ms. Kurtz's terrestrials include such full-sun perennials as swamp milkweed, butterfly weed, several coreopsis, coneflower, and goldenrods and such full-sun to part-shade selections as marginal turtle heads (white, pink, and rose), which require moist soil. Also offers a broad range of plants that are comfortable in partial to full shade. Descriptions include common name, height at maturity, soil preference, color and shape of flowers, and season of bloom. Land-based plants shipped in quart containers. Guarantees true to name and viable; will replace or issue refund. See **Waterscapes.**
Shipping Season: May and June. August through October.

WE-DU NURSERY
1981
Dr. Richard E. Weaver and Rene A. Duval
Catalog: $2, 50 pp., illustrations
We-Du sits on a thirty-acre site abundant in water and with diverse terrain in Marion, North Carolina, where Weaver and Duval combine a nursery, display, and personal garden. The emphasis here among their six hundred offerings are nursery-propagated southeastern natives and their oriental counterparts; rare in cultivation and unusual rock and woodland plants. Their personal favorites are ferns, species iris, trillium, and epimedium. Descriptions include botanical and common names, height at maturity, sun/shade and soil preferences, color and form of flower and foliage, and recommendations for garden or woodland use. Guarantees true to name, correctly labeled, and strong and healthy when shipped; will replace. See **Bulbs**, Iris, Perennials.
Shipping season: Mid-February through mid-December.
No Arizona, California, or Hawaii

WILD EARTH NATIVE PLANT NURSERY
1990
Richard Pillar

Catalog: $2, 26 pp. Seed list: LSASE
Mr. Pillar is a certified landscape architect who propagates (from seeds, spores, cuttings, or by division) 140 native wildflowers, a dozen ferns, and 8 grasses. Highlights include a prickly pear cactus that was once common on the eastern coast of the United States, several introductions from the Mount Cuba Center for the Study of Piedmont Flora, and a substantial number of species that are appropriate for moist to boggy soils. Descriptions include botanical and common names, form and color of flower and foliage, growth and cultural habits, and site preferences. Consistent symbols indicate season of bloom, moisture requirement, height/spread, hardiness zones, sun/shade preference, and the size of plant/container being offered. A seed list is prepared at the end of each growing season offering small packets in limited quantities. Guarantees true to name and healthy. See **Grasses**, Seeds.
Shipping season: Plants, April through October. Seed, December through March.

WILD SEED, INC.
1981
Rita Jo Anthony
Catalog: Free, 14 pp.
Ms. Anthony specializes in the seed of native wildflower, tree, shrub, and grass species from the Rocky Mountains, Great Basin, and Sonoran desert. Wild Seed also offers selected noninvasive introduced species that have proven their adaptability in the Southwest. One hundred and forty wildflower varieties, listed by common and botanical names, are available by the packet (seeds per packet not noted) or by weight. Ten mixtures, including "Sonoran Desert," "Catalina Foothills," "Southwestern Desert," "Arid Lands," "Great Basin," and "Mogollon Rim," are also available by the packet or by weight. Component varieties and the number of pounds of seeds needed to cover two thousand square feet are noted for each. In addition, lists the seeds for eighty trees and shrubs and twenty native grasses; also sold by the packet or by weight. Guarantees true to name. See **Booksellers**, Grasses, **Kidstuff**, Seeds, Trees.
Shipping season: All year.
Canada, Mexico, International

WILDSEED FARMS, INC.
1983
John Thomas
Catalog: $2, 46 pp., color photographs

The subtitle of this seed catalog, a "Wildflower Reference Guide," is not just a copywriter's turn of phrase. The catalog provides extensive information about starting from seed, germination and cultural requirements, site considerations, and how to use the maps and photographs provided. Seventy individual varieties are offered; description includes place of origin, flower color and form, sun and soil preferences, a guide to average planting success with each species, height, soil temperature required for germination, sowing depth, season of bloom, seeds per packet and per pound, seeding rate and suggested uses. Hardiness zone information includes photographs of seedlings during their first forty-five to ninety days of development following germination. Seeds sold by the packet or by weight. Wildseed Farms offers six regional mixtures sold by weight, a low-growing meadow mix, and a showy annual mix, and they offer custom-blending services. See Herbs, Seeds.
Shipping season: All year.

WILLIAM DAM SEEDS
See **Booksellers**, **Garlic**, Herbs, **Seeds**, Vegetables.

YUCCA DO NURSERY AT PECKERWOOD GARDENS
1988
John Fairey and Carl Schoenfeld
Catalog: $3, 45 pp.
A nursery using only organic methods in cultivating seeds and cuttings of the natives of Texas, Mexico, and Asia. Most varieties offered are hardy in zones 7, 8, and 9. Offerings include 120 perennials, concentrating on *Bouvardia, Salvia,* and *Thalictrum* as well as *Dahlia* and *Monarda,* which were acquired on expeditions to Mexico by the folks from Yucca Do. Descriptions include location of find and the color and form of flowers and foliage. Guarantees safe delivery; will replace or issue refund if notified within ten days of delivery. See **Cactus, Conifers,** Grasses, Organics, Perennials, **Trees.**
Shipping Season: October through December. January through May.
International

Selected Reading About Wildflowers and Natives

Gardening with Native Wildflowers, by Samuel B. Jones, Jr., and Leonard E. Foote. The authors encourage the use of wildflowers and hardy ferns (native to the eastern and midwestern United States) in the garden. Advice on propagation and cultivation and how to incorporate the species that they suggest in shady, sunny, or wetland settings. Includes over two-hundred color photographs.

Growing and Propagating Wildflowers, by Harry R. Phillips. Step-by-step instructions for raising woodland and native prairie plants from seed or division. Also includes information about designing borders using these plants. Propagation techniques will be useful in most areas, plant suggestions lean toward eastern natives. Includes three hundred black-and-white illustrations and color photographs.

Landscaping with Wildflowers: An Environmental Approach to Gardening, by Jim Wilson. Mr. Wilson, a host of the PBS-television series, *The Victory Garden,* focuses on the use of native prairie, woodland, western, southwestern, high altitude, and meadow wildflowers in the garden setting. Includes information on design and care as well as lists of plants for specific sites. Color photographs.

The Native Plant Primer, by Carol Ottesen. Advice on how to select, grow, and incorporate native plants into the garden, region by region. Includes recommendations of best ornamental grasses, native trees and shrubs, vines, and wildflowers. Five hundred color photographs.

The Natural Garden, by Ken Druse. The design principles and (ideal) plants for low-maintenance natural gardens in urban, suburban, and exurban environments. Four hundred color photographs.

The Prairie Garden: 70 Native Plants You Can Grow in Town or Country, by J. Robert Smith and Beatrice S. Smith. Includes information on planning, site preparation, planting, collecting and preparing seed, rasing your own plants, and prairie garden maintenance. Species are described and compared on charts that include season of bloom and habitat.

HERBS AND SCENTED GERANIUMS

The number of offerings cited in each profile is based on information in the most recent catalog provided by the source. In this section, shipping season is for herbs (seeds and plants) only. A selection of books about growing herbs and scented geraniums appears after the last listing.

QUICK FIND
The following sources are listed in this section:

ABUNDANT LIFE SEED FOUNDATION
See **Booksellers, Garlic,** Heirlooms, Organics, **Seeds,** Vegetables.

ALLEN, STERLING, & LOTHROP
See **Garlic,** Organics, **Seeds, Supplies,** Vegetables.

BARNEY'S GINSENG PATCH
1970
Barney L. Frye
Catalog: $2, 36 pp.
Mr. Frye specializes in ginseng and goldenseal. Offers yearling roots, seed-bearing-size roots, and stratified ginseng seed. His catalog is an eclectic compilation of testimonials about ginseng use and farming ginseng for profit. Includes planting instructions and notes about constructing an artificial

bed and shading structure. Guarantees satisfaction; will repurchase your roots after one year. See **Booksellers.**
Shipping season: September through early December.
Canada, seed only.

BLUEJAY GARDENS HERB FARM
Viola Jay
Catalog: $1, 12 pp.
Ms. Jay is a herbal craft specialist (weddings are her special specialty) as well as the steward of her Victorian-style herb and perennial gardens in the very Victorian town of Haskell, Oklahoma. She offers three hundred potted herbs and numerous dried flowers. Stock is acquired from cold climate nurseries and grown at BlueJay Gardens using

only organic methods, natural fertilizers, mulches, and insect controls. Catalog is organized by botanical name (common name given). Descriptions include life cycle, height at maturity, and intermittent comments about color, growth habit, and cultural preferences. Notes for each listing include whether a plant is useful for culinary purposes, dye making, insect repellent, tea making, medicinal purposes, garden ornamental, cosmetics, or crafts. Also offers living herbal wreaths, and hanging herbal baskets. See **Organics**.

Shipping season: Plants, October through June. Dried and crafts, all year.
International

BOUNTIFUL GARDENS
See **Booksellers**, **Garlic**, Heirlooms, **Kidstuff**, Organics, **Seeds**, **Supplies**, Vegetables.

BROWN'S EDGEWOOD GARDENS
1987
Brandon Brown
Catalog: Free, 16 pp. Expanded version: $2
A retail flower and herb shop, located in Orlando, Florida, that offers potted herbs (grown using only organic methods), organic products, and books by mail. Brown's offers 110 ornamental and culinary herbs. Recent catalogs have emphasized varieties of basil, mint, oregano, sage, and thyme. Plants listed by common name with a very brief description of color or flavor. Guarantees satisfaction; will replace or refund. See **Booksellers**, **Furniture**, Organics, **Supplies**.
Shipping season: All year.

BUCKHORN GINSENG
1945
Ron Dobbs
Catalog: LSASE, 6 pp.
Mr. Dobbs sells stratified ginseng seed. The text of his catalog is devoted, almost entirely, to explaining what ginseng is, and the basic methods for growing it in hardwood forests. Also sells goldenseal plants in the fall. He requests that you inquire about prices when you are ready to order. Seed sold by weight. If you have wild and cultivated ginseng, goldenseal and various other roots to sell he'd like to hear from you too. See **Booksellers**.
Shipping season: September through November.

CARROLL GARDENS
1933

Alan L. Summers
Catalog: $3 (recoverable), 108 pp., illustrations
Carroll Gardens offers herbaceous perennials, ferns, ground covers, ornamental grasses, roses, and rock garden plants. A brief section is devoted to sixty culinary and fragrant herbs organized by common name (ornamental herbs are listed by botanical name with other perennials). This section highlights scented geraniums, mint, oregano, rosemary, sage, savory, and thyme. Brief text describes scent, taste, craft and other quality-of-life uses. Guarantees true to name, ready to grow, and safe arrival (California, Oregon and Washington true to name only); will replace one time only. See **Daylilies, Hosta**, Iris, **Peonies, Perennials, Roses, Trees**.
Shipping season: March through November.
Canada

COMPANION PLANTS
See **Seeds**.

THE COOK'S GARDEN
1983
Ellen and Shepherd Ogden
Catalog: $1, 112 pp., color and black-and-white illustrations
The Cook's Garden has its origin in the Ogdens' work as organic market gardeners. They are the coauthor's of the award-winning seed-to-table book *The Cook's Garden,* and Shepherd Ogden wrote *Step by Step Organic Vegetable Gardening,* and *Step by Step Organic Flower Gardening.* The catalog is brimming with cultural information, gardening tips, and recipes. Four hundred varieties of modern and heirloom seeds for flowering annuals and perennials, cutting gardens, everlastings, herbs, salad greens, cover crops, vegetables, and a small group of edible plants. Descriptions are extensive and precise. Heirloom varieties noted. A large number of collections and mixtures for various growing conditions and purposes are offered. Seeds sold in packets with seed count or weight specified for each. Guarantees satisfaction; will issue refund. See **Booksellers, Garlic**, Heirlooms, **Kidstuff**, Organics, **Seeds, Supplies**, Vegetables.
Shipping season: All year.
Canada

DABNEY HERBS
1986
Davy Dabney
Catalog: $2 (recoverable), 40 pp.

Mr. Dabney's catalog is glorious potpourri (pun intended) of annual and perennial herbs, midwestern natives, books, teas, botanicals, and herbal accessories. Herbs available as potted plants include nine lavenders, sixteen mints, five *Monarda*—including the 1996 herb of the year—nine varieties of oregano, seven types of sage, thirty tender scented geraniums, and twelve kinds of thyme. Descriptions include life cycle, color of flower, height at maturity, suitability for container culture, and a key noting additional uses for the harvested plant: culinary, decorative, good dried flower, dye plant, for scent or potpourri, as a tonic or tea, insect repellent, or as a cosmetic. Guarantees safe arrival. See **Booksellers**, Perennials.
Shipping season: March through June.
September and October.
Canada

DAVIDSON WILSON GREENHOUSES
Barbara Wilson
Catalog: $3, 48 pp., black-and-white
photographs
Davidson Wilson offers eighty-six scented geraniums organized by type of scent: fruity, including apricot, coconut, strawberry, and several lemons; pungent, including musk, fern leaf, giant oak, and southernwood; flowering scents; minty scents, including chocolate mint, peppermint rose, and pungent peppermint; spicy scents: cinnamon, Cody's nutmeg, old spice, and pine; twenty rose scents; and lemon meringue. Also lists thirty exotic and uncommon herb varieties, including heal-all, (*Prunella vulgaris*), French tarragon (*Artemisia Dracunculus*), ashwagandha (*Withania somnifera*), several mints: apple (*Mentha rotundifolia*), Corsican (*M. requienii*), and pennyroyal (*M. Pulegium*), and three varieties of thyme (*Thymus*). Guarantees healthy plants and safe arrival; will replace.
Shipping season: All year.
Canada, Mexico, International

DEGIORGI SEED COMPANY
See **Booksellers, Garlic, Grasses, Kidstuff, Seeds,** Vegetables.

D. LANDRETH SEED COMPANY
See Garlic, Grasses, Heirlooms, **Seeds,** Vegetables.

DOROCO SEED COMPANY
1988
Roselynn Coonse

Catalog: $2 (recoverable), 28 pp.
A charming catalog that includes folk and culinary uses for the herb seeds being offered. Eighty "useful" plants are included in sections on herbs, strawflowers and everlastings, edible and floral hanging baskets, and ornamental grasses. Number of seeds per packet is specified. Guarantees satisfaction; will replace or issue refund at their discretion. See Seeds.
Shipping season: All year.
Canada

DOWN ON THE FARM SEED
See **Garlic,** Heirlooms, **Kidstuff,** Organics, Seeds, **Vegetables.**

EDGEWOOD FARM & NURSERY
1987
Norman Schwartz and Robert Cary
Catalog: $2 (recoverable), 100 pp.
Mr. Schwartz and his son-in-law propagate and grow over four thousand herbs and perennials (tender and hardy) on the 130-acre Edgewood property situated within thirty miles of the home of *the* perpetually young gardener of Monticello. Depth and diversity are both words that apply to this catalog that includes eighteen *Artemisia*, five *Ballota*, nine calamint, twenty-four catmints, four *Cytisus,* forty-two named lavenders, thirty *Origanum*, forty varieties of mint, sixty scented geraniums, thirty *Rosmarinus*, fourteen *Salvia*, fourteen varieties of savory, and one hundred versions of thyme. Descriptions include hardiness zone, height at maturity, color of flowers, color and characteristics of foliage, growth habit, garden and postharvest uses. Includes lists of herbs to complement food and drink, herbs for placement in full sun, and herbs for partial and full shade. A cross-index of common to botanical names is also provided. Guarantees true to name, healthy, and well rooted. See Perennials.
Shipping season: Spring and fall.

ELIXIR FARM BOTANICALS
1989
Lavinia McKinney
Catalog: $2, 6 pp., illustrations and color
photographs
Elixir Farm Botanicals is a partnership of land and plant stewards located in the Missouri Ozarks in a region where the prairie meets the eastern deciduous forest, providing fertile ground for plant diversity. Elixir Farms uses only organic, biodynamic practices in growing their Chinese and indigenous med-

icinal plants, and they harvest seed for thirty varieties (including mugwort, Japanese catnip, *Echinacea*, and quinine) sold by the packet. Information includes botanical, common, and Chinese names, soil and sun preferences, form and habit of plant, and medicinal uses. See **Booksellers**, Organics, Seeds.
Shipping season: Seeds, all year. Roots, April through November.
Canada, Mexico, International

FEDCO SEEDS
See **Booksellers, Garlic,** Heirlooms, Organics, **Seeds,** Vegetables.

FLOATING MOUNTAIN SEEDS
See Garlic, Heirlooms, Seeds, **Vegetables.**

FLOWERPLACE PLANT FARM
See **Perennials.**

FLOWERY BRANCH SEED CO.
See Perennials, **Seeds.**

FOX HOLLOW HERB & HEIRLOOM SEED CO.
1987
Thomas Porter
Catalog: $1, 54 pp., illustrations
Fox Hollow Herb & Heirloom Seed grows much of their own seed stock using organic methods. They winnow, clean, and cure their seeds by hand. Seed stock not grown by Fox Hollow is acquired primarily through seed exchanges. The catalog lists seed for 97 heirloom variety vegetables, 130 nonheirloom types, 36 old-fashioned flowering plants, and 117 herbs. Recent catalogs featured nine types of basil, including dark opal and holy basil; German and Roman chamomile (*Matricaria Chamomilla* and *Anthemis nobilis*), coriander, cumin, lady's washbowl (*Saponaria officinalis*), weld (*Reseda luteola*), blue vervain (*Verbena hastata*), and woad (*Isatis tinctoria*). Organized by common name, descriptions include botanical name, height at maturity, form and color of flower, site and light preferences and postharvest uses. Sells seeds in a sampler packets of thirty seeds and in larger packets with an unspecified number. See Garlic, Heirlooms, Seeds, **Vegetables.**
Shipping season: All year.

THE FRAGRANT PATH
See Heirlooms, Perennials, **Seeds,** Trees.

GARDEN CITY SEEDS
See **Booksellers, Garlic,** Grasses, Organics, **Seeds, Supplies,** Vegetables.

GOODWIN CREEK GARDENS
1977
Jim and Dotti Becker, Laurie and Gracie Richter
Catalog: $1, 39 pp.
Goodwin Creek specializes in the plants (five hundred) and seeds (one hundred) of herbs, everlasting flowers, scented geraniums, and other fragrant plants. The Beckers are the coauthors of *An Everlasting Garden*, and Mr. Becker is the coauthor with Faye Brawner of *Scented Geraniums: Knowing Growing and Using Pelargoniums*. Highlighted in recent catalogs were five *Agastache*, fourteen *Artemisia*, forty-six scented geraniums, 36 lavenders (*Lavandin* and *Lavandula*), twelve *Origanum*, twenty-four *Rosmarinus*, six *Santolinus*, and forty-three types of thyme. Brief descriptions include habit, height at maturity, and life cycle, hardiness for all; postharvest uses for many. Plants are pot-grown and shipped in a soilless medium. Guarantees true to name, pest free, and healthy. See **Booksellers, Perennials, Seeds.**

THE GOURMET GARDENER™
1986
Christopher E. Combest
Catalog: $2, 30 pp.
A catalog for gardeners who insist upon eating what they grow. Known as the "Herb Gathering" catalog from 1986 through 1990, The Gourmet Gardener includes forty herbs, a hundred vegetables, and a selection of edible flower seeds. Selections emphasize European natives and cultivars that are suitable for North American gardens. Herbs and edible flowers organized by common names. Each description includes botanical name, culinary attributes, postharvest uses, height and description of plant and flower, country of origin, and life cycle. Seeds per packet specified. Guarantees satisfaction; will issue credit or refund. See **Booksellers,** Garlic, Seeds, Vegetables.
Shipping season: All year.
Canada, Mexico, International

HALCYON GARDENS HERBS
1989
F.E.A. (Liz) Bair
Catalog: $2, 28 pp.
Halcyon Gardens offers the seed of fifty individual herbs and a number of multi-packet col-

lections for creating a colonial kitchen garden, an herbal tea garden, and of herbs that appear in the works of William Shakespeare. Descriptions specify number of days to germination, color of flower, and season of bloom. Specifies number of seeds per packet. See Seeds.
Shipping season: All year.
Canada, Mexico, International

HARRIS SEEDS
See Garlic, **Seeds, Supplies**, Vegetables.

HEIRLOOM GARDEN SEEDS
See **Booksellers**, Heirlooms, **Kidstuff, Seeds.**

THE HERB GARDEN
1983
Ann Beall
Plant catalog: $4. Products catalog: $2. Both: $5.
This herb farm in Pilot Mountain, North Carolina offers over five hundred varieties of hardy and tender perennial and annual herbs. Symbols indicate life cycle, height and spread at maturity, hardiness zone, sun/shade requirements, and best method of preserving. Well observed descriptions include color and form of foliage and flowers, notes on natural history and postharvest uses. Extensive information about plant culture, seasonal planting, container gardening and growing herbs indoors, fertilizing, pest control, harvesting, and methods of preservation, e.g., candying, drying, and freezing. Shipped in growing pots. Also offers a catalog of potpourri, teas, and seasonings. Guarantees true to name, state inspected, healthy and pest free on arrival; report damages within ten days.
Shipping season: Late April through mid-June. September and October.

HILLARY'S GARDEN
See Organics, **Perennials.**

HOLLAND WILDFLOWER FARM
See **Booksellers**, Seeds, **Wildflowers.**

J. L. HUDSON, SEEDSMAN
See **Booksellers**, Garlic, Heirlooms, **Seeds**, Vegetables.

JOHNNY'S SELECTED SEEDS
See **Booksellers, Garlic,** Grasses, Heirlooms, Organics, **Seeds, Supplies,** Vegetables.

KIDS IN BLOOM™ SPECIALTY SEEDS
See Heirlooms, **Kidstuff**, Seeds, Vegetables.

KILGORE SEED COMPANY
See **Booksellers**, Garlic, **Seeds**, Vegetables.

LE JARDIN DU GOURMET
See Booksellers, Garlic, Seeds, **Vegetables.**

LILY OF THE VALLEY HERB FARM
1982
Paul and Melinda Carmichael
Catalog: $1 (recoverable), 32 pp.
The Carmichaels grow four hundred herbs, eighty scented geraniums, and four hundred perennials and everlastings on their farm in Minerva, Ohio. Herbs and scented geraniums are organized by common name. Areas of concentration include twenty artemisias, eighteen varieties of basil, six kinds of fennel, ten mints, ten oreganos, twenty-six varieties of sage, and twenty-two thymes. Brief descriptions include botanical name, life cycle, sun/shade requirements, and height at maturity. Seed packets (one hundred seeds per packet) are available for a few of their offerings and are so noted. Plants shipped on soilless medium in containers. Guarantees true to name and healthy. See **Perennials**, Seeds.
Shipping season: Mid-April through July.

MERRY GARDENS
1947
Mary Ellen and Ervin Ross
Catalog: $2 (two-year subscription), 26 pp.
The Rosses of Camden, Maine, offer 225 herbs and seventy scented geraniums from among the rose-scented, odoratissima, oak leaf, peppermint, pine-scented, fulgidum, and lemon-scented groups. Descriptions include life cycle, sun/shade requirements, and brief comments pertaining to an offering's desirable characteristics. Plants shipped in their growing pots. Guarantees healthy and well rooted when shipped.
Shipping season: All year.
Canada

NICHOLS GARDEN NURSERY
1950
Rose Marie Nichols McGee
Catalog: Free, 72 pp.
Nichols Garden Nursery sells herbs: 120 varieties as seeds and seventy as live plants. Includes herbs for culinary and other practical uses as well as a selection of ornamental herb seeds for the perennial garden

connoisseur. Also lists best herbs for growing indoors. Herbs organized by common name; information includes botanical name, life cycle, height of mature plant, cultural notes, and postharvest uses. Herbs sold one hundred seeds to a packet unless otherwise noted. Encourages market and craft gardening with one (or more) of five collections: herbs, everlastings, loofa sponge, gourds, and pansies; offers seed and manuals for germinating your enterprise. See **Booksellers, Garlic,** Organics, **Seeds,** Supplies, **Vegetables,** Wildflowers.
Shipping season: Seeds, All year. Plants, April through early June. September to first frost.
No plants to Hawaii.

NORTHWIND FARMS
See **Booksellers.**

OTIS S. TWILLEY SEED COMPANY
See Garlic, **Seeds,** Vegetables.

PARK SEED® CO.
1868
J. Leonard Park and Karen Park Jennings
Catalog: Free, 76 pp., color photographs
Founded by G. W. Park in the living room in of his Libonia, Pennsylvania, home, Park Seed currently describes its business as the oldest and largest family-owned seed company in America. The catalog includes eighty kitchen and landscape herbs (available variously as seeds or plants) from its list of two thousand seed varieties gathered from worldwide sources and developed here. A separate guide supplements individual descriptions with bloom season, germination time, and cultural notations. Specifies number of seeds per packet. Guarantees satisfaction for one year from date of delivery; will replace or issue credit or refund. See Bulbs, **Garlic,** Peonies, Roses, **Seeds, Supplies,** Vegetables.
Shipping season: Seeds, all year. Plants, spring and fall.
Canada

PERENNIAL PLEASURES NURSERY OF VERMONT
1980
Judith and Rachel Kane
Catalog: $3 (recoverable), 64 pp. Complete herb list: LSASE
The Kanes grow heirloom herbs and flowering plants using organic methods. One hundred culinary, medicinal, and ornamental herbs appear in a separate section of their catalog. Herbs

are arranged alphabetically by botanical name; description includes common name, century of introduction or general use in (eastern) American gardens, description of plant, historical notes, postharvest uses, and cultural tips. A seventeenth-century medicinal plant collection, a Revolutionary tea (substitute) garden, and culinary herb, are among the period and specialty assortments offered. Sixty percent shipped as bareroot plants; balance available in packets of one hundred or more seeds. Guarantees true to name and healthy; will replace or issue refund at customer's discretion. See **Booksellers,** Grasses, Heirlooms, Organics, **Perennials, Seeds.**
Shipping season: April and May. September and October. Seeds, all year.
Seeds only to California, Mexico.

PINETREE GARDEN SEEDS
See **Booksellers,** Garlic, **Kidstuff,** Organics, **Seeds, Supplies, Vegetables.**

P. L. ROHRER & BRO.
See Garlic, Organics, **Seeds,** Supplies, Vegetables.

PUTNEY NURSERY, INC.
See Perennials, Seeds, **Wildflowers.**

REDWOOD CITY SEED COMPANY
See **Booksellers,** Garlic, Heirlooms, **Kidstuff,** Seeds, **Vegetables.**

R. H. SHUMWAY, SEEDSMAN
See **Garlic,** Heirlooms, **Seeds, Vegetables.**

RICHTERS
1969
Conrad Richter
Catalog: $2, 104 pp., color photographs
Richters characterizes itself as being in the tradition of botanical plant explorers of the past, traveling five continents in search of herbs from a mosaic of cultures. Their full-line (many live plants shipped worldwide) herb catalog includes the seeds for six hundred varieties. Seeds obtained from local sources, with established, long-term collection projects in Nepal, India, Ghana, and Mexico. Catalog organized by common name. Brief descriptions emphasize postharvest uses. Information includes botanical name, life cycle, and preferred sowing time. Seeds sold by the packet or by weight. See **Booksellers,** Heirlooms, Organics, Seeds, Vegetables.
Shipping season: All year.

Canada, Mexico, International

THE SANDY MUSH HERB NURSERY
Fairman and Kate Jayne
Catalog: $6, 73 pp., illustrations
The Jaynes offer nine hundred perennials and herbs and eighty scented geraniums from among the rose, lemon, fruit and spice, mint, pungent-scented, and oak-leaf groups. Descriptions include botanical/common name, height at maturity, color of flower, shape and characteristics of leaves, growth habit, season of bloom and harvest, and postharvest uses. Includes diagrams and plant lists for the creation of a little kitchen border, a butterfly and bee garden, a fragrant garden, a geometric culinary garden, a sixteenth-century style knot garden, and a Victorian-style goosefoot garden. Guarantees true to name, healthy when shipped; will replace (for the cost of shipping) or refund. See **Bookseller**, Seeds.
Shipping season: All year.

SEEDS BLÜM
See **Booksellers**, **Garlic**, Heirlooms, **Kidstuff**, **Seeds**, Vegetables, Wildflowers.

SHEPHERD'S GARDEN SEEDS
See **Booksellers**, **Garlic**, Heirlooms, **Kidstuff**, **Seeds**, **Supplies**, **Vegetables**.

SOUTHERN EXPOSURE SEED EXCHANGE®
See **Booksellers**, **Garlic**, Heirlooms, Seeds, **Supplies**, **Vegetables**.

SOUTHERN PERENNIALS & HERBS
1987
Barbara and Michael Bridges
Retail Catalog: $3 (recoverable), 22 pp.
The Bridges specialize in herbaceous plants, including one hundred herbs for the deep South. Almost all of their plants are propagated at their Gulf South nursery in Tylertown, Mississippi. Descriptions are sensitive to performance in the South in addition to not-ing height, habit, season and profusion of bloom, and cultural requirements. Symbols denote sun/shade requirements, dry site and bog plants, attractive to hummingbirds or butterflies, and if a plant is useful as a cut flower. See **Perennials**.
Shipping season: All year. (Not all types of plants available throughout the year. Check for availability.)

"SOW ORGANIC" SEEDS
See Garlic, Heirlooms, Organics, Seeds, **Vegetables**.

SUNNYBROOK FARMS
See **Hosta**, Perennials.

TERRITORIAL SEED COMPANY
See **Booksellers**, **Garlic**, **Kidstuff**, Organics, Seeds, **Supplies**, **Vegetables**.

TINMOUTH CHANNEL FARM
See **Kidstuff**, Organics, Seeds.

VERMONT BEAN SEED COMPANY
See Garlic, Heirlooms, Seeds, **Vegetables**.

VESEY'S SEEDS LTD.
See **Booksellers**, **Garlic**, Seeds, **Supplies**, Vegetables, Wildflowers.

VILENIKI: AN HERB FARM
See **Booksellers**.

WEISS BROTHERS PERENNIAL NURSERY
See Grasses, **Perennials**.

WILDSEED FARMS, INC.
See Seeds, **Wildflowers**.

WILLIAM DAM SEEDS
See **Booksellers**, **Garlic**, Seeds, Vegetables, Wildflowers.

Selected Readings About Herbs and Scented Geraniums

The American Gardening Guides: Herb Gardening, compiled by Cornell Plantations, University of California Botanical Garden, and Mathhei Botanical Gardens (Patricia Hopkinson, Diane Miske, Jerry Parsons, and Holly Shimizu). The herb volume is a series of books that is a collaborative effort by experts from key arboretums and horticultural institutions includes definitions, history and botany, and basic gardening philosophies from a panel of experts. The plant selector section contains more than two hundred color photographs of herbs with detailed descriptions that include size, coloration, growing cycle, maintenance, and care. Includes a section on herb garden design and planting and maintenance techniques. Also explains new methods for growing particular types of herbs in desert climates, tiny spaces, and cold and windy areas, as well as specific advice for gardeners with physical limitations. Three hundred black-and-white and color photographs.

Complete Book of Herbs: A Practical Guide to Growing and Using Herbs, by Lesley Bremness. Includes information on herbal folklore, propagation, growing, harvesting, and postharvest uses: for fragrance, flavoring, health, beauty, and as a material in crafts. Color photographs.

The Encyclopedia of Herbs and Their Uses, by Deni Brown. An ambitious reference work that includes information about a thousand herbs. Includes historical background, growing, harvesting, and postharvest uses. Special attention is also given to planning and growing herb gardens. Includes detailed descriptions and photographs for each listing. Includes fifteen hundred color photographs.

Growing Herbs from Seed, Cutting, and Root: An Adventure in Small Miracles, by Thomas DeBaggio. Step-by-step instructions for creating vigorous viable herb starts by an expert grower. Includes information about best methods for starting each herb, transplanting, taking cuttings, and making divisions. Germination charts illustrate ideal conditions and predict germination times for many popular herbs. Color photographs.

The Herbal Tea Garden: Planning, Planting, Harvesting and Brewing, by Marietta Marshall Marcin. Includes over seventy herbal teas that soothe, invigorate, and help heal. Includes material on the history of tea, cultivation, benefits of specific herbs, and storage.

Landscaping with Herbs, by Jim Wilson. The host of the PBS-television series, *The Victory Garden* encourages the use of herbs as an integral part of garden design and form. Discusses herbs for perennial and mixed borders, fragrant gardens, silver and gray gardens, stone walls, stone paths, and in traditional kitchen gardens. Color photographs.

Rodale's Illustrated Encyclopedia of Herbs, edited by Claire Kowalchik and William Hylton. A highly regarding in-depth work that includes entries for 140 herbs. Covers herb history and lore, cultivation, postharvest uses, and storage. Over 225 illustrations and color photographs.

Scented Geraniums: Knowing Growing and Using Pelargoniums, by Jim Becker and Faye Brawner. The authors describe what they consider the seventy best scented geraniums. Incudes chapters on cultivation, propagation, pruning, and landscape uses. Color photographs.

Using Herbs in the Landscape, by Debra Kirkpatrick. The author, a landscape architect and horticulturist, offers insightful observations and practical advice for choosing and using herbs in the landscape. Includes information about foliage, form, fragrance, ornamental value, site preference, sun and soil requirements, spacing, and light. Includes plans and plant lists for over twenty gardens, and over two hundred black-and-white illustrations.

$\mathcal{V}$EGETABLES

$\mathcal{T}$he annual course of events for the typical North American gardener begins somewhere in January with the deluge of catalogs and subsequent purchase of seeds and concludes well after the first frost with the last squash going down the hatch, so to speak. Many gardeners apparently think, and some actually speak, in terms of cycles: annual (solar), botanical (plant growing), and entomological (insect life cycle). And why shouldn't they? Gardening is, after all, intensive biological activity.

The gardener coaxes vegetables out of the soil to provide salad greens or to assure an ample supply of vegetables for the off-season. Yet there is another, higher level of gardening to please and challenge all those who are willing to add to their earthy skills bank. After the fruits and vegetables are safely canned, frozen, dried, or cellared, the modern gardener has two garden-related choices for the next cycle: go back to the newly freshened rack of seed catalogs and reorder favorites and experiment with new varieties or select varieties of heirloom seed that can be saved from year to year.

There are two fairly common mistakes that new heirloom gardeners make. First, and certainly the most common mistake of new "open-pollinated" gardeners, is not keeping it simple. As Albert Einstein said, "Everything should be made as simple as possible, but not simpler." As a horticulturist new to seed saving, the beginner has to learn basic, easy-to-understand plant biology.

Unless you believe in immaculate conception for plants, the pollen has to come from somewhere to fertilize the egg, or, as it is more properly known in the plant world, the ovule or female part of the flower. Pollen is moved by three basic agents, wind, insects, and "self." The last is most interesting because among those plants that self-pollinate are some of the easiest for beginning heirloom seed savers.

Tomatoes and beans are the best and simplest examples of garden vegetables to acquaint the novice seed saver. They are good because they both are monoecious (literally, "one house") species and they self-pollinate. They are known for bearing "perfect flowers" that are pollinated by the time the flower blooms. In most cases, the fruit, and the seed inside bearing the germ for the next generation, has been isolated from foreign pollen. Tomatoes and beans produced from these heirloom seeds will *usually* reproduce true to the parent generation and therefore supply the gardener with seeds for the following growing season.

The second most common mistake that the beginner makes is going too far in the excitement and zeal of heirloom gardening, replacing all the tried-

and-true hybrid seeds with new heirloom varieties. This is intrinsically a bad move. Hidden within this changeover are far too many details about too many new plants to be comprehensible. The heirlooms have somewhat less predictable maturation dates and require the new heirloom gardener to keep track of details formerly deemed insignificant. For example, the whole process of "rouging" (pulling out plants that show the wrong characteristics) needs to be performed with diligence by someone armed with knowledge. The first-timer needs to perform this practice of rouging and other new techniques on just a few varieties until the freshly learned skills are under the belt.

There is great satisfaction to be gained from heirloom gardening even if it is carried out on the most rudimentary level. For gardeners willing to accept the challenge, the demands on one's knowledge, skill, and patience will be rewarded similarly. Heirloom gardening requires the earth tiller to become more attentive to the weather in addition to other kinds of daily, weekly, and seasonal changes. At times, hours count for a lot in the practice of seed saving. Life cycles of blossoms and bugs take on new meaning when saving the seed from the produce and matter nearly as much as the fruits and vegetables themselves. Saving the seeds for next year's plot binds the gardener closer still to the earth.

—*Steve Miller*

(Steve Miller is the Curator of Agricultural History of the Heirloom Seed Project at the Landis Valley Museum. The HSP and its historic gardens program are nonprofit organizations oriented toward education on environmental and cultural living history. The project was the recipient in 1991 of the American Association for State and Local History's Award of Merit.)

The number of offerings cited in each profile is based on information in the most recent catalog provided by the source. In this section, shipping season is for vegetable seed and plants only. A selection of books about growing vegetables appears after the last listing.

QUICK FIND
The following sources are listed in this section:

ABUNDANT LIFE SEED FOUNDATION
See **Booksellers**, **Garlic**, Heirlooms, Herbs, Organics, **Seeds**.

ALFREY SEEDS
1977
Evelyn Alfrey
Catalog: LSASE, 5 pp., black-and-white photographs
Sells seeds for thirty-four varieties of hot and sweet peppers, five types of okra, a dozen types of tomato, and Korean, Chinese, and smooth loofah sponges. Descriptions includes plant size and taste of vegetable. See Seeds.
Shipping season: All year.
Canada, Mexico

ALLEN, STERLING, & LOTHROP
See **Garlic**, Herbs, Organics, **Seeds**, **Supplies**.

BERLIN SEEDS
See **Booksellers**, **Fruit**, **Garlic**, Grasses, **Kidstuff**, Organics, **Seeds**, **Supplies**.

BOUNTIFUL GARDENS
See **Booksellers**, **Garlic**, Heirlooms, Herbs, **Kidstuff**, Organics, **Seeds**, **Supplies**.

BUTTERBROOKE FARM
1978
Tom Butterworth
Catalog: LSASE, 4 pp.
Butterbrooke is a seed co-op that specializes in

rapidly maturing, chemically untreated, pure-line vegetable varieties. All of their production is derived from raised beds using biodynamic, intensive growing methods. Seventy-five varieties are listed by name only. Packets are offered in two sizes: one for twenty feet of land, the other for sixty to eighty feet. Beginners garden kit includes plans, how-to booklet, and fifteen packets. Co-op members receive a quarterly newsletter, a supplemental list of heirloom varieties, and a 20 percent discount on seed orders. Membership is not required to make a purchase. Certified organic. See **Booksellers**, Organics, Seeds.
Shipping season: All year.
Canada, International

THE COOK'S GARDEN
See **Booksellers**, Garlic, Heirlooms, **Herbs**, **Kidstuff**, Organics, **Seeds**, **Supplies**.

DAN'S GARDEN SHOP
See **Booksellers**, Organics, **Seeds**, **Supplies**.

DEGIORGI SEED COMPANY
See **Booksellers**, Garlic, Grasses, Herbs, **Kidstuff**, **Seeds**.

DIXONDALE FARMS
See **Garlic**.

D. LANDRETH SEED COMPANY
See Garlic, Grasses, Heirlooms, Herbs, **Seeds**.

DOWN ON THE FARM SEED
1990
Ruth A. Guth
Catalog: Free, 52 pp., illustrations
The Guths are organic farmers who sell untreated seed, preserve heirloom varieties, and provide a free seed search service for gardeners. Their catalog includes 140 vegetable varieties. Cultural tips, brief descriptions, number of days to maturity, number of row feet each packet will sow, and seeds per packet for vegetable offerings. Many selections also available by weight. Notes heirloom varieties. Twenty-five basic herbs and twenty types of flowering annuals and perennials sold by the packet; seeds per packet not specified. See **Garlic**, Heirlooms, Herbs, **Kidstuff**, Organics, Seeds.
Shipping season: All year.
Canada, Mexico, International

FARMER SEED AND NURSERY
1888
Don Prodoehl
Catalog: Free, 64 pp., color photographs
Farmer's offers northern-grown plants and their seeds for 165 types of vegetables. Notes number of days to maturity, awards won, description of mature vegetable, and culinary attributes. Seeds sold by the packet or by the ounce. Guarantees satisfaction; will replace or issue credit or refund. See **Garlic**, Perennials, Seeds.
Shipping season: Seeds, all year. Plants, March through June.

FEDCO SEEDS
See **Booksellers**, **Garlic**, Heirlooms, Herbs, Organics, **Seeds**.

FISHER'S GARDEN STORE
See **Garlic**, Seeds.

FLOATING MOUNTAIN SEEDS
1985
Roger Lemstrom
Catalog: $2, 26 pp., illustrations
Mr. Lemstrom offers 110 older and heirloom varieties of seed for vegetables and grains. He also offers two dozen culinary herbs and a dozen flowering plants. Information includes number of days to maturity and date of introduction when known. There are some varieties that he simply refers to as "ancient." Descriptions are informal, occasionally including the general area where a particular type of vegetable was first cultivated. Culinary attributes and intermittent descriptions of the plant itself also included. Seeds sold by the packet; number of seeds not specified. Guarantees seed; will replace or issue refund. See Garlic, Heirlooms, Herbs, Seeds.
Shipping season: All year.

FOX HOLLOW HERB & HEIRLOOM SEED CO.
1987
Thomas Porter
Catalog: $1, 54 pp., illustrations
Fox Hollow Herb & Heirloom Seed grows much of their own seed stock using organic methods. They winnow, clean, and cure their seeds by hand. Seed stock not grown by Fox Hollow is acquired primarily through seed exchanges. The catalog lists seed for 97 heirloom variety vegetables, 130 nonheirloom types, 117 herbs, and 36

old-fashioned flowering plants. Descriptions of eatables include number of days to maturity, form and flavor of vegetable, growth and yield habit, and size for most. Includes botanical names for herbs and flowers and number of days required for germination at ideal soil temperature. Sells seeds in sampler packets of thirty seeds and in larger packets with an unspecified number. Heirloom varieties not available in samplers. See Garlic, Heirlooms, **Herbs**, Seeds.
Shipping season: All year.
Canada, Mexico, International

GARDEN CITY SEEDS
See **Booksellers, Garlic, Grasses**, Herbs, Organics, **Seeds**, Supplies.

GEORGE'S PLANT FARM
See **Garlic**.

GIANT WATERMELONS
See Fruit, **Seeds**.

GLECKLER'S SEEDMEN
1947
George L. Gleckler
Catalog: Free, 12 pp., photographs
Originally a contract seed grower serving large mail-order houses, Gleckler's has been selling vegetable seeds (and, more recently, plants), including numerous heirlooms, through their own catalog since 1947. Among the two hundred varieties of beans, eggplant, mustard greens, pepper, and tomato are twenty-eight types of American Indian squash, a selection that they believe to be the largest in the world. Descriptions are knowledgeable but inconsistent in the details that they provide. Seeds sold by the packet or by weight; seeds per packet not noted. Forty of Gleckler's two hundred seed varieties are available as organically grown plants. Live plants include sweet pepper, hot pepper, eggplant, and tomato only. Guarantees safe arrival. See Heirlooms, Organics, Seeds.
Shipping season: Seeds, all year. Plants, April through June.
Canada, Mexico, International

THE GOURMET GARDENER™
See **Booksellers**, Garlic, **Herbs**, Seeds.

GURNEY'S SEED & NURSERY CO.
See **Garlic, Kidstuff**, Organics, **Seeds**, Supplies.

HARRIS SEEDS
See Garlic, Heirlooms, **Seeds**, Supplies.

HEIRLOOM SEED PROJECT– LANDIS VALLEY MUSEUM
Steve Miller and Nancy Pippart
Catalog: $2.50, 52 pp., illustrations
The Landis Valley Museum is the largest museum of German rural heritage. In 1991, its Heirloom Seed Project was the recipient of the American Association for State and Local History's Award of Merit. The nonprofit project and its historic gardens program are dedicated to environmental and cultural education. The stated purpose of the catalog is "to bridge the gap between modern hybrid vegetable plants in the historical garden and authenticated (accurate) historical plants in the period garden." The catalog offers eighty-eight types of vegetables (a handful of flowers sneak in here, too) that were in use prior to 1940 and were mentioned in writing or through oral tradition dating to the early 1800s. Seeds are harvested from plants grown using 99.9 percent organic methods. Vegetables are planted and cultivated by hand. Catalog descriptions and information about seed saving are thorough, detailed, and rich in history. Gardeners are limited to one packet per variety per annual order. Number of seeds per packet varies. This is a well-written, realistically encouraging catalog of heirlooms. See **Fruit**, Heirlooms, Organics, Seeds, Trees.
Shipping season: March and April.
Canada

HEIRLOOM SEEDS
1988
Tom Hauch
Catalog: $1 (recoverable), 12 pp.
Mr. Hauch's specialty is open-pollinated, primarily untreated heirloom seeds. One hundred and thirty vegetables and twenty flowering plants offered, many introduced in the seventeenth and eighteenth centuries. Description includes number of days to maturity, height at maturity, growth habit, and postharvest uses. Seeds per packet specified. Guarantees satisfaction; will issue refund. See Heirlooms, Seeds.
Canada

HENRY FIELD'S SEED & NURSERY CO.
1892
Orville Dragoo
Catalog: Free, 87 pp., color photographs

A full-line catalog that offers seeds for 290 vegetables, with a strong selection of beans, cabbage, corn, leaf and head lettuce, peas, peppers, pumpkins, radishes, summer and winter squash, and tomatoes. Also sells tomato, pepper, and rhubarb plants as well as six types of asparagus. Descriptions for vegetables include number of days to maturity, size of fruit, disease resistance, and culinary uses. Vegetables sold by the packet (number of seeds specified) or by weight. See **Fruit, Garlic, Kidstuff**, Organics, Perennials, **Seeds, Supplies, Trees**.
Shipping season: February through June.

HORTICULTURAL ENTERPRISES
1973
Catalog: Free, 6 pp., illustrations
Among the things you learn from this catalog: The first hot peppers were sent back to Europe by Christopher Columbus. The first recorded chili production in America occurred in Santa Fe, New Mexico, in 1598. The Aztec Emperor Montezuma's favorite meal incorporated fish and chilies. Among the things you find in this catalog: the seeds (primarily untreated) for forty-three peppers. Descriptions border on the edible. Also includes brief notes on pepper culture and cultivation. Packets contain an unspecified number of seeds. See Seeds.
Shipping season: All year.

J. L. HUDSON, SEEDSMAN
See **Booksellers**, Garlic, Heirlooms, Herbs, **Seeds**.

JOHNNY'S SELECTED SEEDS
See **Booksellers, Garlic**, Grasses, Heirlooms, Herbs, Organics, **Seeds, Supplies**.

J. W. JUNG SEED & NURSERY CO.
See **Bulbs, Fruit**, Garlic, **Kidstuff**, Perennials, **Seeds**, Supplies, **Trees**.

KALMIA FARM
See **Garlic**.

KIDS IN BLOOM™ SPECIALTY SEEDS
See Heirlooms, Herbs, **Kidstuff**, Seeds.

KILGORE SEED COMPANY
See **Booksellers**, Garlic, Herbs, **Seeds**.

KITAZAWA SEED CO.
1917

Sakae Komatsu
Catalog: Free, 12 pp., color photographs
Kitazawa specializes in the seeds of vegetables traditionally used in oriental cuisine and those specifically developed in Japan. A list of 150 offerings includes Japanese greens and radishes (daikon), oriental mustards, Chinese cabbages, gobo, bitter melon, shishito pepper, Tokyo market turnips, and Shin Kuroda carrots. Number of seeds per packet not specified. See Seeds.
Shipping season: All year.

LE JARDIN DU GOURMET
1954
Paul Taylor
Catalog: $1, 16 pp.
Le Jardin du Gourmet began as a provider of gourmet foods by mail when such delicacies as endive and snails were difficult to come by at local retail outlets. The proliferation of gourmet shops caused Le Jardin's trafficking in culinary seed to emerge as the largest part of its business. Gardeners who wish to grow what they prepare in their kitchen will find 100 kinds of herb seeds and 250 kinds of vegetable, most imported from France. Seeds sold in sampler and standard-sized packets with an unspecified number of seeds. Also offers live herb plants and a selection of books on herbs, food preservation, and cookery. See Booksellers, Garlic, Herbs, Seeds.
Shipping season: All year.
Canada

LOCKHART SEEDS, INC.
1948
Steve Auten
Catalog: $2 (recoverable), 75 pp.
Lockhardt characterizes itself as a catalog seed house serving the home and market gardener. Their catalog has a clear and open design with separate sections for each type of vegetable and descriptions of the varieties that they offer within type; contains detailed information about seed testing and treatment, charts for determining seed coverage, and planting guides. Offers hybrid and open-pollinated seed for 420 vegetables (including orientals), lawn and pasture grasses, legumes and cover crops, and twenty-five flowering plants, representing the harvest from fifty seed-producing companies worldwide. The nature of the information provided varies according to the plant material being described. Includes (as

appropriate) relative days to maturity, shape and color of pods and seeds, plant size, disease tolerance and resistance, leaf type, leaf color, skin and flesh color and texture, and date of introduction or parentage. Seeds sold by the packet or by weight. Guarantees true to description; reports of defective seed must be filed within thirty days of receipt. See **Garlic,** Grasses, Seeds.
Shipping season: All year.
Canada, Mexico, International

LONG ISLAND SEED COMPANY
1978
Catalog: Free, 4 pp.
Long Island Seed specializes in genetically diverse vegetable seed blends. They offer forty (including lettuce, spinach, kale and collard greens, onion and scallion, sweet corn, small and large winter squash, vining summer squash, beans, peas, peppers, and melons), drawn from their seed bank of two thousand untreated varieties. Because their packets contain several named vegetables, descriptions are necessarily broad. Limit one packet per mixture (sufficient to provide transplants for fifteen- to twenty-foot rows). See Garlic, Heirlooms, Seeds.
Shipping season: All year.
Canada, Mexico, International

MOOSE GROWERS SUPPLY
See **Booksellers, Garlic,** Organics, **Supplies.**

NATIVE SEEDS/SEARCH
1983
Angelo Joaquin, Jr.
Catalog: $1, 56 pp.
Native Seeds/SEARCH is a nonprofit seed conservation organization with expertise in the traditional native food plants of the southwestern United States. They distribute 325 varieties of open-pollinated, traditional crop seeds adapted to the desert environments. Recent catalogs include sixty types of corn/maize, twenty gourds, an equal number of chiles/chiltepines, and a dozen desert wildflowers. Description of fruit, culinary uses, cultural and seed-saving advice for each type of crop. Special attention is given to whether a variety is appropriate to low or high desert conditions. Number of seeds per packet noted. Free starter seeds available to Native Americans. See **Booksellers,** Garlic, **Kidstuff,** Seeds, Wildflowers.

Shipping season: All year.
Canada, Mexico, International

NICHOLS GARDEN NURSERY
1950
Rose Marie Nichols McGee
Catalog: Free, 72 pp.
Nichols Garden Nursery sells the seeds for 470 vegetables, 120 varieties of herbs, and 150 garden flowers, everlastings, and wildflowers. Vegetables include a selection of beans, melons, cabbages, cucumbers, kale, oriental vegetables, parsley, radishes, and gourmet baby varieties. Recent additions to their vegetable list include paprika supreme, 'Ambrosia' cantaloupe, and 'Embassy' squash. Their "Competitor's Corner" includes pumpkin, blue squash, 'Carolina Cross' watermelon, and other hybrids that have the potential to grow (no maturity stated) to gargantuan proportions within their type. Information includes number of days to maturity, shape and form of fruit, culinary attributes, and recommendations as to which varieties are appropriate for planting in short and variable season climates. Five collections: herbs, everlastings, loofah sponge, gourds, and pansies; includes seeds and manuals for germinating your enterprise. Offers "Profitable Garden Project" collections to encourage home gardeners to undertake sideline businesses from seed. Seeds sold by the packet or by weight; number of seeds per packet noted. See **Booksellers, Garlic, Herbs,** Organics, **Seeds,** Supplies, Wildflowers.
Shipping season: All year.

NITRON INDUSTRIES, INC.
1977
Frank J. Finger
Catalog: Free, 24 pp., color photographs
Nitron Industries manufactures and sells organic fertilizers, enzyme soil conditioners, and mined minerals. Their catalog includes Seeds of Change brand organic seeds (in packets) organized into collections that include a culinary herb garden, a medicinal herb garden, a salsa garden, and a vegetable garden. See **Kidstuff,** Organics, Seeds, **Supplies.**
Shipping season: All year.
Canada, Mexico, International

ORAL LEDDEN & SONS
See **Garlic,** Grasses, Heirlooms, Seeds, **Supplies.**

OTIS S. TWILLEY SEED COMPANY
See Garlic, Herbs, **Seeds.**

P & P SEED COMPANY
See **Seeds**.

PARK SEED® CO.
See **Bulbs**, **Garlic**, **Herbs**, Peonies, Roses, **Seeds**, Supplies.

THE PEPPER GAL
1978
Betty Payton
Catalog: $1, 16 pp. Seed list: Free
Ms. Payton believes that the Pepper Gal's selection of two hundred varieties of capsicum seeds comprises the largest-known offering of hot, sweet, and ornamental peppers. Brief descriptions include size and shape of pepper for some, uses and habits sprinkled here and there for others, and days to maturity for all. Packets of individual varieties contain twenty-five seeds; mixtures contain twenty-five to thirty per packet. Guarantees true to name. See Seeds.
Shipping season: All year.
Canada, Mexico, International

PIEDMONT PLANT CO.
1906
William Parker, Jr.
Catalog: Free, 16 pp., color photographs
Mr. Parker is the fourth generation in his family to tend to field-grown vegetables. Offers five hybrid and four open-pollinated tomatoes, five hybrid and three open-pollinated peppers, three hybrid eggplants, a selection of sweet potato, kale, collard greens, kohlrabi, brussel sprouts, cabbage, broccoli, cauliflower, leeks, and seven types of onion. Descriptions include climatic conditions for which a variety is best suited, size of fruit, days to maturity, disease resistance, planting and care instructions. Guarantees live plants in good growing condition. See Garlic, Heirlooms.
Shipping season: April and May.

PINETREE GARDEN SEEDS
1979
Dick Meiners
Catalog: Free, 192 pp., illustrations and color photographs
Pinetree offers seven hundred types of hybrid and open-pollinated seeds, primarily in their natural, untreated state, packaged in small-count, inexpensive packets suitable for the home gardener. Areas of concentration include beans,

corn, cucumbers, lettuce, melons, pumpkins, and tomatoes. A section with an international flair includes selections of vegetables for French, Italian, oriental, and Latin American cuisine. Number of seeds per packet, number of days to germination, rich descriptions, and cultural information for vegetable seeds. Additional sections include Native American and culinary herbs. Guarantees satisfaction; will replace or issue refund. See **Booksellers**, Garlic, Herbs, **Kidstuff**, Organics, **Seeds, Supplies**.
Shipping season: All year.

PLANTS OF THE SOUTHWEST
1977
Gail Haggard
Catalog: $3.50, 103 pp., color photographs
Plants of the Southwest offers the seeds and live plants of 450 trees, shrubs, wildflowers, grasses, and traditional southwestern vegetables that are native to or have adapted to the conditions of the American Southwest. Offers the seeds of ninety vegetables, with special attention (just under forty varieties) to chilies. Other highlights include amaranth as food (three types), numerous beans, and traditional corn. Descriptions include sowing and thinning suggestions, color and culinary nature of crop, number of days to maturity, intermittent historical and cultural notes, and postharvest uses. Vegetable seeds sold by the packet with the number of seeds specified. Plants are four- to six-inch starts. Guarantees seeds are viable, true to name, and will grow in your garden if you follow their instructions; will replace if they fail. See **Booksellers**, **Grasses**, Heirlooms, Seeds, Trees, **Wildflowers**.
Shipping season: Seeds, all year. Plants, April through June. September and October.

P. L. ROHRER & BRO.
See Garlic, Herbs, Organics, **Seeds**, Supplies.

REDWOOD CITY SEED COMPANY
1971
Craig and Sue Dremann
Catalog: $1, 28 pp., illustrations. Large-print edition: $3. Supplements (twice yearly): $2
The Dremanns offer three hundred traditional open-pollinated vegetable and herb varieties that have been valued and cultivated by diverse cultures over time. They have acquired most of their seed stock from growers in those cultures.

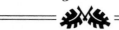
One third of their offering were originally introduced in North America. The catalog is organized by common name. The descriptions benefit from the original research conducted by the Dremanns on plant-related subjects. Information for each heirloom includes botanical name, historical information, and a fully realized description of the plant, its habit, shape, form, and flavor. Seeds sold by the packet. See **Booksellers**, Garlic, Heirlooms, Herbs, **Kidstuff**, Seeds.
Shipping season: All year.
Canada, Mexico, International

R. H. SHUMWAY, SEEDSMAN
1870
Catalog: Free, 55 pp., black-and-white and color illustrations
Shumway's first mail-order catalog was published in 1870 under the name "The Pioneer American Seedsman." Many of the seven hundred offerings are pictured in vintage, or vintage-style engravings. The 550 vegetables offered are a vigorous mix of open-pollinated, heirloom, and hybrid varieties. Descriptions of plant, vegetable, habit, number of days to maturity, and postharvest uses for each. Number of seeds noted within a broad range. Guarantees seeds to grow; will issue onetime refund at seller's discretion. (For three hundred varieties of tomato seed from a division of R. H. Shumway, *see* Totally Tomatoes on page 227.) See **Garlic**, Heirlooms, Herbs, **Seeds**.
Shipping season: All year.
Canada, International

RICHTERS
See **Booksellers**, Heirlooms, **Herbs**, Organics, Seeds.

RONNIGER'S SEED POTATOES
See **Booksellers**, Garlic, Heirlooms, Organics, Seeds.

ROSWELL SEED COMPANY, INC.
1900
Jim and W. L. Gill
Catalog: Free, 28 pp.
One hundred and forty-five hybrid vegetables and melons are described in the Gills' catalog, with those that are particularly strong performers in the Pecos Valley highlighted. Descriptions include number of days to maturity, flesh and skin color and texture, taste of veg-

etable, and typical postharvest use for all listings; number of plants per ounce or acre of seeds indicated for many. The flower and field seeds sections are represented as being adapted to the Southwest. Seeds sold by the packet or by weight. Guarantees true to name. See Garlic, Grasses, Seeds.
Canada, Mexico

SALT SPRING SEEDS
Dan Jason
Catalog: $2.,18 pp.
Mr. Jason, author *of Greening the Garden: A Guide to Sustainable Growing* and the *Salt Springs Seeds Cookbook,* sells 130 types of untreated, open-pollinated vegetable and herb seeds adapted to northern climates. Salt Spring's strong suit has been the one hundred–plus varieties of dry beans that they have offered. Recent additions include heirloom tomatoes. Descriptions are informal and entertaining. A sufficient number of seeds to sow a twenty-five-foot row is contained in each packet. Inquire for their supplemental bean list and price and variety list for fall-planted garlic. Separate price list upon request for live plants (Canada only). See Garlic, Heirlooms, **Kidstuff**, Organics, Seeds.
Shipping season: All year.
Canada, Mexico, International

SEED SAVERS EXCHANGE–SEED SAVER PUBLICATIONS
See **Booksellers**, Heirlooms, **Horticultural Societies**, Seeds.

SEED SHARES™
See Heirlooms, **Seeds**.

SEEDS BLÜM
See **Booksellers**, Garlic, Heirlooms, Herbs, Kidstuff, Seeds, Wildflowers.

SEEDS TRUST: HIGH ALTITUDE GARDENS
Bill McDorman
Catalog: Free, 44 pp.
Seeds Trust is a bioregional company that acquires and tests seeds that are acclimated to cold, short-season use and, in the case of this firm, that will grow at six thousand feet above sea level. Their list includes two hundred open-pollinated vegetable seeds, most of which are grown organically and so marked. The vegetable section with numerous heir-

loom varieties, includes a planting guide denoting minimum soil temperature, soil pH, frost tolerance, spacing of plants in beds and between rows, and planting depth. Descriptions include number of days to maturity, life cycle, seeds per ounce, taste, and form. Seeds sold by weight. Guarantees satisfaction; will replace or issue a refund. See **Booksellers**, Garlic, **Grasses**, Heirlooms, Organics, Seeds, **Wildflowers**.
Shipping season: begins May 20.
Canada, Mexico, International

SENECA HYBRIDS
1920
Bill Carey
Catalog: Free, 8 pp.
Seneca specializes in proprietary hybrid vegetable seeds that mature at different times in the season, including sweet corn, summer squash, yellow squash, winter squash, cucumbers, pumpkins, ornamental corn, and zucchini. See Seeds.
Shipping season: All year.
Canada, Mexico, International

SHEPHERD'S GARDEN SEEDS
1984
Renee Shepherd and Beth Benjamin
Catalog $1, 108 pp., illustrations
Shepherd's positions itself as providing seeds from worldwide sources to the gardener who loves to cook with especially fine-tasting vegetables and culinary herbs. Description of three hundred vegetable varieties includes country of origin, days to maturity, and size of plant, form of vegetable, and are especially rich when suggesting culinary uses. Recipes from Ms. Shepherd's cookbooks appear throughout the catalog. Guarantees satisfaction; will accept seed packets for credit or refund up to six months after purchase. See **Booksellers**, Garlic, Heirlooms, Herbs, **Kidstuff**, Seeds, Supplies.
Shipping season: All year.
Canada

SOUTHERN EXPOSURE SEED EXCHANGE®
1982
Jeff McCormack
Catalog: $3 (recoverable), 62 pp., illustrations
SESE® preserves and sells the seeds of untreated, open-pollinated, pre-1940 heirloom and family

heirloom (handed down privately through several generations) plants. Offers six hundred varieties of vegetables adaptable to the Mid-Atlantic states and areas with similar conditions. Some offerings for short growing seasons. Precise information about regional adaptation, germination testing, and the provenance of the seed from SESE. Descriptions and cultural notes are rich, including shape, form, and taste. Also includes life cycle, hardiness range, light requirements, days for germination and maturity, how to plant, and height of mature plant. Detailed key to disease and pest tolerance for many vegetables. The last page of the catalog is a planting/planning calendar for Mid-Atlantic gardeners. The catalog also contains a brief section of cut flowers, everlastings, fourteen types of sunflower, and fifty kitchen herbs. Notes number of seeds by weight and by the packet; includes germination test results on most packets. Guarantees satisfaction; will replace or issue refund. See **Booksellers, Garlic,** Heirlooms, Herbs, Seeds, **Supplies.**
Shipping season: All year.
Canada

SOUTHERN SEEDS
1987
Wae and Kathy Nelson
Catalog: $1, 40 pp., illustrations
"Some things like it hot" is the motto here. The Nelsons sell two hundred (predominantly open-pollinated) varieties of vegetable seed that are suited to warm to hot climates. Among their special and unusual food plants are Hawaiian super sweet corn, cucuzzi, jicama, passion fruit, tamarillo, and eighteen types of dwarf banana. Descriptions highlight attributes of Southern's selections that make them appropriate for gardening in hot climates. Specifies number of days to maturity and seeds per packet for each. Free fact sheets with general information, growing tips, and recipes for many items are available with order. Guarantees satisfaction; will replace or issue refund. See **Booksellers**, Fruit, Garlic, Organics, Seeds.
Shipping season: All year.
Canada, Mexico, International

"SOW ORGANIC" SEEDS
1979
Alan Venet and Sheryl Lee
Catalog: Free, 17 pp.
Mr. Venet and Ms. Lee grow all of the untreated, open-pollinated seeds that they sell on their certified organic farm. One hundred veg-

etables, fifteen flowers, and fifteen herbs are offered. Descriptions are brief and highlight the culinary uses of their vegetables and herbs. Heirloom varieties are noted. Seeds per packet and total weight of a packet for all. Guarantees true to name. See Garlic, Heirlooms, Herbs, Organics, Seeds.
Shipping season: All year.
Canada, Mexico, International

STOKES SEEDS
See **Garlic, Seeds, Supplies.**

SUNRISE ENTERPRISES
1976
Catalog: $2, 28 pp., black-and-white and color photographs
The focus here is oriental vegetable seeds. The catalog describes the seeds for one hundred hybrid and open-pollinated vegetables, including bitter melon, bok choi, pak choi, daikon (radishes), oriental eggplant, edible gourds, Chinese kale, mitsuba (Japanese parsley), mustard, and pickling melon. Information includes life cycle, size, texture, and form of fruit, number of days to maturity, and culinary uses. Seeds sold by the packet or by weight. See **Booksellers**, Garlic, Seeds.
Shipping season: All year.

TERRITORIAL SEED COMPANY
Tom Johns
Catalog: Free, 95 pp., illustrations and black-and-white photographs
The folks at Territorial are determined "to improve people's self-sufficiency and independence by enabling gardeners to produce an abundance of good-tasting fresh-from-the-garden food twelve months a year." Their meticulously detailed catalog, including over five hundred varieties of vegetables, herbs, and cover crops (and ninety flowers), is clearly written and stuffed with information. Description of vegetable varieties includes culture, vulnerability to specific insects, how to harvest, seed specifications (including soil temperature and number of days to emergence and maturity). Symbols highlight varieties that are well suited to beginners, container gardens, cool climates, and winter gardening. Forty herb descriptions include symbols for postharvest uses: culinary, teas, fresh and dried arrangements. Flower descriptions include life cycle, height and habit of plant, sun/shade re-

quirements, adaptability to container gardening, trellising requirements, usefulness as fresh-cut and dried flowers. Specifies number of seeds by weight and packet. See **Booksellers, Garlic,** Herbs, **Kidstuff**, Organics, Seeds, **Supplies.**
Shipping season: All year.
Canada

THOMPSON & MORGAN
1855
Bruce Sangster
Catalog: Free, 224 pp., color photographs
If you have a passion for seeds, you'd better plan to take a month off from work, ignore your family and friends, and generally dispense with any other responsibilities before sitting down to read the Thompson & Morgan catalog. There are 120 vegetables (and over 900 flowering plants) in this catalog that counts among its inactive customers Charles Darwin and Claude Monet. Information for their A to Z of vegetable seeds includes number of days to maturity, useful traits of particular varieties, evocative descriptions of vegetable, AAS winners, culinary tips, disease resistance, and number of seeds per packet. Guarantees satisfaction; will replace or issue credit. See **Garlic, Grasses,** Heirlooms, **Seeds.**
Shipping season: All year.
Canada, International

TOMATO GROWERS SUPPLY CO.
1984
Linda and Vince Sapp
Catalog: Free, 40 pp., black-and-white illustrations and photographs
The world according to tomatos, and peppers. The Sapps catalog the seed for 250 hybrid and heirloom tomatoes. An essay on starting seeds, preparing the soil, transplanting, watering, fertilizing, culture, and how to know what not to grow will help you plan ahead with some confidence. Plants are characterized as early, mid-, and late-season varieties, beefsteak, processing, yellow and orange, small-fruited plant, and an assortment of others that can't be squeezed under one of these headings. Peppers (one hundred varieties) are listed either as sweet or hot. Descriptions emphasize the traits that distinguish these plants from each other. Information for each listing includes number of days to maturity, growing habit (determinate or indeterminate), disease resistance, nature of

fruit, and postharvest uses. Specifies number of seeds per packet. Guarantees satisfaction for one year; will replace or issue refund. See **Booksellers**, Heirlooms, Seeds, **Supplies**.
Shipping season: All year.

TOTALLY TOMATOES
1992
Catalog: Free, 63 pp., illustrations and color photographs
Also the world according to tomatoes and peppers. The TT catalog weighs in with 279 types of tomato and 120 peppers. Organized loosely by size of fruit, information includes size, weight, and form of fruit, number of days to maturity, growth habit (determinate or not), and postharvest uses. Solid information on germination, site preparation, transplanting, culture, and care. Precise number of seeds per packet or available by weight. Guarantees true to name and your satisfaction; will replace or issue refund. See **Supplies**, Seeds.
Shipping season: All year.
Canada, Mexico, International

VERMONT BEAN SEED COMPANY
1975
Catalog: Free, 96 pp., illustrations and color photographs
The world according to beans (ninety-five kinds), four hundred vegetables, and fifty herbs. The company's offerings are weighted toward hybrids: cantaloupe, cabbage, cauliflower, eggplants, rhubarb, squash, tomatoes, and more. Many choices for northern and other short-season gardeners. Cultural information and tips abound in this decidedly vegetarian catalog. Number of days to maturity, disease resistance, site preference, nature of fruit, and cultural information for each listing.

Highlights varieties that fare well in a wide range of conditions. See **Garlic**, Heirlooms, Herbs, Seeds.
Shipping season: All year.

VESEY'S SEEDS LTD.
See **Booksellers**, **Garlic**, Herbs, **Seeds**, Supplies, Wildflowers.

WILLHITE SEED CO.
1920
Don Dobbs
Catalog: Free, 60 pp., color photographs
Willhite offers many new hybrid vegetables and some older varieties among the four hundred listings in their catalog. Much of what they offer is for the farmer and market gardener; however, they note those types of vegetables that are appropriate for backyard cultivation. Highlights All America selections. Their specialties include cantaloupes and watermelons, French vegetables, and a selection from the Indian subcontinent. Planting chart indicates the amount of seed required for hundred-foot rows and per acre, planting distance in rows, and distance between rows, approximate number of seeds per measure, and days for germination. Descriptions are straightforward and fully realized, characterizing the texture, shape, color, flavor, uses, and disease resistance of each selection. See **Garlic**, Seeds.
Shipping season: All year.
Canada, Mexico, International

WILLIAM DAM SEEDS
See **Booksellers**, **Garlic**, Herbs, **Seeds**, Wildflowers.

WOOD PRAIRIE FARM
See **Garlic**, Seeds.

Selected Reading About Vegetables

The American Gardening Guides: Vegetables, by Callaway Gardens (David Chambers and Lucinda Mays with Laura C. Martin). The vegetable volume in a series of books that is a collaborative effort by experts from key arboretums and horticultural institutions including The New York Botanical Garden, The Holden Arboretum, Royal Botanical Garden, Chicago Botanic Garden, Cornell Plantations, Matthaei Botanical Gardens, University of Nebraska Horticulture Department, Desert Botanical Garden of Phoenix, and Fetzer Organic Garden. Includes definitions, history, botany, and basic gardening philosophies from a panel of experts. The plant selector section contains more than two hundred color photographs of vegetables with detailed descriptions that include size, coloration, growing cycle, maintenance, and care. Also includes a section on design and vegetable gardening techniques. Three hundred black-and-white and color photographs.

Breed Your Own Vegetable Varieties: Popbeans, Purple Peas and Other Innovations from the Backyard Garden, by Carol Deppe. An easy-to-understand (and follow) guide to developing your own vegetables, written for the home gardener. Includes entertaining and inspirational stories of amateur breeders, along with a wealth of detailed instructions and suggestions for finding and evaluating germplasm, genetics and plant parenthood, chromosome doubling, crossing, and domesticating wild plants. Includes a section on the breeding procedures for specific vegetables such as tomatoes, lettuce, peas, onions, squash, and pumpkins.

Cornucopia: A Source Book of Edible Plants, by Stephen Facciola. Lists international sources for over three thousand vegetables, fruit-and nut-bearing plants, herbs, edible flowers and grains.

Designing and Maintaining Your Edible Landscape Naturally, by Robert Kourik. A whole-earth approach that recommends edible plants that add fertility to your soil, attract beneficial insects, minimize the effects of erosion, and includes techniques for enriching your soil and other strategies for providing food through the cultivation of low-maintenance plants.

Garden Seed Inventory (fourth edition), by Kent Whealy. A landmark inventory of sources for 6,800 standard, open-pollinated vegetables.

Home Growing, by Edwin F. Steffek. An A to Z reference for fruit and vegetable gardening. Strong on how to encourage your plants to be healthy and bountiful, using such techniques as forcing, pinching back, pruning etc.

How to Grow More Vegetables, Fruits, Nuts, Berries, Grains, and Other Crops Than You Ever Thought Possible on Less Land Than You Can Imagine, by John Jeavons. The step-by-step instruction manual for sustainable organic biointensive gardening as developed and practiced by Ecology Action (Bountiful Gardens).

Lazy-Bed Gardening, by John Jeavons and Carol Cox. "Lazy Bed" is an Irish term for a deeply dug bed whose growing area can produce substantially more than the equivalent area planted in less deeply dug rows. A step-by-step guide for using this technique in food gardening.

Rodale's Garden Problem Solver: Vegetables, Fruits and Herbs, by Jeff Ball. Lists the symptoms, causes, organic solutions, and preventative measures for seven hundred problems facing your edibles. Color photographs.

Square Foot Gardening: A New Way to Garden in Less Space with Less Work, by Mel Bartholomew. So it's not so new anymore (first published in 1981), but this book has worked wonders for vegetable gardeners on a land budget. Includes sixty drawings and thirty-seven photographs.

GARLIC, POTATOES, ONIONS, AND MUSHROOMS

The number of offerings cited in each profile is based on information in the most recent catalog provided by the source. In this section, shipping season is for garlic, potatoes, onions, and mushrooms only. A selection of books about these plant materials appears after the last listing.

QUICK FIND

The following sources are listed in this section:

ABUNDANT LIFE SEED FOUNDATION
1975
Susan Herman
Catalog: $2 (recoverable), 64 pp., black-and-white photographs
A nonprofit organization that acquires, propagates, and preserves native and naturalized seed, ALSF also disseminates information about seed culture and use. Offers three types of bunching onions, two yellow storage types, two red storage types, Walla Walla for overwintering, and purplette for pickling. Descriptions include number of days to maturity, disease resistance, and postharvest uses. Guarantees true to name; will exchange or issue refund. See **Booksellers**, Heirlooms, Herbs, Organics, **Seeds**, Vegetables.
Shipping season: All year.
Canada, Mexico, International

ALLEN, STERLING, & LOTHROP
1911
Catalog: $1 (recoverable), 40 pp., illustrations
Included among AS&L's seed offerings that have adapted to the New England climate are early yellow globe Danvers, large red Wethersfield, yellow sweet Spanish, and white or green bunching onions. Seed sold by packet. Number of seeds not specified. Guarantees true to name. See **Herbs**, Organics, **Seeds**, **Supplies**, Vegetables.
Shipping season: All year.

BECKER'S SEED POTATOES
1985
Catalog: Free, 12 pp.
Becker's sells Elite seed potatoes of true heritage (fifty years and older), as well as more re-

cent cultivars. Their catalog is organized by season of maturity for thirty regular and four specialty varieties (all blue, all red, banana salad fingerling, and German fingerling). Description indicates whether eyes only or whole seeds are shipped, number of days to maturity, color, disease resistance, and culinary information. Also offers three "Garden Pac" assortments (ten eyes each of assorted, red, or heritage varieties). Whole seed sold by the pound; eyes are twenty-five to a package. Guarantees healthy stock. See **Booksellers**.
Shipping season: Spring (order deadline, April 30).
Canada only

BERLIN SEEDS
1984
Edward and Brenda Beachy
Catalog: Free, 60 pp., illustrations, black-and-white and color photographs
The Beachys offer yellow and white onion sets, and seeds for sweet sandwich and Walla Walla onions. Sets (not described) are sold by the pound. Descriptions for seeds include number of days to maturity, yield, storage, form, and taste. Seeds packed 250 to a packet and in bulk by the quarter ounce. Warrants purity and vitality of seeds. Guarantees seeds to grow; will issue credit or refund. See **Booksellers, Fruit,** Grasses, **Kidstuff,** Organics, **Seeds, Supplies,** Vegetables.
Shipping season: Seeds, after mid-February. Sets, please inquire.
Canada

BOUNTIFUL GARDENS
1972
Bill and Betsy Bruneau
Catalog: Free, 72 pp. rare seeds catalog: $2, 30 pp.
The Bountiful Gardens catalog is published by Ecology Action, a nonprofit organization that practices and teaches organic biointensive methods. In the vegetable section of the main catalog are seeds for ten types of onions, scallions, and chives. Notes weeks to maturity and harvest, approximate yield, and necessary spacing. Size and shape of bulb, flavor, and postharvest use also described. Number of seeds per packet indicated. Guarantees that seeds are vital at time of shipment and meet or exceed federal minimum germination standards. See **Booksellers,** Heirlooms, Herbs, **Kidstuff,** Organics, **Seeds, Supplies,** Vegetables.

Shipping season: All year.
Canada, Mexico, International

THE COOK'S GARDEN
1983
Ellen and Shepherd Ogden
Catalog: $1, 112 pp., illustrations
The Cook's Garden has its origin in the Ogdens' work as organic market gardeners. Offers four varieties of onion and shallot seeds, "Atlantic" and "Success" shallot sets, and Walla Walla seedlings. Offers four kinds of potatoes from Wood Prairie Farm (see page 239). Planting, cultural, and culinary information included for all. Seeds sold in packets, with seed count or weight specified for each. Shallots sold by the pound; onion seedlings sold in groups of 150 plants. Guarantees satisfaction; will issue a refund. See **Booksellers,** Heirlooms, **Herbs,** Kidstuff, Organics, **Seeds, Supplies,** Vegetables.
Shipping season: Seeds, all year. Sets and seedlings, please inquire. Potatoes, March and April.
Seeds only to Canada and Hawaii

DeGIORGI SEED COMPANY
1905
Duane and Monte Thompson
Catalog: $2 (recoverable), 75 pp.
The DeGiorgi catalog contains fourteen hundred varieties of seeds for flowering annuals, perennials, herbs, regional wildflowers, ornamental grasses, and vegetables. Selection includes seeds for fourteen types of onion and red German garlic. Indicates number of days to maturity and describes plant, culinary uses, and storage capabilities. Specifies number of seeds per packet; garlic sold by the pound. Guarantees satisfaction; will replace or issue a refund. See **Booksellers,** Grasses, Herbs, **Kidstuff,** Seeds, Vegetables.
Shipping season: Garlic, September. Onion seeds, all year.

DIXONDALE FARMS
1913
Jeanie Martin Frasier and Pam Martin
Catalog: Free, 6 pp., color photographs
These fourth-generation onion growers work a two-thousand-acre farm. In the home gardener's version of their catalog, Ms. Frasier and Ms. Martin offer eight of the seventy plant varieties that they supply to commercial growers. Tips on variety selection, planting, and harvesting in

catalog; planting guide sent with order. Description includes recommendations for cultivars by region and culinary uses. Sold in bunches of sixty plants. Guarantees unconditionally; will issue credit or refund. See Vegetables.

Shipping season: January through April.

D. LANDRETH SEED COMPANY
See Grasses, Heirlooms, Herbs, **Seeds**, Vegetables.

DOWN ON THE FARM SEED
1990
Ruth A. Guth
Catalog: Free, 52 pp., illustrations
The Guths are organic farmers who sell untreated seed, preserve heirloom varieties, and provide a free seed search service for gardeners. Selection includes seed for early yellow globe, red Wethersfield, Southport red, and white globe onions. Cultural tips, brief descriptions, number of days to maturity, number of row feet each packet will sow. See Heirlooms, Herbs, **Kidstuff**, Organics, Seeds, **Vegetables**.
Shipping season: All year.
Canada, Mexico, International

FARMER SEED AND NURSERY
1888
Don Prodoehl
Catalog: Free, 64 pp., color photographs
Farmer's offers northern-grown plants and seeds. Five varieties of storage, sweet, and bunching onion seeds available. Brief descriptions of bulbs and uses. Also offers garlic, elephant garlic, yellow and white table onions, and yellow shallot sets. Seeds (number not noted) sold by the packet or by weight. Garlic and onion plants sold by weight; elephant garlic by the clove. Guarantees plants for one year; will replace or issue credit or refund. See Perennials, Seeds, **Vegetables**.
Shipping season: Seeds, all year. Plants, March through June.
No onion plants to California or Idaho. No garlic plants to Idaho

FEDCO SEEDS
See **Moose Growers Supply**.

FILAREE FARM
1977
Ron Engeland

Catalog: $2, 42 pp.
Ron, Watershine, Minot, and Brianna grow 350 strains of organic, gourmet-quality garlic, including numerous heirlooms. Filaree Farm is a Washington State–certified organic grower and vendor, listed as a Seed Saver's Exchange "Garlic Curator," Ron is a self-described "small scale farmer who makes his living growing garlic," and the author of the highly regarded book *Growing Great Garlic*. Plant material is organized by nine named strains. Seventy varieties are described in detail; numerous others, including specialty strains, are listed as available. The catalog is grounded in a substantial amount of information pertaining to garlic history, culture, growth, use, and storage, as well as classification systems, including maturity groups. Garlic bulbs sold by weight. Also offers four assortments to appeal to varying tastes and growing expertise. Filaree does not recommend their garlic for areas below thirty-two degrees north latitude. Guarantees bulb size and quality; will issue refund. See **Booksellers**, Organics.
Shipping season: September and October.

FISHER'S GARDEN STORE
1957
Kenneth J. Fisher and Judy Fisher
Catalog: Free, 19 pp., black-and-white photographs
Mr. Fisher breeds and grows hybrid and open-pollinated seeds suitable for high altitudes and short growing seasons. Offers six types of seeds for mild onions. Descriptions include number of days to maturity, size, color, and shape. Seeds available by the packet or by weight. See **Seeds**, Vegetables.
Shipping season: All year.
Canada

FLOATING MOUNTAIN SEEDS
See Heirlooms, Herbs, Seeds, **Vegetables**.

FOX HOLLOW HERB & HEIRLOOM SEED CO.
See Heirlooms, **Herbs**, Seeds, **Vegetables**.

FUNGI PERFECTI
1979
Paul Stamets
Catalog: $3, 80 pp., illustrations and black-and-white photographs
The specialty of Fungi Perfecti is the cultivation of

high-quality certified organic (Washington State) gourmet and medicinal mushrooms. Half of FP's catalog is tailored to the home gardener, the balance for the professional cultivator. Mr. Stamets, the author of *Growing Gourmet and Medicinal Mushrooms* and coauthor (with Jeff Chilton) of *The Mushroom Cultivator*, has written "A Simplified Overview of Mushroom Cultivation Strategies" for this catalog. Nine preinoculated mushroom patches (including shiitake, nameko, pearl oyster, and enokitake) are offered for indoor cultivation, eleven varieties including morel, reishi/ling chi, shiitake, and maitake) for outdoor cultivation. Descriptions and cultural information for each variety. Sold by the plug. Guarantees mushroom kits. See **Booksellers, Kidstuff,** Organics, **Supplies.**
Canada, Mexico, International

GARDEN CITY SEEDS
1982
Susan Wall-MacLane
Catalog: $1, 75 pp.
Garden City Seeds (specializing in northern-acclimated seeds, roots, and tubers) is a subsidiary of the nonprofit Down Home Project, Inc., which supports self-reliant living. Offerings include three strains of certified organic garlic, four varieties of onion seeds, three onion sets, and eleven types of potato. Descriptions include cultural, soil temperature, and composition preferences, susceptibility to pests and solutions, and storage tendencies. Garlic and potatoes sold by weight, onions by sets of one hundred, and seeds by the packet or by weight. The catalog includes articles on mulching, storing the harvest, seed saving for garlic, and a "Green Resource Guide" listing sources of information about sustainable agriculture. Guarantees true to name and satisfaction; will issue refund. See **Booksellers,** Grasses, Herbs, Organics, **Seeds, Supplies,** Vegetables.
Shipping Season: Garlic, September. Onion sets and potatoes, April. Seeds, all year.
Canada

GEORGE'S PLANT FARM
1985
George Vinson and Donna Dellinger
Catalog: LSASE, 2 pp.
Offers sweet potato plants from the hills of Tennessee. Among the varieties recently offered were Oklahoma reds, 'Nancy Hall', Georgia 'Jets', and red nuggets. Descriptions include skin and flesh color, texture, taste, postharvest uses, plant habit (vine or bush type), and days to maturity for most. Guarantees healthy rooted plants; will issue refund. See Vegetables.
Shipping season: April through June.

THE GOURMET GARDENER™
See **Booksellers,** Herbs, Seeds, Vegetables.

GOURMET MUSHROOMS
Catalog: $1., 4 pp.
Offers Morel Habitat Kit®for outdoor growing in areas covering at least five square feet. Self-contained Mushroom Pot® for indoor growing available with shiitake, hericium, or pleurotus spawn. See **Booksellers.**
Shipping season: All year.

GURNEY'S SEED & NURSERY CO.
1866
Donald L. Kruml
Catalog: Free, 64 pp., color photographs
This generalist's catalog includes yellow, white, and red onion sets, eight onion types available as plants or seeds, and the seeds (by the packet or by weight) of six others. Also offers eleven potato sets, four sweet potato plants, an unspecified strain of garlic, and elephant garlic. White and tan mushroom kits arrive with spawn inoculated in compost. Guarantees seeds and plants for one year from date of shipment; will issue credit or refund. See **Kidstuff,** Organics, **Seeds, Supplies,** Vegetables.
Shipping season: Seeds, all year. Plants, February through mid-June. September through November.
Canada, Mexico, International

HARDSCRABBLE ENTERPRISES
1985
Paul Goland
Catalog: $3 (recoverable), 4 pp.
Mr. Goland started raising shiitake mushrooms after being enticed by a magazine article describing their taste. Convinced that he would enjoy them, he ordered some spawn, cut a few logs, and started growing mushrooms. Unfortunately, it took two years for his maiden mushroom to appear because "I did everything wrong the first time." To increase the likelihood of his customers getting their first crop in six to eighteen months, Mr. Goland provides complete growing information in his shiitake starter kit containing dowel

spawn for twelve to fifteen (four- by forty-inch) logs. Also offers dowel spawn kits (for larger yield) and sawdust spawn. See **Booksellers, Supplies.**
Shipping season: All year.

HARRIS SEEDS
See Herbs, **Seeds, Supplies,** Vegetables.

HENRY FIELD'S SEED & NURSERY CO.
1892
Orville Dragoo
Catalog: Free, 87 pp., color photographs
A full line nursery and seed catalog that includes white button and royal tan mushroom kits (including growing container), fifteen types of onion (including Vidalia sweet, Walla Walla sweet, red hamburger, white Bermuda, and red burgermaster) available as seeds or plants, and three types of onion sets (white, red, and yellow). Also offers ten northern-hardy (Shenandoah, Iowa) potato sets (including russet Burbank, Norgold russet, red Pontiac, Kennebec, and Yukon gold). Descriptions include number of days for seeds (onions), number of seeds per packet or sets per offer, culinary uses, flavor, size, and color. Guarantees plants will grow; will replace or issue refund. See **Fruit, Kidstuff,** Organics, Perennials, **Seeds, Supplies, Trees, Vegetables.**
Shipping season: February through June.

J. L. HUDSON, SEEDSMAN
See **Booksellers,** Heirlooms, Herbs, **Seeds,** Vegetables.

JOHNNY'S SELECTED SEEDS
1973
Robert L. Johnston, Jr.
Catalog: Free, 136 pp., color photographs
Seeds offered by JSS are grown using primarily organic methods and nonchemical pest deterrents at their Albion, Maine, farm. The catalog is deep in cultural information, helpful hints, and charts. Offers five types of certified Maine seed potatoes and five that are "double certified," having also passed muster as certified organic. Offers seeds of thirteen hard-storage, sweet-mild, bunching, and mini onions sold by the packet or by weight (notes number of seeds); germination standards included for all seeds. Guarantees satisfaction; will replace or issue refund. See **Booksellers,** Grasses, Heirlooms, Herbs, Organics, **Seeds, Supplies,** Vegetables.
Shipping season: All year.

Canada, Mexico, International

J. W. JUNG SEED AND NURSERY CO.
See **Bulbs, Fruit, Kidstuff,** Perennials, **Seeds, Trees,** Vegetables.

KALMIA FARM
1982
Ken Klotz
Catalog: Free, 14 pp., black-and-white photographs
Mr. Klotz says that Kalmia Farm was first to reintroduce the potato onion and its relatives to American gardeners. The potato onion produces green bunching onions in the spring and again in the fall, as well as large bulbs for long-term storage. This variety also produces its own sets for future planting. Kalmia's selection includes yellow potato onions (Richmond Hill), Catawissa and Egyptian top onions, shallots (pear, gray, yellow Dutch, and French red), and garlic (German, Spanish red topsetting, and white). Onions available in sets, shallots by weight, and garlic variously by the clove or weight. See Vegetables.
Shipping season: Limited in March. Prefers September through mid-November.

KILGORE SEED COMPANY
See **Booksellers,** Herbs, **Seeds,** Vegetables.

LE JARDIN DU GOURMET
See Booksellers, Herbs, Seeds, **Vegetables.**

LOCKHART SEEDS, INC.
1948
Steve Auten
Catalog: $2 (recoverable), 75 pp.
Lockhardt characterizes itself as a catalog seed house serving the home and market gardener. Their catalog has a clear and open design, with separate sections for each type of vegetable and descriptions of the varieties that they offer within type; contains detailed information about seed testing and treatment, charts for determining seed coverage, and planting guides. Offers hybrid and open-pollinated seed for 420 vegetables (including orientals), representing the harvest from fifty seed-producing companies worldwide. The catalog includes thirty varieties of onion. Groups of onions are organized as "short day," "medium day," and "long day," and within each group hybrids and open-pollinated types are presented separately. Includes

relative days to maturity, shape and color of onion, size of fruit, skin color, flesh feel and smell, and suitability for storage. Seed sold by the packet or by weight. Guarantees true to description; reports of defective seeds must be filed within thirty days of receipt. See Grasses, Seeds, **Vegetables**.
Shipping season: All year.
Canada, Mexico, International

LONG ISLAND SEED COMPANY
See Heirlooms, Seeds, **Vegetables**.

MOOSE GROWERS SUPPLY
1970
Bill Getty and Gene Frey
Catalog: $1, 10 pp.
Formerly known as Moose Tubers, this division of Fedco now specializes in seed potatoes (forty varieties), onion sets (Stuttgarter, Braunsweiger red, and Dutch shallots), and sunchokes, all sold by weight. Potatoes organized by number of days to maturity. Listing includes description, culinary uses, yield expressed in number of pounds harvested to number of pounds planted, and disease vulnerability and resistance. Notes varieties that are certified organic. Also offers accessories and supplies. Guarantees satisfaction; will replace or issue refund. See **Booksellers**, Organics, **Supplies**, Vegetables.
Shipping season: April.

MUSHROOMPEOPLE
1976
Albert Bates
Catalog: Free, 8 pp., black-and-white photographs
This mail-order mushroom emporium sells tools, spawn, and books and tapes for the mushroom enthusiast. Offerings include ten shiitake strains: various wide-range types (indoors and outdoors); warm-weather, cold-weather, and sawdust strains. Also offers maitake spawn, oysters (*Pleurotus ostreatus*) for log or stump culture, hen-of-the-woods (*Polyporus frondosus*) for stumps, giant morel (*Morchella angusticeps*) for soil, lion's mane (*Hericium erinaceus*), and reishi (*Ganoderma lucidum*). See **Booksellers**, Supplies.
Shipping season: All year.
Canada, International

NATIVE SEEDS/SEARCH
See **Booksellers**, **Kidstuff**, Seeds, **Vegetables**, Wildflowers.

NICHOLS GARDEN NURSERY
1950
Rose Marie Nichols McGee
Catalog: Free, 72 pp.
Nichols Garden Nursery boasts a broad range of seeds for vegetables (470 varieties) flowers (150) and herbs (120, plus seventy shipped as live plants). According to Ms. McGee, this was the nursery that introduced *Allium ampeloprasum* to the American gardener and named it elephant garlic. Also sells Nichols silverskin garlic, both sold by weight. Nichols top set garlic (Rocambole) sold as bulblets. Offers Egyptian (walking) onions as starts and Walla Walla sweet as plants. Offers nine onion varieties as seeds, by the packet or by the half ounce. Descriptions include cultural requirements and growth habits, and the number of days to maturity for seeds. See **Booksellers**, Herbs, Organics, **Seeds**, Supplies, **Vegetables**, Wildflowers.
Shipping season: Seeds, all year. Elephant garlic, August through mid-October. Rocambole garlic, onion starts, and plants, September to first frost in Albany, Oregon.

ORAL LEDDEN & SONS
1904
Don Ledden
Catalog: Free, 55 pp., black-and-white photographs
A traditional family-owned and -operated seed house that stocks new hybrids, and many hard-to-find heirloom varieties acquired from diverse sources. Vidalia, Walla Walla, and white and yellow sweet Spanish onions are available at approximately seventy-five plants to the bunch. Offers three globe onion sets and one unspecified white garlic set. Seed for red burgermaster, yellow sweet Spanish, white sweet Spanish, and 'First Edition' onion seeds sold by the packet, or by weight (number of seeds per packet indicated). Ten types of seed potato are listed but not described. Guarantees safe arrival; will replace or issue refund. See **Grasses**, Heirlooms, **Seeds**, **Supplies**, Vegetables.
Shipping season: Onion plants and sets, please inquire. Potatoes, March and April. Seeds, January through December.
Canada, Mexico, International

OSC SEEDS
See **Seeds**.

OTIS S. TWILLEY SEED COMPANY
See Herbs, **Seeds**, Vegetables.

PARK SEED® CO.
1868
J. Leonard Park and Karen Park Jennings
Catalog: Free, 76 pp., color photographs
Founded by G. W. Park in the living room of
his Libonia, Pennsylvania, home, Park Seed
currently describes its business as the oldest
and largest family-owned seed company in
America. Offers a button mushroom farm kit
with spawn planted in compost and topsoil,
and a biodegradable "log" inoculated with shiitake spawn, both for indoor growing. Onions
available as seed: Sweet Georgia Brown (a
short-day variety), crystal wax pickling, and
granex hybrid; as sets: yellow, red, and white;
and as plants: granex, yellow Spanish, white
Bermuda, and red Mac hybrids. Also offers
minituber seed potatoes: Desiree, gold rush
russett, Redsen, and yellow Finn. Specifies
number of seeds and tubers per packet. Guarantees satisfaction for one year from date of delivery; will replace or issue credit or refund. See
Bulbs, **Herbs**, **Peonies**, Roses, **Seeds**, **Supplies**, Vegetables.
**Shipping season: Mushrooms, through May.
Onion seeds, all year. Onion sets, through
mid-May. Onion plants, through the end of
spring. Potatoes, through the end of spring.
Canada**

PEACEFUL VALLEY FARM & GARDEN
SUPPLY
1976
Kathleen Fenton
**Catalog: Free, 120 pp., illustrations and
black-and-white photographs**
This full-service catalog is packed with seeds, supplies, and tools for organic gardeners and farmers.
Potatoes carried by Peaceful Valley are organically
grown certified seed stock from Idaho. Their offerings have included Burbank russet, Davis purple, Kennebec, Pontiac red, red Norland, and
Yukon gold. Descriptions include color, nature of
skin, set of eyes, relative size of vine, and reliability for storage. See **Booksellers**, **Grasses**, Organics, Seeds, **Supplies**, **Wildflowers**.
**Shipping season: October and November.
Canada**

PIEDMONT PLANT CO.
See Heirlooms, **Vegetables**.

PINETREE GARDEN SEEDS
See **Booksellers**, Herbs, **Kidstuff**, Organics,
Seeds, **Supplies**, **Vegetables**.

P. L. ROHRER & BRO.
See Herbs, Organics, **Seeds**, Supplies, Vegetables.

REDWOOD CITY SEED COMPANY
See **Booksellers**, Heirlooms, Herbs, **Kidstuff**,
Seeds, **Vegetables**.

R. H. SHUMWAY, SEEDSMAN
1870
**Catalog: Free, 55 pp., black-and-white and
color illustrations .**
Shumway's first mail-order catalog was published in
1870 under the name "The Pioneer American
Seedsman." Many of the seven hundred offerings
are pictured in vintage or vintage-style engravings.
Offers field-grown onion plants (red hamburger,
yellow sweet Spanish, white sweet Spanish, and Vidalia varieties), sets of red, white, and yellow onions,
shallots, and garlic cloves (German red Rocambole,
jumbo elephant, California white, and a newly introduced Chinese red-and-white). Spud fanciers
can purchase eyes for Kennebec, red Pontiac, and
russet Norkotah potatoes. Guarantees seeds to
grow; will issue onetime refund at their discretion.
See Heirlooms, Herbs, **Seeds**, **Vegetables**.
**Shipping season: Onion plants and sets,
February through early June. Potatoes,
February through late April. Garlic, all year.
Canada, International**

RONNIGER'S SEED POTATOES
David Ronniger
**Catalog: $2, 40 pp., black-and-white
photographs**
The Ronnigers believe Sir John Sinclair got it
perfectly right when in 1828 he wrote, "There
is no species of human food that can be con-
sumed in a greater variety of modes than the
potato." In pursuit of that consumption, this
family farm in Idaho's Kootenai River valley offers eighty-five types of certified organic (by the
Idaho State Department of Agriculture) seed
potatoes. Varieties are organized by time of maturation: early–sixty-five days (Bison, Irish Cob-
bler, and red Norland), midseason–eighty days
(all-blue, all-red, Feldeslohn, Kerr's pink, and
'Island Sunshine'), and late season–ninety days
(German butterball, Lemhi russet, and Nook-
sack). Also offers fingerlings and yellow potato

onions. Easy-to-digest cultural information about potatoes and potato growing, and a potato comparison chart enumerating desirable traits such as best keepers, heat tolerance adapted to the southern United States, and scab resistance. Descriptions include limit of purchase, current availability, color, shape, taste, provenance, and response to storage. All sold by weight. Offers a senior citizen and master gardener discount. Guarantees satisfaction; will resolve problems. See **Booksellers**, Heirlooms, Organics, Seeds, Vegetables.
Shipping season: Mid-February through mid-June. September through early November.

ROSWELL SEED COMPANY, INC.
See Grasses, Seeds, **Vegetables**.

SALT SPRING SEEDS
See Heirlooms, **Kidstuff**, Organics, Seeds, **Vegetables**.

SEEDS BLÜM
1981
Jan Blüm
Catalog: $3 (first-class mail, $4.50), 99 pp., illustrations
Ms. Blüm's catalog integrates cultural and practical information about seeds, seed saving, and growing with a strong message about biodiversity and cooperative self-reliance. The catalog includes nine hundred varieties of open-pollinated, nonhybrid, seeds. Offers seventeen varieties of yellow, white, blue, lavender, and pink seed potatoes by the pound; twenty varieties of onion seed, shallot plants, and Egyptian onion bulblets; a strain of silverskin; and elephant garlic sold by the clove. Listings include evocative but precise descriptions, pollination information, genus and species, when to plant, number of days to harvest, spacing, rows, number of seeds per packet, and a notation for heirlooms that have been on record for at least one hundred (a few, seventy-five) years. Ms. Blüm contracts with small-scale growers for seeds, and maintains a "garden to garden network" for home gardeners to test and cultivate seeds. See **Booksellers**, Heirlooms, Herbs, **Kidstuff, Seeds**, Vegetables, Wildflowers.
Shipping season: All year.
Canada, Mexico, International

SEEDS TRUST: HIGH ALTITUDE GARDENS
See **Booksellers**, Heirlooms, **Grasses**, Organics, Seeds, Vegetables, Wildflowers.

SHEPHERD'S GARDEN SEEDS
1984
Renee Shepherd and Beth Benjamin
Catalog: $1, 108 pp., illustrations
Shepherd's positions itself as providing seed from worldwide sources to the gardener who loves to cook with especially fine-tasting vegetables and culinary herbs. Shepherd's potato selection includes heirlooms with unique colors, shapes, and superior flavor. Recent catalogs included Caribe, red ruby, and Maine Kennebec potatoes, gold rush baking potatoes, and all-blues. Offers four collections (potato patches) for those who can't make up their minds. Potato minitubers, packaged ten to a bag, are certified virus free and grown without pesticides or herbicides. Onion plants (Walla Walla sweet, Vidalia sweets, Stockton reds, "Northern Rainbow" and "Southern Rainbow" collections shipped directly from Dixondale Onion Ranch [see Dixondale Farms]. Onion seeds (pearl baby onions from Israel, white Lisbon, and an heirloom, Boretanna Italian cipollini) are offered in packets of eight hundred seeds. Shepherd's purple-skinned Italian heirloom garlic and white-skinned Gilroy (California) garlic are available as cloves. Guarantees satisfaction; will accept seed packets for credit or refund up to six months from purchase. See **Booksellers**, Heirlooms, Herbs, **Kidstuff**, Seeds, **Supplies, Vegetables**.
Shipping season: Potatoes, January through May. Onion plants. January through April. Onion seeds, all year. Garlic cloves, September and October.
No seed potatoes to Alaska, Hawaii, or Canada
No garlic or onion sets to Idaho or Canada

SOHN'S FOREST MUSHROOMS
1983
Eileen and Ray Sohn
Catalog: Free, 8pp.
The Sohns' offer seven strains of shiitake and four of oyster mushrooms, including several that will produce in cool or cold weather. Dowels sold in units of five hundred and in kits suitable for inoculating ten to twelve logs. Sawdust spawn for twenty logs sold in four-quart bags. See **Booksellers, Supplies**.
Shipping season: All year.
Canada, Mexico, International

SOUTHERN EXPOSURE SEED EXCHANGE®
1982

Jeff McCormack
Catalog: $3 (recoverable), 62 pp., illustrations
SESE® preserves and sells the seeds of untreated, open-pollinated, pre-1940 heirloom and family heirloom (handed down through several generations) plants. Offers six hundred varieties of vegetables adaptable to the Mid-Atlantic states and areas with similar conditions. Sells thirteen strains of soft-neck and hard-neck garlic in starter packages of specified weight. Rich descriptions include cultural information, yields, hardiness, provenance, and taste. Also offers garlic keeper and garlic crusher. Sells multiplier onions by weight and nine varieties of bunching and dry bulb onions as seeds. Notes number of seeds by packet or by weight. Prints germination results on most packets. Guarantees satisfaction; will replace or issue refund. See **Booksellers,** Heirlooms, Herbs, Seeds, **Supplies, Vegetables.**
Shipping season: Garlic and multiplier onions, September and October. Seeds, all year.
Seeds only to Canada

SOUTHERN SEEDS
See **Booksellers,** Fruit, Organics, **Seeds,** Vegetables.

"SOW ORGANIC" SEEDS
See Heirlooms, Herbs, Organics, Seeds, **Vegetables.**

STOKES SEEDS
1881
Catalog: Free, 112 pp., color photographs
Stokes is a seed catalog to savor. There are nineteen hundred varieties of flowers and vegetables (including oriental and gourmet types). The catalog is steeped in cultural information for groups of vegetables and flowers, as well as information specific to individual hybrids and open-pollinated varieties. For onions, offers the seed for twelve spring and early summer white bunching varieties, and two overwintering types: Beltsville, and hardy white. Stokes own hybrids for early, main, and late season crops are sold variously by weight and by seed count. Also offers a number of Spanish (including Kelsae Sweet Giant, a world weight record holder at seven pounds, seven ounces) and hybrid Spanish varieties. Rich full descriptions are precise and include specifications for sowing, germination, number of days to matu-

rity, texture and color of skin, and preferred soil conditions. Number of seeds per packet and by weight are specified. See **Seeds, Supplies,** Vegetables.
Shipping season: All year
Canada, Mexico, International

SUNRISE ENTERPRISES
See **Booksellers,** Seeds, **Vegetables.**

TERRITORIAL SEED COMPANY
Tom Johns
Catalog: Free, 95 pp., illustrations and black-and-white photographs
The folks at Territorial are determined "to improve people's self-sufficiency and independence by enabling gardeners to produce an abundance of good tasting fresh from the garden food twelve months a year." Included in this extensive seed catalog are four mushroom kits ("Pearl Oyster" and "Shiitake" for indoor cultivation, "Maitake" and "King Stropharia" for outdoors). All certified organic and guaranteed. See **Booksellers,** Herbs, **Kidstuff,** Organics, Seeds, **Supplies, Vegetables.**
Shipping season: All year.
Canada

THOMPSON & MORGAN
1855
Bruce Sangster
Catalog: Free, 224 pp., color photographs
A very serious seed catalog, T&M has counted among its customers Claude Monet and Charles Darwin. Onion sets include "Ebenezer" (an early-maturing white) and "Stuttgarter" (a high-yielding, long-term keeper). Dutch shallots include golden gourmet and red. Offers a highly decorative and mild-tasting elephant garlic. Also offers ten varieties of onion and shallots from seed. Descriptions include number of days to maturity, shape, color, and texture, and propensity for high yield and storage. Sets sold by weight, the rest per packet (number of seeds specified). Guarantees satisfaction; will issue refund. See **Grasses,** Heirlooms, **Seeds, Vegetables.**
Shipping season: Seeds, all year. Onion and shallot sets, March. Garlic, October through December. March through May.
Limited delivery to Hawaii.
Canada, International

VERMONT BEAN SEED COMPANY
1975

Catalog: Free, 96 pp., illustrations and color photographs

You'll need some flavor enhancers for the five hundred vegetables (including one hundred types of beans) that you're growing from this company's seed catalog. Onions might be an answer. They offer seed (early yellow globe, Ailsa Craig exhibition, red Wethersfield, and He-Shi-Ko), onion sets (red, white, and yellow), and plants (Vidalia, yellow sweet Spanish, white sweet Spanish, and red hamburger). Their selection of organically grown seed potatoes include Yukon gold, rosy pink, and all-blue. Descriptions include number of days to maturity for seeds and flavor, size, color and storage capacity for all. Seeds sold by the packet, sets by weight, plants by the bunch, and potatoes by weight. See Heirlooms, Herbs, Seeds, **Vegetables**.

Shipping season: Seeds, all year. Onion sets and plants, February through May. Potatoes, mid-March through April.

VESEY'S SEEDS LTD.
1939
Allen Perry
Catalog: Free, 126 pp., black-and-white and color photographs.

A purveyor of seeds (primarily untreated) specializing in varieties for short growing seasons. Trial gardens and germination tests on-site on Prince Edward Island. Vesey's offer six varieties of onion seeds, and three sets ("Jet Set," "Stuttgarter," and "Spanish") four types of Elite seed potatoes from PEI (sometimes known as Spud Island): Jemseg, superior, Yukon gold, and russet Burbank; and spring- and fall-planted white garlic sets. Rich descriptions include soil, feeding, water, light, and spacing requirements as well as information on planting and harvest times, pests, and problems. Seeds by the packet or by weight, onion sets by count or weight, garlic by the bulb, and potatoes by weight. See **Booksellers**, Herbs, **Seeds**, **Supplies**, Vegetables, Wildflowers.

Shipping season: Seeds, all year. Garlic sets, January through May. September. Onion sets, January through May. Potatoes, April and May.
Canada

WILLHITE SEED CO.
1920
Don Dobbs
Catalog: Free, 60 pp. color photographs
Willhite offers the seed for four hundred veg-

etables in their catalog. Their onion selection includes seven open-pollinated varieties: evergreen white bunching, red burgundy, white Bermuda (recommended for home gardeners), New Mexico yellow grano, sweet Spanish yellow, sweet Spanish white, and Texas grano (suited for the southern United States). Descriptions are clear and accessible, including information about storage, flavor, size, and whether a variety requires a short or long day. Seeds sold in several sized packets, from a quarter ounce to a pound. See Seeds, **Vegetables**.

Shipping season: All year.
Canada, Mexico, International

WILLIAM DAM SEEDS
1949
Rene W. Dam
Catalog: $2., 63 pp., color photographs
Offers over one thousand varieties of vegetable, herb, flower, tree, shrub, and vine seeds. Over half of the catalog is devoted to hybrid short-season vegetable seeds from Canada, the United States (including All America selections), and Europe (including Fleuroselect Medal winners). Information includes varieties that are best for selling at market, best for preserving, seeds per gram, seeds per packet, number of days to maturity outdoors, and substantial cultural information. Offers four onion and shallot sets, and the seeds for ten varieties. Also offers an unspecified white garlic bulb. See **Booksellers, Herbs, Seeds,** Vegetables, Wildflowers.

Shipping season: Seed, all year. Sets and bulbs, fall.
Canada. International (seeds only)

WOOD PRAIRIE FARM
1976
Jim and Megan Gerritsen
Catalog: Free, 15 pp., photographs
The Gerritsens are the stewards of Wood Prairie Farm, a diversified family business in Aroostook County, Maine, where the first bluenose potatoes were grown by Joseph Houlton in 1807. The Gerritsens' crops are certified by the Maine Organic Farmers and Gardeners Association. You can sample their harvest through their "Potato-of-the-Month" program, or, if you are inclined to break the soil yourself, they offer certified garden seed potatoes. Among their offerings for early, mid-, and late-season harvesting are Onaway, Yukon gold, Reddale, cranberry red, rose gold, Kerry blue, all-blue, and Butte.

They also offer three mid- to late-season finger-lings. Tips for your potato patch are noted in their catalog, and organic cultural instructions accompany each order. Descriptions are brief and clear, taking into account color, shape, disease issues, amount of yield, and ease of storage. Potatoes sold by the pound. See Seeds, Vegetables.

Shipping season: September through May.

WORM'S WAY INDIANA
1985
Michael Dick and Martin Heydt

Catalog: Free, 64 pp., color photographs
Worm's Way began as a small, one-man operation offering organic and natural alternatives to conventional gardening techniques. Included in their wide ranging mix of items are kits for the indoor cultivation of shiitake and pearl oyster mushrooms, and outdoor kits for giant morel and garden giant mushrooms from Mushroom Patch®. Guarantees satisfaction; will accept items for exchange, credit, or refund within thirty days of receipt. See **Booksellers**, Organics, **Supplies**.
Shipping season: All year.
Canada, Mexico, International

Selected Reading About Garlic, Potatoes, Onions, and Mushrooms

Growing Great Garlic, by Ron Engeland. The author, a self-described small-scale organic farmer who makes his living growing garlic at Filaree Farm, wrote and published this work, which is considered the best book available on how to do it. Explains which strains to plant, when to plant, site and soil preparation, when to fertilize (and when not to), when to prune flower stalks, and when and how to harvest. Also contains material about bringing garlic to market.

The Mushroom Cultivator: A Practical Guide to Growing Mushrooms at Home, by Paul Stamets and J. S. Chilton. A respected work on how to get them started and growing. Stamets is also the author of *Growing Gourmet and Medicinal Mushrooms*. The two works together offer a near encyclopedic overview and practical guide to mushroom farming for personal pleasure or on a commercial scale.

Mushrooms Demystified, by David Arora. A field and identification guide to two thousand species. Eight hundred photographs.

The Potato Garden: A Grower's Guide, by Maggies Oster. Profiles two hundred potato varieties. Includes growing and cultural information in a beautiful and entertaining volume.

FURNITURE AND ORNAMENT

This section includes sources for garden furniture, lighting, ornament, sculpture, statuary, decorative planters, greenhouses, arbors, gazebos, and other structures for plants, birds, wildlife, and humans. Sources ship items year-round unless otherwise noted.

QUICK FIND
The following sources are listed in this section:

ADAMS & ADKINS, INC.
Bob Adams and Dorcas Adkins
Catalog: Free, 1p., color photographs
Adams & Adkins are the creators of the Water Flute™ fountain. This self-contained, tranquility-inducing fountain does not require plumbing and is capable of supporting recommended varieties of plant life. Available in three indoor/outdoor models of rough-sawn western red cedar and an indoor version finished in lacquered birch. Guarantees satisfaction; will issue refund.
Canada, International

ADIRONDACK DESIGN
1981
George Griffith
Catalog: Free, 8 pp., color photographs
A nonprofit business created to provide work training for developmentally disabled adults. The redwood used by Adirondack is gathered almost entirely from second-growth trees in state-regulated forests. Furniture crafted at Adirondack Design includes a potting bench, an arbor, display

planters, light risers, Adirondack chairs, love seats, footrests, and swings. Guarantees satisfaction; will issue refund for goods returned within thirty days.

ALPINE MILLWORKS
1989
Kent Struble
Catalog: Free, 6 pp., color and black-and-white photographs.
Alpine manufactures and sells garden and lawn furniture in mahogany and teak. Designs include Devon chairs, Adirondack chairs, benches, and footrests, and British swings in widths of four, five, and six feet. Alpine's own designs include square planters in three sizes and a chaise longue.
Canada, Mexico

ANDERSON DESIGN
Richard L. Anderson
Catalog: Free, 2 pp., illustrations
Mr. Anderson designs and manufactures garden arches made of kiln-dried western cedar in four variations: the "Rose," the "Clematis," the "Ming Tree," and the "Wisteria." Also offers

complementary seats, lattices, gates, and fences. Plans and instructions can be purchased without wood, too. Mr. Anderson will custom-design and -build arbors and trellises. Guarantees satisfaction; will replace or issue credit or refund for goods returned within thirty days.
Canada, Mexico, International

BAMBOO & RATTAN WORKS, INC.
1880
Suzanne Maison
Catalog: Free, 7 pp., black-and-white photographs
B&RW sells custom-made bamboo fencing, reed fencing in stock sizes, bamboo poles (in eighteen sizes), and guadua poles (four sizes) for creating your own fence.
Canada, Mexico, International

BERRY HILL LIMITED
1950
Catalog: Free, 68 pp., black-and-white photographs
A hobby farm equipment and country living catalog that reads like the shelves and old-fashioned general store. Ornamental garden products include greenhouses, weather vanes, wind chimes, birdhouses, and bird feeders. See **Booksellers, Kidstuff, Supplies.**
Canada, International

BOW BENDS
1971
John J. Rogers
Catalog: $3 (recoverable), 30 pp., color photographs
Bow Bends is an offshoot of Bow House, which makes a reproduction house kit. Bow Bends's high-end bridges, fences, railings, and gazebos can be constructed using their design or yours. Material varies according to the product. Mr. Rogers believes that "nature abhors a straight line"; therefore, most of his projects are finished with curved surfaces and details.
Canada, Mexico, International

BRIDGEWORKS
1992
Paul Swain
Catalog: Free, 6 pp., illustrations
Mr. Swain builds bridges in four basic models, including a faithful reproduction of Monet's Japanese-style bridge at Giverny. Uses primar-

ily water-resistant, pressure-treated pine but will use cypress, oak, teak, or the wood of your choice. Bridges available in several spans and widths. Offers beams only, too.
Canada, Mexico, International

BROWN'S EDGEWOOD GARDENS
1987
Brandon Brown
Catalog: Free, 16 pp. Expanded version: $2
Edgewood Gardens is a retail flower and herb shop begun in 1949 by Ruth Brown. Brandon Brown's mail-order operation was launched in 1987. In addition to herb plants, books, and organic supplies, he offers various types of herb garden markers: hand-painted, glazed and fired, clay, stoneware with stake (can be custom-painted), and terra-cotta. See **Booksellers, Herbs**, Organics, **Supplies.**

BRUCE BARBER BIRD FEEDERS, INC.
1970
Ron O'Kane
Catalog: Free, 8 pp., illustrations
BBBF offers twenty-seven handcrafted bird feeders and houses made of kiln-dried western red cedar. Offers unmounted, mounted, and free-hanging styles, including fly-through and platform designs. Catalog includes models designed to attract such specific bird types as barn swallows, bluebirds, cardinals, chickadees, finches, hummingbirds, larks, nuthatches, siskins, tanagers, thrushes, towhees, waxwings, wrens, and several multilevel dwellings for martins. Descriptions include type of mounting, dimensions and weight, and seed capacity for feeders.
Canada, Mexico, International

CHARLESTON BATTERY BENCH, INC.
1929
Phil and Andrew Slotin
Catalog: Free, 4 pp., black-and-white photographs
The Charleston Battery Bench® is made with the original mold pattern (illustrating the flora and fauna of South Carolina) created by the J. F. Riley Iron Works in the mid-nineteenth century. Benches are constructed with hand-sanded cypress wood slats and cast-iron sides.
Canada

CIELI
1989
Joyce Converse

Catalog: $3 (recoverable), 6 pp., color photographs

Ms. Converse is an artist who draws her inspiration from the realm of folktales and the garden. Ornaments are laser-cut from steel and aluminum (either powder coated or permitted to rust naturally) that take the form of fairies, hares, and dinosaurlike creatures known among the Cieli as "Dinonybugs." Descriptions are as cheerful and well humored as the faces and poses of her creature creations while at the same time including such serious things as composition and measurements.

CLASSIC & COUNTRY CRAFTS
1989
Sue Siekierski
Catalog: Free, 2 pp., color photograph
Ms. Siekierski fashions handmade copper landscape lights in natural or patina finishes in over half a dozen styles. Specifications include height, width, and strength of bulb required.
Canada

COUNTRY CASUAL
1977
Bobbie Lopatin
Catalog: Free, 71 pp., color photographs
Country Casual is a designer and importer of garden and site furnishings. Ms. Lopatin's catalog overflows with images and descriptions of benches, tables, chairs, modular architectural trelliswork, arbors, and planters made from a variety of materials, including teak, painted mahogany, and wrought iron. Guarantees products against defects in workmanship and materials for six months from date of purchase.

DAVID BACON WOODWORKING
1975
David Bacon
Catalog: Free, 6 pp., color photographs
A one-man shop making window box and freestanding planters. Planters available in cedar or recycled wood include removable liners. Mr. Bacon's English garden gate is made of cedar and measures $34^{1}/2$ inches high by $37^{1}/2$ inches wide to allow for the easy passage of most garden carts and wheelbarrows.
Canada, Mexico, International

DUNCRAFT
1952

Kathryn Wright
Catalog: Free, 40 pp., color photographs
This catalog presents a cornucopia of feeders, baths, and specialty seed for birds and wildlife. Duncraft offers twenty-four bird feeders and accessories that have been endorsed by the National Audubon Society, including numerous items designed to attract and maintain specific species (bluebirds, finches, hummingbirds, orioles, etc.). Descriptions are rich and informative. Guarantees satisfaction for one year; will exchange, credit, or issue refund. See **Supplies.**
Canada, Mexico, International

EARTHLY GOODS LTD.
1990
Ann Streckfus and Stephen Brown
Catalog: $2 (recoverable), 17 pp., illustrations
Bat roosting boxes, songbird nesting boxes, bird feeders, and squirrel feeders made from 100 percent reclaimed hardwood. Guarantees satisfaction; will issue refund up to thirty days from date of purchase. See Grasses, Seeds, **Wildflowers.**
Canada, Mexico, International

EARTHWORKS
1990
Len Sherwin
Catalog: Free, 1 p.
Mr. Sherwin started Earthworks with the intent of supplying avid rock gardeners with hypertufa containers for growing rare and difficult alpine plants. He expanded his mail-order business as it became apparent that small perennials would also thrive in these troughs. Offers hand-cast troughs in a deep oval-shaped basin and two rectangular models.
Canada

ESCORT LIGHTING
1989
Mike Hartman
Catalog: Free, 8 pp., color photographs
Mr. Hartman is a landscape designer by trade. Faced with what he perceived as a lack of choices in "quality garden lights at reasonable prices," he developed a series of solid copper ornamental lights and garden accents with such self-describing names as "Toadstool," "Mushroom," and the conical-hooded "Firefly." Fixtures come in a variety of diameters and heights and are finished in patinas of mill, verde green, and antique

black. Lightbulbs, wired to operate at your choice of standard or low voltage, are included with fixtures. Will quote for made-to-order fixtures.

Canada

FARM WHOLESALE GREENHOUSES–
HOMESTEAD CARTS
1987
Mike Perry
Catalog: Free, 16 pp., color photographs
Mike and Bev Perry are the creators and manufacturers of the Farm Wholesale corrugated polyethylene greenhouse. Their greenhouse, made of steel-reinforced PVC frame and recyclable corrugated plastic, is offered in four freestanding models and a lean-to model. See **Supplies**.
Canada, Mexico, International

FLORENTINE CRAFTSMEN, INC.
1923
Graham G. Brown II
Catalog: $5 (recoverable), 40 pp., color and black-and-white photographs
A third-generation maker of classic-style outdoor furniture, garden ornaments, fountains, statuary, and accessories made from lead, bronze, iron, aluminum, and stone. Catalog pictures all items with specifications. Welcomes inquiries for custom work.
Canada, Mexico, International

GARDENERS EDEN
Catalog: Free, 39 pp., color photographs
A stylish catalog that strives to render functional objects beautiful. Offerings include etageres, patio furniture, fiberglass re-creations of bronze and stone ornaments and planters, teak garden furniture, English-style freestanding and window-box containers, topiary forms, and dozens of other pieces. Guarantees satisfaction; will issue refund. See **Supplies**.

GARDENER'S SUPPLY COMPANY
1983
Will Raap and Meg Smith
Catalog: Free, 64 pp., color photographs
Gardener's Supply provides a wide range of furniture, ornament, and accessories. Offerings include planters, trellises, lighting, and garden furniture. Guarantees satisfaction; will issue refund. See Organics, **Supplies**.

GENIE HOUSE
Catalog: $3, 37 pp., color photographs
Handcrafted reproductions of historically significant lighting fixtures: garden lights, lampposts, and welcome lights from the colonial, federal, Georgian, and other periods. Each item is pictured and described with technical specifications. See Heirlooms.

GOTHIC ARCH GREENHOUSES
1946
W. H. "Buzz" Sierke, Jr.
Catalog: $5 (recoverable), 4 pp., color photographs. Includes 10-page booklet, "A Practical Guide to Greenhouse Selection"
The curved Gothic arch greenhouse is available in five basic freestanding models. Frames are made from heart redwood and western cedar. Glazing panels (available in two weights) are fiberglass-reinforced, acrylic-modified plastic. Also offers lean-to models, appropriate climate controls. Guarantees satisfaction; will issue refund.
Canada, Mexico, International

GRANITE IMPRESSIONS
1989
Belinda Vos
Catalog: $1, 8 pp., black-and-white photographs
Belinda and Bob Vos make five types of lanterns, five types of water basins, a signpost, pedestals in two sizes, a birdbath, a bench, and three bonsai pots in the traditional Japanese style. Each piece is hand-cast and finished to emulate stone.

GREEN ENTERPRISES
1972
Dwight Green
Catalog: $1, 6 pp., color photographs
Mr. Green and company specialize in the fabrication and restoration of models, prototypes, and museum exhibits of Victorian furniture. Their one-of-a-kind pieces have been made for the National Smithsonian Institution, Epcot Center, and the Alexander Graham Bell House. For those of us who wish to use furniture in the garden, the catalog includes Victorian-style natural oak and maple (painted white) porch swings, gliders, stools, tables, and benches. Guarantees satisfaction; will replace or issue refund up to thirty days after receipt.
Canada, Mexico, International

HERITAGE GARDEN HOUSES
(City Visions, Inc.)
1991
Robert J. Morris
Catalog: $3., 12 pp., illustrations
Mr. Morris describes himself as "a preservation-ist, adaptive reuser, and restoration builder." HGH offers garden buildings modeled on classical precedent in Ionic, Doric, Corinthian, Tuscan, Greek Revival, Italianate, Gothic, Second Empire, Stick, Queen Anne, Tudor, Craftsman, Prairie, and Japanese styles. Buildings, furniture, and ornament include garden houses (one- and two-story structures), pavilions, gazebos, colonnades, pergolas, toolsheds, cabinets, seats, cupolas, spires, belfries, and gates. Components are built of seasoned poplar and select pine, cut and assembled, and primed twice. HGH estimates that their precutting, casing, trimming, and drilling of pilot holes make it possible for you to erect their kits in two days. See Heirlooms.

IDAHO WOOD
1975
Catalog: Free, 20 pp., color photographs
Manufactures garden and outdoor lighting in original modern designs. Offers post, street-, and area lights, bollards, and landscape lights, made from clear western cedar and clear northern states red oak. Descriptions include type of finish, dimensions, and type and strength of bulb.
Canada, Mexico, International

IVYWOOD GAZEBO
1981
John L. Huganir
Catalog: $3, 15 pp., black-and-white illustrations and photographs
Ivywood builds gazebos from western red cedar and pressure-treated southern pine in four standard sizes. Also offers a lightweight line of Chelsea gazebos in two sizes. All structures are shipped partially assembled. Mr. Huganir believes these structures can be erected on your site by a crew of two in under five hours. Catalog includes cupolas with either aluminum or copper tops, a rose arbor, and bird feeders that have the appearance of miniature gazebos. Welcomes inquiries for custom orders.
Canada, Mexico, International

KAREN HARRIS
1991
Karen Harris
Catalog: Free, 1 p.
Ms. Harris creates irregularly shaped hypertufa troughs for herbs and small perennials. Guarantees satisfaction; will refund up to fourteen days after receipt.

KENNETH LYNCH & SONS
1930
T. A. Lynch
Catalog: Inquire for current price, 400 pp., black-and-white photographs and illustrations.
Lynch's main catalog, "The Book of Garden Ornament," includes over two thousand items in 150 categories including bronze and lead sculpture, bird baths, curbing stone, finials, fountains, garden benches, Japanese stone lanterns, Oriental planters, pedestals, pools and pool systems, spheres, stone figures and vases, stone walls, sundials, topiary frames, and weathervanes. Descriptions include identification of materials, size of item, and various notes about its use. Virtually every item is pictured in a photograph or an illustration. Specialty catalogs include "The Book of Benches," "The Book of Sundials & Spheres," and "The Book of Weathervanes and Cupolas."

KINSMAN COMPANY
1981
Graham Kinsman
Catalog: Free, 88 pp., color photographs
A full-line catalog of ornament and supplies including arbors, Versailles tubs, troughs, illusion trellises, expandable plastic trellises, edging tile, wall plaques, Chamber's baskets, pot feet, and birdhouses and birdfeeders. See **Kidstuff, Supplies.**

LANGENBACH
1989
Gail Stokes
Catalog: Free, 48 pp., color photographs
A collection of two hundred garden items, with an emphasis on tools, accessories, and supplies. In the areas of furniture and ornament, you will find stylish planters, garden arches, pillars, tables and chairs, a palladian arch trellis, freestanding trellises, and plaques. Guarantees satisfaction; will issue refund. See **Supplies.**

LAZY HILL FARM DESIGNS
1987
Betty Baker
Catalog: $1, 10 pp., color photographs
Ms. Baker's birdhouses, feeders, and nesting boxes are made of cedar and cypress and topped with cypress shingles or a copper roof. Each piece is assembled by "local ladies from our small town" (Colerain, North Carolina). Structures come in a number of original styles and are made with martins, bluebirds, and small songbirds in mind. All houses, except for the bluebird, come with a mounting bracket. Also sells seven-foot posts with chamfered corners.
Canada

MELLINGER'S
1927
Jean Steiner
Catalog: Free, 104 pp., color photographs
Mellinger's home, farm, and garden catalog describes over four thousand garden-related items, seed, and nursery stock. Half of their catalog contains a full line of accessories, ornaments, and supplies, including greenhouses, trellises, birdhouses, bird feeders, and pots and containers.
See **Booksellers**, **Kidstuff**, Perennials, **Seeds**, **Supplies**, Wildflowers.
Canada, Mexico, International

OUT OF THE REDWOODS
1989
Ernie and Philippa Platt
Catalog: Free, 6 pp., black-and-white photographs
The Platts manufacture sleeves for potted plants from California redwood. Sleeves will slip over and conceal standard two- or five-gallon nursery containers. All-weather nylon stretch cord and hardwood beads separate the redwood slats. Available in natural, variegated, and oak-stained finishes. Also offers mats in the same material and finishes.
Canada, International

OUTWARD SIGNS
1986 (under the name of Good Directions)
Lucy Corsaro
Catalog: Free, 16 pp., color photographs
Outward Signs offers 150 weathervanes made from pure copper, brass, and "blacksmith quality" iron. Numerous motifs are available in ma-chine-molded, hand-hammered, or silhouette vanes. Also offers mounting brackets for decorative use, roof mountings, cupolas, sundials, and bird feeders. Guarantees satisfaction; will replace or issue refund.
Canada, Mexico, International

PARK PLACE
1983
C. Phillip Mitchell
Catalog: $2, 62 pp., color photographs
Park Place's catalog includes numerous articles on planning, design, and the nature of various woods, metals, fabrics, and resins that are used to create the brand-name products that they sell. They offer a large selection of classic garden furniture: benches and dining sets, recliners, chaise longues, Victorian benches, streetlamps, planters, urns, and mailboxes. Porch furniture including handcrafted oak swings, gliders, rockers, outdoor wicker, market umbrellas, fountains, birdbaths, sundials, and statuary.
Canada, Mexico, International

THE PINCHED POT
Catalog: Free, 2 pp., color photograph
The Pinched Pots "Herbs in Clay©" collection is composed of hand-painted stoneware items that are decorated with named herbs. The collection includes round "hang-ups" for drying individual varieties, drying racks in two lengths, and herb garden markers.

ROBERT COMPTON LTD.
1972
Robert and Christine Compton
Catalog: $1, 12 pp., color photographs
The Comptons' studio, adjoining their home in a farming valley, housed cows for many generations before being converted to pottery. Their stoneware Watersculptures® are tiered fountains, some cup shaped, some pitcher shaped, that combine sculptural ornament with the movement of water. Each piece is signed, numbered, and dated by the artist. Matching planters and mushroom Watersculptures® are among the variations (many also suitable for placement indoors) that they offer.

SANTA BARBARA GREENHOUSES
1972
Victor West
Catalog: Free, 14 pp., color photographs
Mr. West's firm manufactures greenhouses ex-

pressly for the home gardener with fiberglass coverings, tempered glass sides, and redwood frames. Freestanding models are available in seventeen sizes, lean-to models in twenty, and redwood benches come in six lengths and are sold in pairs. Kits are available as precut, predrilled parts or with glazed panels ready to be bolted together. Also sells appropriate climate controls. Guarantees satisfaction; will issue refund. See Supplies.
Canada, Mexico, International

SMITH & HAWKEN
1979
Catalog: Free, 62 pp., color photographs
A visually rich catalog that includes special and specialty furniture and ornament: Whichford terra-cotta pots, teak planters, a redwood trellis system, the Giverny® bench and chair, and other garden furniture. See **Kidstuff**, Organics, **Supplies.**

SUN GARDEN SPECIALTIES
1990
Tony Bishop
Catalog: Free, 6 pp., illustrations and black-and-white photographs
Mr. Bishop worked with master sign makers in Kyoto, Japan, before opening the Sun Garden. He creates wooden benches, signs, and posts, with the phrase of your choice translated into Japanese painted on. Mr. Bishop's furniture and ornaments are replicas of original examples found in the gardens of Kyoto and Nara.
International

SUNGLO SOLAR GREENHOUSES
1978
Joseph Pappalardo
Catalog: Free, 8 pp., color photographs
Sunglo Therma Truss® acrylic Plexiglas greenhouses employ a curved design supported by aluminum frames. Freestanding and lean-to models are available in fourteen standard sizes each. A sample package including a small section of wall panel, and a video is available for a refundable charge. Guarantees against problems caused by sunlight for ten years; guarantees against other problems for sixty days from receipt of unassembled product. See **Supplies.**
Canada

TAYLOR RIDGE FARM
1992

Gunnar Taylor
Catalog: $3 (recoverable), 8 pp., color photographs
Mr. Taylor builds Victorian-inspired arbors, rose columns, trellises, and gazebos constructed from copper plumbing pipe, steel reinforcement bar, and steel conduit. Peaked and rounded styles are made in a number of standard sizes. Steel ornaments can be ordered in black, white, and green finishes; copper pieces are either finished and protected or polished without protection to allow for a naturally evolving patina. Inquiries for custom work are encouraged.

TEXAS GREENHOUSE CO., INC.
1948
Catalog: $4 (recoverable), 32 pp., color photographs
This is the manufacturer of the American Classic Greenhouse. Their original models were constructed of cypress, later superseded by California redwood. They discontinued the use of wood altogether in 1991 and currently offer greenhouses constructed with an exclusive process using aluminum shells supported by hot-dipped galvanized steel frames. Fiberglass and polycarbonate panels are also available. The freestanding greenhouse is offered in four models with twenty-six variations. They also offer a lean-to and a bayview version. Guarantees their own products for one year against faulty workmanship and defective parts; other items are subject to original manufacturer's guarantee. See **Supplies.**
Canada, Mexico, International

THE THOMAS JEFFERSON CENTER FOR HISTORICAL PLANTS
1987
Catalog: $1, 4 pp., black-and-white illustrations and photographs
The TJCHP, operating from Jefferson's home in Monticello, collects, preserves, and distributes historic plant varieties and promotes an appreciation for the origins of garden plants. In their annual newsletter, "Twinleaf," they offer a garden plaque with a quote by Jefferson, replicas of forcing pots that he purchased in 1821, modern adaptations of terra-cotta nesting pots unearthed in archaeological digs at Monticello, and a sundial in the tradition of one in George Washington's courtyard at Mount Vernon. See **Booksellers**, Heirlooms, **Seeds.**

WIND & WEATHER
1977
Marcie Schorg
Catalog: Free, 40 pp., color photographs
Two thirds of this catalog describes and illustrates garden ornaments and accessories: handcrafted and manufactured copper and aluminum weathervanes, cupolas, wind chimes, sculpture, fountains, and sundials created by a wide range of artists and manufacturers. Guarantees satisfaction; will exchange or issue refund. See **Supplies**.

WINDLEAVES®
1976
Bart Kister
Catalog: $1 (recoverable), 3 pp., photographs
Mr. Kister, who worked in the forestry service, designed his first weathervane as an assemblage of twelve leaves. Simplicity and harmony with nature synthesized over time so that the Windleaves® thirty-five-inch, copper-and-brass weathervanes he now offers are composed of a single maple, holly, aspen, tulip tree, white oak, ginkgo, or a dogwood (with optional blossom) leaf. A ground post is provided with each weathervane. Custom orders for other species can be requested.
Canada, International

WOOD CLASSICS, INC.®
1982
Barbara and Eric Goodman
Catalog: Free, 24 pp., color photographs
The Goodmans and the artisans at Wood Classics create and build every component of their extensive line of garden, patio, and lawn furniture. Designs include heavyweight estate, British, Chippendale, mission, and Adirondack styles. Pieces are made from either first European-quality teak or Honduran mahogany. Construction is with mortise-and-tenon joinery, and, wherever appropriate, joints are glued and screwed together. Kits can be shipped anywhere in the continental United States; finished pieces are delivered by Wood Classics in their own vehicles in the areas of southern Maine through northern Virginia and as far west as Ohio. Guarantees satisfaction; will issue refund for items returned within thirty days of receipt.

WOOD INNOVATIONS OF SUFFOLK LTD.
1990
Hank Harms
Catalog: Free, 6 pp., color photographs
A manufacturer of wishing wells, landscape bridges, arbors, fan-shaped trellises, hexagonal and rectangular planters—all made from cedar. Mr. Harms encourages inquiries for custom-made pieces.
Canada, Mexico, International

WOODBROOK FURNITURE MANUFACTURERS
Catalog: Free, 8 pp., black-and-white photographs
Woodbrook builds garden and lawn furniture on a made-to-order basis. Pieces for outdoor use are contructed from kiln-dried cypress and other woods as requested. Woodbrook's line includes chairs, benches, tables, and planters in Lutyens, Chelsea, Chippendale, Victorian, Hyde Park, and other designs. Guarantees workmanship and materials for six months from date of delivery for outdoor furniture, one year for indoor pieces.

WOODSTOCK CANOE CO.
Dave Donahue
Catalog: Free, 6 pp.
The "bird stuff" division of the Woodstock Canoe Company builds houses for birds (four styles) and a shelter for bats. The boards, constructed of one-inch, rough-sawn white cedar, provide insulation and a textured surface that makes it easier for birds to use. The entrance holes are said to be ideal for bluebirds and chickadees yet small enough to deter predators. Guarantees satisfaction; will work to resolve problems.

Supplies and Tools

This section includes sources who provide hand tools, power tools, clothing, carts, composting supplies, watering and irrigation components and systems, Integrated Pest Management (IPM) programs and products, hydroponic systems and accessories, seed starting and propagation supplies, fertilizers, and soil amendments. Sources ship items year-round unless otherwise noted.

QUICK FIND
The following sources are listed in this section:

AGE-OLD ORGANICS
Chris Munley
Catalog: Free, 10 pp.
Chris Munley oversees the manufacture of fertilizers, natural pest controls, and products for composting that are available in both small and large quantities. For fertilizing he offers liquid kelp, fish, bat guano, blood meal, cottonseed meal, green sand, rock dust, and worm castings. For pests, products such as diatomaceous earth, grasshopper control, and ladybugs. Supplies and tools for composting include hybrid redworms, bioactivated accelerator, Age-Old's own Hot Sticks that eliminate turning, and a fifty-five-gallon leverage-operated tumbler. Products are color coded for nitrogen, phosphorous, and trace mineral content. See **Organics**.
Canada, Mexico, International

ALLEN, STERLING, & LOTHROP
1911
Catalog: $1 (recoverable), 40 pp., illustrations
Twenty percent of the Allen, Sterling, & Lothrop catalog features supplies: seed-starting paraphernalia, soil mixtures, small hand tools, baskets, organic fertilizers, and insecticides.
See **Garlic**, **Herbs**, Organics, **Seeds**, Vegetables.

ALSTO'S HANDY HELPERS
Mike Voyles
Catalog: Free, 64 pp., color photographs
This general home appliance and tool catalog devotes one quarter of its pages to garden implements. Offers brand-name power garden tools: shredders, pole pruners, and grass shears. Also sells handheld pruners, extension fruit pickers, gloves, compost bins, and watering devices.
Canada, Mexico, International

A. M. LEONARD, INC.
1885
Catalog: $1, 79 pp., black-and-white photographs

This catalog is, at its heart, for professionals—nurserymen and -women, landscapers, foresters, arborists, contractors—with the index listing thirty-six categories of tools and supplies. However, there are myriad products that are appropriate for the home gardener. Most items are pictured and all thoroughly described.
Canada

AQUACIDE COMPANY
See **Waterscapes**.

AQUAMONITOR
1971
Bob Whitener
Catalog: Free, 8 pp.
Mr. Whitener, a licensed professional engineer, is an inventor who holds forty-four U.S. patents. Aquamonitor, a watering control system that can be used in the greenhouse or out-of-doors, "treats" the precise needs of plants, cuttings, and seeds. Guarantees satisfaction. Parts and workmanship guaranteed for two years; will issue refund if item returned in thirty days.
Canada, Mexico, International

ARBICO
1978
Richard C. Frey and Sheri Herrera de Frey
Catalog: Free, 56 pp.
Arizona Biological Control, Inc., specializes in sustainable environmental alternatives, producing and marketing beneficial insects. The Arbico catalog includes soil amendments, botanicals, traps, disease control, beneficial predators, and products for fly control and pet care. The do-it-yourself section and the pest problem-solver chart are useful for developing an understanding of, and a practical strategy for maintaining the health of your garden as a living organism. Descriptions of products are rich and precise. See **Booksellers**, Organics.
Canada, Mexico, International

BERLIN SEEDS
1984
Edward Beachy
Catalog: Free, 60 pp., illustrations, black-and-white and color photographs
The Beachys offer commercial-quality seeds for the home gardener. One third of their catalog includes brand-name fertilizers, plastic mulches, row covers, seed-starting supplies, dust, sprays, wettable powders, and solar panels. See **Booksellers, Fruit, Garlic**, Grasses, **Kidstuff**, Organics, **Seeds**, Vegetables.
Canada

BERRY HILL LIMITED
1950
Catalog: Free, 68 pp., black-and-white photographs
A hobby farm equipment and country living catalog that reads like the shelves of an old-fashioned general store. Supplies and tools offered here include an apple cider press, cultivators, seeders, and hand tools. See **Booksellers, Furniture, Kidstuff**.
Canada, International

BETTER YIELD INSECTS AND GARDEN HOUSES
Catalog: $1, 6 pp.
Biocontrols for home gardener's IPM programs. Catalog clearly illustrates problems and pests, then proposes solutions that Better Yield can supply: live insects (including material for their maintenance), horticultural oils, natural fungicides, insecticides, sticky traps, and pest barriers. See Organics.
International

BIOLOGIC COMPANY
1985
Dr. Albert E. Pye
Catalog: LSASE, 4 pp.
BioLogic is a producer of beneficial nematodes including Scanmask™ for the control of a variety of lawn-invasive and wood-boring insects. Their brochure contains extensive descriptive and prescriptive material about their IPM products. See Organics.
Canada, Mexico, International

BOUNTIFUL GARDENS
1972
Bill and Betsy Bruneau
Catalog: Free, 72 pp., black-and-white photographs

The Bountiful Gardens catalog is published by Ecology Action, a nonprofit organization that practices and teaches organic biointensive methods. "Tools for Biointensive Gardening" briefly highlights human-powered hand tools used at Bountiful and offered for sale, including a D-handled digging tool that functions as a spade or a fork, a transplanting trowel, a widger, a seed-saver kit, and redwood seed flats. Also offers compost activator and earthworms, natural plant protection (including beneficials), nontoxic pest traps, and repellents. See **Booksellers, Garlic**, Heirlooms, Herbs, **Kidstuff**, Organics, **Seeds**, Vegetables.
Canada, Mexico, International

BOZEMAN BIO-TECH, INC.
1986
Dr. E. Wayne Vinje
Catalog: Free, 49 pp., illustrations
Bozeman Bio-Tech was formed to provide pest control products with low toxicity "for which ease of use has been clearly demonstrated in scientific tests." Descriptions of what a product does, and how it does it, are clear and reassuring. Offerings include cultural and mechanical insect controls, beneficial insects, biological pesticides, soaps, oils, abrasives, and botanical insecticides. Also describes products for weed and plant disease control, organic fertilizers, and soil conditioners. Catalog includes a "solution versus the pest" index for quick reference. See **Booksellers, Kidstuff**, Organics.

BRONWOOD WORM FARMS
1975
Jerry Seymour
Catalog: Free, 2 pp.
Sells redworms (including breeders) sorted by size. Also offers bed-run redworms in mixed unsorted sizes. Worms sold by count of one thousand up to one hundred thousand. Guarantees count and live delivery (with some restrictions); will accept return if dissatisfied. See Organics.
Canada

BROWN'S EDGEWOOD GARDENS
1987
Brandon Brown
Catalog: Free, 16 pp. Expanded version: $2
Edgewood Gardens is a retail flower and herb shop begun in 1949 by Ruth Brown. Brandon Brown's mail-order operation was launched in

1987. In addition to herb plants, books, and markers, Mr. Brown offers thirty organic products: soil enhancers, pest and insect controls, worm castings, and compost activator. Three percent of the sales from the purchase of organic products will be donated to a nature preservation group of your choice from the six that he lists. Guarantees satisfaction; will issue refund. See **Booksellers, Furniture, Herbs,** Organics.

CAPE COD WORM FARM
1974
Maggie Pipkins
Price list: Free, 1 p.
The Cape Cod Worm Farm began in the basement of Ms. Pipkin's home as a pilot program to test the feasibility of raising earthworms for commercial purposes. Extensive reading and experimentation over the past twenty-odd years has led her to the production of chemical-free plant food from worm castings (a by-product of earthworms) and an awareness of the work earthworms do in creating loam from kitchen and yard waste. She sells Red Wiggler worms in multiples of a thousand, screened castings in ten-pound measures, and non-screened castings in hundred-pound measures. See Organics.
Canada, Mexico, International

CART WAREHOUSE
1986
Peter D. Reimuller
Catalog: Free, 11 pp., black-and-white photographs
Sells Fold-It, Garden Way®, Homestead, and Carry-It brand carts. All products are well described. Guarantees satisfaction for two years or will buy back cart.
Not all carts to Alaska or Hawaii.
Canada

CATAMOUNT CART
1991
Jim Picardi
Catalog: Free, 2 pp.
Jim Picardi, a cabinetmaker, uses solid ash with mortise-and-tenon joinery and stainless steel hardware to produce handsome carts in sizes that have load capacities of three hundred and four hundred pounds. Guarantees wheels and tires for one year, hardwood and hardware for three; will replace any part that fails free of charge.
Canada, Mexico, International

C. K. PETTY & CO.
1990
Chris Petty
Catalog: Free, 1 p., photograph
Petty will send you an oversized postcard suggesting nine reasons to purchase a Superior Cut nonmotorized lawn mower with optional grass catcher. Guarantees satisfaction.

THE COOK'S GARDEN
1983
Ellen and Shepherd Ogden
Catalog: $1, 112 pp., color photographs and illustrations
The Cook's Garden has its origin in the Ogden's work as organic market gardeners. Their catalog is brimming with cultural information, gardening tips, and recipes; about 7 percent contains supplies. Among the items that they carry are soil builders (including their own brand of organic fertilizers for vegetable and flower gardens), seed-starting systems, harvest baskets, Womanswork® garden gloves, Fiskers® cutting tools, and prints and cards created by the catalog's artist, Mary Azarian. Guarantees satisfaction; will issue refund. See **Booksellers, Garlic,** Heirlooms, Herbs, **Kidstuff,** Organics, **Seeds,** Vegetables.
Canada

THE CRAFTER'S GARDEN
1992
Crowell family
Catalog: Free, 21 pp., illustrations
A homey catalog with a carefully chosen selection of mechanical (human-powered) garden tools, and earth-friendly supplies. Each item is illustrated and its use described. Carries heat-treated steel and ash garden tools of Maine, composters and accessories, mechanical shears, Garden Master aprons, pads, carriers, and buckets, Felco pruners, miserly watering devices, Womanswork® gardening gloves (and some for men, too), organic fertilizers and plant foods, and a dozen types of plant markers. See Organics.

CROP KING®, INC.
1982
Dan Brentlinger
Catalog: $3 (recoverable), 41 pp., black-and-white photographs

Crop King's "Hydroponic Gardening Catalog" offers starter kits and over 150 types of supplies and components for the hobbyist who wishes to grow plants without soil, either indoors or out. The catalog includes an explanation of hydroponic techniques and thorough descriptions of all products. See **Booksellers.**
Canada, Mexico, International

THE DAFFODIL MART
1904
Brent and Becky Heath
Catalog: Free, 56 pp.
The Heaths are third-generation bulb growers. Among the supplies to be found in their catalog are ten types of fertilizer (including one derived primarily from cricket manure) that are particularly useful for daffodils and other bulb plants; they also carry bulb pans, storage bags, and bulb savers. The tools that they recommend and sell include a heavy-duty tubular daffodil planter, a "naturalizing tool," bulb trowels, and an auger. See **Booksellers, Bulbs.**
Shipping season: March and April. September through November.

DAN'S GARDEN SHOP
1977
Dan Youngberg
Catalog: Free, 30 pp., illustrations
Twenty percent of this mixed seed catalog is given over to an eclectic mix of accessories. Descriptions are smart and clear. Supplies offered include peat pots in several sizes, plant starter pellets, assorted plastic pots, nozzles, watering cans, a cold frame, and a row marker. See **Booksellers,** Organics, **Seeds,** Vegetables.

DAVE & SUE'S AQUARIUMS & GREENHOUSE
1983
David Lowman
Catalog: $1 (recoverable), 18 pp., illustrations and black-and-white photographs
Mr. Lowman is a potter and a bonsai artist. His catalog (no fish to be found) includes a large selection of stoneware pottery, particularly suited to this type of cultivation, that he creates from clay. Also offers Artstone planting slabs and planting stones, bonsai tools, and stands. All supplies and tools are shown; descriptions are meticulous. Guarantees satisfaction; will issue refund. See **Booksellers, Trees.**
Canada, Mexico, International

DAY-DEX CO.
1954
Kim Motsinger
Catalog: Free, 2 pp., black-and-white photographs
This is the manufacturer of Day's Tier Bench, which is a set of galvanized wire shelves constructed in step fashion to increase the number of plants that can be placed in a given space. Offers nine variations and a canopy for shade.

DIRT CHEAP ORGANICS
1980
Pallette Amalia
Catalog: Free, 8 pp.
Dirt Cheap offers sixteen types of organic fertilizers, fourteen amendments, ecological pest controls, and live worms. They describe the composition and uses of many of their products. See Organics.

DOROTHY BIDDLE SERVICE
1936
Lynne Johnson Dodson
Catalog: 2 FCS, 20 pp., black-and-white photographs
Ms. Dodson is the granddaughter of the company's founder, Dorothy Biddle, a nationally known flower arranger. The DBS catalog includes 150 tools and accessories for cut-flower arrangement and preservation, including scissors, pruners, snips, hairpin- and needlepoint-style holders, floral foams, work and gardening gloves, and books. See **Booksellers.**

DRAMM CORPORATION
1945
Howard Zimmerman
Catalog: Free, 4 pp., color photographs
John G. Dramm designed and engineered the #400 Waterbreaker, a full-flow showerhead nozzle, in the early 1940s. After receiving numerous requests, he began manufacturing it in the basement of his home; the current generation of Dramm's watering devices is not made in anyone's basement. In addition to the Waterbreaker, the catalog describes the rain wand (for flower beds and shrubs), a hanging basket wand, patio plant wand, seedling nozzle, and a fog-it nozzle. Dramm also markets plastic watering cans with long spouts with two- to ten-liter capacities.
Canada, Mexico, International

DUNCRAFT
1952
Kathryn Wright
Catalog: Free, 40 pp., color photographs
A cornucopia of feeders, baths, and specialty seed for birds and wildlife, this catalog offers birdseed by weight and a customized automatic shipment program for seed, suet, and corn. Descriptions are rich and informative. See **Furniture**.
Canada, Mexico, International

EARLEE, INC.
1974
Mary and Earl Stewart
Catalog: Free, 6 pp.
Here are 150 organic products (most under the brand name of Natures Way®) for enriching the soil, defending against pests, and maintaining healthy plants. A page is devoted to products that are particularly useful for container and window box gardening and for African violets. Descriptions are spare but clear. See **Organics**.

ECO ENTERPRISES
1972
Terri Mitchell
Catalog: Free, 53 pp.
Eco Enterprises, manufacturers of Ecogrow and Ecobloom, sell supplies and materials for growing plants in soilless cultures. Their "Hydroponic Guidebook and Catalog" is packed with background, scientific, evaluative, and cultural information to introduce you to this alternative growing method. There are descriptions of hundreds of products (hydroponic systems, growing mediums, nutrients, lighting, measuring equipment, seed starting supplies) that are rich in detail and written in clear, accessible language. See **Booksellers**.
Canada, Mexico, International

EDMUNDS' ROSES
1949
Kathy and Phil Edmunds
Catalog: Free, 20 pp., color photographs
This family of rosarians specialize in modern garden roses, European, and exhibition varieties, and AARS prizewinners. Supplies include a "Glorious Gardens" rose kit and an easy-to-assemble drip irrigation system, using Dial-a-Flow emitters that can be adjusted to correctly water each plant in your garden. Also offers goatskin gloves and an assortment of Felco brand pruning shears. See **Roses**.
Canada, Mexico, International

EMI MEADE IMPORTERS
1981
Emi Meade
Catalog: Free, 6 pp., black-and-white photographs
Jollys® washable gardening shoes with a removable molded cork insole are characterized as particularly useful for wet and muddy conditions. They are constructed in the traditional shape of a Dutch shoe. According to Gene Meade, worn-out pairs can find a second life as hanging planters. See **Kidstuff**.
Canada

EON INDUSTRIES
1936
Dale E. Leininger
Catalog: Free, 6 pp., illustrations
A family-owned and -operated manufacturer making eight types of garden markers constructed with steel standards and with zinc labels.
Canada

ERTH-RITE
1961
Ellen R. Ranck
Catalog: Free, 6 pp.
Erth-Rite, specializing in organic regenerative agriculture, was founded on the principles of Pennsylvania Dutch stewardship. Erth-Rite products are compost-based fertilizers intended to decompose organic matter, release minerals, and fix nitrogen from the air in order to revitalize soil and provide food for plants. The company will perform soil tests by mail to determine the current condition and needs of your soil. Their basic fertilizer and specialized products are described in detail to aid in choosing those that are best suited for bulbs, evergreens, flowering plants, fruit trees, roses, and vegetables. See **Organics**.
Canada, Mexico, International

FARM WHOLESALE
GREENHOUSES–HOMESTEAD CARTS
1987
Mike Perry
Catalog: Free, 16 pp., color photographs
Mike and Bev Perry are the creators and man-

ufacturers of the Farm Wholesale corrugated polyethylene greenhouse. Greenhouse accessories include sprinkler, programmable timer, tie-down kit, thermometer, fan and heater with thermostat, solar-powered vent opener, and base vents. They also offer their own 10–14 Day Compost Bin, compost turner, pik/pak harvest bins for fruit, rose blankets, tree wraps, and two sizes of Homestead carts. See **Furniture**.
Canada, Mexico, International

FLORIAN RATCHET-CUT™ PRUNING TOOLS
1937
Nat and Stella Florian
Catalog: Free, 8 pp., color photographs
Florian's Ratchet-Cut™ hand pruners, loppers, pole pruning systems, and pole saws are of particular interest to gardeners with diminished hand and arm capabilities. The Florian mechanism multiplies the effect of your natural hand strength, thereby reducing the pressure to complete the cut. Also manufactures diamond sharpening stones. Guarantees against defective parts for one year; will repair or replace.
Canada, Mexico, International

FUNGI PERFECTI
1979
Paul Stamets
Catalog: $3, 80 pp., illustrations and photographs
The specialty of Fungi Perfecti is the cultivation of high-quality, certified-organic gourmet and medicinal mushrooms. A brief section in the catalog includes dried mushroom products: tea, maitake tablets, shiitake rice, and an assortment of mushrooms. Apparel for mushroom hunting includes illustrated T-shirts and sweatshirts. Mushroom cultivating supplies, primarily for the professional, occupy half the catalog. See **Booksellers, Garlic, Kidstuff**, Organics.
Canada, Mexico, International

GARDEN CITY SEEDS
1982
Susan Wall-MacLane
Catalog: $1, 75 pp., illustrations and photographs
Garden City Seeds is a subsidiary organization of the nonprofit Down Home Project, Inc., which supports self-reliant living. The catalog includes a comprehensive chart for safe pest control that

includes cultural, mechanical, biological, and botanical solutions, as well as a "Green Resource Guide" for obtaining information about sustainable agriculture. Supplies include organic and soil fertility ingredients and natural pest controls, including beneficial insects. They also carry a handheld seed sower and a seed-saving storage system. See **Booksellers, Garlic**, Grasses, Herbs, Organics, **Seeds**, Vegetables.
Canada

GARDENERS EDEN
See **Furniture**.

GARDENER'S SUPPLY COMPANY
1983
Will Raap and Meg Smith
Catalog: Free, 64 pp., color photographs
Gardener's Supply provides a very wide range of tools, organic fertilizers and pest controls, watering devices, composters, raised bed- and path-making kits, cold climate and season-extending equipment. They have a separate catalog for irrigation equipment. Guarantees satisfaction; will issue refund. See **Furniture**, Organics.

GARDENS ALIVE!®
1983
Catalog: Free, 47 pp., color photographs
Gardens Alive!® offers an assortment of organic solutions and aids under their own brand names to reduce weeds, diminish pests, enhance plant and lawn growth, produce tastier vegetables, and create richer soil. Descriptions are upbeat and illuminating. See Organics.

THE GREAT AMERICAN RAIN BARREL CO.
1990
George Gehelein
Catalog: Free, 4 pp.
The sixty-gallon-capacity Great American Rain Barrel™, available in three colors, is made of recycled polyethylene. The complete barrel comes with a spigot, overflow fitting, drain plug, and screw-on cover. GARBCo also offers a device to redirect the water from your downspout into the barrel. Guarantees satisfaction; will issue refund.

THE GUANO COMPANY INTERNATIONAL, INC.
Larry Pozarelli

Catalog: Free, 8 pp., black-and-white photographs

On August 18, 1856, the U.S. Congress passed an act authorizing any citizen who discovers guano on an unclaimed island, rock, or key to take possession of that property. Mr. Pozarelli saves you an expedition into uncharted waters by offering unblended, fossilized, and semifossilized seabird guano as well as desert bat guano. His brochure includes historical and cultural information and recommended dosage and usage for each mixture. See Organics.

GURNEY'S SEED & NURSERY CO.
1866
Donald L. Kruml
Catalog: Free, 64 pp., color photographs

Ten percent of this diverse catalog is devoted to supplies. Selection features seed-starting and composting aids, their own brand of plant foods for specific crops, fertilizers, and IPM products, including beneficial insects. Guarantees satisfaction; will replace or issue refund or credit. See **Garlic**, **Kidstuff**, Organics, **Seeds**, **Vegetables**.

Canada, Mexico, International

HAPPY VALLEY RANCH
Wanda and Ray Stagg
Catalog: $1, 15 pp., color photographs

The Staggs hand-craft cider and fruit presses from hardwood framed in cast iron and steel. Single-tub cider/wine press and double-tub cider mill and wine press are available assembled or in kit form.

Canada, Mexico, International

HARDSCRABBLE ENTERPRISES
1985
Paul Goland
Catalog: $3 (recoverable), 4 pp.

This purveyor of shiitake mushroom spawn also sells cultivation equipment: a dehydrator, humidity blanket, spawn plunger, and specialized drills and bits. Serves as a clearinghouse for an oak log exchange, matching mushroom growers who want fresh-cut wood with loggers who can supply it. See **Booksellers, Garlic**.

HARLANE COMPANY, INC.
1964
June Benardella
Catalog: Free, 3 pp.

Sells removable, interchangeable Garden Guide plastic nameplates. Blank plates with or without stakes. Will custom-print rose names only. Also sells gardening gloves and nine models of Felco pruning shears.

HARMONY FARM SUPPLY AND NURSERY
1980
Kate Burroughs and David Henry
Catalog: $2, 127 pp., illustrations

This full-service catalog started when Ms. Burroughs and Mr. Henry conceived of Harmony as a source of organic materials, methods, and tools. Irrigation systems were added in 1982, and the range of products has grown from there. Current areas of concentration include drip, sprinkler, and other irrigation systems and supplies, organic fertilizers, ecological pest controls (beneficials and biorational pesticides), pheromone traps, tools (hand tools, rototillers, mowers, shredders, grafting and pruning equipment, food-processing aids), lawn and cover crop seed, and laboratory and consulting services. There are articles on irrigation troubleshooting, solar pumps, a chart for pest control, and other useful information throughout the catalog. Descriptions and specifications are clear and precise. See **Booksellers, Kidstuff**, Organics.
Canada

HARRIS SEEDS
1879
Richard (Dick) Chamberlin
Catalog: Free, 82 pp., color photographs

Founder Joseph Harris was the editor of *The Genesee Farmer* and *The Rural New Yorker* and in 1867 the first head of the Department of Agriculture at Cornell University. The business remained in his family for a hundred years until the death of his grandson (and namesake) in 1979. Twenty percent of the Harris catalog is devoted to accessories and supplies; its strength is the comprehensiveness of their seed-starting supplies: growing stands, light fixtures, Jiffy® trays, pots, planting media, pellets, strips, tabletop and windowsill plant trays and domes, plastic plant labels, a self-watering seed starter tray, soil control heating system, mulch roll, Wall O' Water® plant protector, and cold frames. See Garlic, Herbs, **Seeds**, Vegetables.

HENRY FIELD'S SEED & NURSERY CO.
1892
Orville Dragoo

Catalog: Free, 87 pp., color photographs
The Henry Field's catalog offers a wide range of seed, plant material, garden tools, and supplies. Ten percent of their catalog is devoted to seed-starting media and accessories, fertilizer, beneficials and other organic insect controls, weed treatments, and pest and rodent controls. See **Fruit, Garlic, Kidstuff,** Perennials, Organics, **Seeds, Trees, Vegetables.**

HERMITAGE GARDENS
See **Waterscapes.**

HOFFCO, INC.
1949
John D. Hedges
Catalog: Free, 34 pp., illustrations
Sells outdoor power equipment, including eight models of gas-powered brush cutters, trimmers, edgers, and eight tillers and cultivators and their attachments. Guarantees for two years if purchased for noncommercial use.

HOMESTEAD CARTS
1979
Bev Perry
Catalog: Free, 2 pp., black-and-white and color photographs
Homestead Carts began as a well-balanced alternative to wheelbarrows. The carts are made of high-quality plywood and feature handles covered in rubber to protect hands in hot and cold weather. Oversized pneumatic wheels are designed to roll over rough terrain without shifting or tipping. Carts are built in a twenty-inch model with a three-hundred-pound load capacity and a twenty-six-inch model holding up to four hundred pounds. Optional steel bed liner and rear-end gate available. Guarantees against defective parts and workmanship for one year.
Canada, Mexico, International

HYDROFARM
1977
Stuart R. Dvorin
Catalog: Free, 28 pp., color photographs
For Mr. Dvorin, it all began during a drought. Restricted water use, and a friend who bought an expensive hydroponic setup, inspired him to find a way to build his own. The growing season at an end, his wife, Emily, suggested that rather than forgo the continuing pleasure of his plants he should move his garden in-

doors. Deficiencies in lighting made the results less than ideal. Another friend, a tree pruner by trade, reported that recently installed Halide streetlights had provoked faster than usual growth in the trees he trimmed. With a smaller version of the lights in place, Hydrofarm was born. This well-detailed catalog contains complete starter and advanced systems, accessories, environmental controls, and other material to put you into hydroponic nirvana twelve months a year. Guarantees unconditionally for thirty days; guarantees workmanship and parts for one year. See **Booksellers.**
Canada

HYDRO-GARDENS, INC.
1968
Stan Benson
Catalog: Free, 91 pp.
The Hydro-Gardens catalog, referred to by some as the most instructional and complete catalog of its kind ever published, is an education in hydroponic greenhouse growing. You will find a homeowner's minicatalog in the back of this book that offers a kit for a family-sized greenhouse that requires a minimum of sixty square feet. HGI's catalog also includes a tabletop wick feed hydro-greenhouse with a planting bed that measures 9 by 14 inches by $2^{1}/_{4}$ inches deep. The bulk of this catalog, however, was crafted with the commercial vegetable grower in mind.
Canada

I.F.M. PRODUCTS FOR NATURAL AGRICULTURE
1983
Phillip Unterschuetz
Catalog: Free, 55 pp.
I.F.M. produces a detailed catalog of products and information to further the use of ecologically sound growing practices. Although much of what is contained in the catalog is for orchardists and organic farmers, there is a generous range of products in sizes suitable for the home gardener. Selections include beneficial insects and predators, organic pest and disease controls, soil amendments, foliar sprays, compost activators, and dusters and grafting supplies. Descriptions of problems, product usage, and dosage requirements are excellent. See **Booksellers,** Organics.
Canada, Mexico, International

**IRRIGRO® INTERNATIONAL IRRIGATION
SYSTEMS**
1975
R. L. Neff
Catalog: Free, 6 pp.
International Irrigation Systems manufactures and markets a microporous drip tubing made of DuPont Tyvek® that is said to deliver watering uniformity, longevity, resistance to clogging, and water savings. Pressure-compensating flow controllers and surface conduits permit maintenance-free operation. The brochure fully describes systems and components from Irrigro®, including the T-Kit for small gardens that waters an area of two hundred square feet. They also offer a Master Gardener system that can water two thousand square feet, and they will customize systems for even larger areas.
Canada, Mexico, International

JOHNNY'S SELECTED SEEDS
1973
Robert L. Johnston, Jr.
Catalog: Free, 136 pp., color photographs
Twenty percent of this seed farmer's catalog is supplies and tools: seed-starting supplies (trays, pots, domes, warmers, soil block makers), row covers, mulches, season extenders, fertilizers and soil maintenance aids, testers, composting accessories, seeders and cultivators, hand tools, biological and botanical insecticides, sprayers and dusters, weather instruments, and kitchenware for preparing harvest meals. Guarantees satisfaction; will replace or issue refund. See **Booksellers, Garlic,** Grasses, Heirlooms, Herbs, Organics, **Seeds,** Vegetables.
Canada, Mexico, International

J. W. JUNG SEED & NURSERY CO.
See **Bulbs, Fruit,** Garlic, **Kidstuff,** Perennials, Seeds, **Trees,** Vegetables.

KADCO USA, INC.
1990
Tom Petherick
Catalog: Free, 5 pp., black-and-white and color photographs
Sells four models of Carry-It carts, including a hitch kit, an extension kit, and a tool caddie. Also sells Compos-It garden composter made of recycled polyethelene. See Organics.
Canada, Mexico, International

KINSMAN COMPANY
1981
Graham Kinsman
Catalog: Free, 88 pp., color photographs
A full-line catalog of supplies and ornament including plant markers, topiary forms, link and loop stakes, Womanswork® garden gloves, Maine, Samuel Parkes, Stockton Heath, and Wilkinson Sword gardening tools, and English zinc and plastic watering cans. See **Kidstuff, Furniture.**

THE LADYBUG CO.
(FORMERLY BIO-CONTROL PRODUCTS)
1959
Julie Steele
Catalog: Free, 4 pp.
A brief but thoroughly described assortment of beneficials: convergent ladybugs, green lacewings, trichogramma, and Chinese praying mantis eggs. Offers Bi-Control Honydew™ to attract and retain a strong population of beneficials. Describes use, release rates and techniques, and care guidelines for all products.
Shipping season: Old ladybugs, January through May. Young ladybugs, June through December. Praying mantis eggs, January through May. Other items, all year.

LANGENBACH
1989
Gail Stokes
Catalog: Free, 48 pp., color photographs
A collection of two hundred garden items, with an emphasis on tools, accessories, and supplies both practical and stylish: watering cans, gloves, Florian and Felco pruners and cutters, power pruning systems, power trimmers, sprayers, carts, composters, gardener's pads and totes, assorted digging implements, etc. Guarantees satisfaction; will issue refund. See **Furniture.**

LEE VALLEY TOOLS LTD.
Leonard G. Lee
Catalog: Free, 52 pp., color photographs
Garden and outdoor leisure supplies both practical and stylish. The Lee Valley catalog includes bird supplies, carts, garden wear, composting supplies, frost protectors, pest and weed controls, propagation and pruning supplies and implements, test kits, and irrigation supplies. Items manufactured in Canada are highlighted. Guarantees satisfaction; will re-

place or issue refund for ninety days from date of receipt. See **Organics**.
Canada

LEHMAN'S
1955
Galen Lehman
Catalog: $2 (recoverable), 128 pp., illustrations and black-and-white photographs
Lehman's old-fashioned "general store" caters locally to a large Mennonite and Amish population. Their catalog of over one thousand nonelectric household tools and work savers includes a number of charming, practical, and hard-to-find items for garden work: reel mowers, scythes, high wheel cultivators, rotary and handheld hoes, trencher-cultivators, planter picks and axes, precision seeders, bulb planters, weeders, trowels, heavy-duty carts, and a one-legged oak garden stool.
Canada, Mexico, International

LILYPONS WATER GARDENS®
See **Booksellers**, **Waterscapes**.

LITTLE'S GOOD GLOVES, INC.
1893
Mark and Beth Dzierson
Catalog: Free, 6 pp., illustrations
Elmer Little's turn-of-the-century manufacturing company for fine dress gloves has since 1987 been involved exclusively in the business of garden and work gloves; four styles, including Mark Dzierson's Work-Lite®, are offered. Each style of glove's features and the tasks for which it is best suited are described. Guarantees satisfaction; will replace or issue refund.
Canada, International

LIVING WALL™ GARDEN CO.
F. Wesley Moffett
Catalog: $5, 27 pp., color photographs
Living Wall™ components are building block container gardens (with planting holes) that are filled with a specially formulated inorganic growing medium. A soluble fertilizer formulated for this system acts in concert with the medium to create plant growth. Accessories for the construction of numerous patterns and shapes, permit the cultivation of flowers and vegetables without the use of arable land. The catalog and price sheets include a full line of components and fertilizer to create small or large Living Wall™ gardens.

Canada, Mexico, International

MacKENZIE NURSERY SUPPLY
1977
Bill Burr
Catalog: Free, 56 pp., illustrations and photographs
A comprehensive catalog of brand-name nursery and gardening tools, supplies, and products in seventy-five categories: carts, dollies, wagons, chopping tools, fencing, fertilizer, flats, gloves, growing mediums, hand pruners, tools, shears, irrigation supplies, spades, shovels, hoes, plant labels, flats, pole pruners, wheelbarrows, wire baskets, etc.
Canada, Mexico, International

MAESTRO-GRO
Catalog: Free, 6 pp., color photographs
Manufactures and sells organic fertilizers formulated for a variety of uses, including grasses, roses, flowering plants, fruiting plants and shrubs, bulb plants, and herbs. Also offers fourteen types of soil conditioners and amendments, including fish and kelp products. See **Organics**.

MAINLINE OF NORTH AMERICA
1938
Daniel K. Davis
Catalog: Free, 12 pp., color photographs
Mainline is a manufacturer of gear-drive power equipment. Their Insta-adapt system permits the rotary tiller to function with additional attachments as a lawn mower, snow remover, irrigation tool, log splitter, or sickle bar mower. Also offers a chipper/shredder. Guarantees parts and labor for three years for home gardeners; guarantees transmission case for life of the machine.
Canada

MALLEY SUPPLY
1988
Allan Garofalow
Catalog: $1 (recoverable), 15 pp., black-and-white photographs
Mr. Garofalow established Malley Supply in order to provide the home gardener and small commercial grower with access to the supplies and equipment that are usually available only in quantities appropriate to the large-scale grower. Catalog includes plastic bowls, growing containers, nursery containers, hanging baskets, seedling trays, flats and inserts, Jiffy®

peat pots, growing media, and plastic labels.

MANTIS
1980
Robert C. Bell
Catalog: Free, 4 pp., color photographs
The lightweight, gasoline-powered Mantis tiller/cultivator functions as a planter/furrower, border edger, lawn de-thatcher, walkway edger, and hedge trimmer. Guarantees satisfaction; will accept returns for one year.
Canada, Mexico, International

THE MARUGG COMPANY, INC.
1873
John Baggenstoss
Catalog: Free, 4 pp., black-and-white photographs
Christian Marugg, a pioneer settler of the Swiss colony called Gruetli in Grundy County, Tennessee, brought the first European scythes there in the early 1860s. The company bearing his name continues to specialize in the manufacture of European-style snaths for scythes. They also import Austrian scythes, sickles, and such sharpening accessories as whetstone holders, hammers, and anvils. Blades made to fit steel, aluminum, or hickory snaths are available in nine sizes, from sixteen to twenty-eight inches in length. Guarantees satisfaction; will issue refund for unsatisfactory products returned within ten days of receipt.
Canada

MAXIMUM
1968
Nat Bishop
Catalog: Free, 15 pp., color photographs
Maximum manufactures and sells weather instruments: thermometers, digital rain gauges, barometers, and a weather processor. Guarantees for five years.
Canada, Mexico, International

MEDINA® AGRICULTURE PRODUCTS COMPANY, INC.
1962
Stuart Franke
Catalog: Free, 4 pp., illustrations
Medina manufactures and sells a biological soil activator, liquid lawn food and plant food, compost starter and compost nutrients, and liquid humus. Offers sampler basket of their organic "Bio-basics" products geared to home gardeners.

Descriptions of all products include tips on use and the results to expect. Other products include a tree protector, spike sprinkler, sprayer, and drip irrigation hose. See Organics.

MELLINGER'S
1927
Jean Steiner
Catalog: Free, 104 pp., illustrations and color photographs
Mellinger's home, farm, and garden catalog describes over four thousand garden-related items, seeds, and nursery stock. Half their catalog contains a full line of supplies and accessories: watering devices, organic and chemical controls, beneficials, dusters, sprayers, lights, budding and grafting supplies, seed-starting materials, garden markers, tools, seeders, augers, planters, composting systems, and greenhouse supplies. See **Booksellers, Furniture, Kidstuff,** Perennials, **Seeds,** Wildflowers.
Canada, Mexico, International

MOOSE GROWERS SUPPLY
1970
Bill Getty and Gene Frey
Catalog: $1, 40 pp.
Previously known as Moose Tubers, this division of Fedco now specializes in seed potatoes, onion sets, and accessories. One third of the catalog includes seed-starting supplies (inoculants, seed pots, labels, trays, domes), synthetic mulches, tools (carts, seeders, diggers, thermometers), soil amendments and fertilizers, and such gardener care items as Avena botanicals, insect repellents, and Womanswork® gloves. Guarantees satisfaction; will replace or issue refund. See **Booksellers,** Garlic, Organics, Vegetables.
Shipping season: February and April.

MORCO PRODUCTS
1992
Robert C. Morrow
Catalog: Free, 6 pp., black-and-white photograph
The Turn Easy Composter is a new, black, fifty-five gallon rigid plastic barrel holding approximately seven dry bushels that sits on a tubular metal stand. All metal parts are coated with zinc or made from aluminium. Each end of the barrel has its own axle; there are three handles placed in such a way that it is possible to turn the barrel or rock it back and forth to aid in the mixing. See Organics.

Shipping season: March through October
Canada

MOTHER NATURE'S WORM CASTINGS
1972
Ed and Hazel Soillant
Catalog: Free, 8 pp.
The naturalist Gilbert White wrote, "The earth without worms would soon become cold, hardbound and void of fermentation, and consequently sterile," and the Soillants couldn't agree more. Their brochure sings the praises of worm castings, and they'll be happy to sell them to you by the twenty-five-pound measure. See Organics.
Canada, Mexico, International

MUSHROOMPEOPLE
See Booksellers, Garlic.

NATURAL GARDENER'S CATALOG
1985
John Dromgoole, Maggie Burnett, and Dolores Nice
Catalog: $1, 48 pp., black-and-white illustrations and photographs
John Dromgoole was hosting a radio call-in show on organic gardening when he realized that there was a lack of readily available, safe garden products on the market. The Natural Gardener's catalog, featuring products by Garden-ville, serves as an answer to that need. Selection includes organic and natural fertilizers, microbial and growth stimulants, soil amendments, cover crop seed, composting supplies, pest controls, and gardener-powered tools. See Booksellers, Organics.
Canada, Mexico, International

NATURE'S CONTROL
1981
Leanne Williams
Catalog: 50¢, 21 pp., illustrations
Nature's control specializes in beneficials, with an emphasis on those types that are most useful in greenhouse and other indoor environments. The catalog is organized into "What's Eating My Plants?" and a corresponding "Good Bugs to the Rescue" that makes it easy to identify the pest by recognizing the type of damage it inflicts and proceed with the appropriate solution. Beneficials include spidermite predators, whitefly parasites, aphid predators

and parasites, green lacewing eggs and pre-hatched larvae, pirate bugs, predator nematodes, and housefly and caterpillar parasites. Also carries sticky traps, diatomaceous earth, and Snail-Barr copper stripping. Descriptions of habits, life cycles, and the interrelationships between the bad bugs and the good bugs are thorough and clear. Guarantees live delivery. See Organics.
Shipping season: All year. Praying Mantis egg cases, February through July   .

NICHOLS GARDEN NURSERY
See Booksellers, Garlic, Herbs, Organics, Seeds, Vegetables, Wildflowers.

NITRON INDUSTRIES, INC.
1977
Frank J. Finger
Catalog: Free, 24 pp., color photographs
Nitron Industries manufactures and sells 100 percent organic fertilizers, enzyme soil conditioners, and mined minerals. In addition to products that aid in maintaining general soil and plant health, they offer solutions formulated specifically for vegetables, tomatoes, roses, flowers, trees, and hydroponic mediums. Descriptions of product composition, use, and intended results are presented in detail and phrased in a reassuring tone. Their technical department is available to answer questions regarding conversion from chemical to organic methods and to help you plan organic fertilization and natural pest control programs. Guarantees satisfaction. See Kidstuff, Organics, Seeds, Vegetables.
Canada, Mexico, International

NIWA TOOLS
1981
Kayoko Kuroiwa
Catalog: $4, 20 pp., illustrations
Niwa garden and bonsai tools are individually crafted in Japan by artisans who are members of small family businesses. For use in the garden, are silky pruning saws, hedge shears, pruners, grafting knives, hatchets and bamboo splitters; for the care of bonsai, there are scissors, shears, branch cutters, plant tweezers, branch benders, palm rope, and other specialized accessories. Niwa welcomes inquiries about custom made-to-order tools.
Canada, Mexico, International

NORTHWIND NURSERY AND ORCHARDS
1983

Frank Foltz
Catalog: $1 (recoverable), 35 pp., illustrations
The Foltz family are growers of northern-hardy, organically grown fruit trees. Ten percent of their catalog is devoted to brand-name orcharding tools: pruners, lopers, razor-tooth saws, grafting pliers, knives, and shears. They also carry natural insect and disease controls. See **Booksellers**, **Fruit**, Organics, Trees.
Canada, Mexico, International

NORWAY INDUSTRIES
1983
Brian Hanson
Catalog: Free, 3 pp.
The Carry-All and its companion, the Carryette, are front-dumping carts with plywood sides and tele-scoping handles that can be adjusted for balance. Both are described as having load-bearing capacities of four hundred pounds, the Carry-All distributing this weight within a 13.6 cubic-foot space, the Car-ryette within 9.2 cubic feet. Guarantees against de-fects for one year; will provide replacement or issue credit.

ORAL LEDDEN & SONS
1904
Don Ledden
Catalog: Free, 55 pp., black-and-white photographs
A traditional family-owned and -operated seed house, twenty-five percent of Ledden's catalog is given over to supplies: bulk quantities of plastic pots with and without saucers, plantable fiber containers, Jiffy® pots, bedding plant contain-ers, and growing mediums. Organic and chem-ical insecticides, fungicides, weed killers, and fertilizers are also offered. Guarantees safe ar-rival; will replace or issue refund. See **Garlic**, Grasses, Heirlooms, **Seeds**, Vegetables.
Canada, Mexico, International

ORCON
(DIVISION OF ORGANIC CONTROL, INC.)
Paula White
Catalog: Free, 26 pp., illustrations
A source for beneficials: *Aphytis melinus*, *Cryp-tolaemus*, decollate snails, *Encarsia formosa*, fly parasites, green lacewings, predatory mites, ne-matodes, trichogramma, as well as earthworms and their castings. The Orcon catalog devotes an individual page to each species, covering use, release techniques and timing, recommen-dations for most effective control, and life

cycle of the beneficial. See Organics.

OZARK HANDLE & HARDWARE
1977
Eddie Silver
Catalog: $2 (refundable), 20 pp., illustrations
If you are inclined to repair or construct your own tools, OH&H has a handle on you. Offers two grades of ash handles for shovels, spades, scoops, hoes, rakes, wheelbarrows, posthole diggers, and plows. Also includes tool storage containers and boxes, a rain gauge, tarpaulins, and assorted pest traps. Guarantees satisfaction; will issue refund for merchandise returned within thirty days.

PARADISE WATER GARDENS
See **Booksellers**, **Waterscapes**.

PARK SEED® CO.
1868
J. Leonard Park and Karen Park Jennings
Catalog: Free, 76 pp., color photographs
Park's flower and vegetable seed catalog in-cludes Park Starts® seed-starting kits, seed-starting pots, bedding plant kits, grow mix, seedling shelves and lights, soil heating cables, tomato and bean towers, netting, cold frames, deer repellent sachet, and Wall O' Water® in-sulation. See **Bulbs**, **Garlic**, **Herbs**, Peonies, Roses, **Seeds**, Vegetables.
Canada

PAW PAW EVERLAST LABEL CO.
1962
A. Arens
Catalog: Free, 6 pp., black-and-white photograph
Manufacturer of Everlast metal plant labels and garden markers. Offers eleven designs, including hairpin, plant/shrub, cap style, rose, tall display, flag, miniature, etc. All of their markers and la-bels have galvanized steel standards and zinc nameplates. Descriptions include size and use. Will quote for custom-printed markers upon re-quest. Guarantees satisfaction; will exchange items returned within thirty days of receipt.
Canada, Mexico, International

PEACEFUL VALLEY FARM & GARDEN SUPPLY
1976
Kathleen Fenton
Catalog: Free, 120 pp.
This full-service catalog is packed with sup-

plies, tools, and seed for organic gardeners and farmers of all sizes. Offers over one thousand items, including natural fertilizers, cover crops, natural pest controls (including beneficial insects), season extenders, garden tools, tillers, chipper-shredders, sprayers, farm equipment, compost supplies, soil tests, and much more. See **Booksellers, Garlic, Grasses,** Organics, Seeds, **Wildflowers.**
Canada, Mexico, International

PEN Y BRYN NURSERY
1946
Catalog: $2.95, 58 pp., illustrations
A nursery for pre-bonsai, exotic trees, and Satsuki azaleas. Offers bonsai starter kits, sheet moss, shears, and assortment of figurines and clay pots. See **Booksellers,** Conifers, **Rhododendrons, Trees.**

PINETREE GARDEN SEEDS
1979
Dick Meiners
Catalog: Free (outside U.S., $1.50), 192 pp., illustrations and color photographs
Pinetree began by offering small-sized packets of vegetable seeds for the home gardener. Their merchandise mix now includes gardening accessories, small tools, season extenders, compost amendments, organic fertilizer, insecticides, pesticides, and herbicides. Guarantees satisfaction; will replace or issue refund. See **Booksellers,** Garlic, Herbs, **Kidstuff,** Organics, **Seeds, Vegetables.**

PLANT COLLECTIBLES (GROWING WITH LIGHTS)
1983
Marsellie Luxenberg
Catalog: 2 FCS., 20 pp., illustrations and black-and-white photographs
Plant Collectibles offers several hundred indoor-outdoor gardening and greenhouse supplies: pots, hanging baskets, markers, flats, cell packs, humidity domes, nursery containers, Jiffy® products, fiber paks, fertilizers, and watering devices. The catalog includes an insert from their Growing With Lights division, which sells carts and lighting for displaying plants and developing seedlings. Plant Collectibles guarantees satisfaction through manufacturer's warranty; will issue refund for any item returned within ten days of purchase. Growing With Lights guarantees merchandise for one year.
Canada, Mexico, International

PLASTIC PLUMBING PRODUCTS, INC. (ENVIROGATION DIVISION)
1979
Craig Pisarkiewicz
Catalog: $1, 28 pp., illustrations
The Envirogation Division of PPP sells drip irrigation components and designs systems for greenhouses, home gardens, and commercial use. A six-page guide in their catalog provides definitions and explanations about design basics in reassuring language. Products offered include emitters and foggers, mini-sprinklers and sprays, polyethylene and PVC tube, irrigation fittings, filters, valves, controllers, and other accessories. Mr. Pisarkiewicz welcomes phone inquiries regarding system design and sizing and will send you an "Irrigation System Design Questionnaire" upon request.
Canada, Mexico, International

P. L. ROHRER & BRO.
1919
Jim Gamber
Catalog: Free, 40 pp., illustrations and color photographs
Rohrer & Bro. describes their selection of seed for farmers and home gardeners as typical to the area in which they are situated, Lancaster County's Pennsylvania Dutch country. Ten percent of their catalog includes house and garden plant care products: rooting compound, lawn soil testers, systemic care products, garden seeders and spreaders, insecticides, orchard sprays, and natural/biological controls for insects and pests. See Garlic, Herbs, Organics, **Seeds,** Vegetables.

REOTEMP INSTRUMENT CORP.
1934
Kathy M. Martin
Catalog: Free, 7 pp., black-and-white photographs
Most ReoTemp thermometers and moisture meters are geared in performance and price for the commercial compost industry. However, if you have a garden-variety compost pile or bin, request information about their backyard compost thermometer. See Organics.
Canada, Mexico, International

RESOURCE CONSERVATION TECHNOLOGY, INC.
See **Waterscapes.**

ROCKY MOUNTAIN INSECTARY
Catalog: Free, 8 pp., illustrations

Sells Pedio™ wasps by the carton (appropriate for five hundred square feet of beans) to control the Mexican bean beetle. Flyer charts the month-by-month life cycle of this beneficial and describes its intended prey. See Organics.

ROYALL RIVER ROSES AT FOREVERGREEN FARM
1983
David King
Catalog: $1, 48 pp., black-and-white photographs
Included in the Royall River catalog is a selection of supplies and tools for the rose enthusiast: suede gardening gloves, goatskin work gloves, beeswax hand cream, rose hips, rose water, a pruner, hand hoe, and weeder, rose ties, zinc markers, fish fertilizer, and soil conditioner formulated for roses, etc. See **Booksellers**, Heirlooms, **Roses**.
Canada

SANTA BARBARA GREENHOUSES
See **Furniture**.

SHEPHERD'S GARDEN SEEDS
1984
Renee Shepherd and Beth Benjamin
Catalog: $1, 108 pp., illustrations
A focused selection of products: seed-starting flats, natural wooden labels, propagation mats, own-brand starting mix, agrofabric floating row cover, wire compost cage, bioactivator, Gardena soft-spray wand, woven oak herb basket, and Womanswork® gardening gloves. See **Booksellers, Garlic**, Heirlooms, Herbs, **Kidstuff**, Seeds, **Vegetables**.
Canada

SMITH & HAWKEN
1979
Catalog: Free, 62 pp., color photographs
A visually rich catalog of special and specialty tools and supplies including Haws watering cans, hoes, rakes, perennial spades, and shovels, Sandvik lopers, a cold frame made from reclaimed redwood, beneficials, composters, compost tools, and gardener's clothing. See **Furniture, Kidstuff**, Organics.

SOHN'S FOREST MUSHROOMS
1983
Eileen and Ray Sohn
Catalog: Free, 8pp.

The Sohns sell shiitake and oyster spawn. Also offer mushrooming supplies, including growing, spawn run, and humidity blankets, inoculation drill bits, aluminum record tags, and sealing wax. See **Booksellers, Garlic**.
Canada, Mexico, International

SOUTHERN EXPOSURE SEED EXCHANGE®
1982
Jeff McCormack
Catalog: $3 (recoverable), 62 pp., illustrations
This source for heirloom seeds carries an extensive selection of labels, markers, tags, seed-saving supplies, pollination barriers and netting, grafting/container sealant, moisture-proof vials, empty packets, polybags, corn shellers, and rice huskers. Guarantees satisfaction; will replace or issue refund. See **Booksellers, Garlic**, Heirlooms, Herbs, Seeds, **Vegetables**.
Canada

STIGALL WATER GARDENS
See Booksellers, **Waterscapes**.

STOKES SEEDS
1881
Catalog: Free, 112 pp., color photographs
Stokes is a seed catalog to savor. There are almost two thousand varieties of annuals, perennials, cut flowers, everlastings, and vegetables. Within the main catalog the twelve page "Stokes Collection" contains tools and accessories: English traditional galvanized steel watering cans, multi-pattern spray wands, floating vegetable row covers, cold frames, seed starter kits, boots, and gardener's aprons. See Garlic, **Seeds**.
Canada

SUBMATIC IRRIGATION SYSTEMS
1970
Dale Brown
Catalog: Free, 24 pp., illustrations
SIS specializes in sprinkler, drip, and subsurface irrigation systems. Their catalog includes step-by-step instructions on how to plan an irrigation system. The catalog emphasizes the needs of home gardeners and the use of Submatic's technology for lawn care. Mr. Brown will design a system for you free of charge, provided all the necessary information is furnished including a sketch drawn to scale. There are hundreds of individual items, as well as kits, in this catalog for creating, maintaining, or upgrading a watering system.

Mexico, International

Sunglo Solar Greenhouses
1978
Joseph Pappalardo
Catalog: Free, 8 pp., color photographs
This manufacturer of greenhouses also sells power panels, heater kits, compact gas heaters, propagation chambers, axial fans, and related accessories. See **Furniture.**
Canada

Territorial Seed Company
Tom Johns
Catalog: Free, 95 pp.
Fifteen percent of Territorial's extensive seed catalog includes natural fertilizers, composting aids, IPM (beneficial insects, natural insecticides, traps and lures), hand tools, seed-starting supplies, garden markers, and watering and drip irrigation equipment. See **Booksellers,** Garlic, Herbs, **Kidstuff,** Organics, **Seeds, Vegetables.**
Canada

Texas Greenhouse Co., Inc.
1948
Catalog: $4 (recoverable), 32 pp., color photographs
The manufacturer of the American Classic Greenhouse, TGC offers a full line of greenhouse accessories, including benches, cold frames, cooling, heating, ventilating, and monitoring systems and components, fiberglass and polycarbonate panels, lighting fixtures, propagation mats, soil cables, shading materials, and watering devices. They also offer a lean-to and a bay-view version. Guarantees their own products for one year against faulty workmanship and defective parts; other items are subject to original manufacturer's guarantee. See **Furniture.**
Canada, Mexico, International

Tomato Growers Supply Company
1984
Linda and Vince Sapp
Catalog: Free, 40 pp., illustrations and black-and-white photographs
The focus of this catalog is the seed for 250 varieties of guess what and one hundred types of peppers. The Sapps also offer a brief complementary list of supplies: chemicals and fertilizers formulated for vegetables and tomatoes, tomato-growing pens and towers, Dustin Mizer, soil test kit, seed-starting supplies, and T-shirt with the

TGSC logo. Guarantees for one year; will replace or issue refund. See **Booksellers,** Heirlooms, **Seeds,** Vegetables.

Totally Tomatoes
1992
Catalog: Free, 64 pp.
Totally Tomatoes offers a total of 279 varieties of tomato and 120 varieties of pepper. The supply list includes brand-name organic growing aids, seed-starting media and accessories, a nylon trellis in five sizes, a flexible plastic tomato web, wire growing cages, and an original design T-shirt. Guarantees satisfaction; will replace or issue refund.
See Seeds, **Vegetables.**
Canada, Mexico, International

Troy-Bilt®
Dean Leith, Jr.
Catalog: Free, 8 pp.
This division of Garden Way manufactures (and markets primarily directly to gardeners) chippervacs and tiller-composters in sizes from three horsepower through eight horsepower. Tiller attachments for other tasks include hiller/furrower, dozer/snow blade, row marker, chipper/shredder, and V-sweep cultivator.

TumbleBug®
1992
Henry Artis
Catalog: Free, 4 pp., black-and-white photographs
The TumbleBug® is a geodesic compost bin. Composting is accomplished by turning the bin, one side at a time, onto one of its twenty faces. Clippings and waste material can be loaded and then deposited by rolling the bin to the desired location. Mr. Artis states that the critical mass achieved by this system raises the internal temperature to 130 degrees Fahrenheit, converting grass clippings in as little as two weeks and leaves in four to six weeks. The TumbleBug® is available in 85-gallon (9.3 bushels), 140-gallon (15.5 bushels), and 193-gallon (21 bushels) sizes. Guarantees satisfaction for five years. See Organics.
Canada, International

Unique Insect Control
1980
Jeanne Houston
Catalog: Free, 6 pp.
According to Ms. Houston, her family's business

is the largest supplier of ladybugs in the United States. She writes, "We are the company that actually gathers them from the Sierra foothills." Also offers whitefly parasites, lacewing eggs, praying mantis egg cases, trichogramma, fly parasites, predatory mites, earthworms, and beneficial nematodes. The descriptions of these beneficials, how they aid in suppressing populations of unwanted pests, and their release rates are clear and informative. Guarantees live delivery. See Organics.
Shipping season: All year. Praying Mantis egg cases, January through June.
Import permit required for Canada.

VALLEY OAK TOOL CO.
1990
David Grau
Catalog: Free, various 2 pp. to 6 pp., black-and-white photographs
Mr. Grau, an organic farmer, makes a rubber-wheeled hoe with an eight-inch blade that is designed to reduce back strain while allowing for cutting close to plant rows. He also makes a stake puller, stake pounder, and a four-tine cultivator. Guarantees unconditional satisfaction for one year; will issue refund.
Canada

VAN NESS WATER GARDENS
See **Booksellers, Waterscapes.**

VESEY'S SEEDS LTD.
1939
Allen Perry
Catalog: Free, 126 pp., black-and-white and color photographs
Vesey's specializes in seeds for short seasons. Ten percent of their catalog includes baskets, bird feeders, composting tools and aids, natural pest controls, soil enhancers, seed-starting supplies, season extenders, Vesey's logo hats, and sunflower shirts. See **Booksellers, Garlic,** Herbs, **Seeds,** Vegetables, Wildflowers.
Canada

VISTA PRODUCTS
1991
Onni and Hilkka Kilpelaine, Gerry and Ritva Vadeboncoeur
Catalog: Free, 4 pp., black-and-white photographs
If you don't have a fruit tree, the Eezy-picker just might encourage you to plant one, or two,

or even a whole grove. This harvesting tool has no moving parts and requires only two sets of movements, which allows you to keep both hands on the handle and both feet on the ground. First, the fruit is caught in the bag at the end of the pole; a second pulling action cuts the fruit (with stationary blades) from the branch while letting it remain safely cradled in the bag. Appropriate for lemons, oranges, peaches, plums, apples, walnuts, etc.
Canada, Mexico, International

WATERFORD GARDENS
See **Booksellers, Waterscapes.**

THE WATERWORKS®
See **Booksellers, Waterscapes.**

WHITE FLOWER FARM
See **Bulbs,** Fruit, **Perennials, Roses,** Trees, **Waterscapes.**

WICKLEIN'S WATER GARDENS
See Booksellers, Iris, **Waterscapes.**

WIKCO INDUSTRIES, INC.
1979
Brandon S. Ideen
Catalog: Free, 126 pp., black-and-white photographs
Wikco is a catalog retailer specializing in commercial grounds maintenance equipment. If your garden and property routinely confront you with large challenges and tasks, here are hundreds of items to contemplate. Categories of equipment and supplies include aerators, backhoes, blades, brush chippers, gloves, irrigation machines, lawn vacuums, mowers, netting and fencing materials, plows, post drivers, power blowers, sprayers, spreaders, stump grinders, sweepers, trimmers, utility carts, and water-removal equipment. Guarantees satisfaction for thirty days; all other guarantees or warranties are subject to the manufacturers' terms.
Canada

WIND & WEATHER
1977
Marcie Schorg
Catalog: Free, 40 pp., color photographs
One third of this catalog describes and illustrates weather stations and systems: electronic and traditional thermometers, rain gauges, barometers, and hygrometers. Guarantees satisfaction; will exchange or issue refund. See **Furniture.**

WINDY OAKS AQUATICS
See **Waterscapes**.

WOMANSWORK®
1985
Nancy Bennett Phillips
Catalog: Free, 24 pp., black-and-white
photographs
Womanswork®—"strong women building a
gentle world"—was founded when Karen Smi-
ley designed a pair of work gloves that fit her
own hands properly. These gloves are said to become more comfortable with wear and have an
excellent reputation for durability. They are offered in eight styles for women and men. They
also sell Womanswork® work aprons, pail
aprons, log carriers, tarp carriers, work boots,
tote bags, caps, visors, T-shirts, and sweatshirts.
Describes material and nature of construction.
The proceeds from 1 percent of their catalog
sales are donated to groups working against do-

mestic violence. Guarantees satisfaction; will replace or issue a refund. See **Kidstuff**.

WORM'S WAY INDIANA
1985
Michael Dick and Martin Heydt
Catalog: Free, 64 pp., color photographs
Worm's Way began as a small, one-man operation offering organic and natural alternatives
to conventional gardening techniques. Worm's
Way now offers hundreds of brand-name
items in the following categories: aquatic gardens, beneficials, composting, fertilizers, hydroponic systems, irrigation and watering
tools, lighting systems, pest and weed control,
propagation, hand tools, and a T-shirt and cap
with the WW logo. Guarantees satisfaction;
will accept items for exchange, credit, or refund within thirty days of receipt. See **Booksellers, Garlic**, Organics.
Canada, Mexico, International

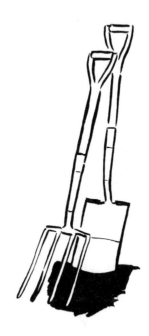

GREAT GARDEN READS

Great Garden Reads

The literature of the garden offers almost as much variety and abundance as the plant world that informs it. The composition of this section is neither all encompassing nor scientifically derived. "For the Sheer Pleasure" is a sampling of books that I have found delightful and enriching, and "To Refer to Again, and Again, and . . ." lists books I have found to be essential (or in some instances quintessential) allies and mentors in tending the soil and the plants in our garden.

For the Sheer Pleasure

The Garden Makers: The Great Tradition of Garden Design from 1600 to the Present Day, by George Plumptre. A grand historical tour of the personalities that shaped English and American gardening and the gardens they created and inspired. The book is divided into periods: "the First Professionals of the Seventeenth Century"; "the Emergence of English Style From 1690 through 1740"; "the Landscape Movement of 1740–1820" "the High Victorian Era through 1880"; "the Period of International Influences from 1880–1920"; "British and American Styles from the end of World War I through 1950"; and "Contemporary Garden Makers." Over seventy influential gardeners are profiled in a book that is beautiful to behold (with forty color photographs) and provides a salient connection to those people who created and influenced our gardening heritage.

Innisfree: An American Garden, by Lester Collins. A tour in words and images that is almost as fulfilling as an afternoon walk through the two-hundred-acre oasis imagined and created (from 1920 through 1960) by Walter and Marion Beck in Millbrook, New York. The grounds at Innisfree include a series of self-contained "cup gardens" inspired by eighth-century Chinese scroll paintings that serve as meditative stops along this unique garden's path. Mr. Collins, a landscape architect, spent decades enhancing and extending Innisfree, which he describes with intimacy. The forty-five color photographs include Mr. Collins's own and the work of other artists that were commissioned for this book.

The Inward Garden: Creating a Place of Beauty and Meaning, by Julie Moir Messervy. Although this is a book of practical lessons about design and composition that can be applied to creating what is very much a garden of one's own, it is through Ms. Messervy's writing (and Sam Abell's photographs) ultimately a book of transcendence. The essence of this journey of garden dream weaving quickly fills the reader's senses. Even if you never apply the lessons given, this book can guide you to deeper levels of your interior landscape.

Monet's Garden: Through the Seasons at Giverny, by Vivian Russell. "Monet wove all the strands of his creative life into Giverny, so that they became the very fabric of the garden, always imaginative, often unique." So too has Ms. Russell, through her writing and photographs, brought to the reader a living garden changing with the seasons and the artist's eye, in book form.

Perennials: Toward Continuous Bloom, edited by Ann Lovejoy. An impassioned symposium (in book form) by thirty-two gardeners moderated by Ms. Lovejoy on one deceptively unsimple topic, the placement of perennials in the garden. Gardeners from across the United States share information and inspiration about design, color, and other considerations in the planting and care of perennials. Includes an index to over seven hundred plants.

Tasha Tudor's Garden, by Tovah Martin. A guided tour of the garden within the magical realm created by Ms. Tudor in the style of the 1830s. The garden, its plants, and inhabitants, blend with the characters and landscape of Ms. Tudor's own books in a work that can only serve as strong encouragement to anyone who wishes to create a garden statement of his or her own. Includes one hundred color photographs by Richard Brown, coauthor (with Ms. Tudor) of an earlier work, *The Private World of Tasha Tudor*.

To Refer to Again. and Again. and . . .

The American Horticultural Society Encyclopedia of Gardening: The Definitive Practical Guide to Gardening Techniques, Planting and Maintenance, Editor-in-Chief Christopher Brickell, Editor-in-Chief American Horticultural Society Elvin McDonald. You do have to know how to read to use this book to its fullest but the three thousand color photographs and illustrations (many of which are sequenced to illustrate step-by-step methods and techniques) are so effective that you may often find yourself getting "it" before you read the text. This encyclopedia is made up of two sections: "Creating the Garden," which includes detailed information about garden planning and design, and chapters on major plant groups, which specify soil preparation, planting, routine care, pruning, and propagation. The section on "Maintaining the Garden" includes tools and materials, soil and climate characteristics in different regions of the United States, as well as construction projects, and pest and disease control.

Botany for Gardeners: An Introduction and Guide, by Brian Capon. How do plants work? What is photosynthesis? How did plants evolve and how do they adapt to environmental stress? Mr. Capon's accessible style makes botany from a gardener's point-of-view an enlightening journey that adds to your understanding of how and why plants do what they do. Fifty-three illustrations and 121 color photographs.

Gardener's Latin, by Bill Neal. A to Z definitions in a language that has more currency in the garden than in any other form of daily tasks or discourse. Bits of garden lore and literature are scattered throughout making this more fun than a book in Latin has a right to be.

Gardening in Deer Country, by Karen Jescavage-Bernard. If the deer eat at your home more often than you do this is a smart little guide for you. Ms. Jescavage-Bernard has a common-sense solution or two including a list of plants that the deer do not like, because if they don't like the way it tastes they're not going to eat it. This volume may not get cheers from tulip growers but its likely to get at least an honorable mention from daffodil societies.

Index of Garden Plants, by Mark Griffiths. A condensed one-volume index based on the Royal Horticultural Society's four-volume *Dictionary of Gardening*. Includes sixty thousand ornamentals, a brief description, range of hardiness, common names and superseded botanical names for thirty thousand cultivars.

Sequence of Bloom of Perennials, Biennials, and Bulbs, by Mower and Lee. Whether you're going to mix the border or simply want to anticipate when which plant you put where will do what, this is a quick reference to when blossoms will appear, height at maturity, and color for almost three hundred often-grown plants.

Taylor's Master Guide to Gardening, Editor-In-Chief Frances Tenenbaum; edited by Rita Buchanan and Roger Holmes. A major reference work for North American gardeners that includes an encyclopedic listing of three thousand species, with where-to-use and how-to-grow information for each; color photographs in landscape and garden settings of a thousand recommended trees, shrubs, perennials, annuals, bulbs, herbs, succulents, ferns, and other types of plants cross-referenced to the encyclopedia; a highly accessible section on creating a garden including design basics and features such as paths, beds and borders, ground covers, meadows, rock gardens, terraces, and other elements that are accompanied by two hundred photographs of garden settings; and a detailed guide to soils, compost, plant acquisition, propagating, pruning, watering, fertilizing, and lawn care.

Booksellers and Computer Software Sellers

Sources will ship books, software, and videos year-round unless otherwise noted.

QUICK FIND
The following sources are listed in this section:

ABRACADATA®
ABUNDANT LIFE SEED FOUNDATION
A. C. BURKE & CO.
ACRES, U.S.A.®
AGACCESS BOOK CATALOG
AMBERGATE GARDENS
THE AMERICAN BOTANIST, BOOKSELLERS
THE ANTIQUE ROSE EMPORIUM
ARBICO
BARBARA FARNSWORTH, BOOKSELLER
BARNEY'S GINSENG PATCH
BEAR CREEK NURSERY
BECKER'S SEED POTATOES
BERLIN SEEDS
BERRY HILL LIMITED
BETH L. BIBBY, BOOKS
BOOK ARBOR
BOOK ORCHARD
BOUNTIFUL GARDENS
BOZEMAN BIO-TECH, INC.
BROOKS BOOKS
BROWN'S EDGEWOOD GARDENS
BUCKHORN GINSENG
BUTTERBROOKE FARM
CAPABILITY'S BOOKS®
CAROL BARNETT, BOOKS
THE COOK'S GARDEN
COUNTRY WETLANDS NURSERY AND CONSULTING
CROP KING, INC.
DABNEY HERBS
THE DAFFODIL MART
DAN'S GARDEN SHOP
DAVE & SUE'S AQUARIUMS & GREENHOUSE
DAYLILY DISCOUNTERS
DEGIORGI SEED COMPANY
DOROTHY BIDDLE SERVICE
ECO ENTERPRISES
ELIXIR FARM BOTANICALS
FAR NORTH GARDENS
FEDCO SEEDS
FEDCO TREES
FILAREE FARM
FUNGI PERFECTI

GARDEN CITY SEEDS
GARDEN WORKS
GARDENIMPORT
GARY WAYNER, BOOKSELLER
GARY W. WOOLSON, BOOKSELLER
GOODWIN CREEK GARDENS
GOSSLER FARMS NURSERY
THE GOURMET GARDENER™
GOURMET MUSHROOMS
GREEN HORIZONS
GREER GARDENS
HARDSCRABBLE ENTERPRISES
HARMONY FARM SUPPLY AND NURSERY
HEIRLOOM GARDEN® SEEDS
HEIRLOOM OLD GARDEN ROSES
HENRIETTA'S NURSERY
HOLLAND WILDFLOWER FARM
HYDROFARM
I.F.M. PRODUCTS FOR NATURAL AGRICULTURE
J. L. HUDSON, SEEDSMAN
JOHNNY'S SELECTED SEEDS
K & L CACTUS & SUCCULENT NURSERY
KILGORE SEED COMPANY
KLEHM NURSERY
LANDSCAPE BOOKS
LARNER SEEDS
LE JARDIN DU GOURMET
LILYPONS WATER GARDENS®
LOUISIANA NURSERY
MCALLISTER'S IRIS GARDEN
MATRIX GROUP, INC.
MELLINGER'S
MILAEGER'S GARDENS
MOOSE GROWERS SUPPLY
MOUNTAIN MAPLES
MUSHROOMPEOPLE
MYRON KIMNACH–BOOKS ON SUCCULENTS
NATIVE AMERICAN SEED
NATIVE SEEDS/SEARCH
NATURAL GARDENER'S CATALOG
NEW ENGLAND WILD FLOWER SOCIETY
NICHOLS GARDEN NURSERY
NORTH STAR GARDENS

NORTHWIND FARMS
NORTHWIND NURSERY AND ORCHARDS
PARADISE WATER GARDENS
PEACEFUL VALLEY FARM & GARDEN SUPPLY
PEN Y BRYN NURSERY
PERENNIAL PLEASURES NURSERY OF VERMONT
PINETREE GARDEN SEEDS
PLANTS OF THE SOUTHWEST
PRAIRIE MOON NURSERY
PRAIRIE NURSERY
PRAIRIE SEED SOURCE
RAINBOW GARDENS BOOKSHOP
RAINTREE NURSERY
RARE CONIFER FOUNDATION– RARE CONIFER NURSERY
RAYMOND M. SUTTON, JR.
REDWOOD CITY SEED COMPANY
RESOURCES: BOOKS FOR PLANT COLLECTORS AND SEED SAVERS
RICHTERS
RONNIGER'S SEED POTATOES
ROSLYN NURSERY
ROYALL RIVER ROSES AT FOREVERGREEN FARM
ST. LAWRENCE NURSERIES
THE SANDY MUSH HERB NURSERY
SAROH
SEED SAVERS EXCHANGE–SEED SAVER PUBLICATIONS
SEEDS BLÜM
SEEDS OF CHANGE®
SEEDS TRUST: HIGH ALTITUDE GARDENS
SELECT SEEDS–ANTIQUE FLOWERS
SHADY OAKS NURSERY
SHEPHERD'S GARDEN SEEDS
SISKIYOU RARE PLANT NURSERY
SOHN'S FOREST MUSHROOMS
SOUTHERN EXPOSURE SEED EXCHANGE®
SOUTHERN SEEDS
SQUAW MOUNTAIN GARDENS
STIGALL WATER GARDENS
STRONG'S ALPINE SUCCULENTS
SUNRISE ENTERPRISES

TERRITORIAL SEED COMPANY

THE THOMAS JEFFERSON CENTER FOR HISTORICAL PLANTS

TIMBER PRESS

TOMATO GROWERS SUPPLY COMPANY

TRANS-PACIFIC NURSERY

VAN NESS WATER GARDENS

VAN VEEN NURSERY

VESEY'S SEEDS LTD.

VILENIKI: AN HERB FARM

WARREN F. BRODERICK

WATERFORD GARDENS

THE WATERWORKS®

THE WAUSHARA GARDENS

WAVECREST NURSERY AND LANDSCAPING

WICKLEIN'S WATER GARDENS

WILD SEED, INC.

WILLIAM DAM SEEDS

WOOD VIOLET BOOKS

WORM'S WAY INDIANA

ABRACADATA®
1985
Catalog: Free, 12 pp., color photographs
A source of plan-making software, including Design Your Own Home™ Landscape, which allows you to plan, choose, and see your plantings mature, and Sprout!™, a program for vegetable gardening and maintenance that includes an editable plant database for seven climate regions, adjustable planting and harvest times, yield, soil pH, plant and row spacing, and other features.
Canada, Mexico, International

ABUNDANT LIFE SEED FOUNDATION
1975
Susan Herman
Catalog: $2 (recoverable), 64 pp., black-and-white photographs
A nonprofit organization that acquires, propagates, and preserves native and naturalized seeds. Book section includes eighty titles on the practical side of alternative agriculture, organic, native, and natural gardening, herbs, seedmanship, and self-sufficiency skills. See **Garlic**, Heirlooms, Herbs, Organics, **Seeds**, Vegetables.
Canada, Mexico, International

A. C. BURKE & CO.
1991
Andrew Burke
Catalog: Free, 24 pp., black-and-white photographs
Burke specializes in "intelligent tools" for gardeners on how-to, planning, and design. One hundred current videos, books, and software emphasizing skills and techniques are pictured and described. Guarantees satisfaction; will issue refund. See **Kidstuff**.
Canada, Mexico, International

ACRES, U.S.A.®
1970
Fred C. Walters

Catalog: Free, 71 pp.
Mr. Walters vigorously describes current works on ecological agriculture, economic policies, and alternative human health care published by Acres, U.S.A.® Also carries two hundred titles from other sources on agriculture, pest and insect control, organic gardening, country skills, market gardening, gardening and ecology for young people, herbology, and natural medicine. Separate section of 175 audiotapes recorded since 1970 of "eco-leaders" speaking at Acres, U.S.A.® conferences. See **Kidstuff**.
Canada, Mexico, International

agAccess BOOK CATALOG
1985
Karen Van Epen
Catalog: Free, 47 pp.
A source for new books on agriculture and horticulture, from water and irrigation to specialty crops. While emphasizing the agricultural, agAccess also carries books on gardening, forestry, and natural history. Five hundred books in the catalog are described in detail. They have an additional twelve thousand titles on a database and welcome specific inquiries.
Canada, Mexico, International

AMBERGATE GARDENS
1985
Mike and Jean Heger
Catalog: $2, 68 pp., illustrations and color photographs
The Hegers, based in Waconia, Minnesota, offer two hundred uncommon and/or unusual native and exotic perennials hardy in zone 4. They offer a brief, focused selection of books, including *Garden Revisions* by Jack Streed, *Ornamental Grasses for Cold Climates* by Meyer, White, and Pellet, *Perennial Gardening Guide* by John Valleau, *Perennials A to Z* by Ambergate co-owner Michael Heger, and *Pictorial Guide to Perennials* by M. Jane Coleman

Helmer and Karla Decker. See **Grasses, Perennials.**
Canada

THE AMERICAN BOTANIST, BOOKSELLERS
1983
D. Keith Crotz
Catalog: $2
The American Botanist, Booksellers, sells out-of-print and previously owned rare books on agriculture, olericulture, garden history, and related fields. The 260 books described in each issue of the catalog are generally characterized as "one of a kind." Want lists are kept for customers who seek specific titles. Mr. Crotz also publishes a series of reprints of out-of-print nineteenth-century books on American horticulture and agricultural history, with new introductions and essays to place these works in perspective. See Heirlooms.
Canada, Mexico, International

THE ANTIQUE ROSE EMPORIUM
1983
G. Michael Shoup
Catalog: $5, 80 pp., color photographs
Mr. Shoup is a charter member of the Texas Rose Rustlers, coauthor (with Liz Druitt) of *Landscaping with Antique Roses* and is passionate about the reintroduction of old garden roses. His catalog includes thirty books and videos on perennials, wildflowers, herbs, and landscaping with an emphasis, understandably, on roses. Recent catalogs included *Landscaping with Antique Roses* by Mr. Shoup and Liz Druitt, *The Art of Gardening with Roses* by Graham Stuart Thomas, *Classic Roses* by Peter Beales, *The Heritage of the Rose* by David Austin, *Heritage Roses and Old Fashioned Crafts* by Elizabeth Culpeper, *The Illustrated Encyclopedia of Roses* by Mary Moody and Peter Harkness, and *In Search of Lost Roses* by Thomas Christopher.
See Heirlooms, **Roses.**

ARBICO
1978
Richard C. Frey and Sheri Herrera de Frey
Catalog: Free, 56 pp.
Arizona Biological Control produces and markets beneficial insects. The education section of their catalog contains a mix of forty titles on ecological pest management, biodynamic agriculture, and organic methods. About half of the titles are appropriate for the home gardener, including titles on composting, problem solving, insect identification, and chemical-free lawns. See Organics, **Supplies.**
Canada, Mexico, International

BARBARA FARNSWORTH, BOOKSELLER
1978
Barbara Farnsworth
Catalog: $3, 60 pp.
Ms. Farnsworth is the proprietor of a large general book store carrying forty thousand used, rare, and out-of-print books. The "Printed Side of Gardening" catalog includes seven hundred titles organized by subject, listed alphabetically by author name. Topics include biography, horticultural history, design and gardening, trees and shrubs, gardens of China and Japan, books for children, the kitchen garden, orchard and vineyard, agriculture, herbs and herbals, botany, plant hunters and naturalists, floras and wildflowers, botanical illustration, and country living. Guarantees satisfaction; will issue refund. See Heirlooms, **Kidstuff.**
Canada, Mexico, International

BARNEY'S GINSENG PATCH
1970
Barney L. Frye
Catalog: $2, 36 pp., illustrations
Six instructive books and pamphlets about growing, using, and selling ginseng, goldenseal, and other medicinal herbs, including *The Book of Ginseng* by Sarah Harriman, *Ginseng and Other Medicinal Plants* by A. R. Harding, and *The Herb Collector's Manual* by Kelly. See **Herbs.**
Canada

BEAR CREEK NURSERY
1977
Hunter and Donna Carleton
Catalog: $1 (recoverable), 80 pp., illustrations
The Carletons recently added a carefully selected group of books to their catalog of fruiting (and other useful) plants and trees. Their recommendations include *The Book of Apples* by Joan Morgan and Alison Richards, *The Experts Book of Garden Hints* by the Editors of Rodale Press, *The Backyard Orchardist* by Stella Otto, and *Acorns and Eat'em* by Suellen Ocean. See **Fruit,** Heirlooms, **Trees.**

BECKER'S SEED POTATOES
1985
Catalog: Free, 12 pp.

Becker's sells Elite seed potatoes of true heritage, as well as more recent cultivars, to the home gardener. They also offer three potato cookbooks: *Stuffed Spuds* by Jeanne Jones, *The International Spud,* by Mara Reid Rogers, and *One Potato, Two Potato, A Cookbook* by Constance Bollen and Marlene Blessing. See **Garlic.**
Canada

BERLIN SEEDS
1984
Edward and Brenda Beachy
Catalog: Free, 60 pp., illustrations, black-and-white and color photographs
The Beachys sell commercial-quality seed to the home gardener. Catalog includes a brief, carefully selected offering of books on mulching, composting, companion planting, seed starting, pruning, organic methods, and natural pest control. Carries *Garden Way* guides to butterfly gardening, cold frames, and growing strawberries and blueberries. See **Fruit, Garlic,** Grasses, **Kidstuff,** Organics, **Seeds, Supplies,** Vegetables.
Canada

BERRY HILL LIMITED
1950
Catalog: Free, 68 pp., black-and-white photographs
A hobby farm equipment and country living catalog that reads like the shelves of an old-fashioned general store. Offers seventy books on family farming, poultry and game birds, rabbits, wild birds, gardening, cooking and preserving what you grow, and a hundred *Country Wisdom Bulletins* from Garden Way. Titles that are of interest to home gardeners in recent catalogs included *Bugs, Slugs, and Other Thugs* by Rhonda Massingham, *Carrots Love Tomatoes* and *Roses Love Garlic* by Louise Riotte, *Building Healthy Gardens* by Catherine Osgood Foster, and *The Mulch Book* by Stu Campbell. See **Furniture, Kidstuff, Supplies.**
Canada, International

BETH L. BIBBY, BOOKS
1965
George A. Bibby
Catalog: $3 (one-year subscription, recoverable), 12 pp.
Three hundred new, out-of print, imported, and rare books on gardening, horticulture, and natural history for people Mr. Bibby characterizes as "working gardeners." Emphasis on

reference and how-to. Guarantees satisfaction; will issue credit or refund.
Canada, International

BOOK ARBOR
1990
Judith M. Bloomgarden
Catalog: Free, 17 pp.
Ms. Bloomgarden's general catalog lists 240 previously owned hardbound volumes covering a wide range of gardening subjects. Inquire about specialty catalogs such as one of nineteenth-century farm and garden titles. Guarantees satisfaction; will issue refund. See Heirlooms.
Canada

BOOK ORCHARD
1991
Raminta Jautokas
Catalog: Free, 6 pp.
Books for gardeners in the western United States, including titles on California, the desert Southwest, the Rocky Mountain states, and the Northwest. Book Orchard also carries an extensive selection of books on drought-tolerant and native plants and organic gardening techniques, as well as garden-to-table, regional, and general interest gardening books.
Canada, Mexico, International

BOUNTIFUL GARDENS
1972
Bill and Betsy Bruneau
Catalog: Free, 72 pp. Rare seeds catalog: $2
One quarter of this catalog is devoted to books, pamphlets, papers, and videotapes about the biointensive method of gardening practiced by Ecology Action, the parent organization of Bountiful Gardens. Also in this section are sixty titles on seed saving and planting, composting and soil fertility, as well as general reference works, with an emphasis on organic and self-sustaining gardening, weather and irrigation, garden planning, market gardening, food storage and preparation, nonchemical plant protection, fruit trees, and herbs. Featured titles in Bountiful's selection have included *How To Grow More Vegetables Fruits, Nuts, Berries, Grains, and Other Crops Than You Ever Thought Possible on Less Land Than You Can Imagine* by John Jeavons and *Lazy-Bed Gardening: The Quick and Dirty Guide* by John Jeavons and Carol Cox. Guarantees satisfaction; will issue refund.
See **Garlic,** Heirlooms, Herbs, **Kidstuff,** Organics,

Seeds, Supplies, Vegetables.
Canada, Mexico, International

BOZEMAN BIO-TECH, INC.
1986
Dr. E. Wayne Vinje
Catalog: Free, 49 pp.
This purveyor of pest control products with low toxicity also offers eight books. Titles for IPM include *Common Sense Pest Control* by Olkowski, Daar, and Olkowski and *The Color Handbook of Garden Insects* by Carr. A four-volume organic gardener's series includes individual works on basic methods, composting, edible plants, and annuals. See **Kidstuff**, Organics, **Supplies**.

BROOKS BOOKS
1986
Phil and Martha Nesty
Catalog: $1, 32 pp.
The Nestys specialize in previously owned out-of-print books on ornamental horticulture, botany, and herbs. Catalog lists five hundred of the five thousand volumes that they stock. Also carries selected hard-to-find new and recent works. Free book search service. See Organics.
Canada, Mexico, International

BROWN'S EDGEWOOD GARDENS
1987
Brandon Brown
Catalog: Free, 16 pp. Expanded version: $2
A retail flower and herb shop that offers potted herbs, organic products, and books by mail. Recent catalogs listed ten books, including *Rodale's Illustrated Encyclopedia of Herbs, Taylor's Pocket Guide to Herbs and Edible Flowers*, and *Southern Herb Growing* by Hill and Barclay. See **Furniture, Herbs**, Organics, **Supplies**.

BUCKHORN GINSENG
1945
Ron Dobbs
Catalog: LSASE., 6 pp.
A Wisconsin purveyor of northern-grown stratified ginseng seed who also offers *All About Ginseng* and *Ginseng and Other Medicinal Plants*. See **Herbs**.
Canada, Mexico, International

BUTTERBROOKE FARM
1978
Tom Butterworth
Catalog: LSASE, 4 pp.

Butterbrooke is a certified organic seed co-op that specializes in rapidly maturing, chemically untreated, pure-line vegetable varieties. Six of Mr. Butterworth's gardening guides—*How to Save Seed from Your Own Garden Produce, How to Build a Passive Solar Heated Plant Growth Chamber, How to Build and Use a Root Cellar, How to Maximize Garden Yields with Raised Beds, How to Improve Soil Through Composting*, and *How to Save Energy (Work) with Mulch*—are described in the catalog. A two-hour video, *How to Grow Healthy Veggies*, filmed at the farm, is available for sale or rental. See Organics, Seeds, **Vegetables**.
Canada, International

CAPABILITY'S BOOKS®
1978
Paulette Rickard and Kristen Gilbertson
Catalog: Free, 72 pp., color and black-and-white photographs. Supplements throughout the year
As the story is told, once upon a time iris borers were destroying a beloved planting of Ms. Rickard's. Unable to find the appropriate solution at her local bookshop, she assumed other gardeners were source poor, too; shortly thereafter, she launched Capability's as a books-by-mail business. The annual master catalog includes one thousand titles organized into 120 indexed subjects. Midyear updates supplement the master list. All titles are thoroughly described; most are pictured. Capability's also publishes original and classic titles under their own imprint, providing, as ever, information that appears to be otherwise unavailable.
Canada, Mexico, International

CAROL BARNETT, BOOKS
1980
Carol Barnett
Catalog: Free, 12 pp.
One hundred and seventy-five previously owned volumes on botany and gardening are offered by Ms. Barnett; selections on the history, construction, and renovation of old gardens are particularly strong. Scholarly books are also featured. Guarantees satisfaction; will issue refund. See Heirlooms.
Canada, Mexico, International

THE COOK'S GARDEN
1983
Ellen and Shepherd Ogden
Catalog: $1, 112 pp., color and black-and-

white illustrations

A seed catalog with a judicious assortment of gardening and cookbooks emphasizing organic methods and freshly harvested fare. Among the titles offered is the award-winning seed-to-table book *The Cook's Garden,* written by the Ogdens, and Shepherd Ogden's *Step-by-Step Organic Vegetable Gardening* and *Step-by-Step Organic Flower Gardening.* See **Garlic,** Heirlooms, **Herbs, Kidstuff,** Organics, **Seeds, Supplies,** Vegetables.
Canada

COUNTRY WETLANDS NURSERY AND CONSULTING
1987
Jo Ann Gillespie
Catalog: $2, 16 pp.
Ms. Gillsepie's firm provides consultation, design, and plant material for wetland restoration and management. The ten books and brochures in this catalog emphasize the flora and fauna of Minnesota, Wisconsin, and the greater Midwest. Includes works on ornamental grass, identifying and gardening with midwestern wildflowers, and *Sedges* by Ms. Gillespie. See Grasses, Seeds, Waterscapes, **Wildflowers.**

CROP KING, INC.
1982
Dan Brentlinger
Catalog: $3 (recoverable), 41 pp.
Crop King's hydroponic gardening catalog offers over 150 products for gardening without soil. Includes an introductory video on home hydroponics and a dozen practical titles describing various methods and techniques for this type of cultivation. See **Supplies.**
Canada, Mexico, International

DABNEY HERBS
1986
Davy Dabney
Catalog: $2 (recoverable), 40 pp.
Mr. Dabney's catalog is glorious potpourri (pun intended) of annual and perennial herbs, midwestern native wildflowers, books, teas, botanicals, and herbal and garden accessories. He offers eighty books (two calendars, and a video) on native plants and wildflowers, herbs, cookery, natural health, crafts, and how-to. Recently featured titles included *Growing and Using Scented Geraniums* by Mary Pedie and

Judy and John Lewis, *The New England Herb Gardener* by Patricia Turcotte, *It's About Thyme* by Marge Clark, *The Healing Herbs* by Michael Castleman *(tambien en Espanol, Las Hierbas qui Curan),* and *Southern Herb Growing* by Madeline Hill and Gwen Barclay. See **Herbs,** Perennials.
Canada

THE DAFFODIL MART
1904
Brent and Becky Heath
Catalog: Free, 56 pp.
These third-generation bulb growers offer eighteen titles that are appropriate for home gardeners and collectors concerning bulb plants. Among the titles that they carry are: *The International Checklist for Hyacinths and Miscellaneous Bulbs* compiled by the Royal Dutch Bulb Growers Association, the Royal Horticultural Society's *International Daffodil Checklist,* Katherine Whiteside's *Classic Bulbs: Hidden Treasures for the Modern Garden, Daffodils for Show and Garden* by the American Daffodil Society, *Narcissus* by M. J. Brown, and a book that the Heaths coauthored, *Daffodils For American Gardeners.* See **Bulbs, Supplies.**

DAN'S GARDEN SHOP
1977
Dan Youngberg
Catalog: Free
Twenty-one titles, most published by Rodale Press, on organic methods, seed starting, natural insect and disease control, ornamental grasses, and fruit-bearing plants. Guarantees satisfaction; will issue refund. See Organics, **Seeds, Supplies,** Vegetables.

DAVE & SUE'S AQUARIUMS & GREENHOUSE
1983
David Lowman
Catalog: $1 (recoverable), 18 pp., illustrations and black-and-white photographs
This catalog of supplies, tools, and plant material for the bonsai artist and enthusiast includes over a dozen books—some instructive, some appreciative—on bonsai. Selections include *Successful Bonsai Growing* by Peter Adams, *The Complete Book of Bonsai* by Harry Tomlinson, and *The Essentials of Bonsai* by the editors of Shufunomoto. Guarantees satisfac-

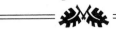
tion; will issue refund. See **Supplies, Trees.**
Canada, Mexico, International

DAYLILY DISCOUNTERS
1988
Tom Allin and Doug Glick
Catalog: $1, 76 pp., color photographs
The focus here is on two hundred daylily culti-
vars. They also offer four books about hemerocal-
lis: *A Passion for Daylilies* by Sidney Eddison,
Daylily Encyclopedia edited by Steve Webber,
Hemerocallis: The Daylily by R. W. Munson, Jr.,
and *Daylilies: The Perfect Perennial* by Lewis and
Nancy Hill. See **Daylilies.**
Mexico, International

DEGIORGI SEED COMPANY
1911
Duane Thompson
Catalog: $2 (recoverable), 75 pp.
The Thompsons offer ten titles in their exten-
sive seed catalog, including *Broccoli & Com-
pany, The Carrot Cookbook, Corn: Meal &
More, Glorious Garlic, The Elegant Onion,* and
The New Zucchini Cookbook. See **Garlic,**
Grasses, Herbs, **Kidstuff,** Seeds, Vegetables.

DOROTHY BIDDLE SERVICE
1936
Lynne Johnson Dodson
**Catalog: 2 FCS, 20 pp., black-and-white
photographs**
Ms. Dodson is the granddaughter of the company's founder, Dorothy Biddle, a nationally
known flower arranger. The catalog includes
eighteen practical titles on cut and dried flower
arranging, design, techniques, and crafts. See
Supplies.

ECO ENTERPRISES
1972
Terri Mitchell
Catalog: Free, 53 pp.
Eco Enterprises' *Hydroponic Guidebook and
Catalog* includes twenty books about growing
plants in soilless cultures. Titles include *Hy-
droponics Simplified* by Tom Colcheedas, *Hy-
droponics–Soilless Gardening: A Beginner's
Guide* by Richard Nicholls, *Hydroponic Home
Food Gardens* by Howard M. Resh, and *More
Food From Your Garden* by Jacob R. Mittleider.
Also offers two videotapes on hydroponic
methods and a dozen plans for creating sys-
tems, including one whose major component is

empty coffee cans. See **Supplies.**
Canada, Mexico, International

ELIXIR FARM BOTANICALS
1989
Lavinia McKinney
**Catalog: $2, 6 pp., illustrations and color
photographs**
Elixir Farm Botanicals is an organic biodynamic partnership (that describes their methods, too) of land
and plant stewards located in the Missouri Ozarks.
Elixir Farm's focus is Chinese and indigenous medicinal plants. Features six titles, including *Herbal Emis-
saries* (a guide to gardening, herbal wisdom, and
well-being), *Herbal Renaissance,* and *Echinacea,* all by
Steven Foster. See **Herbs, Organics, Seeds.**
Canada, Mexico, International

FAR NORTH GARDENS
1962
K. J. Combs
Catalog: $2 (recoverable), 52 pp.
The "Better Books for Better Gardeners" section
includes eighteen how-to and cultural titles on
rock gardening, alpines, ferns, shade gardening,
and perennials, as well as twenty volumes from
the Brooklyn Botanic Garden's Handbook series.
Botany for Gardeners, Seeds of Woody Plants, and
The Bernard Harkness Seedlist Handbook are
among the reference books frequently thumbed
by Ms. Combs and described in a separate section
of her catalog. See **Bulbs,** Grasses, Perennials,
Seeds, Wildflowers.
Canada, Mexico, International

FEDCO SEEDS
1979
Joann Clark
Catalog: $2, 46 pp., illustrations
The book and poster section of this horticultural
and agricultural cooperative's catalog includes
twenty-five titles, including practical works on
seedmanship, market gardening, and organic
techniques and practices. See Heirlooms, Garlic,
Herbs, Organics, **Seeds,** Vegetables.

FEDCO TREES
1979
Roberta and John Bunker
Catalog: $2, 32 pp., illustrations
The book section of this catalog from the
Fedco co-op includes twenty titles about trees,
fruits, and berries for the home orchardist and
gardener, *A Garden of Conifers: Introduction*

and Selection by Robert A. Obrizok, *The Grafter's Handbook* by R. J. Garner, and *One Hundred Tree Myths* by Dr. Alex Shigo. See **Conifers, Fruit,** Heirlooms, Trees.
Shipping season: February and April

FILAREE FARM
1977
Ron Engeland
Catalog: $2, 42 pp.
Ron Engeland grows garlic using organic methods. The Filaree catalog features four titles, including his own highly regarded growing and cultural guide *Growing Great Garlic* (and a thirty-two-page supplement published in 1995). Other titles offered: *A Garlic Testament* by Stanley Crawford, *Onions and Garlic Forever* by Louis Van Denven, and Fulder and Blackwood's *Garlic: Nature's Original Remedy.* Also sells reproductions of Jim Anderson's illustrations from earlier Filaree catalogs. See **Garlic,** Organics.
Canada, Mexico, International

FUNGI PERFECTI
1979
Paul Stamets
Catalog: $3, 80 pp., black-and-white illustrations and photographs
Fungi Perfecti cultivates high-quality, certified organic gourmet and medicinal mushrooms. The catalog offers thirty titles, including books about growing mushrooms (Mr. Stamets's *Growing Gourmet and Medicinal Mushrooms* among them), cookbooks, field identification and taxonomy guides, general interest books, and technical works. See **Garlic, Kidstuff,** Organics, **Supplies.**
Canada, Mexico, International

GARDEN CITY SEEDS
1982
Susan Wall-MacLane
Catalog: $1, 75 pp.
Garden City Seeds is a subsidiary organization of the nonprofit Down Home Project, Inc., which supports self-reliant living. The catalog includes sixteen titles on seedmanship, organic methods of gardening in cold climates, sustainable agriculture, and nonchemical pest control. See **Garlic,** Grasses, Herbs, Organics, **Seeds, Supplies,** Vegetables.
Canada

GARDEN WORKS
1978
Robin Wilkerson
Catalog: $1, 24 pp.
Garden Works lists five hundred previously owned, out-of-print gardening and landscape design books. Guarantees satisfaction; will issue a refund.
Canada, Mexico, International

GARDENIMPORT
Dugald Cameron
Catalog: $4, 52 pp. color photographs
A Canadian perennial nursery that offers a brief selection of books, notably *Practical Guide to Gardening in Canada,* created by the Royal Horticultural Society and edited by Trevor Cole for Canadian gardeners. See **Bulbs,** Grasses, **Peonies,** Perennials.
Canada

GARY WAYNER, BOOKSELLER
1976
Gary Wayner
Catalog: $1, 12 pp.
Mr. Wayner specializes in books of technical natural history with an emphasis on floristics. His catalog of 625 titles (updated quarterly) is organized alphabetically by author. Guarantees satisfaction; will issue refund.
Canada, Mexico, International

GARY W. WOOLSON, BOOKSELLER
1966
Gary W. Woolson
Catalog: Free, 8 pp.
A Maine bookseller who specializes in books on the state but who also gives the rest of us a nod of recognition with a list of 155 previously owned hardbound volumes on horticulture, gardening, and art with the garden as its subject. Guarantees satisfaction; will issue refund.

GOODWIN CREEK GARDENS
1977
Jim and Dotti Becker
Catalog: $1, 39 pp.
Goodwin Creek's "Gardener's Bookshelf" in their plant and seed catalog includes twenty-five titles. Led by *An Everlasting Garden,* coauthored by the Beckers, subjects include growing herbs, postharvest uses of herbs (culinary, domestic, and medicinal), gardening to attract wildlife, and five of the handbooks published by the Brooklyn Botanic Garden. See **Herbs, Perennials, Seeds.**

GOSSLER FARMS NURSERY
See **Trees**.

THE GOURMET GARDENER™
1986
Christopher E. Combest
Catalog: $2, 30 pp.
The "Book Nook" of this seed catalog for gardeners who like to eat what they grow offers a dozen titles. Features harvest-related condiment and sauce cookbooks that use herbs, edible flowers, and vegetables as key ingredients. Titles have included *The Forgotten Art of Flower Cookery* by Leona Woodring Smith, *Pestos! Cooking with Herb Paste* by Dorothy Rankin, and *Natural Herb Gardening* by Marie-Louise Kreuter. See Garlic, **Herbs**, Seeds, Vegetables.
Canada, Mexico

GOURMET MUSHROOMS
Catalog: $1, 4 pp.
Offers three mushroom titles: *A Morel Hunter's Companion,* by Nancy Smith Weber, *Mushrooms Demystified* by David Arora, and *The Mushroom Feast* by Jane Grigson. See **Garlic**.

GREEN HORIZONS
1970
Sherry Miller
Catalog: LSASE., 12 pp.
Specialists in the seeds of Texas wildflowers, their booklist reflects their botanical interests. Green Horizons lists thirty practical works about how to cultivate wildflowers, garden flowers, cacti, herbs, trees, shrubs, woody vines, fruits, vegetables, and grasses in the Lone Star State. Also field and identification guides to the flora of Texas and Louisiana. See Grasses, Seeds, **Wildflowers**.
Canada, Mexico, International

GREER GARDENS
1955
Harold E. Greer
Catalog: $3, 148 pp., illustrations and color photographs
This nursery's catalog includes 180 books and two dozen videos. Areas of concentration: rhododendrons and azaleas (including *Azaleas* by Fred Galle, and *Rhododendron Species: Volumes I - IV* by H. H. Davidian), bonsai culture (*Keep Your Bonsai Alive and Well* by Herb L. Gustafson), gardens to visit (*Complete Guide to North American Gardens: The Northeast* by William Mulligan), perennials, garden and landscape design (*Right Plant, Right Place* by Nicola Ferguson), propagation and pruning, rock gardening, trees and shrubs (*Manual of Woody Landscape Plants: Their Identification, Ornamental Characteristics, Culture, and Propagation* by Dr. Michael A. Dirr and *Plants That Merit Attention, Volume I: Trees* edited by Janet Meakin Poor III), and water and shade gardening. See **Conifers**, **Grasses**, **Peonies**, Fruit, Perennials, **Rhododendrons**, **Trees**.
Canada, Mexico, International

HARDSCRABBLE ENTERPRISES
1985
Paul Goland
Catalog: $3 (recoverable), 4 pp.
This specialist in shiitake mushroom spawn kits offers an information package and several books, including *Shiitake Growers Handbook, Growing Shiitake Mushrooms in a Continental Climate, Year-Round Shiitake Cultivation in the North,* and *Mushrooms Demystified* by David Arora. See **Garlic**, **Supplies**.

HARMONY FARM SUPPLY AND NURSERY
1980
Kate Burroughs and David Henry
Catalog: $2, 127 pp.
Ms. Burroughs and Mr. Henry publish a full-range catalog for the organic gardener and farmer. The book section describes over 120 titles in agriculture, general gardening, xeric gardening, books of special interest to gardeners in the West, organic methods, natural pest control, fruit, nut, and berry culture, herbs, and horticultural practices. See **Kidstuff**, Organics, **Supplies**.
Canada

HEIRLOOM GARDEN® SEEDS
1979
Warren Raysor
Catalog: Free, 37 pp., illustrations and black-and-white photographs
A seed house for heirloom herbs and flowers that also offers a dozen books. Recent selections included *The Heirloom Garden* by Jo Ann Gardner, *Saving Seeds: The Gardener's Guide to Growing and Storing Vegetable and Flower Seeds* by Marc Rogers, and *Flowers That Last Forever* and *Growing and Using Herbs Successfully* by Betty E. M. Jacobs. See Heirlooms, Herbs, **Kidstuff**, Seeds.
Canada

HEIRLOOM OLD GARDEN ROSES
1986
John and Louise Clements
Catalog: $5, 112 pp., color photographs
The Clement's catalog offers 650 heirloom and old garden roses. Their comprehensive rose book section includes *The Rose Expert* by Dr. D. G. Hessayon, *Roses* by Peter Beales, *In Search of Lost Roses*, by Christopher Thomas, *The Heritage of the Rose* by David Austin, *Landscaping with Antique Roses* by Liz Druitt and G. Michael Shoup, and *Roses of America: The Brooklyn Botanic Garden's Guide to Our National Flower* by Stephen Scaniello and Tanya Blayard. See Heirlooms, **Roses**.

HENRIETTA'S NURSERY
1958
Jerry and Sylvia Hardaway
Catalog: $1, 48 pp., black-and-white photographs
The Hardaways grow twelve hundred types of cactus and succulents. They offer twelve titles for the enthusiast and the specialist, including *Cactaceae* by Britton and Ross, *Cacti of the Southwest* by Earle, *Cacti of the United States and Canada* by Lyman Benson, and *The Sansevieria Trifasciata Varieties* by Juan Chahinian. See **Cactus**.

HOLLAND WILDFLOWER FARM
1985
Bob and Julie Holland
Catalog: $4.25, 32 pp., illustrations
Price list: LSASE (with 2 FCS), 4 pp.
The Hollands sell nursery propagated wildflowers and seeds, grown and harvested on their farm in the Ozarks. Their "Flower Books We Love" (and sell) section includes four general interest books for the identification and cultivation of wildflowers, and a pair of books for their area: *Trees, Shrubs, and Vines of Arkansas* and *Wildflowers of Arkansas*, by Carl G. Hunter. See Herbs, Seeds, **Wildflowers**.
Canada, Mexico, International

HYDROFARM
1977
Stuart R. Dvorin
Catalog: Free, 28 pp., color photographs
This catalog, preaching the gospel according to hydroponics, includes *Hydroponics for the Home Gardener* by Stuart Kenyon, and four other titles about growing plants without soil.

See **Supplies**.
Canada

I.F.M. PRODUCTS FOR NATURAL AGRICULTURE
1983
Phillip Unterschuetz
Catalog: Free, 55 pp.
I. F. M. specializes in ecologically sound practices for garden, farm, and orchard; its catalog's book section includes *Growing Organically* by Paul Lanphere and *Common Sense Pest Control* by Olkowski, Daar, and Olkowski. The balance of the list, including University of California IPM manuals, presupposes an avid interest in specific crops. See Organics, **Supplies**.
Canada, Mexico, International

J. L. HUDSON, SEEDSMAN
1911
Catalog: $1, 95 pp., illustrations. Four supplements (published at irregular intervals): $2
Hudson's catalog offers fifteen hundred varieties of open-pollinated seed for flowers, vines, herbs, shrubs, vegetables, and other plant material (much of it rare or unusual) from worldwide sources. Their booklist, like their seed lists is a blend of the common, the esoteric, and the exotic. Recent listings among their two dozen titles included *How Plants Get Their Names* by L. H. Bailey, *How to Grow More Vegetables* by John Jeavons, *Ethnobotany of the Hopi* by A. F. Whiting, *Seed Propagation of Native California Plants* by Dara Emery, and *The Useful Plants of West Tropical Africa* by J. M. Dalziel. See Garlic, Heirlooms, Herbs, **Seeds**, Vegetables.

JOHNNY'S SELECTED SEEDS
1973
Robert L. Johnston, Jr.
Catalog: Free, 136 pp., color photographs
Within this extensive seed and supply catalog is "Johnny's Library," a selection of three dozen titles that includes practical modern works on gardening basics: seed starting, organic methods, vegetable breeding, composting, market gardening, field guides to pests, and developing and using cutting and herb gardens. Guarantees satisfaction; will replace or issue refund. See Garlic, Grasses, Heirlooms, Herbs, Organics, **Seeds**, **Supplies**, Vegetables.
Canada, Mexico, International

K & L CACTUS & SUCCULENT NURSERY
1970
Keith and Lorraine Thomas
Catalog: $2 (recoverable), 28 pp., black-and-white and color photographs
The Thomases specialize in flowering desert and jungle cactus and succulents. Their catalog includes fourteen titles that they consider to be the best works in these areas including *The Encyclopedia of Cacti* by Gotz and Groner, *Haworthia and Astrolaba* by John Pilbeam, and *Cacti and Succulents* by Clive Innes. See **Cactus**, Seeds.
Canada, Mexico, International

KILGORE SEED COMPANY
1918
J. H. Hunziker
Catalog: $1 (recoverable), 24 pp.
Kilgore specializes in bulbs and seeds for gardeners in Florida and areas with similar growing conditions. The catalog includes nine identification guides and how-to works on the state's flora and fauna written by Lewis Maxwell. See Garlic, Herbs, **Seeds**, Vegetables.
Canada, Mexico, International

KLEHM NURSERY
1852
Kit C. Klehm
Catalog: $4 (recoverable), 104 pp., color illustrations and photographs
Five generations of Klehms have tilled the soil and tended plants. Their catalog is a work of art blending full-color photographs, watercolors, and exceptional design. Offers twenty-two titles on practical, cultural, and design considerations in the garden, including works on particular perennials, daylilies, hybrid and tree peonies, and hosta. See **Daylilies, Hosta, Peonies**, Perennials.
Canada, Mexico, International

LANDSCAPE BOOKS
1972
Jane W. Robie
Catalog: $5, 112 pp.
Ms. Robie is a certified landscape designer and bookseller. Her catalog includes twelve hundred hard-to-find new, out-of-print, scarce, and rare books on landscape architecture and garden history. Will search for books and help in establishing and completing collections. See Heirlooms.
Canada, Mexico, International

LARNER SEEDS
1978
Judith Lowry
Catalog: $2, 45 pp., illustrations
The publication section includes forty titles. Emphasis is on the natural history of California, edible plants, and traditional wisdom rooted in the native landscape. Books published by the Redwood City Seed Company and Larner Seeds' own "Notes on Natives" pamphlets are included. Larner's original series contains individual titles on California wildflowers, native grasses, food plants, wild-crafting, and coastal gardening. See **Grasses**, Seeds, **Trees, Wildflowers**.

LE JARDIN DU GOURMET
See Garlic, Herbs, Seeds, **Vegetables**.

LILYPONS WATER GARDENS®
1930
Charles Thomas
Catalog: Free, 100 pp., color photographs
The Lilypons catalog, a compendium of supplies and live material for water gardening offers seventeen books and videos including *Water Gardens* by Charles B. Thomas and Jacqueline Heriteau and *Water Gardens for Plants and Fish* by Charles B. Thomas, Lilypons' president. Other selections include *Water Gardening Basics* by William Uber, *The Hobbyists Guide to Successful Pond Keeping* by David A. Pool, *The Tetra Encyclopedia of Koi* edited by Anne McDowall, and two original videos about installing, stocking, and maintaining ponds. See Supplies, **Waterscapes**.

LOUISIANA NURSERY
1950
Dalton E. Durio
Bamboo and ornamental grass catalog: $3, 12 pp., Crinums and other rare bulbs: $3.50, 72 pp. Daylilies, Louisiana iris, and other irises: $4, 100 pp. Hydrangeas: $3.50. Magnolias: $6, 146 pp. Fruiting trees: $3.50, 60 pp. (all recoverable)
Louisiana Nursery occupies a fifty-six-acre complex that was founded by Ken Durio. Five family members, all trained horticulturists, are currently involved in the business. The Durios publish six specialty catalogs. "Bulbs" lists nine titles. "Daylilies," offers nineteen books, including *Daylilies: Everything You Always Wanted to Know About Daylilies* published by the American Hemerocallis Society, *The Louisiana Iris:*

The History and Culture of Five Native American Species and Their Hybrids by Marie Caillet and Joseph K. Mertzweiller, and *Passalong Plants* by Steve Bender and Felder Rushing. "Fruiting Trees" lists fourteen books, including *Citrus: How To Select, Grow and Enjoy* by Richard Ray and Lance Walheim, *Growing Fruits and Nuts in the South: The Definitive Guide* by William D. Adams and Thomas R. Leroy, *Temperate-Zone Pomology* by Melvin N. Westwood, and *Uncommon Fruits Worthy of Attention: A Gardener's Guide* by Lee Reich. "Magnolias" lists thirty books, including *The Encyclopedia of Ornamental Grasses: How To Grow and Use Over 250 Beautiful and Versatile Plants* by John Greenlee and Derek Fell, *Japanese Maples* by J. D. Vertrees, *The Trees of Georgia and Adjacent States* by Claud L. Brown and Katherine Kirkman, and *The World of Magnolias* by Dorothy Calloway. See **Bulbs, Daylilies, Fruit, Grasses, Iris,** Trees.
Canada, Mexico, International

MCALLISTER'S IRIS GARDEN
1991
Sharon McAllister
Catalog: $1 (recoverable), 24 pp.
Ms. McAllister's catalog of 150 irises is primarily for collectors and aspiring hybridizers. She lists two thirty-two-page Iris booklets that she has written, "Hybridizing" and "Varietal Tips for Hybridizers." See **Iris.**
Canada, International

MATRIX GROUP, INC.
1985
James T. Orrico
Catalog: Free
Matrix offers thirty half-hour videocassettes in The Home Gardener series, hosted by John Lenanton. This telecourse includes individual segments on soils, plant foods, growing vegetables, landscape design, lawns and ground covers, water usage, shrubs and vines, trees, roses, pests, diseases, shade gardens, fruiting plants and trees, propagation, bulbs and succulents, and greenhouses. A companion book, *The Home Gardener,* written by Mr. Lenanton, is characterized as an adjunct to the series or as a stand-alone reference.
Canada, International

MELLINGER'S
1927

Jean Steiner
Catalog: Free, 104 pp., color photographs
Mellinger's home, farm, and garden catalog describes over four thousand garden-related items, seed, and nursery stock. The sixty titles in their "Books Make a Difference in Gardening Success" section include: general reference, greenhouse culture, nursery operation, organic gardening, hydroponics, propagation, perennials, herbs, and twenty titles in the "Garden Way Country Wisdom Bulletin" series. See **Furniture, Kidstuff,** Perennials, **Seeds, Supplies,** Wildflowers.
Canada, Mexico, International

MILAEGER'S GARDENS
1960
Kevin D. Milaeger
Catalog: $1, 84 pp., color photographs
Milaeger's "Perennial Wishbook" includes eleven hundred plant varieties and thirty books dealing primarily with perennials and their myriad garden uses. Recent catalogs featured *Bloom's Hardy Perennials* by Alan Bloom, *Gardening with Color* by Mary Keane, *The American Mixed Border* by Ann Lovejoy, *Perennials for American Gardens* by Ruth Clausen and Nicolas Ekstrom, *Designing with Perennials* and *Color Echoes* both by Pamela J. Harper, *American Border Gardens* by Melanie Fleischmann, *The Gardener's Guide to Growing Hellebores* by Graham Rice and Elizabeth Strangman, and *Wall Plants & Climbers* by Ursula Buchan. See **Grasses, Kidstuff,** Peonies, **Perennials.**

MOOSE GROWERS SUPPLY
1970
Bill Getty and Gene Frey
Catalog: $1, 40 pp.
Formerly Moose Tubers, this division of Fedco continues to offer seed potatoes but also sells books, supplies, and cover crops. Nine titles offered, including *Feed the Soil* by Edwin McLeod, *The Potato Field Manual* edited by Ulrich, Kleinschmidt, and Sandvol, *Natural Insect and Disease Control* by Ellis and Bradley, and *Solar Gardening* by Leandre and Gretchen Vogel Poisson. See **Garlic,** Organics, **Supplies,** Vegetables.

MOUNTAIN MAPLES
1989
Don and Nancy Fiers
Catalog: $1, 36 pp.
The Fierses specialize in *Acer palmatum,* cultivars

of other *Acer* species, beech trees, and Chinese tree peonies. They offer a select group of books and videos including *Japanese Maples* by J. D. Vertrees, *Maples of the World* by D. M. van Gelderen et al., *Bonsai: Its Art, Science, History, and Philosophy* by Deborah Koreshoff, and *Dream Window: Reflections on the Japanese Garden*, a video coproduced by the Smithsonian Institution and Kajimavision, Tokyo. See **Peonies**, **Trees**.

MUSHROOMPEOPLE
1976
Albert Bates
Catalog: Free, 8 pp.
This mail-order mushroom emporium sells tools, spawn, books, and videos for the home mushroom enthusiast. Their "Mushroomer's Bookshelf" describes (in varying degrees of detail) over one hundred books and tapes including *The Shiitake Way* by Jennifer Snyder, *Growing Shiitake in a Continental Climate* by Joe Krawczyck and Mary Ellen Kozak, *The Shiitake Growers Handbook* by Paul Przybylowicz and John Donoghue, and Paul Stamets's *The Mushroom Cultivator* (co-authored with J. S. Chilton) and *Growing Gourmet and Medicinal Mushrooms*. Also rents audio and videotapes from their own "Masters of Modern Shiitake" series. See **Garlic**, Supplies.
Canada, International

MYRON KIMNACH–BOOKS ON SUCCULENTS
1984
Myron Kimnach
Catalog: Free, 28 pp.
A bookseller whose field of concentration is cactus and other succulents, Mr. Kimnach offers 350 new and used books, a substantial number of journals, and out-of-print catalogs from specialty nurseries.
Canada, Mexico, International

NATIVE AMERICAN SEED
1986
Jan and Bill Neiman
Catalog: $1, 20 pp., color photographs
The Neimans specialize in the native seed of wildflowers and grasses harvested from the gene pool of the Texas-Oklahoma bioregion. They offer thirteen books, including *Wildflowers of Texas* by Greyata Ajilvsgi, *Wildflowers of the Texas Hill Country* by Marshall Enquist, *Native Texas Plants Landscaping: Region by Region*, by

Sally Wasowski and Andy Wasowski, and *Texas Range Plants* by Stephan L. Hatch and Jennifer Pluhar. See Grasses, Seeds, **Wildflowers**.

NATIVE SEEDS/SEARCH
1983
Angelo Joaquin, Jr.
Catalog: $1, 56 pp.
Native Seeds/SEARCH is a nonprofit seed conservation organization with expertise in the traditional native food plants of the Southwest. The publications section offers forty titles, including specialty cookbooks utilizing the crops of this area and books on gardening and seed saving that emphasize desert and drought gardening and ethnobiology. See Garlic, **Kidstuff**, Seeds, **Vegetables**, Wildflowers.
Canada, Mexico, International

NATURAL GARDENER'S CATALOG
1985
John Dromgoole, Maggie Burnett, and Dolores Nice
Catalog: $1, 48 pp.
The "Organic Library" section of this catalog describes twenty titles of interest to the organically minded gardener on seed starting, composting, companion planting, and *Lessons in Nature* by Malcolm Beck, founder of Garden-ville. Also offer twenty-four titles in the "Garden Way Country Wisdom" series. See Organics, **Supplies**.

NEW ENGLAND WILD FLOWER SOCIETY
1900
Catalog: $2.50, 22 pp.
NEWFS promotes the conservation of temperate North American plants through horticulture, education, research, habitat preservation, and advocacy. In addition to the native (to eastern North America) seeds and spores in their catalog, they offer thirty books covering general interest gardening, wildflower/native plant identification, and wildflower/native plant gardening. A selection of their own publications include *The Garden in the Woods Cultivation Guide* by William E. Brumback and David R. Longland, *Meadows and Meadow Gardening* by the NEWFS staff, *Propagation of Wild Flowers* by Will C. Curtis, and *Easy Native Plants* by the NEWFS staff. See **Horticultural Societies**, **Kidstuff**, Seeds, **Wildflowers**.

NICHOLS GARDEN NURSERY
1950
Rose Marie Nichols McGee

Catalog: Free, 72 pp.
The "Rural Bookstore" section of this eclectic catalog of herbs (seeds and plants)and vegetable and flower seeds includes an appropriately eclectic selection of fifty books such as: *Deer Resistant Ornamental Plants for the Northern United States* by Pamela Gehn Stephens, *Drip Irrigation* by Robert Kourik, *Herbs: How To Select Grow and Enjoy* by Norma Jean Lathrop, *Knott's Handbook for Vegetable Growers* by Oscar A. Lorenz and Donald N. Maynard, and *The Scented Lavender Book* by Lois Vickers. See **Garlic, Herbs,** Organics, **Seeds,** Supplies, **Vegetables,** Wildflowers.

NORTH STAR GARDENS
See **Fruit.**

NORTHWIND FARMS
1983
Paula C. Oliver
Catalog: $1. Brochure: LSASE
Ms. Oliver is the publisher of a bimonthly trade journal, *The Business of Herbs.* The Northwind Farms catalog offers sixty-five titles, reviewed in rich detail, on growing herbs, the medicinal, domestic, and therapeutic use of herbs, the market gardening of herbs and other plants, aromatherapy, flower crafts, and the selling of crafts created from natural materials. Recent offerings have included *Artistically Cultivated Herbs* by Elise Felton, *The Complete Geranium: Cultivation, Cooking and Crafts* by Susan Conder, *Growing Great Garlic* by Ron Engeland, *The Herbal Tea Garden: Planning, Planting, Harvesting and Brewing* by Marietta Marshall Marcin, and *Using Herbs in The Landscape* by Debra Kirkpatrick. See **Herbs.**
Canada, Mexico, International

NORTHWIND NURSERY AND ORCHARDS
1983
Frank Foltz
Catalog: $1 (recoverable), 35 pp., illustrations
The Foltz family (nine at last count) raise northern-hardy, organically grown fruit trees. Their book section includes fifty titles concerning organic gardening, insect and disease control, seedmanship, orcharding and fruit growing, propagation, grafting, pruning, herbs, harvest storage, fresh-fare cookbooks, and self-sufficiency skills. See **Fruit,** Organics,

Supplies, Trees.
Canada, Mexico, International

PARADISE WATER GARDENS
1950
Paul Stetson, Jr.
Catalog: $3 (recoverable), 66 pp., color illustrations, black-and-white and color photographs
This New England water gardener offers twenty-nine books and videos on water gardening (plants, construction, design, and fish), including a dozen titles published by TetraPress. See Supplies, **Waterscapes.**
Canada

PEACEFUL VALLEY FARM & GARDEN SUPPLY
1976
Kathleen Fenton
Catalog: Free, 120 pp., illustrations and black-and-white photographs
Peaceful Valley's specialty is tools (information being a tool, too) and supplies for organic gardeners and farmers. There are two book sections in the catalog: natural pest management includes *Shepherd's Purse Organic Pest Control Handbook* by Pest Publications, among its seven titles; the general list includes twenty-two titles on biodynamic culture, soil management, and organic methods, including *Start with the Soil* by Grace Gershuny, *The New Organic Grower* and *Four Season Harvest* by Eliot Coleman, and *The Chemical Free Lawn* by Warren Schultz. See **Garlic,** Grasses, Organics, Seeds, **Supplies, Wildflowers.**
Canada

PEN Y BRYN NURSERY
1946
Catalog: $2.95, 58 pp., illustrations
A nursery for pre-bonsai, exotic trees, and Satsuki azaleas. Offers fifteen appropriate titles including *A Brocade Pillow: Azaleas of Old Japan* translated by John Greech, *Bonsai with American Trees* by Masakuni Kawasumi, *The Bonsai Workshop* and *Keep Your Bonsai Alive and Well* by Herb Gustafson, and six books published by the Brooklyn Botanic Garden. See Conifers, **Rhododendrons, Supplies, Trees.**

PERENNIAL PLEASURES NURSERY OF VERMONT
1980
Judith and Rachel Kane

Catalog: $3 (recoverable), 64 pp.

The Kanes are period garden specialists. The book section of their seed and plant catalog includes twenty-eight titles, reference and practical works pertaining to garden history, historic re-creation, growing herbs, gardening in special conditions, and gardening for special uses, e.g., plant dyes, fragrances. See Grasses, Heirlooms, Herbs, Organics, **Perennials, Seeds**.

PINETREE GARDEN SEEDS
1979
Dick Meiners
Catalog: Free (outside U.S., $1.50), 192 pp.
Pinetree began as a company offering vegetable seeds for the home gardener. Their catalog now includes 225 titles from general and specialty publishers on gardening, country craft, cookery, and self-sufficiency. Also carries seventy "Country Wisdom Bulletins" published by Garden Way. See Garlic, **Herbs, Kidstuff**, Organics, **Seeds, Supplies, Vegetables**.

PLANTS OF THE SOUTHWEST
1977
Gail Haggard
Catalog: $3.50, 103 pp., color photographs
Plants of the Southwest offers the seeds and live plants of 450 trees, shrubs, wildflowers, chilies, vegetables, and ornamental grasses that are native to or have adapted to the conditions of the American Southwest. Ms. Haggard offers fifty books and videos organized into three categories: guides, ecology, and growing and design. Among the titles offered are *Flowers of the Southwest Mountains* by Amberger and Janish, *Woody Plants of the Southwest* by Samuel H. Lamb, *Wildflowers of the Western Plains* by Zoe Merriman Kirkpatrick, *Gathering the Desert* by Gary Paul Nabhan, *Gardening Success with Difficult Soils* by Scott Ogden, *How to Grow Native Plants of Texas and the Southwest* by Jill Nokes, *The Xeriscape Flower Gardener* by Jim Knopf, and an Australian-made video series, *The Global Gardener*, with Bill Mollison. See **Grasses**, Heirlooms, Seeds, Trees, **Vegetables, Wildflowers**.

PRAIRIE MOON NURSERY
1982
Alan Wade
Catalog: $2, 30 pp.
The book section of the Prairie Moon catalog contains twenty-three titles on the culture and care of species indigenous to Minnesota and the upper midwestern United States. Mr. Wade's selection includes *Edible Plants of the Prairie* and *Medicinal Wild Plants of the Prairie* by Kelly Kindscher, *Ferns of Minnesota* by Rolla Tryon, *Grasses of Wisconsin* and *Spring Flora of Wisconsin* by Norman Fassett, *Sunflower Species of the United States* by Charlie Rogers, Tommy Thompson, and Gerald Seiler, *How To Manage Small Prairie Fires* by Wayne R. Pauly, and *Landscaping for Wildlife* by Carol L. Henderson. See **Grasses**, Organics, Seeds, Trees, **Wildflowers**.

PRAIRIE NURSERY
1972
Neil Diboll
Catalog: $3, 48 pp., color photographs
Mr. Diboll propagates and preserves native wildflowers, grasses, and shrubs, with emphasis on those found in the upper Midwest. Prairie's "Best of the Books" contains seventeen reference and how-to titles on tallgrass prairie gardening, landscaping with natives, identification guides for wildflowers, and regional titles for Illinois and Wisconsin. Featured titles include *Wildflowers of the Tallgrass Prairie* by Sylvan T. Runkel and Dean M. Roosa, *Grasses: An Identification Guide* by Lauren Brown, *Prairie Propagation Handbook* by Harold W. Rock, *Tallgrass Prairie Wildflowers: A Field Guide* by Doug Ladd and Frank Oberle, and *Landscaping with Wildflowers: An Environmental Approach to Gardening* by Jim Wilson. See Grasses, Seeds, **Wildflowers**.
Canada

PRAIRIE SEED SOURCE
1974
Robert Ahrenhoerster
Catalog: $1, 18 pp.
Mr. Ahrenhoerster's specialty is the seeds of southeastern Wisconsin prairie genotypes and related ecosystem members. The books he offers are *A Sand County Almanac* by Aldo Leopold, *The Prairie World* by David F. Costello, *How to Manage Small Prairie Fires* by Wayne Pauly, *The Prairie Garden* by J. Robert and Beatrice S. Smith, and a pamphlet Mr. Ahrenhoerster coauthored with Trelen Wilson, "Prairie Restoration for the Beginner." See Grasses, Seeds, **Wildflowers**.
Canada, International

RAINBOW GARDENS BOOKSHOP
1977
Charles H. Everson
Catalog: Free, 26 pp. (specify new or out-of-print titles)

Mr. Everson believes Rainbow Gardens to be the largest retail mail-order operation for books on cactus and succulents: bromeliads, sansevierias, orchid cactus, hoyas, baja and desert natives, and the plants of South Africa. Rainbow Gardens issues an annual catalog of four hundred current titles, as well as a separate list of previously owned and out-of-print titles.
Canada, Mexico, International

RAINTREE NURSERY
1974
Sam Benowitz
Catalog: Free, 74 pp., black-and-white and color photographs
This grower of fruits, nuts, berries, and bamboo offers books (and the occasional video) that support the nursery stock that they offer. Titles featured in recent catalogs include *Designing and Maintaining Your Edible Landscape Naturally* by Robert Kourik, *Bamboos* by Recht and Wetterwald, *Uncommon Fruit Worthy of Attention* by Lee Reich, *Grow the Best Blueberries, Grow the Best Strawberries* and *Berries–Raspberry and Black* by Louise Riotte, and *Small Fruits for the Home Garden* by Charles Brun. See **Fruits, Grasses.**

RARE CONIFER FOUNDATION–RARE CONIFER NURSERY
1991
Darshan Mayginnes
Catalog: Free, 28 pp.
The Rare Conifer Foundation is a public charity that works to protect conifers in their native habitats. Six titles selected from the RCF reading list are available through the nursery. Reference works include *Seeds of Woody Plants in North America, The Manual of Cultivated Conifers* by Gerd Krussman, and its pictorial companion, *Conifers.* See **Conifers, Kidstuff, Trees.**
Canada, Mexico, International

RAYMOND M. SUTTON, JR.
1986
Raymond M. Sutton, Jr.
Catalog: Free, 78 pp.
Mr. Sutton's catalog of twelve hundred used, rare, and out-of-print titles is organized by subject. He features fine and illustrated books, as well as works on gardening, bulbs, roses, orchids, wildflowers and florals, trees and shrubs (including forestry), landscaping, garden history, herbals, poisonous plants and medical botany, agriculture and eco-

nomic botany, plant hunting, bibliography, and biography. Under each subject, titles are listed alphabetically by author's name. Supplementary bulletins offer two hundred more titles. Guarantees satisfaction; will issue refund. See Heirlooms.
Canada, Mexico, International

REDWOOD CITY SEED COMPANY
1971
Craig and Sue Dremann
Catalog: $1 (large print, $3), 29 pp.
The Dremanns offer traditional open-pollinated vegetable and herb varieties that have been valued and cultivated by diverse cultures for extended periods of time. Their publications list includes thirty-eight tiles. Leaflets and pamphlets, based on their original research include "Chili Peppers in California," "Peppers Seed Cleaning," and "Radical Vegetable Gardening" by Craig Dremann, and "Peppers: Pickled, Sauces and Salsas" and "Ristras" by Sue Dremann. Books from other sources include *Shifting* by Paul Krapfel, *Sturtevant's Edible Plants of the World.* See Garlic, Heirlooms, Herbs, **Kidstuff**, Seeds, **Vegetables.**
Canada, Mexico, International

RESOURCES: BOOKS FOR PLANT COLLECTORS AND SEED SAVERS
1971
John E. Perkins
Catalog: Free, 24 pp.
A bookseller whose catalog includes seventy titles on sources, seed history and diversity, propagation, names and nomenclature, botany, period gardens, herbs, plant lore, botanical illustration, and plant identification. Recent featured titles included *Cornucopia: A Source Book of Edible Plants* by Stephen Facciola, *The Gardener's Guide to Plant Conservation* by Nina T. Marshall, *Seeds of Change: Five Plants that Transformed Mankind* by Henry Hobhouse, *The Grafter's Handbook* by Robert J. Garner, and *A Garden of Wildflowers: 101 Native Species and How to Grow Them* by Henry W. Art. See Heirlooms.

RICHTERS
1969
Conrad Richter
Catalog: $2, 104 pp., color photographs
Mr. Richter describes himself (and his business) as being in the tradition of botanical plant explorers of the past, traveling five continents in search of herbs from a mosaic of cul-

tures. In addition to six hundred varieties of herb seeds and plants, he offers a comprehensive selection of ninety books and five videos on herb cultivation, preservation, herbalism, and crafts. Recently featured videos included *Cooking with Edible Flowers & Culinary Herbs* by Dr. Sinclair Philip et al., *The Way of Herbs* by Michael Tierra, and *Native American Medicine* by Estela Roman, Patsy Clark, and Theresa Barnes. Books included *The Encyclopedia of Herbs and Their Uses* by Deni Brown, *Growing Herbs from Seed, Cutting, and Root* by Thomas DeBaggio, and *The Herbal Tea Garden: Planning, Planting, Harvesting and Preparing* by Marietta Marshall Marcin. See Heirlooms, **Herbs**, Organics, Seeds, Vegetables.
Canada

RONNIGER'S SEED POTATOES
David Ronniger
Catalog: $2, 40 pp., black-and-white photographs
Ronniger's book section includes *The Potato Garden: A Grower's Guide* by Maggies Oster, *One Potato, Two Potato: A Cookbook* by Constance Bollen and Marlene Blessing, *A Passion for Potatoes* by Lydie Marshall, *Warm Climate Gardening* by Barbara Pleasant, *Successful Cold Climate Gardening* by Lewis Hill, and *Root Cellaring: Natural Cold Storage of Fruits and Vegetables* by Mike and Nancy Bubel. See **Garlic**, Heirlooms, Organics, Seeds, Vegetables.

ROSLYN NURSERY
1984
Dr. Philip Waldman
Catalog: $3, 76 pp., color photographs
Roslyn nursery hybridizes and cultivates rhododendrons and azaleas and grows two thousand varieties of conifers, trees, shrubs, perennials, and grasses. They carry sixty-five titles, with special attention to books about rock gardening, rhododendrons and azaleas, shrubs and trees, and perennials. Highlights for the rhododendron and azalea aficionado (and the aficionado in training) include *Cox's Guide to Choosing Rhododendrons* by Peter A. Cox and Kenneth N. E. Cox, *Rhododendrons* by John Street, *Rhododendron Hybrids* by Homer Salley and Harold Greer, *Getting Started with Rhododendrons and Azaleas* by J. Harold Clarke, *Success with Rhododendrons and Azaleas* by H. Edward Reiley, *Rhododendron Portraits* by D. M. van Gelderen and J.R.P. van Hoey Smith, the three-volume *Rhododendron Species* by H. H. Davidian, *The Larger Rhododendron Species* by Peter A.

Cox, *Azaleas* by Christopher Fairweather, and *Azaleas* by Fred C. Galle. See **Conifers, Perennials, Rhododendrons, Trees.**
Canada, Mexico, International

ROYALL RIVER ROSES AT FOREVERGREEN FARM
1983
David King
Catalog: $1, 48 pp., black-and-white photographs
The Kings of Royall River offer 325 roses in this specialty catalog. Their book and video section is also focused on the genus *Rosa*. Recommended reading for sale includes *The Rose Book* by Maggie Oster, *Easy Roses* by Georgeanne Brennan, and *The Quest for the Rose* and *The Random House Guide to Roses* by Roger Phillips and Martyn Rix. Videos include *Growing Good Roses* by Rayford Clayton Redell, and *The Great Gardens of England,* produced through the courtesy of the National Trust for England. See Heirlooms, **Roses, Supplies.**
Canada

ST. LAWRENCE NURSERIES
1920
Bill and Diana MacKentley
Catalog: Free, 30 pp., illustrations and black-and-white photographs
The MacKentleys, located in Potsdam, New York, grow northern-hardy fruit and nut trees using organic methods. Their catalog lists fourteen titles for home orchardists, including *Designing and Maintaining Your Edible Landscape Naturally* by R. Kourik, *Growing Fruit in the Upper Midwest* by Don Gordon, *Growing Grapes in Minnesota* by the Minnesota Grape Growers Association, *The Orchard Almanac: A Seasonal Guide to Healthy Fruit Trees* by S. Page and J. Smille, *Modern Fruit Science* by N. F. Childers, and *Training and Pruning Apple Trees* by C. G. Forsley. See **Fruit**, Heirlooms, Organics, Trees.
Canada, International

THE SANDY MUSH HERB NURSERY
Fairman and Kate Jayne
circa 1976
Catalog: $6, 73 pp., illustrations
The Jaynes complement their herb and perennial plants and seeds with a small assortment of note cards, herbal accessories, and eighty books covering herb, perennial, and wild-

flower gardening, cookbooks, reference works, reprints of classic herbals, and craft and dye making. Among the titles that they represent are *The Herb Information Handbook* by Ruth D. Wrensch (for the Boerner Botanical Gardens), *Park's Success with Herbs* by Gertrude B. Foster and Rosemary Louden, *The Complete Book of Topiary* by Barbara Gallup and Deborah Reich, and *The Wreath Book* by Rob Pulleyn, which includes many wreaths crafted at Sandy Mush. See **Herbs**, Seeds.

SAROH
1990
George L. Lang
Catalog: Free, 2 pp.

Saroh, providing storage and retrieval of data concerning the care and use of ornamentals, is a multidisk database and search program containing ten thousand plants including eighteen hundred trees, four thousand shrubs, and over four thousand nonwoody plants. Individual listings include current scientific names, previous scientific names, common names, life cycle, foliage cycle, hardiness zones, height at maturity, best site conditions, soil, light, and water requirements, postharvest uses, growth habit, pruning needs, propagation methods, and temperature at which germination should occur.
Canada, Mexico, International

SEED SAVERS EXCHANGE–SEED SAVER PUBLICATIONS
1975
Kent and Diane Whealy
Catalog: $1, 6 pp., black-and-white photographs

Seed Saver Publications is the imprint of Seed Savers Exchange, a nonprofit, grassroots organization of gardeners who are working to save heirloom and endangered vegetable varieties from extinction. Several books are offered, including *Garden Seed Inventory, Seed to Seed: Seed Saving Techniques for the Vegetable Gardener, Fruit, Berry and Nut Inventory, Seed Savers Exchange: The First Ten Years* (articles selected from their membership publications, 1975 through 1985), *The New Organic Grower: A Master's Manual of Tools and Techniques for the Home and Market Gardener* by Eliot Coleman*, and The Vegetable Garden* by Vilmorin-Andrieux, a reprint of a classic work first published in 1885. See Heirlooms, Horticultural Societies, Seeds, Vegetables.

SEEDS BLÜM
1981
Jan Blüm
Catalog: $3 (first-class mail, $4.50), 99 pp.

Ms. Blüm's catalog integrates cultural and practical information about seeds, seed saving, and seedmanship with a strong message about biodiversity and cooperative self-reliance. Ms. Blüm sells 120 titles that are as well described and carefully selected as the seeds she offers. They cover a wide range of topics for growing flowers and vegetables, with a pronounced strength in garden-to-table cookbooks (and other postharvest uses), indigenous crops and methods, organic methods, and specialty gardens. Most titles are found in the section corresponding to their use. See **Garlic**, Heirlooms, Herbs, **Kidstuff**, **Seeds**, Vegetables, Wildflowers.
Canada, Mexico, International

SEEDS OF CHANGE®
Frank Connelly
1989
Catalog: Free, 64 pp., color photographs

Seeds of Change® positions itself as the only national company whose seeds are 100 percent organically grown. The "General Store" section of their catalog offers eight books celebrating the growing of food, organic methods, and cultivating vegetables, including *Seeds of Change: The Living Treasure,* which is the story of this company and the biodiversity movement. Also offered are the back issues of the *Peace Seeds Research and Resource Journal,* featuring the writings of Alan Kapuler. See Heirlooms, Organics, **Seeds**.
Canada, Mexico, International

SEEDS TRUST: HIGH ALTITUDE GARDENS
1984
Bill McDorman
Catalog: Free, 44 pp.

Seventeen practical works on seedmanship, including, Mr. McDorman's *Basic Seed Saving*, organic vegetable gardening, gardening in cold climates, sustainable gardening, and titles of regional interest for the Mountain West. See Garlic, **Grasses**, Heirlooms, Organics, Seeds, **Vegetables**, **Wildflowers**.
Canada, International

SELECT SEEDS–ANTIQUE FLOWERS
1986
Marilyn Barlow

Catalog: $3 (first-class mail, $3.75), 27 pp.
Twenty-two titles, primarily on heirloom and antique gardening and including practical information for the restoration gardener, are available through this flower seed company. Facsimiles of nineteenth-century books in the "America Blossoms" series and reprints of works by Elizabeth Lawrence and Louise Beebe Wilder are among the featured volumes. See Heirlooms, **Seeds**.
Canada

SHADY OAKS NURSERY
1980
Dr. Clayton Oslund
Catalog: $1 (first-class mail, $2.50), 46 pp., color photographs
Shady Oaks offers a brief list of perennial shade gardening books, including *The Genus Hosta* by W. George Schmid, *The Hosta Book* by Paul Aden, *Hostas* by Sandra Bond, *Ferns to Know & Grow* by F. Gordon Foster, and *The Complete Shade Gardener* by George Schenk. See Grasses, **Hosta, Perennials**.

SHEPHERD'S GARDEN SEEDS
1984
Renee Shepherd and Beth Benjamin
Catalog: $1, 108 pp., illustrations
Shepherd and Raboff's *Recipes from a Kitchen Garden* and *More Recipes from a Kitchen Garden* are the featured volumes in this substantial vegetable and flower seed catalog. See **Garlic**, Heirlooms, Herbs, **Kidstuff**, Seeds, Supplies, **Vegetables**.
Canada

SISKIYOU RARE PLANT NURSERY
1963
Baldassare Mineo
Catalog: $2 (recoverable), 74 pp.
Siskiyou lists over eight hundred rock garden and alpine perennials, shrubs, wildflowers, ferns, and dwarf conifers of the four thousand plants under cultivation at the nursery. Offered in the catalog are nine book titles, including *Botany for Gardeners* by Brian Capon, *Miniature Gardens* by Joachim Carl and *Rock Gardening*, by H. Lincoln and Laura Louise Foster. An extensive list of titles about specific genera is available for an LSASE. See **Conifers, Perennials**, Trees.
Canada

SOHN'S FOREST MUSHROOMS
1983
Eileen and Ray Sohn
Catalog: Free, 8 pp.
The ten titles offered in the Sohns' catalog include Przybylowicz and Donohue's *Shiitake Growers Handbook* and pamphlets entitled "Shiitake Inoculation," "Oyster Inoculation," and "Shiitake Indoor Inoculation Wrap Method," all by Ray Sohn. Also offers *Hope's Mushroom Cookbook* by Hope Miller and *The Edible Mushroom* by Margaret Leibenstein. See **Garlic, Supplies**.
Canada, Mexico, International

SOUTHERN EXPOSURE SEED EXCHANGE®
1982
Jeff McCormack
Catalog: $3 (recoverable), 62 pp., illustrations
SESE® features seeds of untreated, open-pollinated, pre-1940 heirloom and family heirloom plants. Offers twenty-five books on starting and saving seeds, plant breeding and propagation, market gardening, livestock, garden-to-table, and vegetable gardening. Selection includes reprints of nineteenth-century works on kitchen gardening. Carries titles from Seed Saver Publications and the American Minor Breeds Conservancy. See **Garlic**, Heirlooms, Herbs, Seeds, **Supplies, Vegetables**.
Canada

SOUTHERN SEEDS
1987
Wae Nelson
Catalog: $1, 40 pp., illustrations
Mr. Nelson specializes in seeds for gardeners in warm to hot climates. Nineteen titles on gardening in Florida and other areas with warm climates, including growing and harvesting plants that produce exotic foods, as well as *The Complete Book of Bananas*. Also carries popular titles on seedmanship, raising vegetables, and organic methods. See Fruit, Garlic, Organics, Seeds, Vegetables.
Canada, Mexico, International

SQUAW MOUNTAIN GARDENS
1983
Joyce Hoekstra, Janis and Arthur Noyes
Catalog: Free, 44 pp.
The Squaw Mountain catalog includes twenty reference works (dictionaries, encyclopedias,

and monographs) on the horticulture and botany of alpine plants and other plants suitable for rock gardens. See **Cactus**.
Canada, International

STIGALL WATER GARDENS
See Supplies, **Waterscapes**.

STRONG'S ALPINE SUCCULENTS
See **Cactus**.

SUNRISE ENTERPRISES
1976
Catalog: $2, 28 pp., black-and-white and color photographs
Sunrise specializes in the seed of oriental vegetables. Their booklist (sixty titles) emphasizes vegetable gardening, garden-to-table cookbooks, the use of herbs, and bilingual (English/Chinese) cookbooks. Featured gardening books include *Grow Your Own Chinese Vegetables* by Geri Harrington, *Tips for the Lazy Gardener* by Linda Tilgner, *Bible Plants for American Gardens* by Eleanor King, and *A to Z Hints for the Vegetable Gardener* by Robert Sanders. See Garlic, Seeds, **Vegetables**.

TERRITORIAL SEED COMPANY
Tom Johns
Catalog: Free, 95 pp.
Territorial's "Bookshelf" holds twenty-four titles, including their own *Territorial Seed Company Gardener's Cookbook*. Their selection covers starting and saving seeds, vegetable gardening, organic methods, growing and using herbs, and postharvest preservation of flowers, fruits, and vegetables. Also offers fifteen low-priced pamphlets published by Cortesia Press covering such gardening basics as design, soil preparation, natural fertilizers, raised beds, beneficial insects, use of cover crops, and how to plant a tree. See **Garlic**, Herbs, **Kidstuff**, Organics, Seeds, **Supplies**, Vegetables.
Canada

THE THOMAS JEFFERSON CENTER FOR HISTORICAL PLANTS
1987
Catalog: $1, 4 pp., black-and-white illustrations and photographs
The TJCHP, operating from Jefferson's home, in Monticello, collects, preserves, and distributes historic plant varieties and promotes an appreciation for the origins of garden plants.

Their annual newsletter, "Twinleaf," features twenty-one books. The book list features reprints of Jefferson's gardening and natural history writings, and of the works of his peers, including Bernard McMahon, author of *The American Gardener's Calendar*, who supplied Jefferson with plants, seeds, and bulbs; pioneer plant hunter William Bartram; and Mary Randolph, sister-in-law of Martha Jefferson. They also offer modern writings about Jefferson, Monticello, and the plants and herbs of eighteenth- and nineteenth-century America. See **Furniture**, Heirlooms, **Seeds**.

TIMBER PRESS
Robert B. Conklin
Catalog: Free, 62 pp., color photographs
Timber Press publishes books on gardening, horticulture, and botany for the advanced gardener and the professional. Their annual catalog (supplements issued seasonally) is written for the home gardener, the nursery, and the book trade. Their 180 titles include works on trees, plant selection, general gardening culture and practices, individual plant species, alpine and rock gardening, landscaping and garden history, noted practitioners, ethnobotany, bonsai, propagation, plant identification, and regional guides for the Pacific Northwest.
Canada

TOMATO GROWERS SUPPLY COMPANY
1984
Linda and Vince Sapp
Catalog: Free, 40 pp., black-and-white illustrations and photographs
The Sapps' seed catalog includes a bushel of tomes about tomatoes: *Terrific Tomatoes* by Mimi Lubberman, *Tomato Diseases*, by John C. Watterson, *The Tomato in America* by Andrew F. Smith, *Tomatoes* by the editors of Garden Way Publishing, *Tomatoes: A Country Garden Cookbook* by Jesse Ziff Cool, and *The Texas Gardener's Guide to Growing Tomatoes* by Mary G. Rundell. See Heirlooms, Seeds, **Supplies**, Vegetables.

TRANS-PACIFIC NURSERY
Jackson Muldoon
Catalog: $2, 44 pp.
Mr. Muldoon specializes in rare, unusual, hard-to-find, and exotic specimens from all over the world, with an emphasis on the south-

ern hemisphere and Pacific Rim. Books, primarily from Timber Press, are below suggested retail cover price. A selection of eighty titles includes general horticultural and gardening reference, orchids and tropicals, trees and shrubs, alpine and rock gardening, ethnobotany, bonsai culture, and works on specific plants. Some of the titles offered by Trans-Pacific include *Dictionary of Plant Names* by Allen J. Coombes, *Gardening With Perennials Month by Month* by Joseph Hudak, *The 500 Best Garden Plants* by Patrick Taylor, *Willows: The Genus Salix* by Christopher Newsholme, and *The Rock Garden and Its Plants* by Graham Stuart Thomas. See Bulbs, Perennial, **Trees**, **Waterscapes**.
Canada, Mexico, International

VAN NESS WATER GARDENS
1932
William C. Uber
Catalog: $2, 55 pp., color photographs
This specialist's catalog includes *Water Gardening Basics* by Van Ness's president William C. Uber, *The Atlas of Garden Ponds* by Axelrod, Spalding, and Kelsey-Wood, *Water in the Garden* by James B. Allison, and nine titles on raising and maintaining fish and turtles. See Supplies, **Waterscapes**.
Canada, Mexico, International

VAN VEEN NURSERY
1926
Ted Van Veen
Catalog: $5 (recoverable), 15 pp.
Price list: Free
Van Veen Nursery is a wholesale grower of rhododendrons who will as a courtesy fulfill retail orders for ARS members. They offer three publications: *Rhododendrons in America* by Ted Van Veen, *American Rhododendron Hybrids,* and *Getting Started with Rhododendrons and Azaleas* by J. Harold Clarke. See **Rhododendrons**, Trees.

VESEY'S SEEDS LTD.
1939
Allen Perry
Catalog: Free, 126 pp., black-and-white and color photographs
A seed-house specializing in varieties for short growing seasons. Offers twenty practical titles on companion planting, organic gardening, and gardening with limited time and space. Carries seven titles in Dr. D.G. Hessayon's "Expert" se-

ries, and thirty "Country Wisdom Bulletins," published by Garden Way. Guarantees satisfaction; will issue refund. See **Garlic**, Herbs, **Seeds**, **Supplies**, Vegetables, Wildflowers.
Canada

VILENIKI: AN HERB FARM
1979
Gerry Janus
Catalog: $2, 14 pp.
The Vileniki booklist is short on description but long on selection. Six hundred titles, organized alphabetically by title within category, include nine sections for herbs: Chinese/oriental, cooking and food, gardening and growing, magical, medicinal/herbals, Native American, reference, spiritual, and teas. Separate sections for general gardening (reference and how-to), farming, foraging, wildflowers, and plants. Also sixteen video- and audiotape selections. See Herbs.
Canada

WARREN F. BRODERICK
1977
Warren F. Broderick
Catalog: $1, 30 pp.
Mr. Broderick deals in out-of-print books from circa 1850 to the present. Five hundred and sixty titles dealing with garden history and lore, garden design and home landscaping, monographs on specific genera, colorplate books and books on botanical illustration, field guides, early garden catalogs, and ephemera. Catalog is organized into broad subject areas; titles listed alphabetically by author's name under each subject. Guarantees satisfaction; will issue refund. See Heirlooms.
Canada, Mexico, International

WATERFORD GARDENS
1895
John A. Meeks
Catalog: $5, 40 pp., color photographs
William Tricker, one of the earliest propagators of water lilies in the United States, established this wet nursery at the turn of the last century. Books offered by Waterford include *The Water Gardener* by Anthony Archer-Wills, *Waterscaping* by Judy Glattstein, and *The Complete Book of the Water Garden* by Philip Swindells and David Mason, and ten other reference and how-to vol-

umes for water gardeners and pond keepers. See Supplies, **Waterscapes.**
Canada, Mexico, International

THE WATERWORKS®
1975
Todd Schaffer
Catalog: $4 (recoverable), 36 pp., illustrations and black-and-white photographs
This catalog for water gardeners includes *Water Gardens for Plants and Fish* by Charles B. Thomas, *Water Gardening Basics* by William Uber, *Ponds and Water Gardens* (revised 2nd edition) by Bill Heritage, *The Tetra Encyclopedia of Koi* edited by Anne McDowall, and *Practical Koi Keeping: Volumes I and II* edited by the Associated Koi Clubs of America. See Supplies, **Waterscapes.**

THE WAUSHARA GARDENS
1924
George Melk
Catalog: $1, 16 pp.
A gladiolus catalog written for the home gardener and the small commercial grower. Individual volumes on gladiolus, lilies, and callas are among the eight titles on cut flower growing and selling. See **Bulbs.**

WAVECREST NURSERY AND LANDSCAPING
1959
Carol T. Hop
Catalog: $1 (recoverable), 24 pp.
Wavecrest offers a sampling of conifers, trees, shrubs, vines, perennials, and ornamental grasses. Ms. Hop's catalog lists two dozen books, including *Alba: The Book of White Flowers* by D. Brown, *The Bamboos of China* by Wang Dajun and Dhen Shap-Jin, *The Grafters Handbook* by R. J. Garner, *Japanese Maples* by J. D. Vertrees, *The Manual of Herbaceous Ornamental Plants* by Steven M. Still, *Pond and Water Gardens* by Bill Heritage, and six title in the Random House "Book of . . . " gardening series. See **Conifers, Grasses,** Perennials, **Trees.**
Canada, Mexico, International

WICKLEIN'S WATER GARDENS
See Iris, Supplies, **Waterscapes.**

WILD SEED, INC.
1981
Rita Jo Anthony
Catalog: Free, 14 pp.
Wild Seed specializes in the native plants of the

Rocky Mountains, Great Basin, and Sonoran desert. They sell six booklets written under the auspices of the Arizona Native Plant Society. Topics include desert trees, desert shrubs, desert ground covers and vines, desert wildflowers, desert grasses, and desert accent plants. See Grasses, **Kidstuff,** Seeds, Trees, **Wildflowers.**
Canada, Mexico, International

WILLIAM DAM SEEDS
1949
Rene W. Dam
Catalog: $2., 63 pp., color photographs
Offers over one thousand varieties of vegetable, herb, flower, tree, shrub, and vine seeds from Canada, the United States, and Europe, including All America and Fleuroselect Medal winners. The Dam catalog has a dozen books on gardening basics, including *Annuals: How to Select, Grow, and Enjoy* by Derek Fell, *Flowers That Last Forever* by Betty A. M. Jacobs, *Rodale's Color Handbook of Garden Insects* edited by Claire Kowalchik and William H. Hylton, and *In Your Greenhouse* by Grace Heinen. See **Garlic,** Herbs, **Seeds,** Vegetables, Wildflowers.
Canada, International

WOOD VIOLET BOOKS
1984
Debbie Cravens
Catalog: $2, 55 pp.
Ms. Cravens describes in detail 275 new and recent titles organized alphabetically by title within category. Subjects include journals (diaries and calendars), plant lore, country living, landscape and garden design, flowers and foliage, trees and shrubs, indoor and container gardening, herbs, garden-to-table and other cookbooks, herb and flower craft, and field guides. Fifty-five titles, including "herb" murder mysteries by Susan Wittig Albert, and works by the pseudonymous Ellis Peters, are also listed. Wood Violet also offers a search service for out-of-print and rare gardening titles. Guarantees satisfaction; will issue a refund.
Canada, Mexico, International

WORM'S WAY INDIANA
1985
Michael Dick and Martin Heydt
Catalog: Free, 64 pp., color photographs
Worm's Way began as a small, one-man operation offering organic and natural alternatives to conventional gardening techniques. Ten percent

of their catalog, which now includes hundreds of brand-name items, consists of one hundred books. The list leans hard toward the practical, with emphasis on organic methods, greenhouse and hydroponic culture, and market gardening. Also carries twenty "Country Wisdom Bul-letins" and videos entitled *Inside Hydroponics* and *Hydroponics Explained.* Will accept items for refund, exchange, or credit within thirty days of receipt. See **Garlic**, Organics, **Supplies**. **Canada, Mexico, International**

KIDSTUFF

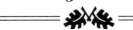
Gardening time is often family time. The companies in this section offer products and services with your child in mind. Kidstuff includes books, tools, clothing, toys, special assortments of seeds, contests, and programs intended to enhance your child's gardening experience. Sources ship year-round unless otherwise noted. A selection of books for young gardeners appears after the last listing.

QUICK FIND
The following sources are listed in this section:

A. C. BURKE & CO.
1991
Andrew Burke
Catalog: Free, 24 pp., black-and-white photographs
Burke specializes in "intelligent tools" for gardeners on how-to, planning, and design. The catalog includes *Linnea's Windowsill Garden* by Christina Bjork and Lena Anderson, *Get Growing! Exciting Indoor Plant Projects for Kids* by Lois Walker, and the *Get Ready, Get Set, Grow!* video from the Brooklyn Botanic Garden among others. Guarantees satisfaction; will issue refund. See **Booksellers**.
Canada, Mexico, International

ACRES, U.S.A.®
1970
Fred C. Walters
Catalog: Free, 71 pp.
This publisher and bookseller's catalog includes seven hard-to-find titles on environmental awareness, natural foods, "ecologically sane" arts and crafts, and organic gardening for children and young readers. See **Booksellers**.
Canada, Mexico, International

AMERICAN FORESTS: FAMOUS AND HISTORIC TREES
1875
Susan T. Corbett
Catalog: Free, 16 pp., illustrations and black-and-white photographs
American Forests, a nonprofit citizen's conservation organization, sponsors the Famous and Historic Trees project. The project grows trees (from seed) that are direct descendants of those that are associated with significant people or historic events. Among the specimens listed are those from George Washington's home at Mount Vernon, and his field headquarters at White Plains, New York; maple and catalpa from Thomas Jefferson's home at Monticello; overcup oak and black walnut from Abraham Lincoln's birthplace; numerous specimens from Civil War battlefields; an oleander from Thomas Edison's winter home in Fort Myers, Florida; a green ash from George Washington Carver's birthplace in Diamond Grove, Missouri; a water oak that Helen Keller climbed at her home in Tuscumbia, Alabama; and trees that shaded Thoreau's cabin at Walden Pond. Historical notes about the trees and their significance abound in this catalog. Information organized in chart form includes

flower, desirable foliage traits, soil requirements, tolerance to high heat, tolerance to shade, spread, and rate of growth. Each tree kit includes a one- to three-foot container plant, planting instructions, a photodegradable tree shelter, fertilizer, bird safety net, certificate of authenticity, and instructions for overwintering indoors. Also offers a historic grove package of twenty trees that includes certificates of authenticity, photodegradable tree shelters, a support stake, bird net, decals to note planting dates, written planting instructions and a video starring "George Washington," educational support material, and a fiberglass grove marker. Guarantees tree will grow for one year; will replace for shipping charges. See Conifers, Heirlooms, **Trees**.
Shipping season: All year
Canada

BARBARA FARNSWORTH, BOOKSELLER
1978
Barbara Farnsworth
Catalog: $3, 60 pp.
Ms. Farnsworth's "The Printed Side of Gardening" catalog includes a section of a dozen or so nineteenth- and twentieth-century books on gardening and natural history written for the younger reader. Previous catalogs have included Louisa May Alcott's *Flower Fables* and Celia Thaxter's *Stories and Poems for Children.* Guarantees satisfaction; will issue refund. See **Booksellers**, Heirlooms.
Canada, Mexico, International

BERLIN SEEDS
Edward Beachy
Catalog: Free, 60 pp.
Berlin conducts an annual children's garden contest. They will send enough seed for a ten-foot row of flowers or vegetables with ten cents added to an adult's order. They publish several letters in their catalog from children describing their gardening experience. See **Booksellers**, **Fruit**, **Garlic**, Grasses, Organics, **Seeds**, **Supplies**, Vegetables.

BERRY HILL LIMITED
1950
Catalog: Free, 68 pp., black-and-white photographs
This hobby farm equipment and country living catalog has a "Just for Kids" page that features diminutive True Temper® tools, a garden set that includes a cotton canvas bag, a work apron, and nylon hand tools, and a bird feeder in a schoolhouse design. Activity sets include

bird book and feeder, garden book and miniature greenhouse, pond book and pail, and bug book and bottle. See **Booksellers**, **Furniture**, **Supplies**.
Canada, International

BOUNTIFUL GARDENS
1972
Bill and Betsy Bruneau
Catalog: Free, 72 pp., illustrations and black-and-white photographs
The Bountiful Gardens catalog is published by Ecology Action, a nonprofit organization that practices and teaches organic biointensive methods. Three of the diversions that they offer are appropriate for kids of many ages: wild food cards (includes color photographs, maps, and tips on foraging and nutrition), chili pepper bandanna, and five ecologically sane rubber stamps. Also offers *Vegetarian . . . (with Children)* by Robin Jeavons, a handmade cookbook with a self-describing title. See **Booksellers**, **Garlic**, Heirlooms, Herbs, Organics, **Seeds**, **Supplies**, Vegetables.
Canada, Mexico, International

BOZEMAN BIO-TECH, INC.
1986
Dr. E. Wayne Vinje
Catalog: Free, 49 pp.
This purveyor of pest control products with low toxicity also offers three seed kits with kids in mind: a sunflower, vegetable, and rain forest garden, each including seeds, growing medium, pine crate, and thematic accessories. See **Booksellers**, Organics, **Supplies**.

THE COOK'S GARDEN
1983
Ellen and Shepherd Ogden
Catalog: $1, 112 pp., color and black-and-white illustrations
The "Family Garden" section of this catalog contains separate flower and vegetable garden sets that include seeds that are easy to grow and large enough for small hands to handle with comfort. Each set includes untreated wooden plant markers. The Ogdens also offer a flower press, child-sized garden gloves, and a small selection of garden-related books for kids. See **Booksellers**, **Garlic**, Heirlooms, **Herbs**, Organics, **Seeds**, **Supplies**, Vegetables.
Canada

DeGiorgi Seed Company
1905
Duane and Monte Thompson
Catalog: $2 (recoverable), 75 pp.
Among the collections offered by the Thompsons are seed packets for a children's starter garden that include flowering annuals and vegetables. Children's gloves in three sizes are also available. Guarantees satisfaction; will replace or issue refund. See **Booksellers, Garlic,** Grasses, Herbs, **Seeds,** Vegetables.

Down on the Farm Seed
1990
Ruth A. Guth
Catalog: Free, 52 pp., illustrations
The Guths, purveyors of untreated seeds for organic growing, have prepared small, inexpensive collections of flower and vegetable seeds for gardening tykes. See **Garlic,** Heirlooms, Herbs, Organics, Seeds, **Vegetables.**
Canada, Mexico, International

Emi Meade Importers
1981
Emi Meade
Catalog: Free, 6 pp., black-and-white photographs
Carries children's sizes of Jollys® brand washable gardening shoes, with a removable molded cork insole, recommended for wet and muddy conditions. See **Supplies.**
Canada

Fungi Perfecti
1979
Paul Stamets
Catalog: $3, 80 pp., illustrations and black-and-white photographs
The specialty of Fungi Perfecti is the cultivation of high-quality certified organic gourmet and medicinal mushrooms. They also offer the Children's Mushroom Garden™. This clear domed cylinder with spawn comes with an instruction booklet and a watering calendar. Guarantees satisfaction. See **Booksellers, Garlic,** Organics, **Supplies.**
Canada, Mexico, International

Gardens for Growing People
1992
Ruth Lopez
Catalog: Free, 8 pp., illustrations
A newsletter and catalog with suggestions for involving children in gardening and nature activities. Tools for kids, including a wheelbarrow, child-sized gloves, and a hand pruner. Offers theme seed kits containing heirloom varieties, including a colonial garden, Native American garden, a window box garden, and one called "Land of the Giants." Guarantees satisfaction; will issue refund.

Gurney's Seed & Nursery Co.
1866
Donald L. Kruml
Catalog: Free, 64 pp., color photographs
A general mail-order nursery catalog. The "Just for Kids" section features a giant jumble packet of flower and vegetable seeds for a penny with any adult order and nylon vegiforms that create a variety of faces and shapes on vegetables as they mature. Pumpkin carving kit described in seed section of catalog. See **Garlic,** Organics, **Seeds, Supplies,** Vegetables.
Canada, Mexico, International

Harmony Farm Supply and Nursery
1980
Kate Burroughs and David Henry
Catalog: $2, 127 pp.
Ms. Burroughs and Mr. Henry publish a full-range catalog for the organic gardener and farmer. The book section includes three volumes for young gardeners and their adult companions. *Blue Potatoes, Orange Tomatoes* by Rosalind Creasy, *Children's Gardens* by Bremner and Pusey, and *Let's Grow with Children* by Linda Tilgner. See **Booksellers,** Organics, **Supplies.**
Canada

Heirloom Garden® Seeds
Warren Raysor
1979
Catalog: Free, 37 pp., illustrations and black-and-white photographs
Among the theme collections prepared by this seed source is a children's garden. The collection includes fountain plant, jumping jewel balsam, broomcorn, loofah sponge, cup-and-saucer flower, birdhouse gourd, lamb's-ears, snapdragons, and teasel heads—the emphasis being unusual and amusing plant characteristics and names. Guarantees true to name, untreated, and disease free. See **Booksellers,** Heirlooms, Herbs, **Seeds.**
Canada

Henry Field's Seed & Nursery Co.

1892
Orville Dragoo
Catalog: Free, 87 pp., color photographs
The "Mighty Mix" seed packet (flowers and vegetables) is available to kids for a penny when it is added to an adult's seed order. See **Fruit**, **Garlic**, Organics, Perennials, **Seeds**, **Supplies**, **Trees**, Vegetables.
No California

J. W. JUNG SEED AND NURSERY CO.
1907
Richard J. Zondag
Catalog: Free, 76 pp., color photographs
This seed and nursery catalog for a wide range of interests offers a children's garden collection of seed packets appropriate for sowing into a ten-by-ten-foot plot. Includes vegetables, mixed flowers, and a gift certificate toward future purchases. See **Bulbs**, **Fruit**, Garlic, Perennials, **Seeds**, Supplies, **Trees**, **Vegetables**.

KIDS IN BLOOM™ SPECIALTY SEEDS
1990
Kay L. Grimm
Catalog: $1, 28 pp., illustrations
Ms. Grimm's catalog is filled with heirloom "Living History Seeds," including many varieties that are not available commercially. The catalog descriptions and the seed packets (illustrated by a teenage artist) include histories and stories pertaining to each variety that she offers. Vegetables and fruiting plants include beans (twenty-three types), beets, cantaloupe/muskmelons, sweet corn, popcorn, ornamental corn, carrots, cucumber, lettuce, gourds, pepper, pumpkin, radishes, squash, sunflowers, tomatoes, watermelons, and what she describes as "Oddballs & Edibles": devil's claw unicorn plant, Job's tears, and colonial broom corn. Among the flowers and herbs are globe amaranth, bachelor's buttons, black-eyed Susans, calendula, calliopsis, harvestburst, balsam, cleome, clock-eye Susan vine, evening stock, love-in-a-mist, mignonette, and tithonia. Theme collections include "Hoosier Heirloom," "Traditional Native American Medicine Kit," "Butterfly Food," "Thomas Jefferson's Totally Terrific Tomatoes," and a "Global Garden" with cosmos native to Mexico, Santa Cruz amaranth, mignonette from the time of Napoleon, and Florence fennel. Seeds sold in packets described as generous but number not specified. See Heirlooms, Herbs, Seeds, Vegetables.

KINSMAN COMPANY
1981
Graham Kinsman
Catalog: Free, 88 pp., color photographs
This full-line tool and supply catalog sets apart a small section that features children's upright and oval watering cans and four solid-forged garden tools suitable for children ages five through twelve. See **Furniture**, **Supplies**.

MELLINGER'S
1927
Jean Steiner
Catalog: Free, 104 pp., color photographs
A garden catalog for year-round living is how Mellinger's describes their book. Merchandise with the young gardener in mind includes a child-sized wheelbarrow, garden tools, and gloves, activity books, cartoon character bird feeders, and a worm farm. See **Booksellers**, **Furniture**, Perennials, **Seeds**, **Supplies**, Wildflowers.
Canada, Mexico, International

MILAEGER'S GARDENS
1960
Kevin D. Milaeger
Catalog: $1, 84 pp., color photographs
Milaeger's "Perennial Wishbook" includes eleven hundred plant varieties and thirty books dealing primarily with perennials and their myriad garden uses. They offer three child's garden collections for the sun and one for the shade made up of five, ten, or fifteen plants hardy within zones 5 to 8. The collections feature an assortment of such curiously named plants as false dragonshead, rattlesnake master, spotted dog, toad lily, and turtlehead. See **Booksellers**, **Grasses**, Peonies, **Perennials**.
Shipping season: April through September.

NATIVE SEEDS/SEARCH
1983
Angelo Joaquin, Jr.
Catalog: $1, 56 pp.
A nonprofit seed conservation organization with expertise in the traditional native food plants of the southwestern United States. They offer four books for children: two about the culture and history of Native Americans, and two written in English and Spanish: *Carlos and the Squash Plant* and *Carlos and the Cornfield*. See **Booksellers**, Garlic, Seeds, **Vegetables**, Wildflowers.
Canada, Mexico, International

NEW ENGLAND WILD FLOWER SOCIETY
1900
Catalog: $2.50, 22 pp.
NEWFS promotes the conservation of temperate North American plants through horticulture, education, research, habitat preservation, and advocacy. Among the seeds, spores, and publications that they offer through the mail are five books for young readers: *Look Inside a Tree, Roger Tory Peterson's Field Guide Coloring Books* (*Birds, Butterflies,* and *Wildflowers*), and *Best Kids Love the Earth Activity Book*. See **Booksellers, Horticultural Societies,** Seeds, **Wildflowers.**

NITRON INDUSTRIES, INC.
1977
Frank J. Finger
Catalog: Free, 24 pp., color photographs
Nitron Industries manufactures and sells 100 percent organic fertilizers, enzyme soil conditioners, and mined minerals. The details of their national "Junior Gardener" program for young people ages twelve to sixteen can be requested free of charge through their toll-free telephone number. See Organics, Seeds, **Supplies, Vegetables.**
Canada, Mexico, International

PINETREE GARDEN SEEDS
1979
Dick Meiners
Catalog: Free, 152 pp., illustrations and
black-and-white photographs
What began from seed has grown into a full-line catalog. Books for kids include *Cunningham's New England Flowers* coloring book by Jim and Maggie Cunningham, *Plant Survival: Adapting to a Hostile World* by Brian Capon, *Let's Grow: 72 Gardening Adventures With Children* by Linda Tilgner, *Keepers of Life: Discovering Plants Through Native American Stories and Earth Activities for Children* by Michael J. Caduto and Joseph Bruchac, *The Victory Garden Vegetable Alphabet Book* by Jerry Pallotta and Bob Thompson, and two editions of *The Secret Garden* by Frances Hodgson Burnett, one with illustrations by Tasha Tudor. See **Booksellers,** Garlic, Herbs, Organics, **Seeds, Supplies, Vegetables,**
Canada, Mexico, International

THE RARE CONIFER FOUNDATION–RARE CONIFER NURSERY
1991
Darshan Mayginnes
Catalog: Free, 28 pp.

The Rare Conifer Foundation, a public charity that protects conifer species in their native habitats, conducts the "Trees for Schools" program. Inquire for details. See **Booksellers, Conifers,** Trees.
Canada, Mexico, International

REDWOOD CITY SEED COMPANY
1971
Craig and Sue Dremann
Catalog: $1, 28 pp., illustrations. Large-print edition: $3. Supplements (twice yearly): $2
The Dremanns will send two free packets of seed to any young gardener who requests them in his or her own handwriting. Send two first-class stamps for the return trip. See **Booksellers,** Garlic, **Herbs,** Seeds, **Vegetables.**
Canada, Mexico, International

SALT SPRING SEEDS
Dan Jason
Catalog: $2, 18 pp.
Salt Spring Seeds sells untreated, open-pollinated vegetable and herb seeds adapted to northern climates. "Child's Delight" is a collection of early maturing bush beans with unique and playful colors and patterns. See Garlic, Heirlooms, Organics, Seeds, **Vegetables.**
Canada, Mexico, International

SEEDS BLÜM
1981
Jan Blüm
Catalog: $3 (first-class mail $4.50), 99 pp.
Seeds Blüm offers "Pollination" and seven other nature card games, and a "Garden Giants" seed collection that includes two-hundred-pound pumpkins, three-foot-tall parsley, and pole beans that can grow to thirty feet. Three "Rainbow Garden" collections promise to provide a surprising array of colors in your child's vegetable garden. See **Booksellers, Garlic,** Heirlooms, Herbs, **Seeds,** Vegetables, Wildflowers.
Canada, Mexico, International

SHEPHERD'S GARDEN SEEDS
1984
Renee Shepherd and Beth Benjamin
Catalog: $1, 108 pp., illustrations
The seeds for eight varieties of vegetables and flowers, including carving-sized pumpkins and mammoth sunflowers, to grow a special garden for children comes with a six-page instruction booklet. See **Booksellers, Garlic, Heirlooms,** Herbs, **Seeds,** Supplies, Vegetables.
Canada

SMITH & HAWKEN
1979
Catalog: Free, 62 pp., color photographs
This stylish catalog includes Japanese farmer pants, clogs, caps, T-shirts, steel-and-wood gardening tools, a watering can, a red wheelbarrow, and a special selection of seeds for the young gardener. See **Furniture**, Organics, **Supplies**.

TERRITORIAL SEED COMPANY
Tom Johns
Catalog: Free, 95 pp.
Territorial's "Little Gardeners" department includes a special "ABC" seed assortment, steel-and-wood gardening tools, and child-sized gloves. See **Booksellers**, **Garlic**, Herbs, Organics, Seeds, **Supplies**, **Vegetables**.
Canada

TINMOUTH CHANNEL FARM
1976
Carolyn Fuhrer and Kathleen Duhnoski
Catalog: $2, 34 pp.
Ms. Fuhrer and Ms. Duhnoski are the stewards of a small herb farm certified by the Vermont Organic Farmer's Association. Their herb garden collection for children has been assembled from the favorite plants of the students from their local kindergarten who visit Tinmouth Channel Farm each year. This selection combines seeds that germinate quickly with live plants, offering an entertaining variety of scents, sights, and textures and requiring only a small space in your garden. Guarantees plant material to be true to name, free from pest and disease, and safe arrival; will replace plants or issue refund. See **Herbs**, Organics, Seeds.
Shipping season: April through October.

WILD SEED, INC.
1981
Rita Jo Anthony
Catalog: Free, 14 pp.
Ms. Anthony specializes in native seed, from the Rocky Mountains, Great Basin, and Sonoran desert. An easy-to-grow wildflower mixture for a child's garden including snapdragons, bubblegum plants, lemon mint, Maximilian sunflowers, owl's clover, five-spot, and Mexican hats is available by the packet or by weight. Guarantees true to name. See **Booksellers**, Grasses, Seeds, Trees, **Wildflowers**.
Canada, Mexico, International

WISCONSIN WAGON CO., INC.
1978
Albert and Lois Hough
Catalog: Free, 8 pp., color photographs
The Houghs make full-sized and scale model oak and maple replicas of early-twentieth-century wheelbarrows, sized appropriately (two to four years old, five to seven, and eight and older), to use while helping in the garden or simply playing. They also build oak replicas of four styles of the original (1900–1934) Janesville Ball Bearing Coaster Wagon.

WOMANSWORK®
1985
Nancy Bennett Phillips
Catalog: Free, 24 pp., black-and-white photographs
Womanswork®, strong women building a gentle world, markets a child-sized collection to complement the Womanswork® line. Kidswork® products include gloves, mittens, a work apron, watering can, and a log carrier. Describes material and nature of construction. The proceeds from 1 percent of their catalog sales are donated to groups working against domestic violence. Guarantees satisfaction; will replace or issue refund. See **Supplies**.

Selected Reading for Young Gardeners

Gardening Wizardry for Kids, by L. Patricia Kite. Includes 300 indoor and outdoor plant growing projects. Includes plant legends, plant crafts, and a canvas gardening belt with three tools. Illustrations.

Gardens from Garbage: How to Grow Indoor Plants From Recycled Kitchen Scraps. For the organic gardener (and recycler) in training. How to grow the next generation of apples, corn, citrus fruits, garlic, white potatoes, and sunflowers from the food you have just eaten. Illustrations.

Grow a Totally Weird Garden, by Joanna Poncavage. Ms. Poncavage answers the basic questions with humor and clarity: What is a seed, a plant, a leaf, a root, a flower, and dirt? Information about when to start your seedlings indoors and out. Seed packets include "living stones," walking stick cabbage, and monster pumpkins.

KidsGardening: A Kid's Guide to Messing Around in the Dirt, by Kevin Raftery and Kim Gilbert Raftery. Gardening basics in separate sections for growing your own vegetables, flowers, and herbs. Includes information about growing lots of stuff to eat, and, for those who would rather not, there is a section on making a scarecrow and creating a worm farm. Includes seed packets. Illustrations.

Sunflower Houses: Gardening Discoveries for Children of All Ages by Sharon Lovejoy. This impressionistic book blends Ms. Lovejoy's fond and sensitive reminiscences, poetry, and songs about gardens and gardening. Projects and practical information too, including plans for planting a flower garden clock based on "The Garden of Hours" created by Carl Linnaeus. Illustrations and paintings.

HORTICULTURAL
SOCIETIES

QUICK FIND

The following horticultural societies and groups are listed in this section:

ALABAMA WILDFLOWER SOCIETY

ALASKA NATIVE PLANT SOCIETY

AMERICAN ASSOCIATION OF FIELD BOTANISTS

THE AMERICAN BEGONIA SOCIETY

THE AMERICAN BOXWOOD SOCIETY

AMERICAN CAMELLIA SOCIETY

THE AMERICAN CONIFER SOCIETY

THE AMERICAN DAFFODIL SOCIETY

THE AMERICAN FERN SOCIETY

AMERICAN FORESTS

THE AMERICAN FUCHSIA SOCIETY

AMERICAN GLOXINIA AND GESNERIAD SOCIETY

AMERICAN GOURD SOCIETY

THE AMERICAN HEMEROCALLIS SOCIETY

AMERICAN HIBISCUS SOCIETY

AMERICAN HOSTA SOCIETY

THE AMERICAN IRIS SOCIETY

THE AMERICAN IVY SOCIETY

THE AMERICAN PENSTEMON SOCIETY

AMERICAN PEONY SOCIETY

AMERICAN POMOLOGICAL SOCIETY

THE AMERICAN RHODODENDRON SOCIETY

AMERICAN ROCK GARDEN SOCIETY

AMERICAN ROSE SOCIETY

AMERICAN WILLOW GROWERS NETWORK

AMHERST MUSEUM WILDFLOWER SOCIETY

ARIZONA NATIVE PLANT SOCIETY

ARKANSAS NATIVE PLANT SOCIETY

BOTANICAL CLUB OF WISCONSIN

BOTANICAL SOCIETY OF WASHINGTON

BOTANICAL SOCIETY OF WESTERN PENNSYLVANIA

BOWMAN'S HILL STATE WILDFLOWER PRESERVE

THE CACTUS AND SUCCULENT SOCIETY OF AMERICA

CALIFORNIA BOTANICAL SOCIETY

CALIFORNIA NATIVE PLANT SOCIETY

THE CALOCHORTUS SOCIETY

CANADIAN WILDFLOWER SOCIETY

CHILE INSTITUTE

COLORADO NATIVE PLANT SOCIETY

CONNECTICUT BOTANICAL SOCIETY

EL PASO NATIVE PLANT SOCIETY

FLORIDA NATIVE PLANT SOCIETY

THE FLOWER AND HERB EXCHANGE

FRIENDS OF ELOISE BUTLER WILDFLOWER GARDEN

FRUIT TESTING ASSOCIATION NURSERY, INC.

GEORGIA BOTANICAL SOCIETY

GREAT PLAINS BOTANICAL SOCIETY

THE HARDY FERN FOUNDATION

THE HARDY PLANT SOCIETY: MID-ATLANTIC GROUP

THE HARDY PLANT SOCIETY OF OREGON

HAWAII BOTANICAL SOCIETY

THE HAWORTHIA SOCIETY

THE HERB SOCIETY OF AMERICA

THE HERITAGE ROSE GROUP

THE HYDROPONIC SOCIETY OF AMERICA

IDAHO NATIVE PLANT SOCIETY

ILLINOIS NATIVE PLANT SOCIETY

INTERNATIONAL DWARF FRUIT TREE ASSOCIATION

INTERNATIONAL GERANIUM SOCIETY

INTERNATIONAL GOLDEN FOSSIL TREE SOCIETY (THE GINKGO SOCIETY)

INTERNATIONAL LILAC SOCIETY, INC.

INTERNATIONAL OLEANDER SOCIETY

INTERNATIONAL ORNAMENTAL CRABAPPLE SOCIETY

INTERNATIONAL WATER LILY SOCIETY

JOSSELYN BOTANICAL SOCIETY

KANSAS WILDFLOWER SOCIETY

KENTUCKY NATIVE PLANT SOCIETY

LONG ISLAND BOTANICAL SOCIETY

LOUISIANA NATIVE PLANT SOCIETY

LOUISIANA PROJECT WILDFLOWER

MARIGOLD SOCIETY OF AMERICA

MARYLAND NATIVE PLANT SOCIETY

MICHIGAN BOTANICAL CLUB

MINNESOTA NATIVE PLANT SOCIETY

MISSISSIPPI NATIVE PLANT SOCIETY

MISSOURI NATIVE PLANT SOCIETY

THE MOHAVE NATIVE PLANT SOCIETY

MONTANA NATIVE PLANT SOCIETY

MUHLENBERG BOTANICAL SOCIETY

NATIONAL HOT PEPPER ASSOCIATION

NATIONAL WILDFLOWER RESEARCH CENTER

THE NATIVE PLANT SOCIETY OF NEW JERSEY

NATIVE PLANT SOCIETY OF NEW MEXICO

NATIVE PLANT SOCIETY OF NORTHEASTERN OHIO

NATIVE PLANT SOCIETY OF OREGON

NATIVE PLANT SOCIETY OF TEXAS

NEW ENGLAND BOTANICAL CLUB

NEW ENGLAND WILD FLOWER SOCIETY

NEW YORK FLORA ASSOCIATION

NEWFOUNDLAND CHAPTER–CANADIAN WILDFLOWER SOCIETY

NIAGARA FRONTIER BOTANICAL SOCIETY

NORTH AMERICAN FRUIT EXPLORERS (NAFEX)

NORTH AMERICAN GLADIOLUS COUNCIL

NORTH AMERICAN HEATHER SOCIETY

NORTH AMERICAN LILY SOCIETY

NORTH CAROLINA WILD FLOWER PRESERVATION SOCIETY, INC.

NORTHERN NEVADA NATIVE PLANT SOCIETY

NORTHWEST HORTICULTURAL SOCIETY

THE NORTHWEST PERENNIAL ALLIANCE

NOVA SCOTIA WILDFLOWER SOCIETY

OHIO NATIVE PLANT SOCIETY

OKLAHOMA NATIVE PLANT SOCIETY

PENNSYLVANIA NATIVE PLANT SOCIETY

PHILADELPHIA BOTANICAL CLUB

RHODE ISLAND WILD PLANT SOCIETY

THE RHODODENDRON SPECIES FOUNDATION

SEED SAVERS EXCHANGE

SOCIETY FOR JAPANESE IRISES

SOCIETY FOR LOUISIANA IRISES

SOCIETY FOR SIBERIAN IRISES

SOIL AND WATER CONSERVATION SOCIETY OF AMERICA

SOUTHERN APPALACHIAN BOTANICAL CLUB

SOUTHERN CALIFORNIA BOTANISTS

THE SPECIES IRIS GROUP OF NORTH AMERICA (SIGNA)

SYRACUSE BOTANICAL CLUB

TENNESSEE NATIVE PLANT SOCIETY

THE TOMATO CLUB

UNIVERSITY BOTANICAL GARDENS AT ASHVILLE, INC.

UTAH NATIVE PLANT SOCIETY

VERMONT BOTANICAL AND BIRD CLUB

VIRGINIA NATIVE PLANT SOCIETY

WASHINGTON NATIVE PLANT SOCIETY

WESTERN CAROLINA BOTANICAL CLUB

WILDFLOWER ASSOCIATION OF MICHIGAN

THE WILDFLOWER SOCIETY

WORLD PUMPKIN CONFEDERATION

WYOMING NATIVE PLANT SOCIETY

ALABAMA WILDFLOWER SOCIETY
Dottie Elam
240 Ivy Lane
Auburn, AL 36830-5771

ALASKA NATIVE PLANT SOCIETY
P.O. Box 141613
Anchorage, AK 99514-1613

AMERICAN ASSOCIATION OF FIELD BOTANISTS
P.O. Box 23542
Chattanooga, TN 37422

THE AMERICAN BEGONIA SOCIETY
1932
P.O. Box 231129
Encinitas, CA 92023-1129
Phone: 707-764-5407
Newsletter: *The Begonian*
Benefits: Fifty-two branches in the United States (at-large membership for those without local branch), exchange program, slides, bookstore, shows, research, begonia-collecting field trips

THE AMERICAN BOXWOOD SOCIETY
1961
Joan Butler
P.O. Box 85
Boyce, VA 22620

(Headquarters: University of Virginia, Orland E. White Arboretum, Blandy Farm, Boyce) Nonprofit organization to disseminate information about the genus *Buxus*.
Newsletter: *The Bulletin* (four issues per year)
Publications: *Boxwood Buyer's Guide, The Boxwood Handbook, Index of the Bulletin*
Benefits: Annual convention, garden tours, workshops, special publications

AMERICAN CAMELLIA SOCIETY
Ann Blair Brown
1 Massee Lane
Fort Valley, GA 31030
Phone: 912-967-2358/967-2722
Fax: 912-967-2083
Maintains 160-acre Massee Lane Gardens, national headquarters for the genus *Camellia* (all camellias registered in the United States registered here).
Newsletter: *The Camellia Journal* (four issues per year)
Publications: *Camellia Culture for Beginners, The American Camellia Yearbook*
Benefits: Membership in forty-six states and twenty-six countries, free admission to Massee Lane Gardens, on-premises use of library

THE AMERICAN CONIFER SOCIETY
1983
Nancy Akehurst

P.O. Box 314
Perry Hall, MD 21128
Phone: 410-256-5595/Fax: 410-256-5595
Newsletter: *ACS Bulletin* (four issues per year)
Benefits: Annual convention, regional groups, lecture and slide programs, plant auctions, seed exchange programs, local area information days
See Conifers.

THE AMERICAN DAFFODIL SOCIETY
1954
Mary Lou Gripshover
1686 Grey Fox Trails
Milford, OH 45150
Newsletter: *The Daffodil Journal* (four issue per year)
Benefits: Society library, annual convention

THE AMERICAN FERN SOCIETY
1893
David B. Lellinger
Smithsonian Institution
Department of Botany
Washington, DC 20560
International organization for those interested in ferns and allied plants.
Newsletters: *The Fiddlehead Forum* (six issues per year), *The American Fern Journal* (four issues per year; published since 1910)
Benefits: Spore exchange program, field trips

AMERICAN FORESTS
1875
R. Neil Sampson
P.O. Box 2000
Washington, DC 20013
Phone: 202-667-3300/Fax: 202-667-7751
American Forests Global Releaf
1516 P Street NW
Washington, DC 20005
Phone: 202-667-3300
Publications: *American Forests* (six issues per year), *Urban Forests* (six issues per year), *Resource Hotline*, *The Global Releaf Report* (four issues per year)
Benefits: Global releaf program, urban and community forestry program, conservation advocacy, forest policy center, national register of big trees, information and education programs
See **Kidstuff, Trees.**

THE AMERICAN FUCHSIA SOCIETY
1948
Virginia D. Feldmann

County Fair Building
9th Avenue and Lincoln Way
San Francisco, CA 95122
13 Robert Place
Millbrae, CA 94030
Newsletter: *Bulletin* (six issues per year)
Benefits: Library, shows, annual convention, registration service

AMERICAN GLOXINIA AND GESNERIAD SOCIETY
The Horticultural Society of New York
128 West 58th Street
New York, NY 10019-2103
Phone: 718-884-5120/Fax: 718-884-5120
Newsletter: *The Gloxinian* (six issues per year)
Benefits: Seed exchange program, round-robin correspondence, training for judges, annual convention, slide programs

AMERICAN GOURD SOCIETY
1970
P.O. Box 274
Mount Gilead, OH 43338
Newsletter: *The Gourd* (four issues per year)
Benefits: Shows, meetings

THE AMERICAN HEMEROCALLIS SOCIETY
Elly Launius
1454 Rebel Drive
Jackson, MS 39211
Newsletter: *The Daylily Journal* (four issues per year)
Publications: Specific topics
Benefits: Round-robin correspondence, regional meetings, annual convention, garden tours, clinics, invitation to exhibit at local AHS flower shows, an extensive network of display gardens, slide and video library

AMERICAN HIBISCUS SOCIETY
1950
Jeri Grantham
P.O. Box 321540
Cocoa Beach, FL 32932-1540
Phone: 407-783-2576/Fax: 407-783-2576
Newsletter: *Seed Pod* (four issues per year)
Benefits: Wholesale and library discounts, training for judges, seed exchange program, meetings, annual convention

AMERICAN HOSTA SOCIETY
Robyn Duback
7802 N.E. 63rd Street

Vancouver, WA 98662
Newsletter: *The Hosta Journal* (two issues per year)
Benefits: Annual convention, garden tours, regional activities, registration of new cultivars, back issue publications, slide and speaker programs.
See Hosta.

THE AMERICAN IRIS SOCIETY
Marilyn Harlow
P.O. Box 8455
San Jose, CA 95155-8455
Newsletter: *AIS Bulletin* (four issues per year)
Benefits: Membership in twenty-four regions of AIS, annual convention, garden tours, round-robin correspondence, regional publications, test gardens, exhibits, training for judges, vote in annual popularity poll, publications, technical assistance, youth program
See Iris.

THE AMERICAN IVY SOCIETY
1973
P.O. Box 2123
Naples, FL 33939-2123
Phone: 813-261-0388/In Ohio: 513-434-7069
For those interested in the genus *Hedera*.
Newsletter: *Between the Vines* (three issues per year), *Ivy Journal* (annual)
Benefits: Publications, information about culture, use and the history of ivy, ivy identification, source list of growers and catalogs, annual convention

THE AMERICAN PENSTEMON SOCIETY
1946
1569 South Holland Court
Lakewood, CO 80232
For those interested in the genus *Penstemon*.
Newsletter: *The Bulletin of APS* (two issues per year)
Publications: *Manual for Beginners with Penstemons* and others
Benefits: Seed exchange program, round-robin correspondence, slides

AMERICAN PEONY SOCIETY
1903
Greta M. Kessenich
250 Interlachen Road
Hopkins, MN 55343
Newsletter: *APS Bulletin* (four issues per year)
Benefits: Seed bank, annual convention, exhibits
See Peonies.

AMERICAN POMOLOGICAL SOCIETY
1848
R. M. Crasweller
103 Tyson Building
University Park, PA 16802-4200
The oldest organization in United States dedicated to fruit.
Newsletter: *The Fruit Varieties Journal* (four issues per year)
Benefits: Publications, awards

THE AMERICAN RHODODENDRON SOCIETY
1945
P.O. Box 1380
Gloucester, VA 23061
Phone: 804-693-4433
Newsletter: *Journal* (four issues per year)
Benefits: Annual convention, seed exchange program, pollen bank, slide programs, book discounts, speaker's bureau, plant registration

AMERICAN ROCK GARDEN SOCIETY
1934
Jacques Mommens
P.O. Box 67
Millwood, NY 10546
Newsletter: *Bulletin* (four issues per year)
Benefits: Thirty local chapters, meetings and lectures, seed exchange program, slides, library loan service, book discount, access to experts in the field

AMERICAN ROSE SOCIETY
P.O. Box 30,000
Shreveport, LA 71130
Phone: 318-938-5402/Fax: 318-938-5405
Publications: *American Rose Magazine* (twelve issues per year), *ARS Annual, ARS Handbook for Selecting Roses* (annual), and *Roses in Review* (annual).
Benefits: local consulting rosarians, lending library, slide programs, book discounts
See Roses.

AMERICAN WILLOW GROWERS NETWORK
1988
Bonnie Gale
R.F.D. 1, Box 124-A
South New Berlin, NY 13843-9653
Phone: 607-847-8264
Benefits: Network survey, willow basketry classes

AMHERST MUSEUM WILDFLOWER
SOCIETY
3755 Tonawanda Creek Road
East Amherst, NY 14051

ARIZONA NATIVE PLANT SOCIETY
P.O. Box 41206, Sun Station
Tucson, AZ 85717-1206

ARKANSAS NATIVE PLANT SOCIETY
P.O. Box 250250
Little Rock, AR 72225

BOTANICAL CLUB OF WISCONSIN
Wisconsin Academy of Arts, Sciences and
Letters
1922 University Avenue
Madison, WI 53705

BOTANICAL SOCIETY OF WASHINGTON
Smithsonian Institution
Department of Botany, NHB 166
Washington, DC 20560

BOTANICAL SOCIETY OF WESTERN PENN-
SYLVANIA
Robert F. Bahl
401 Clearview Avenue
Pittsburgh, PA 15205

BOWMAN'S HILL STATE WILDFLOWER
PRESERVE
Washington Crossing Historic Park
P.O. Box 103
Washington Crossing, PA 18977
See Seeds, **Wildflowers.**

THE CACTUS AND SUCCULENT SOCIETY
OF AMERICA
1535 Reeve Street
Los Angeles, CA 90035
Phone: 310-556-1923
See Cactus.

CALIFORNIA BOTANICAL SOCIETY
University of California
Department of Botany
Berkeley, CA 94720

CALIFORNIA NATIVE PLANT SOCIETY
1722 J Street, Suite 17
Sacramento, CA 95814-2931

THE CALOCHORTUS SOCIETY
1989
H. P. McDonald and Karin R. Stokkink
P.O. Box 1128
Berkeley, CA 94701-1128
Newsletter: *Mariposa* (four issues per year)
Benefits: Historical information on the genus
Calochortus

CANADIAN WILDFLOWER SOCIETY
John Craw
4981 Highway 7 East
Unit 12A, #228
Markham, Ontario, Canada L3R 1N1

CHILE INSTITUTE
New Mexico State University
P.O. Box 3-Q
Las Cruces, NM 88030
Newsletter: (four issues per year)

COLORADO NATIVE PLANT SOCIETY
P.O. Box 200
Fort Collins, CO 80522-0200

CONNECTICUT BOTANICAL SOCIETY
Margaret Taylor
10 Hillside Circle
Storrs, CT 06268

EL PASO NATIVE PLANT SOCIETY
7760 Maya
El Paso, TX 79912

FLORIDA NATIVE PLANT SOCIETY
P.O. Box 680008
Orlando, FL 32868

THE FLOWER AND HERB EXCHANGE
Diane Whealy
3076 North Winn Road
Decorah, IA 52101
Priviliges: Members receive the annual seed
exchange list
See Seeds.

FRIENDS OF ELOISE BUTLER
WILDFLOWER GARDEN
P.O. Box 11592
Minneapolis, MN 55412

FRUIT TESTING ASSOCIATION NURSERY,
INC.
1918

Helen Van Arsdale
P.O. Box 462
Geneva, NY 14456
Phone: 315-787-2205/Fax: 315-787-2216
Nonprofit cooperative established to test varieties developed at the New York State Agricultural Experiment Station (Geneva) and cultivars developed at other testing stations throughout the United States.
See **Fruit**, Trees.

GEORGIA BOTANICAL SOCIETY
Daisy S. Arrington
6700 Peachtree, B-5
Doraville, GA 30360

GREAT PLAINS BOTANICAL SOCIETY
P.O. Box 461
Hot Springs, SD 57747

THE HARDY FERN FOUNDATION
Jocelyn Horder
P.O. Box 166
Medina, WA 98039-0166
Newsletter: (four issues per year)
Benefits: Display garden in conjunction with the Rhododendron Species Foundation Garden, information packet, instructions on growing ferns from spore, current spore list, directory of fern gardens in the United States

THE HARDY PLANT SOCIETY: MID-ATLANTIC GROUP
Pat Horwitz
801 Concord Road
Glen Mills, PA 19342

THE HARDY PLANT SOCIETY OF OREGON
Mary Hoffman
P.O. Box 5090
Oregon City, OR 97045
Newsletter: (six issues per year)
Publication: Twice-yearly bulletin
Benefits: Annual garden tour book, lectures, demonstrations, plant sales at two-day trade show

HAWAII BOTANICAL SOCIETY
University of Hawaii
Botany Department
3190 Maille Way
Honolulu, HI 96822

THE HAWORTHIA SOCIETY
Lois Burks

P.O. Box 1207
Benton, AR 72015-1207
Phone: 501-794-3266
Newsletter: *Haworthiad* (four issues per year)
See Cactus.

THE HERB SOCIETY OF AMERICA
1933
9019 Kirtland Chardon Road
Mentor, OH 44060
Phone: 216-256-0514/Fax: 216-256-0514
Newsletter: *The Herbarist*
Benefits: Tours and symposiums, annual convention, access to national headquarters library, slide rentals

THE HERITAGE ROSE GROUP
925 Galvin Drive
El Cerrito, CA 94530
Newsletter: *Heritage Rose Letter*

THE HYDROPONIC SOCIETY OF AMERICA
1980
P.O. Box 3075
San Ramon, CA 94583
Phone: 510-743-9605/Fax: 510-743-9302
For those interested in growing plants without soil.
Newsletter: (six issues per year)
Benefits: Annual convention, book discounts, library

IDAHO NATIVE PLANT SOCIETY
P.O. Box 9451
Boise, ID 83707-3451

ILLINOIS NATIVE PLANT SOCIETY
Forest Glen Preserve
R.R. 1, Box 495A
Westville, IL 61883

INTERNATIONAL DWARF FRUIT TREE ASSOCIATION
Charles J. Ax, Jr.
14 South Main Street
Middleburg, PA 17842
Phone: 717-837-1551/Fax: 717-837-0090
Newsletter: *Compact News* (periodic)
Publication: *Compact Fruit Tree* (annual)
Benefits: Annual convention, orchard tour, research and extension publications, specialized help and education

INTERNATIONAL GERANIUM SOCIETY
1953
Betty Tufenkian
P. O. Box 92734
Pasadena, CA 91109-2734
Newsletter: *Geraniums Around the World* (four issues per year)
Benefits: Annual convention and banquet, seed exchange program

INTERNATIONAL GOLDEN FOSSIL TREE SOCIETY (THE GINKGO SOCIETY)
1978
Clayton Fawkes
201 West Graham Avenue
Lombard, IL 60148
Newsletter: *Newsletter* (four issues per year)

INTERNATIONAL LILAC SOCIETY, INC.
Walter W. Oakes
11 Pine Street
Dixfield, ME 04224-9561

INTERNATIONAL OLEANDER SOCIETY
1967
Elizabeth S. Head
P.O. Box 3431
Galveston, TX 77552-0431
Newsletter: *Nerium News* (four issues per year)
Benefits: Seeds and cuttings, answers to inquiries about oleanders, speakers' list, registrar for the species *Nerium*, annual convention

INTERNATIONAL ORNAMENTAL CRABAPPLE SOCIETY
1985
Dr. Thomas L. Green
Western Illinois University
208 Waggoner Hall
Macomb, IL 61455
Phone: 309-298-1160/Fax: 309-298-2280
Newsletter: *Malus* (two issues per year)

INTERNATIONAL WATER LILY SOCIETY
Edward L. Schneider
Santa Barbara Botanical Garden
1212 Mission Canyon Road
Santa Barbara, CA 93105
Phone: 805-682-4726
Newsletter: *Water Garden Journal* (four issues per year)
Benefits: Annual convention, library, research on hybridization, propagation, and disease control, speakers, slides and videos, classes, directory and handbook
See Waterscapes.

JOSSELYN BOTANICAL SOCIETY
Marilyn Dwelley
P.O. Box 41
China, ME 04926

KANSAS WILDFLOWER SOCIETY
Washburn University
Mulvane Art Center
17th and Jewell Streets
Topeka, KS 66621

KENTUCKY NATIVE PLANT SOCIETY
Dr. Douglas N. Reynolds
Eastern Kentucky University
Department of Natural Science
Richmond, KY 40475

LONG ISLAND BOTANICAL SOCIETY
P.O. Box 905
Levittown, NY 11756

LOUISIANA NATIVE PLANT SOCIETY
Richard Johnson
Route 1, Box 195
Saline, LA 71070

LOUISIANA PROJECT WILDFLOWER
Lafayette Natural History Museum
637 Girard Park Drive
Lafayette, LA 70503-2896

MARIGOLD SOCIETY OF AMERICA
1978
Jeannette Lowe
P.O. Box 112
New Britain, PA 18901
Newsletter: (four issues per year)
Benefits: Annual convention, information exchange

MARYLAND NATIVE PLANT SOCIETY
P.O. Box 4877
Silver Spring, MD 20914

MICHIGAN BOTANICAL CLUB
Dr. Peter Kaufman
University of Michigan
Department of Biology
Ann Arbor, MI 48109-1048

MINNESOTA NATIVE PLANT SOCIETY
University of Minnesota
220 Biological Science Center
1445 Gortner Avenue
St. Paul, MN 55108-1020

MISSISSIPPI NATIVE PLANT SOCIETY
P.O. Box 2151
Starkville, MS 39759

MISSOURI NATIVE PLANT SOCIETY
P.O. Box 20073
St. Louis, MO 63144-0073

THE MOHAVE NATIVE PLANT SOCIETY
8180 Placid Street
Las Vegas, NV 89123

MONTANA NATIVE PLANT SOCIETY
P.O. Box 992
Bozeman, MT 59771-0992

MUHLENBERG BOTANICAL SOCIETY
Franklin and Marshall College
North Museum
P.O. Box 3003
Lancaster, PA 17604

NATIONAL HOT PEPPER ASSOCIATION
1991
400 N.W. 20th Street
Fort Lauderdale, FL 33311
Phone: 305-565-4972/Fax: 305-566-2208
Newsletter: (four issues per year)
Benefits: Starter seeds, membership card and
certificate

**NATIONAL WILDFLOWER RESEARCH
CENTER**
2600 FM-973 North
Austin, TX 78725-4201

**THE NATIVE PLANT SOCIETY OF NEW
JERSEY**
Cook College
P.O. Box 231
New Brunswick, NJ 08903-0231

**NATIVE PLANT SOCIETY OF NEW MEX-
ICO**
P.O. Box 5917
Santa Fe, NM 87502

**NATIVE PLANT SOCIETY OF NORTHEAST-
ERN OHIO**
2651 Kerwick Road
University Heights, OH 44118

NATIVE PLANT SOCIETY OF OREGON
1961
Jan Dobak
P.O. Box 902
Eugene, OR 97440
Newsletter: *Bulletin* (twelve issues per year)
Publication: *Kalmiopsis* (annual)
Benefits: Annual convention, regular local
meetings and field trips, workshops, flower
shows, plant lists, discount on sale items

NATIVE PLANT SOCIETY OF TEXAS
1980
Dana Tucker
P.O. Box 891
Georgetown, TX 78627-0891
Phone: 512-863-9685
Newsletter: *NPSOT News* (six issues per year)
Benefits: Annual convention, educational
symposium, field trips, plant and seed ex-
change program, lectures and demonstrations

NEW ENGLAND BOTANICAL CLUB
22 Divinity Avenue
Cambridge, MA 02138

NEW ENGLAND WILD FLOWER SOCIETY
1900
Garden in the Woods
180 Hemingway Road
Framingham, MA 01701-2699
Phone: 508-877-7630/617-237-4924
Coordinates the New England Plant Preservation Program (NEPCoP), promotes conservation of plants through five programs, and
maintains forty-five-acre Garden in the
Woods, wildflower sanctuary.
Newsletter: *Newsletter*
Benefits: Subscription to program and events
brochure, discounts on courses, workshops,
and trips, unlimited free admission to Garden
in the Woods, priority mailing of seed and
book catalog, discounts on seed orders, gifts,
books, and plants, discounts on library bor-
rowing privileges
See **Booksellers**, **Kidstuff**, Seeds, **Wildflowers**.

NEW YORK FLORA ASSOCIATION
New York State Museum

3132 CEC
Albany, NY 12230

NEWFOUNDLAND CHAPTER–CANADIAN
WILDFLOWER SOCIETY
Oxen Pond Botanical Park
St. John's, Newfoundland, Canada A1C 557

NIAGARA FRONTIER BOTANICAL SOCIETY
Buffalo Museum of Science
Humboldt Parkway
Buffalo, NY 14211

NORTH AMERICAN FRUIT EXPLORERS
(NAFEX)
1967
Jill Vrobeck
Route 1, Box 94
Chapin, IL 62628
A network throughout the United States and
Canada devoted to the cultivation of fruit and
nuts.
Newsletter: *The Pomona* (four issue per year)
Benefits: Access to lending library by mail, free
advertising for members seeking propagation
material, annual convention, regional work-
shops, interest groups, access to experts in the
field

NORTH AMERICAN GLADIOLUS COUNCIL
Mrs. William Strawser
701 South Hendricks Avenue
Marion, IN 46953
Seventy participating societies throughout the
United States and Canada.
Newsletter: *Quarterly Bulletin*
Publications: "GladioGrams" by Dr. Robert
O. Magie, article on growing gladiolus for the
local market

NORTH AMERICAN HEATHER SOCIETY
1977
Pauline Croxton
3641 Indian Creek Road
Placerville, CA 95667
Newsletter: *Heather News* (four issues per year)
Benefits: Annual convention, regional chapter
meetings, information exchange

NORTH AMERICAN LILY SOCIETY
Dr. Robert Gilman
P. O. Box 272
Owatonna, MN 55060

NORTH CAROLINA WILD FLOWER
PRESERVATION SOCIETY, INC.
1951
Nancy C. Julian
1933 Gaston Street
Winston-Salem, NC 27103
Totten Garden Center 3375, UNC
North Carolina Botanical Garden
University of North Carolina
Chapel Hill, NC 27599-3375
Promotes conservation of native plants and
their habitats through education, protection,
and propagation.
Newsletter: *Society Newsletter* (two issues per
year)
Benefits: Spring and fall meetings, field trips,
society scholarship fund, research

NORTHERN NEVADA NATIVE PLANT
SOCIETY
Margaret Williams
P.O. Box 8965
Reno, NV 89507

NORTHWEST HORTICULTURAL SOCIETY
University of Washington, GF-15
Isaacson Hall
Seattle, WA 98195
Phone: 206-527-1794
Newsletter: *Pacific Horticulture* (four issues
per year)
Benefits: Lecture series, annual fern and plant
sale, seed exchange program, garden tours,
field trips, exhibits, education fund

THE NORTHWEST PERENNIAL ALLIANCE
P.O. Box 45574 University Station
Seattle, WA 98145
A nonprofit organization dedicated to peren-
nials; affiliated with the Hardy Plant Society of
Great Britain.
Newsletter: *The Perennial Post* (four issues per
year)
Benefits: Quarterly meetings, plant sale, gar-
den tours, seed exchange program, book sales,
border projects at the Good Shepherd Center
in Seattle and the Bellevue Botanical Gardens

NOVA SCOTIA WILDFLOWER SOCIETY
6360 Young Street
Halifax, NS, Canada B3L 2A1

OHIO NATIVE PLANT SOCIETY
Ann K. Malmquist

6 Louise Drive
Chagrin Falls, OH 44022
Newsletter: *Trillium* (four issues per year)
Benefits: Annual field trip, classes, lectures

OKLAHOMA NATIVE PLANT SOCIETY
Tulsa Garden Center
2435 South Peoria
Tulsa, OK 74114-1350

PENNSYLVANIA NATIVE PLANT SOCIETY
P.O. Box 281
State College, PA 16804-0281

PHILADELPHIA BOTANICAL CLUB
Academy of Science
19th and Parkway
Philadelphia, PA 19103

RHODE ISLAND WILD PLANT SOCIETY
12 Sanderson Road
Smithfield, RI 02917-2606

THE RHODODENDRON SPECIES FOUNDA-
TION
1964
Deanna Hallsell
P.O. Box 3798
Federal Way, WA 98063-3798
Phone: 206-838-4646/Fax: 206-838-4686
Newsletter: *The Rhododendron Species Foun-
dation* (four issues per year)
Benefits: Plant and seed offerings, free admis-
sion to botanical garden, annual convention

SEED SAVERS EXCHANGE
1975
Kent and Diane Whealy
3076 North Winn Road
Decorah, IA 52101
See **Booksellers**, Heirlooms, Seeds, Vegetables.

SOCIETY FOR JAPANESE IRISES
Carol Warner and Carol Ramsey
16815 Falls Road
Upperco, MD 21155
6518 Beachy Avenue
Wichita KS 67206
See Iris.

SOCIETY FOR LOUISIANA IRISES
P.O. Box 40175 USL Station
Lafayette, LA 70504

1812 Broussard Road East
Lafayette, LA 70508-7847
See Iris.

SOCIETY FOR SIBERIAN IRISES
N75, W 14257 North Point Drive
Menomonee Falls, WI 53051-4325
See Iris.

SOIL AND WATER CONSERVATION SOCI-
ETY OF AMERICA
7515 Northeast Ankeny Road
Ankeny, IA 50021
Phone: 515-289-2331/800-THE-SOIL
Newsletter: *Conservogram*
Publications: *Journal of Soil and Water Conservation*
and *Sources of Native Seeds and Plants*
Benefits: Workshops and seminars, public service
projects, educational programs for schools, access
to technical knowledge

SOUTHERN APPALACHIAN BOTANICAL
CLUB
Cynthia Aulbach-Smith
University of South Carolina
Department of Biological Sciences
Columbia, SC 29208

SOUTHERN CALIFORNIA BOTANISTS
California State University
Department of Biological Sciences
Fullerton, CA 92634

THE SPECIES IRIS GROUP OF NORTH
AMERICA (SIGNA)
Florence Stout
Newsletter: *Signa* (two issues per year)
Part of the American Iris Society.
Benefits: Round-robin correspondence, seed
exchange, slides
See **Iris**.

SYRACUSE BOTANICAL CLUB
Janet Holmes
101 Ambergate Road
DeWitt, NY 13214

TENNESSEE NATIVE PLANT SOCIETY
P.O. Box 856
Sewanee, TN 37375

THE TOMATO CLUB
114 East Main Street
Bogota, NJ 07603

Phone: 201-488-2231/Fax: 201-489-4609
Newsletter: *The Tomato Club* (nine issues per year)

UNIVERSITY BOTANICAL GARDENS AT ASHEVILLE, INC.
151 W. T. Weaver Boulevard
Asheville, NC 28804

UTAH NATIVE PLANT SOCIETY
P.O. Box 520041
Salt Lake City, UT 84152-0041

VERMONT BOTANICAL AND BIRD CLUB
Deborah Benjamin
Warren Road, Box 327
Eden, VT 05652

VIRGINIA NATIVE PLANT SOCIETY
1982
Route 1, Box 381
Delaplane, VA 22025
Phone: 703-364-3066
Nonprofit organization dedicated to wild plants and their habitats.
Newsletter: *Bulletin* (four issues per year)
Benefits: Wildflower and fern checklists, nursery source information, conservation guidelines, discount publications

WASHINGTON NATIVE PLANT SOCIETY
A. R. Kruckeberg
University of Washington
Department of Botany, AJ-30
Seattle, WA 98195
Newsletter: *Douglasia* (four issues per year)
Publications: "Occasional Papers" featuring indepth studies of native flora

Benefits: Field trips, workshops, study weekends, special project committees

WESTERN CAROLINA BOTANICAL CLUB
Dick Smith
6 Tenequa Drive, Connestee Falls
Brevard, NC 28712

WILDFLOWER ASSOCIATION OF MICHIGAN
P.O. Box 80527
6011 West Joseph Street, Suite 403
Lansing, MI 48908-0527

THE WILDFLOWER SOCIETY
Goldsmith Civic Garden Center
750 Cherry Road
Memphis, TN 38119-4699

WORLD PUMPKIN CONFEDERATION
Ray Waterman
14050 Route 62
Collins, NY 14034
Phone: 716-532-5995/Fax: 716-532-5690
Newsletter: *CucurBits* (four issues per year)
Benefits: Entry forms for weigh-offs, record information for giant pumpkins, squash watermelon, round-robin correspondence

WYOMING NATIVE PLANT SOCIETY
Robert Dorn
Box 1471
Cheyenne, WY 82003

Numerous listings for wildflower and native plant societies were provided courtesy of the New England Wildflower Society.

HEIRLOOMS AND RESTORATION GARDENING

The sources listed in this section provide plant materials or information pertaining to heirloom plants and restoration gardening. Chapter titles displayed in boldface type indicate that narrative information about the source and the product or service offered appears in that chapter. Chapters not in boldface indicate that a source offers materials in this area but additional information is not included. A selection of books about heirloom and restoration gardening appears after the last listing.

ABUNDANT LIFE SEED FOUNDATION
Booksellers, **Garlic**, Herbs, Organics, **Seeds**, Vegetables

THE AMERICAN BOTANIST, BOOKSELLERS
Booksellers

AMERICAN FORESTS: FAMOUS AND HISTORIC TREES
Conifers, **Kidstuff**, **Trees**

AMES' ORCHARD & NURSERY
Fruit, Trees

THE ANTIQUE ROSE EMPORIUM
Booksellers, **Roses**

ARENA ROSE COMPANY
Roses

BARBARA FARNSWORTH, BOOKSELLERS
Booksellers, **Kidstuff**

BEAR CREEK NURSERY
Booksellers, **Fruit**, **Trees**

BLOSSOMS & BLOOMERS
Roses

BLUEBIRD HAVEN IRIS GARDEN
Iris

BOOK ARBOR
Booksellers

BOUNTIFUL GARDENS
Booksellers, **Garlic**, Herbs, **Kidstuff**, Organics, **Seeds**, **Supplies**, Vegetables

BRAND PEONY FARM
Peonies, Perennials

BURFORD BROTHERS
Fruit, Trees

CAROL BARNETT, BOOKS
Booksellers

THE COOK'S GARDEN
Booksellers, **Garlic**, **Herbs**, **Kidstuff**, Organics, **Seeds**, **Supplies**, Vegetables

DAISY FIELDS
Perennials

D. LANDRETH SEED COMPANY
Garlic, Grasses, Herbs, **Seeds**, Vegetables

DOWN ON THE FARM
Garlic, Herbs, **Kidstuff**, Organics, Seeds, **Vegetables**

FEDCO SEEDS
Booksellers, **Garlic**, Herbs, Organics, **Seeds**, Vegetables

FEDCO TREES
Booksellers, **Conifers**, **Fruit**, Trees

FLOATING MOUNTAIN SEEDS
Garlic, Herbs, Seeds, **Vegetables**

FOWLER NURSERIES, INC. GARDEN CENTER
Fruit, Trees

FOX HOLLOW HERB & HEIRLOOM SEED CO.
Garlic, **Herbs**, Organics, Seeds, **Vegetables**

THE FRAGRANT PATH
Herbs, Perennials, **Seeds**, Trees

GENIE HOUSE
Furniture

GILBERT H. WILD AND SON, INC.
Daylilies, **Iris**, **Peonies**, Perennials

GILES RAMBLIN' ROSES
Roses

GLECKLER'S SEEDMEN
Organics, Seeds, **Vegetables**

GREENMANTLE
Fruit, Organics, **Roses**, Trees

HEARD GARDENS, LTD.
Trees

HEIRLOOM GARDEN® SEEDS
Booksellers, **Herbs**, **Kidstuff**, **Seeds**

HEIRLOOM OLD GARDEN ROSES
Booksellers, **Roses**

HEIRLOOM SEED PROJECT—LANDIS VALLEY MUSEUM
Fruit, Organics, Seeds, Trees, **Vegetables**

HEIRLOOM SEEDS
Seeds, **Vegetables**

HERITAGE GARDEN HOUSE
Furniture

HERITAGE ROSE GARDENS
Roses

HISTORICAL ROSES
Roses

HOLLY LANE IRIS GARDENS
Daylilies, Hosta, Iris

INGRAHAM'S COTTAGE GARDEN
Roses

THE IRIS POND
Iris

JACKSON & PERKINS
Perennials, Roses

J.L. HUDSON, SEEDSMAN
Booksellers, Garlic, Herbs, Seeds, Vegetables

JOHNNY'S SELECTED SEEDS
Booksellers, Garlic, Grasses, Herbs, Organics, Seeds, Supplies, Vegetables

JOHNSON NURSERY
Fruit, Trees

KIDS IN BLOOM™ SPECIALTY SEEDS
Herbs, Kidstuff, Seeds, Vegetables

LANDSCAPE BOOKS
Booksellers

LAWSON'S NURSERY
Fruit, Trees

LIVING TREE NURSERY
Fruit, Trees

LONG HUNGRY CREEK NURSERY
Fruit, Organics, Trees

LONG ISLAND SEED COMPANY
Garlic, Seeds, Vegetables

LOWE'S OWN-ROOT ROSES
Roses

MENDOCINO HEIRLOOM ROSES
Organics, Roses

MILLER NURSERIES
Fruit, Trees

OLD HOUSE GARDENS
Bulbs

ORAL LEDDEN & SONS
Garlic, Grasses, Seeds, Supplies, Vegetables

PERENNIAL PLEASURES NURSERY OF VERMONT
Booksellers, Grasses, Herbs, Organics, Perennials, Seeds

THE PERFECT SEASON
Herbs, Perennials

PICKERING NURSERIES, INC.
Roses

PIEDMONT PLANT CO.
Garlic, Vegetables

PLANTS OF THE SOUTHWEST
Booksellers, Grasses, Seeds, Trees, Vegetables, Wildflowers

RAYMOND M. SUTTON, JR.
Booksellers

REDWOOD CITY SEED COMPANY
Booksellers, Garlic, Herbs, Kidstuff, Seeds, Vegetables

RESOURCES: BOOKS FOR PLANT COLLECTORS AND SEED SAVERS
Booksellers

R. H. SHUMWAY
Garlic, Herbs, Seeds, Vegetables

RICHTERS
Booksellers, Herbs, Organics, Seeds, Vegetables

RONNIGER'S SEED POTATOES
Booksellers, Garlic, Organics, Seeds, Vegetables

ROSES & WINE
Roses

ROSES OF YESTERDAY AND TODAY
Roses

ROSES UNLIMITED
Roses

ROYALL RIVER ROSES AT EVERGREEN FARM
Booksellers, Roses, Supplies

ST. LAWRENCE NURSERIES
Booksellers, Fruit, Organics, Trees

SALT SPRING SEEDS
Garlic, Kidstuff, Organics, Seeds, Vegetables

SCHLABACH'S NURSERY
Fruit, Trees

SEED SAVERS EXCHANGE–SEED SAVERS PUBLICATIONS
Booksellers, Horticultural Societies, Seeds, Vegetables

SEED SHARES™
Seeds, Vegetables

SEEDS BLÜM
Booksellers, Garlic, Herbs, Kidstuff, Seeds, Vegetables, Wildflowers

SEEDS OF CHANGE
Booksellers, Organics, Seeds

SEEDS TRUST: HIGH ALTI-
TUDE GARDENS
Booksellers, Garlic, **Grasses,**
Organics, **Seeds, Vegetables,**
Wildflowers

SELECT SEEDS–ANTIQUE
FLOWERS
Booksellers, Seeds

SHEPHERD'S GARDEN
SEEDS
Booksellers, Garlic, Herbs,
Kidstuff, Seeds, Supplies,
Vegetables

SISTERS' BULB FARM
Bulbs

SONOMA ANTIQUE APPLE
NURSERY
Fruit, Organics, Trees

SOUTHERN EXPOSURE
SEED EXCHANGE®
Booksellers, Garlic, Herbs,
Seeds, **Supplies, Vegetables**

SOUTHMEADOW FRUIT
GARDENS
Fruit, Trees

"SOW ORGANIC" SEEDS
Garlic, Herbs, Organics,
Seeds, **Vegetables**

STANEK'S NURSERY
Roses

SUNNYRIDGE GARDENS
Daylilies, Iris

THE THOMAS JEFFERSON
CENTER FOR HISTORICAL
PLANTS
Booksellers, Furniture, Seeds

THOMPSON & MORGAN
Garlic, **Grasses, Seeds,**
Vegetables.

TOMATO GROWERS SUP-
PLY COMPANY
Booksellers, Seeds, Supplies,
Vegetables

THE URBAN HOMESTEAD
Fruit, Trees

VERMONT BEAN SEED
COMPANY
Garlic, Herbs, **Seeds,**
Vegetables

VINTAGE GARDENS
Roses

WARREN F. BRODERICK
Booksellers

WAYSIDE GARDENS
Fruit, Grasses, Perennials,
Roses

YORK HILL FARM
Daylilies, Grasses, **Hosta,**
Iris, Perennials

Reading About Restoration, Period, and Heirloom Gardening

Early American Gardens: For Meate or Medicine (17th Century)
American Gardens in the 18th Century: For Use or For Delight
American Gardens in the 19th Century: For Comfort and Affluence
All three works by Ann Leighton comprise a sweeping source of information about the history of American gardening. Each includes accounts contemporary to the periods covered and a detailed list of plants authentic to use in each period.

For Every House a Garden: A Guide for Reproducing Period Gardens, by Rudy and Joy Favretti. Includes a wide range of period garden plans, photographs and illustrations. Includes extensive lists of authentic plants divided into sections which include plants in common use during distinct periods, such as: Flowers, 1600–1699; Shrubs, Trees, and Vines, 1600–1699; Vegetables and Field Crops, 1600–1699, through Trees, Shrubs, and Vines,1850–1900.

Landscape & Gardens for Historic Buildings, by Rudy and Joy Favretti. Includes historical information from the colonial period through 1930. Explains how to research, plan, develop, and maintain a restored landscape. Includes plant lists and some other overlapping material from *For Every House a Garden,* also by the Favrettis.

The Heirloom Garden: Selecting & Growing Over 300 Old-Fashioned Ornamentals, by Jo Ann Gardner. Includes concise descriptions, plant portraits, photographs, histories, cultural advice, and growing information. Includes commercial and noncommercial source lists, plant societies and preservation organizations, and historical gardens to visit.

The Historical Gardener: Plants and Garden Practices of the Past. A quarterly newsletter featuring new (original and reprints) and vintage articles and period pieces about heirloom and historical gardening. Includes sources in each issue for heirloom plant materials and historical information. Contact Kathleen McClelland, The Historical Gardener, 1910 North 35th Place, Mount Vernon, WA 98273-8981.

The Southern Heirloom Garden: The Heritage, the Plants, the Designs, by William Welch and G. Grant. A survey of the gardening heritage of the South, including the influences of diverse cultures and individual plantsmen. Includes a separate section about particular plants, as well as practical information on restoration and re-creation. Illustrated.

For books about heirloom and open pollinated seeds, *see* **Seeds**. For books about antique and old garden roses, *see* **Roses**.

ORGANICS

*M*y first garden failed not because I did anything wrong, but because I didn't do much at all. I did turn sod and plant seeds, then waited patiently, thinking the next step would be quite simply to harvest food. Considering the rude introduction, it's a minor miracle I ever tried gardening again.

Perhaps I thought the organic method would be a kind of solution to gardening problems. Instead, I discovered it was a series of rather meandering pathways never clearly labeled either right or wrong; but I also realized eventually that all these paths really led in the same basic direction.

Today, I would say the organic gardener's eternal task is to help the garden build topsoil. Soil building is a pioneering effort whose work is never quite finished. Our culture prides itself on shortcuts and, indeed, we can improve on nature's normal forty to one hundred years to create one inch of new topsoil. Average soils may take a mere two to six years to regenerate the energy, organic matter, and microbial communities, which then make their organic owners look masterful. This two- to six- year sentence may sound harsh, but we need to stay put to be successful organic gardeners.

Of course, gardening requires more than soil. A healthy garden is a complex community of sun and air, soil and water, plants and animals, especially microscopic animals. Healthy organic gardens literally glow with life, and the real meaning of organic gardening might be in the nurture and cultivation of life rather than mere harvesting of food.

Our current home is a far cry from the early years of transition when we struggled to grow food at the same time we were creating an organic environment from a run-down farm. Patient struggling paid off. By way of analogy, one might say we planted seed that not only survived but blossomed into a community now thriving mostly of its own accord.

In fact, as the abundance of life gradually increased in our garden we found that other people were increasingly attracted as well. The soil and plant community lost its well-defined boundaries and grew to include a human community of good friends and eager helpers.

Today, my wife and I raise over one hundred apple varieties in an orchard that hasn't required a pesticide (other than a dormant fish oil in early spring) in over three years. Our 340 strains of garlic live in fields that haven't seen pesticide in over fifteen years. We improve each year by better anticipating the needs of the garden, but the garden also seems to need less each year. Our worst pests are now occasional potato beetles and tomato hornworms, which we usually handpick.

Each year we promise to be more timely with weeding. We manage best

those years when we lay a good mulch, especially if we grew weeds out of the soil with green manure crops in previous years. We're not weed free (and don't want to be), but green manure allows us to use weeds to benefit soil rather than destroy them as garden enemies.

Each year we do a better job of green manuring. We don't harvest half the garden before buckwheat is already flowering in part of it, and no garden soil goes one full year without growing either vetch or clover in addition to our own food plants. In short, we put at least one crop back in the soil for every crop we take ourselves. Soil building is the fundamental process in which garden and gardener are equal partners. Harvestable food is a happy by-product of our endeavor.

Books and magazines abound with information about crop rotation, green manure crops, sanitation, prevention, recycling of organic matter, use of disease-resistant and locally adapted plants, etc. But books are a poor place to learn patience, tolerance, timeliness, foresight, cooperation with nature, and simple awareness of all the life around us.

What changes must take place for our gardens to become organic? Changes in the soil, and changes in ourselves, both of which produce abundant change around us. My organic garden has been one of the best teachers I ever had, and I can't recall a single moment of drudgery or boredom in the last twenty-two years of learning.

Like this essay, my introduction to organic gardening was a bit awkward, but it led to strong bonds and fine friendships. Now my problem is not knowing how to stop. I never harvest and then think of myself as finished with anything. The organic garden never ends.

—*Ron L. Engeland*

(Ron L. Engeland is a self-described small scale organic farmer who makes his living growing garlic. Ron and Watershine Engeland operate Filaree Farm which is listed as a Seed Saver's Exchange "Garlic Curator." Ron is the author of *Growing Great Garlic*.)

The sources listed in this section provide plant materials cultivated through organic methods, or materials, supplies, and information that are useful in implementing organic practices. Chapter titles displayed in boldface type indicate that narrative information about the source and the product or service offered appears in that chapter. Chapters not in boldface indicate that a source offers materials in this area but additional information is not included. A selection of books about organic methods and practices appear after the last listing.

ABUNDANT LIFE SEED
FOUNDATION
Booksellers, Garlic,
Heirlooms, Herbs, **Seeds,**
Vegetables

AGE-OLD ORGANICS
Supplies

ALLEN, STERLING, &
LOTHROP
Garlic, Herbs, **Seeds,**
Supplies, Vegetables

ARBICO
Booksellers, Supplies

BERLIN SEEDS
Booksellers, Fruit, Garlic,
Grasses, **Kidstuff,** Seeds,
Supplies, Vegetables

BETTER YIELD INSECTS
AND GARDEN HOUSES
Supplies

BIOLOGIC
Supplies

BLOOMINGFIELDS FARM
Daylilies

BLUEJAY GARDENS HERB
FARM
Herbs

BOOTHE HILL WILDFLOW-
ERS
Seeds, **Wildflowers**

BOUNTIFUL GARDENS
Booksellers, Garlic, Heirlooms, Herbs, **Kidstuff,**

Seeds, **Supplies,** Vegetables

BOZEMAN BIO-TECH
**Booksellers, Kidstuff, Sup-
plies**

BRONWOOD WORM FARMS
Supplies

BROOKS BOOKS
Booksellers

BROWN'S EDGEWOOD
GARDENS
Booksellers, Herbs, **Furni-
ture, Supplies**

BUTTERBROOKE FARM
Booksellers, Seeds, **Vegetables**

CAPE COD WORM FARM
Supplies

THE COOK'S GARDEN
Booksellers, Garlic, Heir-
looms, **Herbs, Kidstuff,**
Seeds, **Supplies,** Vegetables

THE CRAFTER'S GARDEN
Supplies

DAN'S GARDEN SHOP
**Booksellers, Seeds, Supplies,
Vegetables**

DIRT CHEAP ORGANICS
Supplies

DOWN ON THE FARM SEED
Garlic, Heirlooms, Herbs,
Kidstuff, Seeds, **Vegetables**

EARLEE, INC.
Supplies

ELIXIR FARM BOTANICALS
Booksellers, Herbs, Seeds

ERTH-RITE
Supplies

FEDCO SEEDS
Booksellers, Garlic, Heir-
looms, Herbs, **Seeds,**
Vegetables

FILAREE FARM
Booksellers, Garlic

FOX HOLLOW HERB &
HEIRLOOMS SEED CO.
Garlic, Heirloom, **Herbs,**
Seeds, **Vegetables**

FUNGI PERFECTI
**Booksellers, Garlic, Kidstuff,
Supplies**

GARDEN CITY SEEDS
Booksellers, Garlic, Grasses,
Herbs, **Seeds, Supplies,**
Vegetables

GARDENER'S SUPPLY CO.
Furniture, Supplies

GARDENS ALIVE!
Supplies

GARDENS NORTH
Grasses, **Seeds,** Wildflowers

GLECKLER'S SEEDMEN
Heirlooms, Seeds, **Vegetables**

GREENMANTLE NURSERY
Fruit, Heirlooms, **Roses**, Trees

THE GUANO COMPANY INTERNATIONAL, INC.
Supplies

GURNEY'S SEED & NURSERY CO.
Garlic, Kidstuff, Seeds, Supplies, Vegetables

HARMONY FARM SUPPLY & NURSERY
Booksellers, Kidstuff, Supplies

HEIRLOOM SEED PROJECT, LANDIS VALLEY MUSEUM
Fruit, Heirlooms, Seeds, Trees, **Vegetables**

HENRY FIELD'S SEED & NURSERY CO.
Fruit, Garlic, Kidstuff, Perennials, **Seeds, Supplies, Trees, Vegetables**

HILLARY'S GARDEN
Herbs, **Perennials**

I.F.M. PRODUCTS FOR NATURAL AGRICULTURE
Booksellers, Supplies

JASPERSON'S HERSEY NURSERY
Daylilies, Iris, Perennials

JOHNNY'S SELECTED SEEDS
Booksellers, Garlic, Grasses, Heirlooms, Herbs, **Seeds**, Supplies, Vegetables

KADCO USA, INC.
Supplies

THE LADYBUG CO.
Supplies

LEE VALLEY TOOLS LTD.
Supplies

LONG HUNGRY CREEK NURSERY
Fruit, Heirlooms, Trees

MAESTRO-GRO
Supplies

MEDINA AGRICULTURE PRODUCTS COMPANY, INC.
Supplies

MENDOCINO HEIRLOOM ROSES
Heirlooms, **Roses**

MOOSE GROWERS SUPPLY
Booksellers, Garlic, Supplies, Vegetables

MORCO PRODUCTS
Supplies

MOTHER NATURE'S WORM CASTINGS
Supplies

THE NATURAL GARDENER'S CATALOG
Booksellers, Supplies

NATURE'S CONTROL
Supplies

NICHOLS GARDEN NURSERY
Booksellers, Garlic, Herbs, Seeds, Supplies, Vegetables, Wildflowers

NITRON INDUSTRIES
Kidstuff, Seeds, **Supplies**, Vegetables

NORTHWIND NURSERY AND ORCHARDS
Booksellers, Fruit, Supplies, Trees

ORCON
Supplies

PEACEFUL VALLEY FARM & GARDEN SUPPLY
Booksellers, Garlic, Grasses, Seeds, **Supplies**, Wildflowers

PERENNIAL PLEASURES NURSERY OF VERMONT
Booksellers, Grasses, Heirlooms, **Herbs, Perennials**, Seeds

PINETREE GARDEN SEEDS
Booksellers, Garlic, Herbs, **Kidstuff, Seeds, Supplies, Vegetables**

P. L. ROHRER & BRO.
Garlic, Herbs, **Seeds**, Supplies, Vegetables

PLUMTREE NURSERY
Fruit

PRAIRIE MOON NURSERY
Booksellers, Grasses, Seeds, Trees, **Wildflowers**

REOTEMP INSTRUMENT CORP.
Supplies

RICHTERS
Booksellers, Heirlooms, **Herbs**, Seeds, Vegetables

ROCKY MOUNTAIN INSECTARY
Supplies

RONNIGER'S SEED POTATOES
Booksellers, Garlic, Heirlooms, Seeds, Vegetables

ST. LAWRENCE NURSERIES
Booksellers, Fruit, Heirlooms, Trees

SALT SPRING SEEDS
Garlic, Heirlooms, **Kidstuff**, Seeds, **Vegetables**

SEEDS OF CHANGE®
Booksellers, Heirlooms, Seeds

SEEDS TRUST: HIGH
ALTITUDE GARDENS
Booksellers, Garlic, **Grasses**,
Heirlooms, Seeds,
Vegetables, Wildflowers

SMITH & HAWKEN
Furniture, Kidstuff, **Supplies**

SONOMA ANTIQUE APPLE
NURSERY
Fruit, Heirlooms, Trees

SOUTHERN SEEDS
Booksellers, Fruit, Garlic,
Seeds, Vegetables

"SOW ORGANIC" SEEDS
Garlic, Heirlooms, Herbs,
Seeds, Vegetables

TERRITORIAL SEED COM-
PANY
Booksellers, Garlic, Herbs,
Kidstuff, Seeds, **Supplies**,
Vegetables

THOMAS GARDENS
Daylilies

TINMOUTH CHANNEL
FARM
Herbs, Kidstuff, Seeds

TUMBLEBUG®
Supplies

UNIQUE INSECT CONTROL
Supplies

WORM'S WAY INDIANA
Booksellers, Garlic, Supplies

YUCCA DO NURSERY AT
PECKERWOOD GARDENS
Cactus, Conifers, Grasses,
Perennials, **Trees,**
Wildflowers

Reading About Organic Methods

Designing and Maintaining Your Edible Landscape Naturally, by Robert Kourik. A whole earth approach that recommends edible plants that add fertility to your soil, attract beneficial insects, and minimize the effects of erosion, offers techniques for enriching your soil, and other strategies for providing food through the cultivation of low-maintenance plants.

Fruit Trees, by Jennifer Bennett. Ms. Bennett's book is most useful for home gardeners in the northern half of the United States. She explains site selection, landscape considerations, planting, pruning, pest control, and container culture while emphasizing ecological soundness and an organic grower's point of view.

How to Grow More Vegetables, Fruits, Nuts, Berries, Grains, and Other Crops Than you Ever Thought Possible on Less Land Than You Can Imagine, by John Jeavons. The step-by-step instruction manual for sustainable organic biointensive gardening as developed and practiced by Ecology Action (Bountiful Gardens).

Lazy-Bed Gardening, by John Jeavons and Carol Cox. An Irish technique for a deeply prepared bed whose growing area can produce substantially more than the equivalent area planted in less deeply developed rows. A step-by-step guide for using this technique in food gardening.

Let It Rot, by Stu Campbell. Creating compost is a natural act. Campbell's home gardener's guide demystifies composting and offers practical advice on how to encourage nature to take its course while letting your plants and soil be the beneficiaries.

Let's Get Growing, by Crow Miller. A dirt-under-nails primer on raising vegetables, fruits and flowers by organic methods. Includes extensive general information on how to grow the soil and specifics on caring for numerous varieties of edible and ornamental plant material.

The Mulch Book, by Stu Campbell. How to use bark, hay, stone, compost, and other materials to effectively minimize and deter weeds while letting beneficial elements nurture your plantings. Advice on when to mulch, how to make mulch, and the most useful types of mulch for varied plant life.

The New Organic Grower's Four-Season Harvest, by Eliot Coleman. A practical and informative manual and guide for extending the harvest by succession planting and crop protection using low-tech, home-gardener-friendly devices and natural methods.

The Orchard Almanac: A Spraysaver's Guide, by Steve Page and Joe Smillie. A handbook organized by season that offers organic and IPM solutions that stress low toxicity in maintaining the health of your home orchard. Also includes a wealth of tips on planting, pruning, fertilization, restoring old trees, harvesting, and storage.

Rodale's All New Encyclopedia of Organic Gardening, by the editors of the Rodale Press. The A to Z of gardening following nature's way. Over four hundred entries cover the full spectrum of gardening tasks and pleasures following true organic methods.

Rodale's Garden Problem Solver: Vegetables, Fruits and Herbs, by Jeff Ball. Lists the symptoms, causes, organic solutions, and preventative measures for seven hundred problems facing your edibles.

Rodale's Landscape Problem Solver: A Plant-by-Plant Guide, by Jeff and Liz Ball. The organic solutions and preventative measures for insect and animal pest problems facing shrubs, trees, ground covers, foliage plants, and lawns.

Rodale's Flower Garden Problem Solver: Annuals, Perennials, Bulbs, and Roses, by Jeff and Liz Ball. Lists the symptoms, causes, organic solutions, and preventative measures for six hundred problems facing flowering plants.

Shepherd's Purse Organic Pest Control Handbook, by Pest Publications. A widely recommended (slim) volume for identifying and controlling pests through nonchemical methods.

Start with the Soil: The Organic Gardener's Guide to Improving Soil for Higher Yields, More Beautiful Flowers, and Healthy Easy-Care Gardens, by Grace Gershuny. A hands-on guide to creating and maintaining healthy garden soil.

GEOGRAPHICAL
INDEX
TO SOURCES

ALABAMA

AUBURN 36830-5771

Alabama Wildflower Society
240 Ivy Lane
Dottie Elam

BIRMINGHAM 35206

Steve Ray's Bamboo Gardens
909 79th Place South
Steve and Janie Ray
Phone: 205-833-3052
On-site: Retail
By appointment.

FORT PAYNE 35967-9501

Gary Wayner, Bookseller
1002 Glenn Boulevard S.W.
Gary Wayner
Phone: 205-845-7828
Fax: 205-845-2070
On-site: Retail
By appointment.

JASPER 35501

T & M Gardens
Route 4, Box 417
Terah George and Mae Snow
Phone: 205-387-8897
On-site: Retail
April through October.
Sunday, 1:00–5:00. Monday
through Saturday, 8:00–6:00.
By appointment.

MOBILE 36633-1564

Gothic Arch Greenhouses
Division of Trans-sphere
Trade, Inc.
P.O. Box 1564

W. H. "Buzz" Sierke, Jr.
Phone: 205-432-7529,
800-628-4974
Fax: 205-433-4570
NOTP

NEWVILLE 36353

Kirkland Daylilies
P.O. Box 176
Street address: Union Springs
Road
Marjorie C. Kirkland
Phone: 205-889-3313
On-site: Retail and wholesale
May through July. Sunday
through Saturday, 8:00–5:00.
By appointment.

TRUSSVILLE 35173

**Woodbrook Furniture Man-
ufacturers**
P.O. Box 175
Street address: 7209 High-
way 11 North
Phone: 800-828-3607
On-site: NOTP

ALASKA

ANCHORAGE 99514-1613

Alaska Native Plant Society
P.O. Box 141613

KENAI 99611

**Baldwin Seed Co.–
Seeds of Alaska**
P.O. Box 3127
Richard Baldwin
NOTP

ALBERTA

CALGARY T2H 251

Lee Valley Tools, Ltd.
7261-11th Street
Phone: 403-253-2066
(See also Ottawa, Ontario)
On-site: Retail
Monday through Wednesday,
9:00–6:00. Thursday and
Friday, 9:00–9:00. Saturday,
9:00–5:00.

EDMONTON T5S 129

Lee Valley Tools, Ltd.
10103 175th Street N.W.
Phone: 403-444-6153
(See also Ottawa, Ontario)
On-site: Retail
Monday through Wednesday,
9:00–6:00. Thursday and
Friday, 9:00–9:00. Saturday,
9:00–5:00.

ARIZONA

GLENDALE 85311-0337

Homan Brothers Seed, Inc.
P.O. Box 337
Nathan Young
Phone: 602-244-1650
Fax: 602-435-8777
NOTP

PARKS 86018

Strong's Alpine Succulents
P.O. Box 50115
Shirley Strong
Phone: 520-526-5784
NOTP

PHOENIX 85003

Arena Rose Company
536 West Cambridge Avenue
John Arena, Sylvester Arena
Phone: 602-266-2223
Fax: 602-266-4335
NOTP

PHOENIX 85051

Shepard Iris Garden
3342 West Orangewood
Don and Bobbie Shepard
Phone: 602-841-1231
On-site: Retail
April. Every day, 9:00–5:00.
By appointment.

TEMPE 85285

Wild Seed, Inc.
P.O. Box 27751
Rita Jo Anthony
Phone: 602-345-0669
Fax: 602-276-3524
On-site: Wholesale
By appointment.

TUCSON 85703

Southwestern Native Seeds
P.O. Box 50503
Sally and Tim Walker
NOTP

TUCSON 85705

Living Stones Nursery
2936 North Stone Avenue
Jane Evans and Gene Joseph
Phone: 520-628-8773
Retail store and nursery:

Plants for the Southwest
50 East Blacklidge
On-site: Retail and wholesale
Wednesday, Thursday, Friday, and Saturday,
9:00–5:30. By appointment.

TUCSON 85717-1206

Arizona Native Plant Society
P.O. Box 41206
Sun Station

TUCSON 85719

Native Seeds/SEARCH
Garden: 2509 North Campbell Avenue #325
Office: Tucson Botanical Gardens
2150 North Alvernon
Angelo Joaquin, Jr.
Phone: 520-327-9123
Fax: 520-327-5821
On-site: Retail
September through July.
Tuesday and Thursday,
10:00–4:00. Other times by appointment.

TUCSON 85738-1247

Arbico
P.O. Box 4247 CRB
Street address: 18701 North Lago Del Oro Parkway
Tucson 85737
Richard C. Frey and Sheri Herrera de Frey
Phone: 520-825-9785,
800-827-BUGS
Fax: 520-825-2038
On-site: Retail
Tours only. By appointment.

ARKANSAS

AUGUSTA 72006

Cooley's Strawberry Nursery
P.O. Box 472
Street address: 105 First Street
James Cooley
Phone: 501-347-2026,
501-724-5630
On-site: Retail and wholesale
January through May. Monday through Friday,
7:00–4:00. Or by appointment.

BENTON 72015-1207

Burk's Nursery
P.O. Box 1207
Lois Burks
Phone: 501-794-3266
NOTP

The Haworthia Society
c/o Burk's Nursery
P.O. Box 1207
Lois Burks
Phone: 501-794-3266

ELKINS 72727

Holland Wildflower Farm
290 O'Neal Lane
Bob and Julie Holland
Phone: 501-643-2622
On-site: Retail and wholesale
April through November 15.
Tuesday through Saturday,
9:30–6:00.

EUREKA SPRINGS 72632

Ozark Handle & Hardware
P.O. Box 390
Street address: 91 South

Main Street
Eddie Silver
Phone: 501-253-6888
NOTP

FAYETTEVILLE 72701

Ames' Orchard & Nursery
18292 Wildlife Road
Guy and Carolyn Falge Ames
Phone: 501-443-0282
(evenings)
Orders: 800-443-0283
On-site: Retail
By appointment.

FAYETTEVILLE 72702-1447

Nitron Industries, Inc.
P.O. Box 1447
Street address:
4605 Johnson Road
Johnson, AR 72741
Frank J. Finger
Phone: 800-835-0123
Fax: 501-750-3008
On-site: Retail and wholesale
All year. Monday through
Friday, 8:00–5:30. Saturday,
9:00–1:00.

FOUKE 71837

Enoch's Berry Farm
Route 2, Box 227
A. B. Enoch
Phone: 501-653-2806
On-site: Retail
November through April.
Monday through Friday.

HOPE 71801

Giant Watermelons
P.O. Box 141
NOTP

LITTLE ROCK 72225

**Arkansas Native Plant
Society**
P.O. Box 250250

MOUNTAINBURG 72946

Boston Mountain Nurseries
Route 2, Box 405-A
Gary Pense
Phone: 501-369-2007
Fax: 501-369-2007
On-site: Retail and wholesale
$100 pick up.

Pense Nursery
16518 Marie Lane
Phillip D. Pense
Phone: 501-369-2494
Fax: 501-369-2494
On-site: Retail and wholesale
October through May. Mon-
day through Friday,
8:00–5:00. By appointment.

PETTIGREW 72752

Highlander Nursery
P.O. Box 177
Phone: 501-677-2300
NOTP

SPRINGDALE 72766-6670

Maestro-Gro
P.O. Box 6670
NOTP

BRITISH
COLUMBIA

GANGES V0S 1E0

Salt Spring Seeds
Box 33
Dan Jason
Phone: 604-537-5269
On-site: Retail
By appointment.

GRAND FORKS V0H 1H0

Hardy Roses for the North
Box 2048
Street address:
5680 Hughes Road
U.S: Box 273
Danville, WA 99121-0273
Barry Poppenheim
Phone 604-442-8442
Fax: 604-442-2766
On-site: Retail
By appointment.

VANCOUVER V6P 523

Lee Valley Tools, Ltd.
1098 S.W. Marine Drive
Phone: 604-261-2262
(See also Ottawa, Ontario)
On-site: Retail
Monday through Wednesday,
9:00–6:00. Thursday and
Friday, 9:00–9:00. Saturday,
9:00–5:00.

CALIFORNIA

ALBION 95410

Digging Dog Nursery
P.O. Box 471
Street address:
31101 Middle Ridge Road
Deborah Whigham and Gary
Ratway
Phone: 707-937-1130
Fax: 707-937-4389
On-site: Retail and wholesale
All year. Tuesday through
Saturday, 9:00–4:00. By
appointment.

AZUSA 91720

Myron Kimnach/Books on Succulents
5508 North Astell Avenue
Myron Kimnach
Phone: 818-334-7349
Fax: 818-334-0658
NOTP

BERKELEY 94701-1128

The Calochortus Society
P.O. Box 1128
H. P. McDonald and
Karin R. Stokkink

BERKELEY 94702

Niwa Tools
1333 San Pablo Avenue
Kayoko Kuroiwa
Phone: 510-524-3700,
800-443-5512
Fax: 510-524-3423
On-site: Retail and wholesale
June through August. By
appointment.

BERKELEY 94709-5082

Living Tree Nursery
P.O. Box 10082
Jesse Schwartz
Phone: 510-420-1440
NOTP

BERKELEY 94720

California Botanical Society
Dept. of Botany
University of California

BERRY CREEK 95916

The Ladybug Company
8706 Oro-Quincy Highway
Julie Steele
Phone: 916-589-5227
NOTP

BOLINAS 94924

Larner Seeds
P.O. Box 407
Street address: 235 Fern Road
Judith Lowry
Phone: 415-868-9407
On-site: Retail and wholesale
All year. Tuesday, Wednesday,
and Friday.
By appointment.

BRANSCOMB 95417

Heritage Rose Gardens
40350 Wilderness Road
Virginia Hopper and
Joyce Demits
Phone: 707-964-3748
On-site: Retail
Summer. By appointment.

BUENA PARK 90620-2698

Malley Supply
7439 LaPalma Avenue,
Suite 514
Allan Garofalow
NOTP

CARPINTERIA 93014

Moon Mountain Wildflowers
P.O. Box 725
Street address: 5690 Casitas
Pass Road
Becky L. Schaff
Phone: 805-684-2565
Fax: 805-684-2565
On-site: Retail
By appointment.

CASTRO VALLEY 94546

Clyde Robin Seed Co., Inc.
P.O. Box 2366
Street address: 3670
Enterprise Avenue

Stew Atwoun
Phone: 510-785-0425
Fax: 510-785-6463
NOTP

CHICO 95926

Valley Oak Tool Co.
448 West Second Avenue
David Grau
Phone: 916-342-6188
On-site: Retail
By appointment.

CHULA VISTA 91910

Pacific Tree Farms
4301 Lynwood Drive
William L. Nelson
Phone: 619-422-2400
Fax: 619-422-2400
On-site: Retail and wholesale
All year. Monday through
Saturday, 8:30–5:00. Sunday,
9:00–3:00.

CHULA VISTA 92010

Tiny Petals Nursery
483 Minot Avenue
Patrick and Susan O'Brien
Phone: 619-422-0385
On-site: Retail and wholesale
All year. Thursday through
Monday, 9:00-5:00.

CITRUS HEIGHTS 95621

Unique Insect Control
5504 Sperry Drive
Jeanne Houston
Phone: 916-961-7945
Fax: 916-967-7082
On-site: Retail
By appointment.

CONCORD 94521

Brooks Books
P.O. Box 21473
Street address:
1343 New Hampshire Drive
Phil and Martha Nesty
Phone: 510-672-4566
Fax: 510-672-3338
On-site: Retail
By appointment.

Classic & Country Crafts
5100 1-B Clayton Road,
Suite 291
Sue Siekierski
Phone: 510-672-4337
Fax: 510-672-4337
NOTP

CORTE MADERA 94925

Dirt Cheap Organics
5645 Paradise Drive
Pallette Amalia
Phone: 415-924-0369
On-site: Retail
All year. Monday through
Saturday, 8:00–4:00.

DAVIS 95617

agAccess Book Catalog
P.O. Box 2008
Street address:
603 Fourth Street
Davis 95616
Karen Van Epen
Phone: 916-756-7177
Fax: 916-756-7188
On-site: Retail
By appointment.

EL CAJON 92021-2328

Blossom Valley Gardens
15011 Oak Creek Road
Sanford Roberts
Phone: 619-443-7711
NOTP

EL CERRITO 94530

Heritage Rose Group
925 Galvin Drive
NOTP

ENCINITAS 92023-1129

**The American Begonia
Society**
P.O. Box 231129
John Ingles
Phone: 707-764-5407

ENCINITAS 92024

Jim Duggan Flower Nursery
1452 Santa Fe Drive
Jim Duggan
Phone: 619-943-1658
On-site: Retail
Daily, 8:30–5:00.

FELTON 95018

Shepherd's Garden Seeds
6116 Highway 9
Renee Shepherd and
Beth Benjamin
Phone: 408-335-6910
Fax: 408-335-2080
On-site: Retail
May through October.
Thursday and Saturday,
10:00–12:00.
By appointment.

FORT BRAGG 95437

Adirondack Design
Cypress Street Center
350 Cypress Street
George Griffith
Phone: 800-222-0343
Fax: 707-964-2701
On-site: Retail

All year. Monday through
Friday, 9:00–3:00.

FREMONT 94539

**Four Winds True Dwarf
Citrus Growers**
P.O. Box 3538,
Mission San Jose District
Don and Mary Ann Dillon
Phone: 510-656-2591
Fax: 510-656-1360
On-site: Retail and wholesale
Weekdays, 8:00–5:00.

FRESNO 93722-5899

Henrietta's Nursery
1345 North Brawley
Jerry and Sylvia Hardaway
Phone: 209-275-2166
Fax: 209-275-6014
On-site: Retail and wholesale
Monday through Saturday,
10:00–4:00.

FRESNO 93726

Pacific Coast Seed Company
3999 North Chestnut,
Suite 256
Fax: 209-225-5606
NOTP

FULLERTON 92634

**Southern California
Botanists**
Dept. of Biological Sciences
California State University

GARBERVILLE 95542

Greenmantle Nursery
3010 Ettersburg Road
Ram and Marissa Fishman
Phone: 707-986-7504
On-site: Retail
By appointment.

**Peaceful Valley Farm &
Garden Supply**
P.O. Box 2209
Street address:
110 Spring Hill Drive
Kathleen Fenton
Phone: 916-272-4769
Fax: 916-272-4794
On-site: Retail
All year. Tuesday through
Saturday, 9:00–5:00.

**Weiss Brothers
Perennial Nursery**
11690 Colfax Highway
Store: 10120 Joerschke
Martin Weiss
Phone: 916-272-7657
Fax: 916-272-3578
On-site: Retail
Seven days. Does not carry
all varieties offered in catalog.

GRAFTON 95444

Gourmet Mushrooms
P.O. Box 515
Phone: 707-829-7301
Fax: 707-823-1507
NOTP

**Harmony Farm Supply
& Nursery**
P.O. Box 460
Nursery: 3244 Gravenstein
Highway North
Sebastopol 95472
Kate Burroughs and David
Henry
Phone: 707-823-9125
Fax: 707-823-1734
On-site: Pick up
Mid-January through mid-
February. Monday through
Sunday, 9:00–5:00.

GUERNEVILLE 95446

Emi Meade Importers
16000 Fern Way
Emi Meade
Phone: 707-869-3218
On-site: Retail
By appointment.

Heirloom Garden® Seeds
P.O. Box 138
Warren Raysor
NOTP

HEALDSBURG 95448

**Sonoma Antique Apple
Nursery**
4395 Westside Road
Carolyn and Terry Harrison,
John Hooper and
Harry Hull
Phone: 707-433-6420
Fax: 707-433-6479
On-site: Wholesale
January through March.
Monday through Friday,
9:00–4:00.

IONE 95640

**K & L Cactus & Succulent
Nursery**
9500 Brook Ranch Road East
Keith and Lorraine Thomas
Phone: 209-274-0360
NOTP

LA HONDA 94020

Cieli
P.O. Box 151
Street address:
36 Ventura Avenue
Joyce Converse
Phone: 415-369-2129,
800-876-3006
Fax: 415-369-2082
NOTP

LAWNDALE 90260-6320

Lagenbach
Dept. L6311, P.O. Box 1420
Gail Stokes
Phone: 800-362-1991,
800-362-4410
Fax: 800-362-4490
NOTP

LAYTONVILLE 95454-1329

Mountain Maples
54561 Registered Guest Road
P.O. Box 1329
Don and Nancy Fiers
Phone: 707-984-6522
Fax: 707-984-7433
On-site: Retail and wholesale
By appointment.

LEMON GROVE 91945

McDaniel's Miniature Roses
7523 Zemco Street
Carol L. Gladson
Phone: 619-469-4669
On-site: Retail
All year. Monday through
Saturday, 9:00–5:00. By
appointment.

LOS ANGELES 90019

**Orcon
Division of Organic
Control, Inc.**
Box 781147
Street address:
5132 Venice Boulevard
Paula White
Phone: 213-937-7444
Fax: 213-937-0123
NOTP

LOS ANGELES 94720

**The Cactus and Succulent
Society of America**
1535 Reeve Street
Phone: 310-556-1923

MARINA DEL REY 90291

A. C. Burke & Co.
2554 Lincoln Boulevard,
Suite 1058
Andrew Burke
Phone: 310-574-2770
Fax: 310-574-2771
NOTP

MENDOCINO 95460

Mendocino Heirloom Roses
P.O. Box 670
Alice Flores and Gail Daly
Phone: 707-877-1888
Fax: 707-937-0963
On-site: Retail and wholesale
By appointment.

MENDOCINO 95460-2320

Wind & Weather
P.O. Box 2320
Store address: Albion Street
Water Tower
Marcie Schorg
Phone: 707-964-1284,
800-922-9463
Fax: 707-964-1278
On-site: Retail
All year. Seven days,
10:00–5:00.

MORGAN HILL 95037

Schulz Cactus Growers
1095 Easy Street
Ernst Schulz
Phone: 408-683-4489
On-site: Retail
By appointment.

NEVADA CITY 95959

David Bacon Woodworking
P.O. Box 1034
David Bacon

Phone: 916-273-8889
Fax: 916-273-8889
NOTP

NEWCASTLE 95658-9627

**Fowler Nurseries, Inc.,
Garden Center**
525 Fowler Road
Dick Fowler
Phone: 916-645-8191
Fax: 916-645-7374
On-site: Retail and wholesale
All year. Monday through
Saturday, 8:00–5:00.
Sunday, 9:30–4:00.

NORTHRIDGE 91325-1341

Northridge Gardens
9821 White Oak Avenue
Phone: 818-349-9798
On-site: Retail and wholesale
Saturday, 10:00–4:00. Other
times, by appointment.

OROVILLE 95965

Canyon Creek Nursery
3527 Dry Creek Road
Susan Whittlesey
Phone: 916-533-2166
On-site: Retail
By appointment.

OXNARD 93030

Santa Barbara Greenhouses
721 Richmond Avenue
Victor West
Phone: 805-482-3765,
483-4288
Fax: 805-483-0229
On-site: Retail and wholesale
All year. Monday through

Friday, 8:00–5:00. Saturday
and Sunday, by appointment.

PALO ALTO 94306

**Common Ground
Garden Supply**
(Store for **Bountiful Gardens**)
2225 Camino Real
Phone: 415-328-6752
On-site: Retail
Tuesday through Saturday,
10:00–5:00. Sunday in the
spring.

PASADENA 91109-2734

**International Geranium
Society**
P.O. Box 92734
Betty Tufenkian

PLACERVILLE 95667

Forest Seeds of California
1100 Indian Hill Road
Bob Graton
Phone: 916-621-1551
Fax: 916-621-1040
On-site: Retail and wholesale
By appointment.

**North American Heather
Society**
3641 Indian Creek Road
Pauline Croxton

POINT ARENA 95468

Cart Warehouse
P.O. Box 3
Street address: 45500
Schooner Gulch Road
Peter D. Reimuller
Phone: 800-655-9100

Fax: 707-882-2488
On-site: Retail
All year. Monday through
Friday, 8:00–5:00.

POINT REYES 94956

Gardens for Growing People
P.O. Box 630
Ruth Lopez
Phone: 415-663-9433
NOTP

POMONA 91766

Greenlee Nursery
301 East Franklin Avenue
John Greenlee
Phone: 714-629-9045
Fax: 909-620-9283
On-site: Retail and wholesale
Monday through Friday,
9:00–5:00. By appointment.

POTTER VALLEY 95469

**Rare Conifer Foundation–
Rare Conifer Nursery**
P.O. Box 100
Darshan Mayginnes
Phone: 707-462-8068
Fax: 707-462-6139
NOTP

RAMONA 92065

Ramona Gardens
2178 El Paso Street
Linda Moore
Phone: 619-789-6099
On-site: Retail and wholesale
By appointment.

REDDING 96001-3008

**Maxim's Greenwood
Gardens**
2157 Sonoma Street
Georgia Maxim
Phone: 916-241-0764

On-site: Retail
All year. Seven days.

REDWOOD CITY 94064

J. L. Hudson, Seedsman
P.O. Box 1058
J. L. Hudson
NOTP

**Redwood City Seed
Company**
P.O. Box 361
Craig and Sue Dremann
Phone: 415-325-SEED
NOTP

SACRAMENTO 95824-2931

**California Native Plant
Society**
1722 J Street, Suite 17

SACRAMENTO 95829

Roris Gardens
8195 Bradshaw Road
Phone: 916-689-7460
Fax: 916-689-5516
On-site: Retail
Iris fair: Mid-April through
early May. Daily, 8:00–5:00.
After May 2, Monday
through Friday.

SAN DIEGO 92121

ReoTemp Instrument Corp.
1568 Sorrento Valley Road,
Suite 10
Kathy M. Martin
Phone: 619-481-7737,
800-648-7737
Fax: 619-481-7150
On-site: Retail and wholesale
By appointment.

SAN FRANCISCO 94120-7307

Gardeners Eden
P.O. Box 7307
Phone: 800-822-9600
Customer Service: 800-822-
1214
Fax: 415-421-5153
NOTP

SAN FRANCISCO 95122

**The American Fuchsia
Society**
County Fair Building
9th Avenue and Lincoln Way
Virginia D. Feldmann

SAN JOSE 95125

Maryott's Gardens
1073 Bird Avenue
Bill Maryott and
Marilyn Harlow
Phone: 408-971-0444
Fax: 408-971-6072
On-site: Retail and wholesale
Mid-April to mid-May.
Monday through Sunday,
9:00–6:00.

SAN JOSE 95126

Kitazawa Seed Co.
1111 Chapman Street
Sakae Komatsu
Phone: 408-243-1330
On-site: Retail
All year. By appointment.

SAN JOSE 95155

The American Iris Society
P.O. Box 8455
Marilyn Harlow

SAN MARCOS 92079-2017

Cordon Bleu Farms
P.O. Box 2017
Street address:
418 Buena Creek Road
Bob Brooks
On-site: Retail
All year. Wednesday through
Saturday, 9:00–4:00.

SAN PEDRO 90732

Book Orchard
1379 Park Western Drive,
Suite 306
Raminta Jautokas
Phone: 310-548-4279
Fax: 310-548-4279
NOTP

SAN RAFAEL 94901

Hydrofarm
Street address:
3135 Kerner Boulevard
Phone: 800-634-9999
All year. Monday through
Friday, 10:00–6:00. Saturday,
10:00–3:00.

SAN RAMON 94583

**The Hydroponic Society
of America**
2819 Crow Canyon Road,
Suite 218
Phone: 510-743-9605
Fax: 510-743-9302

SANTA BARBARA 93105

**International Water Lily
Society**
c/o Santa Barbara

Botanical Garden
1212 Mission Canyon Road
Edward L. Schneider
Phone: 805-682-4726

SANTA CRUZ 95060

Bay View Gardens
1201 Bay Street
Joseph Ghio
Phone: 408-423-3656
NOTP

SANTA CRUZ 95062

Antonelli Brothers
2545 Capitola Road
Skip Antonelli
Phone: 408-475-5222
On-site: Retail and wholesale
All year. Seven days,
9:00–5:00.

SANTA MARGARITA 93453

Las Pilitas Nursery
Las Pilitas Road
Celeste Wilson
Phone: 805-438-5992
On-site: Retail and wholesale
All year. Saturday, 9:00–5:00.
By appointment.

SEBASTOPOL 95472

Miniature Plant Kingdom
4125 Harrison Grade Road
Don and Becky Herzog
Phone: 707-874-2233
Fax: 707-874-2233
On-site: Retail and wholesale
Monday, Tuesday, Thursday
through Saturday, 9:00–4:00.
Sunday, 12:00–4:00.

Vintage Gardens
2833 Gravenstein
Highway South
Gregg Lowery
Phone: 707-829-2035
Fax: 707-829-5342
On-site: Retail
By appointment.
Tuesday through Sunday,
9:00–5:00

SHINGLE SPRINGS 95682

Roses & Wine
6260 Fernwood Drive
Wayne and Barbara Procissi
Phone: 916-677-9722
Fax: 916-676-4560
On-site: Retail
All year. By appointment.

SOMERSET 95684

Bluebird Haven Iris Garden
6940 Fairplay Road
Mary and John Hess
Phone: 209-245-5017
On-site: Retail
Mid-April through mid-May.
Tuesday through Sunday,
10:00–5:00. By appoint-
ment.

STOCKTON 95201

Lockhart Seeds, Inc.
P.O. Box 1361
Store: 3 North Wilson Way
Steve Auten
Phone: 209-466-4401
Fax: 209-466-9766
On-site: Retail and wholesale
By appointment.

STOCKTON 95205

Stockton Iris Gardens
P.O. Box 55195
Street address:
451 North Lillian
Stockton 95215
James McWhirter
Phone: 209-462-8106
On-site: Retail
April through May 15.
Monday through Friday,
9:00–5:00. By appointment.

TOMALES 94971

Mostly Natives Nursery
27235 Highway 1, Box 258
Walter Earle and
Margaret Graham
Phone: 707-878-2009
Fax: 707-878-2009
On-site: Retail and wholesale
All year. Tuesday through
Saturday, 9:00–4:00. Sunday,
11:00–4:00.

UKIAH 95482

Evergreen Gardenworks
P.O. Box 1357
Street address:
430 North Oak Street
Brent Walston
Phone: 707-462-8909
On-site: Retail
March through Thanksgiv-
ing. Tuesday through Satur-
day, 9:00–3:00. By
appointment.

UPLAND 91784-1199

Van Ness Water Gardens
2460 North Euclid Avenue
William C. Uber
Phone: 909-982-2425

Fax: 909-949-7217
On-site: Retail and wholesale
All year. Tuesday through
Saturday, 9:00–4:00.

VENTURA 93003

Vista Products
1245 Prairie Dog Place
Onni and Hilkka
Kilpelainen, Gerry and
Ritva Vadeboncoeur
Phone: 805-659-4389
NOTP

VISALIA 93292

**Sequoia Nursery –Moore
Miniature Roses**
2519 East Noble Avenue
Phone: 209-732-0190
Fax: 209-732-0192
On-site: Retail and Whole-
sale
All year. Monday through
Friday, 8:30–4:30. Saturday
and Sunday, 10:00–4:00.

VISTA 92084

Grigsby Cactus Gardens
2354 Bella Vista Drive
M. Lee
Phone: 619-727-1323
Fax: 619-727-1578
On-site: Retail and wholesale
All year, except in extreme
weather. Tuesday through
Saturday, 8:00–3:30.

**Rainbow Gardens Bookshop
& Nursery**
1444 East Taylor
Charles H. Everson
Phone: 619-758-4290
Fax: 619-945-8934
On-site: Retail and wholesale

All year. Tuesday through
Friday, 9:30–4:00. Saturday,
by appointment.

WATSONVILLE 95076

**Roses of Yesterday and
Today**
803 Brown's Valley Road
Patricia Stemler Wiley and
Kathryn Wiley Minier
Phone: 408-724-2755,
724-3537
Fax: 408-724-1408,
800-980-ROSE
On-site: Retail
All year. Seven days,
9:00–3:00.

WILLITS 95490

Bountiful Gardens
18001 Shafer Ranch Road
Street address:
5798 Ridgewood Road
Bill and Betsy Bruneau
Phone: 707-459-6410
Fax: 707-459-6410
(6 p.m. to 10 p.m.)
On-site: Ecology Action
by appointment or for
scheduled activity
On-site: Retail outlet, see
Palo Alto, Common Ground.

COLORADO

BAYFIELD 81122-9758

**Edge of the Rockies
"Native Seeds"**
P.O. Box 1218
Susan Komarek
Phone: 303-884-9003
NOTP

BOULDER 80306

Age-Old Organics
P.O. Box 1556
Chris Munley
Phone: 303-499-0201,
800-748-3474
Fax: 303-499-3231
On-site: Wholesale
All year. By appointment.

Long's Garden
P.O. Box 19
Street address:
3240 Broadway
Catherine Long Gates
Phone: 303-442-2353
On-site: Retail
May and June. Seven days,
10:00–6:00. Other times,
by appointment.

COLORADO SPRINGS 80936

Hydro-Gardens, Inc.
P.O. Box 25845
Street address:
8765 Vollmer Road
Colorado Springs 80908
Phone: 719-495-2266,
800-634-6363
Fax: 719-531-0506
On-site: Retail
All year. Monday through
Friday, 8:00–5:00.

DENVER 80211

**Bruce Barber Bird
Feeders, Inc.**
4600 Jason Street
Ron O'Kane
Phone: 800-528-2794
Fax: 303-368-9616
NOTP

ENGLEWOOD 80110

Alpine Millworks
1231 West Lehigh
Kent Struble
Phone: 303-761-6334
NOTP

FORT COLLINS 80522-0200

**Colorado Native Plant
Society**
P.O. Box 200

LAKEWOOD 80232

**The American Penstemon
Society**
1569 South Holland Court
Ann Bartlett

KIOWA 80117

Alplains
32315 Pine Crest Court
Alan D. Bradshaw
Phone: 303-621-2247
Fax: 303-621-2864
On-site: Retail
By appointment.

PALISADE 81526

Rocky Mountain Insectary
P.O. Box 152
NOTP

CONNECTICUT

AVON 06001

**Mother Nature's Worm
Castings**
P.O. Box 1055
Ed and Hazel Soillant
Phone: 203-673-3029
NOTP

BANTAM 06750

John Scheepers, Inc.
P.O. Box 700
Jan S. Ohms
Phone: 203-567-0838
Fax: 203-567-5323
NOTP

DEEP RIVER 06417

Ericaceae
P.O. Box 293
Kelsey Hill Road and Mathias C. Zack
Phone: 203-526-5100
(evenings)
On-site: Retail
By appointment.

GAYLORDSVILLE 06755-0005

Bloomingfields Farm
Lee and Diana Bristol
Street address:
9 Route 55
Sherman 06784
Phone: 203-354-6951
On-site: Retail
June through August. Friday,
Saturday, and Sunday,
12:00–5:00. Other times,
by appointment.

GREENWICH 06836-7584

Schipper & Company
Box 7584
Tim Schipper
Phone: 800-877-8637
Fax: 203-862-8909
NOTP

HAMDEN 06518

Broken Arrow Nursery
13 Broken Arrow Road
Richard A. Jaynes

Phone: 203-288-1026
Fax: 203-287-1035
On-site: Retail and wholesale
All year.

LITCHFIELD 06759-0050

White Flower Farm
Plantsmen
P.O. Box 50
Steve Frowine
Phone: 860-496-9624
Fax: 860-496-1418
On-site: Retail
April through October.
Monday through Friday,
10:00–5:00. Saturday and
Sunday, 9:00–5:30.

OXFORD 06478-1529

Butterbrooke Farm
78 Barry Road
Tom Butterworth
Phone: 203-888-2000
On-site: Retail
All year. Weekends.

PLANTSVILLE 06479

**Florian Ratchet-Cut™
Pruning Tools**
P.O. Box 325
Street address:
157 Water Street
Southington 06489
Nat and Stella Florian
Phone: 203-628-9643 Or-
ders: 800-275-3618
Fax: 203-628-6036
NOTP

RIVERSIDE 06878

Outward Signs
1117 East Putnam Avenue
Lucy Corsaro
Phone: 203-348-0243,
800-346-7678

Fax: 203-357-0092
On-site: Retail and wholesale
All year. Monday through
Saturday, 9:30–5:30.

SOUTHPORT 06490

Matrix Group, Inc.
P.O. Box 1176

STORRS 06268

**Ledgecrest Greenhouses and
Garden Center**
1029 Storrs Road, Route 195
Paul Hammer
Phone: 203-487-1661
On-site: Retail
All year. Monday through
Saturday, 9:00–5:30. Sunday,
11:00–5:00.

**Connecticut Botanical
Society**
10 Hillside Circle
Margaret Taylor, Secretary

UNION 06076-4617

**Select Seeds–Antique
Flowers**
180 Stickey Road
Marilyn Barlow
Phone: 203-684-9310
Fax: 203-684-9310
NOTP

WEST CORNWALL 06796

**Barbara Farnsworth,
Bookseller**
P.O. Box 9
Street address:
Route 128
Barbara Farnsworth
Phone: 203-672-6571
Fax: 203-672-3099
On-site: Retail

Saturday, 9:00–5:00.
Or by appointment.

**WEST HARTFORD
06133-0058**

Sunrise Enterprises
P.O. Box 33058
Phone: 203-666-8071
Fax: 203-665-8156
NOTP

WILTON 06897

Kenneth Lynch & Sons
P.O. Box 488
Street address:
84 Danbury Road
Phone: 203-762-8363
Fax: 203-762-2999
NOTP

DELAWARE

HOCKESSIN 19707

Banyai Hostas
11 Gates Circle
Bruce and Lois Banyai
Phone: 302-239-0887
On-site: Retail and wholesale
Saturdays and Sundays. By
appointment.

DISTRICT OF COLUMBIA

WASHINGTON, DC 20007

Park Place
2251 Wisconsin Avenue N.W.
C. Phillip Mitchell
Phone: 202-342-6294
Fax: 202-342-9255
On-site: Retail and wholesale
All year. February through

October, Monday through Sunday.
Mid-October through mid-February, 6:00–9:00. Saturday, 10:00–5:00. Sunday, 12:00–5:00.

WASHINGTON, DC 20013

American Forests
P.O. Box 2000
R. Neil Sampson
Phone: 202-667-3300
Fax: 202-667-7751

WASHINGTON, DC 20560

Botanical Society of Washington
Dept. of Botany, NHB 166
Smithsonian Institution

FLORIDA

ALACHUA 32615

Chestnut Hill Nursery
Route 1, Box 341
R. D. Wallace
Phone: 904-462-2820,
800-669-2067
Fax: 904-462-4330
On-site: Retail
Monday through Friday.
8:00–4:00. By appointment.

Daylily Discounters
1 Daylily Plaza
Tom Allin and Doug Glick
Phone: 904-462-1539 Orders: 800-DAYLILY
Fax: 904-462-5111
On-site: Retail
Memorial Day weekend open house.

Wimberlyway Gardens
1 Daylily Plaza
Ida and Bill Munson and Betty Hudson
Phone: 904-462-1539
Fax: 904-462-5111
On-site: Retail
March through August

BROOKSVILLE 34601-1319

Johnson Daylily Garden
70 Lark Avenue
Jeff and Linda Johnson
Phone: 352-544-0330
On-site: Retail and wholesale
By appointment.

CLEARWATER 34616

Garden Path Daylilies
1196 Norwood Avenue
Jean Duncan
Phone: 813-442-4730
On-site: Selection for future delivery
April and May.

COCOA BEACH 32932-1540

American Hibiscus Society
P.O. Box 321540
Jeri Grantham
Phone: 407-783-2576
Fax: 407-783-2576

DAVIE 33325-4217

Garden of Delights
14560 S.W. 14th Street
Murray Corman
Phone: 305-370-9004
Fax: 305-370-9004
On-site: Retail and wholesale
By appointment.

EUSTIS 32726

The Pepper Gal
P.O. Box 23006
Betty Payton
Phone: 305-537-5540
Fax: 305-566-2208
NOTP

FORT LAUDERDALE 33311

National Hot Pepper Association
400 N.W. 20th Street
Phone: 305-565-4972
Fax: 305-566-2208

FORT MYERS 33902

Tomato Growers Supply Co.
P.O. Box 2237
Linda and Vince Sapp
Phone: 941-768-1119
Fax: 941-768-3476
NOTP

JACKSONVILLE 32219

American Forests: Famous and Historic Trees
8555 Plummer Road
Susan T. Corbett
Phone: 904-765-0727,
800-677-0727
Fax: 904-768-2298
On-site: Retail and Wholesale
By appointment.

MELBOURNE 32902

Southern Seeds
P.O. Box 2091
Wae Nelson
Phone: 407-727-3662

Fax: 407-728-8493
NOTP

MIAMI 33142

Day-Dex Co.
4725 N.W. 36th Avenue
Kim Motsinger
Phone: 305-635-5241, -5259
On-site: Retail and wholesale
All year. Monday through
Friday, 7:30–4:00.

NAPLES 33939-2123

The American Ivy Society
P.O. Box 2123
Daphne Pfaff
Phone: 513-434-7069
(Ohio), 941-261-0388
(Florida)

OKEECHOBEE 34974

Giles Ramblin' Roses
2968 State Road 710
James and Mary Giles
Phone: 941-763-6611
On-site: Retail
All year. Monday through
Friday, 8:00–4:00. Saturday,
8:00–2:00.

ORLANDO 32803

Brown's Edgewood Gardens
2611 Corrine Drive
Brandon Brown
Phone: 407-896-3203
Fax: 407-898-5792
On-site: Retail
Seven days.

ORLANDO 32868

Florida Native Plant Society
P.O. Box 680008

SANFORD 32771

Kilgore Seed Company
1400 West First Street
J. H. Hunziker
Phone: 407-323-6630
NOTP

SANFORD 32771-8315

Floyd Cove Nursery
725 Longwood-Markham
Road
Pat and Grace Stamile
Phone: 407-324-9229
Fax: 407-321-3238
On-site: Retail
By appointment.

SANFORD 32772-1612

Daylily World
P.O. Box 1612
David Kirchoff, Morton
Morse, and Dorothy West-
cott
Phone: 407-322-4034
Fax: 407-322-8629
On-site: Retail
March through July. Wednes-
day through Saturday,
10:00–5:00. Other times, by
appointment.

WINTER HAVEN 33884-1932

Slocum Water Gardens
1101 Cypress Gardens
Boulevard
Phone: 813-293-7151
Fax: 813-299-1896
On-site: Retail and wholesale
All year. Monday through
Friday, 8:00–12:00,
1:00–4:00.

WINTER SPRINGS 32708

Lady Bug Beautiful Gardens
857 Leopard Trail, Tuscawilla
Ra Hansen
Phone: 407-699-0172
On-site: Retail
Monday through
Thursday, 7:30–2:45.
Or by appointment.

GEORGIA

ALBANY 31703

Piedmont Plant Co.
P.O. Box 424
Street address: 807 North
Washington Street
William Parker, Jr.
Phone: 912-883-7029
Fax: 912-432-2888
NOTP

ATHENS 30605-4905

Classic Groundcovers
405 Belmont Road
Wilbur C. Mull
Phone: 706-543-0145,
800-248-8424
Fax: 706-369-9844
On-site: Wholesale
All year. Monday through
Friday.

ATLANTA 30312

The American Fern Society
456 McGill Place
Richard L. Hauke

AUGUSTA 30903-1626

Totally Tomatoes
P.O. Box 1626
Phone: 803-663-0016
Fax: 803-663-9772
NOTP

BALL GROUND 30107

Lawson's Nursery
Route 1, Box 472
Street address:
Yellow Creek Road
James and Bernice Lawson
Phone: 770-893-2141
On-site: Retail
September through May.
Monday through Saturday,
8:00–5:00.

BRONWOOD 31726

Bronwood Worm Farms
P.O. Box 28
Street address:
305 East Main Street
Jerry Seymour
Phone: 912-995-5994
NOTP

CAIRO 31728

Emily Gandy's Daylilies
Route 2, Box 453
Emily Gandy
Phone: 912-377-4056
On-site: Retail
All year. Seven days,
8:00 A.M. till dark, except
Sunday.

COVINGTON 30209

Alcovy Daylily Farm
775 Cochran Road
Jesse and Mary Lois Burgess
Phone: 404-787-7177
On-site: Retail and wholesale
April through October.
By appointment.

DORAVILLE 30360

Georgia Botanical Society
6700 Peachtree Ind., B-5
Daisy S. Arrington

DUBLIN 31027

**Thundering Springs
Daylily Garden**
1056 South Lake Drive
Elmer and Ivelyn Brown
Phone: 912-272-1526
Fax: 912-272-1526
On-site: Retail
May through October. Seven
days, 9:00 A.M. till sundown.

EDISON 31746-9410

Monarch Daylily Garden
Garden Route 2, Box 182
George and Melba Fain
Phone: 912-835-2636
On- Site: Retail
April through October.
Monday through Friday,
8:00–5:30. Saturday, by
appointment.

ELLIJAY 30540

Johnson Nursery
Route 5, Box 29-J,
Highway 52-E
Elisa and Bill Ford
Phone: 706-276-3187
Fax: 706-276-3186
On-site: Retail and wholesale
January and February.
Monday through Friday,
8:00–5:00. Saturday and
Sunday, hours variable.

FLOWERY BRANCH 30542

The Flowery Branch Seed Co.
P.O. Box 1330
Dean Pailler
Phone: 770-536-8380
Fax: 770-532-7825
NOTP

FORT VALLEY 31030

American Camellia Society
One Massee Lane
Ann Blair Brown
Phone: 912-967-2358,
967-2722
Fax: 912-967-2083

OAKWOOD 30566

Pinegarden
5358 Forest South Place
Patricia Seaman
Phone: 404-536-8614
On-site: Retail and wholesale
June and July. By appointment.

UPATOI 31829

Oak Haven Farms Nursery
12727 Upatoi Lane
Glenn and Yolanda
"Lonnie" Ward
Phone: 706-561-6546
On-site: Retail and wholesale
April through November.
Wednesday through Sunday.
By appointment.

**WARNER ROBINS
31095-7686**

Swanns' Daylily Garden
P.O. Box 7686
Street address: 119 Mack Lane
Jean and Mark Swann
Phone: 912-953-4778
On-site: Retail
All year, dawn to dusk.
Bloom season is May
through October.
No sales on Sunday.

HAWAII

HONOLULU 96822

Hawaii Botanical Society
Botany Dept., University of
Hawaii
3190 Maille Way

IDAHO

BOISE 83702

TumbleBug®
2029 North 23rd Street
Henry Artis
Phone: 208-368-7900,
800-531-0102
Fax: 208-368-7900
NOTP

BOISE 83706

Seeds Blüm
H.C. 33, Idaho City Stage
Jan Blüm
Fax: 208-338-5658
NOTP

BOISE 83707-3451

Idaho Native Plant Society
P.O. Box 9451

HAILEY 83333-1048

Seeds Trust:
High Altitude Gardens
P.O. Box 1048
Bill McDorman
Phone: 208-788-4363,
208-788-4419
Fax: 208-788-3452
NOTP

MOSCOW 83843-1607

Northplan/Mountain Seed
P.O. Box 9107
Loring M. Jones
Phone: 208-286-7004,
882-8040
Fax: 208-882-7446
On-site: Retail
Spring and early summer.
Monday through Friday,
mornings. By appointment.

MOYIE SPRINGS 83845

Ronniger's Seed Potatoes
Star Route Road 73
David Ronniger
Fax: 208-267-3265
On-site: Retail and wholesale
March. Monday through
Thursday, 7:00–4:00. By
appointment.

SANDPOINT 83864

Habitat Plants
9730 Center Valley Road
Greg Smith
Phone: 208-265-5873
On-site: Retail and wholesale
By appointment.

Idaho Wood
P.O. Box 488
Street address: 3425 McGhee
Road
Susie Lewis
Phone: 800-635-1100
Fax: 208-263-3102
On-site: Retail and wholesale
All year. Monday through
Friday, 7:00–4:00.

TWIN FALLS 83301

Plantasia Cactus Gardens
867 Filer Avenue West
LaMar N. Orton
Phone: 208-734-7959
On-site: Retail
April through October.
By appointment.

ILLINOIS

BLOOMINGTON 61704

Farmer Seed and Nursery
Division of Plantron, Inc.
Reservation Center
1706 Morrissey Drive
Don Prodoehl
Phone: 507-334-1623
Fax: 507-334-1624
On-site: Retail
March through June.

BOURBONNAIS 60914-0003

Pampered Plant Nursery
P.O. Box 3
Douglas Armstrong
Phone: 815-937-9387
(evenings and weekends)
NOTP

CHAMPAIGN 61821

Klehm Nursery
4210 North Duncan Road
Kit C. Klehm
Phone: 800-533-3715
Fax: 217-373-8403
On-site: Wholesale
All year. Monday through
Friday, 7:00–4:00.

CHAPIN 62628

North American Fruit Explorers (NAFEX)
Route 1, Box 94
Jill Vrobeck

CHILLICOTHE 61523

The American Botanist, Booksellers
P.O. Box 532
Street address:
1103 West Truitt Avenue
D. Keith Crotz
Phone: 309-274-5254
On-site: Retail
By appointment.

DOWNERS GROVE 60517

Laurie's Landscape
2959 Hobson Road,
Box HGS
Laurie Skrzenta
Phone: 708-969-1270
On-site: Retail
May through October.
By appointment.

GALESBURG 61402

Alsto's Handy Helpers
P.O. Box 1267
Benjamin Alsto and
Mike Voyles
Phone: 309-343-6181,
800-447-0048
Fax: 309-343-5785
NOTP

GRANITE CITY 62040

The Flower Lady's Garden
1560 Johnson Road

Agnes Miller
Phone: 618-877-2983
Fax: 618-877-5746
On-site: Retail and wholesale
March to October. By appointment.

HAMBURG 62045

Springvale Farm Nursery
Box 200, Department HGS
Street address:
Mozier Hollow Road
Will and Jeanne Gould
Phone: 618-232-1108
On-site: Retail
April through September,
9:00–2:00. Appointments
for groups or travelers; request map.

HILLSBORO 62049

Bluestem Prairie Nursery
R.R. 2, Box 106-A
Ken Schaal
Phone: 217-532-6344
On-site: Retail
By appointment.

LOMBARD 60148

International Golden Fossil Tree Society (The Ginkgo Society)
201 West Graham Avenue
Clayton Fawkes

The Species Iris Group of North America (SIGNA)
150 North Main Street
Florence Stout

MACOMB 61455

International Ornamental Crabapple Society
208 Waggoner Hall
Western Illinois University
Dr. Thomas L. Green
Phone: 309-298-1160
Fax: 309-298-2280

PEORIA 61632

Breck's
U.S. Reservation Center
6523 North Galena Road
Hans Van Amstel
Phone: 309-689-3862 Orders: 800-722-9069
Fax: 309-689-3803
NOTP

PEORIA 61632-1758

Spring Hill Nurseries
6523 North Galena Road
Street address:
110 West Elm Street
Tipp City, OH 45371
Theresa W. Lusch
Phone: 309-689-3800
Fax: 309-691-5152
On-site: Retail
Seven days.

RIVERWOODS 60015

The Bulb Crate
2560 Deerfield Road
Alice Hosford
Phone: 847-317-1414
Fax: 847-317-1414
NOTP

ROCKTON 61072

Midwest Wildflowers
Box 64
Leroy and Diane Busker
NOTP

SPRINGFIELD 62791

Saroh
P.O. Box 8375
George L. Lang
Phone: 217-546-5917
NOTP

TREMONT 61568

Lee Gardens
P.O. Box 5
Street address:
25986 Sauder Road
Janis Lee
Phone: 309-925-5262
Fax: 309-925-5010
On-site: Retail
April and May: Monday
through Friday, 10:00–6:00.
Saturday, 10:00–3:00. Sun-
day, 12:00–3:00. June
through first frost: Monday
through Friday, 10:00–5:00.
Saturday, 10:00–3:00. Other
times, by appointment.

WESTVILLE 61883

Illinois Native Plant Society
Forest Glen Preserve
R.R. 1, Box 495A

INDIANA

BLOOMINGTON 47401-9111

Worm's Way Indiana
3151 South Highway 446
Michael Dick
Phone: 812-331-0300,
800-274-9676
Fax: 812-331-0854
On-site: Retail and wholesale
All year. Monday through
Saturday, 10:00–6:00.

**CRAWFORDSVILLE
47933-9426**

**Davidson Wilson
Greenhouses**
R.R. 2, Box 168, Dept. 11
Barbara Wilson
Phone: 317-364-0556
Fax: 800-276-3691
On-site: Retail and wholesale
All year. Monday through
Saturday, 9:00–5:00. April
through June, Sundays,
1:00–5:00.

FLOYDS KNOB 47119

Pinecliffe Daylily Gardens
6604 Scottsville Road
Donald C. and Kathy Smith
Phone: 812-923-8113
Fax: 812-923-9618
On-site: Retail and wholesale
Peak bloom, mid-June
through mid-August.
By appointment.

HUNTINGBURG 47542

Indiana Berry and Plant Co.
5218 West 500 South
Carol Chappell and
Jeff Altmeyer
Phone: 812-683-3055,
800-295-2226
Fax: 812-683-2004
On-site: Retail and wholesale
All year. Monday through
Friday, 8:00–5:00. Saturdays,
April and May, 8:00–12:00.

INDIANAPOLIS 46217

Soules Garden
5809 Rahke Road
Marge Soules
Phone: 317-786-7839

On-site: Retail
By appointment.

INDIANAPOLIS 46240

Windleaves
7560 Morningside Drive
Bart Kister
Phone: 317-251-1381
On site: Retail
By appointment.

JAMESTOWN 46147-9010

**Resources: Books for Plant
Collectors and Seed Savers**
9267 West 200 Street
John E. Perkins
Phone: 317-676-5289
NOTP

JEFFERSONVILLE 47130-3556

Earlee, Inc.
2002 Highway 62
Mary and Earl Stewart
Phone: 812-282-9134
Fax: 812-282-2640
On-site: Retail and wholesale
All year. Monday through
Friday, 8:30–5:30. Saturday,
8:30–2:30.

LAWRENCEBURG 47025

Gardens Alive!
5100 Schenley Place
Phone: 812-537-8650,
537-8651
Fax: 812-537-5108
On-site: Retail
All year. Monday through
Saturday, 9:00–5:00.
Sunday, 12:00–5:00.

NEW ALBANY 47150

Earthly Goods Ltd.
P.O. Box 614
Ann Streckfus and
Stephen Brown
Phone: 812-944-3283
NOTP

NEW SALISBURY 47161

**Rocky Meadow Orchard
& Nursery**
360 Rocky Meadow Road,
N.W.
Ed Fackler
Phone: 812-347-2213
On-site: Retail and wholesale
All year. By appointment.

RICHMOND 47374-2297

Hoffco, Inc.
358 N.W. F Street
John D. Hedges
Phone: 317-966-8161,
800-999-8161
Fax: 317-935-2346

SOUTH BEND 46615

C. K. Petty and Co.
203 Wildemere Drive
Chris Petty
Phone: 219-232-4095
Fax: 219-288-3229
NOTP

VALPARAISO 46383

Coburg Planting Fields
573 East 600 North
Philipp Brockington and
Howard J. Reeve, Jr.
Phone: 219-462-4288

On-site: Retail
June through September.
Seven days, 9:00–5:00.

WINAMAC 46996

Iris Acres
T. Sanders
Phone: 219-946-4197
On-site: Retail
By appointment.

ZIONSVILLE 46077

**Kids in Bloom™
Specialty Seeds**
P.O. Box 344
Kay L. Grimm
Phone: 317-290-6996
NOTP

IOWA

ANKENY 50021

**Soil and Water Conservation
Society of America**
7515 N.E. Ankeny Road
Phone: 515-289-2331,
800-THE-SOIL

CEDAR RAPIDS 52403

The Blooming Hill
615 Rosedale Road S.E.
Jerry and Lela Hadrava
Phone: 319-362-1375
On-site: Retail
May through July, seven
days, 10:00–6:00.
April and August through
September. Monday through
Saturday, 10:00–6:00.

CHARLES CITY 50616

Smith Nursery Company
P.O. Box 515
Street address:
9th and Allison Streets
Bill Smith
Phone: 515-228-3239
On-site: Retail and wholesale
All year. Monday through
Saturday, 8:00–12:00,
1:00–5:00.

DECORAH 52101

**The Flower and Herb Ex-
change**
3076 North Winn Road
Diane Whealy
On-site: Garden Tours at
Heritage Farm
June through September,
9:00–5:00

**Seed Savers Exchange—
Seed Saver Publications**
3076 North Winn Road
Kent Whealy
Phone: 319-382-5872
Fax: 319-382-5872
On-site: Garden tours at
Heritage Farm
June through September,
9:00–5:00.

JOHNSTON 50131

Heard Gardens, Ltd.
5355 Merle Hay Road
Mary Anne Rennebohm
Phone: 515-276-4533
Fax: 515-276-8322
On-site: Retail
April through September.
Monday through Friday,

8:00–6:00. Sunday,
12:00–4:00.
Saturdays in October,
8:00–5:00. September
through March, Monday
through Friday, 8:00–5:00.

KELLEY 50134

**Dave & Sue's Aquarium and
Greenhouse**
R.R. 1, Box 97
David Lowman
Phone: 515-769-2446,
800-528-2827
On-site: Retail and
some wholesale
All year, 9:00–9:00.
By appointment.

SHEFFIELD 50475

Iowa Prairie Seed Co.
P.O. Box 228
Street address:
1740 220th Street
Daryl F. Kothenbeutel
Phone: 515-892-4111
Fax: 515-995-2372
On-site: Retail
By appointment.

SHENANDOAH 51602

**Henry Field's Seed and
Nursery Co.**
415 North Burnett
Orville Dragoo
Phone: 605-665-4491,
665-9391
Fax: 605-665-2601
NOTP

KANSAS

BURLINGTON 66839-0187

Huff's Garden
P.O. Box 187
Street address:
617 Juniatta Street
The Huffs
Phone: 800-279-4675
On-site: Retail and wholesale
February through July.

HEALY 67850

Sharp Bros. Seed Co.
P.O. Box 140
Street address:
212 South Sycamore
Gaile Sharp
Phone: 800-4-NATIVE
Fax: 316-398-2220
On-site: Retail and wholesale
By appointment.

OVERLAND PARK 66210

The Gourmet Gardener ™
8650 College Boulevard,
Dept. 205-SK
Christopher E. Combest
Phone: 913-345-0490
Fax: 913-451-2443
NOTP

PAOLA 66071

Happy Valley Ranch
16577 West 327th
Wanda and Ray Stagg
Phone: 913-849-3103
Fax: 913-849-3104
On-site: Retail
By appointment.

TOPEKA 66621

Kansas Wildflower Society
Mulvane Art Center
Washburn University
17th and Jewell Street

WICHITA 67206

Society for Japanese Irises
6518 Beachy Avenue
Carol Ramsey
NOTP

KENTUCKY

FLORENCE 41022-6900
Smith & Hawken
P.O. Box 6900
Street address:
Two Arbor Lane
Phone: 800-776-3336 Customer Service:
800-776-5558
Fax: 606-727-1166
NOTP

FRANKFORT 40601

Shooting Star Nursery
444 Bates Road
Sherri Evans
Phone: 502-223-1679
Fax: 502-875-2319
On-site: Retail
April through October.
Monday through Friday,
by appointment.

LOUISVILLE 40252

Dabney Herbs
P.O. Box 22061
Davy Dabney
Phone: 502-893-5198
Fax: 502-893-5198
NOTP

RICHMOND 40475

**Kentucky Native
Plant Society**
Dept. of Natural Science
East Kentucky University
Douglas N. Reynolds

WILLIAMSBURG 40769-0330

Raymond M. Sutton, Jr.
P.O. Box 330
Street address: 430 Main Street
Raymond M. Sutton, Jr.
Phone: 606-549-3464
Fax: 606-549-3469
NOTP

LOUISIANA

BASTROP 71220

Jaggers Bayou Beauties
15098 Knox Ferry Road
Leroy and Fran Jaggers
Phone: 318-283-2252
On-site: Retail
By appointment.

COVINGTON 70433

Bridgeworks
306 Lockwood Street
Paul Swain
Phone: 504-892-6640
NOTP

LAFAYETTE 70503-2896

**Louisiana Project
Wildflower**
Lafayette Natural History
Museum
637 Girard Park Drive

LAFAYETTE 70508-7847

Society for Louisiana Irises
1812 Broussard Road East
Elaine Borque
NOTP

METAIRIE 70011

Acres, U.S.A.
P.O. Box 8800
Street address:
2617-C Edenborn Avenue
Fred C. Walters
Phone: 504-889-2100,
800-355-5313
Fax: 504-889-2777
On-site: Retail and wholesale
All year. By appointment.

OPELOUSAS 70570

Louisiana Nursery
Route 7, Box 43
Dalton E. Durio
Phone: 318-948-3696
Fax: 318-942-6404
On-site: Retail
All year. Monday through
Saturday, 9:00–12:00,
1:00–5:00. Appointment
anytime.

PRAIRIEVILLE 70769

Crochet Daylily Garden
P.O. Box 425
Street address:
17032 Old Jefferson Highway
Clarence J. and Beth Crochet
Phone: 504-673-8491
On-site: Retail and wholesale
March through November.
Monday through Saturday,
9:00–5:00.

Hobby Garden, Inc.
38164 Monticello Drive
Lee E. Gates and
Mary C. Schexnaydre
Phone: 504-673-3623
On-site: Retail and wholesale
All year. Monday through
Saturday, 8:00–6:00. April
through June, seven days,
8:00–6:00.

SALINE 71070

**Louisiana Native Plant
Society**
Route 1, Box 195
Richard Johnson

SHREVEPORT 71130

The American Rose Society
P.O. Box 30,000
Phone: 318-938-5402
Fax: 318-938-5405

SHREVEPORT 71133-7800

Donovan's Roses
P.O. Box 37800
Tom and Kathy Schimschock
Phone: 318-861-6693
NOTP

MAINE

ALBION 04910-9731

Johnny's Selected Seeds
Foss Hill Road
Barbara Kennedy
Phone: 207-437-9294
Fax: 207-437-2165
On-site: Retail
March through December.
Monday through Saturday,
8:30–5:00.

ALNA 04535

Barth Daylilies
Nelson Road, P.O. Box 54
Nicholas Barth
Phone: 207-586-6455
Fax: 207-586-6455
On-site: Retail and wholesale
May through August, days
and hours variable. By
appointment.

BRIDGEWATER 04735

Wood Prairie Farm
R.F.D. 7, Box 164
Jim and Megan Gerritsen
Phone: 207-429-9765,
800-829-9765
Fax: 800-829-9765
NOTP

CALAIS 04619-6102

Vesey's Seeds Ltd.
P.O. Box 9000
Allen Perry
Phone: 902-368-7333,
800-368-7333
Fax: 902-566-1620
(See Prince Edward Island)

CAMDEN 04843

Merry Gardens
P.O. Box 595
Mechanic Street
Mary Ellen and Ervin Ross
Phone: 207-236-9064
On-site: Retail
All year. Monday through
Saturday, 9:00–4:00.

CHINA 04926

Josselyn Botanical Society
P.O. Box 41
Marilyn Dwelley

DIXFIELD 04224-9561

**International Lilac
Society, Inc.**
11 Pine Street
Walter W. Oakes

FALMOUTH 04105

Allen, Sterling, & Lothrop
191 U.S. Route 1
Phone: 207-781-4142
Fax: 207-781-4143
On-site: Retail and wholesale
April through September.
Monday through Saturday,
8:00–5:30.

GEORGETOWN 04548

Eastern Plant Specialties
P.O. Box 226
Street address:
Bay Point Road
Mark Stavish
Phone: 207-371-2888,
800-WILL-GRO
On-site: Retail and wholesale
Mid-April through Novem-
ber. By appointment.

HAMPDEN 04444

**Gary W. Woolson,
Bookseller**
R.R. 1, Box 1576
Gary W. Woolson
Phone: 207-234-4931
NOTP

LITCHFIELD 04350-9503

Daystar
Route 2, Box 250
Street address:

Hollowell Road
Marjorie Walsh
Phone: 207-724-3369
On-site: Retail and wholesale
May through October.
By appointment.

NEW GLOUCESTER 04260

Pinetree Garden Seeds
Box 300
Dick Meiners
Phone: 207-926-3400
Fax: 207-926-3886
NOTP

NORTH YARMOUTH 04097

**Royall River Roses at
Forevergreen Farm**
70 New Gloucester Road
David King
Phone: 207-829-5830
Fax: 207-829-6512
On-site: Retail
April through November.
Monday through Saturday,
10:00–5:00.

SOUTH HARPSWELL 04079

Eartheart Gardens
R.R. 1, Box 847
Sharon Hayes Whitney
Phone: 207-833-6327

SURRY 04684

Surry Gardens
P.O. Box 145
Street address: Route 172
James M. Dickinson
Phone: 207-667-4493,
207-667-5589
On-site: Retail and wholesale
All year. Seven days,
8:00–5:00.

VASSALBORO 04989-9713

Fieldstone Gardens, Inc.
620 Quaker Lane
Steven D. Jones
Phone: 207-923-3836
Fax: 207-923-3836
On-site: Retail
April through November.
Tuesday through Sunday,
9:00–5:00.

WATERVILLE 04903

Fedco Seeds
(See also Moose Growers
Supply)
P.O. Box 520
Joann Clark
Phone: 207-873-7333
Fax: 207-426-9005
On-site: Pick up of
preorders. Dates vary
from year to year

Moose Growers Supply
P.O. Box 520
Bill Getty and Gene Frey
On-site: Pick up of pre-
orders. Dates vary from
year to year

YORK 03909-0543

Womanswork®
Little Big Farm
P.O. Box 543
Nancy Bennett Phillips
Phone: 207-363-0804,
800-639-2709
Fax: 207-363-0805
NOTP

MARYLAND

BALDWIN 21013

Wicklein's Water Gardens
P.O. Box 9780
Street address: 1820
Cromwell Bridge Road
Baltimore 21234
Walt Wicklein
Phone: 410-823-1335
Orders: 800-382-6716
Fax: 410-823-1427
On-site: Retail and wholesale
All year. Monday through
Saturday, 11:00–4:00. Sun-
days, April 15 through Sep-
tember 15.

BALDWIN 21013-9523

Kurt Bluemel, Inc.
2740 Greene Lane
Phone: 410-557-7229
Fax: 410-557-9785
On-site: Retail
Late spring through early fall.
By appointment.

BALTIMORE 21209-9998

Book Arbor
P.O. Box 20885
Judith Bloomgarden
Phone: 410-367-0338
NOTP

BALTIMORE 21218

**Resource Conservation
Technology, Inc.**
2633 North Calvert Street
Phone: 410-366-1146
Fax: 410-366-1202
On-site: Retail and wholesale

All year. Monday through
Friday, 8:30–5:00. By
appointment.

BALTIMORE 21230

D. Landreth Seed Company
P.O. Box 6426
Street address:
Ostend and Ledenhall Streets
Phone: 410-727-3922,
727-3923
Fax: 410-244-8633
On-site: Retail and wholesale
By appointment.

BUCKEYSTOWN 21717-0010

Lilypons Water Gardens®
P.O. Box 10
Street address:
6800 Lilypons Road
Charles Thomas
Phone: 800-999-5459
Fax: 301-874-2959
On-site: Retail and wholesale
April through September,
seven days, 9:30–5:30. Octo-
ber through March, Monday
through Saturday, 9:30–4:30.

CROWNSVILLE 21032

Bridgewood Gardens
P.O. Box 800
Chick
Phone: 410-849-3916,
800-858-6671
Fax: 410-849-3427
NOTP

DAYTON 21036

Native Seeds, Inc.
14590 Triadelphia Mill Road
James A. Saunders
Phone: 301-596-9818
NOTP

FREDERICK 21701

Dan's Garden Shop
5821 Woodwinds Circle
Dan Youngberg
Phone: 301-695-5966
NOTP

FRUITLAND 21826-0310

Allen Plant Company
P.O. Box 310
Street address: Spearin Road
Phone: 410-742-7122
Fax: 410-742-7120
On-site: Retail
Pick up by appointment.

GERMANTOWN 20874-2999

Country Casual
17317 Germantown Road
Bobbie Lopatin
Phone: 301-540-0040,
800-284-8325
Fax: 301-540-7364
NOTP

JARRETTSVILLE 21084

Maryland Aquatic Nurseries, Inc.
3427 North Furnace Road
Kelly Billing
Phone: 410-557-7615
Fax: 410-692-2857
On-site: Retail and wholesale
April through September.
Saturday, 9:00–4:00.

OWING MILLS 21117

Bundles of Bulbs
112 Green Spring Valley
Road

Kitty Washburne
Phone: 410-363-1371
On-site: Retail
April. By appointment.

PERRY HALL 21128

The American Conifer Society
Box 314
Phone: 410-256-5595
Fax: 410-256-5595
Nancy Akehurst

SALISBURY 21802-2538

Brittingham Plant Farms, Inc.
P.O. Box 2538, Dept. HGS
Wayne I. Robertson
Phone: 410-749-5153
Fax: 410-749-5148
On-site: Retail and wholesale
NOTP

SILVER SPRING 20914

Maryland Native Plant Society
P.O. Box 4877

UPPERCO 21155

Society for Japanese Irises
16185 Falls Road
Carol Warner
NOTP

WEST FRIENDSHIP 21794

Friendship Gardens
2590 Wellworth Way
Joan and Ken Roberts
Phone: 410-442-1197
NOTP

WESTMINSTER 21157

Carroll Gardens
P.O. Box 310
Street address:
444 East Main Street
Alan L. Summers
Phone: 410-848-5422 Orders: 800-638-6334
Fax: 410-857-4112
On-site: Retail and wholesale
Monday through Saturday,
8:30–7:00. Sunday,
10:30–7:00.

MASSACHUSETTS

AGAWAM 01001

Pleasant Valley Glads and Dahlias
P.O. Box 494
Street address:
163 Senator Avenue
Roger Adams, Sr., and
Gary Adams
Phone: 413-786-9146,
789-0307 (evenings)
On-site: Retail and wholesale
July through September. By
appointment.

BOLTON 01740-0900

Bow Bends
P.O. Box 900
Street address:
92 Randall Road
John J. Rogers
Phone: 508-779-2271
Fax: 508-779-2272
On-site: Retail
All year. Monday through
Friday, 8:00–5:00. By
appointment.

BUZZARDS BAY 02532

Cape Cod Worm Farm
30 Center Avenue
Maggie Pipkins
Phone: 508-759-5664
On-site: Wholesale
By appointment.

CAMBRIDGE 02138

New England Botanical Club
22 Divinity Avenue

CARLISLE 01741-0733

R. Seawright
P.O. Box 733
Street address: 201 Bedford Road
Bob and Love Seawright
Phone: 508-369-2172
On-site: Retail
May through August. Seven days, 9:00–5:00. By appointment when closed.

EAST BOSTON 02128

The Great American Rain Barrel Co.
295 Maverick Street
George Gehelein
Phone: 800-251-2352
Fax: 800-251-2352
On-site: Retail and wholesale
All year. Monday through Friday, 8:00–4:00. By appointment.

EAST SANDWICH 02537

Briarwood Gardens
14 Gully Lane
Kevin Shinn
Phone: 508-888-2146
Fax: 508-888-2146
On-site: Retail and wholesale

May through September. Monday through Friday. Other times, by appointment.

EDGARTOWN 02539

Donaroma's Nursery and Landscape Services
P.O. Box 2189
Street address:
Upper Main Street
Mike Donaroma
Phone: 508-627-8366, 627-8595
Fax: 508-627-7855
On-site: Retail
All year. Monday through Saturday, 8:00–5:00.

FALMOUTH 02540

Cape Cod Vireyas
405 Jones Road
Richard Chaikin
Phone: 508-548-1613 (evenings)
Fax: 617-742-4749
On-site: Retail
All year. Sunday through Tuesday. By appointment.

FRAMINGHAM 01701-2699

New England Wild Flower Society
Garden in the Woods
180 Hemenway Road
Phone: 508-877-7630, 617-237-4924

GEORGETOWN 01833

York Hill Farm
18 Warren Street
Darlyn C. Springer
Phone: 508-352-6560
On-site: Retail
After May 15. Thursday,

Friday and Saturday, 12:00–6:00. Sunday, by appointment.

IPSWICH 01938

Messelaar Bulb Co.
P.O. Box 269
Street address:
County Road, Route 1-A
Phone: 508-356-3737
On-site: Retail and wholesale
September through December 15.

LINCOLN 01773

Garden Works
31 Old Winter Street
Robin Wilkerson
Phone: 617-259-1110
On-site: Retail and wholesale
All year. By appointment.

NEW BEDFORD 02745-1200

Maximum
30 Samuel Barnet Boulevard
Street address:
New Bedford Industrial Park
Nat Bishop
Phone: 508-995-2200
Fax: 508-998-5359
On-site: Retail and wholesale
All year. Monday through Friday, 9:00–5:00.

PEABODY 01961-3194

The Crafter's Garden
P.O. Box 3194
Crowell Family
Phone: 508-535-1142
NOTP

PEPPERELL 01463

The Onion Man
30 Mt. Lebanon Street
Mark McDonough
Phone: 508-433-8549
NOTP

REHOBOTH 02769-1395

Tranquil Lake Nursery
45 River Street
Philip Boucher and
Warren Leach
Phone: 508-252-4002
Fax: 508-252-4740
On-site: Retail and wholesale
May through September,
Wednesday through Sunday.
July and August, seven days.
By appointment for groups
with special requirements.

ROCKPORT 01966

New England Bamboo Co.
P.O. Box 358
Phone: 508-546-3581
On-site: Pick up by
appointment.

ROWLEY 01969

Nor' East Miniature
Roses, Inc.
P.O. Box 307
Street address:
58 Hammond Street
Barbara Blackhall
Phone: 508-948-7964
Fax: 508-948-5487
On-site: Retail and wholesale
All year, gardens in spring
and summer. Seven days,
8:00–4:00. By appointment.

SHELBURNE FALL 01370

Catamount Cart
P.O. Box 365
Street address:
27 Rand Road
Jim Picardi
Phone: 413-625-6063,
800-444-0056
On-site: Retail
By appointment.

SOUTH DEERFIELD 01373

Nourse Farms, Inc.
41 River Road
Mary and Tim Nourse
Phone: 413-665-2658
Fax: 413-665-7888
On-site: Retail and wholesale
By appointment.

SOUTHAMPTON 01073

Tripple Brook Farm
37 Middle Road
Phone: 413-527-4626
NOTP

WESTFORD 01886

Burt Associates Bamboo
P.O. Box 719
Street address:
3 Landmark Road
Albert Adelman
Phone: 508-692-3240
Fax: 508-692-3240
On-site: Retail
May through September.
Wednesday through Sunday,
10:00–5:00.

WHITMAN 02382

Paradise Water Gardens
14 May Street
Paul Stetson, Jr.
Phone: 617-447-4711,
447-8595
Fax: 800-966-4591
On-site: Retail and wholesale
All year. Monday through
Friday, 8:00–6:00. Saturday,
8:00–5:00. Sunday,
1:00–5:00.

MICHIGAN

ALTO 49302

Flowers N' Friends
Miniature Roses
9590 100th Street S.E.
Dick and Kathy Gruenbauer
Phone: 616-891-1226
NOTP

ANN ARBOR 48103-4957

Old House Gardens
536 Third Street
Phone: 313-995-1486
Scott G. Kunst
NOTP

ANN ARBOR 48109-1048

Michigan Botanical Club
Department of Biology,
University of Michigan
Peter Kaufman

COOPERSVILLE 49404

Bluebird Orchard Nursery
429 East Randall Street
Tim Strickler
Phone: 616-837-9598
NOTP

EDWARDSBURG 49112

SeedScapes
P.O. Box 295
Karen Tefft and Kathryn
Alexander
Phone: 616-663-8601
NOTP

FERNVILLE 49408

**Wavecrest Nursery and
Landscaping**
2509 Lakeshore Drive
Carol T. Hop
Phone: 616-543-4175
Fax: 616-543-4100
On-site: Retail and wholesale
March 15 through December
25. Monday through Satur-
day, 9:00–5:00. Sunday,
12:00–5:00.
Other times by appointment.

FOWLERVILLE 48836

Arrowhead Alpines
P.O. Box 857
Street address:
1310 North Gregory Road
Bob and Brigitta Stewart
Phone: 517-223-3581
Fax: 517-223-8750
On-site: Retail and wholesale
All year. Wednesday through
Sunday, 11:00–7:00. Whole-
sale, Monday and Tuesday.

FREE SOIL 49411-9752

Cold Stream Farm
2030 Free Soil Road
Mike Hradel
Phone: 616-464-5809
On-site: Retail
Pick ups, by appointment.
Closed April and November.

GALESBURG 49053

Ensata Gardens
9823 East Michigan Avenue
Bob Bauer and John Coble
Phone: 616-665-7500
On-site: Retail
June and July. Seven days,
daylight hours.

HARTLAND 48353

Growers Service Co.
10118 Crouse Road
John K. Riordan
Phone: 810-632-6525
Fax: 810-632-6566
NOTP

HOLLAND 49424

Veldheer Tulip Gardens, Inc.
12755 Quincy Street and
U.S. Highway 31 North
Phone: 616-399-1900
On-site: Retail and wholesale
All year, in season. Monday
through Sunday, 8:00–6:00.
Off season, Monday through
Friday, 8:00–5:00.

HOPKINS 49328

Englearth Gardens
2461 22nd Street
Herrema Family
Phone: 616-793-7196
On-site: Retail and wholesale
June through August.
Monday through Friday,
9:00–5:00. Saturday,
9:00–3:00.

KALAMAZOO 49019-0425

Oikos Tree Crops
P.O. Box 19425
Ken Asmus
Phone: 616-624-6233
Fax: 616-342-2759
On-site: Retail and wholesale
June through August. By
appointment.

LAKESIDE 49116

Southmeadow Fruit Gardens
P.O. Box SM
Phone: 616-469-2865
NOTP

LANSING 48908-0527

**Wildflower Association of
Michigan**
P.O. Box 80527
6011 West St. Joseph,
Suite 403

LANSING, 48933

**Heritage Garden House
City Visions, Inc.**
Robert J. Morris
311 Seymour Street
NOTP

METAMORA 48455

Metamora Country Gardens
1945 Dryden Road
Pat and Larry Salk
Phone: 810-678-3519
On-site: Retail
July and August. By
appointment.

NEW HUDSON 48165

Far North Gardens
P.O. Box 126
Karen J. Combs
Phone: 810-486-4203
Fax: 810-486-4203
NOTP

PAW PAW 49079-0093

Paw Paw Everlast Label Co.
P.O. Box 93-C
Street address: 47161 M-40
Mrs. A. Arens
Phone: 616-657-4921
NOTP

PERRY 48872

Van Dyke Zinnias
5910 Corey Road
Mrs. Mickey Van Dyke
Phone: 517-468-3894
On-site: Retail
June through September.
Seven days, 9:00–7:00.
By appointment.

SOUTH HAVEN 49090

DeGrandchamp's Blueberry Nursery
15575 77th Street
Mike DeGrandchamp
Phone: 616-637-3915
Fax: 616-637-2531
On-site: Retail and wholesale
March 15 through November. Monday through Friday,
8:00–5:00.

VULCAN 49892

Reath's Nursery
County Road 577, Box 247
R. Scott Reath

Phone: 906-563-9777
Fax: 906-563-9777
On-site: Retail
By appointment.

MINNESOTA

ALBERT LEA 56007

Wedge Nursery
R.D. 2, Box 114
Bradford D. Wedge
Phone: 507-373-5225
NOTP

BATTLE LAKE 56515

Swedberg Nurseries, Inc.
P.O. Box 418
Phone: 218-864-5526
Fax: 218-864-5055
On-site: Retail
Mid-April through
mid-June. 8:00–6:00.
By appointment.

BLOOMING PRAIRIE 55917

Blooming Prairie Gardens
R.R. 1, Box 194
J.D. Madison
Phone: 612-813-1278
Fax: 612-813-1279
On-site: Retail
August and September.
Seven days, 9:00–12:00,
1:00–5:00.

BLUE EARTH 56013

Feder's Prairie Seed Co.
Route 1, Box 41
Wayne and Lynda Feder
Phone: 507-526-3049
On-site: Retail
By appointment.

COKATO 55321-3601

Busse Gardens
5873 Oliver Avenue S.W.
Ainie Busse
Phone: 612-286-2654
Orders: 800-544-3192
Fax: 612-286-2654
On-site: Retail and wholesale
Display gardens: June
through August
Retail garden center: May
through September

DUNDAS 55019

Morco Products
P.O. Box 160
Robert C. Morrow
Phone: 507-645-4277
NOTP

EDINA 55439-1249

Savory's Gardens, Inc.
5300 Whiting Avenue
Bob, Arlene, and
Dennis Savory
Phone: 612-941-8755
Fax: 612-941-3750
On-site: Retail and wholesale
May through September.
Monday through Sunday,
9:00-5:00.
Last six weeks of season,
12:00–4:00.

FARIBAULT 55021

Tischler Peony Garden
1021 East Division Street
R. W. Tischler
Phone: 507-334-7242
On-site: Retail
All year. Seven days, daylight
hours.

St. Paul 55108-2337

Landscape Alternatives, Inc.
1465 North Pascal Street
Karl Ruser
Phone: 612-488-3142
Fax: 612-488-3142
On-site: Retail and wholesale
April through first frost.
Hours variable.

St. Paul 55116

Wee Gems
2197 Stewart Avenue
Ted LeBoutillier
Phone: 612-699-2694
NOTP

Waconia 55387-9616

Ambergate Gardens
8015 Krey Avenue
Mike and Jean Heger
Phone: 612-443-2248
Fax: 612-443-2248
On-site: Retail
Tuesday through Sunday,
9:00–5:00. Closed Monday.

Waseca 56093

Shady Oaks Nursery
112 10th Avenue S.E.
Display garden:
700 19th Avenue N.E.
Dr. Clayton Oslund
Phone: 507-835-5033
Fax: 507-835-8772
On-site: Retail and wholesale
May through first frost.
Monday through Saturday,
9:00–4:00.

White Bear Lake
55110-0626

Cascade Daffodils
P.O. Box 10626
Street address:
6788 132nd Street North
White Bear Lake
55110-6029
Dave and Linda Karnstedt
Phone: 612-426-9616
On-site: Retail
By appointment.

White Bear Lake
55110-0748

Aquacide Company
P.O. Box 10748
Street address: 1627 9th Street
Mr. Marhoe
Phone: 612-429-6742,
800-328-9350
Fax: 612-429-0563
On-site: Retail
All year. Monday through
Friday, 8:00–4:30.

Winona 55987

Prairie Moon Nursery
Route 3, Box 163
Alan Wade
Phone: 507-452-1362
Fax: 507-454-5238
On-site: Retail
By appointment preferably
during June through August

MISSISSIPPI

Jackson 39211

**The American
Hemerocallis Society**
1454 Rebel Drive
Elly Launius

Meridan 39304

Flowerplace Plant Farm
P.O. Box 4865
Gail Barton, Richard Lowery,
and Karen Partlow
Phone: 800-482-5686
On-site: Retail
March through June, Sep-
tember through November.
Thursday through Saturday,
9:30–4:00. Other times, by
appointment.

Starkville 39759

**Mississippi Native
Plant Society**
P.O. Box 2151

Tylertown 39667

**Southern Perennials &
Herbs**
98 Bridges Road
Barbara and Michael Bridges
Phone: 601-684-1769
Fax: 601-684-3729
On-site: Wholesale
May through October. First
Saturday of every month.

MISSOURI

Brixey 65618

Elixir Farm Botanicals
General Delivery
Lavinia McKinney
Phone: 417-261-2393
Fax: 417-261-2355
On-site: Retail
By appointment.

CALIFORNIA 65018

Adamgrove
Route 1, Box 1472
Eric and Bob Tankesley-Clarke
NOTP

CAPE GIRARDEAU 63701

Cape Iris Gardens
822 Rodney Vista Boulevard
Dave Niswonger
Phone: 314-334-3383
On-site: Retail
By appointment.

CLINTON 64735

**Sharp Bros. Seed Co.
Wildflower Division**
396 S.W. Davis-Ladue
Judith Rogers
Phone: 800-451-3779
Fax: 816-885-8647
On-site: Retail
By appointment.

ELK CREEK 65464

**Hamilton Seeds and
Wildflowers**
16786 Brown Road
Rex and Amy Hamilton
Phone: 417-967-2190
Fax: 417-967-2190
On-site: Retail and wholesale
March through June. By
appointment.

GOWER 64454

**Comanche Acres Iris
Gardens**
R.R. 1, Box 258
Jim and Lamoyne Hedgecock
Phone: 816-424-6436
Order: 800-382-IRIS
On-site: Retail and wholesale
Mid-April through May.

GRAIN VALLEY 64029

**American Daylily and
Perennials**
P.O. Box 210
Jack and Jo Roberson
Phone: 816-224-2852
Fax: 816-443-2849
NOTP

GROVER 63040

**Plastic Plumbing
Products, Inc. (Envirogation
Division)**
17005 Manchester R,
P.O. Box 186
Craig Pisarkiewicz
Phone: 314-458-2226
Fax: 314-458-2760
On-site: Retail and wholesale
All year. Monday through
Friday, 8:00–4:30. Saturday,
9:00–1:00.

HOLT 64048

Arborvillage Farm Nursery
P.O. Box 227
Street address:
15604 County Road C.C.
Lanny, Sue, and
Derrick Rawdon
Phone: 816-264-3911
On-site: Retail and wholesale
By appointment.

IONIA 65335-9325

Apsher's Perennial Haven
R.R. 1, Box 57
Vern and Helen Apsher
Phone: 816-668-4757
On-site: Retail and wholesale
May through October. Most
days, 9:00–6:00.

JEFFERSON CITY 65109

**Missouri Wildflowers
Nursery**
9814 Pleasant Hill Road
Mervin Wallace
Phone: 573-496-3492
On-site: Retail
March 20 through June.
Monday through Saturday,
9:00–5:00. Sunday,
12:00–5:00. Other times,
by appointment.

KANSAS CITY 64114

Stigall Water Gardens
7306 Main Street
Trent Stigall
Phone: 816-822-1256
NOTP

KANSAS CITY 64133

Lenington Gardens
7007 Manchester Avenue
Robert L. Lenington
Phone: 816-358-6666
On-site: Retail
May through August.
Wednesday through Sunday,
10:00–6:00. Monday and
Tuesday, by appointment.

LOUISIANA 63353-0010

Stark Bro.'s
P.O. Box 10
Street Address:
Highway 54 West
Walter C. Logan II
Phone: 800-325-4180
Fax: 314-754-5290
On-site: Retail and wholesale
February through December.
Monday through Friday,
8:00–4:00. Hours seasonal.

MONTGOMERY CITY 63361

Barney's Ginseng Patch
Route 2, Highway Box 43
Barney L. Frye
Phone: 314-564-2575
On-site: Retail and wholesale
By appointment.

NEW MELLEM 63365

Midwest Cactus
P.O. Box 163
Street address:
4547 Hopewell Road
Wentzville 63385
Chris Smith
Phone: 314-828-5389
On-site: Retail
By appointment.

OWENSVILLE 65066

Homestead Farms
Route 2, Box 31-A
Ron Vitoux
Phone: 314-437-4277
On-site: Retail
April through October.
Tuesday through Saturday,
9:00–5:00. Sunday,
1:00–5:00.

ST. JOSEPH 64507

Butner's Old Mill Nursery
806 South Belt Highway
Charles E. Amtil
Phone: 816-279-7434
On-site: Retail
All year. Six days, 9:00–5:00.

ST. LOUIS 63128

Amberway Gardens
5803 Amberway Drive
Sue and Ken Kremer
Phone: 314-842-6103
On-site: Retail

April through June, September and October. Seven days,
8:00–8:00.

ST. LOUIS 63144-0073

**Missouri Native Plant
Society**
P.O. Box 20073

SARCOXIE 64862-0338

**Gilbert H. Wild and
Son, Inc.**
1112 Joplin Street
Greg Jones
Phone: 417-548-3514
Fax: 417-548-6831
On-site: Retail
When in bloom. Monday
through Saturday, 7:30–4:00.

MONTANA

BELGRADE 59714

Fisher's Garden Store
P.O. Box 326
Street address:
20750 Frontage Road
Kenneth J. Fisher and
Judy Fisher
Phone: 406-388-6052
On-site: Retail
Monday through Saturday,
9:00–5:00.

BILLINGS 59108-0131

DoRoCo Seed Co.
P.O. Box 80131
Roselynn Coonse
NOTP

BOZEMAN 59715

Sourdough Iris Gardens
109 Sourdough Ridge Road
Maurine K. Blackwell
Phone: 406-586-6233 (no
phone orders)
On-site: Retail and wholesale
Mid-June through flowering.
Days variable. By
appointment.

BOZEMAN 59715-9338

Artemis Gardens
170 Moss Bridge Road
Cynthia E. Hyde
NOTP

BOZEMAN 59771-0992

**Montana Native Plant
Society**
P.O. Box 992

BOZEMAN 59772

Bozeman Bio-Tech, Inc.
P.O. Box 3146
Street address:
1612 Gold Avenue
E. Wayne Vinje
Phone: 406-587-5891,
800-289-6656
Fax: 406-587-0223
NOTP

TERRY 59349

The Seed Shop
P.O. Box 533
Jim and Barbara Linaburg
Phone: 406-637-5865
NOTP

VICTOR 59875-9713

Garden City Seeds
1324 Red Crow Road
Store address:
778 Highway 93-N
Hamilton 59840
Susan Wall-MacLane
Phone: 406-961-4837
Fax: 406-961-4877
On-site: Retail
Monday through Saturday,
9:00–5:00.

NEBRASKA

FORT CALHOUN 68023

The Fragrant Path
P.O. Box 238
E. R. Rasmussen

LEXINGTON 68850-9304

Hildenbrandt's Iris Gardens
H.C. 84, Box 4
Les and Toni Hildenbrandt
Phone: 308-324-4334
On-site: Retail and wholesale
April through September.
Visitors welcome anytime.

LINCOLN 68507-3101

Wikco Industries, Inc.
4930 North 57th Street
Brandon S. Ideen
Phone: 800-872-8864
Fax: 402-464-2289
NOTP

MURDOCK 68407-2350

Stock Seed Farms, Inc.
28008 Mill Road
Lyle and Margaret Stock
Dave and Linda Stock
Phone: 402-867-3771
NOTP

OMAHA 68117-1634

DeGiorgi Seed Company
6011 N Street
Duane Thompson
Orders: 402-731-3901,
800-858-2580
Fax: 402-731-8475
On-site: Retail and wholesale
All year. Seven days, 9:00–5:00.

PONCA 68770

Maple Tree Garden
Larry L. Harder
Phone: 409-755-2615
On site: Retail
By appointment.

WAYNE 68787

Garden Perennials
Route 1
Gail Korn
Phone: 402-375-3615
On-site: Retail
April through November.
Monday through Saturday,
10:00–6:00. Sunday,
2:00–6:00.

WISNER 68791-3536

Spruce Gardens
2317 3rd Road
Cal Reuter
Phone: 402-529-6860
On-site: Retail
May and June. Seven days,
9:00 till dark.

NEVADA

RENO 89507

Northern Nevada Native
Plant Society
P.O. Box 8965
Margaret Williams

RENO 89523

Comstock Seed
8520 West 4th Street
Ed and Linda Kleiner
Phone: 702-746-3681
Fax: 702-746-3681
On-site: Retail and wholesale
All year. Monday through
Friday, 8:00–4:30.

LAS VEGAS 89123

The Mohave Native
Plant Society
8180 Placid Street

NEW HAMPSHIRE

EXETER 03833

Landscape Books
P.O. Box 483
Jane W. Robie
Phone: 603-964-9333
NOTP

NASHUA 03062

Lowe's Own-Root Roses
6 Sheffield Road
Mike Lowe
Phone: 603-888-2214
On-site: Retail
April 15 to November.
Seven days, 8:00–5:00.
By appointment.

PENACOOK 03303-9020

Duncraft
P.O. Box 9020
Street address:
102 Fisherville Road
Concord 03303

Kathryn Wright
Phone: 603-224-0200
Fax: 603-226-3735
On-site: Retail
By appointment.

WALPOLE 03608

Berry Hill Herb Gardens
Box 85, R.R. 2
Old Keene Road
Lois Kenyon
Phone: 603-756-9813
On-site: Retail and wholesale
May through October. Monday through Saturday,
10:00–4:00.

WOODSTOCK 03293

Woodstock Canoe Co. •
P.O. Box 118
Dave Donahue
Phone: 800-362-8804
NOTP

NEW JERSEY

ADELPHIA 07710-0200

Dutch Gardens
P.O. Box 200
Henk van der Voort
Phone: 800-818-3861
Fax: 908-780-7720
NOTP

BOGOTA 07603

The Tomato Club
114 East Main Street
Phone: 201-488-2231
Fax: 201-489-4609

FREEHOLD 07728

Wild Earth Native Plant Nursery
49 Mead Avenue
Street address:
Wright DeBow Road, Jackson Township
Richard Pillar
Phone: 908-308-9777
Fax: 908-308-9777
On-site: Retail and wholesale
April through October.
10:00–5:00. By appointment.

GLASSBORO 08028

Summerville's Gladiolus World-Wide
1330 Ellis Mill Road
Alex Summers
Phone: 609-881-0704
NOTP

GREENWICH 08323

Fairweather Gardens
P.O. Box 330
Robert Hoffman and
Robert Popham
Phone: 609-451-6261
Fax: 609-451-6261
NOTP

JACKSON 08527

Thompson & Morgan
P.O. Box 1308
Street address:
Farraday and Gramme Avenues
Bruce Sangster
Phone: 800-367-7333
Fax: 908-363-9356
NOTP

LAKEWOOD 08701

Bamboo & Rattan Works, Inc.
470 Oberlin Avenue South
Suzanne Maison
Phone: 908-370-0220
Fax: 908-905-8386
On-site: Retail and wholesale
All year. Monday through
Friday, 8:30–4:00.

NEW BRUNSWICK 08903-0231

The Native Plant Society of New Jersey
P.O. Box 231
Cook College

RINGOES 08551-1312

Robin Meadow Farm
46 Van Lieus Road
Ralph H. Maiwaldt
Phone: 609-466-1998
On-site: Retail and wholesale
April through November.
Wednesday through Saturday,
8:00–5:00. Sunday through
Tuesday, by appointment.

SADDLE RIVER 07458

Waterford Gardens
74 East Allendale Road
John A. Meeks
Phone: 201-327-0721
Fax: 201-327-0684
On-site: Retail and wholesale
All year. Monday through
Saturday, 9:00–5:00. Sunday,
April through July.

SEWELL 08080-0007

Oral Ledden & Sons
P.O. Box 7
Street address:
Center and Atlantic Avenues
Don Ledden
Phone: 609-468-1000
Fax: 609-414-0947
On-site: Retail and wholesale
All year. Seven days, daylight
hours.

TAPPAN 07675

Harlane Company, Inc.
266 Orangeburgh Road
June Benardella
Phone: 201-768-0158
NOTP

VINCENTOWN 08088-2478

Genie House
P.O. Box 2478
NOTP

NEW MEXICO

BELEN 87002

Mesa Garden
P.O. Box 72
Steven Brack
Phone: 505-864-3131
Fax: 505-864-3124
NOTP

CHAPARRAL 88021

Pleasure Iris Garden
425 East Luna
Mrs. Henry (Luella) Danielson
Phone: 505-824-4299

On-site: Retail
March through April.
9:00–5:00.

DEMING 88030-5009

Desert Nursery
1301 South Copper
Laszlo and Shirley Nyerges
Phone: 505-546-6264
On-site: Retail
March through September.
Monday through Saturday,
10:00–5:30. Other times, by
appointment.

FAIRACRES 88033

McAllister's Iris Garden
P.O. Box 112
Sharon McAllister
Phone: 505-526-4263,
522-6731
On-site: Retail
Mid-March through early
May. By appointment.

LAS CRUCES 88030

Chile Institute
P.O. Box 3-Q
New Mexico State University
NOTP

ROSWELL 88202-0725

Roswell Seed Company, Inc.
P.O. Box 725
James and W. L. Gill
Phone: 505-622-7701
Fax: 505-623-2885
On-site: Retail
All year. Monday through
Saturday, 8:00–5:00.

SANTA FE 87501

Plants of the Southwest
Agua Fria, Route 6,
Box 11-A
Gail Haggard
Phone: 505-471-2212,
800-788-7333
Fax: 505-438-8800
On-site: Retail and wholesale
March through November.
Regular season, Monday
through Sunday. Off season,
Monday through Friday.
8:30–5:30. Weekend hours
vary.

SANTA FE 87505-2929

A High Country Garden
2902 Rufina Street
Greenhouse address:
2904 Rufina Street.
David, Meg, and Bill Salman
Phone: 505-438-3031,
800-925-9387
Fax: 505-438-9552
On-site: Retail
All year.

SANTA FE 87502

**Native Plant Society of
New Mexico**
P.O. Box 5917

SANTA FE 87506-5700

Seeds of Change®
P.O. Box 15700
Frank Connelly
Phone: 505-438-8080,
800-957-3337
Fax: 505-438-7052
NOTP

VEGUITA 87062

Desert Moon Nursery
P.O. Box 600
Street address:
30 Sunset Road
Hodoba Family
Phone: 505-864-0614
On-site: Retail and wholesale
By appointment.

NEW YORK

ALBANY 12230

New York Flora Association
New York State Museum
3132 CEC

AMSTERDAM 12010-5304

Kadco USA, Inc.
16 De Graff Street
Tom Petherick
Phone: 800-448-5503
Fax: 518-842-0602
On-site: Retail
All year. Monday through
Friday, 8:30–5:00.

BABYLON 11702-0598

Van Bourgondien Bros.
P.O. Box 1000
Deborah Van Bourgondien
Phone: 516-669-3500
Orders: 800-622-9997
Customer Service:
800-622-9959
Fax: 516-669-1228
NOTP

BRIGHTWATERS 11718-0430

**Van Dyck's Flower
Farms, Inc.**
P.O. Box 430
Jan Van Dyck
Phone: 800-248-2852
NOTP

BUFFALO 14211

**Niagara Frontier
Botanical Society**
Buffalo Museum of Science
Humboldt Parkway

BUFFALO 14217

Plant Collectibles
103 Kenview Avenue,
Dept. HGS
Marseille Luxenberg
Phone: 716-875-1221
NOTP

BUFFALO 14240-0548

Stokes Seeds
P.O. Box 548
Phone: 716-695-6980
Fax: 716-695-9649
NOTP

CANANDAIGUA 14424

Miller Nurseries
5060 West Lake Road
John E. Miller
Phone: 716-396-2647,
800-836-9630
Fax: 716-396-2154
On-site: Retail
Garden store: January
through early March.
Monday through Friday,
8:00–4:30.
Mid-March through mid-
June. Monday through
Saturday, 8:00–5:00. Sunday,
9:00–5:00. Late June
through December. Monday
through Friday, 8:00–4:30.

CANASTOTA 13032

Hermitage Gardens
P.O. Box 361
Street address:
West Seneca Avenue, Route 5
Russell A. Rielle
Phone: 315-697-9093
Fax: 315-697-8169
On-site: Retail and wholesale
All year. Seven days,
8:00–5:00. By appointment.

COLLINS 14034

P & P Seed Company
14050 Route 62
Ray Waterman
Phone: 716-532-5995
Fax: 716-532-5690
NOTP

**World Pumpkin
Confederation**
14050 Route 62
Ray Waterman
Phone: 716-532-5995
Fax: 716-532-5690

DEWITT 13214

Syracuse Botanical Club
101 Ambergate Road
Janet Holmes

DIX HILLS 11746

Roslyn Nursery
211 Burrs Lane
Philip Waldman
Phone: 516-643-9347
Fax: 516-484-1555
On-site: Retail and wholesale
All year. Monday through
Saturday, 9:00–5:00. April
and May. Sunday.

EAST AMHERST 14051

**Amherst Museum Wild-
flower Society**
3755 Tonawanda Creek
Road

FAYETEVILLE 13066

Karen Harris
200 East Genesee Street
Karen Harris
Phone: 315-637-8209
NOTP

FLANDERS 11901

Long Island Seed Company
1368 Flanders Road
Phone: 516-369-0257
NOTP

GARDINER 12525

Wood Classics, Inc.®
P.O. Box 291
Street address: Osprey Lane
Barbara and Eric Goodman
Phone: 914-255-7871
Fax: 914-255-7881
On-site: Retail
Monday through Friday,
9:00–5:00. Saturday,
9:00–5:30.

GENEVA 14456

**Fruit Testing Association
Nursery, Inc.**
P.O. Box 462
Helen Van Arsdale
Phone: 315-787-2205
Fax: 315-787-2216
NOTP

HALL 14463-0270

Seneca Hybrids
1 Seneca Circle
Bill Carey
Phone: 716-526-6396
Fax: 716-526-5350
On-site: Retail and wholesale
All year. Monday through
Friday, 8:00–4:30. By ap-
pointment.

HUNTINGTON 11743

Aquamonitor
Box 327
Street address:
20 Tall Tree Court
Cold Spring Harbor 11724
Bob Whitener
Phone: 516-427-5664
NOTP

JOHNSTOWN 12095

Little's Good Gloves, Inc.
P.O. Box 808
Street address:
404 South Market Street
Mark and Beth Dzierson
Phone: 518-762-8051,
736-5014
Fax: 518-762-2980
NOTP

LANSINGBURGH 12182

Warren F. Broderick
P.O. Box 124
Warren F. Broderick
Phone: 518-235-4041
NOTP

LEVITTOWN 11756

**Long Island Botanical
Society**

LONG ISLAND CITY 11101

Florentine Craftsmen, Inc.
46-24 28th Street
Graham G. Brown II
Phone: 718-937-7632,
800-876-3567
Fax: 718-937-9858
On-site: Retail and wholesale
All year. Monday through
Friday, 8:00–4:30.

MEDFORD 11763

**Wood Innovations of
Suffolk Ltd.**
P.O. Box 356
Street address:
265 Middle Island Road
Hank Harms
Phone: 516-698-2345
Fax: 516-698-2396
On-site: Retail
All year. Five days,
7:30–4:30.

NEW PALTZ 12561

Plumtree Nursery
387 Springtown Road
Phone: 914-255-0417
NOTP

MILLWOOD 10546

**American Rock Garden
Society**
P.O. Box 67
Jacques Mommens

NEW YORK 10019-2103

**American Gloxinia and
Gesneriad Society**
c/o The Horticultural Society
of New York
128 West 58th Street
Phone: 212-757-0195
Jimmy D. Dates

NIAGARA FALLS 14304

**Irrigro International
Irrigation Systems**
1555 Third Avenue
R. L. Neff
Phone: 905-688-4090
Fax: 905-688-4093
On-site: Retail
By appointment.

POTSDAM 13676

St. Lawrence Nurseries
325 State Highway 345
Bill and Diana MacKentley
Phone: 315-265-6739
On-site: Retail and wholesale
All year. Seven days. By
appointment.

PUTNAM VALLEY 10579

Shepherd Hill Farm
200 Peekskill Hollow Road
Gerry Bleyer
Phone: 914-528-5917
Fax: 914-528-8343
On-site: Retail
All year. Seven days,
8:00–5:00. By appointment.

ROCHESTER 14624

Living Wall™ Garden Co.
2044 Chili Avenue
F. Wesley Moffett
Phone: 716-247-0070
Fax: 716-247-1033

On-site: Retail
Summer, Monday through
Friday, 8:00–4:00. Saturday
and Sunday, 10:00–5:00.
Winter, Monday through
Friday, 8:00–4:00.

ROCHESTER 14692-2960

Harris Seeds
P.O. Box 22960
Street address:
60 Saginaw Drive
Richard (Dick) Chamberlin
Phone: 716-442-0100
Fax: 716-442-9386
NOTP

SARATOGA SPRINGS 12866

Saxton Gardens
1 First Street
S. E. Saxton
Phone: 518-584-4697
On-site: Retail
June through August.
By appointment.

SOUTH FARMINGDALE 11735

Isabel Hibbard Gardens
4 Nancy Drive
Isabel Hibbard
Phone: 516-694-9682
On-site: Retail
April through October.
Seven days, 9:00–7:30.
By appointment.

**SOUTH NEW BERLIN
13843-9653**

**American Willow Growers
Network**
R.F.D. 1, Box 124-A
Bonnie Gale
Phone: 607-847-8264

SOUTH SALEM 10590

Carlson's Gardens
Box 305
Bob Carlson
Phone: 914-763-5958
On-site: Retail
By appointment.

SPRING VALLEY 10977

Matterhorn Nursery, Inc.
227 Summit Park Road
Matt and Ronnie Horn
Phone: 914-354-5986
Fax: 914-354-4749
On-site: Retail
All year. Monday through
Saturday, 8:00–5:00. Sunday,
10:00–5:00.

TROY 12180

Troy-Bilt®
102nd Street and 9th Avenue
Dean Leith, Jr.
Phone: 518-237-8430, ext.
4429; 800-833-6990
NOTP

WARWICK 10990-0430

Hillary's Garden
P.O. Box 430
John Russo
Phone: 914-987-1175
NOTP

WATER MILL 11976

Water Mill Daylily Garden
56 Winding Way
Dan and Jane Trimmer
Phone: 516-726-9640
On-site: Retail
July and August. Seven days,
10:00–5:00.

NEWFOUNDLAND

St. John's A1C 557

Newfoundland Chapter
Canadian Wildflower
Society
c/o Oxen Pond Botanical
Park

NORTH CAROLINA

Asheville 28804

University Botanical
Gardens at Asheville, Inc.
151 W. T. Weaver Boulevard

Bailey 27807

Finch Blueberry Nursery
P.O. Box 699
Rudy Perry
Phone: 919-235-4664
Orders: 800-245-4662
Fax: 919-235-2411
On-site: Retail and wholesale
All year. Monday through
Friday, 8:00–5:00.

Brevard 28712

Western Carolina
Botanical Club
6 Tenequa Drive,
Connestee Falls
Dick Smith

Bryson City 28713

Arrowhead Nursery
5030 Watia Road,
Dept. HGS
Linda Schneider
On-site: Retail
By appointment.

Chapel Hill 27514

Boothe Hill Tea Co.
and Greenhouse
Boothe Hill Wildflowers
23-B Boothe Hill
Nancy Easterling
Phone: 919-967-4091
On-site: Retail
By appointment.

Chapel Hill 27516

Niche Gardens
1111 Dawson Road
Kim Hawks
Phone: 919-967-0078
On-site: Retail
All year. Tuesday through
Friday, 9:00–5:00. Spring
and fall weekends, by
appointment.

Chapel Hill 27599-3375

North Carolina Wild Flower
Preservation Society, Inc.
Totten Garden Center 3375,
UNC
North Carolina Botanical
Garden
Nancy C. Julian

Charlotte 28216

Cat's Paw Gardens
9414 Stonegate Drive
Tom and Gail Moore
Phone: 704-394-8661
On-site: Retail
June through August.
Seven days, 8:00–8:00.
By appointment.

Colerain 27924

Lazy Hill Farm Designs
P.O. Box 235
Street address:
Lazy Hill Road
Betty Baker
Phone: 919-356-2828
Fax: 919-356-2040
NOTP

Dunn 28334

Jernigan Gardens
Route 6, Box 593
Street address:
840 Maple Grove Church
Road
Winifred Jernigan Williams
Phone: 910-567-2135
On-site: Retail
Mid-April through mid-June.
Friday and Saturday,
9:00–6:00. Mid-June
through September. Tuesday
through Saturday, 9:00–6:00.
August through October, by
appointment.

Durham 27717

Witherspoon Rose Culture
Box 51655
Street address:
3312 Watkins Road
David and Rhonda Pike
Phone: 919-489-4446,
800-643-0315
Fax: 919-490-0623
On-site: Retail
February through May.
Monday through Saturday,
8:30–5:00. June through
January. Monday through
Friday, 8:30–5:00.

FUQUAY-VARINA 27526

Chalybeate Gardens
Route 2, Box 220
George and Cathy Tolar
Phone: 919-552-2235
On-site: Retail
May through July. By appointment.

KINGS MOUNTAIN 28086

Iron Gate Gardens
Route 3, Box 250
Van M. Sellers and
Vic Santa Lucia
Phone: 704-435-6178
(evenings)
Fax: 704-435-HEMS
On-site: Retail
April through July.
Seven days, 9:00–6:00.

LEICESTER 28748-9622

**The Sandy Mush Herb
Nursery**
316 Surrett Cove Road
Fairman and Katie Jayne
Phone: 704-683-2014
On-site: Retail
Thursday through Saturday,
9:00–5:00.

LEICESTER 28748

**Washington Evergreen
Nursery**
P.O. Box 388
Street address:
Brooks Branch Road
Jordan Jack
Phone: 704-683-4518, (April
through October) 803-747-
1641, (November through

March)
On-site: Retail
Mid-April through mid-
October. By appointment.

MARIETTA 28362

Marietta Gardens
P.O. Box 70
John, Faye and
Elizabeth O. Shooter
Phone: 910-628-9466
Fax: 910-628-9933
On-site: Retail and wholesale
All year. Monday through
Sunday, 9:00–6:00.

MARION 28752-9338

We-Du Nursery
Route 5, Box 274
Richard A. Weaver and
Rene A. Duval
Phone: 704-738-8300
On-site: Retail
All year. Monday through
Saturday, 9:00–12:00,
1:00–4:00. By appointment
during shipping season.

MIDDLESEX 27557

Little River Farm Daylilies
7815 N.C. 39
Mel Oliver, Jr.
Phone: 919-965-9507
On-site: Retail
June. By appointment.

PILOT MOUNTAIN 27041

The Herb Garden
P. O. Box 773-SC
Ann Beall
Phone: 910-368-2723
NOTP

PINEOLA 28662

Gardens of the Blue Ridge
P.O. Box 10
Street address:
9056 Pittman's Gap Road
Edward Fletcher
Phone: 704-733-2417
Fax: 704-733-8894
On-site: Retail
All year. Monday through
Friday, 7:30–4:30. Saturday,
7:30–1:00. Tours, by appointment.

PITTSBORO 27312

The Wildwood Flower
Route 3, P.O. Box 165
Thurman Maness
Phone: 919-542-4344
(evenings)
NOTP

PRINCETON 27569

Powell's Gardens
9468 U.S. Highway 70 East
Loleta Kenan Powell
Phone: 919-936-4421
On-site: Retail
All year. Monday through
Saturday, 10:00–6:00. Sundays (April 15 through July
4), 2:00–6:00.

PROSPECT HILL 27314

Love Gardens
P.O. Box 9
Street address:
Highway 86
Bob Love
Phone: 910-562-3380
On-site: Retail
April through October.
Seven days, daylight hours.
By appointment.

RALEIGH 27603

Plant Delights Nursery
9241 Sauls Road
Tony and Michelle Avent
Phone: 919-772-4794
Fax: 919-662-0370
On-site: Retail
Two weekends in spring,
summer, and fall. By ap-
pointment.

SALUDA 28773

Taylor Ridge Farm
P.O. Box 222
Gunnar Taylor
Phone: 704-749-4756
On-site: Retail and wholesale
April through November.
Saturday and Sunday,
10:00–6:00. Or by
appointment.

WEDDINGTON 28173

Renaissance Gardens
1047 Baron Road
Judith and Robert Weston
Phone: 704-843-5370
On-site: Retail
By appointment.

WINSTON-SALEM 27105

**Greenthumb Daylily
Gardens**
1315 East Rollingwood Circle
Bill and Joyce Green
Phone: 910-377-2975
On-site: Retail
May through October.
By appointment.

NOVA SCOTIA

HALIFAX B3L 2A1

**Nova Scotia
Wildflower Society**
6360 Young Street

OHIO

ATHENS 45701

Companion Plants
7247 North Coolville Ridge
Road
Peter Borchard
Phone: 614-592-4643
On-site: Retail and wholesale
March through Thanksgiving.
Thursday through Saturday,
10:00–5:00.
Closed first two weeks
in August.

BEDFORD 44146

Bedford Dahlias
65 Leyton Road
Eugene A. Woznicki
Phone: 216-232-2852
NOTP

BELLBROOK 45305

Serendipity Gardens
3210 Upper Bellbrook Road
Becky Stegall and
Shirley Farmer
Phone: 513-426-6596
On-site: Retail
July and August. Friday and
Saturday, 10:00–6:00. Sun-
day, 1:00–6:00.

BRECKSVILLE 44141-3302

Kuk's Forest Nursery
10174 Barr Road
Bob Kuk
Phone: 216-526-5271
On-site: Retail
May through October.
By appointment.

CHAGRIN FALLS 44022

Ohio Native Plant Society
6 Louise Drive
Ann K. Malmquist

CHESTERLAND 44026

**Homestead Division of
Sunnybrook Farms**
9448 Mayfield Road
Peter and Jean Ruh
Phone: 216-729-9838
On-site: Retail
April 25 through October
15. Saturday and Sunday,
9:00–5:00. By appointment.

Sunnybrook Farms
P.O. Box 6
Street address:
9448 Mayfield Road
Tim Ruh
Phone: 216-729-7232
On-site: Retail
All year. Monday through
Saturday, 9:00–5:00. Sunday,
10:00–4:00.

CLEVELAND 44105

**The Guano Company
International, Inc.**
3562 East 80th Street
Phone: 216-641-1200,
800-4B-GUANO
Fax: 216-641-1310
NOTP

CLEVELAND HEIGHTS 44118

Holly Ridge Nursery
1570 Compton Road
Paul Hanslik and
Lucinda Little
Phone: 216-321-5608
Fax: 216-321-5608
Nursery address:
5925 South Ridge Road
Geneva 44041
Nursery phone:
216-466-0134
On-site: Wholesale
By appointment.

GATES MILLS 44040

Crintonic Gardens
County Line Road
Curt Hanson
Phone: 216-423-3349
On-site: Retail and wholesale
May through September.
By appointment.

GENEVA 44041-0428

Girard Nurseries
P.O. Box 428
Street address:
6839 North Ridge East
Peter Girard, Jr.
Phone: 216-466-2881
Fax: 216-466-3999
On-site: Retail and wholesale
Mid-April through June.
Every day, 8:00–4:30.
July through September 20.
Monday through Saturday,
8:00–4:30.
September 20 through
October. Every day,
8:00–4:30.
November through mid-
April. Monday through
Saturday, 8:00–4:30.

HIRAM 44234

Down on the Farm Seed
P.O. Box 184
Ruth A. Guth
Phone: 216-274-8043
NOTP

INDEPENDENCE 44131

William Tricker, Inc.
7125 Tanglewood Drive
Richard Lee
Phone: 216-524-3491
Fax: 216-524-6688
On-site: Retail
Monday through Saturday,
8:00–6:00. Thursday,
8:00–8:00. Sunday,
12:00–5:00.

KIDRON 44636-0041

Lehman's
P.O. Box 41
Street address:
One Lehman Circle
Galen Lehman
Phone: 216-857-5757,
857-5441
Fax: 216-857-5785
On-site: Retail
All year. Monday through
Saturday, 7:00–5:30. Thurs-
day, 7:00–8:00.

LIBERTY CENTER 43532

EON Industries
P.O. Box 11
Street address:
107 West Maple Street
Dale E. Leininger
Phone: 419-533-4961
On-site: Retail
By appointment.

LONDON 43140

Mainline of North America
P.O. Box 526
Street address:
U.S. Route 40 at
State Route 38
Daniel K. Davis
Phone: 614-852-9733,
852-9734
Fax: 614-852-2045
On-site: Retail and wholesale
All year. Monday through
Friday, 8:00–5:00. Saturday,
8:00–12:00.

MADISON 44057

Bluestone Perennials
7211 Middle Ridge Road
William Boonstra
Phone: 800-852-5243
Fax: 216-428-7198
NOTP

MANSFIELD 44907

Wiley's Nut Grove Nursery
2002 Lexington Avenue
Street address:
1116 Hickory Lane
Mansfield 44905
Robert F. Wiley
Phone: 419-756-0697
On-site: Retail
By appointment.

MEDINA 44258

Crop King, Inc.
P.O. Box 310
Street address:
4930 Chippewa Road
Dan Brentlinger
Phone: 216-725-5656

Fax: 216-722-3958
On-site: Retail
All year. Monday through
Friday, 8:00–5:00. Saturday,
8:00–12:00.

MENTOR 44060

**The Herb Society of
America**
9019 Kirtland Chardon
Road
Phone: 216-256-0514
Fax: 216-256-0514

MENTOR 44061-0388

Garden Place
P.O. Box 388
Street address:
6780 Heisley Road
Kathy Sneary
Phone: 216-255-3705
Fax: 216-255-9535
On-site: Retail
By appointment.

METAMORA 43540

Gleckler's Seedmen
George L. Glecker
Phone: 419-923-5463
NOTP

MILFORD 45150

**The American Daffodil
Society**
1686 Grey Fox Trails
Mary Lou Gripshover

MILLERSBURG 44654

Berlin Seeds
5371 County Road 77

Edward Beachy
Phone: 216-893-2811
NOTP

MILLERSBURG 44654-9104

Schlabach's Nursery
3901 County Road 135
David Schlabach
On-site: Retail and wholesale
March and April. Hours
variable. By appointment.

MINERVA 44657

**Lily of the Valley
Herb Farm**
3969 Fox Avenue
Paul
Phone: 216-862-3920
On-site: Retail
Herb shop: All year.
Monday through
Saturday, 10:00–5:00.
Nursery: Mid-April through
summer. Monday through
Saturday, 10:00–6:00. Sun-
day, 1:00–5:00. Closed
Sundays after June.

MOUNT GILEAD 43338

American Gourd Society
P.O. Box 274

NORTH LIMA 44452-9731

Mellinger's
2310 West South Range
Road
Plants: Phil Steiner
Supplies: Jean Steiner
Phone: 216-549-9861
Orders: 800-321-7444
Fax: 216-549-3716

On-site: Retail
All year. Monday through
Saturday, 8:30–5:00.

PAINESVILLE 44077

Historical Roses
1657 West Jackson Street
Ernest J. Vash
Phone: 216-357-7270
NOTP

PERRY 44081

Gilson Gardens
P.O. Box 277
Street address:
3059 U.S. Route 20
Fax: 216-259-2378
On-site: Retail and wholesale
All year. Seven days,
9:00–5:00. Closed Sundays
in winter.

MacKenzie Nursery Supply
3891 Shepard Road
Bill Burr
Phone: 800-777-5030
Fax: 216-259-3004
On-site: Wholesale
All year. Monday through
Friday, 7:30–5:00. Saturday,
7:30–2:30.

PERRYSVILLE 44864

Charles V. Applegate
3699 Pleasant Hill Road
Charles V. Applegate
Phone: 419-938-3827
On-site: Retail
June through September.
Monday through Saturday,
9:00–6:00. By appointment.

PIQUA 45356-0816

A. M. Leonard, Inc.
P.O. Box 816
Street address:
241 Fox Drive
Phone: 800-543-8955
Fax: 800-433-0633
On-site: Retail and wholesale
By appointment.

SOLON 44139

Cattail Meadows Limited
P.O. Box 39391,
Dept. HGS
Street address:
Montgomery Road
Orwell
Ed Tuhela, and Linda and
Steve Tuhela-Reuning
Phone: 216-248-4581
On-site: Retail
By appointment.

UNIVERSITY HEIGHTS 44118

**Native Plant Society of
Northeastern Ohio**
2651 Kerwick Road

VINCENT 45784

**Dyke's Blueberry Farm and
Nursery, Inc.**
Route 1, Box 251
Jeff Nelson
Phone: 614-678-2192
On-site: Retail and wholesale
All year. Seven days, twelve
hours. By appointment.

OKLAHOMA

BLANCHARD 73010

Contemporary Gardens
Box 534

Street address:
110 North Harrison
Perry Dyer
Phone: 405-485-3302
On-site: Retail
April through July. Seven
days. By appointment.

HASKELL 74436

BlueJay Gardens Herb Farm
Route 2, Box 196
Viola Jay
Phone: 918-482-3465
On-site: Retail and wholesale
All year. Tuesday through
Saturday, 9:00–5:00. Or by
appointment.

OKLAHOMA CITY 73112-
2806

Mid-America Garden
3409 North Geraldine
Paul Black
Phone: 405-946-5743
On-site: Retail
Mid-April through mid-May,
mid-June through mid-July.
By appointment.

TULSA 74114-1350

**Oklahoma Native Plant
Society**
Tulsa Garden Center
2435 S. Peoria

TULSA 74152-0382

Sun Garden Specialties
P.O. Box 52382,
Dept. HGS
Street address:
3722 South Winston Avenue

Tulsa 74135
Tony Bishop
Phone: 918-747-4079
NOTP

ONTARIO

BELLE RIVER N0R 1A0

**Better Yield Insects and
Garden Houses**
1302 Highway 2, R.R. 3
Site 4, Box 48
Phone: 519-727-6108
Fax: 519-727-5989
NOTP

CARLISE L0R 1H0

V. Kraus Nurseries Ltd.
Box 180, 1380 Centre Road
Phone: 905-689-4022
Fax: 905-689-8080
On-site: Retail
By appointment.

DUNDAS L9H 6M1

William Dam Seeds
P.O. Box 8400
Street address:
279 Highway 8
West Flamboro
Phone: 905-628-6641
Fax: 905-627-1729
On-site: Retail
April through June.
Monday through Wednesday,
9:00–6:00. Thursday and
Friday, 9:00–9:00. Saturday,
9:00–5:00.
July through March.
Monday through Friday,
9:00–6:00. Saturday,
9:00–5:00.

EDEN N0J 1H0

Otter Valley Native Plants
Box 31, R.R. 1
Phone: 519-866-5639
On-site: Retail
By appointment.

GOODWOOD L0C 1A0

Richters
Conrad Richter
Phone: 905-640-6677
Fax: 905-640-6641
On-site: Retail
Monday through Sunday,
8:30–5:00.

MARKHAM L3R 1N1

Canadian Wildflower Society
4981 Highway 7 East
Unit 12A, #228
John Craw

MARLBANK K0K 2L0

Golden Bough Tree Farm
Phone: 613-478-5829
NOTP

NIAGARA-ON-THE-LAKE L0S 1J0

Grimo Nut Nursery
979 Lakeshore Road North,
R.R. 3
Phone: 905-935-6887
(evenings)
Fax: 905-934-6887
On-site: Pick up, by
appointment.

NORTH GOWER K0A 2T0

Garden North
5984 Third Line Road North,
R.R. 3
Kristl Walek
Phone: 613-489-0065
Fax: 613-489-0065
On-site: Retail
May and June. Daily
9:00–dusk.

OTTAWA K2A 1T4

Lee Valley Tools Ltd.
P.O. Box 6295, Station J
Store address: 1080 Morrison
Drive
Ottawa K2H 8K7
Leonard G. Lee
Phone: 613-596-0350
Orders: 800-267-8767
Fax: 613-596-6030
On-site: Retail
Monday through Wednesday,
9:00–6:00. Thursday and
Friday, 9:00–9:00. Saturday,
9:00–5:00.

PICKERING L1V 1A6

Pickering Nurseries, Inc.
670 Kingston Road
Phone: 905-839-2111
Fax: 905-839-4807
On-site: Pick up, by
appointment.

ST. THOMAS N5P 3R5

Berry Hill Limited
75 Burwell Road
Phone: 519-631-0480,
800-668-3072
Fax: 519-631-8935

On-site: Retail
Showroom: Monday through
Friday, 8:00–5:00. Saturday,
September through June,
9:00–12:00.

THORNHILL L3T 4A5

Gardenimport
P.O. Box 760
Dugald Cameron
Phone: 905-731-1950
Fax: 905-881-3499
On-site: Pick up, by
appointment.

TROUT CREEK P0H 2L0

Becker's Seed Potatoes
R.R.1
Phone: 705-724-2305
NOTP

TORONTO

Lee Valley Tools Ltd.
Store address:
5511 Steeles Avenue West,
Weston
Phone: 416-746-0850
(See also Ottawa)
On-site: Retail
Monday through Wednesday,
9:00–6:00. Thursday and
Friday, 9:00–9:00. Saturday,
9:00–5:00.

WATERDOWN L0R 2H1

Hortico, Inc.
723 Robson Road
R.R. 1
Bill Vanderkruk
Phone: 905-689-6984,
689-3002
Fax: 905-689-6566
NOTP

WATERLOO N2J 3Z9

OSC Seeds
P.O. Box 144
Store address:
16 King Street South
On-site: Retail

OREGON

ALBANY 97321-4580

Nichols Garden Nursery
1190 Pacific Highway
Rose Marie Nichols McGee
Phone: 503-928-9280
Fax: 503-967-8406
On-site: Retail
Monday through Saturday,
9:00–5:00.

BEAVERTON 97007-5742

**Oregon Miniature
Roses, Inc.**
8285 S.W. 185th Avenue
Nick, Katie, and
Ray Spooner
Phone: 503-649-4482
Fax: 503-649-3528
On-site: Retail
All year. Seven days,
9:00–5:00.

BROOKS 97305

Iris Country
6219 Topaz Street N.E.
Roger R. Nelson
Phone: 503-393-4739
On-site: Retail
By appointment.

CARLTON 97111

Carlton Rose Nurseries
P.O. Box 366
Street address:
320 West Monroe Street
Jerry Strahle
Phone: 503-852-7135
Fax: 503-852-7511
On-site: Retail
Open house Friday and
Saturday one week before
Mother's Day, 10:00–4:00.
All year. By appointment.

CLACKAMAS 97015

Out of the Redwoods
P.O. Box 1972
Ernie and Philippa Platt
Phone: 503-658-4135
NOTP

CLOVERDALE 97112

Louck's Nursery
P.O. Box 102
Street address:
14200 Campground Road
Mert and Marjorie Loucks
Phone: 503-392-3166
On-site: Retail
All year. By appointment.

CORBETT 97019

Bonnie Brae Gardens
1105 S.E. Christensen Road
Jeanie McKillop Driver and
Frank Driver
Phone: 503-695-5190
On-site: Retail
Late March through early
May. By appointment.

Oregon Trail Daffodils
41905 S.E. Louden
Bill Tribe
Phone: 503-695-5513
NOTP

CORVALLIS 97330

Redlo Cacti
2315 N.W. Circle Boulevard
Lorne E. Hanna
Phone: 503-752-2910
On-site: Retail
By appointment.

COTTAGE GROVE 97424

Territorial Seed Company
P.O. Box 157
Street address:
20 Palmer Avenue
Tom Johns
Phone: 541-942-9547
Fax: 541-942-9881
On-site: Various, please
inquire.

DRAIN 97435

**Kelleygreen Rhododendron
Nursery**
P.O. Box 62
Street address:
6924 Highway 38
Jan D. Kelley
Phone: 800-477-5676
On-site: Retail
By appointment.

ESTACADA 97023

Squaw Mountain Gardens
36212 S.E. Squaw Mountain
Road
Joyce Hoekstra and
Janis and Arthur Noyes
Phone: 503-630-5458
Fax: 503-630-5849
NOTP

EUGENE 97401-1794

Greer Gardens
1280 Goodpasture Island
Road
Harold E. Greer
Phone: 503-686-8266
Orders: 800-548-0111
Fax: 503-686-0910
On-site: Retail and wholesale
All year. Monday through
Saturday, 9:00–5:30. Sunday,
8:30–5:30.

EUGENE 97402

Abracadata®
P.O. Box 2440
Phone: 800-451-4871
Fax: 503-683-1925
NOTP

EUGENE 97440

**Native Plant Society of
Oregon**
P.O. Box 902
Jan Dobak

GALES CREEK 97117

The Lilly Place Nursery
9205 N.W. Lilly Lane
Echo Larsen
Phone: 503-357-8613
On-site: Retail
June 15 through August 7.
Most days, 10:00–4:30. By
appointment.

GOLD BEACH 97444

**Tradewinds Bamboo
Nursery**
28446 Hunter Creek Loop
Gib and Diane Cooper
Phone: 503-247-0835
Fax: 503-247-0835
On-site: Retail
February through November.
Tuesday through Saturday,
9:00–4:00. By appointment.

GOLD HILL 97525-9730

Beth L. Bibby, Books
1225 Sardine Creek Road
George A. Bibby
Phone: 503-855-1621
On-site: Retail
By appointment.

HILLSBORO 97123-9051

Daisy Fields
12635 S.W. Brighton Lane
JoAnn Wiltrakis
Phone: 503-628-0315
Fax: 503-628-0315
NOTP

HUBBARD 90732

**Grant E. Mitsch Novelty
Daffodils**
P.O. Box 218
Street address:
6247 South Sconce
Richard and Elise Havens
Phone: 503-651-2742
On-site: Retail
March 10 through April 10.
Seven days, 12:00–5:00. By
appointment.

McMINNVILLE 97128

Trans-Pacific Nursery
16065 Oldsville Road
Jackson Muldoon
Phone: 503-472-6215
Fax: 503-434-1505
On-site: Retail
All year. Sunday through
Friday, 9:00–6:00.

MEDFORD 97501

Jackson & Perkins
P.O. Box 1028
Robert Van Diest
Phone: 800-292-4769,
800-872-7673
Fax: 800-242-0329
NOTP

MEDFORD 97501

Nature's Control
P.O. Box 35
Phone: 541-899-8318
Fax: 800-698-6250
NOTP

Siskiyou Rare Plant Nursery
2825 Cummings Road
Baldassare Mineo
Phone: 541-772-6846
On-site: Retail
March through November.
First and last Saturdays,
9:00–2:00. By appointment.

MILWAUKIE 97222-6117

Hidden Garden Nursery
13515 S.E. Briggs
Wayne and Kathy Lauman
Phone: 503-653-8189,
653-0402
On-site: Retail and wholesale
March through October.
Days and hours variable.
By appointment.

MOLALLA 97038-0250

Wildwood Gardens
P.O. Box 250
Street address: 33326 South
Dickey Prairie Road

Will and Tracy Plotner
Phone: 503-829-3102
On-site: Retail
By appointment.

OREGON CITY 97045

**The Hardy Plant Society
of Oregon**
P.O. Box 5090
Mary Hoffman

PORTLAND 97211-7248

Carol Barnett, Books
3562 N.E. Liberty
Carol Barnett
Phone: 503-282-7036
NOTP

PORTLAND 97225

Timber Press
133 S.W. Second Avenue,
Suite 450
Phone: 800-327-5680
Outside U.S. and Canada:
503-227-2878
Fax: 503-227-3070
Robert B. Conklin
On-site: Retail
Monday through Friday,
8:00–6:00. Saturday,
8:00–12:00.

PORTLAND 97286-0424

Van Veen Nursery
P.O. Box 86424
Yearlings & juniors:
4201 S.E. Franklin Street
Phone: 503-777-1734
Fax: 503-777-2048
Budded plants:
33814 South Meridian Drive

Woodburn 97071
Phone: 503-634-2314
Fax: 503-634-2710
Ted Van Veen
On-site: Wholesale
All year. Five days,
8:00–4:30.

SALEM 97303

**Farm Wholesale Green-
houses–
Homestead Carts**
2396 Perkins Street N.E.
Greenhouses: Mike Perry
Carts: Bev Perry
Phone: 503-393-3973,
800-825-1925
Fax: 503-393-3119
On-site: Retail and wholesale
All year. Monday through
Friday, 8:00–5:00.

SALEM 97303-9720

Schreiner's Iris Gardens
3625 Quinaby Road N.E.
David Schreiner
Phone: 503-393-3232,
800-525-2367
Fax: 503-393-5590
On-site: Retail
Mid-May through early June.
Monday through Friday,
8:00 till dusk.

SALEM 97304

**Russell Graham: Purveyor of
Plants**
4030 Eagle Crest Road N.W.
Yvonne and Russell Graham
Phone: 503-362-1135
On-site: Retail
By appointment.

SALEM 97304-9527

Whitman Farms
3995 Gibson N.W.
Lucile Whitman
Phone: 503-585-8728
Fax: 503-363-5020
On-site: Wholesale
All year. Monday through
Saturday. By appointment.

SALEM 97305

Keith Keppel
P.O. Box 18154
Street address:
4020 Cordon Road N.E.
Keith Keppel
Phone: 503-391-9241
On-site: Retail
Bloom season.
Daylight hours.

SANDY 97055

Coenosium Gardens
P.O. Box 847
Phone: 503-668-3574
On-site: Retail
By appointment.

Porterhowse Farms
41370 S.E. Thomas Road
Don Howse
Phone: 503-668-5834
Fax: 503-668-5834
On-site: Wholesale
All year. Monday through
Sunday, 8:00 till dark.
By appointment.

A Sandy Rhododendron
41610 S.E. Coalman Road
Christopher J. Hoffman
Phone: 503-668-4830
Fax: 503-668-4860
On-site: Retail
By appointment.

SCAPPOOSE 97056

Joy Creek Nursery
20300 N.W. Watson Road
Mike Smith and
Scott Christy
Phone: 503-543-7474
On-site: Retail
Mid-March through October. Saturday and Sunday,
9:00–5:00. Thursday and
Friday, by appointment.

SCOTTS MILLS 97375

Cascade Bulb & Seed Co.
P.O. Box 271
Joseph C. Halinar
Phone: 503-873-2218
NOTP
Garden, by appointment.

Ingraham's Cottage Garden
P.O. Box 126
Street address: 370 Street
Jill and Alan Ingraham
Phone: 503-873-8610
On-site: Retail
By appointment.

Walden West
5744 Crooked Finger Road
Charles Purtymun and
Jay Hyslop
Phone: 503-873-6875
On-site: Retail and wholesale
By appointment.

SHERWOOD 97140

Caprice Farm Nursery
15425 S.W. Pleasant Hill
Road
Dot, Al, and Rick Rogers
and Robin Blue

Phone: 503-625-7241,
873-3515
Fax: 503-625-5588
On-site: Retail and wholesale
April through November.
Monday through Saturday,
10:00–4:00.

SILVERTON 97381-0126

Cooley's Gardens
P.O. Box 126
Richard Ernst
Phone: 503-873-5463,
800-225-5391
On-site: Retail
Peak Bloom Festival: May 20
through May 31. Daily, 8:00
till dusk.

SPRINGFIELD 97478-9691

Gossler Farms Nursery
1200 Weaver Road
Phone: 541-746-3922
Fax: 541-747-0749
On-site: Retail and wholesale
By appointment.

Japonica Water Gardens
36484 Camp Creek Road
William and Ron Howes
Phone: 541-746-5378
On-site: Retail and wholesale
By appointment.

Laurie's Garden
41886 McKenzie Highway
Lorena M. Reid
Phone: 541-896-3756
On-site: Retail
Late April through July.
By appointment.

ST. PAUL 97137

Heirloom Old Garden Roses
24062 Riverside Drive N.E.
John and Louise Clements
Phone: 503-538-1576
Fax: 503-538-5902
On-site: Retail
Monday through Friday,
8:00–4:00. Saturday and
Sunday, 10:00–4:00. Closed
Sundays, November through
January.

TALENT 97540

Granite Impressions
342 Carmen Road
Belinda Vos
Phone: 503-535-6190
On-site: Retail and wholesale
By appointment.

TURNER 97392

Frey's Dahlias
12054 Brick Road
Bob and Sharon Frey
Phone: 503-743-3910
On-site: Retail and wholesale
Garden viewing from August
through October. Monday
through Saturday. By appointment.

WILLIAMS 97544

Goodwin Creek Gardens
P.O. Box 83
Jim and Dotti Becker
Phone: 541-846-7357
On-site: Retail
By appointment.

"Sow Organic" Seeds
1130 Tetherow Road
Alan Venet and Sheryl Lee
Phone: 541-846-7173
On-site: Retail
By appointment.

WILLIAMS 97544-9599

Forestfarm®
990 Tetherow Road
Ray and Peg Pragg
Phone: 541-846-7269
Questions: 541-846-6963
Fax: 541-846-6963
On-site: Retail
By appointment.

WILSONVILLE 97070

Edmunds' Roses
6235 S.W. Kahle Road
Kathy and Phil Edmunds
Phone: 503-682-1476
Fax: 503-682-1275
On-site: Retail and wholesale
September. Monday through
Friday, 9:00–5:00. February
through April. 9:00–5:00.
Off season, by appointment.

Justice Miniature Roses
5947 S.W. Kahle Road
Jerry, June, and Tara Justice
Phone: 503-682-2370
On-site: Retail and wholesale
All year. Seven days,
9:00–3:00.

PENNSYLVANIA

COOPERSBURG 18036

The WaterWorks®
111 East Fairmount Street
Todd Schaffer
Phone: 610-282-4784,

800-360-LILY
Fax: 610-282-1262
On-site: Retail and wholesale
April through October.
Monday through Friday,
10:00–6:00.
Saturday, 9:00–5:00.
Sunday, 10:00–4:00.
November and December.
Monday through Friday,
10:00–5:00.
Saturday, 9:00–5:00.
Sunday, 12:00–4:00.

DOYLESTOWN 18901-9209

Stover Mill Gardens
6043 Stover Mill Road
Arthur M. and Ruth E. Kroll
Phone: 215-297-0296
On-site: Wholesale
By appointment.

EASTON 18045-7819

Netherland Bulb Company
13 McFadden Road
Peter Langeveld
Phone: 610-253-8879,
800-755-2852
Fax: 610-253-9012
On-site: Retail
All year. Five days,
8:30–5:30.

FAIRVIEW VILLAGE 19409

Ivywood Gazebo
P.O. Box 9
John L. Hunganir
Phone: 610-584-9699
Fax: 610-631-0846
NOTP

FORKSVILLE 18616

Pen Y Bryn Nursery
R.R. 1 Box 1313
Phone: 717-924-3377
On-site: Retail
May through October. Satur-
day and Sunday,
1:00–6:00.

GAP 17527

Erth-Rite
R.D. 1, Box 243
Ellen R. Ranck
Phone: 717-442-4171,
800-332-4171
Fax: 717-442-8997
On-site: Retail and wholesale
All year. Monday through
Friday, 8:00–4:30. Saturday,
by appointment. Closed
Sunday.

GREELEY 18425-9799

Dorothy Biddle Service
H.C. 01, Box 900
Lynne Johnson Dodson
Phone: 717-226-3239
Fax: 717-226-0349
NOTP

HANOVER 17331-8849

Thomas Gardens
507 Race Horse Road
Dale Thomas
Phone: 717-624-9020
(evenings)
On-site: Retail
By appointment.

INDIANA 15701-0340

Musser Forests
P.O. Box 430, Dept. S-94G
Nancy Musser
Phone: 412-465-5685,
800-643-8319
Fax: 412-465-9893
Garden center: March 25
through December 23.
Seven days, 9:00–5:00.

LANCASTER 17601-4899

**Heirloom Seed Project–
Landis Valley Museum**
2451 Kissel Hill Road
Steve Miller and
Nancy Pippart
Phone: 717-569-0401
Fax: 717-560-2147
NOTP

LANCASTER 17604

**Muhlenberg Botanical
Society**
Franklin and Marshall College
North Museum
P.O. Box 3003

McGRANN 16236

**Fox Hollow Herb and
Heirloom Seed Co.**
P.O. Box 148
Thomas Porter
Phone: 412-763-8247
NOTP

MIDDLEBURG 17842

**International Dwarf Fruit
Tree Association**
14 South Main Street
Charles J. Ax, Jr.
Phone: 717-837-1551
Fax: 717-837-0090

NEW BRITAIN 18901

Marigold Society of America
P.O. Box 112
Jeannette Lowe

NEW HOPE 18938-9990

Charles H. Mueller Co.
7091 North River Road
Charles A. Fritz III
Phone: 215-862-2033
Fax: 215-862-3696
On-site: Retail
April and May. Seven days,
10:00–5:00.

NORTHAMPTON 18067

Howertown Rose Nursery
1656 Weaverville Road
Allen Township
Jane A. Schrantz
Phone: 610-262-5412
On-site: Retail
April through June. Monday
through Friday, 9:00–6:00.
Saturday and Sunday,
9:00–5:00.

OLYPHANT 18447

Vileniki: An Herb Farm
R.D. 1, Box 345
Street address:
Route 438
Montdale 18447
Gerry Janus
Phone: 717-254-9895
On-site: Retail
May through August.
Tuesday through Sunday,
10:00–4:00.

PEN ARGYL 18072-9670

Windrose
1093 Mill Road
M. Nigel Wright
Phone: 610-588-1037
Fax: 610-252-7062
On-site: Retail
Closed Monday. By
appointment.

PHILADELPHIA 19103

Philadelphia Botanical Club
Academy of Science
19th and Parkway

PHILADELPHIA 19111

Matsu-Momiji Nursery
P.O. Box 11414
Street address:
410 Borbeck Street
Steve Pilacik
Phone: 215-722-6286
On-site: Retail and wholesale
By appointment.

PITTSBURGH 15205

**Botanical Society of Western
Pennsylvania**
401 Clearview Avenue
Robert F. Bahl

POINT PLEASANT 18950

Kinsman Company
River Road
Graham Kinsman
Phone: 800-733-4146
Fax: 215-297-0210
On-site: Retail
All year. Monday through
Friday, 9:00–5:00. Saturday
and Sunday, 10:00–5:00.

PORT MATILDA 16870

Limerock Ornamental Grasses, Inc.
R.D. 1, Box 111-C
Norm and Phyllis Hooven
Phone: 814-692-2272
On-site: Retail and wholesale
Mid-April through mid-October. Monday through
Saturday, 8:00–5:00.

RIMERSBURG 16248-0525

Eccles Nurseries, Inc.
Box Y
Street address: Route 68
Michael A. Birocco
Phone: 814-473-6265
Fax: 814-473-4047
On-site: Retail
April through December.
Monday through Friday,
8:00–5:00. Saturday, by
appointment.

SCOTTDALE 15683

The Primrose Path
R.D. 2, Box 110
Charles and Martha Oliver
Phone: 412-887-6756
On-site: Retail
Nursery pick up, by
appointment.

SINKING SPRING 19608

Escort Lighting
201 Sweitzer Road
Mike Hartman
Phone: 610-670-2517
Fax: 610-670-5170
NOTP

SMOKETOWN 17576

P. L. Rohrer & Bro.
P.O. Box 250
Street address:
2472 Old Philadelphia Pike
Jim Gamber
Phone: 717-299-2571
Fax: 717-299-5347
On-site: Retail and wholesale
All year. Monday through
Friday, 8:00–5:00.

SOUTHAMPTON 18966

Mantis
1028 Street Road
Robert Bell
Phone: 800-366-6268
Fax: 215-364-1409
On-site: Retail
All year. Monday through
Saturday, 9:00–5:00.

STATE COLLEGE 16804-0281

**Pennsylvania Native Plant
Society**
P.O. Box 281

TATAMY 18085-0220

Holland Bulb Farm
P.O. Box 220
Sophie Langeveld
Phone: 215-253-9160,
800-283-5082
Fax: 215-253-9012
NOTP

TREVOSE 19053

**Otis S. Twilley Seed
Company**
P.O. Box 65
Arthur Cobb Abott
Phone: 215-639-8800
Orders: 800-622-7333
Fax: 215-245-1949
NOTP

UNIVERSITY PARK 16802-4200

**American Pomological
Society**
103 Tyson Building
R. M. Crasweller

WASHINGTON CROSSING 18977

**Bowman's Hill Wildflower
Preserve**
P.O. Box 103
Washington Crossing
Historic Park
Street address: Route 32
Tom Stevenson
Phone: 215-862-2924
Fax: 215-493-4820
On-site: Retail
All year. Monday through
Saturday, 9:00–5:00. Sunday,
12:00–5:00.

WAYNESBORO 17268-0082

Appalachian Gardens
P.O. Box 82
Tom McCloud
Phone: 717-762-4312
Fax: 717-762-7532
On-site: Retail
Monday through Friday,
8:00-5:00. Saturday, by
appointment.

WEST ELIZABETH 15088-0245

Heirloom Seeds
P.O. Box 245
Tom Hauch
Phone: 412-384-7816
NOTP

WEXFORD 15090

Halcyon Garden Herbs
P.O. Box 75
F.E.A.(Liz) Bair
Phone: 412-935-2233
Order: 800-362-5860
Fax: 412-935-5515

WILLOW HILL 17271

BioLogic Company
P.O. Box 177
Street address: 18056 Spring-
town Road
Albert E. Pye
Phone: 717-349-2789,
349-2922
Fax: 717-349-2789
On-site: Retail
All year. Seven days, hours
variable.

PRINCE EDWARD ISLAND

YORK, C0A 1P0

Vesey's Seeds Ltd.
Allen Perry
Phone: 902-368-7333,
800-368-7333
Fax: 902-566-1620
On site: All year.
Trial gardens

RHODE ISLAND

SMITHFIELD 02917-2606

**Rhode Island Wild Plant
Society**
12 Sanderson Road

SOUTH CAROLINA

CHARLESTON 29401

Charleston Battery Bench
191 King Street
Phil and Andrew Slotin
Phone: 803-722-3842
Fax: 803-722-3846
On-site: Retail and wholesale
All year. Monday through
Saturday, 9:00–5:30.

COLUMBIA 29208

**Southern Appalachian
Botanical Club**
Dept. of Biological Sciences
University of South Carolina
Cynthia Aulbach-Smith

CROSS HILL 29332

The Mini-Rose Garden
P.O. Box 203
Street address: Austin Street
Michael and Betty Williams
and Valerie Jackson
Phone: 864-998-4331
Orders: 800-996-4647
Fax: 864-998-4947
On-site: Retail and wholesale
All year. Monday through
Saturday, 9:00 till dark.
By appointment.
Outside roses bloom May
through October.

GEORGETOWN 29440-8506

Roycroft Daylily Nursery
305 Egret Circle
Street address:
White Hall Avenue
Route 6, Box 70

Bob Roycroft
Phone: 803-546-3007
Nursery: 803-527-1533
On-site: Retail and wholesale
March through October.
Monday through Saturday,
9:00–5:30. Other months,
by appointment.

GRANITEVILLE 29829-0001

R. H. Shumway, Seedsman
P.O. Box 1
Street address:
571 Whaley Pond Road
Phone: 803-663-9771
Fax: 803-663-9772
On-site: Retail
All year. Monday through
Friday, 8:30–4:00.

GREENWOOD 29647-0001

Park Seed Co.
Cokesbury Road
Phone: 864-223-7333
Fax: 864-941-4206
On-site: Retail
All year. Monday through
Saturday, 9:00–6:00. Tours,
by appointment.

HODGES 29695-0001

Wayside Gardens
1 Garden Lane
Street address: Highway 254
Karen P. Jennings
Phone: 800-845-1124
Fax: 800-457-9712
On-site: Retail
All year. Monday through
Saturday, 9:00–6:00.

LAURENS 29360

Roses Unlimited
Route 1, Box 587
North Deer Wood Drive
Bill Patterson
Phone: 864-682-2455
On-site: Retail
By appointment.

SOUTH DAKOTA

HOT SPRINGS 57747

**Great Plains Botanical
Society**
P.O. Box 461

YANKTON 57079

**Gurney's Seed and
Nursery Co.**
110 Capital Street
Donald L. Kruml
Phone: 605-665-1671
Fax: 605-665-9718
On-site: Retail
Mid-September through
mid-November. Monday
through Friday, 8:00–5:30.
Saturday, 8:00–5:00.
Mid-March through mid-
June. Monday through
Friday, 8:00–8:00. Saturday,
8:00–6:00.
Sunday, 12:00–5:00.

TENNESSEE

ANDERSONVILLE 37705
Sunlight Gardens
174 Golden Lane
Andrea Sessions and
Marty Zenni
Phone: 423-494-8237,
800-272-7396
On-site: Retail and wholesale

April through June, September and October. Wednesday
and Thursday, 10:00–3:00.
By appointment.

CHATTANOOGA 37422

**American Association of
Field Botanists**
P.O. Box 23542

COOKEVILLE 38501

Hidden Springs Nursery
170 Hidden Springs Lane
Hector, Susie, and
Annie Black
Phone: 615-268-9889,
268-2592
On-site: Retail
By appointment.

CORRYTON 37721

Oakes Daylilies
8204 Monday Road
Stewart Oakes
Phone: 423-687-3770
On-site: Retail and wholesale
By appointment.

GREENBACK 37742

Native Gardens
5737 Fisher Lane
Meredith and Ed Clebsch
Phone: 423-856-0220
On-site: Retail
By appointment.

HIXSON 37343

**Chattanooga Daylily
Gardens**
1736 Eagle Drive
Lee and Jean Pickles
Phone: 423-842-4630
On-site: Retail
All year. Weekends and
evenings. By appointment.

HIXSON 37343-1738

**Schild Azalea Gardens and
Nursery**
1705 Longview Street
Joseph E. Schild
Phone: 423-842-9686
On-site: Retail
By appointment.

KINGSPORT 37664

Skyland Gardens
4005 Skyland Drive
Bob Hale
Phone: 423-245-6467
On-site: Retail
June and July. Seven days,
9:00–8:00. By appointment.

KNOXVILLE 37901

Alfrey Seeds
P.O. Box 415
Phone: 423-524-5965
Evelyn Alfrey
NOTP

KNOXVILLE 37914-9725

Sunnyridge Gardens
1724 Drinnen Road
Geraldine Couturier
Phone: 423-933-0723
On-site: Retail
Daily. By appointment.

KNOXVILLE 37938

Beaver Creek Nursery
7526 Pelleaux Road
Mike Stansberry
Phone: 423-922-3961
On-site: Retail
Mid-March through mid-
November. Thursday
through Saturday.

MARTIN 38237

George's Plant Farm
Route 1, Box 194
Vinson and Donna Dellinger
Phone: 901-587-9477
On-site: Retail and wholesale
By appointment.

MCMINNVILLE 37110

The Perfect Season
P.O. Box 191
Street address:
4373 Manchester Highway
Bette Myers
Phone: 615-668-3225
Fax: 615-668-3183
On-site: Retail and wholesale
All year. Monday through
Friday, 8:00–4:00. Saturday,
by appointment.

Savage Nursery Center
P.O. Box 125 SFN
Street address:
6255 Beersheba Highway
Jim Savage
Phone: 615-668-8902
On-site: Retail
October through May. Mon-
day through Saturday,
9:00–3:30.

**Vernon Barnes and Son
Nursery**
P.O. Box 250
Street address: Route 2,
Kesey Ford Lane
James V. Barnes, Jr.
Phone: 615-668-8576
Fax: 615-668-2165
On-site: Retail
Monday through Friday,
7:00–3:00.

MEMPHIS 38119-4699

The Wildflower Society
c/o Goldsmith Civic
Garden Center
750 Cherry Road

OOLTEWAH 37363

Lakeside Acres
8119 Roy Lane
Mary Chastain
Phone: 423-238-4534
On-site: Retail
April through September.
Monday through Saturday,
8:00–6:00. By appointment.

PELHAM 37366

Hollydale Nursery
P.O. Box 69
Street address:
Highway 41 South
Dale Bryan
Phone: 615-467-3600,
800-222-3026
Fax: 615-467-3062
On-site: Retail
January through March.
Monday through Friday,
8:00–4:00. By appointment.

**RED BOILING SPRINGS
37150**

**Long Hungry Creek
Nursery**
Box 163
Jeff Poppen
On-site: Retail
By appointment.

SEWANEE 37375

**Tennessee Native Plant
Society**
P.O. Box 856

SUMMERTOWN 38483-0220

Mushroompeople
P.O. Box 220
Street address:
560 Farm Road
Albert Bates
Phone: 615-964-2200,
800-FUNG195
Fax: 615-964-2200,
800-MYCOFAX
On-site: Retail
All year. Monday through
Friday, 9:00–5:00.
By appointment.

TRACY CITY 37387-1418

The Marugg Company, Inc.
P.O. Box 1418
Street address:
35 Depot Street
John Baggenstoss
Phone: 615-592-5042
NOTP

TEXAS

ALTO 75925

Fults Garden Shop
Route 2, Box 276
Bertha Fults
Phone: 409-858-4995
On-site: Retail and wholesale
By appointment.

AUSTIN 78725-4201

**National Wildflower
Research Center**
2600 FM-973 North

AUSTIN 78735

Natural Gardener's Catalog
8648 Old Bee Caves Road
Maggie Burnett and
Dolores Nice
Phone: 512-288-6115
Fax: 512-288-6114
Supplies: 800-320-0724
On-site: Retail and wholesale
All year. Monday through
Friday, 8:00–5:30. Saturday,
8:00–5:00. Sunday,
10:00–4:00.
Closed Sunday in January.

BEAUMONT 77702-2414

Southern Exposure
35 Minor at Rusk
Bob Whitman
Phone: 409-835-0644
Fax: 409-835-5265
On-site: Retail
April through October.
Saturday through Tuesday,
9:00–12:00. By appointment.

BRENHAM 77833

**The Antique Rose
Emporium**
Route 5, Box 143
G. Michael Shoup
Phone: 800-441-0002
Fax: 409-836-0928
On-site: Retail and wholesale
All year. Seven days,
9:00–6:00.

CARRIZO SPRINGS 78834

Dixondale Farms
P.O. Box 127
Street address:
2007 North First Street
Jeanie Martin Frasier and
Pam Martin

Phone: 210-876-2430
Fax: 210-876-9640
On-site: Retail and wholesale
January through April. Mon-
day through Friday,
9:00–5:00. By appointment.

DALLAS 75381-0082

Horticultural Enterprises
P.O. Box 810082
NOTP

DE LEON 76444-9649

Womack's Nursery Co.
Route 1, Box 80
Nursery: State Highway 6
Larry J. Womack
Phone: 817-893-6497
Fax: 817-893-3400
NOTP

EAGLE LAKE 77434-0308

Wildseed Farms, Inc.
P.O. Box 308
Street address: 1101 Campo
Rosa Road
John Thomas
Phone: 800-848-0078
Fax: 408-234-7407
NOTP

EL PASO 79912

El Paso Native Plant Society
7760 Maya

EL PASO 79926

Desertland Nursery
P.O. Box 26126
David and Lupina Guerra
Phone: 915-858-1130

Fax: 915-858-1560
On-site: Retail and
Wholesale
All year, weather permitting,
seven days. Spring and
summer, 9:00–6:00.
Fall and winter, 9:00–5:00.

FLOWER MOUND 75028

Native American Seed
3400 Long Prairie Road
Mail Order Station
Jan and Bill Neiman
Phone: 214-539-0534
Orders: 800-728-4043
Fax: 817-464-3897
NOTP

FORT WORTH 76107

Texas Greenhouse Co., Inc.
2524 White Settlement Road
Phone: 817-335-5447,
800-227-5447
Fax: 817-334-0818
On-site: Retail
All year. Monday through
Friday, 8:00–5:00. Saturday,
by appointment.

GALVESTON 77552-0431

**International Oleander
Society, Inc.**
P.O. Box 3431
Elizabeth S. Head

GEORGETOWN 78627

**Native Plant Society
of Texas**
P.O. Box 891
Dana Tucker
Phone: 512-863-9685

HONDO 78861

Medina® Agriculture Products Company, Inc.
P.O. Box 309
Street address:
Highway 90 West
Stuart Franke
Phone: 210-426-3011
Fax: 210-426-2288
NOTP

HOUSTON 77282-0874

Brudy's Tropical Exotics
P.O. Box 820874
Mike Stich
Phone: 800-926-7333
Fax: 713-960-7117
NOTP

KERRVILLE 78028

Green Horizons
218 Quinlan #571
Sherry Miller
Phone: 512-257-5141
On-site: Retail and Wholesale
All year. Five days,
9:00–5:00. Wednesday and
Sunday, by appointment.

LEANDER 78641

Sunrise Nursery
13705 Pecan Hollow
Tim and Kathy Springer
Phone: 512-259-1877
On-site: Retail
By appointment.

LUBBOCK 79408

Submatic Irrigation Systems
P.O. Box 246,
719 26th Street
Street address:

611 26th Street
Lubbock 79404
Dale Brown
Phone: 800-692-4100
Fax: 806-747-1800
On-site: Retail
All year. Monday through
Friday, 8:00–5:00. Saturday,
8:00–12:00.

QUEMADO 78877

Kunafin
Route 1, Box 39
Frank and Adele Junfin
Phone: 800-832-1113
Fax: 210-757-1468
NOTP

POOLVILLE 76487

Willhite Seed Co.
P.O. Box 23
Don Dobbs
Phone: 817-599-8656
Fax: 817-599-5843
NOTP

TYLER 75708-9239

Tate Rose Nursery
10306 FM 2767
Bobbie Tate
Phone: 903-593-1020
On-site: Retail and
Wholesale
All year. By appointment.

WALLER 77484

Yucca Do Nursery at Peckerwood Gardens
P.O. Box 655
Carl M. Schoenfeld
Phone: 409-826-6363
NOTP

UTAH

SALT LAKE CITY 84152-0041

Utah Native Plant Society
P.O. Box 520041

WEST BOUNTIFUL 84087

G.R.'s Perennial Farm
465 North 660 West
G. R. Burningham
Phone: 801-292-8237
On-site: Retail and wholesale
Bloom Season: Mid-June
through mid-August, every
day but Wednesday.
Other times: Thursday,
Friday, and Saturday,
9:00–6:00. April through
September, by appointment.

VERMONT

BRISTOL 05443

Robert Compton, Ltd.
Rural Delivery 3, Box 3600
Street address: Route 116
Robert and Christine Compton
Phone: 802-453-3778
On-site: Retail
May through October. Seven
days, 10:00–6:00.

BURLINGTON 05401-2804

Gardener's Supply Company
128 Intervale Road
Meg Smith
Phone: 802-863-1700,
800-863-1700
Fax: 802-660-4600
NOTP

CAVENDISH 05142-0032

Mary Mattison van Schaik
P.O. Box 32
Paula M. Parker
Phone: 802-226-7653
(evenings)
NOTP

CHARLOTTE 05445-0005

Vermont Wildflower Farm
P.O. Box 5
Street address: Route 7
Chy and Ray Allen and
Rob Towne
Phone: 802-425-3500
Fax: 802-425-3504
On-site: Retail
May through October.
Seven days, 10:00–5:00.

EAST HARDWICK 05836

**Perennial Pleasures Nursery
of Vermont**
P.O. Box 147
Street address: 2 Brickhouse
Road
Judith and Rachel Kane
Phone: 802-472-5512
On-site: Retail
May through September 15.
Tuesday through Sunday,
9:00–5:00.

EDEN 05652

**Vermont Botanical and
Bird Club**
Warren Road, Box 327

FAIR HAVEN 05743-0250

Vermont Bean Seed Co.
Garden Lane
Phone: 802-273-3400
NOTP

LONDONDERRY 05148

The Cook's Garden
P.O. Box 535
Ellen and Shepherd Ogden
Phone: 802-824-3400
Fax: 802-824-3027
On-site: Retail
Monday through Friday,
8:00–4:30.
Trial gardens: June through
September. Open house:
August 26.

PITTSFIELD 05762-0565

French's: Bulb Importer
P.O. Box 565
Robin Martin
Phone: 802-746-8148
Fax: 802-746-8148
On-site: Retail
By appointment.

PUTNEY 05346

Putney Nursery, Inc.
Route 5
Ruth and C. J. Gorius
Phone: 802-387-5577
Fax: 802-387-4491
On-site: Retail
April through December 24.
Monday through Saturday,
9:00–5:00. Sunday,
10:00–2:00.

**ST. JOHNSBURY CENTER
05863-0075**

Le Jardin du Gourmet
Paul Taylor
P.O. Box 75
Phone: 800-659-1446
Fax: 802-748-9592
NOTP

SOUTH NEWFANE 05351

Olallie Daylily Gardens
H.C.R. 63, Box 1
Marlboro Branch Road
Chris and Amelia Darrow
Phone: 802-348-6614
Fax: 802-348-6614
On-site: Retail and
Wholesale
May through September.
9:00–6:00. Closed Tuesdays.

TINMOUTH 05773

Tinmouth Channel Farm
Box 428-B,
Town Highway 19
Carolyn Fuhrer and Kathleen
Duhnoski
Phone: 802-446-2812
On-site: Retail
April through mid-October.
Friday and Saturday,
10:00–5:00.

VIRGINIA

AFTON 22920

Edible Landscaping
P.O. Box 77
Street address:
Route 2, Box 485-AA
Michael McConkey
Phone: 804-361-9134
Orders: 800-524-4156
On-site: Retail
All year, 9:00–5:00. By
appointment.

ALEXANDRIA 22304

Adams & Adkins, Inc.
104 South Early Street
Bob Adams and
Dorcas Adkins
Phone: 703-823-3404

Fax: 703-823-5367
On site: Retail
February through December.
By appointment

AMISSVILLE 22002

The Pinched Pot
Route 1, Box 274
Phone: 540-937-4238
NOTP

ANNANDALE 22030

**Virginia Native Plant
Society**
P.O. Box 844

BOYCE 22620

**The American Boxwood
Society**
P.O. Box 85
Joan Butler

BRISTOL 24201

The Urban Homestead
818 Cumberland Street
Tim and Donna Hensley
Phone: 540-466-2931
On-site: Retail
February through December.
Monday through Friday,
9:00–5:00. By appointment.

CHARLOTTESVILLE 22902

**The Thomas Jefferson
Center for Historical Plants**
Monticello, P.O. Box 316
Phone: 804-984-9822
Orders: 804-984-9860
On-site: Retail
Garden shop at Monticello:
Seven days, 9:00–6:00.

**CHARLOTTESVILLE
22903-0881**

Kalmia Farm
P.O. Box 3881
Ken Klotz
Phone: 804-296-1582
Fax: 804-296-0487
NOTP

CRADDOCKVILLE 23341

Sterrett Gardens
P.O. Box 85
Street address:
12324 Island Neck Road
Richard and Rikki Sterrett
Phone: 804-442-4606
On-site: Retail and Whole-
sale
Last two Saturdays in June,
first two in July.
By appointment.

EARLYSVILLE 22936

Seed Shares™
P.O. Box 226
Jeff McCormack
Phone: 804-973-4703
Fax: 804-973-4703
On-site: Retail
June and July. Saturday,
10:00–4:00, by appointment.

**Southern Exposure Seed
Exchange®**
P.O. Box 170
Jeff McCormack
Phone: 804-973-4703
Fax: 804-973-4703
NOTP

FISHERSVILLE 22939

**André Viette Farm and
Nursery**
P.O. Box 1109
Street address:
State Route 608
Mark, André, and
Claire Viette
On-site: Retail and
Wholesale
Phone: 540-943-2315
Fax: 540-943-0782
Mid-April through October.
Monday through Saturday,
9:00–5:00. Sunday,
1:00–5:00.

GLOUCESTER 23061

**American Rhododendron
Society**
P.O. Box 1380
Barbara R. Hall
Phone: 804-693-4433

The Daffodil Mart
7463 Heath Trail
Brent and Becky Heath
Phone: 804-693-3966
Orders: 800-ALL-BULB
Fax: 800-420-2852
On-site: Retail
March and April. Tuesday,
Thursday, and Saturday,
9:00–11:00, 1:00–3:00.
Tours, by appointment.

HAMILTON 22068

Green Enterprises
43 South Rogers Street
Dwight Green
Phone: 540-338-3606
On-site: Retail
All year. Monday through
Friday, 8:00–4:30.

LOCUST GROVE 22508

ForestLake Gardens
H.C. 72 Lake of the Woods,
Box 535
Street address:
306 Birchside Circle
Phone: 540-972-2890
Fax: 540-898-8931
On-site: Retail
June 15 through July 15.
Anytime.

LOVETTSVILLE 22080

Water Ways Nursery
Route 2, Box 247
Sally Kurtz
Phone: 540-822-5994
On-site: Retail
April through June and
August through September.
Thursday through Sunday,
8:30–6:00.

MCLEAN 22101-2001

The Iris Pond
7311 Churchill Road
Clarence Mahan
On-site: Retail
May and June.
By appointment.

MONROE 24574

Burford Brothers
Route 1
Thomas Burford
Phone: 804-929-4950
On-site: Retail
By appointment.

STANARDSVILLE 22973

Edgewood Farm & Nursery
Route 2, Box 303
Street address: Route 667,
Greene County
Norman Schwartz and
Robert Cary
Phone: 804-985-3782
On-site: Retail
Mid-March through October.
Monday through Saturday,
9:00–5:00. Sunday, 1:00-5:00.

SUSSEX 23884-0346

Seymour's Selected Seeds
P.O. Box 1346
James Harrison
NOTP

**WOODS CROSS ROADS
23190**

Dickerson Daylily Garden
Route 612, Millers Landing
Road
Jerry W. Dickerson
Phone: 804-693-5240
On-site: Retail and wholesale
June through August. Sunday
through Wednesday,
9:00–9:00. By appointment.

WASHINGTON

ARLINGTON 98223

Hammonds Acres of Rhodys
25911 70th Avenue, N.E.
Dave and Joan Hammond
Phone: 360-435-9206
On-site: Retail and wholesale
All year. Seven days,
10:00–5:30.

BATTLE GROUND 98604

Collector's Nursery
16804 N.E. 102nd Avenue
Bill Janssen and Diana Reeck
Phone: 360-574-3832
On-site: Retail
All year. By appointment.

BELLEVUE 98005

Foliage Gardens
2003 128th Avenue S.E.
Sue and Harry Olsen
Phone: 206-747-2998
On-site: Retail and
Wholesale
By appointment.

BELLEVUE 98007

The Greenery
14450 N.E. 16th Place
Lynn and Marilyn Wats
Phone: 206-641-1458
On-site: Retail
By appointment.

BELLINGHAM 98227

Anderson Design
P.O. Box 4057-C
Richard L. Anderson
Phone: 800-947-7697
NOTP

BRINNON 98320-0080

**Whitney Gardens and
Nursery**
P.O. Box F
Street address:
306264 Highway 101
Anne Sather
Phone: 360-796-4411

Orders: 800-952-2404
On-site: Retail
February through November.
Seven days, 10:00–5:30.
December and January, by
appointment.

BUCKLEY 98321

**Buckley Nursery Garden
Center**
646 North River Avenue
Don Marlow
Phone: 360-829-1811
On-site: Retail and wholesale
By appointment.

CENTRALIA 98531

Brookesfield Farm
426 Byrd Street
Ric and Cathy Cavness
Phone: 360-736-8209
Fax: 360-330-0669
NOTP

Cedar Valley Nursery
3833 McElfresh Road S.W.
Charles C. Boyd
Phone: 206-736-7490
On-site: Retail and wholesale
By appointment.

EVERSON 98247

Cloud Mountain Farm
6906 Goodwin Road
Tom and Cheryl Thornton
Phone: 360-966-5859
Fax: 360-966-0921
On-site: Retail and wholesale
February through mid-June.
Wednesday through Satur-
day, 10:00–5:00.
Sunday, 11:00–4:00.
September and October.
Thursday through Saturday,
10:00–5:00.

FEDERAL WAY 98063-3798

**The Rhododendron Species
Foundation**
P.O. Box 3798
Deanna Hallsell
Phone: 206-838-4646,
927-6960
Fax: 206-838-4686

GRAHAM 98338-8615

Bijou Alpines
P.O. Box 1252
Street address:
13921 240 Street East
Mark Dusek
Phone: 360-893-6191
On-site: Retail and wholesale
March through July, Septem-
ber through November.
Friday and Saturday. By
appointment.

Mt. Tahoma Nursery
28111 112th Avenue East
Rick Lupp
Phone: 206-847-9827
On-site: Retail and wholesale
All year. Saturday and Sunday, 10:00–6:00. Monday
through Friday,
by appointment.

KINGSTON 98346

Heronswood Nursery, Ltd.
7530 N.E. 288th Street
Daniel Hinkley and
Robert L. Jones
Phone: 360-297-4172
Fax: 360-297-8321
On-site: Retail and wholesale
All year. Thursday, Friday,
and Saturday. By appointment.

LANGLEY 98260

**Frosty Hollow Ecological
Restoration**
Box 53
Steve Erickson and
Marianne Edain
Phone: 360-579-2332
Fax: 360-579-6456
NOTP

MEDINA 98039-0166

The Hardy Fern Foundation
P.O. Box 166
Jocelyn Horder

MORTON 98356

Raintree Nursery
391 Butts Road
Sam Benowitz
Phone: 360-496-6400
Fax: 360-496-6465
On-site: Retail and wholesale
January through May 15.
Wednesday through Friday,
9:00–4:00.
Saturday and Sunday,
10:00–5:00. Summer: First
Saturday of each month,
12:00–4:00.

NORTHPORT 99157

Bear Creek Nursery
P.O. Box 411
Hunter and Donna Carleton
Fax: 509-732-4417
On-site: Retail
Appointments arranged
by letter.

OKANOGAN 98840

Filaree Farm
182 Conconully Highway
Ron Engeland
Phone: 509-422-6940
On-site: Retail and wholesale
By appointment.

OLYMPIA 98507

Fungi Perfecti
P.O. Box 7634
Street address:
S.E. 50 Nelson Road
Shelton, WA 98584
Paul Stamets
Phone: 360-426-9292
Fax: 360-426-9292
NOTP

ONALASKA 98570

**Burnt Ridge Nursery and
Orchards**
432 Burnt Ridge Road
Michael Dolan and Carolyn
Cerling-Dolan
Phone: 360-985-2873
On-site: Retail and wholesale
By appointment.

PORT ANGELES 98362

Floating Mountain Seeds
P.O. Box 1275
Roger Lemstrom
Phone: 360-928-2072
On-site: Retail and wholesale
By appointment.

PORT TOWNSEND 98368

**Abundant Life Seed
Foundation**
P.O. Box 772
Susan Herman

Phone: 360-385-5660
Orders: 360-385-7192
Fax: 360-385-7455
NOTP

PUYALLUP 98372

Fred and Jean Minch
4329 Chrisella Road East
Fred and Jean Minch
Phone: 206-845-8043
Fax: 206-845-5204
On-site: Wholesale
By appointment.

SEATTLE 98144

Northwest Native Seed
915 Davis Place South
Ron Ratko
Phone: 206-329-5804
NOTP

SEATTLE 98145

**The Northwest Perennial
Alliance**
P.O. Box 45574 University
Station

SEATTLE 98155

Eco Enterprises
1240 N.E. 175th Street,
Suite B
Terri Mitchell
Phone: 206-363-9981,
525-4784 (evenings),
800-426-6937
Fax: 206-363-9983
On-site: Retail and wholesale
All year. Monday through
Saturday, 8:00–6:00.

SEATTLE 98195

**Northwest Horticultural
Society**
Isaacson Hall

University of Washington,
GF-15
Phone: 206-527-1794

**Washington Native Plant
Society**
Department of Botany,
AJ-30
University of Washington
A. R. Kruckeberg

SEATTLE 98199

Sunglo Solar Greenhouses
4441 26th Avenue West
Joseph Pappalardo
Phone: 206-284-8900,
800-647-0606
Fax: 206-284-8945
On-site: Retail and wholesale
All year. Monday through
Friday, 8:00–5:00. Other
times, by appointment.

SPOKANE 99202

Lamb Nurseries
101 East Sharp Avenue
Phone: 509-328-7956
On-site: Retail
Monday through Saturday,
9:00–5:00.
Visitors Friday and Saturday

SPOKANE 99207

Blossoms and Bloomers
East 11415 Krueger Lane
Geraldine Krueger
Phone: 509-922-1344
On-site: Retail
May and June. Friday, Satur-
day, and Sunday,
10:00–4:00.

SPOKANE 99223

Stanek's Nursery
2929 East 27th Avenue
Tim and Steve Stanek
Phone: 509-534-2939
Fax: 509-534-3050
On-site: Retail
September through June.
Seven days. July and August,
Monday through Saturday.

VANCOUVER 98662

American Hosta Society
7802 N.E. 63rd Street
Robyn Duback

Robyn's Nest Nursery
7802 N.E. 63rd Street
Robyn Duback
On-site: Retail
Mid-March through June,
September and October.
Thursday and Friday,
10:30–5:30.
Saturday, 10:30–2:00. July
and August, by appointment.

VANCOUVER 98685

**Aitken's Salmon Creek
Garden**
608 N.W. 119 Street
Terry and Barbara Aitken
Phone: 360-573-4472
Fax: 360-576-7012
On-site: Retail
April through September.
Seven days. By appointment.

VASHON ISLAND 98070

Colvos Creek Nursery
P.O. Box 1512

Michael Lee
Phone: 206-463-1509
On-site: Retail
Saturday. Or by
appointment.

WENATCHEE 98801

**I.F.M. Products for Natural
Agriculture**
333-B Ohme Gardens Road
Phillip Unterschuetz
Phone: 509-662-3179,
800-332-3179
On-site: Retail
All year. Monday through
Friday, 8:00–5:00.

WENATCHEE 98807

Van Well Nursery
P.O. Box 1339
Street address:
1000 North Miller
Wenatchee 98801
Pete Vanwell
Phone: 509-663-8189,
800-572-1553
Fax: 509-572-1553
On-site: Retail
All year. Monday through
Friday, 8:00–5:00.

WEST VIRGINIA

CIRCLEVILLE 26804

Hardscrabble Enterprises
H.C. 71, Box 42
Street address:
Main Street at Prehard Lane
Franklin 26807
Paul Goland
Phone: 304-358-2921
On-site: Retail and wholesale
By appointment.

WISCONSIN

BAYFIELD 54814

**Hauser's Superior View
Farm**
Route 1, Box 199
Jim and Marilyn Hauser
and Jim Jr.
Phone: 715-779-5404
On-site: Retail
May through September.
Six days, 9:00–5:00.

DEER PARK 54007

Capability's Books®
2379 Highway 46
Paulette Rickard and
Kristen Gilbertson
Phone: 800-247-8154
Outside U.S.: 715-269-5346
Fax: 715-269-5531
On-site: Retail
Monday through Friday,
8:30–4:30. Saturday, by
appointment.

EAGLE 53119

Windy Oaks
West 377 S-10677 Betts
Road
Marilyn Buscler
Phone: 414-594-3033,
594-2803
Fax: 414-594-3033
On-site: Retail and wholesale
By appointment.

EAST TROY 53120

Clifford's Perennial and Vine
Route 2, Box 320
Phone: 414-968-4040
Fax: 414-968-5525
NOTP

FRIESLAND 53935-0368

McClure & Zimmerman
P.O. Box 368
Street address: 108 West
Winnebago Street
Gloria Tamminga and
Dick Zondag
Phone: 414-326-4220
Fax: 800-692-5864
NOTP

JANESVILLE 53545

Wisconsin Wagon Co., Inc.
507 Laurel Avenue
Albert and Lois Hough
Phone: 608-754-0026
On-site: Retail
February through December.
Monday through Friday,
8:30–12:00, 1:00–4:00.
Or by appointment.

MADISON 53704

Wood Violet Books
3814 Sunhill Drive
Debbie Cravens
Phone: 608-837-7207
NOTP

MADISON 53705

Botanical Club of Wisconsin
Wisconsin Academy of Arts,
Sciences and Letters
1922 University Avenue

MANITOWOC 54221-1960

Dramm Corporation
P.O. Box 1960
Street address:
2000 North 18th Street
Manitowoc 54220
Howard Zimmerman
Phone: 414-684-0227,
800-258-0848

Fax: 414-684-4499
On-site: Retail and wholesale
By appointment.

**MENOMONEE FALLS
53051-4325**

Society for Siberian Irises
N75 W14257 North Point
Drive
Howard Brookins

MILWAUKEE 53224-3109

**North American Gladiolus
Council**
c/o Peter J. Welcenbach
11102 West Calumet Road
Mrs. William Strawser

MT. HOREB 53572-2832

**Prairie Ridge Nursery
(CRM Ecosystems Services,
Inc.)**
9738 Overland Road
Joyce A. Powers
Phone: 608-437-5245
Fax: 608-437-8982
On-site: Retail and wholesale
May through October. Mon-
day through Friday,
8:00–5:00. Saturday,
9:00–1:00, by appointment.

MUSKEGO 53150

**Country Wetlands Nursery
and Consulting**
575 West 20755 Field Drive
Jo Ann Gillespie
Phone: 414-679-1268
Fax: 414-679-1279
On-site: Retail and wholesale
Mid-April through mid-
October. Monday through
Friday, 9:00–4:00.
By appointment.

NORTH LAKE 53064-0083

Prairie Seed Source
P.O. Box 83
Robert Ahrenhoerster
On-site: Retail
By appointment.

PLAINFIELD 54966

Waushara Gardens
North 5491 5th Drive
George Melk
Phone: 715-335-4462
Fax: 715-335-4462
On-site: Retail
Open March through June
10. Monday through Satur-
day, 8:00–4:00.
By appointment.

RACINE 53402-2498

Milaeger's Gardens
4838 Douglas Avenue
Kevin D. Milaeger
Phone: 414-639-2371
Orders: 800-669-9956
Fax: 414-639-1855
On-site: Retail and wholesale
May through September.
Monday through Friday,
8:00–8:00.
Saturday, 8:00–5:00.
Sunday, 9:00–5:00.

RANDOLPH 53957-0001

**J. W. Jung Seed and Nursery
Co.**
335 South High Street
Richard J. Zondag
Phone: 414-326-3121
Fax: 414-326-5769
On-site: Retail and wholesale
All year. Monday through
Saturday.

RICHLAND CENTER 53581

Buckhorn Ginseng
Route 4, Box 336
Ron Dobbs
Phone: 608-647-2244
Fax: 608-647-2244
NOTP

STOUGHTON 53589

Norway Industries
143 West Main
Brian Hanson
Phone: 608-873-8664
On-site: Retail and wholesale
All year. Six days, 9:00–5:30.
By appointment.

WAUNAKEE 53597

Skolaski's Glads & Field Flowers
4821 County Highway Q
Stan and Nancy Skolaski
Phone: 608-836-4822
NOTP

WESTFIELD 53964

Prairie Nursery
P.O. Box 306
Street address:
West 5859 Dyke Avenue
Neil Dibol
Phone: 608-296-3679
Fax: 608-296-2741
On-site: Retail
Garden tours, by appointment.

Sohn's Forest Mushrooms
610 South Main Street
Eileen and Ray Sohn
Phone: 608-296-2456
Fax: 608-296-2456
On-site: Retail
All year. Monday through
Saturday, 10:00–6:00.
By appointment.

WILSON 54027

Jasperson's Hersey Nursery
2915 74th Avenue

Phone: 715-772-4749
On-site: Retail
April through October.
Monday through Friday,
9:00–5:00. Saturday and
Sunday, 12:00–6:00, by
appointment.

WYOMING

CHEYENNE 82003

Wyoming Native Plant Society
Box 1471
Robert Dorn

HYATTVILLE 82428

Earthworks
P.O. Box 67
Len Sherwin
Phone: 307-469-2229
NOTP

ALPHABETICAL
INDEX
TO SOURCES

Abracadatar
P.O. Box 2440
Eugene, OR 97402
Phone: 800-451-4871
Fax: 541-683-1925
Catalog: Free
Check, M.O., M.C., Visa
Booksellers

Abundant Life Seed Foundation
P.O. Box 772
Port Townsend, WA 98368
Phone: 360-385-5660
Orders: 360-385-7192
Fax: 360-385-7455
Catalog: $2
Check, M.O., M.C., Visa
With order. $10 minimum with credit card.
Booksellers, Garlic, Heirlooms, Herbs, Organics, Seeds, Vegetables

A. C. Burke & Co.
2554 Lincoln Boulevard, Suite 1058
Marina Del Rey, CA 90291
Phone: 310-574-2770
Fax: 310-574-2771
Catalog: Free, outside U.S. $2
Check, M.O., M.C., Visa
With order. No minimum.
Booksellers, Kidstuff

Acres, U.S.A.
P.O. Box 8800
Metaire, LA 70011
Phone: 504-889-2100, 800-355-5313
Fax: 504-889-2777
Catalog: Free
Check, M.O., M.C., Visa, Discover
With order. No minimum.
Booksellers, Kidstuff

Adamgrove
Route 1, Box 1472
California, MO 65018
Phone: No/Fax: No

Catalog: $3,
2-year subscription
Check, M.O.
With order. $15 minimum.
Daylilies, Iris

Adams & Adkins, Inc.
104 South Early Street
Alexandria, VA 22304
Phone: 703-823-3404
Fax: 703-823-5367
Catalog: Free
Check, M.C., Visa
With order. No minimum.
Furniture

Adirondack Design
Cypress Street Center
350 Cypress Street
Fort Bragg, CA 95437
Phone: 800-222-0343
Fax: 707-964-2701
Catalog: Free
Check, M.O., M.C., Visa
With order. No minimum.
Furniture

agAccess Book Catalog
P.O. Box 2008
Davis, CA 95617
Phone: 916-756-7177
Fax: 916-756-7188
Catalog: Free
Check, M.O.
With order. No minimum.
Booksellers

Age-Old Organics
P.O. Box 1556
Boulder, CO 80306
Phone: 303-499-0201, 800-748-3474
Fax: 303-499-3231
Catalog: Free
Check, M.O., M.C., Visa
With order. No minimum.
Organics, Supplies

Aitken's Salmon Creek Garden
608 N.W. 119 Street
Vancouver, WA 98685
Phone: 360-573-4472

Fax: 360-576-7012
Catalog: $2
Check, M.O.
With order. $15 minimum.
Iris

Alabama Wildflower Society
240 Ivy Lane
Auburn, AL 36830-5771
Horticultural Societies

Alaska Native Plant Society
P.O. Box 141613
Anchorage, AK 99514-1613
Horticultural Societies

Alcovy Daylily Farm
775 Cochran Road
Covington, GA 30209
Phone: 770-787-7177
Catalog: Free
Check, M.O.
With order. $25 minimum.
Daylilies

Alfrey Seeds
P.O. Box 415
Knoxville, TN 37901
Phone: 423-524-5965
Catalog: LSASE
Check, M.O.
With order. No minimum.
Seeds, Vegetables

Allen Plant Company
P.O. Box 310
Fruitland, MD 21826-0310
Phone: 410-742-7122
Fax: 410-742-7120
Catalog: Free
Check, M.O., M.C., Visa
With order. No minimum.
Fruit

Allen, Sterling, & Lothrop
191 U.S. Route 1
Falmouth, ME 04105
Phone: 207-781-4142
Fax: 207-781-4143
Catalog: $1
Check, M.O.
With order. No minimum.
Garlic, Herbs, Organics, Seeds, Supplies, Vegetables

Alpine Millworks
1231 West Lehigh
Englewood, CO 80110
Phone: 303-761-6334
Catalog: Free
Check, M.O., M.C., Visa
With order. No minimum.
Furniture

Alplains
32315 Pine Crest Court
Kiowa, CO 80117
Phone: 303-621-2247
Fax: 303-621-2864
Catalog: $2
Check, M.O.
With order. No minimum.
Perennials, Seeds, Wildflowers

Alsto's Handy Helpers
P.O. Box 1267
Galesburg, IL 61402
Phone: 309-343-6181,
800-447-0048
Fax: 309-343-5785
Catalog: Free
Check, M.O., M.C., Visa,
Amex, Discover
With order. No minimum.
Supplies

A. M. Leonard, Inc.
P.O. Box 816
241 Fox Drive
Piqua, OH 45356-0816
Phone: 800-543-8955
Fax: 800-433-0633
Catalog: $1
Check, M.O., M.C., Visa,
Discover, Amex
With order. $20 minimum.
Supplies

Ambergate Gardens
8015 Krey Avenue
Waconia, MN 55387-9616
Phone: 612-443-2248
Fax: 612-443-2248
Catalog: $2
Check, M.O., M.C., Visa.
With order. $25 minimum.
Booksellers, Grasses, Perennials

Amberway Gardens
5803 Amberway Drive
St. Louis, MO 63128
Phone: 314-842-6103
Catalog: $1
Check, M.O., M.C., Visa
With order. $15 minimum.
Iris

American Association of Field Botanists
P.O. Box 23542
Chattanooga, TN 37422
Horticultural Societies

The American Begonia Society
P.O. Box 231129
Encinitas, CA 92023-1129
Phone: 707-764-5407
Horticultural Societies

The American Botanist, Booksellers
P.O. Box 532
1103 West Truitt Avenue
Chillicothe, IL 61523
Phone: 309-274-5254
Catalog: $2
Check, M.O., M.C., Visa
With order. $25 minimum
with credit card.
Booksellers, Heirlooms

The American Boxwood Society
P.O. Box 85
Boyce, VA 22620
Horticultural Societies

American Camellia Society
One Massee Lane
Fort Valley, GA 31030
Phone: 912-967-2358,
967-2722
Fax: 912-967-2083
Horticultural Societies

The American Conifer Society
Box 314
Perry Hall, MD 21128
Phone: 410-256-5595
Fax: 410-256-5595
Conifers, Horticultural
Societies

The American Daffodil Society
1686 Grey Fox Trails
Milford, OH 45150
Horticultural Societies

American Daylily & Perennials
P.O. Box 210
Grain Valley, MO 64029
Phone: 816-224-2852
Fax: 816-443-2849
Catalog: $3
Check, M.O., M.C., Visa,
Amex
With order. $15 minimum.
Daylilies, Peonies, Perennials

The American Fern Society
Botany Department
Smithsonian Institution
Washington, DC 20560
Horticultural Societies

American Forests
P.O. Box 2000
Washington, DC 20013
Phone: 202-667-3300
Fax: 202-667-7751
Horticultural Societies

American Forests: Famous and Historic Trees
8555 Plummer Road
Jacksonville, FL 32219
Phone: 904-765-0727,
800-677-0727
Fax: 904-768-2298
Catalog: Free
Check, M.O., M.C., Visa,
Amex
With order. No minimum.
Conifers, Heirlooms, Kidstuff, Trees

American Forests Global Releaf
1516 P Street NW
Washington, DC 20005
Phone: 202-667-3300
Horticultural Societies

The American Fuchsia Society.
County Fair Building
9th Avenue and Lincoln Way
San Francisco, CA 95122
Horticultural Societies

American Gloxinia and Gesneriad Society
c/o The Horticultural Society of New York
128 West 58th Street
New York, NY 10019-2103
Phone: 212-757-0195
Horticultural Societies

American Gourd Society
P.O. Box 274
Mount Gilead, OH 43338
Horticultural Societies

The American Hemerocallis Society
1454 Rebel Drive
Jackson, MS 39211
Daylilies, Horticultural Societies

American Hibiscus Society
P.O. Box 321540
Cocoa Beach, FL 32932-1540
Phone: 407-783-2576
Fax: 407-783-2576
Horticultural Societies

American Hosta Society
7802 N.E. 63rd Street
Vancouver, WA 98662
Horticultural Societies, Hosta

The American Iris Society
P.O. Box 8455
San Jose, CA 95155
Horticultural Societies, Iris

The American Ivy Society
P.O. Box 2123
Naples, FL 33939-2123
Phone: 513-434-7069 (Ohio) 941-261-0388 (Florida)
Horticultural Societies

The American Penstemon Society
1569 South Holland Court
Lakewood, CO 80232
Horticultural Societies

American Peony Society
250 Interlachen Road
Hopkins, MN 55343
Horticultural Societies, Peonies

American Pomological Society
103 Tyson Building
University Park, PA 16802-4200
Horticultural Societies

American Rhododendron Society
P.O. Box 1380
Gloucester, VA 23061
Phone: 804-693-4433
Horticultural Societies

American Rock Garden Society
P.O. Box 67
Millwood, NY 10546
Horticultural Societies

The American Rose Society
P.O. Box 30,000
Shreveport, LA 71130
Phone: 318-938-5402
Fax: 318-938-5405
Horticultural Societies, Roses

American Willow Growers Network
R.F.D. 1, Box 124-A
South New Berlin, NY 13843-9653
Phone: 607-847-8264
Horticultural Societies

Ames' Orchard & Nursery
18292 Wildlife Road
Fayetteville, AR 72701
Phone: 501-443-0282 (evenings),
Orders: 800-443-0283
Catalog: Free
Check, M.O., M.C., Visa
Reserved with 25 percent deposit, balance on shipment.
Fruit, Heirlooms, Trees

Amherst Museum Wildflower Society
3755 Tonawanda Creek Road
East Amherst, NY 14051
Horticultural Societies

Anderson Design
P.O. Box 4057-C
Bellingham, WA 98227
Phone: 800-947-7697
Catalog: Free
Check, M.O., M.C., Visa
Furniture

Anderson Iris Gardens
22179 Keather Avenue North
Forest Lake, MN 55025
Phone: 612-433-5268
Catalog: $1
Check, M.O
With order. No minimum.
Daylilies, Iris, Peonies, Perennials

André Viette Farm and Nursery
P.O. Box 1109
Fishersville, VA 22939
Phone: 540-943-2315
Fax: 540-943-0782
Catalog: $3
Check, M.O., M.C., Visa
With order. No minimum.
Daylilies, Grasses, Hosta, Perennials

The Antique Rose Emporium
Route 5, Box 143

Brenham, TX 77833
Phone: 800-441-0002
Fax: 409-836-0928
Catalog: $5
Check, M.O., M.C., Visa
With order. No minimum.
Booksellers, Heirlooms,
Roses

Antonelli Brothers
2545 Capitola Road
Santa Cruz, CA 95062
Phone: 408-475-5222
Catalog: $1
Check, M.O., M.C., Visa,
Discover
With order. No minimum.
Perennials, Seeds

Appalachian Gardens
P.O. Box 82
Waynesboro, PA
17268-0082
Phone: 717-762-4312
Fax: 717-762-7532
Catalog: $2
Check, M.O., M.C., Visa,
Discover
With order. 4-plant
minimum.
Conifers, Rhododendrons,
Trees

Apsher's Perennial Haven
R.R. 1, Box 57
Ionia, MO 65335-9325
Phone: 816-668-4757
Catalog: $1.50
Check, M.O.
With order. $20 minimum.
Daylilies

Aquacide Company
P.O. Box 10748
1627 9th Street
White Bear Lake, MN
55110-0748
Phone: 612-429-6742,
800-328-9350
Fax: 612-429-0563
Catalog: Free
Check, M.O., M.C., Visa,

Discover
With order. No minimum.
Supplies, Waterscapes

Aquamonitor
Box 327
Huntington, NY 11743
Phone: 516-427-5664
Catalog: Free
Check, M.O.
With order. No minimum.
Supplies

Arbico
P.O. Box 4247 CRB
Tucson, AZ 85738-1247
Phone: 520-825-9785,
800-827-BUGS
Fax: 520-825-2038
Catalog: Free
Check, M.O., M.C., Visa,
Amex, Discover
With order. No minimum.
Booksellers, Organics, Sup-
plies

Arborvillage Farm Nursery
P.O. Box 227
15604 County Road C.C.
Holt, MO 64048
Phone: 816-264-3911
Catalog: $1
Check, M.O., M.C., Visa
With order. $25 minimum
with credit card.
Conifers, Trees

Arena Rose Company
536 West Cambridge Avenue
Phoenix, AZ 85003
Fax: 602-266-4335
Catalog: $5
Check, M.O., M.C., Visa
Heirlooms, Roses

Arizona Native Plant Society
P.O. Box 41206
Sun Station
Tucson, AZ 85717-1206
Horticultural Societies

**Arkansas Native Plant Soci-
ety**
P.O. Box 250250
Little Rock, AR 72225
Horticultural Societies

Arrowhead Alpines
P.O. Box 857
1310 North Gregory Road
Fowlerville, MI 48836
Phone: 517-223-3581
Fax: 517-223-8750
Catalog: Free
Check, M.O.
With order. No minimum.
Conifers, Grasses, Perennials,
Seeds, Trees, Wildflowers

Arrowhead Nursery
5030 Watia Road, Depart-
ment HGS
Bryson City, NC 28713
Catalog: $2
Check, M.O.
With order. No minimum.
Trees

Artemis Gardens
170 Moss Bridge Road
Bozeman, MT 59715-9338
Catalog: $1
Check, M.O
With order. $10 minimum.
Daylilies, Iris

**Baldwin Seed Co.–Seeds of
Alaska**
Box 3127
Kenai, Alaska 99611
Catalog: $3
Check, M.O.
With order. No minimum.
Grasses, Seeds, Wildflowers

**Bamboo & Rattan Works,
Inc.**
470 Oberlin Avenue South
Lakewood, NJ 08701
Phone: 908-370-0220
Fax: 908-905-8386
Catalog: Free
Check, M.O.
Furniture

Banyai Hostas
11 Gates Circle
Hockessin, DE 19707
Phone: 302-239-0887
Catalog: Free
Check, M.O.
With order. $25 minimum.
Hosta

Barbara Farnsworth, Book-sellers
P.O. Box 9
Route 128
West Cornwall, CT 06796
Phone: 203-672-6571
Fax: 203-672-3099
Catalog: $3 to $5 (inquire for specific catalog)
Check, M.O., M.C., Visa
With order. No minimum.
Booksellers, Heirlooms, Kidstuff

Barney's Ginseng Patch
Route 2, Highway B
Box 43 HGS
Montgomery City, MO 63361
Phone: 573-564-2575
Catalog: $2
Check, M.O.
With order. $25 minimum
Booksellers, Herbs

Barth Daylilies
Nelson Road, P.O. Box 54
Alna, ME 04535
Phone: 207-586-6455
Fax: 207-586-6455
Catalog: 1 FCS
Check, M.O.
With order. No minimum.
Daylilies

Bay View Gardens
1201 Bay Street
Santa Cruz, CA 95060
Phone: 408-423-3656
Catalog: $2
Check, M.O.
With order. No minimum.
Iris

Bear Creek Nursery
P.O. Box 411
Northport, WA 99157
Fax: 509-732-4417
Catalog: $1
Check, M.O., M.C., Visa
With order. No minimum.
Booksellers, Fruit, Heir-looms, Trees

Beaver Creek Nursery
7526 Pelleaux Road
Knoxville, TN 37938
Phone: 423-922-3961
Catalog: $1
Check, M.O.
With order. $20 minimum.
Conifers, Grasses, Trees

Becker's Seed Potatoes
R.R.1, Trout Creek
Ontario, P0H 2L0 Canada
Phone: 705-724-2305
Catalog: Free
Check, M.O.
With order. No minimum.
Booksellers, Garlic

Bedford Dahlias
65 Leyton Road
Bedford, OH 44146
Phone: 216-232-2852
Catalog: One F.C.S.
Check, M.O., M.C., Visa
With order. No minimum.
Perennials

Bergeson Nursery
Route 1, Box 184
Fertile, MN 56540
Phone: 218-945-6988
Fax: 218-945-6991
Catalog: Free
Check, M.O.
With order. No minimum.
Conifers, Fruit, Trees

Berlin Seeds
5371 County Road 77
Millersburg, OH 44654
Phone: 216-893-2811
Catalog: Free
Check, M.O.

With order. No minimum.
Booksellers, Fruit, Garlic, Grasses, Kidstuff, Organics, Seeds, Supplies, Vegetables

Berry Hill Limited
75 Burwell Road
St. Thomas, Ontario,
Canada N5P 3R5
Phone: 519-631-0480,
800-668-3072
Fax: 519-631-8935
Catalog: Free
Check, M.O., M.C., Visa
With order. $10 minimum.
Booksellers, Furniture, Kid-stuff, Supplies

Beth L. Bibby, Books
1225 Sardine Creek Road
Gold Hill, OR 97525-9730
Phone: 541-855-1621
Catalog: $3,
1-year subscription
With order. No minimum.
Check, M.O.
Booksellers

Better Yield Insects and Garden Houses
1302 Highway 2, R.R. 3
Site 4, Box 48
Belle River, Ontario, Canada
N0R 1A0
Phone: 519-727-6108
Fax: 519-727-5989
Catalog: $1
Check, M.O., M.C., Visa
With order. No minimum.
Organics, Supplies

Bijou Alpines
P.O. Box 1252
Graham, WA 98338-8615
Phone: 360-893-6191
Catalog: $1
Check, M.O., M.C.
With order. $15 minimum.
Conifers, Perennials, Trees, Waterscapes

BioLogic Company
P.O. Box 177

Willow Hill, PA 17271
Phone: 717-349-2789,
349-2922
Fax: 717-349-2789
Catalog: LSASE
Check, M.O., M.C., Visa
With order. No minimum.
Organics, Supplies

The Blooming Hill
615 Rosedale Road S.E.
Cedar Rapids, IA 52403
Phone: 319-362-1375
Catalog: $1
Check, M.O.
With order. No minimum.
Daylilies, Hosta, Iris

Blooming Prairie Gardens
R.R. 1, Box 194
Blooming Prairie, MN
55917
Phone: 612-813-1278
Fax: 612-813-1279
Catalog: Free
Check, M.O., M.C., Visa
With order. $20 minimum.
Bulbs

Bloomingfields Farm
Gaylordsville, CT 06755
Phone: 203-354-6951
Catalog: Free
Check, M.O., M.C., Visa
With order. No minimum.
Daylilies, Organics

Blossom Valley Gardens
15011 Oak Creek Road
El Cajon, CA 92021-2328
Phone: 619-443-7711
Catalog: $1
Check, M.O.
With order. $25 minimum.
Daylilies

Blossoms and Bloomers
East 11415 Krueger Lane
Spokane, WA 99207
Phone: 509-922-1344
Catalog: $1
Check, M.O.
With order. No minimum.

Heirlooms, Roses

Bluebird Haven Iris Garden
6940 Fairplay Road
Somerset, CA. 95684
Phone: 209-245-5017
Catalog: $2/Antique catalog:
$1
Check, M.O.
With order. $10 minimum.
Heirlooms, Iris

Bluebird Orchard Nursery
429 East Randall Street
Coopersville, MI 49404
Phone: 616-837-9598
Catalog: Free
Check, M.O.
With order, custom upon
delivery. No minimum.
Fruit, Trees

BlueJay Gardens Herb Farm
Route 2, Box 196
Haskell, OH 74436
Phone: 918-482-3465
Catalog: $1
Check, M.O.
With order. $5 minimum.
Herbs, Organics

Bluestem Prairie Nursery
R.R. 2, Box 106-A
Hillsboro, IL 62049
Phone: 217-532-6344
Catalog: Free
Check, M.O.
With order. No minimum.
Grasses, Seeds, Wildflowers

Bluestone Perennials
7211 Middle Ridge Road
Madison, OH 44057
Phone: 800-852-5243
Fax: 216-428-7198
Catalog: Free
Check, M.O., M.C.,Visa,
Amex, Discover
With order. No minimum.
Grasses, Perennials, Trees

Bonnie Brae Gardens
1105 S.E. Christensen Road

Corbett, OR 97019
Phone: 503-695-5190
Catalog: 2 FCS
Check, M.O.
With order. $10 minimum.
Bulbs

Book Arbor
P.O. Box 20885
Baltimore, MD 21209-9998
Phone: 410-367-0338
Catalog: Free. 19th-century
farm and garden catalog: $1
Check, M.O.
With order. No minimum.
Booksellers, Heirlooms

Book Orchard
1379 Park Western Drive,
Suite 306
San Pedro, CA 90732
Phone: 310-548-4279
Fax: 310-548-4279
Catalog: Free
Check, M.O.
With order. No minimum.
Booksellers

**Boothe Hill Tea Co. and
Greenhouse**
Boothe Hill Wildflowers
23-B Boothe Hill
Chapel Hill, NC 27514
Phone: 919-967-4091
Catalog: Free
Check, M.O
With order. $10 minimum.
Organics, Seeds, Wildflowers

Boston Mountain Nurseries
Route 2, Box 405-A
Mountainburg, AR 72946
Phone: 501-369-2007
Fax: 501-369-2007
Catalog: 1 FCS
Check, M.O.
With order. No minimum.
Fruit

Botanical Club of Wisconsin
Wisconsin Academy of Arts,
Sciences and Letters
1922 University Avenue

Madison, WI 53705
Horticultural Societies

Botanical Society of Washington
Department of Botany, NHB 166
Smithsonian Institution
Washington, DC 20560
Horticultural Societies

Botanical Society of Western Pennsylvania
401 Clearview Avenue
Pittsburgh, PA 15205
Horticultural Societies

Bountiful Gardens
18001 Shafer Ranch Road
Willits, CA 95490
Phone: 707-459-6410
Fax: 707-459-6410
Catalog: Free
Rare seeds catalog: $2
Check, M.O., M.C., Visa, Amex
With order. No minimum.
Booksellers, Garlic, Heirlooms, Herbs, Kidstuff, Organics, Seeds, Supplies, Vegetables

Bow Bends
P.O. Box 900
92 Randall Road
Bolton, MA 01740-0900
Phone: 508-779-2271
Fax: 508-779-2272
Catalog: $3
Check, M.O.
50 percent with order,
50 percent prior to delivery.
No minimum.
Furniture

Bowman's Hill Wildflower Preserve
Washington Crossing Historic Park
P.O. Box 103
Washington Crossing, PA 18977
Phone: 215-862-2924

Fax: 215-493-4820
Catalog: $1
Check, M.O.
With order. No minimum.
Horticultural Societies, Seeds, Wildflowers

Bozeman Bio-Tech, Inc.
P.O. Box 3146
1612 Gold Avenue
Bozeman, MT 59772
Phone: 406-587-5891,
800-289-6656
Fax: 406-587-0223
Catalog: Free
Check, M.O., M.C., Visa, Discover
With order. No minimum.
Booksellers, Kidstuff, Organics, Supplies

Brand Peony Farm
P.O. Box 842
St. Cloud, MN 56302
Phone: 612-252-5234
Catalog: $1
Check or M.O.
With order. No minimum.
Heirlooms, Peonies, Perennials

Breck's
U.S. Reservation Center
6523 North Galena Road
Peoria, IL 61632-1758
Phone: 309-689-3850
Orders: 800-722-9069
Fax: 309-689-3803
Catalog: Free
Check, M.O., M.C., Visa, Amex, Discover
With order. No minimum.
Bulbs

Briarwood Gardens
14 Gully Lane, R.F.D. 3
East Sandwich, MA 02537
Phone: 508-888-2146
Fax 508-888-2146
Catalog: $2
Check, M.O., M.C., Visa
With order. No minimum.

Rhododendrons, Trees

Bridgewood Gardens
P.O. Box 800
Crownsville, MD 21032
Phone: 410-849-3916,
800-858-6671
Fax: 410-849-3427
Catalog: Free
Check, M.O., M.C., Visa
With order. No minimum.
Hosta

Bridgeworks
306 Lockwood Street
Covington, LA 70433
Phone: 504-892-6640
Catalog: Free
Certified check, M.O., M.C., Visa
With order. No minimum.
Furniture

Brittingham Plant Farms, Inc.
P.O. Box 2538, Department HGS
Salisbury, MD 21802-2538
Phone: 410-749-5153
Fax: 800-749-5148
Catalog: $1
Check, M.O., M.C., Visa
With order. Or one third deposit, balance prior to shipment.
Fruit

Broken Arrow Nursery
13 Broken Arrow Road
Hamden, CT 06518
Phone: 203-288-1026
Fax: 203-287-1035
Catalog: $2
Check, M.O., M.C., Visa
With order. $22 minimum.
Rhododendrons, Trees

Bronwood Worm Farms
P.O. Box 28
Bronwood, GA 31726
Phone: 912-995-5994
Catalog: Free
Check, M.O., M.C., Visa

With order. No minimum.
Organics, Supplies

Brookesfield Farm
426 Byrd Street
Centralia, WA. 98531
Phone: 360-736-8209
Fax: 360-330-0669
Catalog: Free
Check, M.O.
With order. No minimum.
Bulbs

Brooks Books
P.O. Box 21473
1343 New Hampshire Drive
Concord, CA 94521
Phone: 510-672-4566
Fax: 510-672-3338
Catalog: $1
Check, M.O., M.C., Visa,
Discover
With order. No minimum.
Booksellers, Organics

Brown's Edgewood Gardens
2611 Corrine Drive
Orlando, FL 32803
Phone: 407-896-3203
Fax: 407-898-5792
Basic catalog: LSASE De-
tailed catalog: $2
Check, M.O., M.C., Visa
With order. $10 minimum.
Booksellers, Furniture,
Herbs, Supplies

**Bruce Barber Bird Feeders,
Inc.**
4600 Jason Street
Denver, CO 80211
Phone: 800-528-2794
Fax: 303-368-9616
Catalog: Free
Check, M.O.
With order. No minimum.
Furniture

Brudy's Tropical Exotics
P.O. Box 820874
Houston, TX 77282-0874
Phone: 800-926-7333
Fax: 713-960-7117

Catalog: Free
Check, M.O., M.C., Visa
With order. $15 minimum.
Conifers, Fruit, Seeds, Trees

Buckhorn Ginseng
Route 4, Box 336
Richland Center, WI 53581
Phone: 608-647-2244
Fax: 608-647-2244
Catalog: LSASE
Check, M.O.
With order. No minimum.
Booksellers, Herbs

**Buckley Nursery Garden
Center**
646 North River Road
Buckley, WA 98321
Phone: 360-829-1811
Catalog: Free
Check, M.O., M.C., Visa,
Discover
With order. No minimum.
Fruit, Trees

The Bulb Crate
2560 Deerfield Road
Riverwoods, IL 60015
Phone: 847-317-1414
Fax: 847-317-1414
Catalog: $1
Check, M.O., M.C., Visa
With order. $15 minimum
with credit card.
Bulbs

Bundles of Bulbs
112 Green Spring Valley
Road
Owing Mills, MD 21117
Phone: 410-363-1371
Catalog: $2
Check, M.O., M.C., Visa
With order. No minimum.
Bulbs

Burford Brothers
Route 1
Monroe, VA 24574
Phone: 804-929-4950
Catalog: $2
Detailed book: $12

Check, M.O., M.C., Visa
With order. No minimum.
Fruit, Heirlooms, Trees

Burk's Nursery
P.O. Box 1207
Benton, AR 72015-1207
Phone: 501-794-3266
Catalog: $1
Check, M.O., M.C., Visa
With order. $10 minimum,
$20 with credit card.
Cactus

**Burnt Ridge Nursery and
Orchards**
432 Burnt Ridge Road
Onalaska, WA 98570
Phone: 360-985-2873
Catalog: 1 FCS
Check, M.O.
With order. No minimum.
Fruit, Trees

Burt Associates Bamboo
P.O. Box 719
Westford, MA 01886
Phone: 508-692-3240
Fax: 508-692-3240
Catalog: $1
Check, M.O., M.C., Visa,
Discover
With order. No minimum.
Grasses

Busse Gardens
5873 Oliver Avenue S.W.
Cokato, MN 55321-4229
Phone: 320-286-2654
Orders: 800-544-3192
Fax: 320-286-6601
Catalog: $2
Check, M.O., M.C.,Visa,
Amex, Discover
With order. $25 minimum.
Daylilies, Grasses, Hosta,
Peonies, Perennials, Wild-
flowers

Butner's Old Mill Nursery
806 South Belt Highway
St. Joseph, MO 64507
Phone: 816-279-7434

Catalog: Free
Check, M.O., M.C., Visa
With order. No minimum.
Roses

Butterbrooke Farm
78 Barry Road
Oxford, CT 06478-1529
Phone: 203-888-2000
Catalog: LSASE
Check, M.O.
With order. No minimum.
Booksellers, Organics, Seeds,
Vegetables

**The Cactus and Succulent
Society of America**
1535 Reeve Street
Los Angeles, CA 94720
Phone: 310-556-1923
Cactus, Horticultural Societies

California Botanical Society
Department of Botany
University of California
Berkeley, CA 94720
Horticultural Societies

**California Native Plant
Society**
1722 J Street, Suite 17
Sacramento, CA
95814-2931
Horticultural Societies

The Calochortus Society
P.O. Box 1128
Berkeley, CA 94701-1128
Horticultural Societies

Canadian Wildflower Society
4981 Highway 7 East
Unit 12A, #228
Markham, Ontario,
Canada L3R 1N1
Horticultural Societies

Canyon Creek Nursery
3527 Dry Creek Road
Oroville, CA 95965
Phone: 916-533-2166
Check, M.O.

Catalog: $2
Grasses, Perennials

Capability's Books®
2379 Highway 46
Deer Park, WI 54007
Phone: 800-247-8154
Outside U.S.: 715-269-5346
Fax: 715-269-5531
Catalog: Free
Check, M.O., M.C., Visa,
Amex
With order. No minimum.
Booksellers

Cape Cod Vireyas
405 Jones Road
Falmouth, MA 02540
Phone: 508-548-1613
(evenings)
Fax: 617-742-4749
Catalog: $3
Check, M.O., M.C., Visa
With order. No minimum.
Rhododendrons, Trees

Cape Cod Worm Farm
30 Center Avenue
Buzzards Bay, MA 02532
Phone: 508-759-5664
Check, M.O.
With order. 100-pound
minimum.
Organics, Supplies

Cape Iris Gardens
822 Rodney Vista Boulevard
Cape Girardeau, MO 63701
Phone: 573-334-3383
Catalog: $1
Check
With order. No minimum.
Daylilies, Iris

Caprice Farm Nursery
15425 S.W. Pleasant Hill
Road
Sherwood, OR 97140
Phone: 503-625-7241
Fax: 503-625-5588
Catalog: $2
Check, M.O, M.C, Visa
Retail, with order. Wholesale,

terms. No minimum.
Daylilies, Hosta, Iris, Peonies, Perennials

Carlson's Gardens
Box 305
South Salem, NY 10590
Phone: 914-763-5958
Catalog: $3
Check, M.O., M.C., Visa,
Amex
With order. No minimum.
Rhododendrons, Trees

Carlton Rose Nurseries
P.O. Box 366
Carlton, OR 97111
Phone: 503-852-7135
Fax: 503-852-7511
Catalog: Free
Check, M.O., M.C., Visa
With order. No minimum.
Roses

Carol Barnett, Books
3562 N.E. Liberty
Portland, OR 97211-7248
Phone: 503-282-7036
Catalog: Free
Check, M.O.
With order. No minimum.
Booksellers, Heirlooms

Carroll Gardens
444 East Main Street
P.O. Box 310
Westminster, MD 21157
Phone: 410-848-5422,
800-638-6334
Fax: 410-857-4112
Catalog: $3
Check, M.O., M.C., Visa
With order. $25 minimum
with credit card.
Daylilies, Herbs, Hosta, Iris,
Peonies, Perennials, Roses,
Trees

Cart Warehouse
P.O. Box 3
Point Arena, CA 95468
Phone: 800-655-9100
Fax: 707-882-2488

Catalog: Free
Check, M.O.
With order. No minimum.
Supplies

Cascade Bulb & Seed Co.
P.O. Box 271
Scotts Mills, OR 97375
Phone: 503-873-2218
Catalog: 1 FCS
Check, M.O.
With order. No minimum.
Bulbs, Daylilies, Seeds

Cascade Daffodils
P.O. Box 10626
White Bear Lake, MN
55110-0626
Phone: 612-426-9616
Bulbs

Catamount Cart
P.O. Box 365
Shelburne Falls, MA 01370
Phone: 413-625-6063,
800-444-0056
Catalog: Free
Check, M.O., M.C., Visa
With order. No minimum.
Supplies

Cat's Paw Gardens
9414 Stonegate Drive
Charlotte, NC 28216
Phone: 704-394-8661
Catalog: Free
Check, M.O.
With order. $20 minimum.
Daylilies

Cattail Meadows, Limited
P.O. Box 39391, Department
HGS
Solon, OH 44139
Phone: 216-248-4581
Catalog: Free
Check, M.O.
With order. No minimum.
Grasses, Wildflowers

Cedar Valley Nursery
3833 McElfresh Road S.W.
Centralia, WA 98531

Phone: 360-736-7490
Catalog: Free
Check, M.O.
With order. $20 minimum.
Fruit

Chalybeate Gardens
Route 2, Box 220
Fuquay-Varina, NC 27526
Phone: 919-552-2235
Catalog: Free
Check, M.O.
With order. No minimum.
Daylilies

Charleston Battery Bench, Inc.
191 King Street
Charleston, SC 29401
Phone: 803-722-3842
Fax: 803-722-3846
Catalog: Free
Check, M.O., Amex, M.C., Visa
With order. No minimum.
Furniture

Charles H. Mueller Co.
7091 North River Road
New Hope, PA 18938-9990
Phone: 215-862-2033
Fax: 215-862-3696
Catalog: Free
Check, M.O., M.C., Visa
With order. No minimum.
Bulbs

Charles V. Applegate
3699 Pleasant Hill Road
Perrysville, OH 44864
Phone: 419-938-3827
Catalog: 1 FCS
Check, M.O., M.C., Visa
With order. No minimum.
Daylilies

Chattanooga Daylily Gardens
1736 Eagle Drive
Hixson, TN 37343
Phone: 423-842-4630
Catalog: $2
Check, M.O.

With order. $25 minimum.
Daylilies

Chestnut Hill Nursery
Route 1, Box 341
Alachua, FL 32615
Phone: 904-462-2820,
800-669-2067
Fax: 904-462-4330
Catalog: Free
Check, M.O., M.C., Visa
With order. No minimum.
Fruit, Trees

Chile Institute
P.O. Box 3-Q
New Mexico State University
Las Cruces, NM 88030
Horticultural Societies

Cieli
36 Ventura Avenue
P.O. Box 151
La Honda, CA 94020
Phone: 415-369-2129,
800-876-3006
Fax: 415-369-2082
Catalog: $3
Check, M.O.
With order. No minimum.
Furniture

C. K. Petty and Co.
203 Wildemere Drive
South Bend, IN 46615
Phone: 219-232-4095
Fax: 219-288-3229
Catalog: Free
Check, M.O., M.C., Visa
With order. No minimum.
Supplies

Classic & Country Crafts
5100 1-B Clayton Road,
Suite 291
Concord, CA 94521
Phone: 510-672-4337
Fax: 510-672-4337
Catalog: Free
Check, M.O.
With order. No minimum.
Furniture

Classic Groundcovers
405 Belmont Road
Athens, GA 30605-4905
Phone: 706-543-0145,
800-248-8424
Fax: 706-369-9844
Catalog: Free
Check, M.O., M.C., Visa
With order. No minimum.
Grasses, Perennials

Clifford's Perennial & Vine
Route 2, Box 320
East Troy, WI 53120
Phone: 414-968-4040
Fax: 414-968-5525 (February through October)
Catalog: Free
Check, M.O.
With order. No minimum.
Perennials, Trees

Cloud Mountain Farm
6906 Goodwin Road
Everson, WA 98247
Phone: 360-966-5859
Fax: 360-966-0921
Catalog: $1
Check, M.O., M.C., Visa, Discover
With order. $10 minimum.
Fruit

Clyde Robin Seed Co., Inc.
P.O. Box 2366
3670 Enterprise Avenue
Castro Valley, CA 94546
Phone: 510-785-0425
Fax: 510-785-6463
Catalog: Free
Check, M.O., M.C., Visa, Amex
With order. No minimum.
Seeds, Wildflowers

Coburg Planting Fields
573 East 600 North
Valparaiso, IN 46383
Phone: 219-462-4288
Catalog: $2
Check, M.O.
With order. No minimum.
Daylilies

Coenosium Gardens
P.O. Box 847
Sandy, OR 97055
Phone: 503-668-3574
Catalog: $3
Check, M.O.
With order. $25 minimum.
Conifers, Trees

Cold Stream Farm
2030 Free Soil Road
Free Soil, MI 49411-9752
Phone: 616-464-5809
Catalog: Free
Bank check, C.O.D., M.O.
Prior to shipment. No minimum.
Conifers, Fruit, Trees

Collector's Nursery
16804 N.E. 102nd Avenue
Battle Ground, WA 98604
Phone: 360-574-3832
Catalog: $2
Check, M.O., M.C., Visa
With order. $25 minimum
with credit card.
Conifers, Perennials, Trees

Colorado Native Plant Society
P.O. Box 200
Fort Collins, CO
80522-0200
Horticultural Societies

Colvos Creek Nursery
P.O. Box 1512
Vashon Island, WA 98070
Phone: 206- 463-1509
Catalog: $2
Check, M.O.
With order. $15 minimum.
Conifers, Fruit, Trees

Comanche Acres Iris Gardens
R.R. 1, Box 258
Gower, MO 64454
Phone: 816-424-6436,
800-382-IRIS
Catalog: $3
Check, M.O., M.C., Visa,

Discover
With order. $10 minimum.
Iris

Common Ground Garden Supply
(See **Bountiful Gardens**)

Companion Plants
7247 North Coolville Ridge Road
Athens, OH 45701
Phone: 614-592-4643
Catalog: $3
Check, M.O., M.C., Visa
With order. $15 minimum plants, $6.25 minimum seeds.
Herbs, Seeds

Comstock Seed
8520 West 4th Street
Reno, NV 89523
Phone: 702-746-3681
Fax: 702-746-3681
Check, M.O.
With order. No minimum.
Grasses, Seeds, Trees, Wildflowers

Connecticut Botanical Society
10 Hillside Circle
Storrs, CT 06268
Horticultural Societies

Contemporary Gardens
P.O. Box 534
Blanchard, OK 73010
Phone: 405-485-3302
Catalog: $1
Display list: LSASE
Check, M.O.
With order. $20 minimum.
Daylilies, Iris

The Cook's Garden
P.O. Box 535
Londonderry, VT 05148
Phone: 802-824-3400
Fax: 802-824-3027
Catalog: $1
Check, M.O., M.C., Visa
Booksellers, Garlic, Heir-

looms, Herbs, Kidstuff,
Organics, Seeds, Supplies,
Vegetables

Cooley's Gardens
P.O. Box 126
Silverton, OR 97381-0126
Phone: 503-873-5463,
800-225-5391
Catalog: $4
Check, M.O., M.C., Visa
With order. $15 minimum.
Iris

Cooley's Strawberry Nursery
P.O. Box 472
Augusta, AR 72006
Phone: 501-347-2026,
501-724-5630
Catalog: Free
Check, M.O.
With order. 100-plant
minimum.
Fruit

Cooper's Garden
2345 Decatur Avenue North
Golden Valley, MN 55427
Phone: 612-542-9447
Fax: 612-542-9447
Catalog: $1
Check, M.O.
With order. No minimum.
Daylilies, Iris, Perennials

Cordon Bleu Farms
P.O. Box 2017
San Marcos, CA
92079-2017
Check, M.O., M.C., Visa
With order. $12 minimum,
$50 minimum with credit
card.
Daylilies, Iris

Corn Hill Nursery
R.R. 5, Petitcodiac N.B.
E0A 2H0 Canada
Phone: 506-756-3635,
506-756-1087
Check, M.O., M.C., Visa
Perennials

Country Casual
17317 Germantown Road
Germantown, MD
20874-2999
Phone: 301-540-0040,
800-284-8325
Fax: 301-540-7364
Catalog: Free
Check, M.O., M.C., Visa
With order. No minimum.
Furniture

**Country Wetlands Nursery
and Consulting**
575 West 20755 Field Drive
Muskego, WI 53150
Phone: 414-679-1268
Fax: 414-679-1279
Catalog: Free
Check, M.O.
With order. No minimum.
Booksellers, Grasses, Seeds,
Waterscapes, Wildflowers

The Crafter's Garden
P.O. Box 3194
Peabody, MA 01961-3194
Phone: 508-535-1142
Catalog: Free
Check, M.O., M.C., Visa
With order. No minimum.
Organics, Supplies

Crintonic Gardens
County Line Road
Gates Mills, OH 44040
Phone: 216-423-3349
Catalog: $1
Check, M.O.
With order. $50 minimum.
Daylilies

**CRM Ecosystems Services,
Inc.**
(See **Prairie Ridge Nursery**)

Crochet Daylilies Garden
P.O. Box 425
Prairieville, LA 70769
Phone: 504-673-8491
Catalog: Free
Check, M.O.
With order. $25 minimum.

Daylilies

Crop King, Inc.
P.O. Box 310
Medina, OH 44258
Phone: 216-725-5656
Fax: 216-722-3958
Catalog: $3
Check, M.O., M.C., Visa,
Discover
With order. $25 minimum.
Booksellers, Supplies

Dabney Herbs
P.O. Box 22061
Louisville, KY 40252
Phone: 502-893-5198
Fax: 502-893-5198
Catalog: $2
Check, M.O., M.C., Visa
With order. $30 minimum
with credit card.
Booksellers, Herbs, Perennials

The Daffodil Mart
7463 Heath Trail
Gloucester, VA 23061
Phone: 804-693-3966
Orders: 800-ALL-BULB
Fax: 800-420-2852
Catalog: Free
Check, M.O., M.C., Visa,
Amex, Discover
With order. $25 minimum.
Booksellers, Bulbs, Supplies

Daisy Fields
12635 S.W. Brighton Lane
Hillsboro, OR 97123-9051
Phone: 503-628-0315
Fax: 503-628-0315
Catalog: $2
Check, M.O.
With order. No minimum.
Heirlooms, Perennials

Dan's Garden Shop
5821 Woodwinds Circle
Frederick, MD 21701
Phone: 301-695-5966
Catalog: Free
Check, M.O., M.C., Visa

With order. No minimum.
Booksellers, Organics, Seeds,
Supplies, Vegetables

**Dave & Sue's Aquariums
and Greenhouse**
R.R. 1, Box 96
Kelley, IA 50134
Phone 515-769-2446,
800-528-2827
Catalog: $1
Check, M.O., M.C., Visa
With order. $10 minimum.
Booksellers, Supplies, Trees

David Bacon Woodworking
P.O. Box 1034
Nevada City, CA 95959
Phone: 916-273-8889
Fax: 916-273-8889
Catalog: Free
Check, M.O.
With order. No minimum.
Furniture

**Davidson Wilson Green-
houses**
R.R. 2, Box 168, Depart-
ment 11
Crawfordsville, IN
47933-9426
Phone: 317-364-0556
Fax: 800-276-3691
Catalog: $3
Check, M.O., M.C., Visa,
Amex, Discover
With order. 25-plant
minimum.
Herbs

Day-Dex Co.
4725 N.W. 36th Avenue
Miami, FL 33142
Phone: 305-635-5241,
635-5259
Catalog: Free
Check, M.O.
With order. No minimum.
Supplies

Daylily Discounters
1 Daylily Plaza
Alachua, FL 32615

Canadian orders: Crescent
Nursery, R.R. 4
Rockwood, Ontario N0B 2K0
Phone: 904-462-1539,
800-DAYLILIES
Fax: 904-462-5111
Catalog: $1
Check, M.O., M.C., Visa,
Amex, Discover
With order. $25 minimum.
Booksellers, Daylilies

Daylily World
P.O. Box 1612
Sanford, FL 32772-1612
Phone: 407-322-4034
Fax: 407-322-8629
Catalog: $5
Check, M.O., M.C., Visa.
With order. $30 minimum.
Daylilies

Daystar
Route 2, Box 250
Litchfield, ME 04350-9503
Phone: 207-724-3369
Catalog: $1
Check, M.O., M.C., Visa
With order. No minimum.
Conifers, Perennials, Trees

Deep Diversity Seed Catalog
(See Seeds of Change®)

DeGiorgi Seed Company
6011 N Street
Omaha, NE 68117-1634
Phone: 402-731-3901,
800-858-2580
Fax: 402-731-8475
Catalog: $2
Check, M.O., M.C., Visa
With order. $20 minimum
with credit card.
Booksellers, Garlic, Grasses,
Herbs, Kidstuff, Seeds,
Vegetables

**DeGrandchamp's Blueberry
Nursery**
15575 77th Street
South Haven, MI 49090
Phone: 616-637-3915

Fax: 616-637-2531
Catalog: $1
Check, M.O., M.C., Visa
With order. No minimum.
Fruit

Desert Moon Nursery
P.O. Box 600
Veguita, NM 87062
Phone: 505-864-0614
Catalog: $1
Check, M.O.
With order. $15 minimum
for plants, or 4 packets of
seed.
Cactus, Seeds, Wildflowers

Desert Nursery
1301 South Copper
Deming, NM 88030-5009
Phone: 505-546-6264
Catalog: 1 FCS
Check, M.O.
With order. No minimum.
Cactus

Desertland Nursery
P.O. Box 26126
El Paso, TX 79926
Phone: 915-858-1130
Fax: 915-858-1560
Catalog: $1
Check, M.O., M.C., Visa,
Amex, Discover
With order. No minimum.
Cactus, Seeds

Dickerson Daylily Garden
Woods Cross Roads, VA
23190
Phone: 804-693-5240
Catalog: $2
Check, M.O.
With order. No minimum.
Daylilies

Digging Dog Nursery
P.O. Box 471
Albion, CA 95410
Phone: 707-937-1130
Fax: 707-937-4389
Catalog: $2
Check, M.O., M.C., Visa

With order. $25 minimum.
Grasses, Perennials, Trees

Dirt Cheap Organics
5645 Paradise Drive
Corte Madera, CA 94925
Phone: 415-924-0369
Catalog: Free
Check, M.O., M.C., Visa
With order. No minimum.
Organics, Supplies

Dixondale Farms
P.O. Box 127
Carrizo Springs, TX 78834
Phone: 210-876-2430
Fax: 210-876-9640
Catalog: Free
Check, M.O., M.C., Visa
With order. No minimum.
Garlic, Vegetables

D. Landreth Seed Company
P.O. Box 6426
Ostend and Ledenhall Streets
Baltimore, MD 21230
Phone: 410-727-3922,
727-3923
Fax: 410-244-8633
Catalog: $2
Check, M.O.
With order. No minimum.
Garlic, Grasses, Heirlooms,
Herbs, Seeds, Vegetables

**Donaroma's Nursery and
Landscape Services**
P.O. Box 2189
Edgartown, MA 02539
Phone: 508-627-8366,
627-8595
Fax: 508-627-7855
Catalog: $1
Check, M.O., M.C., Visa
With order. 5-plant
minimum.
Perennials, Wildflowers

Donovan's Roses
P.O. Box 37800
Shreveport, LA 71133-7800
Phone: 318-861-6693
Catalog: Free

Check, M.O.
With order. No minimum.
Roses

Dooley Gardens
210 North High Drive N.E.
Hutchinson, MN 55350
Phone: 612-587-3050
Catalog: Free
Check, M.O.
With order. No minimum.

DoRoCo Seed Co.
P.O. Box 80131
Billings, MT 59108-0131
Catalog: $2
Check, M.O., M.C., Visa
With order. $5 minimum.
Herbs, Seeds

Dorothy Biddle Service
H.C. 01, Box 900
Greeley, PA 18425-9799
Phone: 717-226-3239
Fax: 717-226-0349
Catalog: 2 FCS
Check, M.O., M.C., Visa
With order. No minimum.
Booksellers, Supplies

Down on the Farm Seed
P.O. Box 184
Hiram, OH 44234
Phone: 216-274-8043
Catalog: Free
Check, M.O.
With order. No minimum.
Garlic, Heirlooms, Herbs,
Kidstuff, Organics, Seeds,
Vegetables

Dramm Corporation
P.O. Box 1960
Manitowoc, WI 54221-1960
Phone: 414-684-0227,
800-258-0848
Fax: 414-684-4499
Catalog: Free
Check, M.O., M.C., Visa
With order. No minimum.
Supplies

Duncraft

P.O. Box 9020
Penacook, NH 03303-9020
Phone: 603-224-0200
Fax: 603-226-3735
Catalog: Free
Check, M.O., M.C., Visa,
Amex, Discover
With order. No minimum.
Furniture, Supplies

Dutch Gardens
P.O. Box 200
Adelphia, NJ 07710-0200
Phone: 800-818-3861
Fax: 908-780-7720
Catalog: Free
Check, M.O., M.C., Visa,
Amex, Discover
With order. $25 minimum.
Bulbs, Perennials

**Dyke's Blueberry Farm and
Nursery, Inc.**
Route 1, Box 251
Vincent, OH 45784
Phone: 614-678-2192
Catalog: Free
Check, C.O.D., M.O.
With order. No minimum.
Fruit

Earlee, Inc.
2002 Highway 62
Jeffersonville, IN
47130-3556
Phone: 812-282-9134
Fax: 812-282-2640
Catalog: Free
Check, M.O., M.C., Visa
With order. $2.50 minimum.
Organics, Supplies

Earthly Goods Ltd.
P.O. Box 614
New Albany, IN 47150
Phone: 812-944-3283
Catalog: $2
Check, M.O.
With order. $7.50
minimum.
Furniture, Grasses, Seeds,
Wildflowers

Earthworks
P.O. Box 67
Hyattville, WY 82428
Phone: 307-469-2229
Catalog: Free
Check, M.O.
With order. No minimum.
Furniture

Eastern Plant Specialties
Box 226
Georgetown, ME 04548
Phone: 207-371-2888,
800-WILL-GRO
Catalog: $3
Check, M.O., M.C., Visa
With order. $15 minimum.
Conifers, Fruit, Perennials,
Rhododendrons, Trees,
Wildflowers

Eccles Nurseries, Inc.
Box Y
Rimersburg, PA 16248-0525
Phone: 814-473-6265
Fax: 814-473-4047
Catalog: Free
Check, C.O.D., M.O.,
M.C., Visa, Amex, Discover
25 percent deposit, balance
on shipment
Conifers, Trees

Eco Enterprises
1240 N.E. 175th Street,
Suite B
Seattle, WA 98155
Phone: 206-363-9981,
525-4784 (evenings),
800-426-6937
Fax: 206-363-9983
Catalog: Free
Check, C.O.D., M.O.,
M.C., Visa
With order. No minimum.
Booksellers, Supplies

Ecology Action
(See **Bountiful Gardens**)

**Edge of the Rockies "Native
Seeds"**
P.O. Box 1218

Bayfield, CO 81122-9758
Phone: 303-884-9003
Catalog: $2.50
Check, M.O.
With order. No minimum.
Grasses, Seeds, Wildflowers

Edgewood Farm & Nursery
Route 2, Box 303
Stanardsville, VA 22973
Phone: 804-985-3782
Catalog: $2
Check, M.O., M.C., Visa
With order. No minimum.
Herbs, Perennials

Edible Landscaping
P.O. Box 77
Afton, VA 22920
Phone: 804-361-9134
Orders: 800-524-4156
Catalog: Free
Check, M.O., M.C., Visa,
Amex, Discover
With order. No minimum.
Fruit, Trees

Edmunds' Roses
6235 S.W. Kahle Road
Wilsonville, OR 97070
Phone: 503-682-1476
Fax: 503-682-1275
Catalog: Free
Check, M.O., M.C., Visa
With order. No minimum.
Roses, Supplies

El Paso Native Plant Society
7760 Maya
El Paso, TX 79912
Horticultural Societies

Elixir Farm Botanicals
General Delivery
Brixey, MO 65618
Phone: 417-261-2393
Fax: 417-261-2355
Catalog: $2
Check, M.O., M.C., Visa
With order. $10 seed, $20
root and credit card
minimum.
Booksellers, Herbs, Organics,

Seeds

Emily Gandy's Daylilies
Route 2, Box 453
Cairo, GA 31728
Phone: 912-377-4056
Catalog: Free
Check, M.O.
With order. No minimum.
Daylilies

Emi Meade Importers
16000 Fern Way
Guerneville, CA 95446
Phone: 707-869-3218
Catalog: Free
Check, M.O.
With order. No minimum.
Kidstuff, Supplies

Englearth Gardens
2461 22nd Street
Hopkins, MI 49328
Phone: 616-793-7196
Catalog: $1
Check, M.O.
With order. No minimum.
Daylilies, Hosta, Iris, Peren-
nials

Enoch's Berry Farm
Route 2, Box 227
Fouke, AR 71837
Phone: 501-653-2806
Check, M.O.
With order. No minimum.
Fruit

Ensata Gardens
9823 East Michigan Avenue
Galesburg, MI 49053
Phone: 616-665-7500
Catalog: $2
Check, M.O., M.C., Visa
With order. $10 minimum.
Iris

EON Industries
P.O. Box 11
Liberty Center, OH 43532
Phone: 419-533-4961
Catalog: Free
Check, M.O.
With order. 100-piece

minimum.
Supplies

Ericaceae
P.O. Box 293
Kelsey Hill Road
Deep River, CT 06417
Phone: 203-526-5100
(evenings)
Catalog: Free
Check, M.O.
With order. No minimum.
Rhododendrons, Trees

Erth-Rite
R.D. 1, Box 243
Gap, PA 17527
Phone: 717-442-4171,
800-332-4171
Fax: 717-442-8997
Catalog: Free
Check, M.O.
With order. No minimum.
Organics, Supplies

Escort Lighting
201 Sweitzer Road
Sinking Spring, PA 19608
Phone: 610-670-2517
Fax: 610-670-5170
Catalog: Free
Check, M.O., M.C., Visa
With order. No minimum.
Furniture

Evergreen Gardenworks
P.O. Box 1357
Ukiah, CA 95482
Phone: 707-462-8909
Catalog: $2
Check, M.O., M.C., Visa
With order. No minimum.
Conifers, Fruit, Perennials,
Trees

Fairweather Gardens
P.O. Box 330
Greenwich, NJ 08323
Phone: 609-451-6261
Fax: 609-451-6261
Catalog: $3
Check, M.O., M.C., Visa
With order. $100 minimum

to Arizona, California, Idaho,
Minnesota, Nevada, Oregon,
Utah, Washington.
Conifers, Fruit, Rhododen-
drons, Trees

**Farm Wholesale Green-
houses –Homestead Carts**
2396 Perkins Street N.E.
Salem, OR 97303
Phone: 503-393-3973,
800-825-1925
Fax: 503-393-3119
Catalog: Free
Check, M.O., Visa, M.C.
With order. No minimum.
Furniture, Supplies

Farmer Seed and Nursery
Division of Plantron,
Inc.–Reservation Center
1706 Morrissey Drive
Bloomington, IL 61704
Phone: 507-334-1623
Fax: 507-334-1624
Catalog: Free
Check, M.O., M.C., Visa
With order. No minimum.
Garlic, Perennials, Seeds,
Vegetables

Far North Gardens
P.O. Box 126
New Hudson, MI 48165
Phone: 810-486-4203
Fax: 810-486-4203
Catalog: $2
Check, M.O.
With order. No minimum.
Booksellers, Bulbs, Grasses,
Perennials, Seeds, Wildflow-
ers

Fedco Seeds
Fedco Trees
P.O. Box 520
Waterville, ME 04903
Phone: 207-873-7333
Fax: 207-426-9005
Catalog: $2
Check, M.O.
With order. No minimum.

Booksellers, Conifers, Fruit,
Garlic, Heirlooms, Herbs,
Kidstuff, Organics, Seeds,
Supplies, Trees, Vegetables

Feder's Prairie Seed Co.
Route 1, Box 41
Blue Earth, MN 56013
Phone: 507-526-3049
Catalog: Free
Check, M.O.
With order. No minimum.
Grasses, Seeds, Wildflowers

Fieldstone Gardens, Inc.
620 Quaker Lane
Vassalboro, ME 04989-9713
Phone: 207-923-3836
Fax: 207-923-3836
Catalog: $2
Check, M.O., M.C., Visa
With order. No minimum.
Perennials

Filaree Farm
182 Conconully Highway
Okanogan, WA 98840
Phone: 509-422-6940
Catalog: $2
Check, M.O., M.C., Visa
With order. $10 minimum.
Booksellers, Garlic, Organics

Finch Blueberry Nursery
P.O. Box 699
Bailey, NC 27807
Phone: 919-235-4664
Orders: 800-245-4662
Fax: 919-235-2411
Catalog: Free
Check, M.O., M.C., Visa
With order. No minimum.
Fruit

Fisher's Garden Store
P.O. Box 236
Belgrade, MT 59714
Phone: 406-388-6052
Catalog: Free
Check, M.O.
With order. No minimum.
Garlic, Seeds, Vegetables

Floating Mountain Seeds
P.O. Box 1275
Port Angeles, WA 98362
Phone: 360-928-2072
Catalog: $2
Check, M.O.
With order. No minimum.
Garlic, Heirlooms, Herbs,
Seeds, Vegetables

Florentine Craftsmen, Inc.
46-24 28th Street
Long Island City, NY 11101
Phone: 718-937-7632,
800-876-3567
Fax: 718-937-9858
Catalog: $5
Check, M.O.
With order. No minimum.
Furniture

**Florian Ratchet-Cut™
Pruning Tools**
157 Water Street
Southington, CT 06489
Phone: 203-628-9643,
800-275-3618
Fax: 203-628-6036
Catalog: Free
Check, M.O., M.C.,Visa,
Discover
With order. No minimum.
Supplies

Florida Native Plant Society
P.O. Box 680008
Orlando, FL 32868
Horticultural Societies

**The Flower and Herb Ex-
change**
3076 North Winn Road
Decorah, IA 52101
Catalog: $1
Horticultural Societies, Seeds

The Flower Lady's Garden
1560 Johnson Road
Granite City, IL 62040
Phone: 618-877-2983
Fax: 618-877-5746
Catalog: $2
Check, M.O.

With order. $20 minimum.
Daylilies

Flowerplace Plant Farm
P.O. Box 4865
Meridian, MS 39304
Phone: 800-482-5686
Catalog: $3
Check, M.O.
With order. $10 minimum.
Herbs, Perennials

**Flowers N' Friends Minia-
ture Roses**
9590 100th Street S.E.
Alto, MI 49302
Phone: 616-891-1226
Check, M.O.
With order. No minimum.
Roses

**The Flowery Branch Seed
Co.**
P.O. Box 1330
Flowery Branch, GA 30542
Phone: 770-536-8380
Fax: 770-532-7825
Catalog: $3
Check, M.O.
With order. No minimum.
Herbs, Perennials, Seeds

Floyd Cove Nursery
725 Longwood-Markham
Road
Sanford, FL 32771-8315
Phone: 407-324-9229
Fax: 407-321-3238
Catalog: $2
Check, M.O., M.C., Visa
With order. No minimum.
Daylilies

Foliage Gardens
2003 128th Avenue S.E.
Bellevue, WA 98005
Phone: 206-747-2998
Catalog: $2
Check, M.O.
With order. $15 minimum.
Trees

Forest Seeds of California
1100 Indian Hill Road

Placerville, CA 95667
Phone: 916-621-1551
Fax: 916-621-1040
Catalog: Free
Check, M.O.
With order. No minimum.
Conifers, Seeds, Trees

Forestfarm®
990 Tetherow Road
Williams, OR 97544-9599
Phone: 541-846-7269
Questions: 541-846-6963
Fax: 541-846-6963
Catalog: $3
Check, M.O., M.C., Visa,
Discover
With order. 10-plant
minimum.
Conifers, Fruit, Grasses,
Perennials, Roses, Trees

ForestLake Gardens
H.C. 72, Lake of the Woods,
Box 535
Locust Grove, VA 22508
Phone: 540-972-2890
Fax: 540-898-8931
Catalog: Free
Check, M.O.
With order. No minimum.
Daylilies

**Four Winds True Dwarf
Citrus Growers**
P.O. Box 3538, Mission San
Jose District
Fremont, CA 94539
Phone: 510-656-2591
Fax: 510-656-1360
Catalog: LSASE
Check, M.O.
With order. No minimum.
Fruit, Trees

**Fowler Nurseries, Inc.,
Garden Center**
525 Fowler Road
Newcastle, CA 95658-9627
Phone: 916-645-8191
Fax: 916-645-7374
Catalog: $4

Check, M.O., M.C., Visa
With order. No minimum.
Fruit, Heirlooms, Trees

Fox Hollow Herb and Heirloom Seed Co.
P.O. Box 148
McGrann, PA 16236
Phone: 412-763-8247
Catalog: $1
Check, M.O.
With order. No minimum.
Garlic, Heirlooms, Herbs,
Organics, Seeds, Vegetables

The Fragrant Path
P.O. Box 238
Fort Calhoun, NE 68023
Catalog: $2
Check, M.O.
With order. $5 minimum.
Heirlooms, Herbs, Perennials, Seeds, Trees

Fred & Jean Minch
4329 Chrisella Road East
Puyallup, WA 98372
Phone: 206-845-8043
Fax: 206-845-5204
Catalog: Free
Check, M.O.
With order. No minimum.
Rhododendrons, Seeds, Trees

French's: Bulb Importer
P.O. Box 565
Pittsfield, VT 05762-0565
Phone: 802-746-8148
Fax: 802-746-8148
Catalog: Free
Check, M.O., M.C., Visa
With order. $10 minimum.
Bulbs

Frey's Dahlias
12054 Brick Road
Turner, OR 97392
Phone: 503-743-3910
Catalog: Free
Check, M.O., M.C., Visa
With order. No minimum.
Perennials

Friends of Eloise Butler Wildflower Garden
P.O. Box 11592
Minneapolis, MN 55412
Horticultural Societies

Friendship Gardens
2590 Wellworth Way
West Friendship, MD 21794
Phone: 410-442-1197
Catalog: $1
Iris

Frosty Hollow Ecological Restoration
Box 53
Langley, WA 98260
Phone: 360-579-2332
Fax: 360-579-6456
Catalog: LSASE
C.O.D.
Upon receipt. $20 minimum.
Grasses, Seeds, Trees, Wildflowers

Fruit Testing Association Nursery, Inc.
P.O. Box 462
Geneva, NY 14456
Phone: 315-787-2205
Fax: 315-787-2216
Catalog: Included in $10
membership
Check, M.O., M.C, Visa
With order. No minimum.
Fruit, Horticultural Societies,
Trees

Fults Garden Shop
Route 2, Box 276
Alto, TX 75925
Phone: 409-858-4995
Catalog: LSASE
Check, M.O.
With order. $20 minimum.
Daylilies

Fungi Perfecti
P.O. Box 7634
Olympia, WA 98507
Phone: 360-426-9292
Fax: 360-426-9292
Catalog: $3

Check, M.O., M.C., Visa
With order. $10 minimum.
Booksellers, Garlic, Kidstuff,
Organics, Supplies

Garden City Seeds
1324 Red Crow Road
Victor, MT 59875-9713
Phone: 406-961-4837
Fax: 406-961-4877
Catalog: $1
Check, M.O., M.C., Visa,
Discover
With order. $15 minimum
with credit card.
Booksellers, Garlic, Grasses,
Herbs, Organics, Seeds,
Supplies

Garden of Delights
14560 S.W. 14th Street
Davie, FL 33325-4217
Phone: 305-370-9004
Fax: 305-370-9004
Catalog: $2
Check, M.O.
With order. $60 minimum.
Fruit, Seeds, Trees

Garden Path Daylilies
1196 Norwood Avenue
Clearwater, FL 34616
Phone: 813-442-4730
Catalog: $1
Check, M.O.
With order. $25 minimum.
Daylilies

Garden Perennials
Route 1
Wayne, NE 68787
Phone: 402-375-3615
Catalog: $1
Check, M.O.
With order. No minimum.
Daylilies, Grasses, Perennials

Garden Place
6780 Heisley Road
P.O. Box 388
Mentor, OH 44061-0388
Phone: 216-255-3705
Fax: 216-255-9535

Catalog: $1
Check, M.O., M.C., Visa
With order. $15 minimum.
Grasses, Perennials

Garden Works
31 Old Winter Street
Lincoln, MA 01773
Phone: 617-259-1110
Catalog: $1
Check, M.O.
With order. No minimum.
Booksellers

Gardeners Eden
P.O. Box 7307
San Francisco, CA
94120-7307
Phone: 800-822-9600
Customer service:
800-822-1214
Fax: 415-421-5153
Check, M.O., M.C., Visa,
Amex
With order. No minimum.
Furniture, Supplies

Gardener's Supply Company
128 Intervale Road
Burlington, VT 05401-2804
Phone: 802-660-3500,
800-863-1700
Fax: 800-551-6712
Catalog: Free
Check, M.O., M.C.,Visa,
Amex, Discover
With order. No minimum.
Furniture, Organics, Supplies

Gardenimport
P.O. Box 760
Thornhill, Ontario
L3T 4A5
Phone: 905-731-1950
Fax: 905-881-3499
Catalog: $4
Check, M.O., M.C., Visa
With order. $20 minimum.
Bulbs, Booksellers, Grasses,
Peonies, Perennials

Gardens Alive!
5100 Schenley Place

Lawrenceburg, IN 47025
Phone: 812-537-8650,
537-8651
Fax: 812-537-5108
Catalog: Free
Check, M.O., M.C.,Visa,
Discover
With order. No minimum.
Organics, Supplies

Gardens of the Blue Ridge
P.O. Box 10
Pineola, NC 28662
Phone: 704-733-2417
Fax: 704-733-8894
Catalog: $3
Check, M.O., M.C., Visa
With order. $25 minimum.
Perennials, Trees, Wildflowers

Gardens for Growing People
P.O. Box 630
Point Reyes, CA 94956
Phone: 415-663-9433
Catalog: Free
Check, M.C., Visa
With order. No minimum.
Kidstuff

Gardens North
5984 Third Line Road
North, R.R. 3
North Gower, Ontario K0A
2T0
Phone: 613-489-0065
Fax: 613-489-0065
Catalog: $4
Check, M.O.
With order. No minimum.
Grasses, Organics, Perennials,
Seeds, Wildflowers

Gary Wayner, Booksellers
1002 Glenn Boulevard S.W.
Fort Payne, AL 35967-9501
Phone: 205-845-7828
Fax: 205-845-2070
Catalog: $1
Check, M.O., M.C., Visa,
Discover
With order. No minimum.

Booksellers

Genie House
P.O. Box 2478
Street address:
139 Red Lion Road
Vincentown, NJ 08088-
2478
Catalog: $3
Check, M.O.
With order. No minimum.
Furniture, Heirlooms

George's Plant Farm
Route 1, Box 194
Martin, TN 38237
Phone: 901-587-9477
Catalog: LSASE
Check, C.O.D., M.O.
With order. $10 minimum.
Garlic, Vegetables

Georgia Botanical Society
6700 Peachtree Ind., B-5
Doraville, GA 30360
Horticultural Societies

Giant Watermelons
P.O. Box 141
Hope, AR 71801
Catalog: Free
Check, M.O.
With order. No minimum.
Fruit, Seeds, Vegetables

Gilbert H. Wild and Son, Inc.
1112 Joplin Street
Sarcoxie, MO 64862-0338
Phone: 417-548-3514
Fax: 417-548-6831
Catalog: $3
Check, M.O., M.C., Visa,
Discover
With order. No minimum.
Daylilies, Heirlooms, Iris,
Peonies, Perennials

Giles Ramblin' Roses
2968 State Road 710
Okeechobee, FL 34974
Phone: 941-763-6611
Catalog: LSASE
Check, M.O., M.C., Visa,
Discover

With order. 3-bush minimum.
Heirlooms, Roses

Gilson Gardens
P.O. Box 277
Street address: 3059 U.S.
Route 20
Perry, OH 44081
Fax 216-259-2378
Catalog: Free
Check, M.O.
With order. No minimum.
Conifers, Perennials, Trees

Girard Nurseries
P.O. Box 428
Geneva, OH 44041-0428
Phone: 216-466-2881
Fax: 216-466-3999
Catalog: Free
Check, M.O., M.C., Visa,
Discover
With order. $20 plant mini-
mum, $3 seed minimum.
Conifers, Grasses, Rhodo-
dendrons, Seeds, Trees

Gleckler's Seedmen
Metamora, OH 43540
Phone: 419-923-5463
Catalog: Free
Check, M.O.
With order. $2 minimum.
Heirlooms, Organics, Seeds,
Vegetables

Golden Bough Tree Farm
Marlbank, Ontario, Canada
K0K 2L0
Phone: 613-478-5829
Catalog: $2
Check, M.O.
With order. $50 minimum.
Conifers, Fruit, Trees

Goodwin Creek Gardens
P.O. Box 83
Williams, OR 97544
Phone: 541-846-7357,
800-846-7359
Fax: 541-846-7357
Catalog: $1
Check, M.O., M.C., Visa

With order. 6-perennial or
12-annual minimum.
Booksellers, Herbs, Perennials, Seeds

Gossler Farms Nursery
1200 Weaver Road
Springfield, OR 97478-9691
Phone: 541-746-3922
Fax: 541-747-0749
Catalog: $2
Check, M.O., M.C., Visa
With order. No minimum.
Booksellers, Trees

Gothic Arch Greenhouses
Division of Trans-sphere
Trade, Inc.
P.O. Box 1564
Mobile, AL 36633-1564
Phone: 205-432-7529,
800-628-4974
Fax: 205-433-4570
Catalog: $5
Check, M.O.
With order. No minimum.
Furniture

The Gourmet Gardener™
8650 College Boulevard,
Department 205-SK
Overland Park, KS 66210
Phone: 913-345-0490
Fax: 913-451-2443
Catalog: $2
Check, M.O., M.C., Visa
With order. $20 minimum.
Booksellers, Garlic, Herbs,
Seeds, Vegetables

Gourmet Mushrooms
P.O. Box 515
Grafton, CA 95444
Phone: 707-829-7301
Fax: 707-823-1507
Booksellers, Garlic

Granite Impressions
342 Carmen Road
Talent, OR 97540
Phone: 503-535-6190
Catalog: $1
Check, M.O.

With order. No minimum.
Furniture

**Grant E. Mitsch Novelty
Daffodils**
P.O. Box 218
Hubbard, OR 90732
Phone: 503-651-2742
Catalog: $3
Check, M.O.
With order. No minimum.
Bulbs

**The Great American Rain
Barrel Co.**
295 Maverick Street
East Boston, MA 02128
Phone: 800-251-2352
Fax: 800-251-2352
Catalog: Free
Check, M.O., M.C., Visa
With order. No minimum.
Supplies

**Great Plains Botanical
Society**
P.O. Box 461
Hot Springs, SD 57747
Horticultural Societies

Green Enterprises
43 South Rogers Street
Hamilton, VA 22068
Phone: 540-338-3606
Catalog: $1
Check, M.O., M.C., Visa
With order. No minimum.
Furniture

Green Horizons
218 Quinlan, # 571
Kerrville, TX 78028
Phone: 512-257-5141
Catalog: LSASE.
Check, M.O., M.C., Visa
With order. No minimum.
Booksellers, Grasses, Seeds,
Wildflowers

The Greenery
14450 N.E. 16th Place
Bellevue, WA 98007
Phone: 206-641-1458

Fax: 206-643-3844
Catalog: $2
Check, M.O.
With order. $25 minimum.
Rhododendrons, Trees

Greenlee Nursery
301 East Franklin Avenue
Pomona, CA 91766
Phone: 714-629-9045
Fax: 909-620-9283
Catalog: $5
Check, M.O., M.C., Visa
With invoice. No minimum.
Grasses

Greenmantle Nursery
3010 Ettersburg Road
Garberville, CA 95542
Phone: 707-986-7504
Catalog: $3. Rose list:
LSASE
Check, M.O.
Upon invoice. No minimum.
Fruit, Heirlooms, Organics,
Roses, Trees

Greenthumb Daylily Gardens
1315 East Rollingwood
Circle
Winston-Salem, NC 27105
Phone: 910-377-2975
Catalog: Free
Check, M.O.
With order. $20 minimum.
Daylilies

Greer Gardens
1280 Goodpasture Island
Road
Eugene, OR 97401-1794
Phone: 541-686-8266
Orders: 800-548-0111
Fax: 541-686-0910
Catalog: $3/Outside U.S.: $5
Check, M.O., M.C.,Visa
With order. No minimum.
Booksellers, Conifers, Fruit,
Grasses, Peonies, Perennials,
Rhododendrons, Trees

Grigsby Cactus Gardens
2354 Bella Vista Drive
Vista, CA 92084
Phone: 619-727-1323
Fax: 619-727-1578
Catalog: $2
Check, M.O., M.C., Visa
With order. $15 minimum.
$25 minimum with
credit card.
Cactus

Grimo Nut Nursery
979 Lakeshore Road, R.R. 3
Niagara-on-the-Lake, On-
tario L0S 1J0
Phone: 905-935-6887
(evenings)
Fax: 905-934-6887
Catalog: $2 (recoverable)
Check, M.O.
With order. No minimum.
Fruit, Trees

Growers Service Co.
10118 Crouse Road
Hartland, MI 48353
Phone: 810-632-6525
Fax: 810-632-6566
Catalog: $1.
Subscription: $5
Check, M.O.
With order. No minimum.
Bulbs, Perennials, Water-
scapes

G.R.'s Perennial Farm
465 North 660 West
West Bountiful, UT 84087
Phone: 801-292-8237
Catalog: $1
Check, M.O.
With order. $20 minimum.
Daylilies

**The Guano Company Inter-
national, Inc.**
3562 East 80th Street
Cleveland, OH 44105
Phone: 216-641-1200,
800-4B-GUANO
Fax: 216-641-1310

Catalog: Free
Check, M.O.
With order. No minimum.
Organics, Supplies

**Gurney's Seed and Nursery
Co.**
110 Capital Street
Yankton, SD 57079
Phone: 605-665-1671
Order: 665-1930
Fax: 605-665-9718
Catalog: Free
Check, M.O., M.C., Visa,
Discover
With order. No minimum.
Garlic, Kidstuff, Organics,
Seeds, Supplies, Vegetables

Habitat Plants
9730 Center Valley Road
Sandpoint, ID 83864
Phone: 208-265-5873
Catalog: Free
Check, M.O., M.C., Visa
With order. No minimum
Conifers, Trees

Halcyon Garden Herbs
P.O. Box 75
Wexford, PA 15090
Phone: 412-935-2233
Orders: 800-362-5860,
ext. 10
Fax: 412-935-5515
Catalog: $2
Check, M.O., M.C., Visa
With order. $15 minimum
with credit card.
Herbs, Seeds

**Hamilton Seeds and Wild-
flowers**
16786 Brown Road
Elk Creek, MO 65464
Phone: 417-967-2190
Fax: 417-967-2190
Catalog: Free
Check, M.O.
With order. No minimum.
Grasses, Seeds, Wildflowers

Hammond's Acres of Rhodys
25911 70th Avenue N.E.
Arlington, WA 98223
Phone: 360-435-9206
Catalog: $2
Check, M.O.
With order. No minimum.
Rhododendrons, Trees

Happy Valley Ranch
16577 West 327th
Paola, KS 66071
Phone: 913-849-3103
Fax: 913-849-3104
Catalog: $1
Check, M.O., M.C., Visa, Discover
With order. No minimum.
Supplies

Hardscrabble Enterprises
H.C. 71, Box 42
Circleville, WV 26804
Phone: 304-358-2921
Catalog: $3
Check, M.O.
With order. No minimum.
Booksellers, Garlic, Supplies

The Hardy Fern Foundation
P.O. Box 166
Medina, WA 98039-0166
Horticultural Societies

The Hardy Plant Society: Mid-Atlantic Group
801 Concord Road
Glen Mills, PA 19342
Horticultural Societies

The Hardy Plant Society of Oregon
P.O. Box 5090
Oregon City, OR 97045
Horticultural Societies

Hardy Roses for the North
P.O. Box 273
Danville, WA 99121-0273
Phone 604-442-8442
Fax: 604-442-2766
Canada: Box 2048

Grand Forks, British Columbia
V0H 1H0
Catalog: $3
Check, M.O., M.C., Visa
With order. No minimum.
Roses

Harlane Company, Inc.
266 Orangeburgh Road
Old Tappan, NJ 07675
Phone: 201-768-0158
Catalog: Free
Check, M.O.
With order. No minimum.
Supplies

Harmony Farm Supply & Nursery
P.O. Box 460
Grafton, CA 95444
Phone: 707-823-9125
Fax: 707-823-1734
Catalog: $2
Check, M.O., M.C., Visa, Discover
With order. $50 minimum.
$20 minimum with credit card.
Booksellers, Kidstuff, Organics, Supplies

Harris Seeds
P.O. Box 22960
60 Saginaw Drive
Rochester, NY 14692-2960
Phone: 716-442-0100
Fax: 716-442-9386
Catalog: Free
Check, M.O., M.C., Visa, Amex, Discover
With order. $10 minimum with credit card.
Garlic, Herbs, Seeds, Supplies, Vegetables

Hauser's Superior View Farm
Route 1, Box 199
Bayfield, WI 54814
Phone: 715-779-5404
Catalog: Free

Check, M.O.
With order. $25 minimum.
Perennials

Hawaii Botanical Society
Botany Department, University of Hawaii
3190 Maille Way
Honolulu, HI 96822
Horticultural Societies

The Haworthia Society
c/o Burk's Nursery
P.O. Box 1207
Benton, AR 72015-1207
Phone: 501-794-3266
Cactus, Horticultural Societies

Heard Gardens Ltd.
5355 Merle Hay Road
Johnston, IA 50131
Phone: 515-276-4533
Fax: 515-276-8322
Catalog: $2
Check, M.O., M.C., Visa
With order. No minimum.
Heirlooms, Trees

Heirloom Garden® Seeds
P.O. Box 138
Guerneville, CA 95446
Catalog: Free
Check, M.O., M.C., Visa
With order. $25 minimum with credit card.
Booksellers, Heirlooms, Herbs, Kidstuff, Seeds

Heirloom Old Garden Roses
24062 Riverside Drive N.E.
St. Paul, OR 97137
Phone: 503-538-1576
Fax: 503-538-5902
Catalog: $5
M.C., Visa, Check, M.O.
With order. No minimum.
Booksellers, Heirlooms, Roses

Heirloom Seed Project–Landis Valley Museum
2451 Kissel Hill Road

Lancaster, PA 17601-4899
Phone: 717-569-0401
Fax: 717-560-2147
Catalog: $4
Check, M.O., M.C., Visa
With order. No minimum.
Fruit, Heirlooms, Organics,
Seeds, Trees, Vegetables

Heirloom Seeds
P.O. Box 245
West Elizabeth, PA
15088-0245
Phone: 412-384-7816
Catalog: $1
Check, M.O.
With order. No minimum.
Heirlooms, Seeds, Vegetables

Henrietta's Nursery
1345 North Brawley
Fresno, CA 93722-5899
Phone: 209-275-2166
Fax: 209-275-6014
Catalog: $1
Check, M.O., M.C., Visa
With order. $20 minimum
with credit card.
Booksellers, Cactus

**Henry Field's Seed and
Nursery Co.**
415 North Burnett
Shenandoah, IA 51602
Phone: 605-665-4491,
665-9391
Fax: 605-665-2601
Catalog: Free
Check, M.O., M.C., Visa,
Discover
With order. No minimum.
Fruit, Garlic, Kidstuff, Organics, Perennials, Seeds,
Supplies, Trees, Vegetables

The Herb Garden
P. O. Box 773-SC
Pilot Mountain, NC
Phone: 910-368-2733
Catalog: Plants, $4, products
$2, both $5.
Check, M.O.

With order. $15 minimum
Herbs

The Herb Society of America
9019 Kirtland Chardon
Road
Mentor, OH 44060
Phone: 216-256-0514
Fax: 216-256-0514
Horticultural Societies

**Heritage Garden Houses
City Visions, Inc.**
311 Seymour Street
Lansing, MI 48933
Catalog: $3
Check, M.O., C.O.D.
Furniture, Heirlooms

Heritage Rose Gardens
40350 Wilderness Road
Branscomb, CA 95417
Phone: 707-964-3748
Catalog: $1.50
Check, M.O.
With order. No minimum.
Heirlooms, Roses

Heritage Rose Group
925 Galvin Drive
El Cerrito 94530
Horticultural Societies, Roses

Hermitage Gardens
P.O. Box 361
Canastota, NY 13032
Phone: 315-697-9093
Fax: 315-697-8169
Catalog: $1
Check, M.O.
With order. No minimum.
Supplies, Waterscapes

Heronswood Nursery, Ltd.
7530 N.E. 288th Street
Kingston, WA 98346-9502
Phone: 360-297-4172
Fax: 360-297-8321
Catalog: $4
Check, M.O., M.C., Visa
With order. No minimum.
Conifers, Fruit, Grasses,
Perennials, Rhododendrons,

Trees

Heschke Gardens
11503 77th Street South
Hastings, MN 55033
Phone: 612-459-8381
Catalog: Free
Check, M.O.
With order. $25 minimum.
Daylilies, Hosta, Grasses,
Peonies, Perennials

Hidden Garden Nursery
13515 S.E. Briggs
Milwaukie, OR 97222-6117
Phone: 503-653-8189,
653-0402
Catalog: LSASE
Check, M.O.
With order. 5-plant
minimum.
Roses

Hidden Springs Nursery
170 Hidden Springs Lane
Cookeville, TN 38501
Phone: 615-268-9889,
268-2592
Catalog: $1
Check, M.O.
With order. $15 minimum.
Fruit, Trees

A High Country Garden
2902 Rufina Street
Santa Fe, NM 87505-2929
Phone: 505-438-3031,
800-925-9387
Fax: 505-438-9552
Catalog: Free
Check, M.O., M.C., Visa
With order. 6-plant minimum.
Cactus, Grasses, Perennials

Highlander Nursery
P.O. Box 177
Pettigrew, AR 72752
Phone: 501-677-2300
Catalog: Free
Check, M.O.
Fruit, Trees

Hildenbrandt's Iris Gardens
H.C. 84, Box 4
Lexington, NE 68850-9304
Phone: 308-324-4334
Catalog: 2 FCS
Check, M.O.
With order. No minimum.
Hosta, Iris, Peonies, Perennials

Hillary's Garden
P.O. Box 430
Warwick, NY 10990-0430
Phone: 914-987-1175
Catalog: $3
Check, M.O., M.C., Visa, Discover
With order. No minimum.
Herbs, Organics, Perennials

Historical Roses
1657 West Jackson Street
Painesville, OH 44077
Phone: 216-357-7270
Catalog: LSASE
Check, M.O.
With order. No minimum.
Heirlooms, Roses

Hobby Garden, Inc.
38164 Monticello Drive
Prairieville, LA 70769
Phone: 504-673-3623
Catalog: $1
Check, M.O.
With order. $25 minimum.
Daylilies

Hoffco, Inc.
358 N.W. F Street
Richmond, IN 47374-2297
Phone: 317-966-8161,
800-999-8161
Fax: 317-935-2346
Catalog: Free
Check, M.O.
Supplies

Holland Bulb Farms
P.O. Box 220
Tatamy, PA 18085-0220
Phone: 800-283-5082
Fax: 610-253-9012

Catalog: Free
Check, M.O., M.C., Visa, Discover
With order. No minimum.
Bulbs

Holland Wildflower Farm
290 O'Neal Lane
Elkins, AR 72727
Phone: 501-643-2622
Catalog: 2 FCS
Check, M.O., M.C., Visa, Discover
With order. $25 minimum with credit card.
Booksellers, Herbs, Seeds, Wildflowers

Holly Lane Iris Gardens
10930 Holly Lane
Osseo, MN 55369
Phone: 612-420-4876
Catalog: $1
Check, M.O.
With order. No minimum.
Daylilies, Heirlooms, Hosta, Iris

Holly Ridge Nursery
1570 Compton Road
Cleveland Heights, OH 44118
Phone: 216-321-5608
Fax: 216-321-5608
Catalog: Free
Check, M.O.
With order. No minimum.
Trees

Hollydale Nursery
P.O. Box 69
Pelham, TN 37366
Phone: 615-467-3600,
800-222-3026
Fax: 615-467-3062
Catalog: Free
Check, M.O.
With order. $35 minimum.
Fruit, Trees

Homan Brothers Seed, Inc.
P.O. Box 337
Glendale, AZ 85311-0337

Phone: 602-244-1650
Fax: 602-435-8777
Price list: Free
Check, M.O., M.C., Visa
With order. No minimum.
Grasses, Seeds, Trees, Wildflowers

Homestead Carts
2396 Perkins Street N.E.
Salem, OR 97303
Phone: 503-393-3973,
800-825-1925
Fax: 503-393-3119
Catalog: Free
Check, M.O., M.C., Visa
With order. No minimum.
Supplies

Homestead Division of Sunnybrook Farms
9448 Mayfield Road
Chesterland, OH 44026
Phone: 216-729-9838
Catalog: $2/Outside U.S.: $3.50
Check, M.O.
With order. $25 minimum.
Hosta

Homestead Farms
Route 2, Box 31-A
Owensville, MO 65066
Phone: 314-437-4277
Catalog: Free
Check, M.O., M.C., Visa
With order. No minimum.
Daylilies, Hosta, Iris, Peonies, Perennials

Hortico, Inc.
723 Robson Road (R.R. 1)
Waterdown, Ontario L0R 2H1
Phone: 905-689-6984,
689-3002
Fax: 905-689-6566
Catalog: $3
Check, M.O., M.C., Visa
With order. 10-plant minimum.
Grasses, Perennials, Roses, Trees, Waterscapes

Horticultural Enterprises
P.O. Box 810082
Dallas, TX 75381-0082
Catalog: Free
Check, M.O.
With order. No minimum.
Seeds, Vegetables

Howertown Rose Nursery
1656 Weaverville Road
Allen Township
Northampton, PA 18067
Phone: 610-262-5412
Catalog: Free
Check, M.O.
With order. No minimum.
Roses

Hydrofarm
3135 Kerner Boulevard
San Rafael, CA 94901
Phone: 800-634-9999
Catalog: $2
Check, M.O., M.C., Visa
With order. No minimum.
Booksellers, Supplies

Hydro-Gardens, Inc.
P.O.Box 25845
Colorado Springs, CO
80936
Phone: 719-495-2266,
800-634-6363
Fax: 719-531-0506
Catalog: Free
Check, M.O., M.C., Visa
With order. $25 minimum.
Supplies

Hydroponic Society of America
2819 Crow Canyon Road,
Suite 218
San Ramon, CA 94583
Phone: 510-743-9605
Fax: 510-743-9302
Horticultural Societies

Idaho Native Plant Society
P.O. Box 9451
Boise, ID 83707-3451
Horticultural Societies

Idaho Wood
P.O. Box 488
Sandpoint, ID 83864
Phone: 800-635-1100
Fax: 208-263-3102
Catalog: Free
Check, M.O., M.C., Visa
With order. No minimum.
Furniture

I.F.M. Products for Natural Agricultural
333-B Ohme Gardens Road
Wenatchee, WA 98801
Phone: 509-662-3179,
800-332-3179
Catalog: $2
Check, M.O.
With order. No minimum.
Booksellers, Organics, Supplies

Illinois Native Plant Society
Forest Glen Preserve
R.R. 1, Box 495A
Westville, IL 61883
Horticultural Societies

Indiana Berry and Plant Co.
5218 West 500 South
Huntingburg, IN 47542
Phone: 812-683-3055,
800-295-2226
Fax: 812-683-2004
Catalog: Free
Check, M.O., M.C., Visa,
Discover
With order. No minimum.
Fruit

Ingraham's Cottage Garden
P.O. Box 126
Scotts Mills, OR 97375
Phone: 503-873-8610
Catalog $1
Check, M.O.
With order. No minimum.
Heirlooms, Roses

International Dwarf Fruit Tree Association
14 South Main Street
Middleburg, PA 17842

Phone: 717-837-1551
Fax: 717-837-0090
Horticultural Societies

International Geranium Society
P.O. Box 92734
Pasadena, CA 91109-2734
Horticultural Societies

International Golden Fossil Tree Society (The Ginkgo Society)
201 West Graham Avenue
Lombard, IL 60148
Horticultural Societies

International Lilac Society, Inc.
11 Pine Street
Dixfield, ME 04224-9561
Horticultural Societies

International Oleander Society, Inc.
P.O. Box 3431
Galveston, TX 77552-0431
Horticultural Societies

International Ornamental Crabapple Society
208 Waggoner Hall
Western Illinois University
Macomb, IL 61455
Phone: 309-298-1160
Fax: 309-298-2280
Horticultural Societies

International Water Lily Society
c/o Santa Barbara Botanical Garden
1212 Mission Canyon Road
Santa Barbara, CA 93105
Phone: 805-682-4726
Horticultural Societies,
Waterscapes

Iowa Prairie Seed Co.
P.O. Box 228
Sheffield, IA 50475
Phone: 515-892-4111
Fax: 515-995-2372
Catalog: $2

Check, M.O.
With order. $15 minimum.
Grasses, Seeds, Wildflowers

Iris Country
6219 Topaz Street N.E.
Brooks, OR 97305
Phone: 503-393-4739
Catalog: $1
Check, M.O.
With order. $10 minimum.
Iris

The Iris Pond
7311 Churchill Road
McLean, VA. 22101-2001
Catalog: Free
Check, M.O.
With order. $25 minimum.
Heirlooms, Iris

Iron Gate Gardens
Route 3, Box 250
Kings Mountain, NC 28086
Phone: 704-435-6178
(evenings)
Fax: 704-435-HEMS
Catalog: $2
Check, M.O., M.C., Visa
With order. $50 minimum
with credit card.
Daylilies, Hosta

Irrigro® International Irrigation Systems
P.O. Box 360
1555 Third Avenue
Niagara Falls, NY 14304
Phone: 905-688-4090
Fax: 905-688-4093
Catalog: Free
Check, M.O., M.C., Visa
With order. No minimum.
Supplies

Isabel Hibbard Gardens
4 Nancy Drive
South Farmingdale, NY
11735
Phone: 516-694-9682
Catalog: $1
Check, M.O.
With order. $15 minimum.

Daylilies

Ivywood Gazebo
P.O. Box 9
Fairview Village, PA 19409
Phone: 610-584-9699
Fax: 610-631-0846
Catalog: $3
Check, M.O.
With order. No minimum.
Furniture

Jackson & Perkins
P.O. Box 1028
Medford, OR 97501
Phone: 800-292-4769,
800-872-7673
Fax: 800-242-0329
Catalog: $3
Check, M.O., M.C., Visa,
Amex, Discover
With order. No minimum.
Heirlooms, Perennials, Roses

Jaggers Bayou Beauties
15098 Knox Ferry Road
Bastrop, LA 71220
Phone: 318-283-2252
Catalog: Free
Check, M.O., M.C., Visa
With order. $25 minimum.
Daylilies

Japonica Water Gardens
36484 Camp Creek Road
Springfield, OR 97478
Phone: 541-746-5378
Catalog: Free
Check, M.O.
With order. $15 minimum.
Waterscapes

Jasperson's Hersey Nursery
2915 74th Avenue
Wilson, WI 54027
Phone: 715-772-4749
Catalog: 75¢
Check, M.O.
With order. $15 minimum.
Daylilies, Iris, Organics,
Perennials

Jernigan Gardens
Route 6, Box 593
Streeet address:
840 Maple Grove Road
Dunn, NC 28334
Phone: 910-567-2135
Catalog: $1
Check, M.O.
With order. $25 minimum.
Daylilies, Hosta

Jim Duggan Flower Nursery
1452 Santa Fe Drive
Encinitas, CA 92024
Phone: 619-943-1658
Catalog: $2
Check, M.O.
With order. $15 minimum.
Bulbs

J. L. Hudson, Seedsman
P.O. Box 1058
Redwood City, CA 94064
Catalog: $1
Check, M.O.
With order. No minimum.
Booksellers, Garlic, Heirlooms, Herbs, Seeds, Vegetables

John Scheepers, Inc.
P.O. Box 700
Bantam, CT 06750
Phone: 203-567-0838
Fax: 203-567-5323
Catalog: Free
Check, M.O.
With order. $25 minimum.
Bulbs

Johnny's Selected Seeds
Foss Hill Road
Albion, ME 04910-9731
Phone: 207-437-9294
Fax: 207-437-2165
Catalog: Free
Check, M.O., M.C., Visa,
Discover
With order. $15 minimum
with credit card.
Booksellers, Garlic, Grasses,
Heirlooms, Herbs, Organics,
Seeds, Supplies, Vegetables

Johnson Daylily Garden
70 Lark Avenue
Brooksville, FL 34601-1319
Phone: 352-544-0330
Catalog: Free
Check, M.O.
With order. $25 minimum.
Daylilies

Johnson Nursery
Route 5, Box 29-J, Highway
52 East
Ellijay, GA 30540
Phone: 706-276-3187
Fax: 706-276-3186
Catalog: Free
Check, M.O., M.C., Visa,
Discover
With order. $12.50
minimum.
Fruit, Heirlooms, Trees

Josselyn Botanical Society
P.O. Box 41
China, ME 04926
Horticultural Societies

Joy Creek Nursery
20300 N.W. Watson Road
Scappoose, OR 97056
Phone: 503-543-7474
Catalog: $2
Check, M.O., M.C., Visa
With order. No minimum.
Grasses, Perennials

**J. W. Jung Seed & Nursery
Co.**
335 South High Street
Randolph, WI 53957-0001
Phone: 414-326-3121
Fax: 414-326-5769
Catalog: Free
Check, M.O.,M.C.,Visa
With order. $15 minimum.
Bulbs, Fruit, Garlic, Kidstuff,
Perennials, Seeds, Supplies,
Trees, Vegetables

Justice Miniature Roses
5947 S.W. Kahle Road
Wilsonville, OR 97070
Phone: 503-682-2370

Catalog: Free
Check, M.O.
With order. No minimum.
Roses

Kadco USA, Inc.
16 De Graff Street
Amsterdam, NY
12010-5304
Phone: 800-448-5503
Fax: 518-842-0602
Catalog: Free
Check, M.O., M.C., Visa
With order. No minimum.
Organics, Supplies

Kalmia Farm
P.O. Box 3881
Charlottesville, VA
22903-0881
Phone: 804-296-1582
Fax: 804-296-0487
Catalog: Free
Check, M.O.
With order. No minimum.
Garlic, Vegetables

Kansas Wildflower Society
Mulvane Art Center
Washburn University
17th and Jewell Street
Topeka, KS 66621
Horticultural Societies

Karen Harris
200 East Genesee Street
Fayeteville, NY 13066
Catalog: Free
Check, M.O.
With order. No minimum.
Furniture

Keith Keppel
P.O. Box 18154
Salem, OR 97305
Phone: 503-391-9241
Catalog: $2.50
Check, M.O.
With order. No minimum.
Iris

**Kelleygreen Rhododendron
Nursery**
P.O. Box 62

Street address: 6924 High-
way 38
Drain, OR 97435
Phone: 800-477-5676
Catalog: $1.50
Check, M.O., M.C., Visa
With order. No minimum.
Rhododendrons, Trees

Kenneth Lynch & Sons
P.O. Box 488
Wilton, CT 06897
Phone: 203-762-8363
Fax: 203-762-2999
Check, M.O.
With order. No minimum.
Furniture

**Kentucky Native Plant
Society**
Department of Natural
Science
East Kentucky University
Richmond, KY 40475
Horticultural Societies

**Kids in Bloom™ Specialty
Seeds**
P.O. Box 344
Zionsville, IN 46077
Phone: 317-290-6996
Catalog: $1
Check, M.O.
With order. No minimum.
Heirlooms, Herbs, Kidstuff,
Seeds, Vegetables

Kilgore Seed Company
1400 West First Street
Sanford, FL 32771
Phone: 407-323-6630
Catalog: $1
Check, M.O.
With order. No minimum.
Booksellers, Garlic, Herbs,
Seeds, Vegetables

Kinsman Company
River Road
Point Pleasant, PA 18950
Phone: 800-733-4146
Fax: 215-297-0210
Catalog: Free

Check, M.O., M.C., Visa
With order. No minimum.
Furniture, Kidstuff, Supplies

Kirkland Daylilies
P.O. Box 176
Street address: Union Springs
Road
Newville, AL 36353
Phone: 205-889-3313
Catalog: Free
Check, M.O
With order. $30 minimum.
Daylilies

Kitazawa Seed Co.
1111 Chapman Street
San Jose, CA 95126
Phone: 408-243-1330
Catalog: Free
Check, M.O.
With order. No minimum.
Seeds, Vegetables

**K & L Cactus & Succulent
Nursery**
9500 Brook Ranch Road East
Ione, CA 95640
Phone: 209-274-0360
Catalog: $2
Check, M.O., M.C., Visa,
Amex, Discover
With order. $20 minimum.
Booksellers, Cactus, Seeds

Klehm Nursery
4210 North Duncan Road
Champaign, IL 61821
Phone: 800-553-3715
Fax: 217-373-8403
Catalog: $4
Check, M.O., M.C.,Visa,
Amex, Discover
With order. $20 minimum
with credit card.
Booksellers, Daylilies, Hosta,
Peonies, Perennials

Kuk's Forest Nursery
10174 Barr Road
Brecksville, OH 44141-3302
Phone: 216-526-5271
Catalog: $2

Check, M.O.
With order. $30 minimum.
Hosta

Kurt Bluemel, Inc.
2740 Greene Lane
Baldwin, MD 21013-9523
Phone: 410-557-7229
Fax: 410-557-9785
Catalog: $3
Check, M.O., M.C., Visa
With order. No minimum.
Grasses, Perennials, Water-
scapes

Lady Bug Beautiful Gardens
857 Leopard Trail, Tuscawilla
Winter Springs, FL 32708
Phone: 407-699-0172
Catalog: $2
Check, M.O.
With order. $35 minimum.
Daylilies

The Ladybug Company
8706 Oro-Quincy Highway
Berry Creek, CA 95916
Phone: 916-589-5227
Catalog: $1
Check, M.O.
With order. No minimum.
Organics, Supplies

Lakeside Acres
8119 Roy Lane
Ooltewah, TN 37363
Phone: 423-238-4534
Catalog: $2
Check, M.O.
With order. $40 minimum.
Daylilies, Hosta, Perennials

Lamb Nurseries
101 East Sharp Avenue
Spokane, WA 99202
Phone: 509-328-7956
Catalog: Free
Check, M.O., M.C., Visa
With order. No minimum.
Grasses, Perennials, Trees

Landscape Alternatives, Inc.
1465 North Pascal Street

St. Paul, MN 55108-2337
Phone: 612-488-3142
Fax: 612-488-3142
Catalog: $2
Check, M.O.
With order. $25 minimum.
Grasses, Wildflowers

Landscape Books
P.O. Box 483
Exeter, NH 03833
Phone: 603-964-9333
Catalog: $5
Check, M.O.
With order. No minimum.
Booksellers, Heirlooms

Langenbach
Department L63100, P.O.
Box 1420
Lawndale, CA 90260-6320
Phone: 800-362-1991,
362-4410
Fax: 800-362-4490
Catalog: Free
Check, M.O., M.C., Visa,
Amex, Discover
With order. No minimum.
Furniture, Supplies

Larner Seeds
P.O. Box 407
Bolinas, CA 94924
Phone: 415-868-9407
Catalog $2
Check, M.O.
With order. No minimum.
Booksellers, Grasses, Seeds,
Trees, Wildflowers

Las Pilitas Nursery
Las Pilitas Road
Santa Margarita, CA 93453
Phone: 805-438-5992
Catalog: $6
Check, M.O.
With order. No minimum.
Grasses, Trees, Wildflowers

Laurie's Garden
41886 McKenzie Highway
Springfield, OR 97478
Phone: 541-896-3756

Catalog: 1 FCS
Check, M.O.
With order. No minimum.
Iris, Perennials, Waterscapes

Laurie's Landscape
2959 Hobson Road,
Box HGS
Downers Grove, IL 60517
Phone: 708-969-1270
Catalog: $1
Check, M.O.
With order. No minimum.
Hosta, Peonies, Perennials,
Trees

Lawson's Nursery
2730 Yellow Creek Road
Ball Ground, GA 30107
Phone: 770-893-2141
Catalog: Free
Check, C.O.D., M.O.,
M.C., Visa
With order. $25 minimum
with credit card.
Fruit, Heirlooms, Trees

Lazy Hill Farm Designs
P.O. Box 235
Lazy Hill Road
Colerain, NC 27924
Phone: 919-356-2828
Fax: 919-356-2040
Catalog: $1
Check, M.O., M.C., Visa
With order. $350 minimum.
Furniture

**Ledgecrest Greenhouses and
Garden Center**
1029 Storrs Road, Route 195
Storrs, CT 06268
Phone: 203-487-1661
Catalog: Free
Check, M.O., M.C., Visa
With order. $20 minimum.
Perennials

Lee Gardens
P.O. Box 5
Tremont, IL 61568
Phone: 309-925-5262
Fax: 309-925-5010

Catalog: $2
Check, M.O., M.C., Visa
With order. $25 minimum.
Daylilies, Hosta, Perennials

Lee Valley Tools Ltd.
P.O. Box 6295, Station J
Ottawa, Ontario, Canada
K2A 1T4
Phone: 613-596-0350
Orders: 800-267-8767
Fax: 613-596-6030
Catalog: Free
Check, M.O., M.C., Visa
With order. No minimum.
Organics, Supplies

Lehman's
P.O. Box 41
Street address:
One Lehman Circle
Kidron, OH 44636-0041
Phone: 216-857-5757,
857-5441
Fax: 216-857-5785
Catalog: $2
Check, M.O., M.C., Visa,
Discover
With order. No minimum.
Supplies

Le Jardin du Gourmet
P.O. Box 75
St. Johnsbury Center, VT
05863-0075
Phone: 800-659-1446
Fax: 802-748-9592
Catalog: 50¢
Check, M.O., M.C., Visa
With order. $15 minimum.
Booksellers, Garlic, Herbs,
Seeds, Vegetables

Lenington Gardens
7007 Manchester Avenue
Kansas City, MO 64133
Phone: 816-358-6666
Catalog: 2 FCS
Check, M.O.
With order. $25 minimum.
Daylilies

Lily of the Valley Herb Farm
3969 Fox Avenue
Minerva, OH 44657
Phone: 216-862-3920
Catalog: $2
Check, M.O., M.C., Visa
With order. $10 minimum.
Herbs, Perennials, Seeds

The Lilly Place Nursery
9205 N.W. Lilly Lane
Gales Creek, OR 97117
Phone: 503-357-8613
Catalog: 1 FCS
Check, M.O.
With order. No minimum.
Daylilies

Lilypons Water Gardens®
P.O. Box 10
Buckeystown, MD
21717-0010
Phone: 800-999-5459
Fax: 301-874-2959
Catalog: Free
Check, M.O., M.C., Visa,
Amex, Discover
With order. No minimum.
Booksellers, Supplies, Water-
scapes

**Limerock Ornamental
Grasses, Inc.**
R.D. 1, Box 111-C
Port Matilda, PA 16870
Phone: 814-692-2272
Catalog: $3
Check, M.O., M.C., Visa
With order. 3-plant
minimum.
Grasses

Little River Farm Daylilies
7815 N.C. 39
Middlesex, NC 27557
Phone: 919-965-9507
Catalog: $2
Check, M.O., Visa, M.C.
With order. $25 minimum.
Daylilies

Little's Good Gloves, Inc.
P.O. Box 808

Street address:
404 South Market Street
Johnstown, NY 12095
Phone: 518-762-8051,
736-5014
Fax: 518-762-2980
Catalog: Free
Check, M.O., M.C., Visa
With order. No minimum.
Supplies

Living Stones Nursery
2936 North Stone Avenue
Tucson, AZ 85705
Phone: 602-628-8773
Catalog: $2
Check, M.O., M.C., Visa
Cactus

Living Tree Nursery
P.O. Box 10082
Berkeley, CA 94709-5082
Phone: 510-420-1440
Catalog: $4
Check, M.O., M.C., Visa
With order. No minimum.
Fruit, Heirlooms, Trees

Living Wall™ Garden Co.
2044 Chili Avenue
Rochester, NY 14624
Phone: 716-247-0070
Fax: 716-247-1033
Catalog: $5
Check, M.O.
With order. No minimum.
Supplies

Lockhart Seeds, Inc.
P.O. Box 1361
Stockton, CA 95201
Phone: 209-466-4401
Fax: 209-466-9766
Catalog: $2
Check, M.O., M.C., Visa
With order. $10 minimum.
Garlic, Grasses, Seeds, Vegetables

Long Hungry Creek Nursery
Box 163
Red Boiling Springs, TN

37150
Catalog: Free
Check, M.O.
With order. No minimum.
Fruit, Heirlooms, Organics,
Trees

Long Island Botanical Society
P.O. Box 905
Levittown, NY 11756
Horticultural Societies

Long Island Seed Company
1368 Flanders Road
Flanders, NY 11901
Phone: 516-369-0257
Catalog: Free
Check, M.O.
With order. No minimum.
Garlic, Heirlooms, Seeds,
Vegetables

Long's Garden
P.O. Box 19
Boulder, CO 80306
Phone: 303-442-2353
Catalog: Free
Check, M.O.
With order. No minimum.
Iris

Louck's Nursery
P.O. Box 102
Cloverdale, OR 97112
Phone: 503-392-3166
Catalog: $1
Check, M.O.
With order. No minimum.
Trees

Louisiana Native Plant Society
Route 1, Box 195
Saline, LA 71070
Horticultural Societies

Louisiana Nursery
Route 7, Box 43
Opelousas, LA 70570
Phone: 318-948-3696
Fax: 318-942-6404
Catalogs: Bamboo and
Ornamental Grasses: $3;

Crinums and Other Rare
Bulbs: $3.50; Daylilies,
Louisiana Iris, and Other
Irises: $4; Hydrangeas:
$3.50; Magnolias: $6; Fruiting Trees: $3.50
Check, M.O., M.C., Visa
With order. $35 minimum.
$75 fruit plant minimum.
Booksellers, Bulbs, Daylilies,
Fruit, Grasses, Iris, Trees

Louisiana Project Wildflower
Lafayette Natural History
Museum
637 Girard Park Drive
Lafayette, LA 70503-2896
Horticultural Societies

Love Gardens
P.O. Box 9, Highway 86
Prospect Hill, NC 27314
Phone: 910-562-3380
Catalog: $2
Check, M.O.
With order. $20 minimum.
Daylilies

Lowe's Own-Root Roses
6 Sheffield Road
Nashua, NH 03062
Phone: 603-888-2214
Catalog: $2
Check, M.O.
20 percent with order.
Heirlooms, Roses

MacKenzie Nursery Supply
3891 Shepard Road
Perry, OH 44081
Phone: 800-777-5030
Fax: 216-259-3004
Catalog: Free
Check, M.O., M.C., Visa
With order. No minimum.
Supplies

McAllister's Iris Garden
P.O. Box 112
Fairacres, NM 88033
Phone: 505-526-4263,
522-6731

Catalog: $1
Check, M.O.
With order. No minimum.
Booksellers, Iris

McClure & Zimmerman
108 West Winnebago Street
P.O. Box 368
Friesland, WI 53935-0368
Phone: 414-326-4220
Fax: 800-692-5864
Catalog: Free
Check, M.O., M.C., Visa
With order. No minimum.
Bulbs

McDaniel's Miniature Roses
7523 Zemco Street
Lemon Grove, CA 91945
Phone: 619-469-4669
Catalog: Free
Check, M.O.
With order. No minimum.
Roses

Maestro-Gro
P.O. Box 6670
Springdale, AR 72766-6670
Catalog: Free
Check, M.O.
With order. No minimum.
Organics, Supplies

Mainline of North America
P.O. Box 526
London, OH 43140
Phone: 614-852-9733,
852-9734
Fax: 614-852-2045
Catalog: Free
Check, M.O., M.C., Visa
With order. No minimum.
Supplies

Malley Supply
7439 LaPalma Avenue,
Suite 514
Buena Park, CA 90620-2698
Catalog: $1
Check, M.O.
With order. No minimum.
Supplies

Mantis

1028 Street Road
Southampton, PA 18966
Phone: 800-366-6268
Fax: 215-364-1409
Catalog: Free
Check, M.O., M.C., Visa,
Amex, Discover
With order. No minimum.
Supplies

Maple Tree Garden
Ponca, NE 68770
Phone: 409-755-2615
Catalog: 50¢
Check., M.O.
With order. No minimum.
Daylilies, Iris

Marietta Gardens
P.O. Box 70
Marietta, NC 28362
Phone: 910-628-9466
Fax: 910-628-9933
Catalog: Free
Check, M.O., Visa, M.C.
With order. No minimum.
Daylilies

Marigold Society of America
P.O. Box 112
New Britain, PA 18901
Horticultural Societies

The Marugg Company, Inc.
P.O. Box 1418
35 Depot Street
Tracy City, TN 37387-1418
Phone: 615-592-5042
Catalog: Free
Check, M.O.
With order. No minimum.
Supplies

Maryland Aquatic Nurseries, Inc.
3427 North Furnace Road
Jarrettsville, MD 21084
Phone: 410-557-7615
Fax: 410-692-2857
Catalog: $5
Check, M.O., M.C., Visa
With order. $25 minimum.
Perennials, Waterscapes

Maryland Native Plant Society
P.O. Box 4877
Silver Spring, MD 20914
Horticultural Societies

Mary Mattison van Schaik
P.O. Box 32
Cavendish, VT 05142-0032
Phone: 802-226-7653
(evenings)
Catalog: $1
Check, M.O.
With order. $10 minimum.
Bulbs

Maryott's Gardens
1073 Bird Avenue
San Jose, CA 95125
Phone: 408-971-0444
Fax: 408-971-6072
Catalog: $1
Check, M.O., M.C., Visa
With order. $15 minimum.
Iris

Matrix Group, Inc.
P.O. Box 1176
Southport, CT 06490
Catalog: Free
Check, M.O.
Booksellers

Matsu-Momiji Nursery
P.O. Box 11414
Philadelphia, PA 19111
Phone: 215-722-6286
Catalog: $2
Check, M.O.
With order. $50 minimum.
Conifers, Trees

Matterhorn Nursery, Inc.
227 Summit Park Road
Spring Valley, NY 10977
Phone: 914-354-5986
Fax: 914-354-4749
Catalog: $5
Check, M.O., M.C., Visa
With order. No minimum.
Conifers, Grasses, Perennials,
Rhododendrons, Trees,
Waterscapes

Maxim's Greenwood Gardens
2157 Sonoma Street
Redding, CA 96001-3008
Phone: 916-241-0764
Catalog: $2
Check, M.O.
With order. No minimum.
Iris

Maximum
30 Samuel Barnet Boulevard
New Bedford, MA
02745-1212
Phone: 508-995-2200
Fax: 508-998-5359
Catalog: Free
Check, M.O., M.C., Visa,
Amex, Discover
With order. No minimum.
Supplies

Medina® Agriculture Products Company, Inc.
P.O. Box 309
Highway 90 West
Hondo, TX 78861
Phone: 210-426-3011
Fax: 210-426-2288
Catalog: Free
Check, M.O., M.C., Visa,
Amex, Discover
With order. No minimum.
Organics, Supplies

Mellinger's
2310 West South Range Road
North Lima, OH
44452-9731
Phone: 216-549-9861,
800-321-7444
Fax: 216-549-3716
Catalog: Free
Check, M.O., M.C., Visa,
Discover.
With order. $10 minimum
with credit card.
Booksellers, Furniture, Kid-
stuff, Perennials, Seeds,
Supplies, Wildflowers

Mendocino Heirloom Roses
P.O. Box 670
Mendocino, CA 95460
Phone: 707-877-1888
Fax: 707-937-0963
Catalog: $1
Check, M.O.
With order. No minimum.
Heirlooms, Organics, Roses

Merry Gardens
P.O. Box 595
Street address: Mechanic
Street
Camden, ME 04843
Phone: 207-236-9064
Catalog: $2
Check, M.O., M.C., Visa
With order. $20 minimum.
Herbs

Mesa Garden
P.O. Box 72
Belen, NM 87002
Phone: 505-864-3131
Fax: 505-864-3124
Catalog: $1
Check, M.O., M.C., Visa
With order. No minimum.
Cactus, Seeds

Messelaar Bulb Co.
County Road, Route 1-A
P.O. Box 269
Ipswich, MA 01938
Phone: 508-356-3737
Catalog: Free
Check, M.O.
Bulbs

Metamora Country Gardens
1945 Dryden Road
Metamora, MI 48455
Phone: 810-678-3519
Catalog: Free
Check, M.O.
With order. $25 minimum.
Daylilies, Hosta, Iris

Michigan Botanical Club
Department of Biology,
University of Michigan
Ann Arbor, MI 48109-1048

Horticultural Societies

Mid-America Garden
3409 North Geraldine
Oklahoma City, OK
73112-2806
Phone: 405-946-5743
Catalog: $3
Check or M.O.
With order. $15 minimum.
Daylilies, Hosta, Iris

Midwest Cactus
P.O. Box 163
New Mellem, MO 63365
Phone: 314-828-5389
Catalog: $1
Check, M.O.
With order. No minimum.
Cactus

Midwest Wildflowers
Box 64
Rockton, IL 61072
Catalog: $1
Check, M.O.
With order. $3 minimum.
Seeds, Wildflowers

Milaeger's Gardens
4838 Douglas Avenue
Racine, WI 53402-2498
Phone: 414-639-2371,
800-669-9956
Fax: 414-639-1855
Catalog: $1
Check, M.O., M.C., Visa,
Discover
With order. $25 minimum.
Booksellers, Grasses, Kid-
stuff, Peonies, Perennials

Miller Nurseries
5060 West Lake Road
Canandaigua, NY 14424
Phone: 716-396-2647,
800-836-9630
Fax: 716-396-2154
Catalog: Free
Check, M.O., M.C., Visa,
Amex, Discover
With order. $10 minimum
with credit card.

Fruit, Heirlooms, Trees

Miniature Plant Kingdom
4125 Harrison Grade Road
Sebastopol, CA 95472
Phone: 707-874-2233
Fax: 707-874-2233
Catalog: $2.50
Check, M.O.
With order. No minimum.
Conifers, Fruit, Grasses,
Perennials, Trees

The Mini-Rose Garden
P.O. Box 203
Cross Hill, SC 29332
Phone: 864-998-4331
Orders: 800-996-4647
Fax: 864-998-4947
Catalog: Free
Check, M.O., M.C., Visa
With order. No minimum.
Roses

**Minnesota Native Plant
Society**
220 Biological Science Center
University of Minnesota
1445 Gortner Avenue
St. Paul, MN 55108-1020
Horticultural Societies

**Mississippi Native Plant
Society**
P.O. Box 2151
Starkville, MS 39759
Horticultural Societies

Missouri Native Plant Society
P.O. Box 20073
St. Louis, MO 63144-0073
Horticultural Societies

Missouri Wildflowers Nursery
9814 Pleasant Hill Road
Jefferson City, MO 65109
Phone: 573-496-3492
Catalog: $1
Check, M.O.
With order. No minimum.
Grasses, Perennials, Seeds,

Wildflowers

**The Mohave Native Plant
Society**
8180 Placid Street
Las Vegas, NV 89123
Horticultural Societies

Monarch Daylily Garden
Route 2, Box 182
Edison, GA 31746-9410
Phone: 912-835-2636
Catalog: Free
Check, M.O.
With order. No minimum.
Daylilies

**Montana Native Plant
Society**
P.O. Box 992
Las Vegas, NV 89123
Horticultural Societies

Moon Mountain Wildflowers
P.O. Box 725
Carpinteria, CA 93014
Phone: 805-684-2565
Fax: 805-684-2565
Catalog: $3
Check, M.O., M.C., Visa
With order. $15 minimum.
Seeds, Wildflowers

Moose Growers Supply
P.O. Box 520
Waterville, ME 04903
Phone: 207-873-7333
Catalog: $1
Check, M.O.
With order. No minimum.
Booksellers, Garlic, Organics, Supplies, Vegetables

Morco Products
P.O. Box 160
Dundas, MN 55019
Phone: 507-645-4277
Catalog: Free
Check, M.O.
With order. No minimum.
Organics, Supplies

Mostly Natives Nursery
27235 Highway 1, Box 258
Tomales, CA 94971
Phone: 707-878-2009
Fax: 707-878-2009
Catalog: $3
Check, M.O., M.C., Visa
With order. $21 minimum.
Grasses, Perennials, Trees,
Wildflowers

**Mother Nature's Worm
Castings**
Box 1055
Avon, CT 06001
Phone: 203-673-3029
Catalog: Free
Check, M.O.
With order. $9.98
minimum.
Organics, Supplies

Mountain Maples
54561 Registered Guest Road
P.O. Box 1329
Laytonville, CA 95454-1329
Phone: 707-984-6522
Fax: 707-984-7433
Catalog: $1
Check, M.O., M.C., Visa,
Discover
With order. No minimum.
Booksellers, Peonies, Trees

Mt. Tahoma Nursery
28111 112th Avenue East
Graham, WA 98338
Phone: 206-847-9827
Catalog: $1
Check, M.O.
With order. No minimum.
Grasses, Perennials

**Muhlenberg Botanical
Society**
Franklin and Marshall College
North Museum
P.O. Box 3003
Lancaster, PA 17604
Horticultural Societies

Mushroompeople
P.O. Box 220
560 Farm Road
Summertown, TN 39493
Phone: 615-964-2200,
800-FUNGI95
Fax: 800-MYCOFAX
Catalog: Free
Check, M.O., M.C., Visa
With order. No minimum.
Booksellers, Garlic, Supplies

Musser Forests
P.O. Box 340, Department
S-94G
Indiana, PA 15701-0340
Phone: 412-465-5685,
800-643-8319
Fax: 412-465-9893
Catalog: Free
Check, M.O., M.C., Visa,
Amex, Discover
With order. No minimum.
Conifers, Fruit, Trees

**Myron Kimnach/Books on
Succulents**
5508 North Astell Avenue
Azusa, CA 91702
Phone: 818-334-7349
Fax: 818-334-0658
Catalog: Free
Check, M.O.
With order. No minimum.
Booksellers

National Hot Pepper Association
400 N.W. 20th Street
Fort Lauderdale, FL 33311
Phone: 305-565-4972
Fax: 305-566-2208
Horticultural Societies

National Wildflower Research Center
2600 FM-973 North
Austin, TX 78725-4201
Horticultural Societies

Native American Seed
3400 Long Prairie Road
Flower Mound, TX 75028

Phone: 214-539-0534
Orders: 800-728-4043
Fax: 817-464-3897
Catalog: $1
Check, M.O., M.C., Visa
With order. $15 minimum.
Booksellers, Grasses, Seeds,
Wildflowers

Native Gardens
5737 Fisher Lane
Greenback, TN 37742
Phone: 423-856-0220
Catalog: $2
Check, M.O.
With order. No minimum.
Grasses, Seeds, Trees, Wild-
flowers

**The Native Plant Society of
New Jersey**
P.O. Box 231
Cook College
New Brunswick, NJ
08903-0231
Horticultural Societies

**Native Plant Society of New
Mexico**
P.O. Box 5917
Santa Fe, NM 87502
Horticultural Societies

**Native Plant Society of
Northeastern Ohio**
2651 Kerwick Road
University Heights, OH
44118
Horticultural Societies

**Native Plant Society of
Oregon**
P.O. Box 902
Eugene, OR 97440
Horticultural Societies

**Native Plant Society of
Texas**
P.O. Box 891
Georgetown, TX 78627
Phone: 512-863-9685
Horticultural Societies

Native Seeds, Inc.

14590 Triadelphia Mill Road
Dayton, MD 21036
Phone: 301-596-9818
Catalog: Free
Check, M.O., M.C., Visa
With order. No minimum.
Seeds, Wildflowers

Native Seeds/SEARCH
Garden: 2509 North Camp-
bell Avenue, #325
Tucson, AZ 85719
Office: Tucson Botanical
Gardens
2150 North Alvernon
Tucson, AZ 85719
Phone: 520-327-9123
Fax: 520-327-5821
Catalog: $1
Check, M.O., M.C., Visa,
Discover
With order. $15 minimum
with credit card.
Booksellers, Garlic, Kidstuff,
Seeds, Vegetables, Wildflow-
ers

Natural Gardener's Catalog
8648 Old Bee Caves Road
Austin, TX 78735
Phone: 800-320-0724
Fax: 512-288-6114
Catalog: $1
Check, M.O., M.C., Visa,
Discover
With order. No minimum.
Booksellers, Organics, Sup-
plies

Nature's Control
P.O. Box 35
Medford, OR 97501
Phone: 541-899-8318
Fax: 800-698-6250
Catalog: 50¢
Check, M.O., M.C., Visa,
Amex
With order. No minimum.
Organics, Supplies

Netherland Bulb Company
13 McFadden Road

Easton, PA 18045-7819
Phone: 610-253-8879,
800-755-2852
Fax: 610-253-9012
Catalog: Free
Check, M.O., M.C., Visa,
Discover
With order. No minimum.
Bulbs

New England Bamboo Co.
P.O. Box 358
Rockport, MA 01966
Phone: 508-546-3581
Catalog: $1
Check, M.O., M.C.,Visa
With order. $50 Minimum
Grasses

**New England Wild Flower
Society**
Garden in the Woods
180 Hemenway Road
Framingham, MA
01701-2699
Phone: 508-877-7630,
617-237-4924
Catalog: $2.50
Check, M.O.
With order. No minimum.
Booksellers, Horticultural
Societies, Kidstuff, Seeds,
Wildflowers

New York Flora Association
New York State Museum
3132 CEC
Albany, NY 12230
Horticultural Societies

**Newfoundland Chapter
Canadian Wildflower Soci-
ety**
c/o Oxen Pond Botanical
Park
St. John's, Newfoundland,
A1C 557
Horticultural Societies

**Niagara Frontier Botanical
Society**
Buffalo Museum of Science
Humboldt Parkway

Buffalo, NY 14211
Horticultural Societies

Niche Gardens
1111 Dawson Road
Chapel Hill, NC 27516
Phone: 919-967-0078
Fax: 919-967-4026
Catalog: $3
Check, M.O., M.C., Visa
With order. $15 minimum.
Perennials, Trees, Wildflow-
ers

Nichols Garden Nursery
1190 Pacific Highway
Albany, OR 97321-4580
Phone: 541-928-9280
Fax: 541-967-8406
Catalog: Free
Check, M.O., M.C., Visa
With order. No minimum.
Booksellers, Garlic, Herbs,
Organics, Seeds, Supplies,
Wildflowers, Vegetables

Nitron Industries, Inc.
P.O. Box 1447
Fayetteville, AR 72702-1447
Phone: 800-835-0123
Fax: 501-750-3008
Catalog: Free
Check, M.O., M.C., Visa
With order. No minimum.
Kidstuff, Organics, Seeds,
Supplies, Vegetables

Niwa Tools
1333 San Pablo Avenue
Berkeley, CA 94702
Phone: 510-524-3700,
800-443-5512
Fax: 510-524-3423
Catalog: $4
Check, M.O., M.C., Visa
With order. No minimum.
Supplies

**Nor' East Miniature Roses,
Inc.**
P.O. Box 307
Rowley, MA 01969
Phone: 508-948-7964

Fax: 508-948-5487
Catalog: Free
Check, M.O., M.C., Visa
With order. $20 minimum
with credit card.
Roses

**North American Fruit Ex-
plorers (NAFEX)**
Route 1, Box 94
Chapin, IL 62628
Horticultural Societies

**North American Gladiolus
Council**
11102 West Calumet Road
Milwaukee, WI 53224-3109
Horticultural Societies

**North American Heather
Society**
3641 Indian Creek Road
Placerville, CA 95667
Horticultural Societies

North American Lily Society
Dr. Robert Gilman
P.O. Box 272
Owatonna, MN 55060
Horticultural Societies

**North Carolina Wild Flower
Preservation Society**
North Carolina Botanical
Garden
Totten Garden Center 3375
University of North Carolina
Chapel Hill, NC 27599-3375
Horticultural Societies

North Star Gardens
19060 Manning Trail North
Marine on St. Croix, MN
55047-9723
Phone: 612-227-9842
Fax: 612-227-9813
Catalog: Free
Check, M.O., M.C., Visa,
Discover
With order. $25 plant
minimum.
Booksellers, Fruit

Northern Nevada Native Plant Society
P.O. Box 8965
Reno, NV 89507
Horticultural Societies

Northplan/Mountain Seed
P.O. Box 9107
Moscow, ID 83843-1607
Phone: 208-286-7004,
882-8040
Fax: 208-882-7446
Catalog: $1
Check, M.O.
With order. No minimum.
Seeds

Northridge Gardens
9821 White Oak Avenue
Northridge, CA 91325-1341
Phone: 818-349-9798
Fax: 818-349-9798
Catalog: $1
Check, M.O., M..C., Visa,
Amex
With order. $20 minimum.
Cactus

Northwest Horticultural Society
Isaacson Hall
University of Washington,
GF-15
Seattle, WA 98195
Phone: 206-527-1794
Horticultural Societies

Northwest Native Seed
915 Davis Place South
Seattle, WA 98144
Phone: 206-329-5804
Catalog: $1 or 3 IRC
Check, M.O.
With order. No minimum.
Seeds, Wildflowers

The Northwest Perennial Alliance
P.O. Box 45574, University
Station
Seattle, WA 98145
Horticultural Societies

Northwind Farms
R.R. 2, Box 246
Shevlin, MN 56676
Phone: 218-657-2478
Fax: 218-657-2447
Catalog: $1/Brochure:
LSASE
Check, M.O.
With order. No minimum.
Booksellers, Herbs

Northwind Nursery and Orchards
7910 335th Avenue N.W.
Princeton, MN 55371-4915
Phone: 612-389-4920
Catalog: $1
Check, M.O.
With order. No minimum.
Booksellers, Fruit, Organics,
Supplies, Trees

Norway Industries
143 West Main
Stoughton, WI 53589
Phone: 608-873-8664
Catalog: Free
Check, M.O., M.C., Visa,
Discover
With order. No minimum.
Supplies

Nourse Farms, Inc.
41 River Road
South Deerfield, MA 01373
Phone: 413-665-2658
Fax: 413-665-7888
Catalog: Free
Check, M.O., M.C.,Visa
With order. No minimum.
Fruit

Nova Scotia Wildflower Society
6360 Young Street
Halifax, Nova Scotia B3L 2A1
Horticultural Societies

Oak Haven Farms Nursery
12727 Upatoi Lane
Upatoi, GA 31829
Phone: 706-561-6546
Catalog: $2

Check, M.O.
With order. $25 minimum.
Daylilies

Oakes Daylilies
8204 Monday Road
Corryton, TN 37721
Phone: 423-687-3770
Catalog: $2
Check, M.O., M.C., Visa
With order. No minimum.
Daylilies

Ohio Native Plant Society
6 Louise Drive
Chagrin Falls, OH 44022
Horticultural Societies

Oikos Tree Crops
P.O. Box 19425
Kalamazoo, MI 49019-0425
Phone: 616-624-6233
Fax: 616-342-2759
Catalog: $1
Check, M.O., M.C., Visa
With order. $20 minimum.
Fruit, Trees

Oklahoma Native Plant Society
Tulsa Garden Center
2435 South Peoria
Tulsa, OK 74114-1350
Horticultural Societies

Olallie Daylilies Gardens
H.C.R. 63, Box 1
Street address: Marlboro
Branch Road
South Newfane, VT 05351
Phone: 802-348-6614
Fax: 802-348-6614
Catalog: $1
Check, M.O., M.C., Visa
With order. $30 minimum.
Daylilies

Old House Gardens
536 Third Street
Ann Arbor, MI 48103-4957
Phone: 313-995-1486
Catalog: $1
Check, M.O.

With order. $20 minimum.
Bulbs, Heirlooms

The Onion Man
30 Mt. Lebanon Street
Pepperell, MA 01463
Phone: 508-433-8549
Catalog: $1
Check, M.O.
With order. No minimum.
Perennials, Seeds

Oral Ledden & Sons
P.O. Box 7
Street address:
Center and Atlantic Avenues
Sewell, NJ 08080-0007
Phone: 609-468-1000
Fax: 609-414-0947
Catalog: Free
Check, M.O., M.C., Visa,
Amex, Discover
With order. No minimum.
Garlic, Grasses, Heirlooms,
Seeds, Supplies, Vegetables

Orcon
Division of Organic Con-
trol, Inc.
Box 781147
5132 Venice Boulevard
Los Angeles, CA 90019
Phone: 213-937-7444
Fax: 213-937-0123
Catalog: Free
Check, M.O.
With order. No minimum.
Organics, Supplies

Oregon Miniature Roses,
Inc.
8285 S.W. 185th Avenue
Beaverton, OR 97007-5742
Phone: 503-649-4482
Fax: 503-649-3528
Catalog: Free
Check, M.O., M.C., Visa
With order. $20 minimum.
Roses

Oregon Trail Daffodils
41905 S.E. Louden
Corbett, OR 97019

Phone: 503-695-5513
Catalog: Free
Check, M.O.
With order. No minimum.
Bulbs

OSC Seeds
P.O. Box 144
Waterloo, Ontario N2J 3Z9
Phone: 519-886-0557
Fax: 519-886-0605
Catalog: Free
Check, M.O., M.C., Visa
With order. No minimum.
Garlic, Seeds

Otis S. Twilley Seed Com-
pany
P.O. Box 65
Trevose, PA 19053-0065
Phone: 215-639-8800
Orders: 800-622-7333
Fax: 215-245-1949
Catalog: Free
Check, M.O., M.C., Visa
With order. $25 minimum
with credit card
Garlic, Herbs, Seeds, Vegeta-
bles

Otter Valley Native Plants
Box 31, R.R. 1
Eden, Ontario
N0J 1H0
Phone: 519-866-5639
Catalog: $2
Check, M.O.
With order. $15 plant mini-
mum. No seed minimum.
Grasses, Seeds, Wildflowers

Out of the Redwoods
P.O. Box 1972
Clackamas, OR 97015
Phone: 503-658-4135
Catalog: Free
Check, M.O., M.C., Visa
With order. No minimum.
Furniture

Outward Signs
1117 East Putnam Avenue
Riverside, CT 06878

Phone: 203-348-0243,
800-346-7678
Fax: 203-357-0092
Catalog: Free
Check, M.O., M.C., Visa
With order. $20 minimum.
Furniture

Ozark Handle & Hardware
P.O. Box 390
Street address: 91 South
Main Street
Eureka Springs, AR 72632
Phone: 501-253-6888
Catalog: $2
Check, M.O., M.C., Visa
With order. No minimum.
Supplies

P & P Seed Company
14050 Route 62
Collins, NY 14034
Phone: 716-532-5995
Fax: 716-532-5690
Catalog: LSASE
Check, M.O., M.C., Visa
With order. No minimum.
Seeds, Vegetables

Pacific Coast Seed Company
3999 North Chestnut,
Suite 256
Fresno, CA 93726
Fax: 209-225-5606
Catalog $1
Check, M.O.
With order. $10 minimum.
Conifers, Seeds, Trees

Pacific Tree Farms
4301 Lynwood Drive
Chula Vista, CA 91910
Phone: 619-422-2400
Fax: 619-422-2400
Catalog: $2
Check, M.O., M.C., Visa
With order. No minimum.
Conifers, Fruit, Trees

Pampered Plant Nursery
P.O. Box 3
Bourbonnais, IL
60914-0003

Phone: (evenings):
815-937-9387
Catalog: LSASE
Check, M.O.
With order. $10 minimum.
Fruit, Trees

Paradise Water Gardens
14 May Street
Whitman, MA 02382
Phone: 617-447-4711,
447-8595
Fax: 800-966-4591
Catalog: $3
Check, M.O., M.C., Visa
With order. No minimum.
Booksellers, Supplies, Water-
scapes

Park Place
2251 Wisconsin Avenue
N.W.
Washington, D.C. 20007
Phone: 202-342-6294
Fax: 202-342-9255
Catalog: $2
Check, M.O.
With order. No minimum.
Furniture

Park Seed® Co.
Cokesbury Road
Greenwood, SC 29647-0001
Phone: 864-223-7333
Fax: 864-941-4206
Catalog: Free
Check, M.O., Discover,
M.C., Visa
With order. No minimum.
Bulbs, Garlic, Herbs, Roses,
Peonies, Seeds, Supplies,
Vegetables

Paw Paw Everlast Label Co.
P.O. Box 93-C
Paw Paw, MI 49079-0093
Phone: 616-657-4921
Catalog: Free
Check, M.O.
With order. No minimum.
Supplies

**Peaceful Valley Farm &
Garden Supply**
P.O. Box 2209
Grass Valley, CA 95945
Phone: 916-272-4769
Fax: 916-272-4794
Catalog: Free
Check, M.O., M.C., Visa
With order. $20 minimum
with credit card.
Booksellers, Garlic, Grasses,
Organics, Seeds, Supplies,
Wildflowers

Pen Y Bryn Nursery
R.R. 1, Box 1313
Forksville, PA 18616
Phone: 717-924-3377
Catalog: $2.95
Check, M.O., M.C., Visa
With order. $25 minimum.
Booksellers, Rhododendrons,
Supplies, Trees

**Pennsylvania Native Plant
Society**
P.O. Box 281
State College, PA
16804-0281
Horticultural Societies

Pense Nursery
16518 Marie Lane
Mountainburg, AR 72946
Phone: 501-369-2494
Fax: 501-369-2494
Catalog: Free
Check, M.O., M.C., Visa
With order. $11 minimum.
Fruit, Trees

The Pepper Gal
P.O. Box 23006
Fort Lauderdale, FL 33307
Phone: 305-537-5540
Fax: 305-566-2208
Catalog: $1
Check, M.O.
With order. No minimum.
Seeds, Vegetables

**Perennial Pleasures Nursery
of Vermont**
P.O. Box 147
2 Brickhouse Road
East Hardwick, VT 05836
Phone: 802-472-5512
Fax: 802-472-6572
Catalog: $3
Check, M.O., M.C., Visa,
Discover
With order. No minimum.
Booksellers, Grasses, Heir-
looms, Herbs, Organics,
Perennials, Seeds

The Perfect Season
P.O. Box 191
McMinnville, TN 37110
Phone: 615-668-3225
Fax: 615-668-3183
Catalog: $2
Check, M.O., M.C., Visa
With order. $15 minimum.
Heirlooms, Herbs, Perennials

Philadelphia Botanical Club
Academy of Science
19th and Parkway
Philadelphia, PA 19103
Horticultural Societies

Pickering Nurseries, Inc.
670 Kingston Road
Pickering, Ontario
L1V 1A6
Phone: 905-839-2111
Fax: 905-839-4807
Catalog: $3
Check, M.O.
With order. 3-plant
minimum.
Heirlooms, Roses

Piedmont Plant Company
P.O. Box 424
Street address: 807 North
Washington Street
Albany, GA 31703
Phone: 912-883-7029
Fax: 912-432-2888
Catalog: Free
Check, M.O., M.C., Visa

With order. No minimum.
Garlic, Heirlooms, Vegetables

The Pinched Pot
Route 1, Box 274
Amissville, VA 22002
Phone: 540-937-4238
Catalog: Free
Check, M.O., M.C., Visa
With order. No minimum.
Furniture

Pinecliffe Daylily Gardens
6604 Scottsville Road
Floyds Knob, IN 47119
Phone: 812-923-8113
Fax: 812-923-9618
Catalog: $2
Check, M.O
With order. $25 minimum.
Daylilies

Pinegarden
5358 Forest South Place
Oakwood, GA 30566
Phone: 770-536-8614
Catalog: $1
Check, M.O.
With order. $35 minimum.
Daylilies

Pinetree Garden Seeds
Box 300
New Gloucester, ME 04260
Phone: 207-926-3400
Fax: 207-926-3886
Catalog: Free
Check, M.O., M.C., Visa,
Amex, Discover
With order. No minimum.
Booksellers, Garlic, Herbs,
Kidstuff, Organics, Seeds,
Supplies, Vegetables

Plant Collectibles
(includes **Growing with
Lights**)
103 Kenview Avenue, Department HGS
Buffalo, NY 14217
Phone: 716-875-1221
Catalog: 2 FCS

Check, M.O.
With order. $10 minimum.
Supplies

Plant Delights Nursery
9241 Sauls Road
Raleigh, NC 27603
Phone: 919-772-4794
Fax: 919-662-0370
Catalog: $2
Check, M.O., M.C., Visa
With order. $25 minimum.
Conifers, Grasses, Hosta,
Perennials, Trees

Plantasia Cactus Gardens
867 Filer Avenue West
Twin Falls, ID 83301
Phone: 208-734-7959
Catalog: LSASE, 2 FCS
Check, M.O.
With order. No minimum.
Cactus

Plants of the Southwest
Agua Fria, Route 6,
Box 11-A
Santa Fe, NM 87501
Phone: 505-471-2212,
800-788-7333
Fax: 505-438-8800
Catalog: $3.50
Check, M.O., M.C, Visa
With order. $20 minimum
with credit card.
Booksellers, Grasses, Heirlooms, Seeds, Trees, Vegetables, Wildflowers

**Plastic Plumbing Products,
Inc. (Envirogation Division)**
17005 Manchester R,
P.O. Box 186
Grover, MO 63040
Phone: 314-458-2226
Fax: 314-458-2760
Catalog: $1
Check, M.O.
With order. No minimum.
Supplies

**Pleasant Valley Glads and
Dahlias**
163 Senator Avenue
P.O. Box 494
Agawam, MA 01001
Phone: 413-786-9146,
789-0307 (evenings)
Catalog: Whatever you please
Check, M.O.
With order. $15 minimum.
Bulbs

Pleasure Iris Garden
425 East Luna
Chaparral, NM 88021
Phone: 505-824-4299
(evenings)
Catalog: $4
Check, M.O.
With order. $15 minimum.
Iris

P. L. Rohrer & Bro.
P.O. Box 250
Smoketown, PA 17576
Phone: 717-299-2571
Fax: 717-299-5347
Catalog: Free
Check, M.O., M.C., Visa
With order. No minimum.
Garlic, Herbs, Organics,
Seeds, Supplies, Vegetables

Plumtree Nursery
387 Springtown Road
New Paltz, NY 12561
Phone: 914-255-0417
Catalog: $1
Check, M.O.
With order. No minimum.
Fruit, Organics

Porterhowse Farms
41370 S.E. Thomas Road
Sandy, OR 97055
Phone: 503-668-5834
Fax: 503-668-5834
Catalog: $4
Check, M.O.
With order. No minimum.
Conifers, Perennials, Trees

Powell's Gardens
9468 U.S. Highway 70 East
Princeton, NC 27569
Phone: 919-936-4421
Catalog: $3.50
Check, M.O.
With order. No minimum.
Conifers, Daylilies, Hosta,
Iris, Peonies, Perennials, Trees

Prairie Moon Nursery
Route 3, Box 163
Winona, MN 55987
Phone: 507-452-1362
Fax: 507-454-5238
Catalog: $2
Check, M.O.
With order. No minimum.
Booksellers, Grasses, Organics, Seeds, Trees, Wildflowers

Prairie Nursery
P.O. Box 306
Westfield, WI 53964
Phone: 608-296-3679
Fax: 608-296-2741
Catalog: $3
Check, M.O., M.C.,Visa,
Discover
With order. $25 minimum.
Booksellers, Grasses, Seeds,
Wildflowers

Prairie Ridge Nursery
(CRM Ecosystems Services,
Inc.)
9738 Overland Road
Mt. Horeb, WI 53572-2832
Phone: 608-437-5245
Fax: 608-437-8982
Catalog: $3
Check, M.O., M.C., Visa
With order. $45 minimum.
Grasses, Perennials, Seeds,
Wildflowers

Prairie Seed Source
P.O. Box 83
North Lake, WI
53064-0083
Catalog: $1
Check, M.O.

With order. No minimum.
Booksellers, Grasses, Seeds,
Wildflowers

The Primrose Path
R.D. 2, Box 110
Scottdale, PA 15683
Phone: 412-887-6756
Catalog: $2
Check, M.O.
With order. No minimum.
Perennials, Wildflowers

Putney Nursery, Inc.
Route 5
Putney, VT 05346
Phone: 802-387-5577
Fax: 802-387-4491
Catalog: Free
Check, M.O., M.C., Visa
With order. $15 minimum.
Herbs, Perennials, Seeds,
Wildflowers

**Rainbow Gardens Bookshop
& Nursery**
1444 East Taylor
Vista, CA 92084
Phone: 619-758-4290
Fax: 619-945-8934
Book catalog: Free/Nursery
catalog: $2
Check, M.O., M.C., Visa
With order. $15 book minimum, $20 plant minimum.
Booksellers

Raintree Nursery
391 Butts Road
Morton, WA 98356
Phone: 360-496-6400
Fax: 360-496-6465
Catalog: Free
Check, M.C., Visa, M.O.
With order. No minimum.
Booksellers, Fruit, Grasses

Ramona Gardens
2178 El Paso Street
Ramona, CA 92065
Phone: 619-789-6099
Catalog: $1
Check, M.O.

With order. No minimum.
Daylilies

**Rare Conifer Foundation–
Rare Conifer Nursery**
P.O. Box 100
Potter Valley, CA 95469
Phone: 707-462-8068
Fax: 707-462-6139
Catalog: Free
Check, M.O.
With order. $25 minimum.
Booksellers, Conifers, Kidstuff, Trees

Raymond M. Sutton, Jr.
P.O. Box 330
Williamsburg, KY
40769-0330
Phone: 606-549-3464
Fax: 606-549-3469
Catalog: Free
Check, M.O., M.C., Visa,
Amex, Discover
With order. No minimum.
Booksellers, Heirlooms

Reath's Nursery
County Road 577, Box 247
Vulcan, MI 49892
Phone: 906-563-9777
Fax: 906-563-9777
Catalog: $2
Check, M.O.
With order. No minimum.
Peony, Perennials

Redlo Cacti
2315 N.W. Circle Boulevard
Corvallis, OR 97330
Phone: 541-752-2910
Catalog: $2
Check, M.O.
With order. No minimum.
Cactus

Redwood City Seed Company
P.O. Box 361
Redwood City, CA 94064
Phone: 415-325-SEED
Catalog: $1/Large print:
$3/Supplement: $2

Check, M.O.
With order. No minimum.
Booksellers, Garlic, Heirlooms, Herbs, Kidstuff, Seeds, Vegetables

Renaissance Gardens
1047 Baron Road
Weddington, NC 28173
Phone: 704-843-5370
Catalog: $1
Check, M.O.
With order. No minimum.
Daylilies

ReoTemp Instrument Corp.
1568 Sorrento Valley Road, Suite 10
San Diego, CA 92121
Phone: 619-481-7737, 800-648-7737
Fax: 619-481-7150
Catalog: Free
Check, M.O., M.C., Visa
With order. No minimum.
Organics, Supplies

Resource Conservation Technology, Inc.
2633 North Calvert Street
Baltimore, MD 21218
Phone: 410-366-1146
Fax: 410-366-1202
Catalog: Free
Check, M.O., M.C., Visa
With order. No minimum.
Supplies, Waterscapes

Resources: Books for Plant Collectors and Seed Savers
9267 West 200 Street
Jamestown, IN 46147-9010
Phone: 317-676-5289
Catalog: Free
Check, M.O.
With order.
Booksellers, Heirlooms

Rhode Island Wild Plant Society
12 Sanderson Road
Smithfield, RI 02917-2606
Horticultural Societies

The Rhododendron Species Foundation
P.O. Box 3798
Federal Way, WA 98063-3798
Phone: 206-838-4646, 927-6960
Fax: 206-838-4686
Horticultural Societies

R. H. Shumway, Seedsman
P.O. Box 1
Graniteville, SC 29829-0001
Phone: 803-663-9771
Fax: 803-663-9772
Catalog: Free
Check, M.O., M.C., Visa, Discover
With order. $15 minimum with credit card.
Garlic, Heirlooms, Herbs, Seeds, Vegetables

Richters
Goodwood, Ontario
L0C 1A0
Phone: 905-640-6677
Fax: 905-640-6641
Catalog: $2
Check, M.O., M.C., Visa
With order. 2-tray, 6-plant, 3-rose minimum.
Booksellers, Heirlooms, Herbs, Organics, Seeds, Vegetables

Robert Compton Ltd.
R.D. 3, Box 3600
Bristol, VT 05443
Phone: 802-453-3778
Catalog: $1
Check, M.O., M.C., Visa
With order. No minimum.
Furniture

Robin Meadow Farm
46 Van Lieus Road
Ringoes, NJ 08551-1312
Phone: 609-466-1998
Catalog: $1
Check, M.O.
With order. $25 minimum.

Daylilies

Robyn's Nest Nursery
7802 N.E. 63rd Street
Vancouver, WA 98662
Catalog: $2
Check, M.O., M.C., Visa
With order. No minimum.
Grasses, Hosta, Perennials

Rocky Meadow Orchard & Nursery
360 Rocky Meadow Road N.W.
New Salisbury, IN 47161
Phone: 812-347-2213
Catalog: $1
Check, M.O.
With order. No minimum.
Fruit, Trees

Rocky Mountain Insectary
P.O. Box 152
Palisade, CO 81526
Catalog: Free
Check, M.O.
With order. No minimum.
Organics, Supplies

Ronniger's Seed Potatoes
Star Route Road 73
Moyie Springs, ID 83845
Fax: 208-267-3265
Catalog: $1
Check, M.O.
With order. $10 minimum.
Booksellers, Garlic, Heirlooms, Organics, Seeds, Vegetables

Roris Gardens
8195 Bradshaw Road
Sacramento, CA 95829
Phone: 916-689-7460
Fax: 916-689-5516
Catalog: $3
Check, M.O., M.C., Visa
With order. $10 minimum.
Iris

Roses & Wine
6260 Fernwood Drive
Shingle Springs, CA 95682
Phone: 916-677-9722

Fax: 916-676-4560
Catalog: LSASE
Check, M.O.
With order. No minimum.
Heirlooms, Roses

Roses of Yesterday and Today
803 Brown's Valley Road
Watsonville, CA 95076
Phone: 408-724-2755,
724-3537
Fax: 408-724-1408, 800-980-ROSE
Catalog: $3
Check, M.O., M.C., Visa,
Amex
With order. $20 minimum
with credit card.
Heirlooms, Roses

Roses Unlimited
Route 1, Box 587
Street address: North Deer
Wood Drive
Laurens, SC 29360
Phone: 864-682-2455
Catalog: Free
Check, M.O.
With order. No minimum.
Heirlooms, Roses

Roslyn Nursery
211 Burrs Lane
Dix Hills, NY 11746
Phone: 516-643-9347
Fax: 516-484-1555
Catalog: $3
Check, M.O., M.C.,Visa,
Discover
With order. No minimum.
Booksellers, Conifers, Perennials, Rhododendrons, Trees

Roswell Seed Company, Inc.
P.O. Box 725
Roswell, NM 88202-0725
Phone: 505-622-7701
Fax: 505-623-2885
Catalog: Free
Check, M.O., M.C., Visa
With order. $5 minimum.

Garlic, Grasses, Seeds, Vegetables

Royall River Roses at Forevergreen Farm
70 New Gloucester Road
North Yarmouth, ME 04097
Phone: 207-829-5830
Fax: 207-829-6512
Catalog: $1
Check, M.O., M.C., Visa
With order. No minimum.
Booksellers, Heirlooms,
Roses, Supplies

Roycroft Daylilies Nursery
305 Egret Circle
Georgetown, SC 29440-8506
Phone: 803-546-3007
Nursery: 527-1533
Catalog: Free/Outside U.S.:
$1
Check, M.O., M.C., Visa
With order. $40 minimum.
Daylilies

Russell Graham: Purveyor of Plants
4030 Eagle Crest Road N.W.
Salem, OR 97304
Phone: 503-362-1135
Catalog: $2
Check, M.O.
With order. $30 minimum.
Perennials, Wildflowers

R. Seawright
201 Bedford Road
P.O. Box 733
Carlisle, MA 01741-0733
Phone: 508-369-2172
Catalog: $2
Check, M.O.
With order. $15 minimum.
Daylilies, Hosta

St. Lawrence Nurseries
325 State Highway 345
Potsdam, NY 13676
Phone: 315-265-6739
Catalog: Free
Check, M.O.

With order. No minimum.
Booksellers, Fruit, Heirlooms, Organics, Trees

Salt Spring Seeds
Box 33
Ganges, British Columbia
V0S 1E0
Phone: 604-537-5269
Catalog: $2
Check, M.O.
With order. No minimum.
Garlic, Heirlooms, Kidstuff,
Organics, Seeds, Vegetables

The Sandy Mush Herb Nursery
316 Surrett Cove Road
Leicester, NC 28748-9622
Phone: 704-683-2014
Catalog: $6
Check, M.O., M.C., Visa,
Discover
With order. $20 minimum
with credit card.
Booksellers, Herbs, Seeds

A Sandy Rhododendron
41610 S.E. Coalman Road
Sandy, OR 97055
Phone: 503-668-4830
Fax: 503-668-4860
Catalog: $2
Check, M.O., M.C., Visa
With order. No minimum.
Rhododendrons, Trees

Santa Barbara Greenhouses
721 Richmond Avenue
Oxnard, CA 93030
Phone: 805-482-3765,
805-483-4288
Fax: 805-483-0229
Catalog: Free
Check, M.O., M.C., Visa
With order. No minimum.
Furniture, Supplies

Saroh
P.O. Box 8375
Springfield, IL 62791
Phone: 217-546-5917
Catalog: Free

Check, M.O.
With order. No minimum.
Booksellers

Savage Nursery Center
P.O. Box 125 SFN
McMinnville, TN 37110
Phone: 615-668-8902
Catalog: Free
Check, M.O., M.C., Visa
With order. No minimum.
Conifers, Fruit, Trees

Savory's Gardens, Inc.
5300 Whiting Avenue
Edina, MN 55439-1249
Phone: 612-941-8755
Fax: 612-941-3750
Catalog: $2
Check, M.O., M.C., Visa
With order. $25 minimum.
$35 minimum with credit
card.
Hosta

Saxton Gardens
1 First Street
Saratoga Springs, NY 12866
Phone: 518-584-4697
Catalog: $1
Check, M.O.
With order. No minimum.
Daylilies

**Schild Azalea Gardens and
Nursery**
1705 Longview Street
Hixson, TN 37343-1738
Phone: 423-842-9686
Catalog: $1
Check, M.O.
With order. $25 minimum.
Rhododendrons, Trees

Schipper & Company
Box 7584
Greenwich, CT 06836-7584
Phone: 800-877-8637
Fax: 203-862-8909
Catalog: Free
Check, M.O., M.C., Visa
With order. $50 minimum.
Bulbs

Schlabach's Nursery
3901 County Road 135
Millersburg, OH
44654-9104
Catalog: Free
Check, M.O.
With order. No minimum.
Fruit, Heirlooms, Trees

Schreiner's Iris Gardens
3637 Quinaby Road N.E.
Salem, OR 97303-9720
Phone: 503-393-3232,
800-525-2367
Fax: 503-393-5590
Catalog: $4
Check, M.O., M.C., Visa
With order. $15 minimum.
Iris

Schulz Cactus Growers
1095 Easy Street
Morgan Hill, CA 95037
Phone: 408-683-4489
Catalog: Free
Check, M.O.
With order. No minimum.
Cactus

**Seed Savers Exchange–
Seed Saver Publications**
3094 North Winn Road
Decorah, IA 52101
Phone: 319-832-5990
Fax: 319-382-5872
Brochure: $1
Check, M.O., M.C., Visa
With order. No minimum.
Booksellers, Heirlooms,
Horticultural Societies,
Seeds, Vegetables

Seed Shares™
P.O. Box 226
Earlysville, VA 22936
Phone: 804-973-4703
Fax: 804-973-4703
Catalog: $2
Check, M.O.
With order. No minimum.
Heirlooms, Seeds, Vegetables

The Seed Shop
P.O. Box 533
Terry, MT 59349
Phone: 406-637-5865
Catalog: $2/international:
$3.50
Check, M.O.
With order. No minimum.
Cactus, Seeds

Seeds Blüm
H.C. 33, Idaho City Stage
Boise, ID 83706
Fax: 208-338-5658
Catalog: $3
(first-class mail: $4.50)
Check, M.O., M.C., Visa
With order. No minimum.
Booksellers, Garlic, Heir-
looms, Herbs, Kidstuff,
Seeds, Vegetables, Wildflow-
ers

Seeds of Alaska
(see **Baldwin Seed Co.**)

Seeds of Change®
P.O. Box 15700
Santa Fe 87506-5700
Catalog: Free
Phone: 505-438-8080,
800-957-3337
Fax: 505-438-7052
Check, M.O., M.C., Visa,
Amex, Discover
With order. No minimum.
Booksellers, Heirlooms,
Organics, Seeds

**Seeds Trust: High Altitude
Gardens**
P.O. Box 1048
Hailey, ID 83333-1048
Phone: 208-788-4363,
208-788-4419
Fax: 208-788-3452
Catalog: Free
Check, M.O., M.C., Visa
With order. No minimum.
Booksellers, Garlic, Grasses,
Heirlooms, Organics, Seeds,
Vegetables, Wildflowers

SeedScapes
P.O. Box 295
Edwardsburg, MI 49112
Phone: 616-663-8601
Catalog: Free
Check, M.O.
With order. No minimum.
Seeds

Select Seeds–Antique Flowers
180 Stickney Road
Union, CT 06076-4617
Phone: 203-684-9310
Fax: 203-684-9310
Catalog: $3
Check, M.O., M.C., Visa
Booksellers, Heirlooms,
Seeds

Seneca Hybrids
1 Seneca Circle
Hall, NY 14463-0270
Phone: 716-526-6396
Fax: 716-526-5350
Catalog: Free
Check, M.O.
With order. No minimum.
Seeds, Vegetables

Sequoia Nursery–Moore Miniature Roses
2519 East Noble Avenue
Visalia, CA 93292
Phone: 209-732-0190
Fax: 209-732-0192
Catalog: Free
Check, M.O., M.C., Visa
With order. No minimum.
Roses

Serendipity Gardens
3210 Upper Bellbrook Road
Bellbrook, OH 45305
Phone: 513-426-6596
Catalog: Free
Check, M.O.
With order. No minimum.
Daylilies

Seymour's Selected Seeds
P.O. Box 1346
Sussex, VA 23884-0346
Catalog: Free
Check, M.O., M.C., Visa,
Discover
With order. No minimum.
Seeds

Shady Oaks Nursery
112 10th Avenue S.E.
Waseca, MN 56093
Phone: 507-835-5033
Fax: 507-835-8772
Catalog: $1
(first-class mail: $2.50)
Check, M.O., M.C., Visa
With order. No minimum.
Booksellers, Grasses, Hosta,
Perennials

Sharp Bros. Seed Co.
Box 140
Healy, KS 67850
Phone: 800-4-NATIVE
Fax: 316-398-2220
Catalog: $4
Check, M.O., M.C., Visa
With order. No minimum.
Grasses, Seeds

Sharp Bros. Seed Co. Wildflower Division
396 S.W. Davis-Ladue
Clinton, MO 64735
Phone: 800-451-3779
Fax: 816-885-8647
Catalog: Free
Check, M.O., M.C., Visa
With order. No minimum.
Seeds, Wildflowers

Shepard Iris Garden
3342 West Orangewood
Phoenix, AZ 85051
Phone: 602-841-1231
Catalog: 2 FCS
Check, M.O., M.C., Visa
With order. No minimum.
Iris

Shepherd Hill Farm
200 Peekskill Hollow Road

Putnam Valley, NY 10579
Phone: 914-528-5917
Fax 914-528-8343
Catalog: Free
Check, M.O.
With order. No minimum.
Conifers, Rhododendrons,
Trees

Shepherd's Garden Seeds
6116 Highway 9
Felton, CA 95018
Phone: 408-335-6910
Fax: 408-335-2080
Catalog: $1
Check, M.O., M.C., Visa,
Amex, Discover
With order. No minimum.
Booksellers, Garlic, Heir-
looms, Herbs, Kidstuff,
Seeds, Supplies, Vegetables

Shooting Star Nursery
444 Bates Road
Frankfort, KY 40601
Phone: 502-223-1679
Fax: 502-875-2319
Catalog: $2
Check, M.O., M.C., Visa
With order. $10 minimum.
$25 minimum with credit
card.
Grasses, Perennials, Seeds,
Waterscapes, Wildflowers

Siskiyou Rare Plant Nursery
2825 Cummings Road
Medford, OR 97501
Phone: 541-772-6846
Catalog: $2
Check, M.O., M.C., Visa
With order. $35 minimum
with credit card.
Booksellers, Conifers, Peren-
nials, Trees

Sisters' Bulb Farm
(see **Old House Gardens**)

Skolaski's Glads & Field Flowers
4821 County Highway Q
Waunakee, WI 53597

Phone: 608-836-4822
Catalog: Free
Check, M.O
Bulbs

Skyland Gardens
4005 Skyland Drive
Kingsport, TN 37664
Phone: 423-245-6467
Catalog: LSASE
With order. $25 minimum.
Daylilies

Slocum Water Gardens
1101 Cypress Gardens Blvd.
Winter Haven, FL
33884-1932
Phone: 941-293-7151
Fax: 941-299-1896
Catalog: $3
Check, M.O., M.C., Visa,
Amex
With order. $15 minimum.
Waterscapes

Smith & Hawken
P.O. Box 6900
Street address: 2 Arbor Lane
Florence, KY 41022-6900
Phone: 800-776-3336
Customer service:
800-776-5558
Fax: 606-727-1166
Catalog: Free
Check, M.O., M.C., Visa,
Amex, Discover
With order. No minimum.
Furniture, Kidstuff, Organics, Supplies

Smith Nursery Company
P.O. Box 515
Charles City, IA 50616
Phone: 515-228-3239
Catalog: Free
Check, M.O.
With order. No minimum.
Fruit, Seeds, Trees

Society for Japanese Irises
16815 Falls Road
Upperco, MD 21155
6518 Beachy Avenue

Wichita KS 67206
Horticultural Societies, Iris

Society for Louisiana Irises
1812 Broussard Road East
Lafayette, LA 70508-7847
Horticultural Societies, Iris

Society for Siberian Irises
N75, W 14257 North
Point Drive
Menomonee Falls, WI
53051-4325
Horticultural Societies, Iris

Sohn's Forest Mushrooms
617 South Main Street
Westfield, WI 53964
Phone: 608-296-2456
Fax: 608-296-2456
Catalog: Free
Check, M.O., M.C., Visa
With order. No minimum.
Booksellers, Garlic, Supplies

**Soil and Water Conservation
Society of America**
7515 Northeast Ankeny
Road
Ankeny, IA 50021
Phone: 515-289-2331,
800-THE-SOIL
Horticultural Societies

**Sonoma Antique Apple
Nursery**
4395 Westside Road
Healdsburg, CA 95448
Phone: 707-433-6420
Fax: 707-433-6479
Catalog: Free
Check, M.O., M.C., Visa
With order. $15 minimum.
Fruit, Heirlooms, Organics,
Trees

Soules Garden
5809 Rahke Road
Indianapolis, IN 46217
Phone: 317-786-7839
Catalog: $2
Check, M.O.
With order. $10 minimum.
Daylilies, Hosta

Sourdough Iris Gardens
109 Sourdough Ridge Road
Bozeman, MT 59715
Phone: 406-586-6233
No phone orders
Catalog: LSASE
Check, M.O.
With order. $6 minimum.
Iris

**Southern Appalachian
Botanical Club**
Department of Biological
Sciences
University of South Carolina
Columbia, SC 29208
Horticultural Societies

**Southern California
Botanists**
Department of Biological
Sciences
California State University
Fullerton, CA 92634
Horticultural Societies

**Southern Exposure Seed
Exchange®**
P.O. Box 170
Earlysville, VA 22936
Phone: 804-973-4703
Fax: 804-973-4703
Catalog: $2
Check, M.O., M.C., Visa,
Discover
With order. No minimum.
Booksellers, Garlic, Heirlooms, Herbs, Seeds, Supplies, Vegetables

Southern Seeds
P.O. Box 2091
Melbourne, FL 32902
Phone: 407-727-3662
Fax: 407-728-8493
Catalog: $1
Check, M.O.
With order. No minimum.
Booksellers, Fruit, Garlic,
Organics, Seeds, Vegetables

Southern Perennials & Herbs
98 Bridges Road
Tylertown, MS 39667
Phone: 601-684-1769
Fax: 601-684-3729
Catalog: $3
Check, M.O.
With order. $25 minimum
Herbs, Perennials

Southmeadow Fruit Gardens
10603 Cleveland Avenue
Baroda, MI 49101
Phone: 616-422-2411
Catalog: $9
Check, M.O.
With order. $15 minimum.
Fruit, Heirlooms, Trees

Southwestern Native Seeds
P.O. Box 50503
Tucson, AZ 85703
Catalog: $1
Check, M.O.
With order. $11 minimum.
Cactus, Seeds, Trees, Wildflowers

"Sow Organic" Seeds
1130 Tetherow Road
Williams, OR 97544
Phone: 541-846-7173
Catalog: Free
Check, M.O.
With order. No minimum.
Garlic, Heirlooms, Herbs, Organics, Seeds, Vegetables

The Species Iris Group of North America (SIGNA)
150 North Main Street
Lombard, IL 60148
Horticultural Societies, Iris

Spring Hill Nurseries
6523 North Galena Road
Peoria, IL 61632-1758
Phone: 309-689-3849,
800-582-8527
Fax: 309-689-3817
Catalog: $2
Check, M.O., M.C., Visa,

Amex, Discover
With order. No minimum.
Roses

Springvale Farm Nursery
Box 200, Department HGS
Street address: Mozier Hollow Road
Hamburg, IL 62045
Phone: 618-232-1108
Catalog: $3
Check, M.O., M.C., Visa
With order. $25 plant minimum.
Conifers, Trees

Spruce Gardens
2317 3rd Road
Wisner, NE 68791-3536
Phone: 402-529-6860
Catalog: $1
Check., M.O.
With order. $10 minimum.
Iris

Squaw Mountain Gardens
36212 S.E. Squaw Mountain Road
Estacada, OR 97023
Phone: 503-630-5458
Fax: 503-630-5849
Catalog: Free
Check, M.O.
Booksellers, Cactus

Stanek's Nursery
2929 East 27th Avenue
Spokane, WA 99223
Phone: 509-535-2939
Fax: 509-534-3050
Catalog: Free
Check, M.O., M.C., Visa,
Amex, Discover
With order. No minimum.
Heirlooms, Roses

Stark Bro.'s
P.O. Box 10
Louisiana, MO 63353-0010
Phone: 800-325-4180
Fax: 314-754-5290
Catalog: Free
Check, M.O., M.C.,Visa,

Amex, Discover
With order. No minimum.
Conifers, Fruit, Trees

Sterrett Gardens
P.O. Box 85
Craddockville, VA 23341
Phone: 804-442-4606
Catalog: Free
Check, M.O.
With order. $20 minimum.
Daylilies, Perennials

Steve Ray's Bamboo Gardens
909 79th Place South
Birmingham, AL 35206
Phone: 205-833-3052
Catalog: $2
Check, M.O.
With order. $20 minimum.
Grasses

Stigall Water Gardens
7306 Main Street
Kansas City, MO 64114
Phone: 816-822-1256
Catalog: Free
Check, M.O., M.C., Visa
With order. No minimum.
Booksellers, Supplies, Waterscapes

Stock Seed Farms, Inc.
28008 Mill Road
Murdock, NE 68407-2350
Phone: 402-867-3771
Catalog: Free
Check, M.O., M.C., Visa
With order. $10 minimum.
Grasses, Seeds, Wildflowers

Stockton Iris Gardens
P.O. Box 55195
Stockton, CA 95205
Phone: 209-462-8106
Catalog: Free
Check, M.O.
With order. $20 minimum.
Iris

Stokes Seeds
P.O. Box 548
Buffalo, NY 14240-0548

Phone: 716-695-6980
Fax: 716-695-9649
Catalog: Free
Check, M.O., M.C., Visa
With order. No minimum.
Garlic, Seeds, Supplies,
Vegetables

Stover Mill Gardens
6043 Stover Mill Road
Doylestown, PA
18901-9209
Phone: 215-297-0296
Catalog: Free
Check, M.O.
With order. $35 minimum.
Daylilies

Strong's Alpine Succulents
P.O. Box 50115
Parks, AZ 86018
Phone: 520-635-1127
Catalog: $2
Check, M.O., M.C., Visa,
Discover
With order. No minimum.
Booksellers, Cactus

Submatic Irrigation Systems
P.O. Box 246
Street address: 719 26th
Street
Lubbock, TX 79408
Phone: 800-692-4100
Fax: 806-747-1800
Catalog: Free
Check, M.O., M.C., Visa
With order. No minimum.
Supplies

**Summerville's Gladiolus
World-Wide**
1330 Ellis Mill Road
Glassboro, NJ 08028
Phone: 609-881-0704
Catalog: Free
Check, M.O.
With order.
Bulbs

Sun Garden Specialties
P.O. Box 52382, Department
HGS

Tulsa, OK 74152-0382
Phone: 918-747-4079
Catalog: Free
Check, M.O., M.C., Visa
With order. No minimum.
Furniture

Sunglo Solar Greenhouses
4441 26th Avenue West
Seattle, WA 98199
Phone: 206-284-8900,
800-647-0606
Fax: 206-284-8945
Catalog: Free
Check, M.O., M.C., Visa
With order. No minimum.
Furniture, Supplies

Sunlight Gardens
174 Golden Lane
Andersonville, TN 37705
Phone: 423-494-8237,
800-272-7396
Catalog: $3 (two-year sub-
scription)
Check, M.O., M.C., Visa
With order. $15 minimum.
Trees, Wildflowers

Sunnybrook Farms
P.O. Box 6
9448 Mayfield Road
Chesterland, OH 44026
Phone: 216-729-7232
Catalog: $1
Check, M.O., M.C., Visa,
Discover
With order. $15 minimum.
Herbs, Hosta, Perennials

Sunnyridge Gardens
1724 Drinnen Road
Knoxville, TN 37914-9725
Phone: 423-933-0723
Catalog: $1.50
Check, M.O.
With order. $20 minimum.
Daylilies, Heirlooms, Iris

Sunrise Enterprises
P.O. Box 33058
West Hartford, CT 06133-
0058

Phone: 203-666-8071
Fax: 203-665-8156
Catalog: $2.
Check, M.O.
With order. $5 minimum.
Booksellers, Garlic, Seeds,
Vegetables

Sunrise Nursery
13705 Pecan Hollow
Leander, TX 78641
Phone: 512-259-1877
Catalog: Free
Check, M.O.
With order. $15 minimum.
Cactus

Surry Gardens
P.O. Box 145, Route 172
Surry, ME 04684
Phone: 207-667-4493,
667-5589
Catalog: Free
Check, M.O., M.C., Visa,
Discover
With order. $25 minimum.
Grasses, Perennials

Swanns' Daylilies Garden
P.O. Box 7686
Warner Robins, GA 31095-
7686
Phone: 912-953-4778
Catalog: Free
Check, M.O.
With order. No minimum.
Daylilies

Swedberg Nurseries, Inc.
P.O. Box 418
Battle Lake, MN 56515
Phone: 218-864-5526
Fax: 218-864-5055
Catalog: Free
Check, M.O., M.C., Visa
With order. $25 minimum
with credit card.
Conifers, Fruit, Trees

Syracuse Botanical Club
101 Ambergate Road
DeWitt, NY 13214
Horticultural Societies

T & M Gardens
Route 4, Box 417
Jasper, AL 35501
Phone: 205-387-8897
Catalog: $1
Check, M.O.
With order. No minimum.
Daylilies

Tate Rose Nursery
10306 FM 2767
Tyler, TX 75708-9239
Phone: 903-593-1020
Catalog: Free
Check, M.O., M.C., Visa
With order. 3-bush
minimum.
Roses

Taylor Ridge Farm
P.O. Box 222
Saluda, NC 28773
Phone: 704-749-4756
Catalog: $3
Check, M.O.
With order. No minimum.
Furniture

TEC
P.O. Box 539
Osseo, MN 55369
Catalog: Free
Check, M.O.
With order. 5-tree minimum.
Conifers, Fruit, Trees

**Tennessee Native Plant
Society**
P.O. Box 856
Sewanee, TN 37375
Horticultural Societies

Territorial Seed Company
P.O. Box 157
Cottage Grove, OR 97424
Phone: 541-942-9547
Fax: 541-942-9881
Catalog: Free
Check, M.O., M.C., Visa
With order. $20 minimum
with credit card.
Booksellers, Garlic, Herbs,
Kidstuff, Organics, Seeds,

Supplies, Vegetables

Texas Greenhouse Co., Inc.
2524 White Settlement Road
Fort Worth, TX 76107
Phone: 817-335-5447,
800-227-5447
Fax: 817-334-0818
Catalog: $4
Check, M.O., M.C., Visa
With order. No minimum.
Furniture, Supplies

Thomas Gardens
507 Race Horse Road
Hanover, PA 17331-8849
Phone: 717-624-9020
(evenings)
Catalog: Free
Check, M.O.
With order. $25 minimum.
Daylilies, Organics

**The Thomas Jefferson
Center for Historical Plants**
Monticello, P.O. Box 316
Charlottesville, VA 22902
Phone: 804-984-9822
Orders: 804-984-9860
Catalog: $1
Check, M.O., M.C., Visa
With order. No minimum.
Booksellers, Furniture, Heir-
looms, Seeds

Thompson & Morgan
P.O. Box 1308
Farraday and Gramme
Avenues
Jackson, NJ 08527-0308
Phone: 800-274-7333
Fax: 908-363-9356
Catalog: Free
Check, M.O., M.C., Visa,
Amex, Discover
With order. No minimum.
Garlic, Grasses, Heirlooms,
Seeds, Vegetables

**Thundering Springs Daylily
Garden**
1056 South Lake Drive
Dublin, GA 31027

Phone: 912-272-1526
Fax: 912-272-1526
Catalog: $1
Check, M.O.
With order. $25 minimum.
Daylilies

Timber Press
The Haseltine Building
133 S.W. Second Avenue,
Suite 450
Portland, OR 97204
Phone: 800-327-5680
Outside U.S. and Canada:
503-227-2878
Fax: 503-227-3070
Catalog: Free
Check, M.O., M.C., Visa,
Amex, Discover
With order. No minimum.
Booksellers

Tinmouth Channel Farm
Box 428-B,
Town Highway 19
Tinmouth, VT 05773
Phone: 802-446-2812
Catalog: $2
Check, M.O., M.C., Visa
With order. 6-plant mini-
mum. $18 minimum with
credit card.
Herbs, Kidstuff, Organics,
Seeds

Tiny Petals Nursery
483 Minot Avenue
Chula Vista, CA 92010
Phone: 619-422-0385
Catalog: Free
Check, M.O., M.C., Visa
With order. No minimum.
Roses

Tischler Peony Garden
1021 East Division Street
Faribault, MN 55021
Phone: 507-334-7242
Catalog: Free
Check, M.O.
With order. No minimum.
Peonies, Perennials

The Tomato Club
114 East Main Street
Bogota, NJ 07603
Phone: 201-488-2231
Fax: 201-489-4609
Horticultural Societies

Tomato Growers Supply Co.
P.O. Box 2237
Fort Meyers, FL 33902
Phone: 941-768-1119
Fax: 941-768-3476
Catalog: Free
Check, M.O., M.C., Visa
With order. $15 minimum.
Booksellers, Heirlooms,
Seeds, Supplies, Vegetables

Totally Tomatoes
P.O. Box 1626
Augusta, GA 30903-1626
Phone: 803-663-0016
Fax: 803-663-9772
Catalog: Free
Check, M.O., M.C., Visa,
Discover
With order. No minimum.
Seeds, Supplies, Vegetables

Tradewinds Bamboo Nursery
28446 Hunter Creek Loop
Gold Beach, OR 97444
Phone: 541-247-0835
Fax: 541-247-0835
Catalog: $2/Price list: LSASE
Check, M.O., M.C., Visa
With order. $40 minimum.
Grasses

Tranquil Lake Nursery
45 River Street
Rehoboth, MA 02769-1395
Phone: 508-252-4002
Fax: 508-252-4740
Catalog: $1
Check, M.O.
With order. $10 minimum.
Daylilies, Iris

Trans-Pacific Nursery
16065 Oldsville Road
McMinnville, OR 97128

Phone: 503-472-6215
Fax: 503-434-1505
Catalog: $2
Check, M.O., M.C., Visa
With order. $10 minimum.
Booksellers, Bulbs, Perennials, Trees, Waterscapes

Tripple Brook Farm
37 Middle Road
Southampton, MA 01073
Phone: 413-527-4626
Catalog: Free
Check, M.O., M.C., Visa,
Amex, Discover, Diner's
Club
With order. No minimum.
Fruit, Grasses, Perennials,
Trees, Wildflowers

Troy-Bilt®
102nd Street and 9th Avenue
Troy, NY 12180
Phone: 518-237-8430, ext.
4429; 800-833-6990
Catalog: Free
Check, M.O., M.C., Visa,
Discover
With order. No minimum.
Supplies

TumbleBug®
2029 North 23rd Street
Boise, ID 83702
Phone: 208-368-7900,
800-531-0102
Fax: 208-368-7900
Catalog: Free
Check, M.O., M.C., Visa,
Discover
With order. No minimum.
Organics, Supplies

Unique Insect Control
5504 Sperry Drive
Citrus Heights, CA 95621
Phone: 916-961-7945
Fax: 916-967-7082
Catalog: Free
Check, M.O.
With order. No minimum.
Organics, Supplies

University Botanical Gardens at Asheville, Inc.
151 W.T. Weaver Boulevard
Asheville, NC 28804
Horticultural Societies

The Urban Homestead
818 Cumberland Street
Bristol, VA 24201
Phone: 540-466-2931
Catalog: Free
Check, M.O.
With order. No minimum.
Fruit, Heirlooms, Trees

Utah Native Plant Society
P.O. Box 520041
Salt Lake City, UT
84152-0041
Horticultural Societies

Valley Oak Tool Co.
448 West Second Avenue
Chico, CA 95926
Phone: 916-342-6188
Catalog: Free
Check, M.O.
With order. No minimum.
Supplies

Van Bourgondien Bros.
P.O. Box 1000
Babylon, NY 11702-0598
Phone: 516-669-3500
Orders: 800-622-9997
Fax: 516-669-1228
Catalog: Free
Check, M.O., M.C.,Visa,
Amex, Discover
With order. No minimum.
Bulbs, Perennials

Van Dyck's Flower Farms, Inc.
P.O. Box 430
Brightwaters, NY
11718-0430
Phone: 800-248-2852
Catalog: Free
Check, M.O., M.C., Visa,
Amex, Discover, Optima
With order. 5-packet minimum.
Bulbs

Van Dyke Zinnias
5910 Corey Road
Perry, MI 48872
Phone: 517-468-3894
Catalog: Free
Check, M.O.
With order. No minimum.
Seeds

Van Ness Water Gardens
2460 North Euclid Avenue
Upland, CA 91784-1199
Phone: 909-982-2425
Fax: 909-949-7217
Catalog: $2
Check, M.O., M.C, Visa
With order. No minimum.
Booksellers, Supplies, Water-
scapes

Van Veen Nursery
P.O. Box 86424
Yearlings and juniors.:
4201 S.E. Franklin Street
Portland, OR 97286-0424
Phone: 503-777-1734
Fax: 503-777-2048
Budded plants:
33814 South Meridian Drive
Woodburn, OR 97071
Phone: 503-634-2314
Fax: 503-634-2710
Catalog: $5. Price list: Free
Check, M.O.
With order. $25 minimum.
Booksellers, Rhododendrons,
Trees

Van Well Nursery
P.O. Box 1339
Wenatchee, WA 98807
Phone: 509-663-8189,
800-572-1553
Fax: 509-662-9336
Catalog: $1
Check, M.O.
With order. No minimum.
Fruit, Trees

Veldheer Tulip Gardens, Inc.
12755 Quincy Street and
U.S. 31 North

Holland, MI 49424
Phone: 616-399-1900
Catalog: Free
Check, M.O., M.C., Visa
With order. No minimum.
Bulbs

Vermont Bean Seed Co.
Garden Lane
Fair Haven, VT 05743-0250
Phone: 802-273-3400
Catalog: Free
Check, M.O., M.C., Visa,
Discover
With order. $20 minimum
with credit card.
Garlic, Heirlooms, Herbs,
Seeds, Vegetables

**Vermont Botanical and Bird
Club**
Warren Road, Box 327
Eden, VT 05652
Horticultural Societies

Vermont Wildflower Farm
P.O. Box 5, Route 7
Charlotte, VT 05445-0005
Phone: 802-425-3500
Fax: 802-425-3504
Catalog: Free
Check, M.O., M.C., Visa
With order. No minimum.
Seeds, Wildflowers

**Vernon Barnes and Son
Nursery**
P.O. Box 250S6
McMinnville, TN 37110
Phone: 615-668-8576
Fax: 615-668-2165
Catalog: Free
Check, M.O., M.C., Visa
With order. $20 minimum
with credit card.
Conifers, Fruit, Trees

Vesey's Seeds, Ltd.
P.O. Box 9000
Calais, ME 04619-6102
Phone: 902-368-7333,
800-368-7333
Fax: 902-566-1620

York, Prince Edward Island
C0A 1P0
Catalog: Free
Check, M.O., M.C., Visa
With order. No minimum.
Booksellers, Garlic, Herbs,
Seeds, Supplies, Vegetables,
Wildflowers

Vileniki: An Herb Farm
Road 1, Box 345
Olyphant, PA 18447
Phone: 717-254-9895
Catalog: $2
Check, M.O., M.C., Visa
With order. $20 minimum.
Booksellers, Herbs

Vintage Gardens
2833 Gravenstein Highway
South
Sebastopol, CA 95472
Phone: 707-829-2035,
Fax: 707-829-5342
Catalog: $5
Check, M.O., M.C., Visa
With order. 2-plant mini-
mum.
Heirlooms, Roses

**Virginia Native Plant
Society**
P.O. Box 844
Annandale, VA 22030
Horticultural Societies

Vista Products
1245 Prairie Dog Place
Ventura, CA 93003
Phone: 805-659-4389
Catalog: Free
Check, M.O.
With order. No minimum.
Supplies

V. Kraus Nurseries Ltd.
Box 180, 1380 Centre Road
Carlise, Ontario
L0R 1H0
Phone: 905-689-4022
Fax: 905-689-8080
With order. No minimum.
Roses

Walden West
5744 Crooked Finger Road
Scotts Mills, OR 97375
Phone: 503-873-6875,
873-3515
Catalog: 50¢
Check, M.O.
With order. No minimum.
Hosta

Warren F. Broderick
P.O. Box 124
Lansingburgh, NY 12182
Phone: 518-235-4041
Catalog: $1
Check, M.O.
Pro forma invoice.
No minimum.
Booksellers, Heirlooms

**Washington Evergreen
Nursery**
P.O. Box 388
Leicester, NC 28748
Phone: 704-683-4518
Catalog: $2
Check, M.O.
With order. $20 minimum.
Conifers, Rhododendrons,
Trees

**Washington Native Plant
Society**
Department of Botany,
AJ-30
University of Washington
Seattle, WA 98195
Horticultural Societies

Waterford Gardens
74 East Allendale Road
Saddle River, NJ 07458
Phone: 201-327-0721
Fax: 201-327-0684
Catalog: $5
Check, M.O., M.C., Visa
With order. No minimum.
Booksellers, Supplies, Water-
scapes

Water Mill Daylily Garden
56 Winding Way
Water Mill, NY 11976

Phone: 516-726-9640
Catalog: Free
Check, M.O.
With order. No minimum.
Daylilies

Water Ways Nursery
Route 2, Box 247
Lovettsville, VA 22080
Phone: 540-822-5994
Catalog: $2
Check, M.O.
With order. $42 minimum.
Waterscapes, Wildflowers

The WaterWorks®
111 East Fairmount Street
Coopersburg, PA 18036
Phone: 610-282-4784
Orders: 800-360-LILY
Fax: 610-282-1262
Catalog: $4
Check, M.O., M.C., Visa
With order. No minimum.
Booksellers, Supplies, Water-
scapes

The Waushara Gardens
North 5491 5th Drive
Plainfield, WI 54966
Phone: 715-335-4462
Fax: 715-335-4462
Catalog: $1
Check, M.O., M.C., Visa
With order. $20 minimum.
Booksellers, Bulbs

**Wavecrest Nursery and
Landscaping**
2509 Lakeshore Drive
Fernville, MI 49408
Phone: 616-543-4175
Fax: 616-543-4100
Catalog: $1
Check, M.O., M.C., Visa
With order. No minimum.
Booksellers, Conifers,
Grasses, Perennials, Trees

Wayside Gardens
1 Garden Lane
Hodges, SC 29695-0001
Phone: 800-845-1124

Fax: 800-457-9712
Catalog: Free
Check, M.O., M.C., Visa,
Discover
With order. No minimum.
Fruit, Heirlooms, Grasses,
Perennials, Roses

We-Du Nursery
Route 5, Box 724
Marion, NC 28752-9338
Phone: 704-738-8300
Fax: 704-738-8131
Catalog: $2
Check, M.O., M.C., Visa,
Discover
With order. $20 minimum.
$25 minimum with credit
card.
Bulbs, Iris, Perennials, Wild-
flowers

Wedge Nursery
R.D. 2, Box 114
Albert Lea, MN 56007
Phone: 507-373-5225
Catalog: Free
Check, M.O., M.C., Visa
With order. No minimum.
Trees

Wee Gems
2197 Stewart Avenue
St. Paul, MN 55116
Phone: 612-699-2694
Check, M.O.
With order. No minimum.
Roses

**Weiss Brothers Perennial
Nursery**
11690 Colfax Highway
Grass Valley, CA 95945
Phone: 916-272-7657
Fax: 916-272-3578
Catalog: Free
Check, M.O., M.C., Visa,
Amex, Discover
With order. No minimum.
Herbs, Grasses, Perennials

**Western Carolina Botanical
Club**

6 Tenequa Drive, Connestee Falls
Brevard, NC 28712
Horticultural Societies

White Flower Farm
Plantsmen
P.O. Box 50
Litchfield, CT 06759-0050
Phone: Orders:
860-496-9624
Fax: 860-496-1418
Catalog: Free
Check, M.O., M.C., Visa,
Amex, Discover
With order. No minimum.
Bulbs, Fruit, Perennials,
Roses, Supplies, Trees, Waterscapes

Whitman Farms
3995 Gibson N.W.
Salem, OR 97304-9527
Phone: 503-585-8728
Fax: 503-363-5020
Catalog: $1
Check, M.O.
With order. $10 minimum.
Fruit, Trees

Whitney Gardens and Nursery
P.O. Box F
306264 Highway 101
Brinnon, WA 98320-0080
Phone: 360-796-4411
Orders: 800-952-2404
Catalog: $4
Check, M.O., M.C., Visa
With order. No minimum.
Rhododendron, Trees

Wicklein's Water Gardens
P.O. Box 9780
Baldwin, MD 21013
Phone: 410-823-1335
Orders: 800-382-6716
Fax: 410-823-1427
Catalog: $2
Check, M.O., M.C., Visa
With order. No minimum.
Booksellers, Iris, Supplies,

Waterscapes

Wikco Industries, Inc.
4930 North 57th Street
Lincoln, NE 68507-3101
Phone: 800-872-8864
Fax: 402-464-2070
Catalog: Free
Check, M.O., M.C., Visa,
Amex, Discover
With order. No minimum.
Supplies

Wild Earth Native Plant Nursery
49 Mead Avenue
Freehold, NJ 07728
Phone: 908-308-9777
Fax: 908-308-9777
Catalog: $2
Check, M.O.
With order. $15 minimum.
Grasses, Seeds, Wildflowers

Wildflower Association of Michigan
P.O. Box 80527
6011 West Street Joseph,
Suite 403
Lansing, MI 48908-0527
Horticultural Societies

The Wildflower Society
c/o Goldsmith Civic Garden Center
750 Cherry Road
Memphis, TN 38119-4699
Horticultural Societies

Wild Seed, Inc.
P.O. Box 27751
Tempe, AZ 85285
Phone: 602-276-3536
Fax: 602-276-3524
Catalog: Free
Check, M.O.
With order. No minimum.
Booksellers, Grasses, Kidstuff, Seeds, Trees, Wildflowers

Wildseed Farms, Inc.
P.O. Box 308

Street address: 1101 Campo Rosa Road
Eagle Lake, TX 77434-0308
Phone: 800-848-0078
Fax: 409-234-7407
Catalog: $2
Check, M.O., M.C., Visa,
Amex, Discover
With order. No minimum.
Herbs, Seeds, Wildflowers

The Wildwood Flower
Route 3, P.O. Box 165
Pittsboro, NC 27312
Phone: 919-542-4344
(evenings only)
Catalog: LSASE
Check, M.O.
With order. No minimum.
Perennials, Trees

Wildwood Gardens
P.O. Box 250
33326 South Dickey Prairie Road
Molalla, OR 97038-0250
Phone: 503-829-3102
Catalog: $2
Check, M.O.
With order. No minimum.
Daylilies, Hosta, Iris

Wiley's Nut Grove Nursery
2002 Lexington Avenue
Mansfield, OH 44907
Phone: 419-756-0697
Catalog: 1 FCS
Check, M.O.
With order. No minimum.
Fruit, Trees

Willhite Seed Co.
P.O. Box 23
Poolville, TX 76487
Phone: 817-599-8656
Fax: 817-599-5843
Catalog: Free
Check, M.O., M.C., Visa
With order. No minimum.
Garlic, Seeds, Vegetables

William Dam Seeds
P.O. Box 8400
Dundas, Ontario L9H 6M1
Street address:
279 Highway 8
West Flamboro
Phone: 905-628-6641
Fax: 905-627-1729
Check, M.O.
With order. No minimum.
Booksellers, Garlic, Herbs,
Seeds, Vegetables, Wildflowers

William Tricker, Inc.
7125 Tanglewood Drive
Independence, OH 44131
Phone: 216-524-3491
Fax: 216-524-6688
Catalog: $3
Check, M.O., M.C., Visa
With order. No minimum.
Waterscapes

Wimberlyway Gardens
1 Daylilies Plaza
Alachua, FL 32615
Phone: 904-462-1539
Fax: 904-462-5111
Catalog: $2
Check, M.O., M.C., Visa,
Amex, Discover
With order. $25 minimum.
Daylilies

Wind & Weather
P.O. Box 2320
Mendocino, CA 95460-2320
Phone: 707-964-1284,
800-922-9463
Fax: 707-964-1278
Catalog: Free
Check, M.O., M.C.,Visa,
Amex, Discover
With order. No minimum.
Furniture, Supplies

Windleaves
7560 Morningside Drive
Indianapolis, IN 46240
Phone: 317-251-1381
Catalog: $1

Check, M.O.
With order. No minimum.
Furniture

Windrose
1093 Mill Road
Pen Argyl, PA 18072-9670
Phone: 610-588-1037
Fax: 610-252-7064
Catalog: $3
Check, M.O., M.C., Visa
With order. $20 minimum.
Perennials, Trees

Windy Oaks Aquatics
W 377 S-10677 Betts Road
Eagle, WI 53119
Phone: 414-594-3033,
594-2803
Fax: 414-594-3033
Catalog: $1
Check, M.O.
With order. No minimum.
Supplies, Waterscapes

Wisconsin Wagon Co., Inc.
507 Laurel Avenue
Janesville, WI 53545
Phone: 608-754-0026
Catalog: Free
Check, M.O., M.C., Visa
With order. No minimum.
Kidstuff

Witherspoon Rose Culture
P.O. Box 51655
Durham, NC 27717-1655
Phone: 800-643-0315
Fax: 919-490-0623
Catalog: Free
Check, M.O., M.C., Visa,
Discover
With order. No minimum
Roses

Womack's Nursery Co.
Route 1, Box 80
DeLeon, TX 76444-9649
Phone: 817-893-6497
Fax: 817-893-3400
Check, M.O.
With order. $25 minimum.
Fruit, Trees

Womanswork®
Little Big Farm
P.O. Box 543
York, ME 03909-0543
Phone: 207-363-0804,
800-639-2709
Fax: 207-363-0805
Catalog: Free
Check, M.O., M.C., Visa,
Amex
With order.
Kidstuff, Supplies

Wood Classics, Inc.
P.O. Box 291
20 Osprey Lane
Gardiner, NY 12525
Phone: 914-255-7871
Fax: 914-255-7881
Catalog: Free
Check, M.O., M.C., Visa
With order. No minimum.
Furniture

Wood Innovations of Suffolk, Ltd.
P.O. Box 356
Medford, NY 11763
Phone: 516-698-2345
Fax: 516-698-2396
Catalog: Free
Check, M.O.
With order. No minimum.
Furniture

Wood Prairie Farm
R.F.D. 7, Box 164
Bridgewater, ME 04735
Phone: 207-429-9765, 800-
829-9765
Fax: 800-829-9765
Catalog: Free
Check, M.O., M.C., Visa,
Amex, Discover, Diners
Club, Carte Blanche
With order. No minimum.
Garlic, Seeds, Vegetables

Wood Violet Books
3814 Sunhill Drive
Madison, WI 53704
Phone: 608-837-7207

Catalog: $2
Check, M.O., M.C., Visa
With order. No minimum.
Booksellers

**Woodbrook Furniture Man-
ufacturers**
P.O. Box 175
Street address: 7209 High-
way 11 North
Trussville, AL 35173
Phone: 800-828-3607
Catalog: Free
Check, M.O.
50 percent with order, bal-
ance due prior to shipment
Furniture

Woodstock Canoe Co.
P.O. Box 118
Woodstock, NH 03293
Phone: 800-362-8804
Catalog: Free
Check, M.O.
With order. No minimum.
Furniture

**Gary W. Woolson, Book-
sellers**
R.R. 1, Box 1576

Hampden, ME 04444
Phone: 207-234-4931
Catalog: Free
Check, M.O.
With order. No minimum.
Booksellers

**World Pumpkin Confedera-
tion**
14050 Route 62
Collins, NY 14034
Phone: 716-532-5995
Fax: 716-532-5690
Horticultural Societies

Worm's Way Indiana
3151 S. State Road
Bloomington, IN 47404-
9477
Phone: 812-331-0300,
800-274-9676
Fax: 800-316-1278
Catalog: Free
Check, C.O.D., M.O.,
M.C., Visa, Amex, Discover
With order. $25 C.O.D.
minimum.
Booksellers, Garlic, Organ-
ics, Supplies

**Wyoming Native Plant
Society**
Box 1471
Cheyenne, WY 82003
Horticultural Societies

York Hill Farm
18 Warren Street
Georgetown, MA 01833
Phone: 508-352-6560
Catalog: $1.50
Check, M.O.
With order. $25 minimum.
Daylilies, Grasses, Heir-
looms, Hosta, Iris, Perennials

**Yucca Do Nursery at Pecker-
wood Gardens**
P.O. Box 655
Waller, TX 77484
Phone: 409-826-6363
Catalog: $3
Check, M.O.
With order. $25 minimum.
Cactus, Conifers, Grasses,
Organics, Perennials, Trees,
Wildflowers

About the Author

Author and photographer SOLOMON M. SKOLNICK'S credits include *The Window-Box Book* and *Simple Gifts: The Shaker Song*. His work has appeared in *The New York Times, People,* and *Fine Gardening*. He lives and gardens in Pleasantville, New York.

About the Type

This book was set in Garamond, a typeface designed by the French printer Jean Jannon. It is styled after Garamond's original models. The face is dignified, and is light but without fragile lines. The italic is modeled after a font of Granjon, which was probably cut in the middle of the sixteenth century.